D1219541

■ Solution-Focused Brief Therapy

Solution-Focused Brief Therapy

A Handbook of Evidence-Based Practice

EDITED BY

Cynthia Franklin

Terry S. Trepper

Wallace J. Gingerich

Eric E. McCollum

OXFORD
UNIVERSITY PRESS

Published in the United States of America by Oxford University Press, Inc.,
198 Madison Avenue, New York, NY, 10016
United States of America

Oxford University Press, Inc., publishes works that further Oxford University's
objective of excellence in research, scholarship, and education

Library of Congress Cataloging-in-Publication Data

Solution-focused brief therapy : a handbook of evidence-based practice / edited by
Cynthia Franklin ... [et al.].
    p. cm.
  Includes bibliographical references and index.
  ISBN 978-0-19-538572-4
1. Solution-focused brief therapy. I. Franklin, Cynthia.
  RC489.S65S65 2012
  616.89'147—dc23   2011017401

9 8 7 6 5 4 3 2 1
Printed in the United States of America on acid-free paper

PREFACE

■ CYNTHIA FRANKLIN, TERRY S. TREPPER,

WALLACE J. GINGERICH, AND ERIC McCOLLUM

Solution-Focused Brief Therapy: A Handbook of Evidence-Based Practice brings together a talented cadre of professionals from the United States, Europe, Canada, and Japan who summarize state-of-the-art solution-focused brief therapy (SFBT) practice and research from around the world. This book offers an evidence-informed review of SFBT for both practitioners and researchers and reviews the current state of the research on solution-focused therapy interventions using diverse research methods, including microanalysis and basic research, experimental designs, meta-analysis, process studies, and the best program evaluations and practice-based research from clinics and other settings. *Solution-Focused Brief Therapy* provides a practice text that reveals that SFBT has considerable empirical support and is an intervention that is firmly grounded in research evidence.

The evidence base of SFBT began with its origin in the Brief Family Therapy Center in Milwaukee, Wisconsin, where practitioners and researchers used systematic observations and qualitative methods to study what works with clients in brief family therapy. The practices of SFBT continued to evolve; today, numerous researchers from around the world have studied its mechanisms of change and its outcomes. Until now, studies on the effective practices of SFBT have existed in disparate international sources; this cutting-edge book has compiled all of this helpful research information in one practice resource. Each chapter offers the best solution-focused practice information and timely resources that are important to the development of solution-focused therapy as an evidence-informed practice. In no other single resource will practitioners find such an integration of SFBT practices and research.

■ WHO HELPED US DEVELOP THE BOOK?

This book was originally envisioned by Insoo Kim Berg and Steve de Shazer, two of the developers of the SFBT model. They wanted all the research evidence on SFBT brought together in one source so that practitioners could easily access this information. Insoo and Steve had a big vision, and while we cannot claim to have reviewed every study on SFBT over the past 30 years, we believe that this book summarizes a large proportion of the research evidence. Our distinguished contributors from around the world have worked together to make this vision a reality. We are pleased that this book covers SFBT research across diverse fields and interests.

Beyond the help of the developers, we also had a group of editorial consultants whose names are listed below. They include practitioners and researchers from various countries, and each was instrumental in helping us develop this book—offering vision and direction, advice and guidance, support and/or valued critiques, and timely reviews of various manuscripts.

■ CONTENTS OF THE BOOK

The contents of this book were generated from a review of the literature and suggestions from the international scholars who served as our editorial consultants. The book has 25 chapters divided into five sections. Section I summarizes the origins and development of SFBT and illustrates the treatment components illustrated in the Solution-Focused

Brief Therapy Association's treatment manual. Section II covers measurement issues, with chapters on the development of a solution-focused fidelity measure; a chapter on standardized, solution-focused, and strengths-based outcome measures; and a chapter on the use of in-session rating scales that help provide continuous monitoring of outcomes in clinical practice. Section III presents systematic reviews and meta-analyses, summaries of process research, and microanalysis research from communication laboratories that support the major theory and constructs of SFBT. Section IV examines the effectiveness of SFBT with several different clinical populations. Finally, Section V reviews innovative SFBT practice programs and the research supporting them, further illustrating the expansion of SFBT into diverse practice areas such as mental health clinics, schools and classrooms, social services, business management, life coaching, and health care. We conclude with an *Epilogue* which offers a review of the current state of the art of research in Solution-focused Brief Therapy and offers suggestions for future research.

The sections and chapters are diverse in content, so complete uniformity across chapters was not possible or even advantageous. However, as editors, we tried to make the book as uniform as possible so that the chapters would be comparable and easy to read. In doing so, we asked all authors to discuss what they have learned so far about their particular topic, to describe the solution-focused interventions being applied, and to cover the research methods being used, as well as the results. We also asked them to offer critiques of the research and indicate future directions for study. Finally, the authors were asked to provide practice guidelines and key findings from their work, along with a list of further learning resources to help practitioners. They have followed these guidelines with great care and expertise, and we believe the result is a book that offers both the best scholarship and the most helpful practice guidelines for SFBT.

■ WHY FOCUS ON EVIDENCE-BASED PRACTICE?

Today's practice contexts demand that therapists and other professionals follow the best evidence-based practices. Busy practitioners, however, often do not have a great deal of time to search for evidence-based practice information. They need summaries and rapid guides to research information in their field. For this reason, we believe that this book about the evidence base of SFBT is overdue. In developing the book, we use a definition for evidence-based practice similar to that of Sackett, Straus, Richardson, Rosenberg, and Haynes (2000) in their work on evidence-based medicine: *Evidence-based practice focuses on integrating the best research evidence available with clinical expertise and with clients' values, preferences, and circumstances.* Although it originated in the medical field, this definition of evidence-based practice has been adopted by most major practice professional organizations, including the American Psychological Association (APA) and the National Association of Social Workers (NASW), as well as other clinical and therapeutic disciplines (Kim, Smock, Trepper, McCollum, & Franklin, 2009). This definition of evidence-based practice offers a process that practitioners can follow in choosing the best treatments for their clients. Importantly, this process also takes into consideration the judgments of skilled clinicians and the viewpoints of their clients, thus giving credibility to the practice-based evidence at hand.

Empirically supported treatment, another term that is important for this book, concerns the process of increasing the quality of studies that support SFBT practices and the evaluation of those studies to see if they meet certain criteria for excellence that would earn them the rating "empirically supported" or "evidence-based." As a practice field, SFBT has been more interested in the process of doing effective therapy with clients than with proving itself to be an empirically supported treatment or evidence-based practice. As this book shows, however, from its very beginning, SFBT has followed evidence-based practice by gathering and using evidence as part of its clinical process and has now developed to the point where considerable empirical support also exists for its practices. This book provides a much needed lens through which the SFBT field can view the state of its research and practices.

■ REFERENCES

Kim, J. S., Smock, S., Trepper, T., McCollum, E. E., & Franklin, C. (2009). Is solution-focused therapy evidence based? *Families in Society*, *91*(3), 301–305.

Sackett, D. L., Straus, S. E., Richardson, W. S., Rosenberg, W., & Haynes, R. B. (2000). *Evidence-based medicine* (2nd ed.), London: Churchill Livingstone.

■ ACKNOWLEDGMENTS

Many people made this book possible and we are not able to mention them all here, but we would like to acknowledge that this book was a collaborative effort involving may professionals in the SFBT field and others who were interested in having it published. First and foremost, we want to thank Oxford University Press for supporting this work. Our deepest gratitude goes to Maura Roessner and her staff and to Joan H. Bossert for their help and guidance throughout this project. We also thank our editorial consultants, who provided the help we needed at just the right point in time, and the authors who worked diligently on each chapter. We want to thank and acknowledge one of our editorial members in particular, Dr. Alasdair MacDonald, for his help with the early envisioning of this book and his work on planning it with Insoo Kim Berg.

Many assistants helped us along the way. We would to thank Katherine Montgomery, MSW, Kristy Lagana Riordan, MSSW, Tiffany Ryan, MSSW, and all the others for their assistance in the preparation and editing of the manuscript. Finally, we would like to thank our families and friends who endured the sacrifice of time and attention that was necessary during the preparation, writing, and editing of this book.

■ EDITORIAL CONSULTANTS

Janet Beavin Bavelas, PhD
Professor Emeritus
Department of Psychology, University of Victoria, Victoria, BC, Canada

Harry Korman, MD
Psychiatrist and Family Therapist
Private Practice
Malmo, Sweden

Stephen Langer, PhD
Clinical Psychologist
Director
Nothwest Brief Therapy Training Center
Olympia, WA

Günter Lueger, PhD
Director
Solution Management Center
Vienna, Austria

Alasdair J. Macdonald, MB ChB, FRCPsych, DPM, DCH
Consultant Psychiatrist
Dorset Primary Care Trust, Dorchester, United Kingdom

■ CONTENTS

■ CONTRIBUTORS

Aneta Y. Anichkina, MD
Psychiatrist
Freelance Practitioner
Sofia, Bulgaria

Victoria Baldwin
Founding Principal
Garza High School
Austin, Texas

Janet Beavin Bavelas, PhD
Professor Emeritus
Department of Psychology
University of Victoria
Research Consultant
Victoria, British Columbia

Robin Bluestone-Miller, LCSW
Director
SFBT/WOWW Training Project
Family and School Partnerships Program
School of Social Work
Loyola University Chicago
Chicago, Illinois

Kaitlin Stewart Brigman, MSW
Social Worker
Valeo Behavioral Health
Lawrence, Kansas

Viktorija Čepukienė, PhD
Clinical Psychologist
Family clinics "Bendrosios medicinos
    praktika" (General Medicine
    Practice)
Lecturer
General Psychology Department
Vytautas Magnus University
Kaunas, Lithuania

Jacqueline Corcoran, PhD
Professor
School of Social Work
Virginia Commonwealth University
Richmond, Virginia

Peter De Jong, PhD, ACSW
Emeritus Professor
Calvin College
Grand Rapids, Michigan

James Derks, LCSW
Posthumous, Psychotherapist
Fredonia, Wisconsin

Yvonne Dolan, MA Psychology
Director
Institute for Solution Focused Therapy
Highland, Indiana

Cynthia Franklin, PhD, LCSW, LMFT
*Stienberg/Spencer Family Professor in
    Mental Health*
School of Social Work
University of Texas at Austin
Austin, Texas

J. Arthur Gillaspy, Jr., PhD
*Associate Professor of Psychology and
    Counseling*
Licensed Psychologist
University of Central Arkansas
Conway, Arkansas

Wallace J. Gingerich, PhD, LISW-S
Professor Emeritus
Mandel School of Applied Sciences
Case Western Reserve University
Cleveland, Ohio

Suzy Green, DPsyc (Clinical)
Adjunct Lecturer
Coaching Psychology Unit
University of Sydney
Sydney, Australia

Mary Beth Harris, PhD, LCSW
Clinical Associate Professor
School of Social Work
University of Southern
    California
San Diego, California

Stéphan Hendrick, PhD
*Clinical Psychologist and
    Family Therapist*
Associate Professor
Director of the Systemic and
    Psychodynamic Department
Mons University

Viv Hogg, DipSW/Ed
Social Work Team Manager
Gateshead Council
Gateshead, England

Luc Isebaert, MD
Senior Consultant
Department of Psychiatry and
    Psychosomatics
St. John's Hospital
Head of Teaching Faculty
Korzybski International
Brugge, Belgium

Chris Iveson, BSc
Solution-Focused Brief Therapist
BRIEF
London, England

Michael S. Kelly, PhD, MSW
Assistant Professor
School of Social Work
Loyola University Chicago
Chicago, Illinois

Johnny S. Kim, PhD, LICSW
Associate Professor
School of Social Welfare
University of Kansas
Lawrence, Kansas

Harry Korman, MD
Child Psychiatrist and Family Therapist
Owner
SIKT
Malmö, Sweden

Marilyn LaCourt, AAMFT, CICSW
Personal Coach and Consultant
Bully Prevention Programs
Brookfield, Wisconsin

Mo Yee Lee, PhD
Professor
College of Social Work
Ohio State University
Columbus, Ohio

Peter Lehmann, PhD
Associate Professor
School of Social Work
University of Texas at Arlington
Arlington, Texas

Eve Lipchik, ACSW, LMFT, LCSW
Psychotherapist
ICF Consultants, Inc.
Milwaukee, Wisconsin

Michele Liscio, LMFT
Family and Marriage Therapist
Private Practice
Parkland, Florida

**Alasdair J. Macdonald, MB ChB,
    FRCPsych, DPM, DCH**
Consultant Psychiatrist
Dorset Primary Care Trust
Children's Services
Dorset, England

Eric E. McCollum, PhD, LCSW LMFT
Professor and Program Director
Marriage and Family Therapy Program
Virginia Tech
Falls Church, Virginia

Jay McKeel, MS
Therapist, Trainer, and Supervisor
Private Practice
Laurel, Maryland

Mark McKergow, PhD, MBA, MSc, BSc
Director
The Centre for Solutions Focus at Work
  (sfwork)
Cheltenham, United Kingdom

Norio Mishima, MD, PhD
Director
Ikemi Memorial Clinic of Mind-Body
  Medicine
Fukuoka City, Japan

Katherine L. Montgomery, MSSW
Doctoral Student
School of Social Work
University of Texas at Austin
Austin, Texas

John J. Murphy, PhD
Professor of Psychology and Counseling
Licensed Psychologist
University of Central Arkansas
Conway, Arkansas

Elam Nunnally, PhD
Posthumous
Professor Emeritus
Helen Bader School of Social
  Welfare
University of Wisconsin-Milwaukee
Milwaukee, Wisconsin

Rytis Pakrosnis, PhD
Clinical Psychologist
Private practice
Consultant
UAB Smarta
Lecturer
General Psychology Department
Vytautas Magnus University
Kaunas, Lithuania

Plamen A. Panayotov, MD
Chief Physician
Rousse Regional Psychiatric Dispensary
Rousse, Bulgaria

Joy D. Patton, PhD, MSSW, MA
Assistant Professor
Counseling and Human Services
University of North Texas Dallas
Dallas, Texas

Katherine Sanchez, PhD,
Assistant Professor
The University of Texas at Arlington,
School of Social Work,
Arlington, Texas

John Sebold, LCSW
Clinical Director
Plumas County Mental Health
Quincy, California

Guy Shennan, BA, MA, MA, CQSW
Solution-Focused Practitioner and Trainer
Guy Shennan Associates
London, England

Lee Shilts, PhD
Professor
Family Therapy Department
Nova Southeastern University
Fort Lauderdale, Florida

Sara A. Smock, PhD
Assistant Professor
Department of Applied and Professional
 Studies
Center for the Study of Addiction and
 Recovery
Texas Tech University
Lubbock, Texas

Geert J. J. M. Stams, PhD
Professor
Department of Forensic Child and Youth
 Care Sciences
Faculty of Social and Behavioral Sciences
University of Amsterdam
Amsterdam, the Netherlands

Sandra M. Stith, PhD
Professor Program Director
Marriage and Family Therapy Program
Kansas State University
Manhattan, Kansas

Boyan E. Strahilov, MD
Coach, Therapist, and Trainer
PIK Center
Sofia, Bulgaria

Sanna J. Thompson, PhD, MSW
Associate Professor
School of Social Work
University of Texas at Austin
Austin, Texas

Cynthia J. Thomsen, PhD
Research Psychologist
Naval Health Research Center
San Diego, California

Terry S. Trepper, PhD
Professor of Psychology
Department of Behavioral Sciences
Purdue University Calumet
Hammond, Indiana

Adriana Uken, LCSW
Trainer and Consultant
Chester, California

Linda Webb, PhD
Principal
Garza High School
Austin, Texas

John Wheeler, BSc, MA
UKCP Registered Systemic
 Psychotherapist
Child and Adolescent Mental Health
 Unit
Queen Elizabeth Hospital
Gateshead, United Kingdom
Independent Trainer, Supervisor, and
 Consultant
John Wheeler Solutions Ltd
Ryton, United Kingdom

Origins and Treatment Manual for Solution-Focused Brief Therapy

1 The Evolution of Solution-Focused Brief Therapy

■ EVE LIPCHIK, JAMES DERKS,
MARILYN LACOURT, AND ELAM NUNNALLY

■ INTRODUCTION

The solution-focused brief therapy (SFBT) model (de Shazer, 1985; de Shazer et al., 1986; Walter & Peller, 1992) evolved out of the brief family therapy (BFT) approach (de Shazer, 1982) between 1978 and 1984, long before the words *evidence-based practice* became an integral part of the medical and mental health vocabulary. However, from its beginning, SFBT was grounded in research about what works in therapy. Subsequently, its practitioners and researchers used a variety of research methods to study the mechanisms of solution-focused change and outcomes. Several examples of these methods are presented in this book, but the chapters do not do justice to the thousands of hours of clinical observations and data collected by those who have both studied and contributed to the model's development.

At the beginning, the team at the Brief Family Therapy Center (BFTC) utilized a research approach that relied on clinical observations and client data to discover which therapeutic techniques would most effectively facilitate behavioral change. Only recently has SFBT been studied through the lens of efficacy research and evidence-based practice.

In this chapter we, the original team members, chronicle how we actually used an evidence-based process to develop the model; how the approach evolved from a brief family therapy model to a therapeutic approach that focuses on future solutions; and the specific theory and interventions that made SFBT both similar to and different from other therapies. The core therapeutic components of SFBT evolved from a collaborative effort by a group of people imbued with the spirit of inquiry that was facilitated by Steve de Shazer. Essentially, the underlying question that drove all our work was "What works in brief therapy?"

Evidence-based practice has been defined as the integration of the best research evidence with clinical expertise and client values. As team members and experienced clinicians, we were dedicated to developing an approach that matched our clients' worldview, and that produced research evidence that the problems that brought our clients to the clinic were alleviated. We borrow here from the main definition used in evidence-based medicine to discuss what we mean by the type of research that we valued from the start. As the preface of this book suggests, this definition remains important to current research on SFBT, including the studies that are reported in this book.

> By best research evidence we mean clinically relevant research often from the basic sciences of medicine, but especially from patient-centered clinical research into the accuracy and precision of diagnostic tests (including the clinical examination), the power of prognosis markers, and the efficacy and safety of therapeutic, rehabilitative and preventive regimens. New evidence from clinical research both invalidates previously accepted diagnostic tests and treatments and replaces them with new ones that are more powerful, more accurate, more efficacious, and safer.
>
> By clinical expertise we mean the ability to use our clinical skills and past experience to rapidly identify each patient's unique health state and diagnosis, their individual risks and benefits of potential interventions, and their personal values and expectations.
>
> By patient values we mean the unique preferences, concerns and expectations each patient brings to a clinical encounter and which must be integrated into clinical decisions if they are to serve the patient.
>
> When these three elements are integrated, clinicians and clients form a diagnostic and therapeutic alliance which optimizes clinical outcomes and quality of life.
>
> —Sackett et al. (2000, p. 1)

■ THE CORE THERAPEUTIC ELEMENTS OF SFBT

This evidence-based approach to the development of SFBT has led to several codifications of the core therapeutic elements of this therapy. In a treatment manual developed to "help standardize the implementation of SFBT by practitioners and increase treatment fidelity of the model," the Research Committee of the Solution-Focused Brief Therapy Association (SFBTA) identified three components as representing SFBT:

1. use of conversations centered on clients' concerns
2. conversations focused on coconstructing new meanings surrounding clients' concerns
3. use of specific techniques to help clients coconstruct a vision of a preferred future and to draw upon past successes and strengths to help resolve issues (Trepper et al., 2008)

Other reviews of SFBT research have identified the following techniques and core components (de Shazer & Berg, 1997; Gingerich & Eisengart, 2000):

1. using a miracle question
2. using a scaling question
3. scheduling a consulting break and giving the client a set of compliments
4. assigning homework tasks
5. looking for strengths or solutions
6. setting goals
7. looking for exceptions to the problem

These descriptions of what constitutes SFBT are a comfortable fit with the world of research. Both the techniques and the change processes of SFBT have been widely applied and studied, but it is less well known how SFBT techniques were created through continuous observations by multiple observers and by the study of brief therapy outcomes with clients. This chapter will describe the evidence-based process used in the early development of SFBT, and will show how clinical and empirical evidence was used to develop and evaluate new techniques and methods as they evolved from the clinical practice of the original group at the BFTC.

Developing the Building Blocks of SFBT

In the early 1970s, Insoo Berg, Jim Derks, Elam Nunnally (a professor of social work at the University of Wisconsin-Milwaukee), Judith Tietyen, Don Norum, and some other social workers were practicing family therapy at Family Service of Milwaukee. At the time, most of the therapists at Family Service favored psychodynamic models of psychotherapy. Insoo, Don, and Jim were graduates of the Family Institute of Chicago, where they had been exposed to the brief therapy approach of the Mental Research Institute (MRI) (Watzlawick & Weakland, 1977; Watzlawick et al 1974). By the mid-1970s, this group of therapists had installed a one-way mirror at Family Service, and had begun to experiment with MRI's ideas. Marilyn LaCourt and Eve Lipchik came to Family Service in 1978 as trainees in Family Service's family therapy training program that was accredited by the American Association for Marriage and Family Therapy (AAMFT).

Steve de Shazer, also a social worker, was living and working in Palo Alto, California, in the 1970s. He, too, was very interested in the work being done at MRI. When Insoo and Jim went to MRI for some training in brief therapy, Insoo and Steve met and recognized that they shared similar interests and goals. Eventually, Steve returned to Milwaukee, his home town, and he and Insoo were married. Steve joined Insoo and her like-minded colleagues at Family Service of Milwaukee. This forward-thinking group read about and discussed the innovative ideas of Haley (Haley, 1963; Haley & Hoffman, 1967), MRI (Watzlawick et al., 1974), and the Milan group (Selvini Palazzoli et al., 1978). They pondered questions like this: "In psychodynamic work, it is said that it takes seven sessions for clients to engage in therapy. How could we tell from observing clients and their reports in the second session whether the first session worked?"

Soon a small group began to meet at Insoo and Steve's house to continue experimenting and discussing new ideas. We did pro bono therapy for experimental purposes. The clients were friends, or friends of friends, who either could not afford therapy elsewhere or were willing to participate in this experiment out of altruism or curiosity. We called our work *brief family therapy* (BFT). Though similar to the MRI approach, BFT was a broader concept. It followed the general systems theory assumption of equifinality: that as long as a problem is considered from a systemic point of view, there are multiple opportunities for intervention rather than just one.

The interviews were conducted in Insoo and Steve's living room by one person while a team observed. The observers and interviewer took a break toward the end of the session in an upstairs bedroom to discuss their observations and developed a message for the clients. The sessions were taped by Marilyn LaCourt, with her video camera, in the corner of the living room, while observers sat on the stairs to the second floor. In keeping with the MRI and Milan models, the observers and the interviewer took a break toward the end of the session (in an upstairs bedroom) to discuss their impressions and ideas and to develop a message for the clients. From the beginning, the goal was to understand what interventions resulted in client satisfaction with the changes.

In 1978, these informal meetings at Insoo and Steve's house were formalized in the establishment of the BFTC, a for-profit, state-certified clinic/think tank/training center with a nonprofit arm that was eligible for grant money. The participants in this venture all contributed close to $1,000 each to get it off the ground. The core staff of this new clinic consisted of Steve, Insoo, Jim Derks, Elam Nunnally, Marilyn LaCourt, and Eve Lipchik. Unfortunately, a number of people who were interested in and had participated in the experimental sessions in the home setting up to this point, were unable to join this core group. It was clear from the start that there would be no salary until a client base was established. Only people who had a partner with an income had the luxury of waiting for that to happen. For example, Don Norum of Family Service, who had written a paper called "The Client Has the Solution" in 1979 (Norum, 2000), and Judith Tietyen, an active group participant, were unable to leave their jobs to work at BFTC because they were the breadwinner of their family. Dr. Marvin Wiener, the only physician who had participated, left Milwaukee at that point. Insoo did not leave Family Service for a year after BFTC was founded because of the need to support Steve and herself.

As predicted, business was slow when BFTC started. However, this situation had the benefit of allowing time for a lot of observation and thought. Steve and Jim Derks staffed the BFTC office by themselves until the core group gathered regularly. This gave them the opportunity to spend a lot of time watching videotapes and asking questions like "What are we doing?" and "Why are we doing it?" Later, when the core group met regularly, we spent at least 4 hours a day discussing cases and watching videotapes to determine what worked. Steve outlined these discussions on the chalkboard.

de Shazer wrote that the model from which SFT developed was "historically rooted in a tradition that starts with Milton H. Erickson and flows through Gregory Bateson (1979) and the group of therapists-thinkers at the MRI" (de Shazer, 1982, p. xi) and that "the influence of Buddhist and Taoist thought upon the epistemology and the model is central" (p. x).

■ **METHODS FOR DEVELOPING SFBT**

In the course of BFT's development, the team always tried to use theory to guide practice and to further test the theory-driven practices with clients. Various theories were tested as a possible framework, and some of them had a big impact on the development of the model. These theories include homeostasis versus morphogenesis (Hoffman, 1971); Heider's balance theory (Heider, 1946); Cronen's "strange" and "charmed loops" (Cronen et al., 1982); catastrophe theory (Thom, 1975); and Axelrod's theory of cooperation (Axelrod, 1984). However, our thinking during these explorations of theory was still ecosystemic and problem focused. After SFBT evolved, the framework of choice became social constructivism. However, one underlying principle that never changed was the dedication to a minimalist philosophy derived from Occam's Razor: "Entities should not be multiplied more than necessary."

The Team That Developed SFBT

Like MRI and the Milan group, the team at BFTC used experienced therapists and researchers to develop its practices. Observing peers, including therapists and interested researchers, were considered consultants. They watched the clinical work from behind a one-way mirror. Thus, the first BFTC office was a large room divided by a narrow room with a mirror facing either side. Sessions were conducted even before the mirrors were installed, and clients saw the silent observers through the hole in which the mirrors were later placed. The observers and the conductor took a break with each other toward the end of the session in a room away from the clients' sight and hearing. After the group composed the intervention message, the conductor rejoined the clients and read the message and homework task to them.

After the mirror was installed, the team sometimes called the conductor out for a conference before the break at the end of the session when one or all members of the team had an idea about taking the interview in a different direction or wanted specific information.

In the early days, the team behind the mirror usually consisted of the core group and students (Alex Molnar, Pat Bielke, Dave Pakenham, Michele Weiner-Davis, John Walter, Jane Peller, and others). Within a few years, it also included research assistants (Wally Gingerich, Gale Miller, and former students like Alex Molnar and Michele Weiner-Davis), invited colleagues from Milwaukee and other parts of the United States (Marilyn Bonjean, Lyman Wynn, Brad Keeney, Bill O'Hanlon, Yvonne Dolan, Carl Tomm, and others), and eventually people from all over the world (Michael White, Michael Durrant, Brian Cade, and others). In 1984, Jim Wilk, an American living in England, joined the group as staff for a brief period. He and Steve studied the hypnotic aspects of our therapeutic process.

We all came from different backgrounds and varied in the perspective we could offer during discussions. Steve had come from a behavioral background; Insoo was from a family systems background; Elam was steeped in both family and communication theory; Marilyn came from a communication background; and Eve had a psychodynamic background. This diversity of views was considered an advantage because we believed that observations from different perspectives would generate more opportunities for useful interventions and homework assignments.

During the time when we at BFTC were still problem focused, the team had the habit of giving cases names, like "The Piano Case," The Wicked Stepmother," and "Picky-Picky." These names had various origins. They were our way of assuring client confidentiality, but they also reflected our reactions to clients: characteristics of their personalities, their appearance, or an issue they were dealing with. For people who eschewed diagnostic categories, our often comic and frequently judgmental names now seem highly inappropriate. However, as we focused more on solutions, this habit fell by the wayside. Now assumptions like "Clients have strengths and resources to help themselves" and "Nothing is all negative" guided us and changed the color of our glasses to a much rosier hue.

Gale Miller, a professor of Social and Cultural Sciences at Marquette University, who sat behind the mirror at BFTC for a year in 1984 and returned in 1989, studied the process at BFTC from the perspective of language and meaning. The following is his impression of life behind the mirror:

> [T]here would be people going in and out of the observations area all the time. The flow of activity was fascinating—there would be people observing a session from beginning to end, and a lot of people coming in and out, conversation about matters others than therapy, Insoo asking about scheduling a client, people would call home to check on

their families. There was a door from the observation room into the main part of the building, so people would go out that door to go to the bathroom. This was kind of home for a lot of therapists who would come for the afternoon and stay till 8 or 9 at night. People would order pizza, eat vegetables, Insoo and others did stretching exercises on the floor. My sense was that the staff put in 12–13 hour days so they had to do something to stay alert!"

—McKergow (2009, pp. 80–81)

Life behind the one-way mirror was irreverent at times and may have seemed disorganized, but if anyone had asked an observer what was going on in front of the mirror, they would have gotten a surprisingly coherent reply. Moreover, everyone involved was intensely interested in the outcome. David Kiser (1995) reported that in 1983, 25% of clients were called randomly and asked whether their problem had been solved by therapy; whether the change had lasted; and whether the change had generalized to any other aspects of their lives. The results showed that seventy-three percent of clients said that their goals had been met or that their problems were significantly reduced; 13 percent reported further changes.

The Interview

We implemented the goal of unbiased observation as a means of understanding clients and finding a way to help them from the start. When clients called for an appointment, the only information they were asked for was basic demographics. Thus, the interviewing therapist (the *conductor*) and the team had no prior information about a case. If the referral was made by another professional who sent case notes, we did not read them before meeting the client. We wanted to keep our observations as untainted as possible. It was more difficult to ignore information provided during telephone referrals, but we all made an effort to do so as much as possible.

At the first appointment, clients were asked for written permission to have their session videotaped for educational purposes. If they were uncertain, the conductor explained the purpose of videotaping again at the start of the session. If clients still refused to be videotaped, we did not tape them. The conductor also explained the use of the one-way mirror and the purpose of the team behind it. At the time, we did not permit clients to meet the team. We believed that the message from the team might be more powerful if it came from a mysterious source. If a client refused to be interviewed in front of the mirror, we referred him or her elsewhere, because we considered every session to be a research opportunity and did not want to deviate from that goal.

Once the introductory formalities were concluded, the conductor's job was to *join* with clients; that meant a few minutes of superficial socializing before asking about the client's reason for the appointment. After that, the conductor's task was to gather information that would enable the team to compose an intervention message and a homework task. The role of the conductor actually reflected our collaborative process, since only an actively participating member of the team could understand what information was necessary for this purpose. In the early days of BFTC, the necessary information was primarily about the clients' perceptions of their problem, their general worldview, and their interactional patterns, which were obtained by asking circular questions (Selvini Pallazoli et al. 1978). For example, a child might be asked, "What does Dad do when you don't brush your teeth?" "What does Mom do?" "What does Mom do when Dad doesn't agree with her?" "What do you do then?"

In the early 1980s, we expanded the number of circular questions to provide better scaffolding for the model (Lipchik & de Shazer, 1986). The questions were now called:

Direct questions, which gather information about how the complaints are viewed at present and how they arose

Constructive questions, which are future-oriented inquiries about possible solutions

Individual questions, which seek information about why a person thinks a problem exists; when he or she thinks it began; what the reasons for it are; and what will have to happen for the situation to change

Systemic questions, which search for information about differences and relationships, such as who is most affected by the problem; how family members react to each other; and how family members will interact differently when the problem no longer exists (Lipchik & de Shazer, 1986)

The conductor also asked questions that the team members wanted answered during the session. This was accomplished early on with a knock on the consultation room door or on the one-way mirror, signaling the conductor to step out, and later by a telephone hookup between the consultation room and the viewing room. Not long after the mirror was in use, a client's request for direct feedback from the observers led to the crumbling of the wall between the clients, the conductor, and the observing team. This signaled the birth of BFT as an ecosystemic approach that viewed the conductor and team members (the therapy team) and the client's family as subsystems of a larger suprasystem that produced change as a result of its ecological connections (de Shazer, 1982, p. xiii).

Much later, when BFT morphed into SFT, the interview rather than the intervention became the primary agent of change. This elevated the role of the conductor to that of interviewing therapist, who utilized techniques (e.g., exception questions, miracle questions, coping questions, and scaling questions) as interventions to elicit and build on clients' experience and resources. This, in turn, affected the team behind the mirror, whose messages and tasks were now designed to reinforce the strengths and resources of clients discovered during the interview, as well as to stimulate more options for solutions between sessions.

The Consultation Break

The purpose of the consultation break was to facilitate the development of the intervention message and the homework task. The format used was similar to that used at MRI and by the Milan group, as well as in the training program at Family Service of Milwaukee before BFTC was founded. The boundary of a one-way mirror offered the team the opportunity to obtain different information than the conductor could obtain. The team was able to have a more detached view as it observed interactional patterns and body language, and its members had the luxury of free communication with each other during the interview. Prior to the development of SFT, our conversations behind the mirror were, more often than not, free associations that ranged from the ridiculous to the sublime as we tried to be creative about interrupting dysfunctional patterns. Nothing was considered off limits for the sake of doing something different. After all, intervening at any point could make "a difference that makes a difference" (Bateson, 1979, p. 109). We might decide to consult the I Ching; ask a fighting couple to hand each other a cookie whenever they felt angry with each other; or suggest to parents that they squirt water at their misbehaving child with a squirt gun.

In accordance with the binocular theory of change (de Shazer, 1982, pp. 7–18), which guided our work at the time, interventions had to be isomorphic with the clients' view of the problem. The word *isomorphic* means that two complex structures can be mapped onto each other in such a way that for each part of one structure there is a cor-responding part in the other structure, where *corresponding* means that the two parts play similar roles in their respective structures. This use of the word *isomorphic* is derived from a more precise notion in mathematics (Hofstadter, 1979, p. 49).

We thought that the different perception clients obtained from the intervention would interrupt their dysfunctional patterns. Consequently, it was important to design interventions that fit the clients' perception of the problem, their interactions, and their worldview. The squirt gun task, for example, was likely to be given to parents who appeared to be fun-loving but who were also quite angry with their child and needed a way to express the anger in a harmless manner.

Conductors, on the other hand, who were face-to-face with clients, obviously observed body language and interactions as well, but focused more intently on verbal interaction with the clients and on making choices about what to ask, what to ignore, and how to respond to answers. When they left clients to come behind the mirror during the consultation break, we greeted them either with a suggested message and task or with the question "So, what do you think?" Then a discussion would ensue in which everyone participated. However, regardless of how messages and tasks were finally developed, the conductors (except for students) had the final say about what they would tell clients upon returning to the consultation room. The reason for this was that the conductors' face-to-face experience with the clients was considered the most telling information of all.

The Intervention Message

Anyone watching from behind the mirror at BFTC in the early 1980s would have described the therapy as strategic and as utilizing paradoxical interventions. After the ecosystemic perspective came to guide our thinking, this situation gradually changed. de Shazer believed that when paradoxical interventions or symptom prescriptions (Soper & L'Abate, 1977; Weeks & L'Abate, 1973) are viewed in an ecosystemic context, they are really a class of isomorphic interventions because they are "a counter double bind, a mirror image, which is appropriate to the structure of the family's pathogenic double bind" (de Shazer, 1982, p. 17). He believed that paradoxical interventions should not be reified and viewed as the actual cause of change, but rather as fitting isomorphically with the family's own paradoxical pattern. From this perspective, seemingly paradoxical intervention messages or homework assignments could be seen as joining, or *cooperating*. This is quite different from MRI's use of these interventions for indirect systemic pattern interruption to allow the system to reorganize in its own way (Watzlawick et al., 1974) and the counterparadoxical prescriptions of the Milan team (Selvini Palazzoli et al., 1978).

de Shazer first described cooperating in 1982 (pp. 9–10) as follows:

Each family (individual or couple) shows a unique way of attempting to cooperate, and the therapist's job becomes first, to describe that particular manner to himself that the family shows and, then, to cooperate with the family's way, and thus, to promote change.

Thus, the conductor's and team's observations about how they believed the family cooperated was essential information for intervention design. This was particularly true of the response to the homework assignment and any information offered about change, for better or for worse. Some clients did the tasks as prescribed; others did the opposite. Some modified them or did not do them at all. Every response was considered the client's way of cooperating and was used as evidence for deciding how to assign subsequent tasks. In *Patterns of Brief Family Therapy*, de Shazer illustrates how clients' patterns of response can be charted to help the therapist decide on the best therapeutic pattern of cooperating (1982, pp. 57–58). He was fond of using decision trees, which he and Alex Molnar developed together throughout the evolution of BFT and SFT to clarify and keep the therapeutic process as simple as possible (de Shazer & Molnar, 1984; Molnar & de Shazer, 1987).

The Importance of Compliments

In both BFT and SFT, the format for the intervention message started with compliments. This was probably due to the influence of positive connotation used by the Milan team, but de Shazer said that "the intention of compliments was to encourage clients to continue therapy . . . that saying nice things to them was more likely to bring them back" (Kiser, 1995, p.126). We had all observed that compliments elicited a change of mood in clients, but before we completely embraced a solution-focused way of working and were still problem focused, our interest was in the negative responses in order to learn what not to do. Jim Derks remembered that "We began to notice that we could encourage more cooperation in clients if we complimented them." Marilyn LaCourt added that "Compliments themselves were frequently a reframe of an attempted solution the clients did not think was working." For example, in response to a client's statement about his child ("I keep telling her not to do X"), the compliment would be "The team is impressed with your willingness to continue to try to persuade your daughter that X is not good for her, even though it isn't working. You must care very deeply about her." The result of giving compliments and observing how clients responded to them was a direct step toward asking clients questions about positives in their lives, as well as strengths and resources, rather than details about their problems.

The hypnotherapist Milton Erickson was very influential in the development of psychotherapy, and BFT used many of his techniques (Havens, 2003). Ericksonian hypnosis had greatly influenced the use of a consultation break, and in particular the effect of compliments. Erickson described five benefits for clients while they wait for the therapist's message during a consultation break (Schmidt & Trenkle, 1985, p. 143):

- It heightens attention on what the therapist will say upon returning.
- It leads to relaxation when the therapist's message expresses acceptance and understanding.
- It offers difference by means of surprise, relief, and distraction from the client's view of the problem.
- It offers continuity because it reflects the client's language and manner of cooperating.
- In a trance-like state, clients are more receptive to information.

We observed that clients began to nod their heads when the conductor started to compliment them. This response is referred to as a sign of the *yes set* (de Shazer, 1982; Erickson & Rossi, 1979; Erickson et al., 1976). The *yes set* led to one of the first research investigations at BFTC. A student was instructed to count and record the number of head nods during the compliments. Some graduate students were also involved in watching videotapes without sound and recording head nods. The objective was to find out whether there was a correlation between the number of client head nods and client compliance with tasks. In his dissertation on SFT, David Kiser quotes Insoo Berg as saying that this was a crucial point. "That was the beginning of thinking about this interactional aspect of a client and therapist. Prior to that, we never thought of looking at what we were doing; [instead] we would study the clients a lot. We didn't study ourselves" (Kiser, 1995, p. 128).

Compliments were followed by a statement called *the clue,* which was based on the therapeutic team's observations of the clients' response to the interview and to previous interventions, as well as reported change or lack of it. Sometimes the message offered information (e.g., about the behavior of children and adolescents) and/or alternative perspectives by means of reframing or normalizing. In the true ecosystemic manner, the team's observations of the clients' reactions to the team's actions were really a metaobservation of the suprasystem (the family system and the therapeutic system) that informed the therapy system how to proceed.

Homework Tasks

The last part of the intervention was the homework task. This was thought of as a pattern interruption at first and was frequently arrived at in many different, often wildly creative ways. Given the importance of the intervention, a great deal of effort and thought was devoted to it.

An early research effort was the accidental result of not having the video camera and the VTR behind the mirror with the team (as it is now). Instead, it was in a separate room, meaning we used a three-room suite which considered of a therapy room, an observation room, and a video room. The video room was also a working office, with a typewriter. Usually the person assigned to videotaping did the job with the sound turned off, while occupied with other tasks.

One day (in 1979) while in the video room, Alex Molnar and Steve de Shazer turned on the sound and watched [a tape]. Their discussion shifted from just talking about their observations and what the intervention might look like to speculating about what kind of intervention the rest of the team (who were in the observation room) might develop. As a lark, they developed an intervention which they planned to compare with the one the therapy team developed. When they later compared their intervention with that of the therapy team, they found it to include the same homework assignment and some of the same compliments. However, as they compared how they had arrived at their interventions, it became clear that their thinking had come from several widely different directions. For a period of time, this comparison activity continued, which greatly contributed to our understanding of where interventions come from.

This research also led to our current routine in situations where two training teams observe the same case. During the intermission, each team goes to its own room and designs an intervention. Later on, the two intervention messages are compared for similarities and differences. This comparison not only helps trainees understand how to construct interventions, but also demonstrates to them the useful notion that *there is no one right intervention.*

—Nunnally et al. (1986, p. 82) (emphasis added.)

Once work at BFTC became solution focused, the intervention messages changed. The team and the interviewing therapist developed compliments together that focused on positive changes they observed; intervention messages aimed at reinforcing reported changes; and tasks that were less complex and outrageous. Tasks also tended to be more open-ended and allowed clients to interpret them in their own way, which in turn provided the therapeutic team with new information about how to help them to build solutions.

Formula First Session Task

Once the ecosystemic foundation had been laid, it was just a small step from BFT to SFT. Like much of the developmental growth of the model, the decisive step occurred in a serendipitous manner. In 1982, a team member behind the mirror suggested that instead of giving the frequently used task at the end of the session that asked clients to make a list of what they *wanted* to change, we should ask them what they *didn't* want to change. The team agreed, as they always did when something was new and different. The clients came back and reported what they did not want to change, but also reported some positive changes in their situation. We recognized immediately that something very significant was happening and that we should explore this question further. The same results occurred when we tested the question several more times. This investigation led to the development of a generic first session task, the formula first session task (FFST):

> Between now and next time we meet, we would like you to observe, so that you can describe to us next time, what happens in your (pick one: family, life, marriage, relationship) that you want to continue to have happen.
>
> —de Shazer (1985, p. 137)

The wording of this task was an improvement on the former one that asked what clients did not want to change, because it was more positive and made an assumption of change. The FFST was given to 100 clients, and the reactions were recorded and studied. Trainees were involved in this study as well. They, as well as the therapists, were instructed to use this task in every case unless they could justify not using it. The reason someone chose not to use it also provided valuable information. For example, the task was usually inappropriate in a first session in which the client had reported having suffered a loss.

David Kiser quotes Marilyn LaCourt as describing the importance of this project:

> And so that piece of research, I think, was an important marker. Up until that time we were looking for a specific solution to a specific problem, but then we noticed that people came back changed, or changing, and that the changes were not necessarily connected to the complaint, but nevertheless they were satisfied or that they were liking the changes. So at any rate, I think that was the beginning or the marker for the next real important piece which is how do you disconnect the solution from the problem and does the

outcome of therapy always have to be that the solution is connected to the problem. And of course the answer is "no."

People reported change from the first session to the second even though we had not asked them to look for change, necessarily. . . . So then when they would come back with something positive that happened, we would ask, "Is that different?" or, "Is that something that's been going on all along?" And then if they would say it was different, well then the next question would be "How did you get that to happen?"

—Kiser (1995, p. 102)

Thus, we suddenly realized that we had transitioned from being problem focused to being solution focused. A review of videotapes of sessions conducted during the past year led to the recognition that the first few sessions during which the complaint was investigated and the problem was defined could be eliminated. A therapist could now move from the clients' statement of the problem directly to their goals and then to solution construction.

■ SFT EMERGES

The focus on solutions opened up more opportunities for investigating the process. Gingerich and colleagues (1988) developed a coding system around 1985 that was used to analyze when and how frequently the therapeutic conversations were about change. They discovered that first sessions contained little *change talk*, whereas subsequent sessions contained significantly more of it. As a result, they developed questions that therapists could ask to elicit change talk as soon as therapy began. For example, they would ask clients, "What, if anything, are you already doing to solve the problem?" Awareness of these dynamics played a big role in the development of the techniques (exception questions, miracle questions, coping questions, and others) for which SFT became known all over the world.

Presession Change

Presession change was another facet of discovering clients' inherent ability to solve their own problems. According to Michele Weiner-Davis, she first got the idea of investigating presession change when a client mentioned at the end of the first session that her son had already begun to try harder at school, and the therapist reinforced that change. She initiated an informal research project during which 30 initial intakes were asked: "Many times people notice in between the time they make the appointment for therapy and the first session that things already seem different. What have you noticed about your situation?"

Twenty clients noticed changes. Michele Weiner-Davis and her research colleagues de Shazer and Gingerich (1987) then found ways to reinforce these pre–first-session exceptions to the problem with questions that helped clients build on these changes, like "What do you need to do to continue these changes?" "What might present an obstacle to these changes 'sticking'?" "How would you overcome these obstacles?"

Assumptions of change created during the interview and with the intervention message were an important part of BFT and continue to be so in SFT. During the interview, the therapist's use of language builds expectations of change—for example, asking "What will be different when . . .?" rather than "What would be different if . . .?"

Kiser (1995, p. 129) quoted LaCourt with regard to the importance of the language of presupposed changed:

Steve, Elam and I were sitting there talking about, really talking about . . . the concept of cooperating and insisting on using the "ing" instead of cooperation. Then the language was very precise and it was very important that the language be precise because I think we were making a very conscious effort to train ourselves to think in terms of change as opposed to stability.

de Shazer (1985, p. 45) described it this way:

Once the therapist has created (or helped create) expectations that things are going to be different, next in importance is what the client expects to be different after the complaint is gone.

The Miracle Question

The miracle question was another building block of SFT. As the story goes, Jim Wilks was observing Steve de Shazer with a client in front of the mirror when Steve suddenly asked a question that was influenced by Milton Erickson's Crystal Ball Technique (Erickson, 1954): "If a miracle happened in the middle of the night when you were asleep and you woke up and the problem had been solved, how would you know that?" Jim had never heard that question before and asked Steve about it later. Steve said he just used it sometimes. Jim felt that this question was of great significance for the model; consequently, everyone was instructed to use it and observe the results. It soon became evident that the miracle question added a new dimension to therapy: a future orientation and an opportunity for people to build on their hopes and dreams for solutions, not only past and present strengths and resources.

Marilyn LaCourt remembers another marker in the road to a future focus. Around 1983, she was sitting behind the mirror when Eve Lipchik asked a question that caught her attention: "How will you know when you don't need to come here anymore?" The useful information this question produced for therapist and client alike led to its integration into the interviewing process.

■ RESEARCH METHODS USED AT THE BFTC

The BFTC was founded as a think tank and a place for research. The research was conceptualized not as we think of efficacy studies or formal outcome research today, but more as exploratory, practice-based research in a clinical setting intended to find new and more effective ways of working with clients. The discoveries from the research at BFTC were a recursive process involving theory, research, and practice that was more in line with the methods of qualitative research. This was a very appropriate method for the beginning stages of model building and the discovery of new techniques.

Thus for therapists at BFTC observing and hypothesizing about therapist–client interactions was research and theory building. Although founders certainly drew from others' ideas and theories, many of their ideas were based on grounded data (i.e. their clinical work and observations, and self-report of clients). Even the ideas they derived from others were often purposefully and directly tested in their clinical work.

—Kiser (1995, p. 98)

The modus operandi for all research completed at the BFTC on SFBT was to observe (live sessions and videotapes of sessions) in order to understand what encourages positive change. As early as 1979, for example, de Shazer reported watching Jim Derks conduct an interview and realizing that something was different—that they had developed a new method of relating one task to the response a family reported to the previous task. Jim said it wasn't different, but "business as usual." Studying tapes made [him] Steve realize they had been working this way for two years (de Shazer, 1982, p. x).

The development of SFT came about as a result of new data that sometimes arose as an "aha" moment but overall was a gradual process. Jim Derks described it recently like "watching rainwater run down a hill and following the flow." As the water flowed, it changed directions with the newly observed data. The perception of the therapist and client as an ecosystem rather than as separate entities occurred when a client asked for the team's feedback one day. Counting head nods during the yes set made us start studying what *we* were doing in relation to clients, not just studying the client. Scoring clients' responses to the delivery of intervention messages to predict clients' compliance with tasks led to the realization that the therapist played a part in client compliance. This realization piqued our curiosity and caused us to look at what the therapist team does, not only at what clients are doing. This led to the death of "resistance" and the birth of "cooperation." Spontaneous reactions like "Let's ask what they don't want to change" opened the gate to the FFST, which in turn led to refocusing from problem to solution. Compliments to start intervention messages shifted the interviewing process toward more questions about positives in clients' lives and away from problem details. A focus on solutions led to research on change talk that modified the routing of the interviewing process. Therapists began to ask about exceptions, strengths, and resources immediately rather than probing the problem first. Pre–first-session change was noticed and asked for as soon as the therapist and client met. Jim Wilks' attention to de Shazer's sudden use of the miracle question one day opened up the path to exploring future possibilities with clients as part of solution construction. Language using the assumption of change was incorporated. Treatment became shorter and more focused on constructing solutions with clients based on their own resources rather than on clever intervention messages and tasks.

■ RESULTS OF RESEARCH ON SFBT FROM THE BFTC

Ultimately, the clinical observations and research conducted at the BFTC resulted in the worldwide dissemination of SFT. Even though the BFTC never produced a controlled outcome study, its therapists made continuous clinical observations, collected data on client satisfaction, and conducted program evaluations as a regular part of their daily work . Above all, most of them wrote about their experiences, which led other therapists to adopt them.

There were also some early clinical studies of SFBT's effectiveness. In 1984, de Shazer and Molnar designed a study to explore the outcomes of the FFST. "The task was given to 56 or 88 new clients. Of these, fifty (89%) reported that something worthwhile had happened, while six (11%) did not report anything happening that they wanted to continue to have happen. Forty-six (82%) new clients reported that at least one of the events they wanted to continue to have happen was new or different" (de Shazer, 1985, p. 155).

In another follow up survey, "treatment outcome was measured by asking clients at 6–18 months follow up to indicate if they had met their goals for therapy or felt that significant progress had been made. de Shazer (1985) reported an 82% success rate on follow up of 28 clients. In 1986, de Shazer, et al. reported a 72% success rate with a 25% sample of 1600 cases" (Gingerich & Eisengart, 2000, p. 478).

■ LOOKING TO THE FUTURE TO UNDERSTAND THE PAST

The authorship of this book reflects the global acceptance SFBT has achieved. The question we can now ask ourselves is: Were the clinical observations and continuous analysis that our pioneering therapy team did part of an evidence-based practice process? We believe that they were and that they can now be more rigorously tested. Our team's dedication to research was certainly a client-centered investigative process conducted with a lot of clinical expertise. Our techniques, while not validated by rigorous efficacy studies or investigations into the mechanisms of change, proved to work in clinical settings with clients, as indicated in the early studies mentioned above. These early studies at the BFTC provided a firm foundation for future studies of SFBT. This book describes research conducted on SFBT from the early days until the present time. When we, the early pioneers, consider this research and think about the future of SFBT, we see a therapy that, from the beginning, was grounded in research and aspired to follow an evidence-based practice process. Undoubtedly, these intentions made it the brief and effective approach it is today.

The formative years of SFT were exciting times—times of creativity, collegiality, and a sense of power. The many hours we spent together thinking, talking, and obsessing about cases were exhilarating and mind-expanding. We frequently expressed the feeling that other therapists could not help their clients as well as we could. This may sound like hubris, and it was, but this attitude spurred us on and kept advancing the work. However, credit for the success of SFT belongs to many people: those who worked at the BFTC on a daily basis for long hours, as well those who may have sat behind the mirror just once and noticed something important or asked a significant question that led to a new direction in our work. Gale Miller sums it up elegantly:

> People made a mistake when they associated all this (BFTC and its creative process and creations) with Steve and Insoo—they owned the place, but the work emerged within the interactions of a lot of creative people. The term I prefer is not to say that Steve and Insoo were the leaders, but eventually they became the ambassadors of SF therapy—the representatives as well as contributing leaders.
>
> —McKergow (2009, p. 81)

■ KEY POINTS TO REMEMBER

- The SFBT model (de Shazer, 1985; de Shazer et al., 1986; Walter & Peller, 1992) evolved out of the BFT approach (de Shazer, 1982) between 1978 and 1984 and was created by a team of experienced social workers and other therapists and researchers that worked at the BFTC in Milwaukee.
- The BFTC was founded as a think tank and a place for exploratory, practice-based research. The discoveries from the research at the BFTC emerged during a recursive process involving theory, research, and practice that was more in line with the methods of qualitative research and discovery than those of experimental designs.

- The team that developed SFBT used continuous observations (live sessions and videotapes of sessions) in order to understand what encouraged positive change in their clients. They also made use of client feedback, satisfaction surveys, and coding systems to understand the impact of SFBT on clients' behavior change.
- The solution-focused techniques developed at the BFTC have spread to several continents and continue to be studied using a variety of research designs including basic research, experimental and quasi-experimental designs, and process and qualitative approaches to research.

■ **FURTHER LEARNING**

Lipchik, E. (2002) Uncovering MRI roots in Solution-focused Therapy. *Ratkes* (4), 9–14. (A Finnish publication that can be contacted at http://www.ratkes.fi)

Lipchik, E. (2003). *Interview: Eve Lipchik with attitude*! Retrieved Oct. 2003, http://www.brieftherapynetwork.com

Lipchik, E. (2009). A solution focused journey. In E. Connie & L. Metcalf (Eds.), *The art of solution focused therapy* (pp. 21–45). New York: Springer.

Lipchik, E., Becker, M., Brasher, B, Derks, J., & Volkmann, J. (2005). Neuroscience: A new direction for solution-focused thinkers? *Journal of Systemic Therapies, 8,* 49–70.

Visser, C. F. (2009). *The think tank that created the solution-focused approach—interview with Eve Lipchik*. Retrieved Nov. 2009 http://interviewscoertvisser.blogspot.com/2009/11/thinktank-that-created-solution-focused.html

■ **REFERENCES**

Axelrod, R. (1984). *The evolution of cooperation*. New York: Basic Books.

Bateson, G. (1979). *Mind and nature: A necessary unity*. New York: Dutton.

Cronen, V., Johnson, K., & Lannamann, J. (1982). Paradoxes, double binds, and reflexive loops: An alternative theoretical perspective. *Family Process, 21,* 91–126.

de Shazer, S. (1982). *Patterns of brief family therapy: An ecosystemic approach*. New York: Guilford Press.

de Shazer, S. (1984). The death of resistance. *Family Process, 23,* 79–93.

de Shazer, S. (1985). *Keys to solution in brief therapy*. New York: Norton.

de Shazer, S., & Berg. I. K. (1997). What works? Remarks on research aspects of solution-focused brief therapy. *Journal of Family Therapy, 19,* 121–124.

de Shazer, S., Berg, I., Lipchik, E., Nunnally, E., Molnar, A., Gingerich, W., & Weiner- Davis, M. (1986). Brief therapy: Focused solution development. *Family Process, 25,* 207–222.

de Shazer, S., & Molnar, A. (1984). Four useful interventions in brief family therapy. *Journal of Marital and Family Therapy, 10,* 297–304.

Erickson, M. H. (1954). Pseudo-orientation in time as a hypnotherapeutic procedure. *Journal of Clinical and Experimental Hypnosis, 2,* 261–283.

Erickson, M. H., & Rossi, E. (1979). *Hypnotherapy: An exploratory casebook*. New York: Irvington.

Erickson, M. H., Rossi, E., & Rossi, S. (1976). *Hypnotic realities*. New York: Irvington.

Fisch, R.,Weakland, J., & Segal, L. (1983). *The tactics of change: Doing therapy briefly*. San Francisco: Jossey-Bass.

Gingerich, W. J., de Shazer, S., & Weiner-Davis, M. (1988). Constructing change: A research view of interviewing. In E. Lipchik (Ed.), *Interviewing* (pp. 21–33). Rockville, MD: Aspen.

Gingerich, W. J., & Eisengart, S. (2000). Solution-focused brief therapy: A review of the outcome research. *Family Process, 39,* 477–498.

Haley, J. (1963). *Strategies of psychotherapy*. New York: Grune & Stratton.

Haley, J., & Hoffman, L. (1967). *Techniques of family therapy*. New York: Basic Books.

Havens, R. A. (2003). *The wisdom of Milton Erickson*. Bethel, CT: Crown House Publishing.

Heider, F. (1946). Attitudes and cognitive organization. *Journal of Psychology, 21*, 107–112.

Hoffman, L. (1971). Deviation-amplifying processes in natural groups. In J. Haley (Ed.), *Changing families*, 285–311, New York: Grune & Stratton.

Hofstadter, D. (1979). *Godel, Escher, Back: An eternal golden braid*. New York: Basic Books.

Kiser, D. J. (1995). *Process and politics of solution-focused therapy theory development: A qualitative analysis*. Unpublished dissertation, Purdue University.

Lipchik, E., & de Shazer, S. (1986). The purposeful interview. *Journal of Strategic and Systemic Therapies, 5*, 88–99.

McKergow, M. (2009). *Gale Miller: The man behind the mirror behind the mirror at BFTC. Interaction (1 and 2)*. Retrieved April 5, 2010, from http://www.asfct.org/documents/journal/2009–05/gale_miller.pdf

Miller, G. (1997). *Becoming miracle workers: Language and meaning in brief therapy*. Hawthorne, NY: Aldine de Guyter.

Molnar, A., & de Shazer, S. (1987). Solution-focused therapy: Toward the identification of therapeutic tasks. *Journal of Marital and Family Therapy, 13*, 349–358.

Norum, D. (2000). The family has the solution. *Journal of Systemic Therapies, 19*, 3–16.

Nunnally, E., de Shazer, S., Lipchik, E., & Berg, I. (1986). A study of change: Therapeutic theory in process. In D. E. Efron (Ed.), *Journeys: Expansion of the strategic-systemic therapies* (pp. 77–97). New York: Brunner/Mazel.

Sackett, D. L., Straus, S. E., Richardson, W. S., Rosenberg, W., & Haynes, R. B.(2000). *Evidence-based medicine: How to practice and teach EBM*. Edinburgh: Churchill Livingstone.

Schmidt, G., & Trenkle, B. (1985). An integration of Ericksonian techniques with concepts of family therapy. In J. K. Zeig (Ed.), *Ericksonian psychotherapy: Volume II. Clinical applications* (pp. 132–155). New York: Brunner/Mazel.

Selvini Palazzoli, M., Cecchin, G., Prata, G., & Boscolo, L. (1978). *Paradox and counterparadox: A new model in the therapy of the family in schizophrenic transaction*. New York: Jason Aronson.

Soper, P., & L'Abate, L. (1977). Paradox as a therapeutic technique. *International Journal of Family Counseling, 5*, 10–21.

Thom, R. (1975). *Structural stability and morphogenesis*. Reading, MA: Benjamin/Cummings.

Trepper, R. S., McCollum, E. E., DeJong, P., Korman, H., Gingerich, W., & Franklin, C. (2008). *Solution-focused therapy treatment manual for working with individuals: Research Committee of the Solution-Focused Brief Therapy Association*. Retrieved May 20, 2008, from http://www.sfbta.org/researchDownloads.html

Walter, J. L., & Peller, J. E. (1992). *Becoming solution-focused in brief therapy*. New York: Brunner/Mazel.

Watzlawick, P., & Weakland, J. (1977). *The interactional view*. New York: Norton.

Watzlawick, P., Weakland, J., & Fisch, R. (1974). *Change: Principles of problem formation and problem resolution*. New York: Norton.

Weiner-Davis, M., de Shazer, W., & Gingerich, W. J. (1987). Building on pretreatment change to construct the therapeutic solution: An exploratory study. *Journal of Marital and Family Therapy, 13*, 359–363.

2 Solution-Focused Brief Therapy Treatment Manual[1]

■ TERRY S. TREPPER, ERIC E. McCOLLUM, PETER
DE JONG, HARRY KORMAN, WALLACE
J. GINGERICH, AND CYNTHIA FRANKLIN

The purpose of this preliminary treatment manual is to offer an overview to the general structure of solution-focused brief therapy (SFBT). Treatment manuals often form the foundation of a psychotherapy approach, providing clinicians and researchers a structured view of the major components, methods, techniques, and interventions of an approach. They also are recommended to be used in any research endeavor so that uniformity in the presentation, timing, and actual interventions is present. Finally, almost all clinical trial studies funded by large agencies such as the National Institute of Mental Health require that the clinical approaches being investigated use treatment manuals to assure replicability in future research.

This manual will follow the standardized format and include each of the components recommended by Carroll and Nuro (1997). The following sections are included: (a) overview, description, and rationale of SFBT; (b) goals and goal setting in SFBT; (c) how SFBT is contrasted with other treatments; (d) specific active ingredients and therapist behaviors in SFBT; (e) nature of the client–therapist relationship in SFBT; (f) format; (g) session format and content; (g) compatibility with adjunctive therapies; (h) target population; (i) meeting the needs of special populations; (j) therapist characteristics and requirements; (j) therapist training; and (k) supervision.

■ OVERVIEW, DESCRIPTION, AND RATIONALE

Solution-focused brief therapy group treatment is based on over 20 years of theoretical development, clinical practice, and empirical research(e.g., de Shazer et al., 1986; Berg, 1994; Berg & Miller, 1992; De Jong & Berg (2008); de Shazer et al., 2007). Solution-focused brief therapy is different in many ways from traditional approaches to treatment. It is a competency-based model that minimizes emphasis on past failings and problems and instead focuses on clients' strengths and previous successes. There is an emphasis on working from the client's understandings of her or his concern/situation and what the client might want to change. The basic tenets that inform SFBT are as follows:

- It is based on solution building rather than problem solving.
- The therapeutic focus should be on the client's desired future rather than on past problems or current conflicts.
- Clients are encouraged to increase the frequency of current useful behaviors.
- No problem happens all the time. There are exceptions—that is, times when the problem could have happened but didn't—that can be used by the client and therapist to coconstruct solutions.
- Therapists help clients find alternatives to current undesired patterns of behavior, cognition, and interaction that are within the clients' repertoire or can be coconstructed by therapists and clients as such.
- Differing from skill building and behavior therapy interventions, the SFBT model assumes that solution behaviors already exist for clients.
- It is asserted that small increments of change lead to large increments of change.
- Clients' solutions are not necessarily *directly* related to any identified problem by either the client or the therapist.
- The conversational skills required of the therapist to invite the client to build solutions are different from those needed to diagnose and treat client problems.

Solution-focused brief therapy differs from traditional treatment in that traditional treatment focuses on exploring problematic feelings, cognitions, behaviors, and/or interactions, providing interpretations, confrontation, and client education (Corey, 1985). In contrast, SFBT helps clients develop a desired vision of the future wherein the problem is solved, and explore and amplify related client exceptions, strengths, and resources to coconstruct a client-specific pathway to making the vision a reality. Thus, each client finds his or her own way to a solution based on his or her emerging definitions of goals, strategies, strengths, and resources. Even in cases where the client comes to use outside resources to create solutions, it is the client who takes the lead in defining the nature of those resources and how they would be useful.

Solution-Focused Therapeutic Process

Solution-focused brief therapy utilizes the same process regardless of the concern that the individual client brings to therapy. The SFBT approach focuses on *how* clients change rather than on diagnosing and treating problems. As such, it uses a language of *change*. The signature questions used in solution-focused interviews are intended to set up a therapeutic process wherein practitioners listen for and absorb clients' words and meanings (regarding what is important to clients, what they want, and related successes), then formulate and ask the next question by connecting to clients' key words and phrases. Therapists then continue to listen and absorb as clients again answer from their frames of reference, and once again formulate and ask the next question by similarly connecting to the client's responses. It is through this continuing process of listening, absorbing, connecting, and client responding that practitioners and clients together coconstruct new and altered meanings that build toward solutions. Communication researchers McGee, Del Vento, and Bavelas (2005) describe this process as creating new common ground between practitioner and client in which questions that contain embedded assumptions of client competence and expertise set in motion a conversation in which clients participate in discovering and constructing themselves as persons of ability with positive qualities who are in the process of creating a more satisfying life. Examples of this therapeutic process are given below when the questions used in SFBT are presented.

General Ingredients of SFBT

Most psychotherapy, SFBT included, consists of *conversations*. In SFBT there are three main general ingredients to these conversations.

First, there are the overall topics. In SFBT, conversations are centered on client concerns: who and what is important to the clients; a vision of a preferred future; clients' exceptions, strengths, and resources related to that vision; scaling of clients' motivational level and confidence in finding solutions; and ongoing scaling of clients' progress toward reaching the preferred future.

Second, as indicated in the previous section, SF conversations involve a therapeutic process of coconstructing altered or new meanings in clients. This process is set in motion largely by therapists asking SF questions about the topics of conversation identified in the previous paragraph and connecting to and building from the resulting meanings expressed by clients.

Third, therapists use a number of specific responding and questioning techniques that invite clients to coconstruct a vision of a preferred future and draw on their past successes, strengths, and resources to make that vision a reality.

■ GOAL SETTING AND SUBSEQUENT THERAPY

The setting of specific, concrete, and realistic goals is an important component of SFBT. Goals[2] are formulated and amplified through SF conversation about what clients want to be different in the future. Consequently, in SFBT, clients set the goals. Once a beginning formulation is in place, therapy focuses on exceptions related to goals, regularly scaling how close clients are to their goals or a solution, and coconstructing useful next steps to reaching their preferred futures.

■ HOW SFBT IS CONTRASTED WITH OTHER TREATMENTS

Solution-focused brief therapy is most similar to competency-based, resiliency-oriented models, such as some of the components of motivational enhancement interviewing (Miller & Rollnick, 2002; Miller et al., 1994). There are also some similarities between SFBT and cognitive-behavioral therapy, although the latter model has the therapist assigning changes and tasks, while the SFBT therapist encourages the client to use more of his or her *own* previous exception behavior and/or test behaviors that are part of the client's description of his or her goal. In addition, SFBT has some similarities to narrative therapy (e.g., Freedman & Combs, 1996) in that both take a nonpathology stance, are client-focused, and work to create new realities as part of the approach. Solution-focused brief therapy is most dissimilar, in terms of underlying philosophy and assumptions, to any approach that requires "working through" or intensive focus on a problem to resolve it, or any approach that is primarily focused on the past rather than the present or future.

■ SPECIFIC ACTIVE INGREDIENTS

Some of the major active ingredients in SFBT include (a) developing a cooperative therapeutic alliance with the client; (b) creating a solution versus a problem focus; (c) setting measurable and changeable goals; (d) focusing on the future through future-oriented questions and discussions; (e) scaling the ongoing attainment of the goals to get the client's evaluation of the progress made; and (f) focusing the conversation on exceptions to the client's problems, especially those exceptions related to what he or she wants to be different; and (g) encouraging the client to do more of what he or she did to make the exceptions happen.

■ NATURE OF THE CLIENT–THERAPIST RELATIONSHIP

With SFBT, the therapist is seen as a collaborator and consultant, there to help clients achieve their goals. Clients do more of the talking, and what they talk about is considered the cornerstone of the resolution of their complaints. Usually, SFBT therapists will use more indirect methods such as extensive questioning about previous solutions and exceptions. In SFBT, the client is the expert, and the practitioner takes the stance of "not knowing" and of "leading from one step behind" through solution-focused questioning and responding.

■ FORMAT AND SESSION STRUCTURE

Much of the following discussion is taken from de Shazer et al. (2007).

Main Interventions

A Positive, Collegial, Solution-Focused Stance. One of the most important aspects of SFBT is the general tenor and stance taken by the therapist. The overall attitude is positive, respectful, and hopeful. There is a general assumption that people are extremely resilient and continuously utilize this resilience to make changes. Further, there is a strong belief that most people have the strength, wisdom, and experience to effect change. What other models view as "resistance" is generally seen as (a) people's natural protective mechanisms or realistic desire to be cautious and go slowly or (b) a therapist error, that is, an intervention that does not fit the client's situation. All of these factors make for sessions that tend to feel collegial rather than hierarchical (although, as noted earlier, SFBT therapists do lead from behind) and cooperative rather than adversarial.

Looking for Previous Solutions. In SFBT, therapists have learned that most people have previously solved many, many problems. This may have been at another time, in another place, or in another situation. The problem may have also come back. The key is that the person had solved the problem, even if only for a short time.

Looking for Exceptions. Even when a client does not have a previous solution that can be repeated, most clients have recent examples of exceptions to their problem.

An *exception* is thought of as a time when a problem could have occurred but did not. The difference between a previous solution and an exception is small but significant. A previous solution is something that the family has tried on their own that has worked, but for some reason they did not continue to use it and probably forgot about it. An exception is something that happens instead of the problem, with or without the client's intention or maybe even understanding.

Questions versus Directives or Interpretations. Questions are an important communication element of all models of therapy. Therapists use questions often with all approaches while taking a history, when checking in at the beginning of a session, and when finding out how a homework assignment went. However, SFBT therapists make questions the primary communication and intervention tool. These therapists tend to make no interpretations, and they very rarely directly challenge or confront a client.

Present- and Future-Focused Questions versus Past-Oriented Questions. The questions that are asked by SFBT therapists are almost always focused on the present or the future, and the emphasis is almost exclusively on what the client wants to have happen in his or her life or on what of what is already happening in the client's life. This reflects the basic belief that problems are best solved by focusing on what is already working and how clients would like their lives to be, rather than on the past and the origin of problems.

Compliments. Compliments are another essential part of SFBT. Validating what clients are already doing well and acknowledging how difficult their problems are encourages clients to change while sending the message that the therapist has been listening (i.e., understands) and cares (Berg & Dolan, 2001, pp. 90–94). Compliments in therapy sessions can help to highlight what the client is doing that is working.

Gentle Nudging to Do More of What Is Working. Once SFBT therapists have created a positive frame via compliments and then have discovered some previous solutions and exceptions to the problem, they gently nudge clients to do more of what has previously worked or to try changes they have brought up that they would like to try—frequently called an *experiment*. It is rare for an SFBT therapist to make a suggestion or give a homework assignment that is not based on the client's previous solutions or exceptions. It is always best if change ideas and assignments emanate from the client at least indirectly during the conversation, rather than from the therapist, because these behaviors are familiar to them.

Specific Interventions

Presession Change. At the beginning or early in the first therapy session, SFBT therapists typically ask, "What changes have you noticed that have happened or started to happen since you called to make the appointment for this session?" This question has three possible answers. First, the client may say that nothing has happened. In this case, the therapist simply goes on and begins the session by asking something like: "How can I be helpful to you today?" or "What would need to happen today to make this a really useful session?" or "How would your best friend notice if/that this session was helpful to you?" or "What needs to be different in your life after this session for you to be able to say that it was a good idea that you came in and talked with me?"

The second possible answer is that things have started to change or get better. In this case, the therapist asks many questions about the changes that have started, requesting a lot of detail. This starts the process of *solution talk*, emphasizing the client's strengths and resiliencies from the beginning, and allows the therapist to ask, "So, if these changes were to continue in this direction, would this be what you would like?" thus offering the beginning of a concrete and positive goal.

The third possible answer is that things are about the same. The therapist might be able to ask something like, "Is this unusual, that things have not gotten worse?" or "How have you all managed to keep things from getting worse?" These questions may lead to information about previous solutions and exceptions, and may move them into a solution-talk mode.

Solution-Focused Goals. As in many models of psychotherapy, clear, concrete, and specific goals are an important component of SFBT. Whenever possible, the therapist tries to elicit smaller goals rather than larger ones. More important, clients are encouraged to frame their goals as the presence of a solution rather than the absence of a problem. For example, it is better to have as a goal "We want our son to talk nicer to us"—which would need to be described in greater detail—rather than "We would like our child to not curse at us." Also, if a goal is described in terms of its solution, it can be more easily scaled (see below).[3]

Miracle Question. Some clients have difficulty articulating any goal at all, much less a solution-focused goal. The miracle question asks for a client's goal in a way that communicates respect for the immensity of the problem and, at the same time, leads to the client's coming up with smaller, more manageable goals. It is also a way for many clients to do a *virtual rehearsal* of their preferred future.

The precise language of the intervention may vary, but the basic wording is as follows:

> I am going to ask you a rather strange question [pause]. The strange question is this: [pause] After we talk, you will go back to your work (home, school) and you will do whatever you need to do the rest of today, such as taking care of the children, cooking dinner, watching TV, giving the children a bath, and so on. It will become time to go to bed. Everybody in your household is quiet, and you are sleeping in peace. In the middle of the night, a miracle happens and the problem that prompted you to talk to me today is solved! But because this happens while you are sleeping, you have no way of knowing that there was an overnight miracle that solved the problem. [pause] So, when you wake up tomorrow morning, what might be the small change that will make you say to yourself, "Wow, something must have happened—the problem is gone!"
>
> —Berg & Dolan (2001, p. 7)

Clients have a number of reactions to the question. They may seem puzzled. They may say that they don't understand the question or that they "don't know." They may smile. Usually, however, given enough time to ponder it and with persistence on the part of the therapist, they start to come up with some things that would be different when their problem is solved. Here is an example of how a couple, both former drug dealers with several years of previous contact with therapists and social workers, who said that they wanted "social services out of our lives," began to answer the miracle question. Insoo Kim Berg is the interviewer. Besides being a good example of how clients begin answering the miracle question, these interview excerpts illustrate SF coconstruction between therapist and clients in which altered or new meanings build as the therapist formulates next questions and responses based on the clients' previous answers and words, here about what will be different when the miracle happens (Berg & De Jong, 2008):

BERG: (Finishing the miracle question with . . .) So when you wake up tomorrow morning, what will be the first small clue to you . . . "whoa, something is different"?

DAD: You mean everything's gone: the kids . . . everything?

MOM: No, no.

BERG: The problem is gone.

DAD: It never happened?

MOM: The problem happened but it's all better.

BERG: It's all handled now.

MOM: To tell you the truth, I probably don't know how . . . we're waiting. I mean, we're waiting on that day. We're waiting on that day when there is just nobody.

BERG: Nobody. No social service in your life.

MOM: Yeah.

BERG: How would you, when you sort of come out of sleep in the morning, and you look around and see, what will let you know . . . "wow, today is different, a different day today, something is different, something happened."

DAD: The gut feeling. The inside feeling. The monkey off the back so to speak.

BERG: Okay.

DAD: When I had a drug problem . . . I guess it's a lot of the time the same feeling. When I had a drug problem I always was searching, and just always something, I never felt good about it. You know.

BERG: (Connecting to clients' words and meanings, ignoring the "complaint statements," and choosing one part of the clients' message that is connected with what they want to feel differently) So, after this miracle tonight, when the miracle happens, the problems are all solved, what would be different in your gut feeling?

DAD: Maybe I'd feel a little lighter, a little easier to move . . . not having to, ah, answer for my every movement.

MOM: Uh huh. Being able to make decisions as husband and wife. As parents of kids. Without having to wonder, "did we make the right decision or are we going to be judged on that decision?"

BERG: Oh.

MOM: I mean, this is what we feel is best, but when we have to answer our decision to somebody else . . .

DAD: Yeah, I mean "try it this way," or "try it that way," well, I mean, it's natural to learn a lot of those things on your own, I mean . . . I mean, you fail and you get back up and you try it another way.

BERG: So you would like to make the decision just the two of you, you were saying, "hmm, this makes sense, let's do it this way" without worrying: "is someone going to look over our shoulder or not."

MOM & DAD: Right.

MOM: And whether we agree or whether we disagree. To have somebody, have somebody taking sides, you know, what is his point, what is my point, and then trying to explain to us, well . . .

DAD: (Referring to social services) It was always having a mediator, I mean . . .

MOM: Yeah, there's always somebody to mediate.

BERG: So the mediator will be gone. Will be out of your life.

MOM & DAD: Right.

BERG: (Connecting again to client words/meanings; accepting and building) Okay. All right. All right. So suppose, suppose all these mediators are out of your life, including me. What would be different between the two of you? (Silence)

DAD: (Sighs)

MOM: Everything. Like I said, being able to look at each other as husband and wife and know that if we have, if we agree on something, that that is *our* decision, and that's the way it's going to be. If we disagree on something, it's a decision that, I mean, that's something we have to work out between us, and we don't have to worry what that third person's opinion is going to be, and I don't have to have a third person saying, "Yes, well, I agree, the way Keith decided it was right." Which makes me feel even *more* belittled.

BERG: All right. So, you two will make decisions regarding your family. What to do about the kids, what to do about the money, going to do whatever, right?

MOM: Right.

BERG: Suppose you were able to do that without second guessing. What would be different between the two of you . . . that will let you know, "Wow! This is different! We are making our own decisions."

MOM: A lot of tension gone I think. . . .

And so forth.

What clients are able to coconstruct with the therapist in answer to the miracle question can usually be taken as the goals of therapy. With a detailed description of how they would like their lives to be, clients often can turn more easily to building enhanced meanings about exceptions and past solution behaviors that can be useful in realizing their preferred futures.

In therapy with couples or families or work groups, the miracle question can be asked to individuals or to the group as a whole. If the question is asked to individual members, each one would give his or her response, and others might react to it. If the question is asked to the family, work group, or couple as a whole, members may "work on" their miracle together. The SFBT therapist, in trying to maintain a collaborative stance among family members, highlights similar goals and supportive statements among family members.

Scaling Questions. Whether the client gives specific goals directly or via the miracle question, an important next intervention in SFBT is to have the client evaluate his or her own progress. The therapist uses the Miracle Questions Scale and asks: "From 1 to 10, where 1 means the time when the initial appointment was arranged and 10 means the day after the miracle, where are things now?" For example, with a couple for whom better communication is the goal, scaling might proceed as follows:

THERAPIST: What I want to do now is scale the problem and the goal. Let's say a 1 is as bad as the problem ever could be; you never talk, only fight, or avoid all the time. And let's say a 10 is where you talk all the time, with perfect communication, never have a fight ever.

HUSBAND: That is pretty unrealistic

T: That would be the ideal. So, where would you two say it was for you at its worst? Maybe right before you came in to see me.

WIFE: It was pretty bad . . . I don't know . . . I'd say a 2 or a 3.

H: Yeah, I'd say a 2.

T: Okay (writing) . . . a 2–3 for you and a 2 for you. Now, tell me what you would be satisfied with when therapy is over and successful.

W: I'd be happy with an 8.

H: Well, of course I'd like a 10, but that is unrealistic. Yeah, I'd agree, an 8 would be good.

T: What would you say it is right now?

W: I would say it is a little better, because he is coming here with me, and I see that he is trying . . . I'd say maybe a 4?

H: Well, that's nice to hear. I wouldn't have thought she'd put it that high. I would say it is a 5.

T: Okay, a 4 for you, a 5 for you. And you both want it to be an 8 for therapy to be successful, right?

There are three major components to this intervention. First, it is an assessment device. That is, when it is used in each session, the therapist and the clients have an ongoing measurement of the clients' progress. Second, it makes it clear that the clients' evaluation is more important than the therapist's. Third, it is a powerful intervention in and of itself, because it focuses the dialogue on previous solutions and exceptions and emphasizes new changes as they occur. Like the changes made before the first session, here are three things that can happen between each session: (a) things can get better, (b) things can stay the same, or (c) things can get worse.

If the scale goes up, the therapist gets long descriptions and details concerning what is different and better and how the client was able to make the changes. The therapist may compliment the client during the session for progress made and/or may comment on the changes in the summary of the session. This supports and solidifies the changes and leads to the obvious nudge to do more of the same. If things stay the same, the client again can be complimented on maintaining the changes or for not letting things get worse. "How did you keep it from going down?" the therapist might ask. It is interesting how often that question will lead to a description of changes that the client has made, in which case the therapist can again compliment, support, and encourage more of those changes.

T: Mary, last week you were a 4 on the scale of good communications. I am wondering where you are this week.

W: [pause] I'd say a 5.

T: A 5! Wow! Really, in just one week.

W: Yes, I think we communicated better this week.

T: How did you communicate better this week?

W: Well, I think it was Rich. He seemed to try to listen to me more this week.

T: That's great. Can you give me an example of when he listened to you more?

W: Well, yes, yesterday, for example. He usually calls me once a day at work, and . . .

T: Sorry to interrupt, but did you say he calls you once a day? At work?

w: Yes.

T: I'm just a little surprised, because not all husbands call their wives every day.

w: He has always done that.

T: Is that something you like? That you wouldn't want him to change?

w: Yes, for sure.

T: Sorry, go on. You were telling me about yesterday when he called.

w: Well, usually it is kind of a quick call. But I told him about some problems I was having, and he listened for a long time, seemed to care, gave me some good ideas. That was nice.

T: So, that was an example of how you would like it to be, where you can talk about something, a problem, and he listens and gives good ideas? Support?

W: Yes.

T: Rich, did you know that Mary liked your calling her and listening to her? That that made you two move up the scale, to her?

H: Yeah, I guess so. I have really been trying this week.

T: That's great. What else have you done to try to make the communication better this week?

This example shows how going over the scale with the couple served as a vehicle for determining their progress. The therapist gathered more and more information about the small changes that the clients made on their own, using the differences on the scale to generate questions. This naturally led to the therapist's suggesting that the couple continue to do the things that were working—in this case, for the husband to continue calling his wife and engaging in the active listening that she found so helpful.

Constructing Solutions and Exceptions. The SFBT therapist spends most of the session listening attentively for talk about previous solutions, exceptions, and goals. When these details are provided, the therapist highlights them with enthusiasm and support. The therapist then works to keep the solution talk in the forefront. This, of course, requires a whole range of different skills from those used in traditional problem-focused therapies. Whereas the problem-focused therapist is concerned about missing signs of what has caused or is maintaining a problem, the SFBT therapist is concerned about missing signs of progress and solutions.

MOTHER: She always just ignores me, acts like I'm not there, comes home from school, just runs into her room. Who knows what she is doing in there.

DAUGHTER: You say we fight all the time, so I just go in my room so we don't fight.

M: See? She admits she just tries to avoid me. I don't know why she can't just come home and talk to me a little about school or something, like she used to.

T: Wait a second, when did she "used to"? Anita, when did you used to come home and tell your mom about school?

D: I did that a lot, last semester I did.

T: Can you give me an example of the last time you did that?

M: I can tell you, it was last week, actually. She was all excited about her science project getting chosen.

T: Tell me more, what day was that . . .?

M: I think last Wednesday.

T: And she came home . . .

M: She came home all excited.

T: What were you doing?

M: I think the usual. I was getting dinner ready. And she came in all excited, and I asked her what was up, and she told me her science project was chosen for the display at school.

T: Wow, that is quite an honor.

M: It is.

T: So then what happened?

M: Well, we talked about it, she told me all about it.

T: Anita, do you remember this?

D: Sure, it was only last week. I was pretty happy.

T: And would you say that this was a nice talk, a nice talk between you two?

D: Sure. That's what I mean; I don't always go in my room.

T: Was there anything different about that time, last week, that made it easier to talk to each other?

M: Well, she was excited.

D: My mom listened, wasn't doing anything else.

T: Wow, this is a great example. Thank you. Let me ask this: if it were like that more often, where Anita talked to you about things that were interesting and important to her, and where Mom, you listened to her completely without doing other things, is that what you two mean by better communication?

D: Yeah, exactly.

M: Yes.

In this example, the therapist did a number of things. First, she listened carefully for an exception to the problem, a time when the problem could have happened but did not. Second, she punctuated that exception by repeating it, emphasizing it, getting more details about it, and congratulating them on it. Third, she connected the exception to their goal (or miracle) by asking the question, "If this exception were to occur more often, would your goal be reached?"

Coping Questions. If a client reports that the problem is not better, the therapist may sometimes ask coping questions such as "How have you managed to prevent it from getting worse?" or "This sounds hard; how are you managing to cope with this to the degree that you are?"

Taking a Break and Reconvening. Many models of family therapy have encouraged therapists to take a break toward the end of the session. Usually this involves a conversation between the therapist and a team of colleagues or a supervision team who have been watching the session and who give feedback and suggestions to the therapist. In SFBT, therapists are also encouraged to take a break near the session's end. If there is a team, they give the therapist feedback, a list of compliments for the family, and some suggestions for interventions based on the clients' strengths, previous solutions, or exceptions. If no team is available, the therapist will still take a break to collect his or her thoughts and then come up with compliments and ideas for possible experiments. When the therapist returns to the session, he or she can offer the family compliments.

T: I just wanted to tell you, the team was really impressed with you two this week. They wanted me to tell you that, Mom, they thought you really seem to care a lot about your daughter. It is really hard to be a mom, and you seem so focused and clear about how much you love her and how you want to help her. They were impressed that you came to the session today, in spite of work and having a sick child at home. Anita, the team also wanted to compliment you on your commitment to making the family better. They wanted me to tell you how bright and articulate they think you are and what a good "scientist" you are! Yes, you seem to be really aware of what small, little things that happen in your family might make a difference. . . . That is what scientists do; they observe things that seem to change things, no matter how small. Anyway, they were impressed with you two a lot!

D: [Seeming pleased.] Wow, thanks!

Experiments and Homework Assignments. While many models of psychotherapy use intersession homework assignments to solidify changes begun during therapy, most of the time the homework is assigned by the therapist. In SFBT, therapists frequently end the session by suggesting a possible experiment for clients to try between sessions if they so choose. These experiments are based on something the clients are already doing (exceptions), thinking, feeling, and so on that is moving them in the direction of their goal. Alternatively, homework is sometimes designed by the client. Both experiments and homework follow the basic philosophy that what emanates from the client is better than what comes from the therapist. This is true for a number of reasons. First, what is usually suggested by the client, directly or indirectly, is familiar. One of the main reasons homework is not accomplished in other models is that it is foreign to the family, and thus takes more thought and work to accomplish (usually thought of as resistance). Second, the clients usually assign themselves either more of what has worked already for them (a previous solution) or something they really want to do. In both cases, the homework is more closely tied to their own goals and solutions. Third, when clients create their own homework assignment, it reduces the natural tendency for clients to resist outside intervention, no matter how good the intention. While SFBT does not focus on resistance (in fact, it sees resistance as a natural protective process that people use to move slowly and cautiously into change rather than as evidence of psychopathology), when clients initiate their own homework, there is a greater likelihood of success.

T: Before we end today, I would like for you two to think about a homework assignment. If you were to give yourselves a homework assignment this week, what would it be?

D: Maybe that we talk more?

T: Can you tell me more?

D: Well, that I try to talk to her more when I come home from school. And that she stops what she is doing and listens.

T: I like that. You know why? Because it is what you two were starting to do last week. Mom, what do you think? Is that a good homework assignment?

M: Yeah, that's good.

T: So let's make this clear. Anita will try to talk to you more when she comes home from school. And you will put down what you are doing, if you can, and listen and talk to her about what she is talking to you about. Anything else? Anything you want to add?

M: No, that's good. I just need to stop what I was doing. I think that it's important to listen to her.

T: Well, that sure seemed to work for you two last week. Okay, so that's the assignment. We'll see how it went next time.

A couple of points should be emphasized here. First, the mother and daughter were asked to make their own assignment rather than have one imposed on them by the therapist. Second, what they assigned themselves flowed naturally from their previous solution and exceptions from the week before. This is very common and is encouraged by SFBT therapists. However, even if the client suggested an assignment that was not based on solutions and exceptions to the problem, the therapist would most likely support it. What is preeminent is that the assignments come from the client.

In cases where the client has not been able to form a clear goal, the therapist may propose that the client think about how he or she wants things to be by, for instance, using the formula first session task (de Shazer, 1992, 1995).

Ideas about what the therapist thinks might be useful for the client to observe may (and will often) be given with the end-of-session message. These will have something to do with what the client described in the miracle.

"So, what is better, even a little bit, since the last time we met?" At the start of each session after the first, the therapist will usually ask about progress, about what has gotten better during the interval. Many clients will report that there have been some noticeable improvements. The therapist will help the clients describe these changes in as much detail as possible. Of course, some clients will report that things have remained the same or have gotten worse. This will lead the therapist to explore how the client maintained things without their getting worse or, if things did get worse, what the client did to prevent them from getting much worse. Whatever the client has done to prevent things from worsening is then the focus and a source for compliments and perhaps for an experiment, since whatever the client did should be continued. During the session, usually after there has been a lot of talk about what is better, the therapist will ask the client how the client would now rate himself or herself on the progress (toward a solution) scale. Of course, when the rating is higher than that in the previous session, the therapist will compliment this progress and help the client figure out how to maintain the improvement.

At some point during the session—possibly at the beginning or perhaps later on— the therapist will check, frequently indirectly, on how the assignment went. If the client did the assignment and it worked—that is, it helped the client move toward his or her goals—the therapist will compliment the client. If the client did not do the assignment, the therapist usually drops the subject or asks what the client did instead that was better.

One difference between SFBT and other homework-driven models, such as cognitive-behavioral therapy, is that the homework itself is not required for change per se, so not completing an assignment is not addressed. If the client does not complete an assignment, it is assumed that (a) something realistic got in the way of its completion, such as work or illness; (b) the client did not find the assignment useful; or (c) it was basically not relevant during the interval between sessions. In any case, no fault is assigned. If the client did the assignment but things did not improve or got worse, the therapist handles this situation in the same way he or she would when problems stay the same or get worse in general.

■ COMPATIBILITY WITH ADJUNCTIVE THERAPIES

Solution-focused brief therapy can easily be used as an addendum to other therapies. One of the original and primary tenets of SFBT—"If something is working, do more of it"—suggests that therapists should encourage their clients to continue with other therapies and approaches that are helpful. For example, clients are encouraged to (a) continue to take prescribed medication, (b) stay in a self-help group if it is helping them to achieve their goals, or (c) begin or continue family therapy. Finally, it is a misconception that SFBT is philosophically opposed to traditional substance abuse treatments. Just the opposite is true. If a client is in traditional treatment or has been in the past and it has helped, he or she is encouraged to continue doing what is working. As such, SFBT could be used in addition to or as a component of a comprehensive treatment program.

■ TARGET POPULATIONS

Solution-focused brief therapy has been found clinically to be helpful in treatment programs in the United States for adolescent and adult outpatients (Pichot & Dolan, 2003) and as an adjunct to more intensive inpatient treatment in Europe. This therapy is being used to treat the entire range of clinical disorders, and is also being used in educational and business settings. Meta-analysis and systematic reviews of experimental and quasi-experimental studies indicate that SFBT is a promising intervention for youth with externalizing behavior problems and those with school and academic problems, showing medium-sized to large effects (Kim, 2008; Kim & Franklin, 2009; Kim et al., 2009).

Many of the other chapters in this book present detailed discussions on the use of SFBT with specific clinical and other populations.

■ MEETING THE NEEDS OF SPECIAL POPULATIONS

While SFBT may be useful as the primary treatment mode for many individuals in outpatient therapy, those with severe psychiatric problems, medical problems, or unstable living situations will most likely need additional medical, psychological, and social services. In those situations, SFBT may be part of a more comprehensive treatment program.

■ THERAPIST CHARACTERISTICS AND REQUIREMENTS

Solution-focused brief therapy therapists should posses the requisite training and certification in a mental health discipline and specialized training in SFBT. The ideal SFBT therapist would possess (a) a minimum of a master's degree in a counseling discipline such as counseling, social work, marriage and family therapy, psychology, or psychiatry and (b) formal training and supervision in SFBT, either via a university class or a series of workshops and training. Therapists who seem to embrace and excel in solution-focused therapy have these characteristics: they (a) are warm and friendly; (b) are naturally positive and supportive (often are told that they "see the good in people"); (c) are open-minded and flexible in using new ideas; (d) are excellent listeners, especially in listening for clients' previous solutions embedded in problem talk; and (e) are tenacious and patient.

■ THERAPIST TRAINING

Therapists who meet the above requirements should receive formal training and supervision in SFBT. A brief outline of such a training program would include:

1. The history and philosophy of SFBT
2. Basic tenets of SFBT
3. Session format and structure of SFBT
4. Video examples of "masters" of SFBT
5. Format of SFBT
6. Role playing
7. Practice with video feedback
8. Training with video feedback

Therapists can be considered trained when they achieve an 85% adherence and competency rating using standardized adherence and competency rating scales. There should also be subjective evaluations by the trainers concerning therapists' overall ability to function reliably and capably as solution-focused therapists.

■ SUPERVISION

Solution-focused brief therapy therapists should be supervised live whenever possible. One of the most common problems is that the therapist slips back into problem talk. It is far better for the therapist-in-training to receive concurrent feedback, via telephone call-in for example, so that this problem can be corrected immediately. Solution talk is far more likely to become natural and accommodated by therapists when they are given immediate feedback, especially early in training. The other advantage of live supervision, of course, is that there is a second set of "clinical eyes," which also will benefit the clients, especially in more difficult cases. When live supervision is not possible, videotape supervision is the best alternative, since the movement and body language of the group are relevant to the feedback that the supervisor will want to give the therapist. Adherence and competency scales should be used as an adjunct to supervision to focus the supervision on balancing the quantity of interventions (adherence) and the quality (competency) and allow for more immediate remediation.

■ ENDNOTES

1. This is the official *Treatment Manual of the Solution-Focused Brief Therapy Association*. It is revised periodically, and the updates are available at http://www.sfbta.org and also from the first author at http://www.solutionfocused.net. Its use in clinical research is encouraged.

2. Goals in SFBT are desired emotions, cognitions, behaviors, and interactions in different contexts (areas of the client's life).

3. Goals connect emotion, cognition, behavior, and interaction. So, if the client says, "I don't want to feel depressed," the therapist will start eliciting goals by asking how the client will notice when things become better and the client might answer, "I'd feel better. I'd be more calm and relaxed." The therapist might then ask in what area of the client's life he or she will start noticing if the client felt more calm and relaxed, and the client might

answer: when he or she is getting the children ready to go to school. The client will then be asked what the children will notice about him or her that shows that the client is more calm and relaxed, and how the children will behave differently when they notice this.

The conversation might then move on to what difference this will make in other areas of the client's life, like the relationship with the client's partner and/or colleagues at work. The therapist will try to create descriptions of cognition, emotion, behavior, and interaction in several different contexts (parts of the client's life) and with people in these contexts.

This is an important part of SFBT: connecting descriptions of both desired and undesired cognitions, emotions, behavior, and interactions with each other in contexts where they make sense.

■ REFERENCES

Berg, I. K. (1994). *Family-based services: A solution-focused approach.* New York: Norton.

Berg, I. K., & De Jong, P. (2008). *"Over the hump:" Families and couples treatment [DVD].* (Available from the Solution-Focused Brief Therapy Association, http://www.sfbta.org/SFBT_dvd_store.html).

Berg, I. K., & Dolan, Y. (2001). *Tales of solutions: A collection of hope-inspiring stories.* New York: Norton.

Berg, I. K., & Miller, S. D. (1992). *Working with the problem drinker: A solution-oriented approach.* New York: Norton.

Carroll, K. M., & Nuro, K. F. (1997). The use and development of treatment manuals. In K. M. Carroll (Ed.), *Improving compliance with alcoholism treatment* (pp. 53–72). Bethesda, MD: National Institute on Alcohol Abuse and Alcoholism.

Corey, G. (1985). *Theory and practice of group counseling* (2nd ed.). Monterey, CA: Brooks/Cole.

De Jong, P., & Berg, I. K. (2008). *Interviewing for solutions* (3rd ed.). Belmont, CA: Thomson Brooks/Cole.

de Shazer, S. (1985). *Keys to solution in brief therapy.* New York: Norton.

de Shazer, S. (1992). *Patterns of brief family therapy.* New York: Guilford Press.

de Shazer, S., Berg, I. K., Lipchik, E., Nunnally, E., Molnar, A., Gingerich, W., & Weiner-Davis, M. (1986). Brief therapy: Focused solution development. *Family Process, 25*(2), 207–221.

de Shazer, S., Dolan, Y. M., Korman, H., Trepper, T. S., McCollum, E. E., & Berg, I. K. (2007). *More than miracles: The state of the art of solution-focused therapy.* New York: Routledge Press.

Freedman, J., & Combs, G. (1996). *Narrative therapy: The social construction of preferred realities.* New York: Norton.

Kim, J. (2008). Examining the effectiveness of solution-focused brief therapy: A meta-analysis. *Research on Social Work Practice, 18,* 107–116.

Kim, J., & Franklin, C. (2009). Solution-focused brief therapy in schools: A review of the literature. *Children and Youth Services Review, 31,* 464–470.

Kim, J., Smock, S., Trepper, T. S., McCollum, E. E., & Franklin, C. (2009). Is solution-focused brief therapy evidenced-based? *Families in Society, 91,* 301–305.

McGee, D. R., Del Vento, A., & Bavelas, J. B. (2005). An interactional model of questions as therapeutic interventions. *Journal of Marital and Family Therapy, 31,* 371–384.

Miller, W. R., & Rollnick, S. (2002). *Motivational interviewing: Preparing people for change* (2nd ed.). New York: Guilford Press.

Miller, W. R., Zweben, A., DiClemente, C. C., & Rychtarik, R. G. (1994). *Motivational enhancement therapy manual: A clinical research guide for therapists treating individuals with alcohol abuse and dependence* (NIH Publication No. 94–3723). Rockville, MD: National Institute on Alcohol Abuse and Alcoholism.

Pichot, T., & Dolan, Y. (2003). *Solution-focused brief therapy: Its effective use in agency settings.* New York: Routledge.

Measuring Solution-Focused Brief Therapy Practice

3 The Development of a Solution-Focused Fidelity Instrument

A Pilot Study

■ PETER LEHMANN AND JOY D. PATTON

■ **INTRODUCTION**

In a recent paper, Kazdin (2008) stated that "the unifying goals of clinical research and practice are to increase our understanding of therapy and to improve patient care" (p. 151). Twenty-five years ago, there was very little evidence that clinical research and practice played much of a role in the growth of psychotherapy. Fortunately, advances in the field of outcome evaluation and in the development of models of practice continue to show that psychotherapy has the potential to alleviate clinical problems. Solution-focused brief therapy (SFBT) has reason to celebrate, as it can be considered one of many contributors to bringing about this change. The worldwide growing interest in SFBT and the growth of professional associations supporting SFBT, in addition to the developing clinical research field, as described in many chapters in this book, highlights the support for its usefulness in many treatment contexts. Further, recognition of SFBT as a "promising" model of practice (OJJDP, 2009) strengthens the importance of providing evidence for the model, thereby shortening the gap for researchers and practitioners.

The purpose of this chapter is to articulate and improve the front-line practitioner's ability to evaluate his or her work and assist in bringing the practice and research of SFBT closer together throught the development of tools that increase adherence to SFBT practice. The growing empirical recognition of SFBT, as noted in this book, should represent a shift bringing researchers and therapists closer together. As the expectation for more thorough and precise evaluations of interventions from local and national funders increases, and as human service providers call for greater sophistication and clarity about how one works in response to clients' needs, the interventions will be expected to demonstrate the specifics of the model being used. Thus, those who research and practice SFBT should be concerned about whether their work with clients represents the clearest intent of the assumptions as represented by the model (Corcoran & Pillai, 2009;de Shazer et al., 2007;). One way to improve a clinician's adherence to the assumptions and practices of SFBT is to follow a treatment manual or set of treatment guidelines for SFBT. Chapter 2 of this presents the official treatment manual developed by the Solution-focused Brief Therapy Association (SFBTA). A second method is to develop adherence or fidelity measures. The development of these methods for improving adherence to SFBT practice is the topic of this chapter.

To begin, the chapter introduces the importance of *fidelity*, also known as *treatment integrity* (e.g. Perepletchikova et al., 2009; Waltz et al., 1993), to SFBT. Since both terms are used interchangeably in the literature, the remainder of this chapter will use the term *fidelity*. A definition of and rationale for the use of fidelity, as well as the background of the current instrument, are provided. Next, the methods and analysis sections highlight the results of a pilot study evaluating the Fidelity instrument in a university training setting for master's-level social work interns. The chapter concludes with a discussion section relevant to SFBT practice and research.

■ **WHAT WE HAVE LEARNED SO FAR**

What Is Fidelity?

Fidelity is defined as "the adherence of actual treatment delivery to the protocol originally developed" (Orwin, 2000, p. 310). Fidelity, can have administrative and research purposes: to determine how well a program model has been implemented (Bond et al., 2000), to determine whether therapists adhere closely to the model procedures (Perepletchikova et al., 2007), or to reassure funders or local stakeholders that services are being implemented as intended to the desired clients (Orwin, 2000). In terms of its relevance to SFBT, a central question for practitioners is whether the outcomes of what is done in sessions are valid; that is, can the practitioner/researcher make inferences about the relationship between using SFBT and outcomes, and are the application and intervention of SFBT delivered in the manner originally designed? As hopes for the precision and usefulness of SFBT in practice grow, fidelity is likely to make a significant contribution.

Fidelity is usually assessed through either direct or indirect means (Perepletchikova et al., 2007). Direct means include such methods as viewing sessions via a one-way mirror; a cotherapist joining the session; or videotaping a session, which can then be rated by experts. Indirect methods can assess fidelity via therapist self-reports, interviews with clients about their experiences, written homework assignments, and data collection. Other indirect methods include mail surveys, reviews of case files, progress reports from supervisors, daily activity sheets, and/or exit interviews (Mowbray et al., (2003).

The importance of fidelity to SFBT is new, but it is also a relatively recent concept in mental health research and practice. In their summary of the history and evolution of fidelity, Mowbray and colleagues (2003) traced the origins of fidelity to the early stages of developing organizations, when innovations within organizations should be adopted with the original model in mind. This pro- fidelity movement was intended to maintain the effectiveness and integrity of programs as well as minimize the chances of their being diluted.

The use of fidelity to assess outcomes within the practice field appears to have been given minimal attention. Researchers (McGrew et al., 1994; Teague et al., 1998) have described steps in establishing fidelity criteria, but to date, few published studies have implemented these ideas within the field. For example, Mowbray and colleagues (2003) surveyed the literature and reviewed published studies that had developed, validated, and/or used fidelity criteria. From 1995 to 2003, the authors found that only 21 studies had followed the recommended procedures. Furthermore, many recommendations have been made for addressing fidelity (e.g., Gresham et al., 2000; Perepletchikova & Kazdin, 2005; Waltz et al., 2003), yet it appears that available guidelines are not followed. More recently, Perepletchikova and colleagues (2007) identified the presence of fidelity in randomized, controlled studies. They found 147 studies that met their criteria, but after careful analysis, it was concluded that only 3.5% of them adequately addressed fidelity/integrity. In a later report, Perepletchikova and colleagues (2009) identified barriers to measuring fidelity, including general lack of knowledge about fidelity; lack of guidelines on how to implement fidelity; the time, financial cost, and labor demand; and lack of editorial requirements for publication. In spite of these modest beginnings, it would seem that good client care has practical and ethical value for those interested in considering fidelity with SFBT.

■ WHY ASSESS FIDELITY IN SFBT?

There are a number of reasons why fidelity is likely to be important to SFBT. If SFBT is to become a model of practice that can be taught (and ultimately researched) as it was intended and replicated by seasoned practitioners and new trainees, a first good reason centers on testing an instrument. Within the SFBT field a number of fidelity-like instruments currently exist (e.g., Chevalier, 1995; De Jong & Berg, 1997; Fiske & Zalter-Minton, 2003; Warner, 2000), but none appear to have undergone psychometric scrutiny. Testing an instrument for fidelity could help determine whether good outcomes are a consequence of the SFBT model and its implementation as intended or whether poor outcomes are linked to the model and improper implementation

A second reason for considering fidelity in SFBT is to be able to highlight the specificity and concreteness of the model in predicting outcomes (Perepletchikova et al., 2007). In this case, being exact about the interventions will be helpful for identifying what works in training and how clients benefit from the approaches used. Gresham et al. (2000) have suggested that the complexity of therapy is inversely related to the level of treatment integrity or fidelity. Evaluators should therefore be able to better define and measure the interventions in a manner that is concrete and exact.

The current gold standard of clinical evaluation is the randomized clinical trial (RCT). In RCT, clients are randomly assigned to SFBT and compared with clients who have received standard treatment or no treatment at all. In many clinical settings, RCT can be impractical, too costly, or possibly unethical. Thus, beyond RCT, there appears to be few or no expectations for "research quality and design" (Mowbray et al., 2003, p. 316). This points to a third reason for fidelity: it can help provide evidence for the effectiveness of SFBT beyond an RCT. Kim (2008) has pointed out that the bulk of SFBT evaluation research has come from real-world rather than clinically controlled research settings. Therefore, using RCT to evaluate the outcomes of SFBT may not be a viable option. Invariably, developing methods of evaluation under less than ideal research conditions will continue; however, practitioners should be able to use fidelity tools to evaluate how they adhere to the interventions, as well as to show how the interventions impact outcomes to provide evidence of effectiveness.

Finally, using fidelity instruments should not be considered a fixed process for detailing specific intervention effectiveness. For example, Barber et al. (2006) found that "both low and high levels of adherence [to treatment protocols] were associated with worse outcomes, whereas an intermediate level of adherence was associated with the best outcomes" (p. 237). Thus, a fourth reason for the importance of fidelity is the need for practitioners and researchers to decide whether fidelity in SFBT requires an exact replication of the model or whether this therapy can also include adaptation by "allowing choice (exact or modification) between alternative pathways to fit local contexts" (Mowbray et al., 2003, p. 336). Since SFBT is a goal-driven model that includes the knowledge, cultural context, and values of each client, it can certainly be flexible. Also, SFBT is now practiced in a variety of settings, such as prisons, child welfare agencies, hospitals, criminal justice and university settings, business and management settings, and others. Consequently, the context will define how the model is used and how it can be adapted. One expectation for SFBT and fidelity, then, will be to measure how the model can be adhered to in various sites of practice and still be evaluated for effectiveness.

As the evidence for psychotherapy outcomes continues to accrue, the SFBT clinician and/or researcher will be required to show how specific interventions make for better client treatment. One way to refocus on the usefulness of SFBT may be through fidelity. Because the delivery of an intervention is critical to assessing the effectiveness of psychotherapy, one central research question for this chapter is: Could criteria that were consistent with many of the underlying assumptions of SFBT be developed into a fidelity instrument?

Background

The initial steps in developing fidelity criteria centered on two procedures supported in the literature. First, criteria could be developed by considering which operations of an existing model have proven successful in the literature (Bond et al., 2000). To this end, books, book chapters, and published articles relating to theoretical development and clinical practice were reviewed (e.g., Berg & Reuss, 1997; De Jong & Berg, 1997; de Shazer, 1985, 1992; de Shazar et al., 1986, 2006). Critical to this process was the search for conceptual clarity and consistency within SFBT. In particular, there was a search for the intervention commonalities and formats that were considered successful and were found in interviews related to the model.

The original fidelity criteria were written by the first author (PL) in January 2006 and compiled in a question format using Likert scaling. Items were measured on a scale of 1 (not at all) to 7 (very clearly and specifically), The rationale for using Likert scaling in this case was purposive; rather than a dichotomous yes/no response, each criterion item was given a range of responses, depending on the context. The first draft of the fidelity criteria yielded 12 items.

This draft was then submitted to the worldwide solution-focused listserv, as well as local and national practitioners considered experts in solution-focused practice. An attempt was made to invite listserv members, practitioners, and experts to comment on factors such as question content, specific wording, and structure. As recommendations for changes came in, the instrument was reworded and configured in accord with the comments, resulting in 18 items. In total, there were nine drafts of the fidelity criteria, resulting in 17 items assessing fidelity and 1 item referring to consistency with previous sessions. This procedure was used because it has been recommended in developing fidelity criteria (Mowbray et al., 2003). Consequently, face and content validity was promoted via the collaborative review and revision of the instrument.

The next phase involved construction of two instruments with 18 mirror items worded for the respondent: Fidelity Instrument Therapist (FIT) and Fidelity Instrument Consumer (FIC). Eleven graduate-level social work students, 1 therapist, and 66 clients at the Community Services Center (CSC) of the University of Texas at Arlington each filled in the appropriate instrument. Using a time series design, with assessments made during the third session and every three sessions thereafter, reliability (internal consistency) and factorial validity were measured. The purpose was to evaluate the consistency of the items and model adherence in response to solution-focused intervention from two sources: the therapist and the client. In sum, valid observations of 70 FITs completed by 11 graduate-level social work students and 1 therapist were compared to 99 FICs completed by 66 clients. An overall alpha coefficient (alpha = .89) was calculated, with a standardized item alpha determined for the 18 items in the parallel forms of the scale across the time series. The analysis also used scores from the first observation in the time series to assure independence of responses with the reliability coefficient remaining stable (alpha = .88).

The final constructed Fidelity instrument included 13 items. Because fidelity would be measured on the sixth session rather than the first, five items were removed from the original instrument. Two items (a and d) were removed because, ordinarily, a therapist in the sixth session with a client might not necessarily be following these items of the intervention protocol. Further, items b and c were considered redundant and removed, and item e had previously been included for CSC administrative purposes and was not needed for the assessment of the Fidelity instrument. The following are the items that were removed:

(a) I asked the client the miracle question.
(b) I asked the client "what else" was better in today's session.
(c) I complimented the family about their contributions as the session ended.
(d) Towards the end of the session, I gave the client a task.
(e) Have your two previous sessions with the client/family been similar to today's session?

The 13 items remaining and included in the analysis of the Fidelity instrument are as follows (also see Figure 3.1):

1. I asked what the client wanted out of today's session.
2. I asked "what's better" in today's session.
3. The client's stated needs for today's session were related to overall goal(s) for therapy.
4. I summarized the client's comments during today's session.
5. I complimented the client's strengths/resources during today's session.
6. I asked exception/difference questions during today's session.
7. I asked amplifying questions during today's session.
8. I asked reinforcing questions (e.g., summarizing/complimenting) of the client's reported change in today's session.
9. I was able to help the client behaviorally describe a next small step of progress.
10. I asked scaling questions during today's session.
11. I asked coping questions related to the client's abilities that emerged during today's session.

Circle the answer which applies to you (Session # _____)

| 1 | 2 | 3 | 4 | 5 | 6 | 7 |

not at all   yes, but not clear enough   yes, clearly   yes, clearly and specifically

1. I asked what the client/family wanted out of today's session

1   2 3 4 5 6   7

2. I asked "what's better" in todays session

1   2 3 4 5 6   7

3. The client's/family's stated needs for today's session were related to overall goal(s) for therapy.

1   2 3 4 5 6   7

4. summarized the client's/family's comments during today's session
1   2 3 4 5 6   7

5. I complimented the client's/family's strengths/resources during today's session

1   2 3 4 5 6   7

6. I asked exception/difference questions during today's session

1   2 3 4 5 6   7

7. I asked amplifying questions during today's session

1   2 3 4 5 6   7

8. I asked reinforcing questions (e.g. summarizing/complimenting) of client's reported change in today's session

1   2 3 4 5 6   7

9. I was able to help the client/family behaviorally describe a next small step of progress towards their goals

1   2 3 4 5 6   7

10. I asked scaling questions during today's session

1   2 3 4 5 6   7

11. I asked coping questions related to the client's/family's abilities that emerged during today's session
1   2 3 4 5 6   7

12. I asked questions to help the client think about how changes will affect the client's family and important others in their life

1   2 3 4 5 6   7

13. I asked for feedback on the helpfulness of the session today from the client/family.
1   2 3 4 5 6   7

Figure 3.1. Solution-Focused Fidelity Instrument v10˚. Permission to reproduce is granted.

12. I asked questions to help the client think about how changes will affect the client's family and important others in their life.
13. I asked for feedback on the helpfulness of the session today from the client.

■ RESEARCH METHODS

The Fidelity instrument used in this study gathered information on the use of SFT from graduate-level social work students completing their internship in the CSC as part of the requirements for graduation. After the completion of specific course work in direct practice, students are assigned a 500-hour internship in their area of interest. Since these interns had little or no previous exposure to SFBT, the Fidelity instrument was used as a way of measuring their use of this intervention protocol.

Data Collection

Interns were instructed to rate themselves on their use of SFBT on the Fidelity instrument at the end of their first, third, sixth, and ninth sessions with each client. This study utilized the data collected from interns in the sixth session for two reasons. First, a major element of treatment adherence is the therapists' skill and proficiency levels. To accurately assess adherence to a given intervention, it is important to take into account the therapist's skills and proficiency in that specific intervention protocol. To be able to determine with reasonable confidence that the intervention was implemented as intended, the individuals being assessed should be well trained in the therapy process as well as in the intervention protocol (Nezu & Nezu, 2008).

The interns in this study were required to successfully complete 9 hours of graduate work in which counseling techniques and the therapy process were learned. While the interns came to the CSC trained in the therapy process, they had little knowledge of the SFBT intervention protocol. Therefore, they were required to complete a 6-hour basic SFBT training seminar before the beginning of their internship in the clinic. Each week, in addition to seeing clients in session, the interns attended a 2-hour supervision session and a 2-hour continued training session in SFBT. By the time the interns had reached their sixth session with a client, they had received sufficient training in SFBT to measure the intervention protocol.

A second reason for using the sixth-session fidelity data had to do with data availability. An analysis of the average number of sessions completed by clients in the clinic revealed that, in general, clients were seen for six sessions. Clients could officially terminate therapy at the sixth session or could simply not return after that session. Thus, in order to give the interns an opportunity to be trained in the SFBT protocol and to have data available for analysis, the sixth session was chosen.

Sample

In using structural equation modeling (SEM), researchers are advised to replicate the assessment of the instrument using multiple samples to provide the basis for stability of the parameter estimates. However, this is usually not feasible (Schrieber et al., 2006). When there is only one sample with which to assess the instrument, sample size becomes the rule for verifying the stability of parameter estimates.

There appear to be two competing approaches in determining sample size when completing an instrument analysis: applying either a minimum total sample size or a ratio of subjects to variables. Most researchers suggest that a minimum total sample size is simplistic and unrealistic when taking into consideration the variance in the types of scales being evaluated. This has led researchers to focus more on the subject-to-variable ratio to determine sample size. Pedhazur (1997) suggests that a ratio of subjects to variables is critical when generalizing the results.

The recommended subject-to-variable ratio ranges from 5:1 (Gorsuch, 1983; Hatcher, 1994) to 10:1 (Nunnally, 1978); some researchers suggest a ratio as large as 30:1 (Pedhazur, 1997). A recent survey (Costello & Osborne, 2003) of 1,076 peer-reviewed, published studies using factor analysis indicated that about 40% of them had a subject-to-variable ratio of less than 5:1 and 60% had a ratio between 5:1 and 10:1.

The data for this sample were collected over 18 months, from August 2007 to March 2009. On average, seven interns were involved in the study during each semester within that period, at varying stages of internship completion. The sample used in this study included completed Fidelity instruments from approximately 23 interns who completed the sixth session with 116 clients. There were no missing data. The subject-to-variable ratio in this study is 9:1, which falls within the reported average range for this ratio in published studies.

■ **RESULTS OF RESEARCH**

Measuring the Fidelity Instrument

The SEM software AMOS 16.0 was used in this pilot study to perform a confirmatory factor analysis (CFA). In SEM, CFA is used to establish that the items of an instrument are measuring the intended construct. In other words, for the current analysis, CFA was used to establish that the 13 items of the Fidelity instrument were indeed measuring the intended construct of Fidelity (adherence to the SFBT; see Figure 3.2). The purpose of the measurement model, then, is to understand how well the indicators (or SFBT criteria) work together as one measurement instrument for the latent variable, Fidelity (Hoyle, 1995).

Maximum likelihood estimation was chosen because the data were normally distributed (see Table 3.1). The data come from 13 items on one Likert scale instrument measuring SFBT adherence. Each item was rated on a 7-point scale ranging from 1 (not at all) to 7 (yes, clearly and specifically). The factor loading matrix was set to reflect loadings on only one factor, thus assuming a single-factor structure to be confirmed in the measurement portion of the model. In this analysis, none of the 13 items were permitted to correlate, nor were the residuals permitted to correlate across factors. This was done in order to maintain the independence of the items measuring Fidelity.

Correlations

Correlations between each of the 13 items of the Fidelity instrument were run to provide essential information regarding the reliability of the items used in the analysis. It is expected that most of the 13 items will correlate with each other. The correlations for each of the 13 items are provided in Table 3.1, along with the mean and standard deviation.

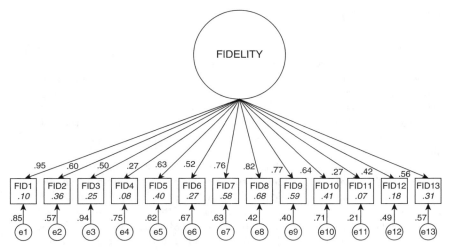

Figure 3.2. Fidelity adherence measure.

Reliability Estimates

Fidelity is conceptualized as the latent variable in the SEM model that is measured by multiple indicators (13 items). Reliability of the indicators is important to establish that the items on the Fidelity scale are indeed measuring the adherence to SFBT. A reliability analysis was conducted to determine the psychometric property of the Fidelity instrument. In this case, the interest lay in the internal consistency of the criteria. Nunnally (1978) states that internal consistency reliabilities should be greater than .70. The reliability of the Cronbach alpha's internal consistency was calculated for the Fidelity instrument, which exceeded the .70 cutoff level. The Cronbach alpha was .83; thus, the 13-item scale appears to be measuring adequately the underlying assumptions of SFBT.

TABLE 3.1. *Correlations with Each Item of the Fidelity Instrument*

	FID1	FID2	FID3	FID4	FID5	FID6	FID7	FID8	FID9	FID10	FID11	FID12	FID13
FID1	1												
FID2	.28**	1											
FID3	.19*	.38**	1										
FID4	.31**	.36**	.36**	1									
FID5	.12	.28**	.30**	.45**	1								
FID6	.19*	.43**	.39**	.51**	.37**	1							
FID7	.27**	.48**	.38**	.52**	.37**	.69**	1						
FID8	.15	.46**	.32**	.43**	.48**	.55**	.65**	1					
FID9	.12	.06	.30**	.22*	.22*	.19*	.16	.17	1				
FID10	.27*	.26**	.18	.24**	.13	.30**	.37**	.25**	.24*	1			
FID11	.14	.27**	.31**	.36**	.29**	.50**	.41**	.43**	.23*	.28**	1		
FID12	.16	.17	.28**	.39**	.24**	.36**	.33**	.16	.13	.15	.19*	1	
FID13	.15	.21*	.27**	.30**	.32**	.38**	.35**	.32**	.20*	.32**	.23*	.39**	1

*Correlation is <.05; **correlation is <.01; M = 76; SD = 10; FID1–FID 13 (see Figure 3.1).

Distribution of Scores

In order to verify the distribution of scores for the 13 Fidelity instrument items, skewness and kurtosis values were computed. Kline (1998) reports that values at or below 3.0 for skewness and 10.0 for kurtosis are reasonable cutoff levels in determining valid results. As shown in Table 3.2, no violations of skewness and/or kurtosis were evident in the 13 items being measured. Additionally, assumptions of multivariate normality and linearity were evaluated through the use of the Statistical Package for the Social Sciences (SPSS) 16.0 using box plots and Mahalanobis distance. The results showed that there were no outliers.

The original model of the Fidelity instrument with the 13 items is presented in Figure 3.2. Standardized parameter estimates are provided within the model. The squared multiple correlations (SMC) values are also provided in italics just below each of the 13 items. The SMC values indicate that item 11 of the Fidelity instrument accounts for the smallest amount of variance in fidelity (7%), while item 8 accounts for the largest amount of variance (68%). No post hoc modifications of the model were made from the analysis because of the good-fit indices (see Table 3.3) as well as because there were no indication of problems from the residual analysis.

In SEM, a chi-square statistic is but one way to determine if the result of the analysis is reliable. Using a combination of chi-square and other goodness-of-fit indices is recommended to determine the fit of the model, as chi-square statistics are vulnerable to

TABLE 3.2. *Means, Standard Deviations, Skewness, and Kurtosis for Fidelity Instrument Items*

Item Number	Mean	Standard Deviation	Skewness	Kurtosis
1	6.08	1.11	−0.93	−0.12
2	6.31	0.95	−1.60	3.15
3	5.99	1.12	−1.18	1.31
4	6.03	1.03	−0.84	0.59
5	6.21	0.96	−0.85	−0.48
6	5.93	1.22	−1.50	2.80
7	5.85	1.15	−1.17	2.01
8	6.02	1.00	−1.33	4.12
9	5.86	1.15	−1.05	0.90
10	5.49	2.10	−1.12	−0.22
11	5.56	1.52	−1.21	1.26
12	5.65	1.48	−1.40	1.76
13	5.33	1.85	−1.10	0.30

TABLE 3.3. *Global Fit Statistics*

Fit Index	Fit Value
Chi-square	75.86
RMSEA	.03
GFI	.97
AGFI	.91
CFI	.97

sample size (Schreiber et al., 2006). A variety of other indices are also used when examining model fit. Common fit indices include the Goodness of Fit Index (GFI), the Adjusted Goodness of Fit Index (AGFI), the Comparative Fit Index (CFI) and the Root Mean Square Error of Approximation (RMSEA), and all play a part in determining the fit of the scale. In establishing whether or not items are reliable, the chi-square results should not be significant. For the Fidelity instrument, χ^2 (65, $N = 116$) was 75.86 ($p = .17$). The GFI, AGFI, and CFI fit indices should all have values of .90 or above, and RMSEA values should be .05 or lower.

For this analysis, chi-square was not significant ($p > .05$), the results of the goodness-of-fit indices were above the recommended .90 level, and RMSEA was below .05. Thus, the results of the correlations, the reliability estimates, and the global fit statistics (see Table 3.3) indicate that the 13-item Fidelity instrument is indeed a good model fit in measuring adherence to the SFBT protocol.

■ DISCUSSION AND APPLICATION TO SFBT AND RESEARCH

In this pilot study, the goal was to determine whether criteria that were consistent with the underlying assumptions of SFBT could be developed into a fidelity instrument. SFBT fidelity criteria were developed as part of a rating scale and were used to determine how well the final 13 items worked together to measure adherence. The results of this study generally indicated that (a) it was possible to develop fidelity criteria from SFBT and that (b) these same criteria could be operationalized and measured as a tool that has the potential to be used for evaluating SFBT.

The findings of this pilot study suggest that the use of fidelity can be regarded as an important beginning step for testing intervention efficacy in SFBT research. As such, the reliability findings of this pilot study may be a step toward the support of SFBT interventions and their intended outcomes. The next step would be to identify convergent validity. The results of the positive relationships found in this pilot study might then be tested for replication in multiple settings to examine convergent validity (e.g., three separate samples of fidelity would show that the Fidelity instrument is theoretically sound and a good fit; Mowbray et al., 2003).

To examine the strength of fidelity in SFBT, it might also be important to call attention to discriminant validity, the notion being that the criteria for SFBT would not correlate highly with the criteria for other practice models such as cognitive behavioral therapy (CBT). For example, consider two therapists, one using CBT and the other using SFBT. These practice models are theoretically based on different concepts of intervention. Cognitive behavioral therapy offers the client a new way of considering emotions and thoughts, and SFBT offers the client a way of determining his or her goals in the context of finding solutions/exceptions to problems. Therefore, it would be important to show that the Fidelity instrument measures SFBT and not CBT. In other words, establishing the discriminant validity of the Fidelity instrument for SFBT would then show that the constructs of SFBT do not overlap greatly with the constructs of other practice models such as CBT; thus, the Fidelity instrument is only measuring the use of SFBT.

The SFBT Fidelity instrument developed in this study might enhance the credibility of research from multiple settings. It is well established that much of SFBT outcome research comes from real- world rather than academic settings (Kim, 2008), where, for example, RCTs are commonly used. Utilizing a fidelity approach may help control for less than ideal conditions (e.g., quasi-experimental designs). For example, adhering to a model by measuring fidelity in these situations could demonstrate the portability of SFBT. In this case, it is entirely possible that the effect sizes (*d*) or the relationship between two variables (SFBT and outcomes) might be strengthened. Furthermore, measuring fidelity in real-world situations could demonstrate that adherence can still occur and be tailored to fit in different contexts, with different populations, and different areas of concern (Hohmann & Shear, 2002).

The use of fidelity could increase funders' support for what constitutes best practice. Including fidelity in research applications may represent a specific and quantifiable approach that highlights better quality control and improved methodological standards when monitoring outcomes, especially given the shrinking dollars in highly competitive funding markets. The very mention of fidelity in reports may provide much greater credence than describing the use of a specific instrument that has had some initial testing (Perepletchikova et al., 2009).

The findings of this pilot study also highlight an important question: Does fidelity have to be the exact replication of a model or can the model be adapted to the context and still be useful (Mowbray et al., 2003)? In this study, we did not include the miracle question or the task question as part of our item construction because of the point in treatment at which we measured fidelity. This should, however, not imply that adapting either question in measuring SFBT outcomes cannot be used in other circumstances or that adherence to SFBT was compromised because either question was omitted. Instead, adhering to fidelity criteria could be measured in phases as an additional way to measure outcomes. For example, it might be perfectly acceptable to revise a fidelity measure in the second session in such a way that the adoption of the miracle question could be included at that point but omitted in later sessions.

Emphasizing fidelity in SFBT has implications for the front-line practitioner. Most importantly, the Fidelity instrument is adaptable to most working environments, inexpensive, and easy to use. Further, it could forge a relationship between the researcher and practitioner on at least two fronts. First, it might be considered a straightforward method of sensitizing the practitioner to research as it measures adherence in real time. The practitioner can see the immediate impact of what he or she does on the research intent. Second, using the Fidelity instrument may be one way the practitioner and researcher can collaborate more closely on technique and its method of delivery (Kazdin, 2008). The utility of SFBT is dependent on the client's needs, goals, and values. Thus, intervention may not be possible unless the practitioner's "clinical judgment, expertise, and context" (Kazdin, 2008, p.156) are contributing to what the client wants.

Using an SFBT Fidelity instrument might also be related to increasing practitioners' competence (Perepletchikova et al., 2009). The instrument in this pilot study should be able to assess the therapist's skill as well as the delivery of the intervention. Consequently, it may be used as a tool in training (see also Fiske, 2008) to assess how, for example, a practitioner handles a difficult situation or a trainee's stage of learning in delivering an SFBT intervention. The literature on training in SFBT is growing (e.g., Cunanan & McCollum, 2006; Nelson, 2005; Smock, 2005; Trepper et al., 2008), and it suggests that trainees consistently view practice, the combination of training and learning, and examining the therapist's own theoretical process of change as steps toward using SFBT. The use of a Fidelity instrument is likely to complement the process of matching the timing and pacing of intervention with the acquisition of new skills.

A second area of practitioner competence using the Fidelity instrument involves supervision. Here we suggest that supervision and the Fidelity instrument may be compatible in that both can attend to increasing professional growth and administrative responsibility. First, the instrument is pragmatic; it should help the practitioner and the supervisor notice what works in solution building while keeping a focus on what the client wants. We argue that this process of goal setting parallels the supervisor's function in improving the practitioner's abilities and skills. Second, as solution-focused therapy continues to move toward greater evidence of its efficacy, the Fidelity instrument could have an important function in measuring practitioners' work as it relates to case auditing or annual performance appraisals. If there is a need to demonstrate clinical or training outcomes that relate to standards of excellence, the Fidelity instrument should be able, at the very least, to demonstrate practitioners' competence at different points in time.

■ LIMITATIONS

Results from this pilot study should be interpreted in light of its limitations. The participants in this study were graduate-level student interns, and their responses may have been different from those of more experienced practitioners. This could limit the generalizability of the findings, and it will be important for future research to address and compare fidelity within these two groups. Additionally, questions might be raised regarding self-ratings and whether there was any bias toward social desirability. To help minimize bias in self-ratings, a consumer Fidelity instrument (FIC) is under construction.

Another limitation is that, while a clinician self-report instrument can be used to monitor fidelity, it does not by itself establish fidelity. According to Stein and colleagues (2007), two major elements should be considered when ascertaining reliable and proficient intervention fidelity: adherence and competence. The SFBT Fidelity instrument in this study aligns most closely with adherence in that it uses the student interns' responses to examine the "extent to which the interventionists' behaviors conform to the treatment protocol" (Stein et al., 2007, p. 4). What needs to be addressed in future research is competence, which involves a "focus on the interventionists' skillfulness in the delivery of the intervention" (p. 4). Markowitz et al. (2000) identified the gold standard test of treatment fidelity as the evaluation of therapists' adherence and competence through observation of videotaped and/or actual sessions. Although more costly and time-consuming, the use of videotaping or of independent raters via one way mirrors could be an alternative way of measuring the use of SFBT with the Fidelity instrument. Consent from both the clinician and the client would first need to be obtained. Next, SFBT-trained observers would be needed to view videotapes of client sessions or to observe through one-way mirrors. Interrater reliability between observers would need to be established before ratings could begin. Finally, using the Fidelity instrument as the rating scale, observers would view videotapes and/or actual sessions and rate the clinician's use of SFBT. The data collected from the observations could then be used to help determine the validity of the instrument.

The nature of this pilot project finally focuses on the need for additional studies to improve reliability and validity. If future work with fidelity is to be pursued, checks and balances need to be established concerning such issues as test-retest reliability and the internal consistency of SFBT criteria, as well as controlling for threats to internal and construct validity. Hohmann and Shear (2002) have argued that the ambiguous or negative findings of outcome research may be the most frequently cited reason for looking into internal validity; that is, for asking whether the independent variable (SFBT) has an effect on the dependent variable (the outcome of therapy). In order for SFBT is to be successfully replicated in various settings using detailed interventions, it will be important to determine if good outcomes are a function of the model as well as adherence to accurate implementation.

▪ CONCLUSION

As the expectation for the evidence of psychotherapy increases, solution-focused therapists will need to develop closer ties with their research peers. To bring the role of clinical practice and research into focus, this chapter has examined the notion of fidelity in relation to SFBT. Fidelity criteria were collected from the SFBT literature and grouped into a 13-item instrument, which was then tested by graduate-level social work interns. Initial pilot testing indicated the Fidelity instrument is a potentially good tool for measuring adherence to SFBT. While the discussion of the findings may be one way to advance SFBT research and practice (Kazdin, 2008), the stated limitations show the need to develop fidelity instrumentation via continued study that demonstrates greater rigor and thoroughness.

▪ REFERENCES

Barber, J. P., Gallop, R., Crits-Christoph, P., Frank, A., Thase, M. E., Weiss, R. D., & Gibbons, M.B.C. (2006). The role of therapist adherence, therapist competence, and alliance in predicting outcome of individual drug counseling: Results from the National Institute Drug Abuse Collaborative Cocaine Treatment Study. *Psychotherapy Research*, *16*, 229–240.

Berg, I. K., & Reuss, N. (1997). *Solutions step by step: A substance abuse treatment manual*. New York: Norton.

Bond, G. R., Evans, L., Salyers, M. P., Williams, J., Kim, H-W. (2000). Measurement of fidelity in psychiatric rehabilitation. *Mental Health Services Research, 2*, 75–87.

Chevalier, A. J. (1995). *On the client's path: A manual to teaching brief solution-focused therapy*. Oakland, CA: New Harbinger.

Corcoran, J., & Pillai, V. (2009). A review of the research on solution-focused therapy. *British Journal of Social Work, 39*, 234–242.

Costello, A. B., & Osborne, J. W. (2003). *Exploring best practices in factor analysis*. Chicago: American Educational Research Association.

Cunanan, E. D., & McCollum, E. E. (2006). What works when learning solution focused brief therapy: A qualitative study of trainee's experiences. *Journal of Family Psychotherapy*, *17*, 49–65.

De Jong, P., & Berg, I. K. (1997). *Interviewing for solutions*. New York: Thompson Learning.

de Shazer, S. (1985). *Keys to solution in brief therapy*. New York: Norton.

de Shazer, S. (1992). *Patterns of brief family therapy*. New York: Guilford

de Shazer, S., Berg, I. K., Lipchik, E., Nunnally, E., Molnar, A., Gingerich, W., & Weiner-Davis, M. (1986). Brief therapy: Focused solution development. *Family Process, 25*, 207–221.

de Shazer. S., Dolan, Y. M., Korman, H., Trepper, T. S., McCollum, E. E., & Berg, I. K. (2007). *More than miracles: The state of the art of solution focused therapy*. New York: Haworth.

Fiske, H. (2008). Solution-focused training: The medium and the message. In T. S. Nelson & F. N. Thomas (Eds.), *Handbook of solution-focused brief therapy: Clinical applications* (pp. 317–341). New York: Haworth.

Fiske, H., & Zalter, B. (2003). *The consultation feedback form.* Toronto: Unpublished document.

Gorsuch, R. L. (1983). *Factor analysis* (2nd ed.). Hillsdale, NJ: Erlbaum.

Gresham, F. M., MacMillan, D. L., Beebee-Frankenberger, M. E., & Bocian, K. M. (2000). Treatment integrities in learning disabilities intervention research: Do we really know how treatments are implemented? *Learning Disabilities Research & Practice, 15,* 198–205.

Hatcher, L. (1994). *A step-by-step approach to using structural equation modeling for factor analysis.* Cary, NC: SAS Institute.

Hohmann, A. A., & Shear, M. K. (2002). Community-based intervention research: Coping with the "noise" of real life in study design. *American Journal of Psychiatry, 159,* 201–207.

Hoyle, R. H. (1995). The structural equation modeling approach: Basic concepts and fundamental issues. In R. H. Hoyle (Ed.), *Structural equation modeling: Concepts, issues and applications* (pp. 1–15). Thousand Oaks, CA: Sage Publications.

Kazdin, A. E. (2008). Evidence-based treatment and practice. *American Psychologist, 63,* 146–159.

Kline, R. B. (1998). *Principles and practice of structural equation modeling.* New York: Guilford Press.

Markowitz, J. C., Spielman, L. A., Scarvalone, P. A., & Perry, S. W. (2000). Psychotherapy adherence of therapists treating HIV-positive patients with depressive symptoms. *Journal of Psychotherapy Practice and Research, 9,* 75–80.

McGrew, J. H., Bond, G. R., Dietzen, L., & Salyers, M. (1994). Measuring the fidelity of implementation of a mental health program model. *Journal of Consulting and Clinical Psychology, 62,* 670–678.

Mowbray, C. T., Holter, M. C., Teague, G. B., & Bybee, D. (2003). Fidelity criteria: Development, measurement, and validation. *American Journal of Evaluation, 24,* 315–340.

Nelson, T. S. (Ed.). (2005). *Education and training in solution-focused brief therapy.* Binghampton, NY: Haworth.

Nezu, A. M., & Nezu, C. M. (2008). Ensuring treatment integrity. In A. M. Nezu & C. M. Nezu (Eds.), *Evidence based outcome research: A practical guide to conducting randomized controlled trials for psychosocial interventions* (pp. 263–284). New York: Oxford University Press.

Nunnally, J. C. (1978). *Psychometric theory* (2nd ed.). New York: McGraw-Hill.

Office of Juvenile Justice and Delinquency Prevention (OJJDP). (2009). *Solution-focused brief therapy.* Washington, DC: U.S. Department of Justice, Office of Justice Programs Retrieved November 27, 2009, from http://www2.dsgonline.com/mpg/mpg_program_detail.aspx?ID=712&title=Solution-Focused%20Brief%20Therapy

Orwin, R. G. (2000). Assessing program fidelity in substance abuse health services research. *Addiction, 95* (Suppl 3), s309—s327.

Pedhazur, E. J. (1997). *Multiple regression in behavioral research: Explanation and prediction.* Fort Worth, TX: Harcourt Brace College.

Perepletchikova, F., Hilt, L. M., Chereji, E., & Kazdin, A. E. (2009). Barriers to implementing treatment integrity procedures: Survey of treatment outcome researchers. *Journal of Consulting and Clinical Psychology, 77,* 212–218.

Perepletchikova, F., & Kazdin, A.E. (2005). Treatment integrity and therapeutic change: Issues and research recommendations. *Clinical Psychology: Science and Practice, 12,* 365–383.

Perepletchikova, F., Treat, T. A., & Kazdin, A. E. (2007). Treatment integrity in psycho-therapy research: Analysis of the studies and examination of the associated factors. *Journal of Consulting and Clinical Psychology, 75,* 829–841.

Schreiber, J. B., Stage. F. K., King, J., Nora, A., & Barlow, E. A. (2006). Reporting structural equation modeling and confirmatory factor analysis results: A review. *Journal of Educational Research, 99,* 323–337.

Smock, S. A. (2005). A student's response to SFBT training meetings: The future looks bright. *Journal of Family Psychotherapy, 16,* 11–13.

Stein, K. F., Sargent, J. T., & Rafaels, N. (2007). Intervention research: Establishing fidelity of the independent variable in clinical trials. *Nursing Research, 56,* 54–62.

Teague, G. B., Bond, G. R., & Drake, R. E. (1998). Program fidelity and assertive community treatment: Development and use of a measure. *American Journal of Orthopsychiatry, 68,* 216–232.

Trepper, T. S., McColum, E. E., De Jong, P., Korman, H., Gingerich, W., & Franklin, C. (2008). *Solution focused therapy treatment manual for working with individuals: Research Committee of the Solution Focused Brief Therapy Association.* Retrieved April 10, 2009, from http://www.sfbta.org/Research.pdf

Waltz, J., Addis, M. E., Koerner, K., & Jacobson, N. S. (1993). Testing the integrity of a psy-chotherapy protocol: Assessment of adherence and competence. *Journal of Consulting and Clinical Psychology, 61,* 620–630.

Warner, R. (2000). *Qualitative self-assessment.* Toronto: Unpublished document.

4 A Review of Solution-Focused, Standardized Outcome Measures and Other Strengths-Oriented Outcome Measures

■ SARA A. SMOCK

■ INTRODUCTION

The recent positive psychology movement has set the stage for increased demand for strengths-based instruments in the field of psychotherapy. The need for reliable and valid measures that capture constructs about positive client traits is vast. Fortunately, numerous instruments exist for this purpose. These instruments are useful for clinicians and researchers who need to quantify their clients' strengths. Due to the philosophical emphasis of solution-focused brief therapy (SFBT) on clients' resources, the availability of various strengths-based instruments will increase the efficacy and effectiveness research on the model. Finally, instruments exist that capture the core elements of SFBT. By using strengths-based assessment to measure treatment progress and outcomes, SFBT will continue to be recognized as an evidence-based practice for specific populations.

The purpose of this chapter is to discuss the development and use of strengths-based instruments in the field of psychotherapy. Chapter 5 also describes assessment and outcome measurement tools that practitoners and researchers can use to measure the effectiveness of SFBT. This chapter will begin by summarizing the positive psychology movement and how it has set the stage for strengths-based instruments. Next, an overview of strengths-based assessments, including their psychometric properties, will be presented. Published research studies using strengths-based assessments will also be covered. The chapter will end by discussing how strengths-based instruments can and should be used in SFBT research, as well as specific suggestions for implementation.

A better understanding of strengths-based assessments and instruments is very important for solution-focused therapists. First, it is important to know the valid and reliable strengths-based instruments available for SFBT therapists to use in a clinical setting. Possessing instruments that align philosophically with SFBT's poststructural stance will aid in providing congruent clinical services. Second, researchers will gain a variety of strengths-based instruments that can be used in conducting research on

SFBT interventions. In order to develop the evidence base of solution-focused therapy, it is important to use instruments that measure constructs aligning with SFBT principles.

■ HISTORY

Throughout the history of psychotherapy, deficits, weaknesses, and pathology have been the focus of treatment. Depression, anxiety, psychosis, and other ailments have been studied intensively in order to decrease the prevalence of such impairments in clients' lives. Recently, a paradigm shift in the field began to occur in the way clients are viewed by their psychotherapists.

The positive psychology movement. Positive psychology is a recent movement reacting to the dominant frame of psychotherapy, which focuses on problems and pathology. In the 2000 special issue of *American Psychology* on positive psychology, Seligman introduced the movement as one that focuses on "valued subjective experiences: wellbeing, contentment, and satisfaction (in the past); hope and optimism (in the future); and flow and happiness (in the present)" (Seligman & Csikszentmihalyi, 2000, p. 5). The positive psychology movement shifts from pathologizing clients to a more preventive and strengths-based approach to mental illness. There are several specific topics within the positive psychology movement. They include one's own positive experience (e.g., Diener, 2000; Kahneman, 1999; Massimini & Delle Fave, 2000; Peterson, 2000), positive personality (e.g., Baltes & Staudinger, 2000; Ryan & Deci, 2000; Vaillant, 2000), and positive communities (e.g., Buss, 2000; Larson, 2000; Myers, 2000), just to name a few.

Numerous studies illustrate the advantage of focusing on clients' abilities and strengths. For example, several studies show the benefit of focusing on strengths and resources due to the connections between mental and physical health (e.g., Salovey et al., 2000; Taylor et al., 2000). In addition, developing excellent qualities in clients such as wisdom (e.g., Baltes & Staudinger, 2000), exceptional intellectual abilities (e.g., Lubinski & Benbow, 2000), and creativity (e.g., Simonton, 2000) shows promise in furthering their health. Theories on positive psychology have also examined the role of positive emotion (Fredrickson, 2004) and postulate the idea of posttraumatic growth (Bannink, 2008; Joseph & Linley, 2008). For clinicians and researchers in the twenty-first century, it is clear that the zeitgeist is one of investigating what is working and how to use strengths to prevent maladies as well as sustain desired futures.

Solution-focused brief therapy. Solution-focused brief therapy is a systemic model used in the fields of social work and marriage and family therapy (see Chapter 1 for an overview of the history of SFBT). While the history of social work has its roots in strengths-based principles, SFBT was one of the first clinical approaches to provide solution-based therapeutic tools for working with clients (De Jong & Berg, 1995). Solution-focused brief therapy emerged as a revolt against the practice of pathologizing individuals and families; it focuses exclusively on clients' ability to build solutions. De Shazer and colleagues (1986) describe the main principle of SFBT as "utilizing what clients bring with them to help them meet their needs in such a way that they can make satisfactory lives for themselves" (p. 208). At the time of its development, SFBT's approach to psychotherapy was revolutionary and has more recently come into its own. Today SFBT is widely used in family therapy (e.g., McCollum & Trepper, 2001) and in treating substance abuse (e.g. Berg & Miller, 1992) and schizophrenia (e.g., Eakes et al., 1997), just to name a few areas of practice.

Although SFBT is not part of the positive psychology movement, some of its principles are similar to those of psychology's strengths-based approaches. For example, SFBT's main premise is solution building. Smock and colleagues (2010) summarize the key components of solution building, which is the main premise of SFBT, as defining the client's preferred future (De Jong & Berg, 1998), increasing the client's awareness of exceptions (De Jong & Berg; de Shazer, 1988, 1991), and the client's hope for the future (Berg & Dolan, 2001). Solution building is similar to the strengths-based approaches in psychology in that they both build on the resources of the client. Thus, SFBT benefits from the popularity of the positive psychology movement and the development of instruments to measure client strengths constructs.

■ STRENGTHS-BASED ASSESSMENT

The emergence of the positive psychology movement has created the need for strengths-based assessments. Epstein and Sharma (1998) define strengths-based assessment as "the measurement of those emotional and behavioral skills, competencies, and characteristics that create a sense of personal accomplishment; contribute to satisfying relationships with family members, peers, and adults; enhance one's ability to deal with adversity and stress; and promote one's personal, social, and academic development" (p. 3).

Strengths-based assessments are instruments that measure constructs found in positive psychology and other strengths-based approaches. To date, these assessments have been used in many areas, such as education (e.g., Epstein et al., 2000), parenting (e.g., Strom & Coolege, 1987), and the development of positive traits (e.g., Snyder, 1995); they also show promise as a way to measure empirically supported treatments. Due to the zeitgeist of focusing on a person's positive characteristics and the growing number of strengths-based measures, strengths-based assessment appears to be here to stay.

■ REVIEW OF STRENGTHS-BASED INSTRUMENTS

A vast number of strengths-based instruments exist. However, the purpose of this chapter is to provide a helpful list of reliable and valid instruments for clinicians and researchers to choose from. This section will begins by providing a brief overview of what constitutes a reliable and valid instrument.

Reliability and Validity

Reliability is one important aspect of an instrument's psychometric properties that needs to be considered when selecting a measure. *Reliability* is defined as how consistent a measure is (i.e., if you administer the measure again and again, it will it yield similar results; Bloom et al., 2005; Fischer & Corcoran, 2007; Graham & Lilly, 1984; Sattler, 1988). It is important for instruments to have good or high reliability to ensure as much as possible that the measure is trustworthy. While different types of reliability computations exist, internal consistency is the one most commonly reported.

Alphas (reported as α =) give a number between 0.00 and 1.00 (e.g., α = .85). The higher the number, the higher the reliability. The cutoff for a reliable instrument varies, but an acceptable level ranges between .6 (Hudson, 1982) and .7 (Abell et al., 2009).

Validity is another important type of psychometric component. *Validity* is defined as the degree to which an instrument measures the construct it is supposed to measure. For example, an instrument to measure self-esteem is valid if and only if it actually measures the level of self-esteem. As with reliability, there are several different types of validity: content, criterion, concurrent, and construct. In *content validity*, each item in an instrument measures the intended construct of the instrument (Hudson, 1981). *Criterion validity* correlates the instrument with an empirical criterion, another known measure of the same construct such as a standardized assessment evaluation (Anastasi, 1996). *Concurrent validity* occurs when an instrument correlates well with a previously established instrument that measures the same construct. *Construct validity* defines how well an instrument coincides with the theoretical concept of the construct being measured (Anastasi, 1996; Bostwick & Kyte, 1988; Rubin & Babbie, 2008; Sattler, 1988). Overall, a valid instrument is one that accurately measures the construct intended to be measured. (For more detailed information on reliability and validity information, see Jordan and Franklin's 2011 book on clinical assessment.)

Inclusion Criteria

Reviews of reliable and valid strengths-based instruments used in clinical and/or research settings will be summarized in this chapter. Each review includes the following: the developer of the instrument, the definition of the measured construct, details about the items, reliability and validity, and clinical and research usefulness. Instruments are categorized by their intended populations (e.g., individual traits and attributes, family, children, and adolescents) or purposes (i.e., measures developed specifically for SFBT). Within each group, measures are listed in descending order; the strongest psychometric properties appear first.

A thorough search for strengths-based instruments found 41 reliable and/or valid measures. All of them are listed in this chapter. Instruments that met the following criteria are *not* included:

1. Measures that are not standardized instruments
2. Measures that appear to be strengths-based from their title but lack enough information about the construct being measured to demonstrate that they are truly strengths-based instruments
3. Measures that have not been translated into English

Tables are also given summarizing the instruments' reliability, validity, and clinical and research appropriateness. Reliability and validity are rated as "yes," "moderate," or "unknown." "Yes" ratings indicate at least one measure of high reliability (i.e., better than .6). A rating of "yes" in the validity column requires at least one stable measure of validity. "Moderate" scores denote acceptable reliability (slightly under .6) and only one modest validity (e.g., promising criterion validity). Evaluations of "unknown" are given when published reports are inconclusive about the measure's reliability and/or validity.

The table columns "Appropriateness in Clinical Settings" and "Appropriateness in Research Settings" provide guidance on how to best use the instruments. *Clinical appropriateness* refers to using an instrument in a clinical setting, with a rating of either "appropriate" or "unknown." An "Appropriate" rating in the clinical category means that the measure was developed to be used or has been successfully used in clinical settings. "Unknown" indicates that the measure is unspecified for clinical populations. The "Appropriateness in Research Settings" column rates instruments for their use in any type of quantitative research (e.g., outcome studies). A rating of "appropriate" is given when an instrument meets the minimum requirements for reliability and validity. A rating of "unknown" indicates that either reliability and/or validity has not been evaluated or is not strong enough for the instrument to be recommended for research purposes. The purpose of this summary is to aid clinicians and researchers in making informed decisions when selecting the best strengths-based measures in their practice and/or research. The sections below briefly review key components of strengths-based assessments that can be used in clinical and/or research settings. Tables 4.1 to 4.4 provide a quick reference to all published assessments that have the potential to quantify characteristics of the solution-focused approach.

TABLE 4.1. *Strengths-Based Individual's Traits and Attributes*

Name of Instrument	Reliable	Valid	Appropriateness in Clinical Settings	Appropriateness in Research Settings
Herth Hope Scale/Index (HHS/HHI)	Yes	Yes	Appropriate	Appropriate
Curiosity and Exploration Inventory (CEI)	Yes	Yes	Unknown	Appropriate
Inspiration Scale (IS)	Yes	Yes	Unknown	Appropriate
Meaning in Life Questionnaire (MLQ)	Yes	Yes	Unknown	Appropriate
State Hope Scale	Yes	Yes	Unknown	Appropriate
Subjective Happiness Scale (SHS)	Yes	Yes	Unknown	Appropriate
Self-Efficacy Scale	Yes	Yes	Unknown	Appropriate
Immediate Outcome Rating Scale (IORS)	Yes	Unknown	Appropriate	Unknown
Gratitude Questionnaire-6 (GQ-6)[1]	Yes	Yes	Unknown	Appropriate
Mindful Attention Awareness Scale (MAAS)[2]	Yes	Yes	Unknown	Appropriate
Personal Growth Initiative Scale (PGIS)[3]	Yes	Yes	Unknown	Appropriate
Transgression-Related Interpersonal Motivations Inventory (TRIM)[4]	Yes	Yes	Unknown	Appropriate
Situational Confidence Questionnaire[5]	Yes	Yes	Unknown	Appropriate
Dispositional Hope Scale (DHS)[6]	Yes	Yes	Unknown	Appropriate
Nowotny Hope Scale[7]	Yes	Unknown	Appropriate	Inconclusive
Life Orientation Test Revised (LOT-R)[8]	Yes	Unknown	Unknown	Inconclusive
Global Self-Esteem Scale[9]	Yes	Unknown	Unknown	Inconclusive
Social Desirability Scale-17[10]	Yes	Unknown	Unknown	Inconclusive

[1] McCullough et al. (2002).
[2] Brown and Ryan (2003).
[3] Robitschek (1998).
[4] McCullough et al.(1998).
[5] Annis and Graham (1988).
[6] Snyder (1995).
[7] Nowotny (1991).
[8] Scheier and Carver (1992).
[9] Robins et al.(2001).
[10] (Stober, 2001).

TABLE 4.2. *Strengths-Based Family Instruments*

Name of Instrument	Reliable	Valid	Appropriateness in Clinical Settings	Appropriateness in Research Settings
Family Assessment Device (FAD)	Yes	Yes	Appropriate	Appropriate
Family Functioning Style Scale (FFSS)	Yes	Yes	Unknown	Appropriate
Parent Perception Inventory	Yes	Yes	Unknown	Appropriate
Developmental Assets Profile (DAP)	Yes	Yes	Unknown	Appropriate
Parent-Adolescent Communication Scale[1]	Yes	Unknown	Appropriate	Inconclusive
Family Assessment Measure (FAM-III)[2]	Yes	Unknown	Appropriate	Inconclusive
Family Resource Scale (FRS)[3]	Unknown	Yes	Unknown	Inconclusive
Family Support Scale (FSS)[4]	Yes	Unknown	Unknown	Inconclusive
Family Empowerment Scale (FES)[5]	Yes	Unknown	Unknown	Inconclusive

[1] Barnes and Olsen (1985).
[2] Skinner et al. (1983).
[3] Dunst and Leet (1987).
[4] Dunst et al. (1988).
[5] Koren et al. (1992).

TABLE 4.3. *Strengths-Based Children and Adolescents*

Name of Instrument	Reliable	Valid	Appropriateness in Clinical Settings	Appropriateness in Research Settings
Behavioral and Emotional Rating Scale (BERS)	Yes	Yes	Unknown	Appropriate
Developmental Assets Profile (DAP)	Yes	Yes	Unknown	Appropriate
Social Skills Rating System (SSRS)[1]	Yes	Moderate	Unknown	Inconclusive
Behavioral Assessment System for Children (BASC)[2]	Yes	Moderate	Unknown	Inconclusive
Multidimensional Student Life Satisfaction Survey[3]	Yes	Moderate	Unknown	Appropriate
School Social Behavior Scale-2 (SSBS-2)[4]	Yes	Moderate	Unknown	Appropriate
California Healthy Kids Survey-Resilience Youth Development Module (RYDM)[5]	Yes	Moderate	Unknown	Appropriate

[1] Gresham and Elliott (1990).
[2] Reynolds and Kamphaus (1992).
[3] Huebner and Gilman (2003).
[4] Merrell (2002).
[5] Constantine et al. (1999).

TABLE 4.4. *Measures Created Specifically for SFBT*

Name of Instrument	Reliable	Valid	Appropriateness in Clinical Settings	Appropriateness in Research Settings
Solution Building Inventory (SBI)	Yes	Yes	Appropriate	Appropriate
Solution Identification Scale (SIS)	Yes	Unknown	Appropriate	Unknown
Solution-Focused Recovery Scale for Trauma Survivors	Yes	Unknown	Appropriate	Unknown
Immediate Outcome Rating Scale (IORS)	Yes	Unknown	Appropriate	Unknown

Individual's Traits and Attributes

The following instruments measure a variety of strengths and positive traits of individuals. This overview contains a broad range of traits and qualities.

Herth Hope Scale/Index (HHS/HHI). The Herth Hope Scale/Index is a 30-item questionnaire developed to assess hope for adults in clinical settings on a 4-point scale (Herth, 1991). It is based on the six dimensions of hope presented in Dufault and Martocchio's Model of Hope (Dufault & Martocchio 1985). Reliability for the HHS/HHI ranges from .75 to .94, with test-retest reliability ranging from .89 to .91. Convergent validity was manifested by a significant negative correlation between the HHS/HHI and the Beck Hopelessness Scale. Factor analysis on the HHS/HHI revealed the following three components: temporality and future, positive readiness and expectancy, and interconnectedness. Thus, the HHS/HHI appears to be a reliable and valid strengths-based instrument in both clinical and research settings.

Curiosity and Exploration Inventory (CEI). The CEI was developed by Kashdan, Rose, and Fincham (2004) and assesses an individual's differences in the pursuit, recognition, and integration of challenging and novel experiences and information. This measure is a seven-item scale that captures both exploration and absorption. The first component, *exploration*, refers to strivings for novel and challenging information and experiences. *Absorption* is defined as the tendency to be deeply engaged in activities. The items are evaluated using a 7-point Likert-type scale. The reliability of the CEI ranges from .63 to .80 and shows moderately large positive relationships with reward sensitivity, openness to experience, intrinsic motivation, and subjective vitality. In terms of validity, the CEI has been shown to measure constructs of positive affect and reward sensitivity.

Inspiration Scale (IS). The IS was published by Thrash and Elliot in 2003. It is a four-item measure of a motivational resource. Although this is a very brief scale, it contains both frequency and intensity subscales that can be pooled into an overall inspiration scale. A strength of this instrument is its favorable psychometric properties. The IS demonstrates internal consistency, a consistent two-factor structure, temporal stability, and measurement consistency across time and across populations. Its reliability is .90, with good test-retest reliability ($r = .77$). The IS also demonstrates strong evidence of construct validity and empirical utility.

Meaning in Life Questionnaire (MLQ). Steger and colleagues (2006) developed the MLQ to assesses both the presence of and the search for meaning in life dimensions. The Presence of Meaning subscale (MLQ-P) measures the level of fulfillment in individual's' lives. The Search for Meaning subscale (MLQ-S) measures individuals' level of engagement and motivation in their effort to find or deepen their understanding of meaning in their lives. This 10-item scale uses a 7-point Likert rating ranging from "absolutely true" to "absolutely untrue." Steger et al. report good reliability for the MLQ-P (.81) and the MLQ–S (.84). The 1-month test-retest reliability coefficients are favorable (MLQ–P = .7; MLQ–S = .73). The MLQ subscales also possess good convergent and discriminant validity when examined across time and across subjects, as well as in comparison with two other meaning scales.

State Hope Scale. The State Hope Scale was developed to measure the goal-directed thinking of a person at a certain point in time (Snyder et al., 1996). This six-item self-report instrument contains two components: agency and pathways thinking. Three items measure each component. The higher the total score on the State Hope Scale, the more state hope exists. Cronbach's alphas range from .79 to .95. The State Hope Scale shows discriminant validity when compared other measures assessing hope.

Subjective Happiness Scale (SHS). Lyubomirsky and Lepper (1999) developed the SHS to measure the concept of global subjective happiness. The SHS is a four-item scale; two items ask individuals to characterize themselves using both absolute ratings and ratings relative to peers, while the other two items offer short descriptions of happy and unhappy individuals and ask respondents to what extent each characterization describes them. Reliability coefficients range from .79 to .94 and indicate that the SHS has high internal consistency. Construct validity, as well as convergent and discriminant validity, have been tested and confirm the SHS's ability to measure the construct of subjective happiness.

Self-Efficacy Scale. The Self-Efficacy Scale was developed by Jerusalem and Schwarzer (1992) to assess a general sense of perceived self-efficacy in a unidimensional measure. Its purpose is to predict the client's ability to cope with daily stressors as well as adaptation after experiencing various stressful life events. The Self-Efficacy Scale contains 10 items preferably added randomly to a larger pool of items that have the same response format. Cronbach's alphas computed on this scale range from .76 to .90. Criterion-related validity has been established in several correlational studies comparing the Self-Efficacy Scale with favorable emotions, dispositional optimism, and work satisfaction.

Family

This section includes systemic measures of positive family qualities. Although numerous systemic instruments exist, the measures listed in this section have at least one section focused on strengths.

Family Assessment Device (FAD). The McMaster family assessment device, also known as the Family Assessment Device, was created by Epstein, Baldwin, and Bishop in 1983. The 53-item instrument measures behavior control, affective responsiveness, problem solving, communication, roles, and affective involvement in families. The FAD has been used in both clinical and nonclinical settings, showing various types of validity as well as reliability. Initially, reports of Cronbach's alpha ranged from .72 to .90 (Epstein, Baldwin, & Bishop, 1983), with many subsequent studies reporting similar results (e.g., Kabacoff et al., 1990). Numerous studies have used the FAD to assess the strengths in family functioning.

Family Functioning Style Scale (FFSS). Trivette and Dunst (1990) developed the FFSS to measure family strengths. The instrument contains 26 items rated on a 5-point scale. The five subscales within the FFSS are Interactional Patterns, Family Values, Coping Strategies, Family Commitment, and Resource Mobilization. Coefficient alpha the split-half reliabilities are .92 on the total FFSS score. Several types of validity are noted. First, criterion validity was assessed by comparing the Family Hardiness Index (FHI) to the FFSS ($r = .62$). Predictive validity, a type of construct validity, was assessed by using two measures of well-being; the Psychological Well-Being Index (PWI), a measure of personal well-being, and the Mastery and Health subscale of the Family Inventory of Resources and Management (FIRM).

Parent Perception Inventory. In 1983, Hazzard, Christensen, and Margolin created the Parent Perception Inventory. This 18-item, 4-point scale is given to children and is intended to measure the child's perceptions of positive and negative parental behaviors.

The data collector administers this scale in an interview format away from the child's parents. Reliability ranges from .78 to .88. Both discriminant and convergent validity have been demonstrated.

Developmental Assets Profile (DAP). The DAP is a 58-item self-report scale rated on a 4-point range (Benson et al., 2004). Eight assets, such as support, empowerment, and positive values, are measured. Reported internal consistency is excellent (.81), as is test-retest reliability (.84–.87). Comparisons between the DAP and several measures demonstrate moderate to strong convergent validity.

Children and Adolescents

Assessments for children and adolescents vary in the setting in which they can be given. The following measures can be given to children and/or adolescents, their parents, and/or their teachers. Be sure to note the specific setting in which each instrument is intended to be given (e.g., home, school). Educators, social workers, and therapists will find this list to be very useful in highlighting the strengths of the children they serve.

The Behavioral and Emotional Rating Scale (BERS). Buckley and Epstein (2004) created the BERS to measure children's behavioral and emotional strengths. Fifty-two items capture an overall strengths quotient as well as the following five subscales: Interpersonal Strengths, Family Involvement, Intrapersonal Strengths, School Functioning, and Affective Strengths. An adult who has known the child for several months completes the BERS. A standard score for the overall measure, as well as a score for each subscale, is computed. Internal consistency of the total scale (strengths quotient) and the subscales is strong, with high test-retest reliabilities. Interrater reliability coefficients range from .83 to .98. Criterion-related validity has been established.

Developmental Assets Profile (DAP). The DAP was developed by the Search Institute (2003) to measure the following eight developmental components: support, empowerment, boundaries and expectations, constructive use of time, commitment to learning, positive values, social competencies, and positive identity. In this 58-item, 4-point Likert scale, internal consistency alpha coefficients average .81 over the eight categories. Construct validity was tested by comparing the DAP to the Search Institute's 40 developmental assets model.

Measures Created Specifically for SFBT

Severalmeasures have been developed to capture principles of solution-focused therapy. While some of these measures do not possess psychometric properties, it seems important to list all of the instruments that have been developed specifically to measure aspects of SFBT.

Immediate Outcome Rating Scale (IORS). Adams, Piercy, and Jurich (1991) created the IORS to assess goal clarity, optimism, and compliance. The IORS asks clients to rate changes in the severity of their current presenting problem. This measure was created because no existing instrument captured "outcome optimism" or "goal clarity" in clients. Ten items were developed using a 5-point Likert scale. Reliability reports of .86 for goal clarity and .81 for optimism were found in the initial analysis.

Solution Building Inventory (SBI). The SBI was developed by Smock, McCollum, and Stevenson (2010) to measure the construct of solution building. This instrument was developed by defining the components of solution building through the scale development procedure of factor analysis. Through statistical computations, the SBI is a unidimensional scale using 14 items to capture the construct of solution building. Sample items include the following: "I am aware of small positive changes that I make," "I have successfully overcome challenges in the past," and "I have made steps towards improving my life." Respondents are asked to respond to each statement on a 5-point Likert scale; responses range from "strongly agree" to "strongly disagree." The SBI possesses high internal consistency (α = .886) as well as good content, convergent, and discriminant validity. The instrument has been tested on a clinical population and has yielded high internal consistency (α = .916) as well as inverse correlations with the Outcome Questionnaire (OQ) 45.2 and the Brief Symptom Inventory (BSI) General Severity Index and positive correlations with the Dyadic Adjustment Scale Revised (DAS-R). These comparisons confirm that as one's solution building increases, less distress (OQ 45.2, DAS-R, and the BSI General Severity Index) occurs (Smock, 2007).

Solution Identification Scale (SIS). The SIS, originally developed by Goldman and Baydanan in 1990, assesses solution-oriented relational behaviors in couples. It contains 30 items, which are scored on a scale from 1 (never) to 10 (always). Total SIS scores range from 30 to 300, with higher scores indicating better relational skills in intimate relationships. Sample items include "expresses feeling other than anger" and "supports spouse's or partner's friendships." Although the authors did not report the reliability and validity of the SIS, Lee et al. (2003), in their study on solution-focused treatment of domestic violent couples, reported a high reliability coefficient of .93.

Solution-Focused Recovery Scale for Trauma Survivors. The Solution-Focused Recovery Scale for Trauma Survivors was developed by Dolan (1991) to measure positive coping skills in individuals who experienced sexual abuse as a child. It consists of 36 items scored on a Likert-type scale from 0 (not at all) to 4 (very much). The higher the score, the more adaptive coping is present. Individuals rate the following behaviors: ability to think/talk about the abuse, ability to go to work/school, ability to hold hands with loved ones, ability to keep self physically safe, and ability to look strangers in the eye. Although psychometric properties were not established by Kruczek and Vitanza (1999) of Dolan's scale, adjusting one item found the reliability to be .69 in their study.

Other solution-focused questions have been used to measure concepts of SFBT. The following questions/measures have been used: questionnaire from a brief family therapy center (Lee, 1997), solution-focused questions (Seagram, 1977), and clients' reports on whether things were better before each session (Reuterlov et al., 2000). In addition, Chapter 3 in this book discusses the details of a fidelity measure.

■ SFBT OUTCOME STUDIES USING STRENGTHS-BASED INSTRUMENTS

Despite the fact that numerous strengths-based instruments exist, few have been used to evaluate SFBT. To date, nine quantitative experimental and quasi-experimental outcome studies, both published and unpublished, in English use strengths-based measures (see Table 4.5). The research designs used in these studies vary from descriptive to experimental. Additional outcome studies conducted on SFBT exist (see other chapters in this book for details) but do not use at least one strengths-based instrument to measure progress.

TABLE 4.5. *SFBT Outcome Studies Using Strengths-Based Instruments*

Name of study	Population	All Outcome Measures Used in the Study
Huang (2001)	Couples	Conflict Tactics Scale, Scaling Questions
Seagram (1997)	Youth offenders	Jesness Behavior Checklist, Carlson Psychological Survey, Solution-focused Questions, Test of Self-Conscious Affect
Bozeman (1999)	Psychiatric patients	Beck Depression Inventory, Nowotny Hope Scale
Leggett (2004)	Students	Coopersmith Self-Esteem Inventory, Children's Hope Scale
Seagram (1997)	Youth offenders	Coopersmith Self-Esteem Inventory
Adams et al. (1991)	Families	Immediate Outcome Rating Scale-Goal Clarity, Optimism, and Compliance
Triantafillou (2002)	Children	Parent-Adolescent Communication Scale, Family Adaptability & Cohesion Scales II
Zimmerman et al. (1996)	Parents	Parent Skills Inventory
Littrell et al. (1995)	Students	Likert Scale Questionnaire assessing changes in students' concerns, goal attainment, intensity of students' feelings

Results

While a few reviews and meta-analyses on SFBT exist, little is known about the results of SFBT studies that include strengths-based instruments. Kim's (2008 meta-analysis on SFBT reported on nine studies that used strengths-based instruments (see Table 4.5). Five of these studies used a quasi-experimental or experimental approach (Adams et al., 1991; Leggett, 2004; Seagram, 1997; Triantafillou, 2002; Zimmerman et al., 1996). Of these five, only one produced a moderate to strong effect size (.70; Adams et al., 1991; Kim, 2008). This study used an experimental design that looked at the effects of the formula first session task (FFST) on families. Participants were measured on three measures, one of which was strengths-based. The Immediate Outcome Rating Scale (IORS) was used to assess overall family functioning and improvements from a strengths perspective. Results from this study indicated that families were more successful in completing the FFST than the problem-focused task. For a more detailed review of the Kim meta-analysis and other systematic reviews of SFBT, see Chapter 6 this volume.

Overall, there are very few SFBT studies that use strength-based instruments. Only one found promising effects for SFBT using a strengths-based measure. More SFBT studies need to be conducted using strengths-based measures to accurately capture the constructs of SFBT.

■ PRACTICE GUIDELINES

Using strengths-based instruments to measure the effectiveness of SFBT is important to both clinicians and researchers. It is important to select instruments that are reliable and valid but that also have clinical utility. If an instrument has good clinical utility, using the measure in practice ". . . makes a difference with respect to the accuracy, outcome, or efficiency of clinical activities" (Hunsley & Mash, 2007, p. 45, cited in Franklin & Parrish, 2011) in press. When choosing an instrument to use, it is important to investigate its clinical utility. *Clinical utility* refers how practical a measure is to use, that is, whether it can help the therapist plan and evaluate therapies. Other issues also come into play, such as whether the instrument is easy to administer and score (Franklin & Parrish). For example, the length of an instrument, whether any training is needed to administer it, and the instrument's ability to enhance services are all important factors to consider when selecting a measure. One also must consider if a measure makes sense, given the particular client's situation. A measure may have excellent psychometric properties (e.g., validity, reliability) but may be too lengthy for a solution-focused practice requiring measures that can be used in brief practice situations and that are sensitive to brief change. In addition, Franklin and Parrish point out that for a measure to meet the demands of evidence-based assessment and to have clinical utility, it must be normed on the client populations (e.g., assess reliability with the specific group using the instrument) and evaluated for its cultural competence (i.e., whether the instrument takes cultural differences into account). For example, child treatment centers located in inner cities should choose instruments that have been normed on children as well as include items that accurately measure constructs regardless of the child's cultural, ethnic/racial, and/or religious background. Both therapists and researchers should evaluate strengths-based instruments with these characteristics in mind.

While this chapter has provided a summary of several potentially useful strengths-based instruments, selecting the appropriate instrument for clinical work and/or research projects should be done on an individual basis. This chapter only provides a starting point to move practitioners in the right direction when selecting appropriate instruments.

■ LIMITATIONS

Despite the increased use of strengths-based instruments, measures focusing on client deficits continue to be used widely in outcome research. Only a few instruments exist to measure SFBT's contructs, and continued validation of these measasures on various populations is needed. In addition, very few outcome studies on SFBT have used strengths-based instruments to meausre its efficacy. Awareness of this need will hopefully motivate more researchers to incorporate SFBT instruments into their studies.

■ FUTURE DIRECTIONS

Although the central construct of SFBT can be best measured by strengths-based instruments, it is also important to pair these measures with well-established non-strengths-based instruments. This allows better communication with researchers and grant reviewers who are not familiar with strengths-based measures. For example, when designing a research study, one can pair a strengths-based instrument, like the State Hope Scale, with the Beck Depression Inventory (BDI). This allows the researcher to test if hope increases when depression decreases. Another method is to give respondents several well-known pathology-oriented instruments (e.g., the Beck Anxiety Inventory) together with several strengths-based instruments (e.g., the Herth Hope Scale/Index [HHS/HHI]) that measure opposite constructs. Correlation tests can be run between instruments to measure and support inverse relationships between problem-focused and strengths-based characteristics, showing that as deficits decrease, positive traits increase. A word of caution: In order to achieve accurate inverse correlations between problem-focused and strengths-based scales, instruments must measure the *polar opposite* constructs. Noninverse correlations will result when the instruments do not measure the ends of the same spectrum (e.g., depression versus hope). Because not all pathologizing instruments have a strengths-based counterpart, it can be difficult to compare measures accurately. As more studies utilize strengths-based instruments, researchers will increase their confidence in nondeficit outcome measures.

While several instruments have been designed to measure principles of SFBT, there is a growing need for additional instruments. The Immediate Outcome Rating Scale (IORS) and the SBI are the only two standardized instruments that measure aspects of SFBT in the general population. The Solution Identification Scale (SIS) and the Solution-Focused Recovery Scale for Trauma Survivors were created for specific populations. Thus, there is a need for more standardized instruments that capture solution-focused concepts.

Another important issue is that strengths-based instruments need to be included in SFBT research as it becomes more widely recognized as an evidence-based model. Kim and colleagues (2010) report that SFBT is recognized by the Office of Juvenile Justice and Delinquency Prevention (OJJDP) as a "promising practice" for juvenile offenders. This rating is based on Newsome's (2004) study on using SFBT groupwork with at-risk junior high students. With continued efforts to recognize SFBT as an empirically validated and evidence-based approach, the need for strengths-based instruments to measure and report its efficacy will grow.

■ CONCLUSION

This chapter has introduced strengths-based instruments and has considered how they can be used to further SFBT practice and research. While several instruments were discussed, it is important to remember that selecting the appropriate measure is always done on a case-by-case basis. With the emergence of SFBT as an evidence-based practice, it will become more and more important to select the appropriate instruments for conducting SFBT and measuring its effectiveness and efficacy.

■ FURTHER LEARNING

Corcoran, J., & Walsh, J. M. (2008). *Mental health in social work: A casebook on diagnosis and strengths-based assessment.* Boston: Allyn & Bacon.
Jordan, C., & Franklin, C. (2011). *Clinical assessment for social workers: Quantitative and qualitative methods* (3rd ed.). Chicago: Lyceum Books.
Roberts, A. R., & Yeager, K. R. (2004). *Evidence-based practice manual.* New York: Oxford University Press.

■ REFERENCES

Abell, N., Springer, D. W., & Kamata, A. (2009). *Developing and validating rapid assessment instruments.* New York: Oxford University Press.
Adams, J. F., Piercy, F. P., & Jurich, J. A. (1991). Effects of solution focused therapy's "formula first session task" on compliance and outcome in family therapy. *Journal of Marital and Family Therapy, 17*(3), 277–290.

American Psychiatric Association practice guidelines, psychiatric evaluation of adults (2nd ed.). Retrieved March 11, 2008, from http://psychiatryonline.com

Anastasi, A. (1996). *Psychological testing* (7th ed.). New York: Macmillan.

Annis, H. M., & Graham, J. M. (1988). *Situational Confidence Questionnaire (SCQ-39) user's guide.* Toronto: Alcoholism and Drug Addiction Research Foundation.

Baltes, P. B., & Staudinger, U. M. (2000). Wisdom: A metaheuristic (pragmatic) to orchestrate mind and virtue toward excellence. *American Psychologist, 55,* 122–136.

Bannink, F. P. (2008). Posttraumatic succsess: Solution-focused brief therapy. *Brief Treatment and Crisis Intervention, 8,* 215–225.

Barnes, H. L., & Olson, D. H. (1985). Parent–adolescent communication and the Circumplex model. *Child Development, 56,* 438–447.

Benson, P. L., Roehlkepartain, E. C., & Sesma, A., (2004). Tapping the power of community: The potential of asset building to strengthen substance abuse prevention efforts. *Search Institute Insights & Evidence, 2,* 1–14.

Berg, I. K., & Dolan, Y. (2001). *Tales of solutions: A collection of hope-inspiring stories.* New York: W. W. Norton.

Berg, I. K., & Miller, S. D. (1992). *Working with the problem drinker: A solution-focused approach.* New York: Norton.

Bloom, M., Fischer, J., & Orme, J. (2005). *Evaluating practice: Guidelines for the accountable professional* (5th ed.). Boston: Allyn & Bacon.

Bostwick, G., & Kyte, N. (1988). Validity and reliability. In R. M. Grinnell, Jr. (Ed.), *Social work research and evaluation* (3rd ed., pp. 111–136). Itasca, IL: Peacock.

Bozeman, B. N. (1999). The efficacy of solution-focused therapy techniques on perceptions of hope in clients with depressive symptoms. *Unpublished doctoral dissertation,* New Orleans Baptist Theological Seminary, New Orleans, LA.

Brown, K. W., & Ryan, R. M. (2003). The benefits of being present: Mindfulness and its role in psychological well-being. *Journal of Personality and Social Psychology, 84,* 822–848.

Buckley, J. A., & Epstein, M. H. (2004). The Behavioral and Emotional Rating Scale-2 (BERS-2): Providing a comprehensive approach to strength-based assessment. *California School Psychologist, 9,* 21–27.

Buss, D. M. (2000). The evolution of happiness. *American Psychologist, 55,* 15–23.

Constantine, N., Benard, B., & Diaz, M. (1999). *Measuring protective factors and resilience traits in youth: The Healthy Kids Resilience assessment.* Paper presented at the seventh annual meeting of the Society for Prevention Research, New Orleans.

DeJong, P., & Berg, I. K. (1998). *Interviewing for solutions.* Pacific Grove, CA: Brooks/Cole.

De Jong, P., & Miller, S. D. (1995). How to interview for client strengths. *Social Work, 40,* 729–735.

de Shazer, S. (1988). *Clues: Investigating solutions in brief therapy.* New York: W.W. Norton.

de Shazer, S., Berg, I. K., Lipchik, E., Nunnaly, E., Molnar, A., Gingerich, W., & et al. (1986). Brief therapy: Focused solution development. *Family Process, 25,* 207–221.

Diener, E. (2000). Subjective well-being: The science of happiness and a proposal for a national index. *American Psychologist, 55,* 34–43.

Dolan, Y. M. (1991). *Resolving sexual abuse: Solution-focused therapy and Ericksonian hypnosis for adult survivors.* New York: Norton.

Dufault, K., & Martocchio, B. C. (1985). Symposium on compassionate care and the dying experience. Hope: Its spheres and dimensions. *Nursing Clinics of North America, 20,* 379–391.

Dunst, C. J., & Leet, H. E. (1987). Measuring the adequacy of resources in households with young children. *Child Care Health Development, 13,* 111–125.

Dunst, C., Trivette, C., & Deal, A. (1988). *Enabling and empowering families:Principles and guidelines for rractice.* Cambridge, MA: Brookline Books.

Eakes, G., Walsh, S., Markowski, M., Cain, H., & Swanson, M. (1997). Family-centered brief solution-focused therapy with chronic schizophrenia: A pilot study. *Journal of Family Therapy, 19*, 145–158.

Epstein N. B., Baldwin, L. M., & Bishop, D. S. (1983). The McMaster Family Assessment Device. *Journal of Marital and Family Therapy, 9*, 171–180.

Epstein, M. H., Rudolph, S., & Epstein, A. A. (2000). Using strengths-based assessment in transition planning. *Teaching Exceptional Children, 32*, 50–54.

Epstein, M. H., & Sharma, J. M. (1998). *Behavioral and Emotional Rating Scale: A strength-based approach to assessment*. Austin, TX: PRO-ED.

Fischer, J., & Corcoran, K. (2007). *Measures for clinical practice: A sourcebook* (Vols. I and II, 4th ed.). New York: Oxford University Press.

Fredrickson, B. L. (2004). The broaden-and-build theory of positive emotions. *Philosophical Transactions: Biological Science (The Royal Society of London), 359*, 1367–1377.

Goldman, J., & Baydanan, M. (1990). *Solution Identification Scale*. Denver, CO: Peaceful Alternatives in the Home.

Graham, J. R., & Lilly, R. S. (1984). *Psychological testing*. Englewood Cliffs, NJ: Prentice-Hall.

Gresham, F. M., & Elliott, S. N. (1990). *Social Skills Rating System manual*. Circle Pines, MN: AGS.

Hazzard, A., Christensen, A., & Margolin, G. (1983). Children's perceptions of parental behaviors. *Journal of Abnormal Child Psychology, 11*, 49–60.

Herth, K. (1991). Development and refinement of an instrument to measure hope. *Scholarly Inquiry for Nursing Practice, 5*, 39–51.

Hudson, W. W. (1981). Development and use of indexes and scales. In R. M. Grinnell, Jr. (Ed.), *Social work research and evaluation* (pp. 130–155). Itasca, IL: Peacock.

Hudson, W. W. (1982). *The clinical measurement package: A field manual*. Homewood, IL: Dorsey.

Huebner, E. S., & Gilman, R. (2003). Toward a focus on positive psychology in school psychology. *School Psychology Quarterly, 18*, 99–102.

Huang, M. (2001). A comparison of three approaches to reduce marital problems and symptoms of depression. Unpublished Dissertation, University of Florida.

Hunsley, J., & Mash, E. J. (2007). Evidence-based assessment. *Annual Review of Clinical Psychology, 3*, 29–51.

Jerusalem, M., & Schwarzer, R. (1992). Self-efficacy as a resource factor in stress appraisal processes. In R. Schwarzer (Ed.), *Self-efficacy: Thought control of action* (pp. 195–213). Washington, DC: Hemisphere.

Jordan, C., & Franklin, C. (2003). *Clinical assessment for social workers: Quantitative and qualitative methods* (2nd ed.). Chicago: Lyceum Books.

Jordan, C. & Franklin, C. (2011). Clinical Assessment for Social Workers: Quantitative and qualitative methods, third edition. Chicago: Lyceum Press.

Joseph, S., & Linley, P. (2008). Trauma, recovery and growth: Positive psychological perspectives on posttraumatic stress. In S. Joseph & P. Linley (Eds.), *Trauma recovery and growth: Positive psychological perspectives on posttraumatic stress* (pp. 339–356). Hoboken, NJ: Wiley.

Kabacoff, R. I., Miller, I. W., Bishop, D. S., Epstein, N. B., & Keitner, G. I. (1990). A psychometric study of the McMaster Family Assessment Device in psychiatric, medical, and nonclinical samples. *Journal of Family Psychology, 4*, 431–439.

Kahneman, D. (1999). Objective happiness. In D. Kahneman, E. Diener, & N. Schwartz (Eds.), *Well-being: The foundations of hedonic psychology* (pp. 3–25). New York: Russell Sage Foundation.

Kashdan, T. B., Rose, P., & Fincham, F. D. (2004). Curiosity and exploration: Facilitating positive subjective experiences and personal growth opportunities. *Journal of Personality Assessment, 82,* 291–305.

Kim, J. S. (2008). Examining the effectiveness of solution-focused brief therapy: A meta-analysis. *Research on Social Work Practice, 18,* 107–116.

Kim, J. S., Smock, S. A., Trepper, T. S., McCollum, E. E., & Franklin, C. (2010). Is solution-focused brief therapy evidence-based? *Families in Society: The Journal of Contemporary Social Sciences, 91,* 300–306.

Koren, P. E., DeChillo, N., & Friesen, B. J. (1992). Measuring empowerment in families whose children have emotional disabilities: A brief questionnaire. *Rehabilitation Psychology, 37,* 305–321.

Kruczek, T. (1999). Treatment effects with an adolescent abuse survivor's group. *Child Abuse & Neglect, 23,* 477–485.

Kruczek, T. & Vitanza, S. (1999). Treatment effects with an adolescent abuse survivor's group. *Child Abuse & Neglect, 23,* 477-485.

Larson, R. W. (2000). Toward a psychology of positive youth development. *American Psychologist, 55,* 170–183.

Lee, M. Y. (1997). A study of solution-focused brief family therapy: Outcomes and issues. *American Journal of Family Therapy, 25,* 3–17.

Lee, M. Y., Sebold, J., & Uken, A. (2003). *Solution-focused treatment of domestic violence offenders: Accountability for change.* New York: Oxford University Press.

Leggett, M. E. S. (2004). The effects of a solution-focused classroom guidance intervention with elementary students. Unpublished Dissertation, Texas A&M University- Corpus Christi.

Littrell, J. M., Malia, J. A., & Vanderwood, M. (1995). Single-session brief counseling ina high school. *Journal of Counseling and Development, 73,* 451–458.

Lubinski, D., & Benbow, C. P. (2000). States of excellence. *American Psychologist, 55,* 137–150.

Lyubomirsky, S., & Lepper, H. S. (1999). A measure of subjective happiness: Preliminary reliability and construct validation. *Social Indicators Research, 46,* 137–155.

Massimini, F., & Delle Fave, A. (2000). Individual development in a bio-cultural perspective. *American Psychologist, 55,* 24–33.

McCollum, E. E., & Trepper, T. S. (2001). *Creating family solutions for substance abuse.* New York: Haworth Press.

McCullough, M. E., Emmons, R. A., & Tsang, J. (2002). The grateful disposition: A conceptual and empirical topography. *Journal of Personality and Social Psychology, 82,* 112–127.

McCullough, M. E., Rachal, K. C., Sandage, S. J., Worthington, E. L., Brown, S. W., & Hight, T. L. (1998). Interpersonal forgiving in close relationships: II. Theoretical elaboration and measurement. *Journal of Personality and Social Psychology, 75,* 1586–1603.

Merrell, K. M. (2002). *School Social Behavior Scales, second edition: User's guide.* Eugene, OR: Assessment-Intervention Resources.

Myers, D. G. (2000). The funds, friends, and faith of happy people. *American Psychologist, 55,* 56–67.

Newsome, W. S. (2004). Solution-focused brief therapy groupwork with at-risk junior high school students: Enhancing the bottom line. *Research on Social Work Practice, 14,* 336–343.

Nowotny, M. L. (1991). Every tomorrow, a vision of hope. *Journaol of Psychosocial Oncology, 9,* 117–125.

Peterson, C. (2000). The future of optimism. *American Psychologist, 55,* 44–55.

Reuterlov, H., Lofgren, T., Nordstrom, K., Ternstrom, A., & Miller, S. D. (2000). What is better? A preliminary investigation of between-session change. *Journal of Systemic Therapies, 19,* 111–115.

Reynolds, C. R., & Kamphaus, R. W. (1992). *Behavior Assessment System for Children (BASC).* Circle Pines, MN: American Guidance Services.

Robins, R. W., Hendin, H. M., & Trzesniewski, K. H. (2001). Measuring global self-esteem: Construct validation of a single-item measure and the Rosenberg Self-Esteem Scale. *Personality and Social Psychology Bulletin, 27,* 151–161.

Robitschek, C. (1998). Personal growth initiative: The construct and its measure. *Measurement and Evaluation in Counseling and Development, 30,* 183–198.

Rubin, A., & Babbie, E. (2008). *Research methods for social work* (6th ed.). Belomont, CA: Thomson Brooks/Cole.

Ryan, R. M., & Deci, E. L. (2000). Self-determination theory and the facilitation of intrinsic motivation, social development, and well-being. *American Psychologist, 55,* 68–78.

Salovey, P., Rothman, A. J., Detweiler, J. B., & Steward, W. T. (2000). Emotional states and physical health. *American Psychologist, 55,* 110–121.

Sattler, J. M. (1988). *Assessment of children* (3rd ed.). San Diego, CA: Jerome M. Sattler.

Scheier, M. F., & Carver, C. S. (1992). Effects of optimism on psychological and physical well-being: Theoretical overview and empirical update. *Cognitive Therapy and Research, 16,* 201–228.

Seagram, B. M. C. (1997). *The efficacy of solution-focused therapy with young offenders.* Unpublished doctoral dissertation, York University, Canada.

Search Institute. (2003). *40 developmental assets for adolescents.* Retrieved January 9, 2004, from http://www.search-institute.org/assets/forty.html

Seligman, M. E. P., & Csikszentmihalyi, M. (2000). Positive psychology. *American Psychologist, 55,* 5–14.

Simonton, D. K. (2000). Creativity: Cognitive, personal, developmental, and social aspects. *American Psychologist, 55,* 151–158.

Skinner, H. A., Steinhauer, P. D., & Santa-Barbara, J. (1983). Family assessment measure. *Canadian Journal of Community Mental Health, 2,* 91–105.

Smock, S. A. (2007, October). *Further development of the Solution Building Inventory.* Poster session presented at the annual meeting of the American Association for Marriage and Family Therapy, Long Beach, CA.

Smock, S. A., McCollum, E., & Stevenson, M. (2010). The development of the solution-focused inventory. *Journal of Marriage and Family Therapy, 34,* 499–510.

Snyder, C. R. (1995). Conceptualizing, measuring, and nurturing hope. *Journal of Counseling and Development, 73,* 355–360.

Snyder, C. R., Sympson, S. C., Ybasco, F. C., Borders, T. F., Babyak, M. A., & Higgins, R. L. (1996). Development and validation of the State Hope Scale. *Journal of Personality and Social Psychology, 2,* 321–335.

Steger, M. F., Frazier, P., Oishi, S., & Kaler, M. (2006). The Meaning in Life Questionnaire: Assessing the presence of and search for meaning in life. *Journal of Counseling Psychology, 53,* 80–93.

Stober, J. (2001). The Social Desirability Scale-17 (SDS-17): Convergent validity, discriminant validity, and relationship with age. *European Journal of Psychological Assessment, 17,* 222–232.

Strom, R., & Cooledge, N. (1987). *Parental strengths and needs inventory research manual.* Tempe: Arizona State University.

Taylor. S. E., Kemeny, M. E., Reed, G. M., Bower, J. E., & Gruenewald, T. L. (2000). Psychological resources, positive illusions, and health. *American Psychologist, 55,* 99–109.

Thrash, T. M., & Elliot, A. J. (2003). Inspiration as a psychological construct. *Journal of Personality and Social Psychology, 84,* 871–889.

Triantafillou, N. (2002). *Solution-focused parent groups: A new approach to thetreatment of youth disruptive behavior.* Unpublished Dissertation, University of Toronto.

Trivette, C. M., & Dunst, C. J. (1990). Assessing family strengths and family functioning style. *Topics in Early Childhood Special Education, 10,* 16–36.

Vaillant, G. E. (2000). Adaptive mental mechanisms: Their role in a positive psychology. *American Psychologist, 55,* 89–98.

Zimmerman, T. S., Jacobsen, R. B., MacIntyre, M. (1996). Solution-focused parenting groups: An empirical study. *Journal of Systemic Therapies, 15*(4), 12–25.

5

Incorporating Outcome and Session Rating Scales in Solution-Focused Brief Therapy

■ J. ARTHUR GILLASPY, JR.

AND JOHN J. MURPHY

However beautiful the strategy, you should occasionally look at the results.

—Sir Winston Churchill

■ INTRODUCTION

In a classic article from the business literature, Levitt (1975) described how several industries, from railroads to movie making, suffered huge losses when they became product-oriented rather than customer-oriented. Railroad leaders in the mid-twentieth century scoffed at the possibility that air travel might eventually become a key player in the transportation business. Movie moguls were caught off guard by television because they wrongly saw themselves in the movie business rather than the entertainment business. Movie executive Darryl Zanuck boldly claimed that the television industry would not last more than 6 months because people would quickly tire of staring at a tiny box every night (Lee, 2000). This arrogant lack of foresight eventually forced the bankrupcy and closure of once-powerful movie studios.

Therapists can fall into a similar trap of acting as if they are in the therapy business rather than the business of helping people change. Our profession's focus on the means of producing change (evidence-based practice) rather than the clients' experience of change (practice-based evidence) sets us up for a fate similar to that of the railroad and movie industries. Most therapists agree that evaluating services is an important task of our profession. However, therapists differ greatly on what to evaluate, how to evaluate it, and who does the evaluating. In solution-focused brief therapy (SFBT), the client is the ultimate authority on the usefulness of services. Scaling questions are commonly used to assess clients' perceptions of problems and goal attainment ("On a scale of 0 to 10, with 0 being the worst it's been with this concern and 10 being where you want it to be, where are things right now?"). Client-based scaling provides instant feedback and privileges the client's voice over all others when it comes to assessing the effectiveness of therapy (Franklin et al., 1997). The importance of client feedback is underscored by the fact that therapists are notoriously inaccurate in evaluating their own effectiveness (Sapyta et al., 2005).

In keeping with the client-driven emphasis of SFBT (de Shazer et al., 2007), this chapter describes (a) an empirical rationale for obtaining systematic, session-by-session client feedback on treatment outcome and the therapeutic alliance, (b) two practical tools for doing so—the Outcome Rating Scale and the Session Rating Scale, (c) empirical evidence on both scales, (d) potential challenges and practical guidelines, and (e) future research directions in client feedback. See Chapter 4 for a discussion of other strengths-based measures that can be used to assess treatment outcomes in solution-focused therapy.

■ WHAT WE HAVE LEARNED SO FAR: RESEARCH ON SYSTEMATIC CLIENT FEEDBACK

Convincing evidence supports the efficacy of obtaining systematic, session-by-session client feedback on treatment outcome and the therapeutic alliance. The majority of research has focused on the Outcome Questionaire Measures, a feedback system developed by Lambert and colleagues (Lambert et al., 2004). At the center of this system is the Outcome Questionnaire 45 (OQ45; Lambert et al., 2004), a 45-item measure of client functioning along three dimensions (symptom distress, interpersonal functioning, and social role functioning). Prior to each session, clients complete the OQ45 via computer, and the results are immediately transmitted to their therapist. The therapist also receives treatment suggestions, depending on the client's progress (improving, no change, or deterioration). In addition, a package of Clinical Support Tools (CSTs) was developed that includes assessment of the therapeutic alliance, stages of change, and social support (Whipple et al., 2003).

The OQ Measure system has been evaluated in five randomized clinical trials (RCTs) (Harmon et al., 2007; Hawkins et al., 2004; Lambert et al., 2001, 2002; Whipple et al., 2003). In all five studies, continuous assessment of client feedback and the provision of that feedback to therapists improved clinical outcomes and decreased treatment dropout for clients at risk for treatment failure (effect sizes ranged from .34 to .92). When feedback about alliance, stage of change, and social support (through the CST) was added to the intervention, the proportion of at-risk clients who achieved clinically significant change doubled. With the exception of the studies by Harmon et al. (2007) and Hawkins et al. (2004), the effect of client feedback on outcomes was limited to those clients at risk for treatment deterioration or failure. In addition, clients in the feedback condition who were not at risk for failure required fewer sessions than those in the no-feedback group, suggesting that client feedback may also improve treatment efficiency (Lambert et al., 2001; Whipple et al., 2003).

Although several measures of client feedback have been developed, most were designed for research purposes and are too long and complex for everyday use. Brown and colleagues (1999) found that most practitioners will not use any measure that takes more than 5 minutes to complete, score, and interpret. This presents a serious obstacle to implementing a continuous feedback system in clinical practice. In response to the need for practical feedback measures, proponents of client-directed, outcome-informed practice developed two ultra-brief tools for monitoring outcome and alliance at every session: the Outcome Rating Scale (ORS; Miller & Duncan, 2000) and the Session Rating Scale (SRS; Miller et al., 2002). The ORS consists of four items corresponding to the OQ45 (Lambert et al., 2004): personal or symptom distress, interpersonal well-being, social relationships, and overall well-being. The SRS consists of four items that assess client perceptions of respect and understanding, relevance of goals and topics, client–practitioner fit, and overall alliance. The ORS is typically given at the start of (or just before) each meeting, and the SRS is completed at the end of the session. Scoring is completed in the presence of clients, and results are immediately discussed. In contrast to expert-driven diagnostic instruments that clients may view as mysterious and inaccessible, the ORS and SRS are transparent tools that become a routine part of therapeutic practice. A more thorough description of administration and scoring instructions is available elsewhere (Duncan, 2010; Miller & Duncan, 2004). The joint use of the ORS and SRS is referred to as the Partners for Change Outcome Management System (PCOMS; Duncan et al., 2004; "Miller et al., 2005).

The ORS and SRS are displayed in Figures 5.1 and 5.2. Both scales use a visual analog format of four 10-centimeter lines. Clients are instructed to place a mark on

Outcome Rating Scale (ORS)

Name _____Age (Yrs):____ Sex: M / F
Session # _____ Date: _____
Who is filling out this form? Please check one: Self_____ Other_____
If other, what is your relationship to this person? _____

Looking back over the last week, including today, help us understand how you have been feeling by rating how well you have been doing in the following areas of your life, where marks to the left represent low levels and marks to the right indicate high levels. *If you are filling out this form for another person, please fill out according to how you think he or she is doing.*

Individually
(Personal well-being)

I----Examination-Copy-Only----I

Interpersonally
(Family, close relationships)

I----Examination-Copy-Only----I

Socially
(Work, school, friendships)

I----Examination-Copy-Only----I

Overall
(General sense of well-being)

I----Examination-Copy-Only----I

The Heart and Soul of Change Project

www.heartandsoulofchange.com

© 2000, Scott D. Miller and Barry L. Duncan

Figure 5.1. Outcome Rating Scale (ORS). *Source*: The Heart and Soul of Change Project. © 2000, Scott D. Miller and Barry L. Duncan. Available at http://www.heartandsoulofchange.com

Session Rating Scale (SRS V.3.0)

Name _____Age (Yrs):_____

ID# _____ Sex: M / F

Session # _____ Date: _____

Please rate today's session by placing a mark on the line nearest to the description that best fits your experience.

Relationship

I did not feel heard, understood, and respected. I---------Examination--Copy--Only------I I felt heard, understood, and respected.

Goals and Topics

We did *not* work on or talk about what I wanted to work on and talk about. I---------Examination--Copy--Only------I We worked on and talked about what I wanted to work on and talk about.

Approach or Method

The therapist's approach is not a good fit for me. I---------Examination--Copy--Only------I The therapist's approach is a good fit for me.

Overall

There was something missing in the session today. I---------Examination--Copy--Only------I Overall, today's session was right for me.

The Heart and Soul of Change Project

www.heartandsoulofchange.com

© 2002, Scott D. Miller, Barry L. Duncan, & Lynn Johnson

Figure 5.2. Session Rating Scale (SRS V.3.0). *Source*: The Heart and Soul of Change Project. © 2002, Scott D. Miller, Barry L. Duncan, and Lynn Johnson. Available at http://www.heartandsoulofchange.com

each line, with low estimates to the left and high estimates to the right. The total score is simply the summation of the marks made by the client to the nearest millimeter on each of the four lines (maximum score of 40). Using a large sample of ORS scores (n = 34,790), Miller and Duncan (2004) set a clinical cutoff score of 25 (77th percentile) to distinguish individuals who typically do not seek therapy (nonclinical) from individuals who do seek treatment (clinical). A change of 5 points or more was also determined to indicate a reliable change. For the SRS, a total score of 36 or any individual item rated below 9 was established as indicative of potential alliance problems (Miller & Duncan, 2004). Regardless of the above clinical cutoffs, scores in any area are strictly means to an end, the end being obtaining and honoring client feedback about therapy services.

The Child-ORS (CORS; Duncan et al., 2003a) and the Child-SRS (CSRS; Duncan et al., 2003b) include simpler language and smiling/frowning faces to assist children in understanding and completing the scales. When caregivers such as parents or teachers are involved, they should complete the same outcome scale given to the child. For example, if the child completes the CORS, then the caregiver would also complete the CORS. This allows for exploration of similarities and differences across perspectives ("James, I noticed that you rated 'Family' a lot lower than your mother. What do you make of that?").

■ SFBT INTERVENTION: PUTTING THE ORS AND SRS INTO ACTION

Shouldn't I be telling you what I think?
—Clarice, a 10-year-old client

This section illustrates how to use the ORS and SRS throughout the therapy process. Additional examples and guidelines can be found in the ORS/SRS manual (Miller & Duncan, 2004).

Before the First Meeting

We inform clients about our interest in their feedback when scheduling the first contact by phone, letter, or e-mail:

To help you reach your goals, I need to ask how things are going for you from meeting to meeting using a couple of short forms. Your feedback will tell us if we're on track or if we need to change something to make things better for you. Is that something you can help me with?

Introducing the ORS/CORS at the First Meeting

ORS: *As I mentioned when we spoke by phone last week, I appreciate you completing a couple of forms about how things are going for you out there and in our meetings. To make the most of our time together and get the best results, we need to make sure we're on the same page about how you are doing and how our meetings are working. Your answers will help us to stay on track and to work on what's most important to you. Are you okay with that?*

CORS: *Here is that paper with the smiley and frowny faces that tells me how you're doing, and it only takes about a minute. I need you to mark each of these lines to tell me how things are going for you. Can you give it a try?*

Discussing ORS/CORS Results

ORS: *From your ORS marks, it looks like you're experiencing some real problems. Or: Your total score is 15. Things must be pretty tough for you. What's going on? Or: From your score, it looks like you're doing okay. Why do you think you were referred for counseling? Or: This mark on personal well-being tells me that you're really having a tough time. Would you like to tell me about it?*

CORS (TO A PARENT IN A FAMILY SESSION): *Your rating of Maria tells me you're quite concerned about her, especially in school and personal well-being. Does this make sense with what you are thinking? Or: Your score on the CORS is 34, which indicates that you think Maria is doing pretty well overall, but that you have some concern about her school performance or behavior. Is that true?*

Therapists may need to help clients (a) connect their experience with their ORS marks and (b) consider what needs to happen to make things better:

ORS: *I need your help to understand what this mark means in your life. Can you help me understand this better? What needs to happen for that mark to move a little bit to the right?*

The last question invites clients to describe concrete signs of improvement, which is an important strategy of SFBT.

CORS (TO A CHILD'S TEACHER): *It sounds like talking out in class is your biggest concern about William. Does that explain your mark of 2.4 on the School scale? Is there anything else that explains your mark? What needs to happen for your mark to move 1 or 2 centimeters to the right?*

Introducing the SRS/CSRS at the First Meeting

SRS: *This form tells me how the meeting went for you. It's like taking the temperature of our meeting today, and I need you to be really honest and tell me exactly what you think.*

CSRS: *Before we wrap up, I'd like you to fill out another short form that has faces on it. You mark it just like you did the other form, with marks over here (pointing to the right) meaning that our meeting was good for you and over here (pointing to the left) meaning not so good. This form tells me how you think I am doing. That's right, you get to grade me! I need you to be very honest about it because that's the only way I'll know how things are working for you. Okay?*

Discussing SRS/CSRS Results

When SRS results are uniformly high (9 or above on each item), we can simply acknowledge it and invite any other comments or suggestions from the client. Since people tend to rate alliance measures highly, we should address any hint of a problem. A total score of less than 36, or below 9 on any item, may signal a concern and warrant further discussion.

SRS: *These marks are way over here to the right, which suggests that we're on the same page, that we are talking about things that are important to you, and that today's meeting was right for you. What else could I do to make sure we're working well together?*

CSRS: *Let me see how you think we are doing. Okay, seems like I am missing the boat somewhere here. Thanks for being honest and giving me a chance to change things. What could I do to make the next meeting better for you?*

The SRS provides a practical and systematic way to address alliance problems as they occur instead of waiting until the client shuts down or drops out. The therapists' nondefensive acceptance of alliance problems and willingness to make adjustments are essential components of repairing alliance problems (Safran & Muran, 2000).

Later Meetings

Each meeting compares the current ORS with previous ratings. Scores serve as prompts to discuss progress and future plans. When scores increase even a little, we can give clients credit and explore their role in the change.

ORS: *Wow, your total score increased 3 points. How did you make that happen?*

CORS (TO A TEACHER): *Your rating of Maria improved to a 24. That's 4 points higher than it was last week. How did you make things better with Maria? What did you learn about yourself or Maria? Where do you think we should go from here?*

When scores decline or remain unchanged, we can discuss what to do differently to improve the situation.

ORS: *So, things haven't changed since our last meeting. What do you make of that? I wonder what we could do differently here.*

When ORS or SRS ratings remain low across several consecutive sessions, we can initiate a discussion along the following lines:

ORS: *These scores suggest that we might need to try something pretty different to make things better. I wonder what that might be.*

SRS: *These scores haven't changed for the past 3 weeks. If we're not working well together, I wonder what I can do to be on the same page with you. If I can't do that, we could consider switching to another counselor who might be more effective with you.*

As illustrated in the above examples, partnering with clients to monitor treatment progress and the alliance promotes responsive and accountable services. The hands-on format of these measures makes it easier for some clients to express dissatisfaction with the therapist or the course of treatment. Murphy (2008) provides additional excerpts of dialogue that illustrate how the ORS and SRS are used within a solution-focused approach. In the next section, we critically review ORS/SRS research methodology.

■ RESEARCH METHODS

Since the introduction of the ORS and SRS in 2000, research has progressed from instrument validation to RCTs. In addition to the ORS/SRS manual (Miller & Duncan, 2004), five instrument development and validation studies have been published (see Table 5.1). Three of the five studies focused on the ORS (Bringhurst et al., 2006; Duncan et al., 2006; Miller et al., 2003), one investigated the SRS (Duncan et al., 2003c), and one included both (Campbell & Hemsley, 2009). A variety of psychometric characteristics have been examined, including internal consistency, test-retest reliability, sensitivity to change, and score validity. These studies featured sample sizes ranging from 65 to 1961 and a wide range of participants including clinical and nonclinical

TABLE 5.1. *Summary of ORS/SRS Psychometric Studies*

Study	Measure	Sample (n)	Alpha	Test-retest Reliability	Validation Measure(s)	r
Miller et al. (2003)	ORS	Nonclinical (86) Clinical (435)	.93	.66	OQ45	−.53 to −.69
Duncan et al. (2003)	SRS	Outpatient clinical (326)	.88	.64	HAQ-II	.48
Bringhurst et al. (2006)	ORS	Nonclinical (98)	.97	.80	OQ45	−.56 to .69
Duncan et al. (2006)	ORS	Clinical adolescents (1,495)	.93	.78	YOQ	−.53
	CORS	Nonclinical children (119)	.84	.60	YOQ	−.43
Campbell & Hemsley (2009)	ORS	Outpatient clinical (65)	.90	—	OQ45	−.74
					QLS	.74
					RSES	.66
					GPES	.53
	SRS		.93	—	WAI-S	.58

GPES = General Perceived Self-Efficacy Scale; HAQ-II = Helping Alliance Questionnaire-II; OQ45 = Outcome Questionnaire 45; ORS = Outcome Rating Scale; QLS = Quality of Life Scale; RSES = Rosenberg Self-Esteem Scale; SRS = Session Rating Scale; WAI-S = Working Alliance Inventory-Short; YOQ = Youth Outcome Questionnaire.

children, adolescents, and adult caretakers. Two studies also compared usage rates of the ORS and SRS to longer alliance and outcome measures.

Four experimental studies[1] of the ORS/SRS system (PCOMS) have been published (Anker et al. 2009; Miller et al., 2006; Reese et al., 2009a). These studies are summarized in Table 5.2. The first (Miller et al., 2006) was a quasi-experimental ABB design; the other three were between-subjects RCTs. In all four studies, use of the ORS/SRS resulted in improved treatment outcomes versus treatment as usual (TAU). Several methodological features bolster confidence in these positive results. For example, the RCTs employed random assignment of participants to the treatment condition, block assignment of therapists to control for therapist effects (with the exception of Reese et al., 2009a), active treatment comparison groups, and therapist training in the use of PCOMS.

All four studies used adequate to large client samples ranging from 74 (Reese et al., 2009a) to 6424 (Miller et al., 2006). Sixty-nine percent of therapists were licensed professionals (primarily master's-level clinicians). Treatment settings included university counseling centers, community-based training clinics and mental health centers, and a telephone-based employee assistance program (EAP). Although three of the four studies focused on individual therapy, Anker et al. (2009) extended evaluation of PCOMS to couples therapy. All studies evaluated treatment outcomes based on reliable change or clinically significant change (Jacobson & Truax, 1991). Cohen's d effect sizes were reported in all studies.

Limitations of ORS/SRS Research

The ORS/SRS research has several limitations. First, with the exception of Anker et al. (2009) and Miller et al. (2006), the fidelity of ORS/SRS implementation was not assessed. Although therapists in these studies received training in PCOMS, whether

TABLE 5.2 *Summary of ORS/SRS Outcome Studies*

Study	Design	N	Clients	Therapists	DV	Results	ES
Miller et al. (2006)	Within- subjects ABB	6424	Adult Employee Assistance Program	n = 75 (LP 45%; LCSW 35%; LMFT 20%)	ORS	Final phase > baseline, 47% vs. 34% of clients experienced reliable change	.79
Anker et al. (2009)	RCT	820 (410 couples)	Adult couples	n = 10 (4 LP, 5 LCSW, 1 LNP	ORS LWMAT	ORS/SRS > TAU; 67% reliable and clinically significant change vs. 39% at 6-month FU	.50 .30
Reese et al. (2009a) Study 1	RCT Clients randomized	74	University students	n = 10 (5 MS-level clinicians, 5 graduate trainees)	ORS	ORS/SRS > TAU; 80% vs. 54% of clients experienced reliable change	.54
Study 2	Therapist randomized	74	Adult community sample	n = 17 (graduate trainees)	ORS	ORS/SRS > TAU; 67% vs. 41% of clients experienced reliable change; ORS/SRS clients achieved reliable change in fewer sessions than TAU	.49

DV = dependent variable; ES = effect size; LCSW = licensed clinical social worker; LMFT = licensed marriage and family therapist; LNP = licensed nurse practitioner; LP = licensed psychologist; LWMAT = Lock Wallace Marital Adjustment Test; ORS = Outcome Rating Scale; RCT = randomized clinical trial; SRS = Session Rating Scale; TAU = treatment as usual.

they implemented the intervention as intended was not evaluated. Second, the literature involves a relatively small number of therapists ($n = 10$–75), limiting generalizability. Third, with the exception of Anker et al. (2009), the ORS was the only measure used to assess treatment outcome. This is problematic since the ORS is also part of the intervention, and outcome is ideally assessed with multiple measures. Fourth, two of the four studies were conducted by developers or advocates of PCOMS. The presence of researcher allegiance effects is a frequent issue in psychotherapy research (Luborsky et al., 1999; Wampold, 2010).

■ RESEARCH RESULTS

The emerging empirical literature on the ORS/SRS is very promising. In this section, we review findings from instrument validation (Table 5.1) and outcome studies (Table 5.2).

The utility of the ORS and SRS depends on the reliability and validity of their scores. Therefore, the psychometric characteristics of ORS/SRS scores are of primary importance. The ORS and SRS scores exhibit impressive internal consistency and test-retest reliability given the ultra-brief nature (four items) of these measures. Across seven studies, average Cronbach's alpha coefficients for ORS scores were .85 (clinical samples) and .95 (nonclinical samples). Duncan et al. (2006) reported that internal consistency for the CORS was .93 for adolescents and .84 for children. These values compare favorably with the ORS's parent instrument, the OQ45. For SRS scores, internal consistency estimates were reported in five studies with an average alpha of .92, range .88 (Duncan et al., 2003c; Reese et al., 2009a) to .96 (Miller & Duncan, 2004). These alpha coefficients suggest that the SRS assesses a single global alliance construct. This is consistent with research on other alliance measures such as the Working Alliance Inventory (WAI; Horvath & Greenberg, 1989).

The ORS and SRS scores also demonstrate adequate test-retest reliability. As an indicator of treatment progress, ORS scores should be expected to be sensitive to change for clinical samples yet stable over time for nonclinical samples. The average test-retest reliability (1 to 3 weeks between administrations) for nonclinical samples was .73 (Bringhurst et al., 2006; Miller et al., 2003). For clinical samples, test-retest reliability was usually assessed between the first and second sessions and ranged from .51 to .72 (Reese et al., 2009a) for adults and .60 to .78 for children and adolescents (Duncan et al., 2006). Statistically significant differences between pretreatment and posttreatment ORS scores further support the ORS's sensitivity to change (Miller et al., 2003). Three studies (Miller & Duncan, 2004; Duncan et al., 2003c; Reese et al., 2009a) reported test-retest reliability of SRS scores from the first to the second session. The average reliability coefficient was .59 (range, .54 to .64), indicating adequate stability.

The concurrent validity of ORS and SRS scores has been examined primarily through correlations with established outcome and alliance measures. The average bivariate correlation between the ORS and OQ45 across three studies (Bringhurst et al., 2006; Campbell & Hemsley, 2009; Miller et al., 2003) was |.62| (range |.53| to |.74|), indicating moderately strong concurrent validity. Campbell and Hemsley (2009) reported moderately strong relationships (.53 to .74) between the ORS and the Depression Anxiety Stress Scale (Lovibond & Lovibond, 1995), Quality of Life Scale (Burckhardt & Amderson, 2003), and Rosenberg Self-Esteem Scale (Rosenberg, 1989). Duncan et al. (2006) found that the CORS also demonstrated moderate concurrent validity with the Youth Outcome Questionnaire (YOQ; Burlingame et al., 2001) for adolescents ($r = |.53|$) and children ($r = |.43|$). In addition, Miller et al. (2003) reported that pretreatment ORS scores distinguished clinical and nonclinical samples, providing further support for the validity of ORS scores.

Two studies have investigated the concurrent validity of SRS scores. Duncan et al. (2003) reported a correlation of .48 between the SRS and the Helping Alliance Questionnaire-II (HAQ-II; Luborsky et al., 1996). Campbell and Hemsley (2009) found that SRS scores correlated .58 with the Working Alliance Inventory-Short (WAI-S; Tracey & Kokotovic, 1989); interitem correlations ranged from .39 (WAI-S Bond–SRS Relationship) to .63 (WAI-S Goal–SRS Approach). These findings indicate moderate concurrent validity with longer alliance measures. Finally, the predictive validity of the SRS was supported by Duncan et al. (2003). Early SRS scores (second or third session) were predictive of posttreatment ORS scores ($r = .29$), which is consistent with previous research linking early client perceptions of alliance with outcome (Horvath & Bedi, 2002).

Another issue relevant to the usefulness of the ORS and SRS is feasibility in clinical practice. In two clinics, one using the ORS and the other using the OQ45, Miller et al. (2003) found that therapists were much more likely to use the ultra-brief ORS (89%) than the longer OQ45 (25%). Duncan et al. (2003c) similarly reported 96% usage for the SRS compared to 29% for the 12-item WAI (Horvath & Greenberg, 1989).

As seen in Table 5.2, four studies have demonstrated the efficacy of PCOMS compared with TAU. In the first study (Miller et al., 2006), PCOMS was implemented in a large ($n = 6424$) Employee Assistance Program (EAP) that provided telephone-based counseling services. The introduction of the ORS and SRS significantly improved client retention and outcome from baseline to 6-month follow-up (ES at baseline = .37; follow-up = .79). Anker et al. (2009) randomized couples seeking therapy ($n = 410$) to PCOMS or TAU. At 6-month follow-up, 67% of couples in the feedback condition reported reliable or clinically significant change versus 39% in TAU ($ES = .50$ after treatment, .44 at follow-up). Greater marital satisfaction was also reported by clients in the PCOMS condition ($ES = .30$). Two clinical trials comparing the PCOMS to TAU were reported by Reese et al. (2009a). Study 1 occurred at a university counseling center ($n = 74$) and Study 2 at a graduate training clinic ($n = 74$). Clients in the PCOMS condition in both studies showed more change than TAU clients (80% vs. 54% in Study 1, 67% vs. 41% in Study 2; ES from .49 to .54). In addition, clients in PCOMS achieved reliable change in significantly fewer sessions than those in TAU. These studies collectively support the effectiveness of PCOMS as a client feedback intervention across various treatment models. The average effect size for PCOMS versus TAU was .52, representing a medium treatment effect. This finding is especially impressive considering that the effect size for differences between treatment models is generally estimated to be around .20 (Wampold, 2001).

■ PRACTICE GUIDELINES, LIMITATIONS, AND CHALLENGES

Until research clarifies the relative impact of formal and informal client feedback, we recommend that practitioners obtain formal feedback on outcome and alliance (PCOMS, OQ Measures). This recommendation is supported by the finding that even the best therapists are effective with only about 7 out of 10 clients (Hansen et al., 2002), and that it is better to know sooner rather than later if clients are not improving.

Integrating formal feedback is easier said than done because most of us have established fairly standardized ways to begin and end therapy sessions. This section outlines practice guidelines for using the ORS and SRS in SFBT along with potential limitations and challenges of doing so. Instead of merely describing each limitation, we offer suggestions for addressing it based on research findings and practice guidelines (Duncan, 2010; Duncan et al., 2004; Murphy & Duncan, 2007) as well as our own clinical practice, training, and supervision.

Potential Limitations and Challenges of Using the ORS and SRS in SFBT

Limitation/Challenge 1. One limitation of the ORS is that it may restrict clients' focus to the areas and descriptors on the scale as opposed to asking open-ended questions such as "What are you most concerned with?" or "What do you want to work on?" The influence of words on clients' perceptions and therapeutic conversations has long been recognized in SFBT (de Shazer, 1985, 1994). Although the ORS items are broad and cover major life domains, they may narrow the client's focus in ways that exclude important perceptions and experiences.

Suggestions. The ORS/SRS manual (Miller & Duncan, 2004) urges therapists to explain each category and cautions against moving too quickly, especially in the first few administrations. In addition, the Overall item taps general well-being and may address any remaining concerns missed on the first three items. More important than the instrument itself is the mind set and manner in which it is presented and discussed with clients. For starters, we explicitly acknowledge that no form is perfect and that the sole purpose of the ORS is to ensure that clients are benefiting from our services. We also address this issue after discussing the ORS by saying, "Before we move on, I want to make sure we haven't missed anything else that you are concerned about or would like to work on. Can you think of anything else?" Similar to informal scaling questions, the client's responses to the ORS provide a foundation for goal development and exception finding: "What will you be doing differently when this mark (pointing to the client's mark of 3.7) moves to 3.8 or 4.0?" "When have you done that, even just a little, during the past couple of weeks?"

Limitation/Challenge 2. As with the ORS, it is possible for clients to become overly form-bound on the SRS at the expense of providing more subjective perspectives on the alliance. The SRS items are derived from theoretical formulations and research-identified aspects of the working alliance (Bordin, 1979; Hatcher & Barends, 1996). However, some investigators have found that clients' understanding and experience of the alliance may differ from therapist-derived definitions of the alliance (Bedi, 2006; Horvath & Bedi, 2002). The challenge is to use the SRS in a way that honors the client's experience of the alliance.

Suggestions. Several suggestions about the ORS apply to the SRS as well. Thus, we recommend concluding the SRS discussion with a catch-all question that invites clients to share any other alliance-related issues: "Is there anything else, anything at all, that I can do differently or we can do differently to click better or make these meetings as useful as possible?"

Limitation/Challenge 3. Adding the ORS and SRS would alter common SFBT protocols for beginning and ending sessions. For example, De Jong and Berg (2008) recommend that practitioners (a) begin each session (after the first one) by asking clients, "What's better since we last met?" and (b) conclude each meeting with a short break and end-of-session feedback comprised of compliments and suggestions. Practitioners of SFBT may wrestle with how to incorporate the ORS and SRS into their standard way of opening and closing sessions. The ORS may be a more nonleading way to begin a session compared to the presuppostional "What's better?," which intentionally prompts clients to describe positive changes. Rather, the ORS invites clients to report changes in either direction. The SRS, while consistent with the client-driven nature of SFBT, may also pose a logistical challenge for practitioners who end sessions in a highly standardized way.

Suggestions (ORS). As noted by de Shazer et al. (2007): "Sometimes SFBT is portrayed as an approach that does not permit the discussion of problems. Nothing could be further from the truth" (p. 153). There is a difference between being solution-focused and solution-forced. There is also a difference between validating clients' experience of a problem and remaining mired in problem talk. As is the case with clients' responses to informal scaling questions, ORS ratings can be explored in a variety of solution-focused ways. When scores are higher from one session to the next, we can ask clients what they did to make things better and encourage them to continue doing what is working. When scores drop, we can validate clients' experience while exploring what was different when things were better as well as asking their opinions on what might help turn things around. When used in this fashion, the ORS is consistent with solution-focused emphases on respecting clients' perceptions and focusing on solutions.

Suggestions (SRS). For practitioners wishing to use the SRS within SFBT protocols, we propose two options for when to use the SRS: right before or right after the end-of-session feedback. Practitioners of SFBT often take a short break prior to giving feedback. Clients could complete the SRS during the break and then discuss it with the therapist. This permits therapists to receive alliance feedback from clients while ending the session as they normally would. Since compliments are part of the SFBT feedback strategy, therapists can thank clients for sharing their perceptions on the SRS as part of the end-of-session compliment. The second option is to have clients complete the SRS at the very end of the meeting. This would allow clients to respond to the entire session, including the feedback message.

Limitation/Challenge 4. Clients' ratings on the SRS may be heavily inflated toward the positive, making it difficult to detect emerging alliance problems. Score inflation is a well-documented limitation of alliance measures (Tyron et al., 2008). Therefore, it is important for practitioners to keep this in mind as they present, interpret, and discuss the SRS.

Suggestions. Practitioners of SFBT should present and discuss the SRS in a way that actively welcomes negative feedback from clients (e.g., "I'm not fishing for high marks. In fact, I need to know about anything that is not working for you in these meetings."). A total score of 36 or below, or less than 9 on any item, should be explored. Even when clients rate every item a 10, we can ask if there is anything else that would make the sessions more useful.

Practitioners of SFBT will ultimately decide if and how to monitor clients' perceptions of treatment progress and the alliance. Therapists develop their own unique styles and ways of soliciting and discussing feedback, and the ORS and SRS can become part of that style. We are confident that practitioners and researchers will continue to refine and develop these measures in ways that will advance our knowledge and practice. We now turn our attention to future directions for ORS/SRS research.

■ FUTURE RESEARCH

Research on client feedback in general, and on the ORS/SRS in particular, is in the beginning stages. Existing research suggests that these tools enhance treatment effectiveness. Additional research is needed to better understand the nature and essential components of this client feedback system.

An issue of particular importance to SFBT practitioners is the differential impact of formal versus informal feedback. Obtaining outcome feedback using informal scaling questions such as "On a scale of 0 (worst) to 10 (best), how would you rate your progress right now?" is a common SFBT strategy. Future studies should compare the relative effect of monitoring client feedback using the ORS versus informal scaling questions.

One limitation of current PCOMS literature is the absence of rigorous treatment integrity checks. Two of the four outcome studies did not assess whether the PCOMS was implemented as intended. There may be important differences in how therapists presented and discussed client feedback. In addition, no studies have empirically examined how best to use the ORS and SRS in sessions: Does treatment outcome vary based on the amount of time spent discussing the ORS and SRS? Is treatment outcome impacted by types of therapist responses to client feedback? What is the impact of adjusting therapy in response to client feedback? How closely does the ORS/SRS match clients' subjective experience and understanding of treatment progress and alliance? Future research should refine guidelines for using PCOMS and employ manipulation checks.

As mentioned earlier, all four treatment outcome studies compared PCOMS to TAU. While this design is typical in the early stages of outcome research, there is much to be gained from a finer-grained analysis of PCOMS. For example, PCOMS involves two discrete components: monitoring treatment outcome and the alliance. Research has not addressed the efficacy of using both measures versus only the ORS or SRS. Component or dismantling studies are appropriate designs for determining the relative and additive contribution of monitoring treatment outcome and the alliance.

The impact of client feedback on training and supervision is another direction for future research. Supervision often does not include systematic evaluation of client progress, leaving trainees confused or unsure about the usefulness of their services. Incorporating outcome and alliance feedback into supervision sessions anchors supervision in client-driven rather than supervisor-driven criteria of trainee effectiveness. In a study of 28 graduate students, Reese et al. (2009b) found that trainees whose supervisors used ORS/SRS feedback in supervision had better outcomes than trainees in the no-feedback condition. Future studies should build on this research to better understand potential uses of client feedback in training and supervision.

Future studies should also investigate the relative efficacy of PCOMS compared to other systems such as the OQ Measures (Lambert et al., 2004). Of particular interest is the finding that in PCOMS studies, all clients (both those at risk for treatment failure and those who were progressing normally) benefited from continuous feedback. However, with the exception of Harmon et al. (2007) and Hawkins et al. (2004), in the OQ studies only clients not on track or at risk showed enhanced outcomes due to feedback. One possible explanation is that PCOMS involves monitoring progress and alliance. Although alliance is included in the CSTs, the OQ system focuses primarily on outcome assessment. The explicit emphasis of PCOMS on alliance feedback may have an additive impact not found in the OQ system. In addition, when PCOMS is used, the ORS and SRS are completed in session in a collaborative manner. Therapists and clients discuss the feedback in the here and now. In contrast, the OQ45 is completed by clients in the waiting area and then discussed with the therapist. Clients provide alliance feedback after the session, and the results are not discussed until the following session. Thus, the immediacy and collaborative nature of soliciting and processing client feedback may be important components of maximizing outcomes. Future studies can address these issues by directly comparing the efficacy of PCOMS with the OQ Measures as well as other client feedback systems.

■ KEY FINDINGS TO REMEMBER

- Research by Lambert and colleagues (see Lambert, 2010) demonstrates that continuous monitoring of client feedback improves client retention and clinical outcomes, especially for clients at risk for treatment failure.
- The ORS and SRS scores exhibit impressive internal consistency and test-retest reliability given their ultra-brief nature.
- The ORS and SRS scores have moderately strong concurrent validity with longer, more established measures of treatment outcome and therapeutic alliance.
- Four studies, including three RCTs, support the efficacy of using the ORS and SRS (PCOMS) as a client feedback intervention across various treatment approaches.

■ KEY POINTS TO REMEMBER

Monitoring client feedback via the ORS and SRS is a natural fit with SFBT practice. Client-driven partnerships are founded on the belief that clients are better positioned than anyone else to inform and evaluate the therapy process in ways that are most beneficial to them. Strong initial evidence suggests that the use of these ultra-brief measures in session with clients improves treatment outcomes. The ORS and SRS provide immediate feedback on what is working and what is not. In addition, monitoring and adjusting treatment via client feedback is a core component of recent definitions of evidence-based practice (EBP). For example, the American Psychological Association's Presidential Task Force on Evidence-based Practice (APA, 2006) defined EBP as ". . . the integration of the best available research with clinical expertise in the context of patient characteristics, culture, and preferences" (p. 273), which includes "the monitoring of patient progress . . . that may suggest the need to adjust the treatment" p. 276). In light of the research reviewed in this chapter, we agree with Kazdin's (2007) recommendation regarding client feedback: "Now that measures are available, . . . their use ought to be strongly encouraged in clinical training and practice" (p. 44).

In closing, we echo Thomas' (2007) reminder that "loyalty to a theory—especially loyalty that goes beyond what reason, history, research, and other critical lenses bring to a therapy approach—does not do SFBT any favors" (p. 394). One of the most admirable features of SFBT is that it has continually evolved and changed in response to new discoveries that offer the promise of improving therapy services for clients. It is in that same spirit of discovery and evolution that we offer this chapter to our SFBT colleagues.

■ **ENDNOTES**

1. Reese et al. (2009a) report two RCTs. Two additional studies using the PCOMS have been published, but are not included in Table 5.2 because they are not independent RCTs. The first (Reese et al., 2009b) involved a subset of data from Reese et al. (2009a) and found that graduate trainees whose supervisors also received feedback about treatment progress and alliance had better outcomes than trainees in a no-feedback condition. The second study (Anker et al., 2010) used data from Anker et al. (2009) to investigate the relationship between alliance and outcome. In this study, early alliance (third-session SRS ratings) predicted client change beyond early symptom change ($d = .25$).

■ **FURTHER LEARNING**

- http://www.heartandsoulofchange.com and http://www.scottmiller.com. All versions of the ORS and SRS are available in several languages without charge for individual use. These Web sites also offer research and training resources.
- http://www.myoutcomes.com and http://www.clientvoiceinnovations.com. These sites offer software and Web-based applications for administering, scoring, and interpreting ORS and SRS scores.
- http://www.drjohnmurphy.com. Information on helping young people and families apply their own ideas, strengths, and resources toward solutions at school and elsewhere is available, along with relevant links and training information.

■ **REFERENCES**

American Psychological Association. (2006). Evidence-based practice in psychology. *American Psychologist, 61*(4), 271–285.

Anker, M. G., Duncan, B. L., & Sparks, J. A. (2009). Using client feedback to improve couple therapy outcomes: A randomized clinical trial in a naturalistic setting. *Journal of Consulting and Clinical Psychology, 77*, 693–704.

Anker, M. G., Owen, J., Duncan, B. L., & Sparks, J. A. (2010). The alliance in couple therapy: Partner influence, early change, and alliance patterns in a naturalistic sample. *Journal of Consulting and Clinical Psychology, 78*, 635–645.

Bedi, R. (2006). Concept mapping the client's perspective on counseling alliance formation. *Journal of Counseling Psychology, 53*, 26–35.

Bordin, E. S. (1979). The generalizability of the psychoanalytic concept of the working alliance. *Psychotherapy: Theory, Research, and Practice, 16*, 252–260.

Bringhurst, D. L., Watson, C. W., Miller, S. D., & Duncan, B. L. (2006). The reliability and validity of the Outcome Rating Scale: A replication study of a brief clinical measure. *Journal of Brief Therapy, 5*, 23–30.

Brown, J., Dreis, S., & Nace, D. (1999). What really makes a difference in psychotherapy outcome? Why does managed care want to know? In M. Hubble, B. Duncan, & S. Miller (Eds.), *The heart and soul of change* (pp. 389–406). Washington, DC: American Psychological Association Press.

Burckhardt, C. S., & Anderson, K. L. (2003). The Quality of Life Scale (QOLS): Reliability, validity and utilization. *Health and Quality of Life Outcomes, 1*(60), 64–70.

Burlingame, G. M., Mosier, J. I., Wells, M. G., Atkin, Q. G., Lambert, M. J., Whoolery, M., & Latkowski, M. (2001). Tracking the influence of mental health treatment: The development of the Youth Outcome Questionnaire. *Clinical Psychology and Psychotherapy, 8*, 361–379.

Campbell, A., & Hemsley, S. (2009). Outcome Rating Scale and Session Rating Scale in psychological practice: Clinical utility of ultra-brief measures. *Clinical Psychologist, 13,* 1–9.

De Jong, P., & Berg, I. K. (2008). *Interviewing for solutions* (3rd ed.). Belmont, CA: Thomson.

de Shazer, S. (1985). *Keys to solution in brief therapy.* New York: Norton.

de Shazer, S. (1994). *Words were originally magic.* New York: Norton.

de Shazer, S., Dolan, Y., Korman, H., Trepper, T., McCollum, E., & Berg, I. K. (2007). *More than miracles: The state of the art of solution-focused brief therapy.* New York: Haworth Press.

Duncan, B. L. (2010). *On becoming a better therapist.* Washington, DC: American Psychological Association.

Duncan, B. L., Miller, S. D., & Sparks, J. A. (2003a). *Child Outcome Rating Scale.* Ft. Lauderdale, FL: Author.

Duncan, B. L., Miller, S. D., & Sparks, J. A. (2003b). *Child Session Rating Scale.* Ft. Lauderdale, FL: Author.

Duncan, B. L., Miller, S. D., & Sparks, J. A. (2004). *The heroic client: A revoluntionary way to improve effectiveness through client-directed outcome informed therapy* (rev. ed.). San Franciso, CA: Jossey-Bass.

Duncan, B. L., Miller, S. D., Sparks, J., Claud, D., Reynolds, L., Brown, J., & Johnson, L. (2003c). The Session Rating Scale: Preliminary psychometric properties of a "working" alliance measure. *Journal of Brief Therapy, 3,* 3–12.

Duncan, B. L., Sparks, J., Miller, S. D., Bohanske, R., & Claud, D. (2006). Giving youth a voice: A preliminary study of the reliability and validity of a brief outcome measure for children, adolescents, and caretakers. *Journal of Brief Therapy, 5,* 66–82.

Franklin, C., Corcoran, J., Nowicki, J., & Streeter, C. L. (1997). Using client self-anchored scales to measure outcomes in solution-focused therapy. *Journal of Systemic Therapies, 10,* 246–265.

Hansen, N. B., Lambert, M. J., & Forman, E. V. (2002). The psychotherapy dose-response effect and its implications for treatment delivery services. *Clinical Psychology: Science and Practice, 9,* 329–343.

Harmon, S. C., Lambert, M. J., Smart, D. W., Hawkins, E. J., Nielsen, S. L., Slade, K., et al. (2007). Enhancing outcome for potential treatment failures: Therapist/client feedback and clinical support tools. *Psychotherapy Research, 17,* 379–392.

Hatcher, R. L., & Barends, A. W. (1996). Patient's view of psychotherapy: Exploratory factor analysis of three alliance measures. *Journal of Consulting and Clinical Psychology, 64,* 1326–1336.

Hawkins, E. J., Lambert, M. J., Vermeersch, D. A., Slade, K., & Tuttle, K. (2004). The effects of providing patient progress information to therapists and patients. *Psychotherapy Research, 14,* 308–327.

Horvath, A. O., & Bedi, R. P. (2002). The alliance. In J. C. Norcross (Ed.), *Psychotherapy relationships that work: Therapist contributions and responsiveness to patients* (pp. 37–70). New York: Oxford University Press.

Horvath, A. O., & Greenberg, L. S. (1989). Development and validation of the Working Alliance Inventory. *Journal of Counseling Psychology, 64,* 223–233.

Jacobson, N. S., & Truax, P. (1991). Clinical significance: A statistical approach to defining meaningful change in psychotherapy research. *Journal of Consulting and Clinical Psychology, 59,* 12–19.

Kazdin, A. E. (2007). Systematic evaluation to improve the quality of patient care: From hope to hopeful. *Pragmatic Case Studies in Psychotherapy, 3,* 37–49.

Lambert, M. J. (2010). Yes, it is time for clinicians to routinely monitor treatment outcome. In B. L. Duncan, S. D. Miller, B. E. Wampold, & M. A. Hubble (Eds.), *The heart and soul of change* (pp. 239–266). Washington, DC: American Psychological Association.

Lambert, M. J., Morton, J. J., Hatfield, D., Harmon, C., Hamilton, S., Reid, R. C., Shimokowa, K., Christopherson, C., & Burlingame, G. M. (2004). *Administration and scoring manual for the Outcome Questionnaire-45.* Salt Lake City, UT: OQMeasures.

Lambert, M. J., Whipple, J. L., Smart, D. W., Vermeersch, D. A., Nielsen, S. L., & Hawkins, E. J. (2001). The effects of providing therapists with feedback on client progress during psychotherapy: Are outcomes enhanced? *Psychotherapy Research*, 11, 49–68.

Lambert, M. J., Whipple, J. L., Vermeersch, D. A., Smart, D. W., Hawkins, E. J., Nielsen, S. L., & Goates, M. K. (2002). Enhancing psychotherapy outcomes via providing feedback on client progress: A replication. *Clinical Psychology and Psychotherapy*, 9, 91–103.

Lee, L. (2000). *Bad predictions*. Rochester, MI: Elsewhere Press.

Levitt, T. (1975, September–October). Marketing myopia. *Harvard Business Review*, 19–31.

Lovibond, P. F., & Lovibond, S. H. (1995). The structure of negative emotional states: Comparison of the Depression Anxiety Stress Scale (DASS) with the Beck depression and anxiety scales. *Behaviour Research and Therapy*, 33, 248–262.

Luborsky, L., Barber, J., Siqueland, L., Johnson, S., Najavits, L., Frank, A., et al. (1996). The Helping Alliance Questionnaire (HAQ-II): Psychometric properties. *The Journal of Psychotherapy Practice and Research*, 5, 260–271.

Luborsky, L., Diguer, L., Seligman, D., Rosenthal, R., Krause, E., Johnson, S., et al. (1999). The researcher's own therapy allegiances: A "wild card" in comparisons of treatment efficacy. *Clinical Psychology: Science and Practice*, 6(1), 95–106.

Miller, S. D., & Duncan, B. L. (2000). *The Outcome Rating Scale.* Ft. Lauderdale, FL: Author.

Miller, S. D., & Duncan, B. L. (2004). *The Outcome and Session Rating Scales: Administration and scoring manuals.* Ft. Lauderdale, FL: Author.

Miller, S. D., Duncan, B. L., Brown, J., Sorrell, R., & Chalk, B. (2006). Using outcome to inform and improve treatment outcomes. *Journal of Brief Therapy*, 5, 5–22.

Miller, S. D., Duncan, B. L., Brown, J., Sparks, J., & Claud, D. (2003). The Outcome Rating Scale: A preliminary study of the reliability, validity, and feasibility of a brief visual analog measure. *Journal of Brief Therapy*, 2, 91–100.

Miller, S. D., Duncan, B. L., Johnson, L. (2002). *The Session Rating Scale 3.0.* Ft. Lauderdale, FL: Author.

Miller, S. D., Duncan, B. L., Sorrell, R., & Brown, G. S. (2005). The Partners for Change Outcome Management System. *Journal of Clinical Psychology*, 61, 199–208.

Murphy, J. J. (2008). *Solution-focused counseling in schools* (2nd ed.). Alexandria, VA: American Counseling Association.

Murphy, J. J., & Duncan, B. L. (2007). *Brief interventions for school problems: Outcome-informed strategies* (2nd ed.). New York: Guilford Press.

Reese, R. J., Norsworthy, L., & Rowlands, S. (2009a). Does a continuous feedback system improve psychotherapy outcomes? *Psychotherapy*, 46, 418–431.

Reese, R. J., Usher, E., Bowman, D., Norsworthy, L., Halstead, J., Rowlands, S., & Chisholm, R. R. (2009b). Using client feedback in psychotherapy training: An analysis of its influence on supervision and counselor self-efficacy. *Training and Education in Professional Psychology*, 3(3), 157–168.

Rosenberg, M. (1989). *Society and the adolescent self-image* (rev. ed.). Middletown, CT: Wesleyan University Press.

Safran, J. D., & Moran, J. C. (2000). *Negotiating the therapeutic alliance: A relational treatment guide.* New York: Guilford Press.

Sapyta, J., Riemer, M., & Bickman, L. (2005). Feedback to clinicians. Theory, research, and practice. *Journal of Clinical Psychology, 61,* 145–153.

Thomas, F. N. (2007). Possible limitations, misunderstandings, and misuses of solution-focused brief therapy. In T. S. Nelson & F. N. Thomas (Eds.), *The handbook of solution-focused brief therapy: Clinical applications* (pp. 391–408). New York: Haworth.

Tracey, T. J., & Kokotovic, A. M. (1989). Factor structure of the Working Alliance Inventory. *Psychological Assessment, 1,* 207–210.

Tryon, G. S., Blackwell, S. C., & Hammel, E. F. (2008). The magnitude of client and therapist working alliance ratings. *Psychotherapy: Theory, Research, Training, 45,* 546–551.

Wampold, B. E. (2001). *The great psychotherapy debate.* Mahwah, NJ: Erlbaum.

Wampold, B. E. (2010). The research evidence for the common factors models: A historically situated perspective. In B. L. Duncan, S. D. Miller, B. E. Wampold, & M. A. Hubble (Eds.), *The heart and soul of change: Delivering what works in therapy* (pp. 49–81). Washington, DC: American Psychological Association.

Whipple, J. L., Lambert, M. J., Vermeersch, D. A., Smart, D. W., Nielsen, S. L., & Hawkins, E. J. (2003). Improving the effects of psychotherapy: The use of early identification of treatment failure and problem solving strategies in routine practice. *Journal of Counseling Psychology, 58,* 59–68.

Reviews of the Research

6 Solution-Focused Brief Therapy Outcome Research

■ WALLACE J. GINGERICH, JOHNNY S. KIM,
GEERT J. J. M. STAMS, AND
ALASDAIR J. MACDONALD

■ INTRODUCTION

It is now about 25 years since Steve de Shazer, Insoo Kim Berg, and their colleagues at the Brief Family Therapy Center (BFTC) in Milwaukee, Wisconsin, first described solution-focused brief therapy (SFBT) in the professional literature (de Shazer et al., 1986). This therapy had been evolving in a context of intellectual curiosity, systematic observation, and creative innovation in what could be described, at least in the early years, as a "therapeutic think tank" (see Lipchik et al. in Chapter 1 of this volume). The primary focus during that time was on the change process itself—finding what worked in sessions and between sessions—rather than on end-of-treatment outcomes. However, the team also conducted several follow-up studies early in the development of the approach because they felt it was important to determine if clients who completed SFBT experienced positive change as a result. The bulk of solution-focused outcome research has been conducted by practitioners and scholars elsewhere in the United States and in Europe; in addition, large, well-funded, controlled investigations of SFBT outcomes have recently appeared.

This chapter reviews the development of SFBT outcome research chronologically, beginning with the first compilation of outcome studies by the European Brief Therapy Association (EBTA) described by Macdonald (1994b). Next, we discuss the first systematic review of controlled SFBT outcome studies published by Gingerich and Eisengart (2000), followed by the meta-analytic reviews of Stams et al. (2006) and Kim (2008). Finally, we discuss several important studies that have appeared since the meta-analyses and conclude with a summary of SFBT outcome research to date.

■ REVIEWS OF RESEARCH

1994 Compilation of Eight Reports

In 1994 the EBTA appointed Dr. Alasdair Macdonald as Research Coordinator to compile and maintain a record of published research on SFBT. Eight published reports existed in 1994; three came from the Brief Family Therapy Center in Milwaukee, two from England, one from Germany, one from the Salamanca team in Spain, and one from California. All of these were naturalistic follow-up studies of clinic populations. Seven of the studies used the criterion of success originally piloted by the Mental Research Institute in Palo Alto, California, namely, that clients had met their goals for therapy or that significant improvement had been made so that further therapy was unnecessary (Watzlawick et al., 1974). Effectiveness reports from these eight studies ranged from 66% to 86% improvement.

The first published reports of follow-up studies came from de Shazer and colleagues in Milwaukee. In 1985 de Shazer reported a 6-month follow-up of 28 cases that had received the formula first session task. After an average of five sessions, 23 cases (82%) had improved and 11 had solved other problems in addition to those that brought them in for treatment (de Shazer, 1985). One year later, de Shazer and colleagues reported a telephone follow-up of 25% of 1,600 cases seen during a 5-year period at the Brief Family Therapy Center; after an average of six sessions, 72% of the cases had improved (de Shazer et al., 1986). In 1991 de Shazer reported a third follow-up study in which 23 of 29 cases (80%) reported that they had either resolved their original difficulty or made significant progress toward resolving it. After 18 months, the success rate had increased to 86%, and 67% of cases reported other improvements as well. Treatment comprised an average of 4.6 sessions in this study, and cases with four or more sessions reported better outcomes.

Perez-Grande, Iveson, and Ratner (1990) conducted a 6-month telephone follow-up of 62 individuals and families seen in their London clinic; 41 (66%) were satisfied with the outcome. Burr (1993) carried out the first study of SFBT published in a peer-reviewed journal. Fifty-five cases referred to a North German child psychiatry clinic were followed up for an average of 9 months. Of the 34 who replied, 26 (77%) reported some improvement. There was a mean of four sessions of treatment. New problems were reported in four cases with improvement and four without. The Milwaukee and London clinic studies are covered in more detail in Chapters 1 and 19 of this book.

Perez-Grande (1991) published a study of 97 cases seen at a family clinic in Salamanca, Spain, 25% of whom were children. After an average of five sessions, 71% regarded themselves as better at the end of therapy. Eighty-one clients were contacted during a follow-up 6 to 35 (mean, 19) months later, at which time 13% had relapsed. However, 38% not only reported improvement but also noted that other problems were also better than before. There were more dropouts if the problem was of long standing.

Morrison and colleagues (1993) used a family systems approach based on solution-focused principles to address behavior and learning problems in an elementary school in the United States. Thirty children (including six from the special education stream) received one to seven sessions of family intervention. Of these, 23 (77%) improved but 7 relapsed later.

The first study of SFBT in adult psychiatric practice was completed by Macdonald and his team in Scotland (Macdonald, 1994a). Forty-one adult cases were followed up for 1 year after a mean of 3.7 sessions. Twenty-nine families or individuals were contacted, of whom 29 (70%) had improved. Clients with long-standing problems (over 4 years' duration prior to therapy) did less well. Importantly, clients from all socioeconomic classes benefited equally from the intervention.

These early follow-up studies of SFBT outcomes consistently showed approximately 70% of clients reporting that their goals had been met or that they had improved significantly. Although these studies provided preliminary evidence that SFBT had a positive impact on client outcomes, more rigorous controlled designs would be needed to establish a stronger evidence base.

The EBTA maintains an updated compilation of studies that, at the time of this writing, included 87 studies. The compilation can be accessed via the EBTA Web site at http://www.ebta.nu and at http://www.solutionsdoc.co.uk. The current list includes 13 randomized controlled trials that show benefit from SFBT, of which six show benefit superior to that of other methods. Of an additional 29 comparison studies, 22 favor SFBT. In addition, effectiveness data are available from more than 3,000 cases in naturalistic studies, with a success rate exceeding 60% and requiring an average of three to five sessions of therapy time. Many of these studies have been included in subsequent reviews of SFBT outcomes.

2000 Qualitative Review of 15 Studies

The first qualitative review of SFBT outcome research was conducted by Gingerich and Eisengart (2000). They systematically searched the bibliographic databases, dissertation abstracts, and bibliographies of identified research studies in an effort to locate all controlled studies of SFBT outcomes appearing in the English literature up to and including 1999. Studies were included in the review if they met all of the following criteria: the intervention was SFBT, some form of experimental control was used, the outcome measure assessed client behavior or functioning, and outcomes were assessed at the end of treatment or later. To be considered SFBT, the intervention had to include one or more of the following core components: (a) a search for presession change, (b) goal setting, (c) the miracle question, (d) a scaling question, (e) a search for exceptions, (f) a consulting break, and (g) a message including compliments and a task. These core components had been identified in the writings of de Shazer and Berg (1997) and Beyebach (1998). Since the term *solution-focused* was already appearing in the literature in reference to other approaches and interventions, the authors included studies in this review only if they referenced the work of the original group at the Brief Family Therapy Center in Milwaukee, Wisconsin.

Fifteen studies had appeared in the literature by 1999. Two of them included all seven core components of SFBT; four included only two or three components. Gingerich and Eisengart also categorized each study according to the degree of experimental control used, based on standards published by the American Psychological Association (Task Force on Promotion and Dissemination of Psychological Procedures, 1995) and modified by Chambless and Hollon (1998). Five studies were classified as well controlled, four as moderately controlled, and six as poorly controlled. The five well-controlled studies used samples of 40 or more employed randomized or matched control group designs, and most used some form of treatment monitoring and established outcome measures.

The five well-controlled studies included a study of depression in college students (Sundstrom, 1993), a study of parenting skills conducted at a university-based facility (Zimmerman et al., 1996), a study of rehabilitation of orthopedic patients (Cockburn et al., 1997), a study of recidivism in a Swedish prison population (Lindforss & Magnusson, 1997), and a study of institutionalized adolescent offenders (Seagram, 1997). All five of these studies reported positive outcomes. The depressed college students showed significant improvement on the Beck Depression Inventory; Parenting Skills Inventory scores for the parenting group improved significantly; the orthopedic rehabilitation patients showed significant between-group differences on the Family Crisis Oriented Personal Evaluation Scales (F-COPES) and the Psychological Adjustment to Illness Scale Revised (PAIS-R) scores in comparison with the usual treatment control group and 68% of the SFBT patients had returned to work within 7 days of discharge compared with 4% of the comparison group. The recidivism rates in both the adult and adolescent offender studies were 30%–50% less than those of the comparison groups who did not receive SFBT.

Gingerich and Eisengart (2000) concluded that the studies provided "preliminary support for the idea that SFBT may be beneficial to clients" (p. 495). All 15 studies purported to show positive outcomes of SFBT, although few if any met the stringent research criteria needed to establish efficacy by current standards. Several of the investigators recognized this by describing their research as "pilot" studies or "preliminary" investigations. Gingerich and Eisengart went on to say that SFBT research seemed to be evolving from simple follow-up "open trials" to more controlled "efficacy" studies.

2006 Meta-analytic Review of 21 Studies

A team of Dutch scholars conducted the first meta-analysis of SFBT outcomes in 2006 to provide quantitative evidence for the efficacy of SFBT (Stams et al., 2006). By this time, meta-analytic review methods were increasingly being used to provide a more systematic means of analysis of study findings by converting study outcomes to a standardized metric called *effect size* so that outcomes could be compared across studies regardless of the outcome measure used. Meta-analysis can account for inconsistencies among study results that may be explained by moderators such as publication characteristics (publication status, impact factor, and year of publication), client characteristics (sex, age, socioeconomic background, type of target group, and types of problems), intervention characteristics (modality, expertise of the therapist, duration of therapy, and number of sessions), and study design characteristics (controlled or noncontrolled study, random assignment or not, type of comparison group, and quality of the study design).

The primary search method involved inspection of the computerized databases Medline, PsycINFO, and ERIC. No specific year was indicated, and the following keywords were used for searching in varying combinations: *solution-focused therapy, brief therapy, SFBT, therapy, solution, intervention*. Only published studies and dissertations were included in the meta-analysis. In the second step, additional studies were located using the ancestry method, that is, inspection of the reference sections of obtained articles, book chapters, and dissertations and the qualitative review of SFBT outcome research that was conducted by Gingerich and Eisengart in 2000.

Studies were considered studies of SFBT if the author described the treatment as such; no further descriptions of the intervention were checked to establish if the criteria for SFBT were met. Stams et al. (2006) included both strong and weak designs in their meta-analysis. Strong designs were controlled studies with pre- and posttest measurements or single-case experimental designs with a multiple baseline; weak designs were noncontrolled studies or controlled studies with posttest measurements only.

The Stams et al. (2006) meta-analysis included 21 studies with $N = 1,421$ participants. The random effects model was used to test for statistical significance of the meta-analytic results. In this model, significance testing is based on the total number of studies in the meta-analysis and results are generalized to the population of studies from which the primary studies were drawn (Rosenthal, 1995).

Stams et al. (2006) used the fail-safe method to examine whether publication bias or a file drawer problem existed by estimating the number of unpublished studies not included in the meta-analysis that could have rendered the overall significant effect size nonsignificant (Durlak & Lipsey, 1991). Meta-analytic findings are considered to be robust if the fail-safe number exceeds the critical value obtained with Rosenthal's (1995) formula of $5 * k + 10$, where k is the number of studies used in the meta-analysis. If the fail-safe number falls below this critical value, a publication bias or file drawer problem may exist. The fail-safe number in their meta-analysis was 444, which exceeded Rosenthal's (1995) critical value ($21 * 5 + 10$), suggesting that there was no file drawer effect.

The combined effect size according to the random effect model was $d = .37$ (95% CI, $19 < d < .55$), $p < .001$ ($Z = 3.94$), indicating a small to medium-sized effect of SFBT. Effect sizes of $d = .20$, $d = .50$, and $d = .80$ are indices of small, medium-sized, and large differences (Cohen, 1988), respectively. However, the sample of studies was found to be heterogeneous, with $Q (20) = 63.87$, $p < .001$, in which case the overall effect size was not a good descriptor of the distribution of individual study effect sizes. Therefore, a series of ANOVAs was conducted to identify moderators accounting for differences in effect size among studies.

The results of the random effect moderator analyses are presented in Table 6.1. The most important finding was that SFBT did have a positive effect compared to no treatment, $d = .57$, $p < .01$, but that the effect was not larger than the effect of treatment as usual, that is, non-evidence-based treatment: $d = .16$, n.s. ($Q = 5.14$, $p < .05$). Furthermore, the effect of SFBT was larger in studies published after Gingerich and Eisengart's 2000 review ($d = .87$) than in those published before ($d = .29$: $Q = 5.71$, $p < .05$). The ANOVA results revealed that adults benefited more from SFBT ($d = .61$) than did children and adolescents ($d = .23$; $Q = 5.05$, $p < .05$). Clients residing in institutions, including delinquents and patients with schizophrenia, benefited more from SFBT ($d = .60$) than did nonresidential clients such as families/couples ($d = .40$) and students ($d = .21$; $Q = 6.06$, $p < .05$). The effect of SFBT proved to be largest for clients with externalizing behavior problems ($d = .61$) compared with clients with marital problems ($d = .55$), internalizing problems ($d = .49$), or mixed problems ($d = .22$; $Q = 8.89$, $p < .05$). Group therapy clients had better outcomes ($d = .59$) than did individual therapy clients ($d = .33$; $Q = 9.17$, $p < .05$). Finally, the effect of SFBT was larger for noncontrolled studies ($d = .84$) than for controlled studies ($d = .25$; $Q = 7.04$, $p < .01$).

Stams et al. (2006) also conducted a multiple regression analysis to examine the unique contribution of each moderator to the combined effect size, controlling for the effect of other moderators. All significant moderators were included in the multiple regression analysis. Moderators with three or more categories were transformed into dichotomous dummy variables. A significant regression equation [$Q (8, 12) = 198.62$, $p < .001$, $R = .38$] explained 65% of the differences of effect sizes among studies. The more recent studies yielded relatively larger effect sizes ($b = .36$, $p < .001$). The effect size for clients who resided in institutions was larger than for that clients in nonresidential treatment settings (standardized regression coefficient $b = .36$, $p < .001$). The effect size for SFBT was larger for externalizing problems (oppositional defiant disorder, attention deficit hyperactivity disorder, delinquent behavior) than for marital problems, internalizing problems (anxiety and depression), and mixed problems ($b = .17$, $p < .05$).

TABLE 6.1. *Random Effects Moderator Analysis ANOVA Results for the Stams et al. (2006) Meta-Analysis*

Moderator Variables	N Number of Subjects	K Number of Studies	Cohen's d (Random Effects)	95% Confidence Interval	Q Statistic Between Studies	Q Statistic within Studies
Publication status					.68	
Journal	1,283	16	.38***	.19 to .55		22.05
Dissertation	130	5	.43	−.06 to .91		3.37
Impact					.84	
Low	682	12	.47**	.17 to .77		14.41
High	731	9	.33**	.08 to .58		10.85
Year of publication					5.71*	
Before 2000	1,196	14	.29***	.11 to .46		16.87
After 2000	217	7	.87**	.33 to 1.41		3.52
Sex					2.45	
Males 60% or more	227	6	.71**	.19 to 1.24		1.30
Females 60% or more	82	2	.52	−.10 to 1.13		.31
Mixed 40% to 60%	583	9	.39**	.14 to .64		10.37
Age					5.05*	
Children and adolescents	617	10	.23*	.05 to .42		5.49
Adults	331	9	.61***	.34 to .88		4.12
SES					3.97	
Lower class	476	3	.26	−.15 to .67		4.90
Mixed	211	5	.47**	.13 to .82		1.24
Upper class	49	1	.64	−.81 to 2.09		0.00
Target group					6.06*	
Students	569	7	.21*	.01 to .40		5.62
Family or couples	558	6	.40*	.02 to .78		9.51
Institutionalized	286	8	.60***	.28 to .93		4.92
Type of problem					8.89*	
Mixed	950	7	.22	−.01 to .45		9.89
Internalizing	98	3	.49	−.17 to 1.14		.27
Marital	82	2	.55*	.10 to 1.00		.29
Externalizing	283	9	.61***	.26 to .96		6.66
Modality					9.17*	
Individual	590	9	.33**	.08 to .58		9.88
Group	322	9	.59***	.29 to .89		1.22
Mixed	501	3	.57	−.44 to 1.57		5.82
Therapist					2.22	
Professional	1,212	15	.31**	.10 to .52		19.47
Nonprofessional	85	3	.53*	.08 to .98		1.24
Duration of therapy					1.69	
6 weeks or less	281	7	.46***	.20 to .72		2.68
More than 6 weeks	522	7	.25*	.05 to .44		5.12
Number of sessions					.03	
6 or more	344	7	.57***	.31 to .84		2.88
Less than 6	313	9	.54**	.19 to .88		5.94
Control group					7.04**	
Yes	1,006	11	.25**	.09 to .41		12.26
No	407	10	.84***	.37 to 1.30		6.80
Random assignment					1.10	
Yes	533	4	.29	−.05 to .63		6.66
No	473	7	.26**	.08 to .44		4.50
Comparison group					5.14*	
Problem focused	872	7	.16	.00 to .31		6.77
No treatment	134	4	.57**	.22 to .93		.34
Design					1.23	
Weak	889	12	.47**	.13 to .80		17.52
Strong	524	9	.30***	13 to .48		7.35

*p < .05.   ** p < .01.   *** p < .001.

Finally, the effect size was smaller for controlled studies than for noncontrolled studies (b = -.61, p < .001).

The meta-analytic results show a positive and small-to-medium effect of SFBT. Publication year, type of target group (families/couples, students, or clients in residential settings), type of problem (marital problems, externalizing and internalizing problems), and study design (noncontrolled or controlled studies) were identified as unique moderators of SFBT efficacy. Stams et al. (2006) concluded that although SFBT does not have a larger effect than standard problem-focused therapy, it does have a positive effect in less time, satisfying the condition of the client's autonomy. Therefore, they considered it reasonable to consider SFBT when it fits the client and the problem.

2008 Meta-analytic Review of 22 Studies

Kim (2008) conducted a second meta-analytic review of SFBT research to synthesize previous research studies examining the effectiveness of SFBT and to determine the magnitude and the treatment effect. This review examined the effectiveness of SFBT separately for different types of outcomes: externalizing behavior problems, internalizing behavior problems, and family or relationship problems.

Kim (2008) extracted published studies through literature searches in various electronic databases for the period 1988 to 2005. In addition, unpublished dissertations were identified through the electronic database UMI Dissertation Abstract using the same keywords. Kim used the SFBT descriptors identified by de Shazer and Berg (1997) as selection criteria for what constituted SFBT:

1. The therapist must ask the miracle question.
2. Scaling questions must be asked at least once.
3. Toward the end of the interview, the therapist must take a break.
4. After the break, the therapist gives the client a set of compliments and sometimes suggestions or homework tasks.

At least one of these components had to be utilized in a study for it to be included in the meta-analysis.

Kim's (2008) meta-analysis included only studies that employed comparison groups, whereas Stams et al. (2006) included single-group pretest-posttest studies (n = 10) as well as comparison group studies (n = 11). When pretest and posttest scores for both groups were available, a single effect size was calculated for each study using the independent-groups pretest-posttest design sample estimator (Morris & DeShon, 2002). Hedges' g (1982) with the unbiased estimate was used if only mean posttest scores were available for both the experimental and control groups. For studies that reported nonsignificant results without providing any detailed statistical information, an effect size of zero was substituted for nonsignificant outcomes (Perry, 1997), providing a conservative pooled point estimate of the effect size. In order to ensure statistical independence of the data (Bangert-Drowns, 1997; Devine, 1997), only one effect size value was used to represent each study in the meta-analysis. This was done by calculating the effect size for each measure used in a single study and then averaging them to derive one overall average effect size for that study. Hierarchical linear modeling software was used to combine the studies under a random effects model.

Twenty-two studies were included in the Kim (2008) meta-analysis, grouped into three categories based on the outcome problem each study targeted: (a) externalizing behavior problems, (b) internalizing behavior problems, and (c) family or relationship problems. Five studies (Franklin et al., 2008; Huang, 2001; Marinaccio, 2001; Seagram, 1997; Triantafillou, 2002) were included in more than one category because they examined more than one outcome problem.

Nine studies of externalizing behavior problems had effect sizes ranging from −.43 to .74 (Table 6.2). Results from the unconditional model showed an overall random effects weighted mean effect size estimate of .13, which is considered a small effect size estimate (Cohen, 1988). While the direction of this effect size estimate is positive (favoring the SFBT group), the magnitude of the effect was not statistically significant, $t(8) = 1.08$, $p= .31$ indicating little real difference in treatment effect between the SFBT group and the comparison group that did not receive SFBT intervention.

For internalizing behavior problems (Table 6.3), 12 SFBT studies were combined; the effect size ranged from −.46 to 1.18. Results from the unconditional model showed an overall random effects weighted mean effect size estimate of .26, a small effect size estimate (Cohen, 1988) but statistically significant nonetheless: $t(11) = 2.51$, $p = .03$.

Eight studies examined family or relationship problems (Table 6.4) and produced effect sizes ranging from −.56 to 1.23. Results from the unconditional model showed an

TABLE 6.2. *Externalizing Behavior Results for the Kim (2008) Review*

Study	Sample	Sample Size	Session Number	Effect Size	CI
Franklin et al. (2007)	Students	85	N/A	.47	(.03, .91)
Gallardo-Cooper (1997)	Mothers and teachers	66	1	−.14	(−.56, .28)
Huang (2001)	Couples	39	8	−.43	(−1.24, .38)
Ingersoll-Dayton et al. (1999)	Elderly	21	7	.32	(−.30, .94)
Marinaccio (2001)	Students, mothers, and teachers	120	4.5	−.25	(−.56, .06)
Franklin et al. (2008)	Students	59	5.8	.74	(.20, 1.28)
Newsome (2004)	Students	52	8	.22	(−.33, .77)
Seagram (1997)	Youth offenders	40	10	.17	(−.47, .81)
Triantafillou (2002)	Children	30	4	.17	(−.59, .93)

CI = 95% confidence interval.
N/A = not available.

TABLE 6.3. *Internalizing Behavior Results for the Kim (2008) Review*

Study	Sample	Sample Size	Session Number	Effect Size	CI
Bozeman (1999)	Psychiatric patients	52	3	.56	(−.01, 1.13)
Cook (1998)	Students	68	6	.28	(−.21, .77)
Huang (2001)	Couples	39	8	.23	(−.58, 1.04)
Leggett (2004)	Students	67	11	.04	(−.45, .53)
Marinaccio (2001)	Students	48	4.5	.06	(−.24, .37)
Franklin et al. (2008)	Students	59	5.8	.74	(.20, 1.28)
Seagram (1997)	Youth offenders	40	10	−.06	(−.70, .58)
Springer et al. (2000)	Students	10	6	.57	(−.91, 2.05)
Sundstrom (1993)	College students	40	1	1.18	(.48, 1.88)
Triantafillou (2002)	Children	30	4	−.46	(−1.23, .31)
Villalba (2002)	Students	59	6	.11	(−.41, .63)
Wettersten (2002)	Adults	65	25	.26	(−.24, .76)

CI = 95% confidence interval.

TABLE 6.4. *Family or Relationship Results for the Kim (2008) Review*

Study	Sample	Sample Size	Session Number	Effect Size	CI
Adams et al. (1991)	Families	40	9.5	.70	(.04, 1.36)
Cockburn et al. (1997)	Orthopedic patients	48	6	1.23	(.30, 2.16)
Eakes et al. (1997)	Families	10	5	.52	(−.38, 1.42)
Huang (2001)	Couples	39	8	.25	(−.56, 1.06)
Sundman (1997)	Adults	200	N/A	0	(−.28, .28)
Triantafillou (2002)	Children	30	4	−.56	(−1.33, .21)
Zimmerman et al. (1996)	Parents	42	6	.17	(−.52, .86)
Zimmerman et al. (1997)	Couples	36	6	.29	(−.20, .78)

CI = 95% confidence interval.

overall random effects weighted mean effect size estimate of .26. While the direction of this small effect size estimate was positive, it did not reach statistical significance: $t(7) = 1.70$, $p = .13$.

Kim's (2008) meta-analysis found that SFBT demonstrated small but positive treatment effects favoring the SFBT groups. However, only the overall weighted mean effect size for internalizing behavior problems was statistically significant at the $p < .05$ level, indicating that the overall treatment effect for the SFBT group was different from that of the control group. In sum, SFBT appears to be effective with internalizing behavior problems such as those involving depression, anxiety, self-concept, and self-esteem while appearing to be less effective with externalizing behavior problem such as hyperactivity, conduct problems, aggression, and family and relationship problems.

Kim's (2008) meta-analysis noted some differences between the individual SFBT studies, which might help explain the overall results. For example, dissertations had much lower effect sizes than published studies. On the one hand, this is somewhat expected since mean effect sizes for doctoral dissertations average about a third smaller than for published studies (Smith, 1980, as cited in Carlberg & Walberg, 1984). On the other hand, what is particularly interesting is that out of all the dissertations ($n = 11$) in all three subgroups, only one study had a moderate effect size (.56) and only one study had a large effect size (1.18); all the rest had either negative or small effect sizes. This is quite different from the published studies ($n = 11$), which had four large or nearly large effect sizes, three moderate effect sizes, and four small effect sizes. Kim noted that these widely varying differences in effect sizes may provide a possible explanation for the small overall mean effect size estimates, with the negative and small effect sizes of doctoral dissertations bringing down the overall mean effect size.

Kim (2008) speculated that the effect size differences between doctoral dissertations and published studies could be explained by the possibly lower intervention fidelity of the dissertations. According to Rubin and Babbie (2005), intervention fidelity involves "the degree to which an intervention being evaluated is actually delivered to clients as intended" (p. 750). Of concern is the type of SFBT training the clinicians received in the dissertation studies prior to the intervention that could affect the quality of SFBT delivered to the experimental group and thereby affect the study results. Six dissertations used therapists with little or no specified SFBT training. In only three dissertation studies did the therapists have 6 or more hours of training in SFBT.

Similarly, seven of the published studies involved clinicians with little or no specified training for implementing the intervention; however, in the four remaining published studies, clinicians had a minimum of 20 hours of training over a period of up to

8 weeks. All four of the doctoral dissertations in which clinicians had training of 20 hours or less had either negative or small effect sizes. In comparison, the two studies that provided 2- and 4-day training had close to large effect sizes (.70 and .74). The one published study that provided 20 hours of training had an effect size of zero; interestingly, the study that provided 8 weeks of training also had an effect size of zero. It could be that providing less than 20 hours of training on SFBT, as in the dissertations that gave this information, is not enough to ensure competence in the delivery of the therapy model and threatens intervention fidelity. While the core components and techniques of SFBT may appear simple, becoming proficient and skilled in delivering this therapy takes practice and ample training. Since it appears that the published studies provided more training in the therapy model than the dissertation studies, this raises questions about intervention fidelity for those dissertations and whether there was sufficient training in the SFBT model. See Chapter 3 for a discussion on how to improve the intervention fidelity of SFBT.

Recent Studies

Two important SFBT outcome studies have appeared since the reviews discussed above. Smock and colleagues (2008) compared six sessions of manualized SFBT group therapy with a 6-week adaptation of the Hazelden model on the mental health functioning of 38 level 1 substance abuse outpatients. Subjects were referred to the study primarily from the probation department and were randomly assigned to groups. Mental health outcomes were assessed using the Beck Depression Inventory and the Outcome Questionnaire 45.2 (OQ-45). The SFBT group showed statistically significant improvement on both measures, with an effect size of .64 for the Beck Depression Inventory and .61 for the OQ-45 Symptom Distress subscale. The Hazelden comparison group showed a positive trend on both measures, but changes were not significant. The SFBT group had higher scores on both measures at pretest, but by posttest the scores of the two groups were roughly comparable; thus, between-group differences at posttest did not reach statistical significance. Both groups were in the normal range of the OQ-45 at both pretest and posttest.

The second recent study was a large-scale randomized comparison of SFBT with two other evidence-based treatments. Knekt, Lindfors, and colleagues compared the effect of SFBT, short-term psychodynamic psychotherapy (SPP), and long-term psychodynamic therapy (LPP) on the work ability and mental health outcomes of patients with depression and anxiety disorders (Knekt & Lindfors, 2004; Knekt et al., 2008a, 2008b). To be included in the study, patients had to meet DSM-IV criteria for anxiety or mood disorders; not have a psychotic disorder, severe personality disorder, substance use disorder, organic disease, or mental retardation; and not have received psychotherapy within the previous 2 years. Of the 459 patients who met inclusion criteria, 326 participated in the study and were randomly assigned to treatment groups.

On average, SFBT patients received 9.8 therapy sessions over a period of 7.5 months; SPP patients received 18.5 sessions over a period of 5.7 months; and LPP patients received 232 sessions over a period of 31.3 months. Solution-focused brief therapists had an average of 9 years of experience in SFBT therapy; SPP therapists had an average of 25 years of experience, and LPP therapists had an average of 18 years. Solution-focused brief therapy was manualized and monitored for adherence; the two psychodynamic psychotherapies were not manualized.

Patients were assessed over a 3-year period for mental health outcomes and work ability. The Beck Depression Inventory, Hamilton Depression Rating Scale, Symptom Check List Anxiety Scale, and Hamilton Anxiety Rating Scale were the primary measures of mental health outcomes. A statistically significant reduction of symptoms was noted for all four measures over the 3-year period for patients in all three treatment groups. Solution-focused brief therapy and SPP produced benefits more quickly (i.e., during the first year) than LPP, and the results were not significantly different from each other. The benefits from LPP caught up with those of the short-term therapies during the second year and exceeded those of the short-term therapies during the third year.

Patients were assessed for work ability using the Work Ability Index, Work subscale of the Social Adjustment Scale, the Perceived Psychological Functioning Scale, the prevalence of working or studying, and the number of sick leave days. Work ability was statistically improved during the 3 years for all therapies; again, SFBT and SPP produced better results during year 1, the three therapies were comparable during year 2, and by year 3 LPP produced better results. The results of SFBT and SPP were not significantly different. There were no differences among the three therapies at the 3-year follow-up on prevalence of individuals working or studying or in number of sick leave days.

Knekt, Lindfors, and their colleagues concluded that "short-term term therapies produce benefits more quickly than long-term psychodynamic psychotherapy but in the long run long-term psychodynamic psychotherapy is superior to short-term therapies" (Knekt et al., 2008a, p. 689). In effect, SFBT and SPP outperformed LPP during year 1 and maintained their gains over the 3-year period, but LPP caught up with them during year 2 and exceeded them during year 3.

The Knekt and Lindfors study conforms more closely to generally accepted standards for effectiveness studies than perhaps any other study appearing to date. It used clear inclusion criteria for the subject sample based on a DSM-IV diagnostic grouping and excluded those who had additional confounding diagnoses or who were receiving other treatment. The study employed a large sample and used random assignment to groups; treatment fidelity was assessed for at least one of the treatments (SFBT). The study employed multiple outcome measures assessing both mental health functioning and work ability (role performance), and outcomes were assessed multiple times over a 3-year period. Therapists delivering the three treatments were all trained in the treatment method and were highly experienced mental health professionals. Solution-focused brief therapy was compared with two other evidence-based treatments. Given these study characteristics, the findings of the Knekt and Lindfors study probably provide the most rigorous test to date of the impact of SFBT on mental health outcomes and role performance.

■ RESULTS OF RESEARCH

The four reviews discussed above, along with the studies by Smock et al. (2008), Knekt and Lindfors (2004), and Knekt et al. (2008a, 2008b) add up to a combined total of 46 unique studies, a sizable body of research on an approach that was first described in the literature in 1986. (The 46 studies included in the four reviews are indicated in the References list by the superscript letters G, Gingerich & Eisengart, 2000; K, Kim, 2008; M, Macdonald, 1994b; and S, Stams et al., 2006.) The very first studies were follow-up studies of clients who had competed SFBT at the Brief Family Therapy Center and several other clinics. Controlled studies began appearing as soon as 1993 (Sundstrom, 1993) and have appeared regularly since then, showing a natural progression in the types and quality of studies.

The Gingerich and Eisengart (2000) qualitative review included the first controlled studies of SFBT outcomes and concluded that there was preliminary evidence of SFBT's effectiveness. Only five of the studies at that time approached a level of control approaching current methodological standards for effectiveness research.

The two meta-analytic reviews used quantitative approaches to summarize SFBT outcomes across a wide range of studies using the metric of effect size, which converts observed differences to a standard score format. The Stams et al. (2006) meta-analysis found an overall effect size of .37 for SFBT, a small to moderate treatment effect by conventional standards. Studies that compared SFBT with no treatment ($n = 4$) yielded an effect size of .57 compared to studies where SFBT was compared to another treatment ($n = 7$), which yielded an effect size of only .16. This result is open to various interpretations, one of which is that SFBT is as good as or slightly better than other accepted treatments, but it is clearly better than no treatment at all. Wampold's (2001) research on common factors suggests that all treatments, when done well, have similar outcomes.

Kim's (2008) meta-analysis looked at the effectiveness of SFBT separately based on different outcome constructs (externalizing, internalizing, and family or relationship problems). The effect size of SFBT was .13 for externalizing problems, .26 for internalizing problems, and .26 for family and relationship problems. Although Kim's analysis included only comparison group studies, he did not separate them based on the type of comparison group due to the small number of studies available, so it is not possible to examine the incremental effect of SFBT for no treatment compared with a standard treatment.

The two recent studies provide a direct comparison of SFBT with an established treatment(s). Smock et al. (2008) found that SFBT produced pretest-posttest effect sizes of .61 and .64 for mental health outcomes and was comparable at posttest to the Hazelden comparison group. Knekt and Lindfors (2004) compared SFBT to evidence-based forms of SPP and LPP. This study used a large sample of subjects in each group who were treated by trained and highly experienced therapists; the three treatments were found to be approximately equal. Solution-focused brief therapy and SPP had equivalent outcomes over the 3 years of the study. TheLPP treatments produced outcomes more slowly, but by the end of 3 years they were better than the two short-term treatments. The LPP treatment consisted of approximately 230 sessions over the 3-year period, however, compared to 10 and 18 sessions, respectively, for SFBT and SPP over a period of approximately 6 months.

■ PRACTICE GUIDELINES

This chapter highlights the natural progression in SFBT research in terms of the types and quality of studies over the past few decades. The Gingerich and Eisengart (2000) review was significant in highlighting the quality of studies conducted on SFBT and what their results found. The two meta-analyses expanded this study by adding more quantitative data to synthesize the differing results found in all the primary studies conducted. Stams et al.'s (2006) meta-analysis calculates the overall effect size of SFBT and uses moderating variables to explain differences in study effect sizes. Kim's (2008) study breaks down the effectiveness of SFBT based on different outcome constructs (externalizing, internalizing, and family or relationship problems) and provides overall effect sizes for each of these treatment problems separately.

■ LIMITATIONS

While the utility of the two meta-analyses lies in combining various SFBT studies to come up with an overall effect size, this statistical analysis approach has some limitations. A limitation that cuts across both studies reviewed in this chapter is the limited number of rigorous SFBT studies available for inclusion. A meta-analysis study is only as good as the studies previously conducted by other researchers. It is clear that SFBT research studies have improved over the years in terms of research methods and design, but they are limited by small sample sizes and lack of randomization. This problem further restricts how specific a meta-analysis study can be in terms of grouping treatment problems, and it forced both SFBT meta-analyses to use broad outcome categories like internalizing and externalizing problems.

Despite these limitations, the research on SFBT continues to improve and show small but positive outcomes for a broad range of topics and populations. This holds value for practitioners who are interested in using SFBT but who want to know if it works and for what problems it is most effective. This information will prove useful when trying to justify SFBT as a promising evidence-based treatment model to clients, supervisors, and reimbursement agencies.

■ FUTURE STUDIES

Meta-analytic reviews of the outcome research to date show SFBT to have a small to moderate positive outcome, however, when SFBT has been compared with established treatments in recent, well-designed studies, it has been shown to be equivalent to other evidence-based approaches, sometimes producing results in substantially less time and at less cost. As this chapter shows, the quality of studies on SFBT is steadily improving and the Knekt et al. (2008a) study is the strongest to date, based on sample size, randomization, treatment fidelity, and standardized measures. The next wave of research on SFBT must continue to improve on the quality of the research design by improving internal validity and incorporating the SFBT treatment manual to enhance treatment fidelity.

■ KEY POINTS TO REMEMBER

- Solution-focused brief therapy was first described in the literature in 1986 (by de Shazer et al.) and the first controlled study of SFBT outcomes appeared in 1993 (by Sundstrom).
- More than 48 studies have appeared to date, as well as two independent meta-analytic reviews. The quality of the studies is steadily improving.
- Overall, SFBT has been shown to have a small to moderate effect size and to be the equivalent of other established treatments.

■ FURTHER LEARNING

- European Brief Therapy Association (EBTA) compilation of SFBT studies: http://www.ebta.nu
- Gingerich SFBT research section: http://www.gingerich.net/SFBT
- Helsinki Psychotherapy Study: http://www.ktl.fi/tto/hps/index.en.html
- Macdonald SFBT Web site: http://www.solutionsdoc.co.uk
- Solution Focused Brief Therapy Association (SFBTA) research page: http://www.sfbta.org/research.html

■ REFERENCES

Superscripts denote whether a particular study was included in one or more of the reviews: G = Gingerich and Eisengart (2000), K = Kim (2008), M = Macdonald (1994b), S = Stams et al. (2006).

KAdams, J. F., Piercy, F. P., & Jurich, J. A. (1991). Effects of solution focused therapy's "formula first session task" on compliance and outcome in family therapy. *Journal of Marital and Family Therapy, 17,* 277–290.

Bangert-Drowns, R. L. (1997). Some limiting factors in meta-analysis. In W. J. Bukoski (Ed.), *Meta-analysis of drug abuse prevention programs* (NIDA Report No. 170, pp. 234–252). Rockville, MD: National Institute on Drug Abuse.

Beyebach, M. (1998). *European Brief Therapy Association Outcome Study: Research definition.* Retrieved December 4, 2009, from http://www.ebta.nu/sfbt-researchdefinition.pdf

SBeyebach, M., Rodriguez-Sanchéz, M. S., & Arribas de Miguel, J. (2000). Outcome of solution-focused therapy at a university family therapy centre. *Journal of Systemic Therapies, 19*(1), 116–128.

KBozeman, B. N. (1999). *The efficacy of solution-focused therapy techniques on perceptions of hope in clients with depressive symptoms.* Unpublished doctoral dissertation, New Orleans Baptist Theological Seminary, New Orleans.

MBurr,W. (1993). Evaluation der Anwendung losungsorientierter Kurztherapie in einer kinder- und jugendpsychiartischen Praxis [Evaluation of the use of brief therapy in a practice for children and adolescents]. *Familiendynamik, 18,* 11–21.

Carlberg, C. G., & Walberg, H. J. (1984). Techniques of research synthesis. *Journal of Special Education, 18,* 11–26.

Chambless, D. L., & Hollon, S. D. (1998). Defining empirically supported therapies. *Journal of Consulting and Clinical Psychology, 66,* 7–18

G,S,KCockburn, J. T., Thomas, F. N., & Cockburn, O. J. (1997). Solution-focused therapy and psychosocial adjustment to orthopedic rehabilitation in a work hardening program. *Journal of Occupational Rehabilitation, 7,* 97–106.

Cohen, J. (1988). *Statistical power analysis for the behavioral sciences* (2nd ed.). Hillsdale, NJ: Erlbaum.

SConoley, C. W., Graham, J. M., Neu, T., Craig, M. C., O'Pry, A., Cardin, S. A., Brossart, D. F., & Parker, R. I. (2003). Solution-focused family therapy with three aggressive and oppositional-acting children: An *N* = 1 empirical study. *Family Process, 42*(3), 361–374.

KCook, D. R. (1998). *Solution-focused brief therapy: Its impact on the self-concept of elementary school students.* Unpublished doctoral dissertation, Ohio University, Athens.

SCorcoran, J. (1997). A solution-oriented approach to working with juvenile offenders. *Journal of Child and Adolescent Social Work, 14*(4), 277–288.

[S]Corcoran, J., & Stephenson, M. (2000). The effectiveness of solution-focused therapy with child behavior problems: A preliminary report. *Families in Society, 81*(5), 468–474.

[M]de Shazer, S. (1985). *Keys to solutions in brief therapy.* New York: Norton.

[M]de Shazer, S. (1991). *Putting differences to work.* New York: Norton.

de Shazer, S., & Berg, I. K. (1997). What works? Remarks on research aspects of solution-focused brief therapy. *Journal of Family Therapy, 19,* 121–124.

[M]de Shazer, S., Berg, I. K., Lipchik, E., Nunnally, E., Molnar, A., Gingerich, W., & Weiner-Davis, M. (1986). Brief therapy: Focused solution development. *Family Process, 25,* 207–222.

Devine, E. C. (1997). Issues and challenges in coding interventions for meta-analysis of prevention research. In W. J. Bukoski (Ed.), *Meta-analysis of drug abuse* (NIDA Report No. 170, pp. 130–146). Rockville, MD: National Institute on Drug Abuse.

Durlak, J. A., & Lipsey, M. W. (1991). A practitioner's guide to meta-analysis. *American Journal of Community Psychology, 19*(3), 291–332.

[G,S,K]Eakes, G., Walsh, S., Markowksi, M., Cain, H., & Swanson, M. (1997). Family centered brief solution-focused therapy with chronic schizophrenia: A pilot study. *Journal of Family Therapy, 19,* 145–158.

[G]Franklin, C., Corcoran, J., Nowicki, J., & Streeter, C. (1997). Using client self-anchored scales to measure outcomes in solution-focused therapy. *Journal of Systemic Therapies, 16,* 246–265.

[K]Franklin, C., Moore, K., & Hopson, L. (2008). Effectiveness of solution-focused brief therapy in a school setting. *Children & Schools, 30,* 15–26.

[K]Franklin, C., Streeter, C. L., Kim, J. S., & Tripodi, S. J. (2007). The effectiveness of a solution-focused, public alternative school for dropout prevention and retrieval. *Children & Schools, 29,* 133–144.

[K]Gallardo-Cooper, M. I. (1997). *A comparison of three different home-school meeting formats conducted by mental health professionals.* Unpublished doctoral dissertation, University of Florida, Gainesville.

[G,S]Geil, M. (1998). *Solution-focused consultation: An alternative consultation model to manage student behavior and improve classroom environment.* Unpublished doctoral dissertation, University of Northern Colorado, Greeley.

[S]Gensterblum, A. E. (2002). *Solution-focused therapy in a residential setting.* Unpublished doctoral dissertation.

[M]George, E., Iveson, C., & Ratner, H. (1990). *Problem to solution.* London: Brief Therapy Press.

Gingerich, W. J., & Eisengart, S. (2000). Solution-focused brief therapy: A review of the outcome research. *Family Process, 39,* 477–498.

Hedges, L. V. (1982). Estimation of effect size from a series of independent experiments. *Psychological Bulletin, 92,* 490–499.

[K]Huang, M. (2001). *A comparison of three approaches to reduce marital problems and symptoms of depression.* Unpublished doctoral dissertation, University of Florida, Gainesville.

[K]Ingersoll-Dayton, B., Schroepfer, T., & Pryce, J. (1999). The effectiveness of a solution-focused approach for problem behaviors among nursing home residents. *Journal of Gerontological Social Work, 32,* 49–64.

Kim, J. S. (2008). Examining the effectiveness of solution-focused brief therapy: A meta-analysis. *Research on Social Work Practice, 18,* 107–116.

Knekt, P., & Lindfors, O. (2004). *A randomized trial of the effect of four forms of psychotherapy on depressive and anxiety disorders* (Studies in Social Security and Health 77). Helsinki, Finland: The Social Insurance Institution.

Knekt, P., Lindfors, O., Härkänen, T., Välikoski, M., Virtala, E., Laaksonen, M. A., Marttunen, M., Kaipainen, M., Renlund, C., & the Helsinki Psychotherapy Study Group. (2008a). Randomized trial on the effectiveness of long- and short-term psychodynamic psychotherapy and solution-focused therapy on psychiatric symptoms during a 3-year follow-up. *Psychological Medicine, 38,* 689–703.

Knekt, P., Lindfors, O., Laaksonen, M. A., Raitasalo, R., Haaramo, P., Järvikoski, A., & the Helsinki Psychotherapy Study Group. (2008b). Effectiveness of short-term and long-term psychotherapy on work ability and functional capacity—A randomized clinical trial on depressive and anxiety disorders. *Journal of Affective Disorders, 107,* 95–106.

G,SLaFountain, R. M., & Garner, N. E. (1996). Solution-focused counselling groups: The results are in. *Journal for Specialists in Group Work, 21*(2), 128–143.

GLambert, M. J., Okiishi, J. C., Finch, A. E., & Johnson, L. D. (1998). Outcome assessment: From conceptualization to implementation. *Professional Psychology: Research and Practice, 29,* 63–70.

SLee, M. Y. (1997). A study of solution-focused brief family therapy: Outcomes and issues. *American Journal of Family Therapy, 25*(1), 3–17.

KLeggett, M. E. S. (2004). *The effects of a solution-focused classroom guidance intervention with elementary students.* Unpublished doctoral dissertation, Texas A&M University–Corpus Christi.

G,SLindforss, L., & Magnusson, D. (1997). Solution-focused therapy in prison. *Contemporary Family Therapy, 19*(1), 89–103.

G,SLittrell, J. M., Malia, J. A., & Vanderwood, M. (1995). Single-session brief counseling in a high school. *Journal of Counseling and Development, 73,* 451–458.

MMacdonald, A. J. (1994a). Brief therapy in adult psychiatry. *Journal of Family Therapy, 16,* 415–426.

Macdonald, A. J. (1994b). *European Brief Therapy Association Research Page.* Retrieved October 31, 1994, from http://www.ebta.nu/

SMacdonald, A. J. (1997). Brief therapy in adult psychiatry—further outcomes. *Journal of Family Therapy, 19,* 213–221.

Macdonald, A. J. (2007). *Solution-focused therapy: Theory, research and practice.* London: Sage Publications.

KMarinaccio, B. C. (2001). *The effects of school-based family therapy.* Unpublished doctoral dissertation, State University of New York at Buffalo.

Morris, S. B., & DeShon, R. P. (2002). Combining effect size estimates in meta-analysis with repeated measures and independent-groups designs. *Psychological Methods, 7,* 105–125.

MMorrison, J. A., Olivos, K., Dominguez, G., Gomez, D., & Lena, D. (1993) The application of family systems approaches to school behaviour problems on a school-level discipline board: An outcome study. *Elementary School Guidance & Counselling, 27,* 258–272.

SNelson, T. S., & Kelley, L. (2001). Qualitative research—solution-focused couples group. *Journal of Systemic Therapies, 20*(4), 47–66.

KNewsome, S. (2004). Solution-focused brief therapy (SFBT) groupwork with at-risk junior high school students: Enhancing the bottom line. *Research on Social Work Practice, 14,* 336–343.

MPerez-Grande, M. D. (1991). Evaluacion de resultados en terapia sistemica breve [Evaluation of results in brief systemic therapy.]. *Cuadernos de Terapia Familiar,* [Family Therapy Notebooks], *18,* 93–110.

Perry, P. D. (1997). Realities of the effect size calculation process: Considerations for beginning meta-analysts. In W. J. Bukoski (Ed.), *Meta-analysis of drug abuse prevention programs* (NIDA Report No. 170, pp. 120–128). Rockville, MD: National Institute on Drug Abuse.

GPolk, G. W. (1996). Treatment of problem drinking behaviour using solution-focused therapy: A single subject design. *Crisis Intervention, 3,* 13–24.

Rosenthal, R. (1995). Writing meta-analytic reviews. *Psychological Bulletin, 188,* 183–192.

Rubin, A., & Babbie, E. (2005). *Research methods for social work* (5th ed.). Belmont, CA: Brooks/Cole-Thomson Learning.

G,S,KSeagram, B. M. C. (1997). *The efficacy of solution-focused therapy with young offenders.* Unpublished doctoral dissertation, York University, Toronto, Canada.

Smith, M. L. (1980). Publication bias and meta-analysis. *Evaluation in Education, 4,* 18–21

Smock, S. A., Trepper, T. S., Wechtler, J. L., McCollum, E. E., Ray, R., & Pierce, K. (2008). Solution-focused group therapy for level 1 substance abusers. *Journal of Marital and Family Therapy, 34,* 107–120.

S,KSpringer, D. W., Lynch, C., & Rubin, A. (2000). Effects of a solution-focused mutual aid group for Hispanic children of incarcerated parents. *Journal for Child and Adolescent Social Work, 17*(6), 431–442.

Stams, G. J. J. M, Dekovic, M., Buist, K., & De Vries, L. (2006). Effectiviteit van oplossings-gerichte korte therapie: een meta-analyse [Efficacy of solution focused brief therapy: A meta-analysis]. *Tijdschrift voor gedragstherapie, 39,* 81–94.

SStoddart, K. P., McDonnell, J., Temple, V., & Mustata, A. (2001). Is brief better? A modified brief solution-focused therapy approach for adults with a developmental delay. *Journal of Systemic Therapies, 20*(2), 24–40.

G,S,KSundman, P. (1997). Solution-focused ideas in social work. *Journal of Family Therapy, 19,* 159–172.

G,S,KSundstrom, S. M. (1993). *Single-session psychotherapy for depression: Is it better to be problem-focused or solution-focused?* Unpublished doctoral dissertation, Iowa State University, Ames.

Task Force on Promotion and Dissemination of Psychological Procedures. (1995). Training in and dissemination of empirically-validated psychological treatments: Report and recommendations. *Clinical Psychologist, 48,* 3–23.

G,KTriantafillou, N. (2002). *Solution-focused parent groups: A new approach to the treatment of youth disruptive behavior.* Unpublished doctoral dissertation, University of Toronto, Canada.

KVillalba, J. A. (2002). *Using group counseling to improve the self-concepts, school attitudes and academic success of limited-English-proficient Hispanic students in English-for-speakers-of-other-languages/English-as-a-second-language programs.* Unpublished doctoral dissertation, University of Florida, Gainesville.

Wampold, B. E. (2001). *The great psychotherapy debate: Model, methods, and findings.* Mahwah, NJ: Erlbaum.

Watzlawick, P., Weakland, J. H.,& Fisch, R. (1974). *Change: Principles of problem formation and problem resolution.* New York: Norton.

KWettersten, K. B. (2002). *Solution-focused brief therapy, the working alliance, and outcome: A comparative analysis.* Unpublished doctoral dissertation, University of Kansas, Lawrence.

G,K,SZimmerman, T. S., Jacobsen, R. B., MacIntyre, M., & Watson, C. (1996). Solution-focused parenting groups: An empirical study. *Journal of Systemic Therapies, 15,* 12–25.

G,K,SZimmerman, T. S., Prest, L., A., & Wetzel, B. E. (1997). Solution-focused couples therapy groups: An empirical study. *Journal of Family Therapy, 19,* 125–144.

7 A Systematic Review of Single-Case Design Studies on Solution-Focused Brief Therapy

■ JOHNNY S. KIM

■ INTRODUCTION

Researchers and solution-focused brief therapy (SFBT) clinicians are finding positive, mixed, and null results on the effectiveness of SFBT on a wide range of problems and populations. The conflicting results and questions concerning the research designs employed in several outcome studies can be a baffling maze of information for researchers, practitioners, and consumers to digest and sort out. A systematic review and meta-analysis can be an effective strategy for handling the differing results gathered from the increasing number of studies on SFBT and discussed in other chapters of this book. Recently, emphasis on the effectiveness of SFBT has focused on experimental and quasi-experimental studies that control for internal and external threats to validity. However, there is a growing body of published empirical studies on the effectiveness of SFBT using single-case designs that has been left out of the overall discussion and evaluation of SFBT as an effective therapy model. This chapter reviews single-case design studies using SFBT and calculates an index of treatment effectiveness using the percentage of nonoverlapping data (PND) method.

■ WHAT WE HAVE LEARNED SO FAR

Early research at the Brief Family Therapy Center consisted of follow-up surveys of clients to see if they had met their goals or felt they had made significant progress (De Jong & Hopwood, 1996). These studies, however, were limited in their research methodology and were criticized for not using more rigorous designs. This led to more research in the 1990s and 2000s that incorporated more experimental designs and larger sample sizes in an attempt to control for threats to validity and reliability. According to Rubin and Babbie (2010), experimental and quasi-experimental designs test hypotheses about the effects of the independent variable by using two identical groups (treatment and control), with the treatment group receiving the intervention or program. With an increase in the number of studies examining the effectiveness of

SFBT using a control group, Gingerich and Eisengart (2000) conducted a systematic review of all controlled outcome studies. Also included in their review were single-case repeated-measures design studies. This study and other systematic reviews of SFBT are described in more detail in Chapter 6.

Single-case design research methodology has been used in many social and behavioral science disciplines such as social work, psychology, and education (Strain et al., 1998). Single-case design studies use repeated measures of a particular outcome on a single individual or a small number of individuals to evaluate an intervention or program (Rubin & Babbie, 2010). The use of single-case designs can be an alternative when clinicians and researchers are unable to conduct group comparisons with large numbers of participants. This approach, unlike group comparison studies, focuses on the individual as the unit of analysis and examines variability within and across individuals rather than examining differences based on group mean scores (Strain et al., 1998).

Single-case designs use repeated measures before the intervention or program is introduced in the baseline phase to serve as a control. Then the repeated measures are obtained after the intervention to assess any changes that occurred shortly after the intervention (Rubin & Babbie, 2010). The most common method for evaluating single-case design results on a particular outcome problem for an individual is to conduct a visual inspection of the graph data before and after the implementation of the intervention to identify shifts of the data points. Unfortunately, this visual analysis procedure can often be difficult to interpret due to ambiguous graphs. An alternative to visual inspection is to use the PND, which is easily computed and offers a good measure for treatment effectiveness (Scruggs et al., 1987). Therefore, the purpose of this chapter is to examine the empirical evidence of SFBT from single-case design studies. To gauge the treatment effectiveness for single-subject design studies, the PND method will be used.

■ RESEARCH METHODS

Published studies (between 1984 to 2006) were identified through literature searches in PsycINFO, Academic Search Premier, and the Behavioral and Social Science Index using the keywords *brief solution-focused brief therapy, solution-focused brief therapy, solution focused therapy*, and *solution-building* (cross referenced with the keywords *outcome* and *evaluation*). In addition, unpublished dissertations were identified through the electronic database UMI Dissertation Abstract using the same keywords and time frame.

Based on the database search, eight single-case design studies using SFBT were identified. The studies were divided and grouped into three categories based on the outcome problem each study targeted: (a) family and relationship problems, (b) externalizing behavior problems, and (c) internalizing behavior problems.

Percentage of Nonoverlapping Data

One common method for systematically analyzing the effective outcome in single-subject graphic displays is to calculate the proportion of overlapping data between baseline and treatment (Scruggs et al., 1987). Calculating the PND that exists between baseline and treatment phases in single-subject graphs yields an index of treatment effectiveness (Strain et al., 1998). To calculate a PND for a particular study, the researcher tabulates the number of treatment data points that exceeds the highest baseline data point in the desired direction and then divides by the total number of treatment data points (Scruggs et al., 1987). If multiple subjects are measured on a particular outcome measure, the median percentage PND score is reported. If the median score for a study's outcome is between two subjects' PND scores, then the average of those two scores is calculated to come up with the median score for that particular measure. A PND above 90 indicates a highly effective treatment, 70–90 indicates a moderately effective treatment, 50–69 indicates a mildly effective treatment, and 49 or below indicates an ineffective treatment (Mathur et al., 1998, as cited in Strain et al., 1998).

Results from the single-subject design studies are provided in Tables 7.1–7.3. However, meta-analytically synthesizing single-subject studies using PND as the metric is not recommended due to concerns about the results being misleading and incorrect (Salzberg et al., 1987; Strain et al., 1998; White, 1987).

Single-case Design Results

Research Designs. Of the eight single-case design studies that examined the effectiveness of SFBT, six (75%) were published in peer-reviewed journals and two (25%) were unpublished dissertations. The most common level of intervention was individual with five studies (62.5%). The rest consisted of single studies that involved small groups (12.5%), family interventions (12.5%), and couples (12.5%) as their level of intervention.

Participants. The eight studies in this systematic review explored the effectiveness of SFBT in a total of 51 participants. The mean sample size was 6.38 participants per study, with a range of 1 to 16 participants. All eight studies reported the mean ages or age range of their sample participants. The reported ages ranged from 8.5 to 45.0 years, with a mean age of 24.2 years. Regarding information on gender, all eight studies reported the percentage of male and female participants. The percentage of male participants ranged from 20% to 100%, with a mean of 55.9%. The percentage of female participants ranged from 0% to 80%, with a mean of 44.1%.

Only one of the studies (12.5%) did not report any information on the ethnicity of the participants. For the seven studies that did provide this information, Caucasians (M = 74.2%) were the highest reported mean percentages, followed by African Americans (M = 65.5%), and Hispanics (M = 62.0%). None of the studies included any Asian Americans, Native Americans, or an "other" category of ethnicity.

Setting. Seven of the studies (87.5%) were conducted in the United States and one study (12.5%) was conducted in a foreign country. Half of the studies did not report the setting of the study. Two studies were conducted in schools (25.0%), one was conducted in a clinic (12.5%), and another was conducted in a social service agency (12.5%). The mean number of sessions was 10, with a range of 4 to 37 sessions.

Treatment Fidelity. All of the studies used some sort of treatment manual or treatment protocol, but only three studies (37.5%) recorded, by video or audio, counseling sessions and rated them to determine treatment fidelity. Only one study (12.5%) used both experienced professional counselors and graduate interns to provide treatment to study participants; another study (12.5%) used only experienced professional counselors. Three studies (37.5%) used only graduate interns, and another three studies (37.5%) did not specify who provided treatment.

Externalizing Behavior Problems. Single-subject design studies examining the effectiveness of SFBT on externalizing behavior problems were the most abundant. Five of the eight single-case design studies measured externalizing behavior problems ranging from attendance report to conduct problems. Polk (1996) examined alcohol drinking behaviors and work attendance rates for adults in an employee assistance program. Results based on the PND method show the median PND of 100% for days abstaining from alcohol use as reported by both the client and the collateral contact. As for the number of work days attended, the median PND score of 66.7% was calculated. These PND scores indicate a highly effective treatment for alcohol abstinence and a mildly effective treatment for work attendance rates, respectively.

A study by Franklin and colleagues (2001) examined externalizing behavior problems among elementary school students using several subscales of the Conners Teacher Rating Scale. Median PND scores for the Hyperactivity Index subscale was 47.65%, which is considered ineffective treatment, but the PND score for the Hyperactivity subscale was 66.7%, which is considered mildly effective treatment. The median PND score for the Daydream Attention subscale was also mildly effective, with a score of 60%. The Asocial and Conduct Problem subscales both had median PND scores in the moderately effective range: 81.3% and 88.9%, respectively.

Yarborough (2004) investigated the effectiveness of SFBT on assignment completion and accuracy rates for six elementary school students. Using the PND on this study produced opposite results for the two externalizing behavior measures. The median PND for assignment accuracy rates was 0%, indicating ineffective treatment, but the median PND for assignment completion rates was 93.8%, reflecting a highly effective treatment.

Franklin and colleagues (1997) used client self-anchored scales to measure externalizing behavior problems in three adolescents. All three identified the externalizing behaviors that they wanted to change during their SFBT sessions. All of them had median PND scores of 100%, indicating highly effective treatment.

A study by Conoley and colleagues (2003) examined the effect of a solution-focused treatment on problem frequency with three children diagnosed with oppositional-aggressive behavior. The median PND score for the parent daily report on problem frequency was 0%, indicating ineffective treatment. For the outcome results of these studies, see Table 7.1.

Internalizing Behavior Problems. Two studies (Franklin et al., 2001; Jakes & Rhodes, 2003) examined internalizing behavior problems. Jakes and Rhodes (2003) examined the effectiveness of SFBT with five adults suffering from delusions. Results based on the PND method show a median PND of 42.7% for conviction percent, 7.1% for preoccupation, and 0% for distress. All three PND scores indicate an ineffective treatment.

Franklin and colleagues (2001) also examined internalizing behaviors with seven students using two subscales of the Conners Teacher Rating Scale. Results based on the PND method show a median PND of 11.1% for the Anxious-Passive subscale, which indicates ineffective treatment. The other subscale, Emotional Indulgence, had a median PND of 66.7%, which indicates a mildly effective treatment. For the outcome results of these studies, see Table 7.2.

Family and Relationship Problem. Using the PND method, Nelson and Kelley's (2001) study examining marital satisfaction produced median PND scores of 50% for the Revised Dyadic Adjustment Scale (RDAS) and 20% for the Kansas Marital

TABLE 7.1. *Single-Subject Design Externalizing Behavior Outcome Results*

Author	Population	Sample Size	Setting	Session Number	Outcome Measure	PND (Median)
Polk (1996)	Adults	1	Employee assistance program	6	Days abstinent	100%
					Days abstinent collateral report	100%
					Attendance report	66.7%
Conoley et al. (2003)	Oppositional aggressive children	3	Unknown	4–5	Parent daily report: problem frequency	0%
Franklin et al. (1997)	Adolescents	3	Youth homeless shelter	5	Self-anchored scale	100%
Franklin et al. (2001)	Students	7	Elementary school	5–10	Conners Teacher Rating Scale: Hyperactivity	66.7%
					Conners Teacher Rating Scale: Hyperactivity Index	47.7%
					Conners Teacher Rating Scale: Asocial	81.3%
					Conners Teacher Rating Scale: Conduct Problem	88.9%
					Conners Teacher Rating Scale: Day Dream Attention	60%
Yarbrough (2004)	Students	6	Elementary school	5	Assignment completion rates	93.8%
					Assignment accuracy rates	0%

TABLE 7.2. *Single-Subject Design Internalizing Behavior Outcome Results*

Author	Population	Sample Size	Setting	Session Number	Outcome Measure	PND (Median)
Jakes and Rhodes (2003)	Adults with delusions	5	Unknown	6–68	Conviction percent	42.7%
					Preoccupation	7.1%
					Distress	0%
Franklin et al. (2001)	Students	7	Elementary school	5–10	Conners Teacher Rating Scale: Emotional Indulgence	66.7%
					Conners Teacher Rating Scale: Anxious Passive	11.1%

Satisfaction Scale (KMSS). Using the guidelines suggested by Mather and colleagues (1998), these PND results ranged from mildly effective (RDAS) to ineffective (KMSS).

Naude's (1999) study on marital problems yielded a median PND of 86.2% for Relationship Thermometer Ratings, indicating a moderately effective treatment. However, the median PND score for goal attainment was 0%, indicating an ineffective treatment. For the outcome results of these studies, see Table 7.3.

TABLE 7.3. *Single-Subject Design Family and Relationship Outcome Results*

Author	Population	Sample Size	Setting	Sessions Number	Outcome Measures	PND (Median)
Nelson & Kelley (2001)	Adult couples	5	Unknown	4	Revised Dyadic Adjustment Scale	50%
					Kansas Marital Satisfaction Scale	20%
Naude (1999)	Adult couples	16	Military clinic	4–8	Relationship Thermometer Ratings	86.2%
					Goal attainment	0%

■ **PRACTICE GUIDELINES**

Single-subject Design Summary. Scruggs and colleagues (1987) recommend calculating the proportion of overlapping data between baseline and treatment phases in single-subject graphs to determine an index of treatment effectiveness. Results for all three outcome measures for the single-subject design studies were mixed using the PND method. In terms of SFBT's effectiveness in treating externalizing problem behavior, Franklin and colleagues (1997) had a PND of 100%, indicating that it was highly effective. Polk (1996) also had two outcome measures with a PND of 100% and one outcome measure with a PND of 66.7%, which is considered mildly effective. Yarbrough (2004) had one outcome measure with a PND of 93.8%, which is considered highly effective, and another outcome measure with a PND of 0%. Franklin and colleagues (2001) had two moderately effective PND scores of 81.3% and 88.9%, two mildly effective PND scores of 66.7% and 60.0%, and one PND score of 47.7%, which is considered ineffective. Conoley and colleagues (2003) reported a PND of 0% for their externalizing behavior problem, which is considered ineffective.

As for internalizing behavior problems, Jakes and Rhodes (2003) had PNDs for all three outcome measures that were considered ineffective. Franklin and colleagues (2001) also had a PND for one outcome measure of 11.1%, which is considered ineffective, but a PND for another outcome measure of 66.7%, which is considered mildly effective.

Finally, family and relationship problems had results similar to those of internalizing problem behaviors. Nelson and Kelley (2001) had one outcome measure with a PND of 20%, which is considered ineffective, but another outcome measure with a PND of 50%, which is considered mildly effective. Naude's (1999) study fared a little better. One outcome measure had a PND of 86.2%, which is deemed moderately effective, and another with a PND of 0%, which is considered ineffective.

Overall, these single-case design studies show mixed results for all three outcomes, with externalizing problem behaviors having the most effective PND scores. Caution, however, is warranted in drawing any definitive conclusions about the effectiveness of SFBT based on these results because of lack of generalizability due to the research design and the limited number of studies reviewed. Rather, these results further add to the empirical base on SFBT and should be viewed in context with other empirical studies and systematic reviews discussed in the other chapters of this book. For example, while Kim's (2008) meta-analysis did not find externalizing problem behaviors to be statistically significant, results from this single-case design review showed that most of the studies' outcomes found highly effective PND scores. Support for the effectiveness of SFBT is consistent with the meta-analysis of Stams and colleagues (2006), which found statistical significance for externalizing problem behaviors as well. As more studies are conducted on SFBT, more definitive conclusions can be drawn on its effectiveness.

■ LIMITATIONS

While single-case designs and the PND method offers a feasible approach to conducting research, there are some limitations. With the single-case design, the major concerns are the limited external validity and the limited ability to generalize to the larger population. Results showing improvement in a particular outcome from a study involving one or a few clients may not necessarily hold true for other clients due to the distinctive nature of a sample involving so few clients and their unique individual characteristics (Rubin & Babbie, 2010). There are also feasibility concerns about practitioners incorporating single-case designs when clients are in crisis, when practitioners have heavy caseloads, when supervisors or agencies don't support research, and when clients resent the extensive self-monitoring involved (Gerdes et al., 1996; Rubin & Babbie, 2010). Additionally, there are times when the PND method is not appropriate for unusual or complex cases, as discussed further by Scruggs and colleagues (1987).

Despite some of these limitations, this chapter provides another useful research design approach to studying SFBT for practitioners interested in doing outcome studies with their clients. Unfortunately, social workers and other counselors have a difficult time trying to incorporate research in their practice due to concerns about large sample sizes and withholding treatment from the control group. Those interested in evaluating how effective SFBT is with their clients can use single-case designs and incorporate visual inspections, as well as calculating a PND score to help interpret the results.

■ FUTURE STUDIES

Solution-focused practitioners can play an integral role in helping to build the empirical base of SFBT through single-case design studies. This not only helps practitioners evaluate their clinical work with clients, which is an important step in developing the evidence-based practice model (Gibbs & Gambrill, 2002), but also generates new studies examining the effectiveness of SFBT. The aggregation of multiple single-case design studies on a similar outcome can help offset the generalizability limitation of this research design. Using single-case research designs can also be an alternative for practitioners working with clients where administrative or ethical concerns prohibit the use of more rigorous randomized, controlled trial designs (Rubin & Babbie, 2010). The flexibility of single-case designs can also be especially useful when trying to assess the effectiveness of SFBT in treating complicated problems like suicidal thoughts and behaviors. Having solution-focused practitioners provide research using single-case designs and calculating PND values helps to increase the empirical base of SFBT, which benefits not only the practitioners but also, ultimately, the clients they serve.

■ KEY FINDINGS TO REMEMBER

- Five single-case design studies examined externalizing problem behaviors; two studies examined internalizing problem behaviors; and two studies examined family and relationship problems.
- Most of the studies examining externalizing problem behaviors reported highly effective PND scores.
- Most of the studies examining internalizing problem behaviors and family and relationship problems reported ineffective or mildly effective PND scores.

■ FURTHER LEARNING

- Jones, W. P., Ed.D. Web site on single-case research and statistical analysis: http://faculty.unlv.edu/pjones/singlecase/scsantro.htm
- Rubin, A. & Babbie, E. (2010). *Research methods for social work* (7th ed.). Belmont, CA: Brooks/Cole.
- Special Issue on single-case designs. *Research on Social Work Practice Journal.* (1996). 6(1), 5–129.

■ REFERENCES

Conoley, C. W., Graham, J. M., Neu, T., Craig, M. C., O'Pry, A., Cardin, S. A., Brossart, D. F., & Parker, R. I. (2003). Solution-focused family therapy with three aggressive and oppositional-acting children: An *N* = 1 empirical study. *Family Process, 42,* 361–374.

De Jong, P., & Hopwood, L. E. (1996). Outcome research on treatment conducted at the Brief Family Therapy Center, 1992–1993. In S. D. Miller, M. A. Hubble, & B. L. Duncan (Eds.), *Handbook of solution-focused brief therapy* (pp. 272–298). San Francisco: Jossey-Bass.

Franklin, C., Biever, J., Moore, K., Clemons, D., & Scamardo, M. (2001). The effectiveness of solution-focused brief therapy with children in a school setting. *Research on Social Work Practice, 11,* 411–434.

Franklin, C., Corcoran, J., Nowicki, J., & Streeter, C. (1997). Using client self-anchored scales to measure outcomes in solution-focused brief therapy. *Journal of Systemic Therapies, 10,* 246–265.

Gerdes, K. E., Edmonds, R. M., Haslam, D. R., & McCartney, T. L. (1996). A statewide survey of licensed clinical social workers' use of practice evaluation procedures. *Research on Social Work Practice, 6,* 27–39.

Gibbs, L., & Gambrill, E. (2002). Evidence-based practice: Counterarguments to objections. *Research on Social Work Practice, 12,* 452–476.

Gingerich, W., & Eisengart, S. (2000). Solution-focused brief therapy: A review of outcome research. *Family Process, 39*(4), 477–496.

Jakes, S. C., & Rhodes, J. E. (2003). The effect of different components of psychological therapy on people with delusions: Five experimental single cases. *Clinical Psychology & Psychotherapy, 10,* 302–315.

Kim, J. S. (2008). Examining the effectiveness of solution-focused brief therapy: A meta-analysis. *Research on Social Work Practice, 18,* 107–116.

Mathur, S. R., Kavale, K. A., Quinn, M. M., Forness, S. R., & Rutherford, R. B. (1998). Social skills intervention with students with emotional and behavioral problems: A quantitative synthesis of single-subject research. *Behavioral Disorders, 23,* 193–201.

Naude, J. H. (1999). *Evaluating the efficacy of solution-focused couple therapy using single case design.* Unpublished doctoral dissertation, Georgia State University: Atlanta.

Nelson, T., & Kelley, L. (2001). Solution-focused couples group. *Journal of Systemic Therapies, 20,* 47–66.

Polk, G. W. (1996). Treatment of problem drinking behavior using solution-focused therapy: A single subject design. *Crisis Intervention, 3,* 13–24.

Rubin, A., & Babbie, E. (2010). *Research methods for social work* (7th ed.). Belmont, CA: Brooks/Cole-Thomson Learning.

Salzberg, C. L., Strain, P. S., & Baer, D. M. (1987). Meta-analysis for single-subject research: When does it clarify, when does it obscure? *Remedial and Special Education, 8,* 43–48.

Scruggs, T. E., Mastropieri, M. A., & Casto, G. (1987). The quantitative synthesis of single-subject research: Methodology and validation. *Remedial and Special Education, 8,* 24–33.

Stams, G. J., Dekovic, M., Buist, K., & de Vries, L. (2006). Effectiviteit van oplossingsgerichte korte therapie; een meta-analyse (Efficacy of solution-focused brief therapy: A meta-analysis). *Gedragstherapie (Behavior Therapy), 39*(2), 81–94.

Strain, P. S., Kohler, F. W., & Gresham, F. (1998). Problems in logic and interpretation with quantitative syntheses of single-case research: Mathur and colleagues (1998) as a case in point. *Behavioral Disorders, 24*(1), 74–85.

White, O. R. (1987). Some comments concerning "the quantitative synthesis of single-subject research." *Remedial and Special Education, 8,* 34–39.

Yarbrough, J. L. (2004). *Efficacy of solution-focused brief counseling on math assignment completion and accuracy in an elementary school.* Unpublished doctoral dissertation, University of Tennessee: Knoxville.

8 Review of Outcomes with Children and Adolescents with Externalizing Behavior Problems

■ JACQUELINE CORCORAN

■ INTRODUCTION

The purpose of this chapter is to discuss the application of solution-focused brief therapy (SFBT) to externalizing behaviors in youth. This represents a broad category of behaviors characterized and described as aggressive, antisocial, or disruptive behavior. The American Psychiatric Association's *Diagnostic and Statistical Manual of Mental Disorders* includes as disruptive behavior disorders attention deficit/hyperactivity disorder (ADHD), oppositional defiant disorder (ODD), and conduct disorder (CD; APA, 2000). These disorders will be briefly described here. Attention deficit/hyperactivity disorder involves a persistent pattern (for 6 months or more) of inattention and/or hyperactivity and impulsive behavior that is more frequent and severe than what is typically observed in others at a comparable developmental level (APA, 2000). Oppositional defiant dissorder involves a pattern (for 6 months or more) of negativistic, hostile, and defiant behaviors toward authority figures such as parents and teachers. Conduct disorder also involves an entrenched pattern of behavior, but in this diagnosis the basic rights of others or major age-appropriate societal norms or rules are violated (APA, 2000). The externalizing behaviors are the most common reason children are seen in both inpatient and outpatient settings.

■ WHAT WE HAVE LEARNED SO FAR

Solution-focused brief therapy has been conceptually applied to both child and teenage problem behaviors in many reports for the past 15 or so years (Clark, 1997; Corcoran, 1997; Selekman, 1993, 1997). Certain aspects of SFBT make it ideally suited to this problem area. First, youth with externalizing problems are typically mandated clients. In other words, other people are more concerned about their behavior than they are, and they are typically referred for services nonvoluntarily. When they are receiving services, such clients do not seem motivated to change. In SFBT, three main types of clients are present: the customer (the voluntary client who wants to make changes); the complainant (who is more interested in change for another person); and the visitor (the involuntary client who has been mandated to attend; De Jong & Berg, 2008). With youth externalizing problems, two types of clients are typically present. Children with behavior problems are usually visitors (Selekman, 1993). They are generally less concerned about their behaviors than others are (their parents, the school system, the courts); their main goal is to terminate treatment.

Parents (and teachers) are the complainant type; they see their children as the problem and want change to come from them. Solution-focused brief therapy has strategies with which to engage both types of clients, using language and questioning to influence the way clients view their problems, the potential for building solutions, and the expectancy for change (Berg & De Jong, 1996).

Second, youth with behavior problems often have a past life filled with failure and adversity. The people close to them are frustrated and disappointed with their behaviors. In SFBT, the practitioner refrains from eliciting detail about a problematic past; in this treatment model, understanding the problem does not necessarily lead to solving it (De Jong & Berg, 2008). Instead, the focus is on *exceptions* to the problem when the youth acts in a prosocial manner. There are countless examples daily of situations in which the child is doing what he or she is supposed to. In SFBT, the construction of solutions from exceptions is seen as easier and ultimately more successful than stopping or changing existing problem behavior. Along with exceptions, another major orientation in SFBT is toward the future without the problem, which helps children, their caregivers, and their teachers envision a way out of the current circumstances rather than being mired in the problem. Solution-focused brief therapy focuses on positives and solutions rather than negative histories, problems, and deviance.

Youth labeled as having ADHD, ODD, or CD can be challenging to work with because of their lack of focus and attention, anger, and defiance. Therefore, a third advantage to using SFBT with this population is that it can help providers gain a more hopeful and empowered view of the helping process. Emphasis is on well-formulated goals that are achievable within a brief time frame. This is in contrast to some long-term therapies that often target relatively fixed and stable characteristics of people, such as their personalities (O'Hanlon & Weiner-Davis, 1989). In an SFBT view, change is more likely to be maximized when specific, concrete behaviors are targeted rather than hypothetical entities (Cade & O'Hanlon, 1993). For example, a youth who has destroyed someone's property or harmed others is easier to influence than a CD; a youth who talks back to teachers is easier to manage than an ODD: and a youth who fails to finish school assignments is easier to deal with than an ADHD.

The focus on small, concrete changes is believed, in SFBT, to stimulate further change. This phenomenon of reciprocal change is also assumed to be responsible for the onset and maintenance of child behavior problems. By the time a family with such a child comes to treatment, a negative pattern has developed: the child "acts out"; the parent views the child negatively; the parent communicates this negative view to the child, who then acts in a manner consistent with this view; and the spiral continues. In solution-focused treatment, the aim is to reverse this pattern so that a positive spiral instead results: specific behaviors the parent wants to see are elicited; the child's positive behavior is attended to and reinforced; the parent views the child more favorably; the child acts more consistently with this view; and the upward spiral continues.

A fourth reason SFBT is suited to externalizing problems involves the fact these clients often have experienced myriad life stressors, such as poverty, overcrowded living conditions, multiple moves, large family size, parental divorce, incarceration of parents, parental substance abuse, community violence, and other difficult life circumstances. An agenda for some helpers is "to process the client's feelings" about all the losses and difficulties he or she has experienced. However, youth often resist such tactics and avoid the discussion by remaining uncooperative or uncommunicative. Rather than getting into a struggle with clients about what they "should be dealing with" and pushing them in a direction that they may find intrusive and irrelevant, SFBT targets the goals that clients need to achieve so that they no longer get into trouble for their behavior and focuses on the resilience and strength youth have used to survive challenging and stressful life events.

■ SFBT INTERVENTION

The following case illustrates some of the techniques of SFBT. An in-home therapist is seeing Clarice, an African American 17-year-old mother of a 2-year-old, who lives with her mother, Samantha. Clarice has a history of truancy, not following rules at home and at school, and poor academic performance. She is now in the ninth grade at an alternative school. She currently resides with her mother and other siblings.

The in-home therapist makes an initial home visit with Samantha and finds that Clarice is not present for the scheduled meeting. Samantha explains, "We all tried calling but she doesn't pick up her phone, doesn't answer texts. She doesn't follow the rules. She doesn't listen. Clarice does what Clarice wants to do. She doesn't care. A while ago she got a ride from her sister and stole money out of the glove compartment."

Joining is the clinician's task of establishing a positive, mutually cooperative relationship (Berg, 1994) so that the client is amenable to working with the practitioner and to change (Cade & O'Hanlon, 1993). Samantha presents with the complainant relationship, with which several SFBT techniques can be used. First, there are *coping questions*: "This sounds very difficult. What have you been doing to manage?" Coping questions convey the therapist's recognition of the hardships involved. They also promote the idea that while the situation is challenging, the mother is drawing on strengths (abilities, skills, resources) to cope (De Jong & Berg, 2008). In this case, Samantha reports that she copes by focusing on taking care of her other children and grandchildren. She says, "I can't waste all my time worrying about Clarice. We do fun things together as a family. We go to the movies, bowling, and laser tag. We don't want her there anyway if she's in a bad mood, ruining it for everyone."

The therapist can then reinforce these strengths by offering a *compliment*. In this case, the therapist says, "So, you focus on the rest of your family and don't let it derail you from taking care of them." Compliments are an ongoing part of the solution-finding process, starting with joining.

Another ongoing process involves the practitioner's awareness of the strengths clients demonstrate in different areas of their lives. In the course of complaining about Clarice, her mother mentions a younger daughter, comparing her favorably to Clarice: "She's on the right track. She's cheerleading and in a higher grade than Clarice." Here the therapist offers an *indirect compliment* using the client's own language: "How have you done things differently with her to make sure she is on the right track?" In indirect complimenting, the practitioner, rather than telling the client she is doing well, poses a question to get the client to figure out for herself the resources and strengths she uses to make that happen (De Jong & Berg, 2008). Compliments are more powerful when clients generate them for themselves and experience the sense of empowerment that comes from them. A more empowered view of oneself is more conducive to change than feeling bad about one's shortcomings. Note also, in this example, the way the therapist uses the same *language* as the client, such as "on the right track." Client, rather than clinical, language is used so that clients feel understood.

Rather than allowing complainants to keep dredging up their difficulties with the youth with behavior problems, SFBT orients them to a *future without the problem* by asking a question, such as "How would you like things to be with your daughter?" By fleshing out the details of what she wants from her daughter, Samantha can move toward this vision instead of being stuck in past problems.

When Samantha answers that she would like the relationship with her daughter to be "perfect," the therapist can use *normalizing* to show that living with teenagers and young children (and life in general) is never going to be perfect. Normalizing is a solution-focused technique to depathologize people's concerns and present them instead as normal life difficulties (Bertolino & O'Hanlon, 2002; O'Hanlon & Weiner-Davis, 1989).

In response to the therapist's question, Samantha says, "When she doesn't lie. Answers her phone when we call her. She says I don't know how to talk to her. She does what she wants. She wants to be a mother, but how can she be? I told her she needs to read the Bible or something." The therapist's task is to seek the presence of concrete positive behaviors rather than the absence of negative behaviors. For instance, Samantha talks about wanting her daughter not to lie; the therapist could ask, "What would you like her to be telling the truth about? How will you respond to that?"

Note the SFBT assumption that the context of the situation drives behavior more than individual traits in the question "How will you respond to that?" When Samantha later comments, "She says I don't know how to talk to her," the focus on the interactional sequence is seen again when the therapist responds, "How are you talking to her when she acts like you want?" In answer, Samantha says, "We just talk, joke around." The therapist then tries to elicit more specific details with questions such as "What kinds of things do you talk about? So, you share a sense of humor? What kind of joking around do you together?" This will get Samantha to focus on the more positive aspects of their relationship and her daughter. The solution-focused assumption is that enlarging these aspects and figuring out the resources that go into these times is more productive than trying to undo problems.

Exception finding, which involves identifying the times that the problem does not occur (or is less urgent) and the circumstances at those times, is the crux of SFBT intervention.

When the therapist eventually meets with Clarice, instead of talking about the problem—the times Clarice was truant from school—she explores the times she attended her classes and what was different then. They then talk about the relationship Clarice has with the father of her child, which has been contentious in the past.

CLARICE: Yeah. But it's better now. We talk about things more.

THERAPIST: You've been able to talk more? How are you able to do that? (indirect complimenting)

s: I don't know. We just talk about what's going on. I have an attitude problem. I would get mad about other stuff and take it out on him. A lot of people tell me I have an attitude.

Hearing the talk about "attitude," the therapist uses the technique of *externalizing*. Rather than viewing an "attitude problem" as a pathological behavior of Clarice, the therapist instead formulates it through the use of language as an external entity that can be changed. Some possible questions are as follows: "When are you able to get control of *the* attitude?" "When is it able to get control of you?" "When can you resist the urge to have *the* attitude tell you what to do?" "When are you able to stand up to *the* attitude and not let it get it in the way of your relationships?"

Once progress has been made—and maintained—on the goals clients have named, termination may follow. Termination in SFBT is geared toward helping clients identify strategies so that the momentum developed will cause further change to occur. At the termination of this case, Samantha has made plans to move from temporary custody of her grandson to permanent full custody. Clarice is now working at a part-time job, and she is studying for a GED degree. Samantha says, "I don't think I could've done it without everyone's help." The therapist gives Samantha credit for her expert knowledge of what she and her family need ("What was most helpful about this work?") and the work that has been done ("How were you able to use the help that was offered to you?"). In response, Samantha says, I've been doing better with talking with her. When she raises her voice, I tell her to calm down."

■ METHODS

Two recent reviews were undertaken on the SFBT treatment outcome research. The Corcoran and Pillai (2009) review involved experimental or quasi-experimental studies conducted from 1985 to 2006 in which the outcome was defined as other than client satisfaction. The review was limited to published studies written in English. A meta-analysis was also recently conducted on SFBT (Kim, 2008). Studies had to have control or comparison groups in order to be included; unpublished studies (dissertations) were also part of the criteria.

■ RESULTS

In the Corcoran and Pillai (2009) review, 3 of the 10 studies meeting inclusion criteria focused on child externalizing problems. See Table 8.1 for details of these three studies. Effect sizes were calculated using a standardized mean difference (Lipsey & Wilson, 2001), but due to the different constructs used to determine outcomes in these studies, an average effect size could not be determined.

Kim (2008) grouped studies with externalizing, internalizing, and relationship outcomes separately. Therefore, externalizing behaviors in children (Franklin et al., 2007, 2008; Newsome, 2004; Seagram, 1997; Triantafillou, 2002) were combined with other studies that used externalizing outcomes with adults and the elderly. Like Corcoran and Pillai (2009), Kim (2008) also found the methodological quality of the studies to be low. Ratings for the child externalizing studies ranged from 3 to 5 (out of 6 on a rating scale). Because of the way studies were synthesized, it is not known how child externalizing problems fared as a result of SFBT. Overall, the externalizing effect size in Kim (2008) was small and not statistically significantly different from zero.

Interestingly, there was no overlap in the child behavior studies in the Corcoran and Pillai (2009) review and the Kim (2008) meta-analysis. The latter contained unpublished doctoral dissertations and an in press article, and Franklin et al. (2008) had yet

TABLE 8.1. *Description of Youth Externalizing Studies in Corcoran and Pillai (2009)*

Author/Population	Intervention	Design/Sample Size	Outcome	Effect Size
Corcoran (2006) Children with behavior problems	Family therapy (average five sessions) provided by social work graduate students	Nonrandom treatment group and comparison group $N = 83$	Connors Parent Rating Scale; Feelings, Attitudes, and Behaviors Scale for Children	$d = 0.178$
Littrell et al. (1995) Teens with school problems	One session of individual therapy provided by school counselors	Random treatment group and comparison group with 2-week and 6-week follow-up $N = 61$	Changes in students' concerns; goals attained; intensity of students' feelings decreased	$d = 0.172$ at posttest $d = 0.113$ at follow-up
Zimmerman et al. (1996) Parents who experience adolescent–parent conflict	Group (average six sessions) provided by marriage and family therapy graduate students	Randomization to treatment group and control group $N = 42$	Parenting Skills Inventory, total score; Family Strength, total score	$d = 0.632$

to be published when Corcoran and Pillai undertook their review. One of the studies had been screened out of the Corcoran and Pillai (2009) review for not having a control/comparison group (i.e., Newsome, 2004). See Chapter 16 for a review of the Franklin et. al (2008) study and other, more recent outcome studies on SFBT's effectiveness with externalizing behavior problems.

■ PRACTICE GUIDELINES FROM THE RESEARCH

In conclusion, the research on SFBT has been sparse, and very little has been collected solely on child externalizing problems. Therefore, there are few practice guidelines to present at this point. In defense of the minimal research base of SFBT in general,and for youth externalizing behaviors in particular, several reasons have been advanced (Corcoran & Pillai, 2009). First, the solution-focused view is that intervention begins at the first contact with initial intervention questions, such as "What needs to happen here so that you know coming here was a success?" In comparison, most of the instruments used to assess outcome in treatment research tend to be problem focused. Therefore, an assessment period devoted to a problem focus would detract from the strengths orientation of solution-focused therapy. However, with the use of strengths-based measures, as described in Chapter 4, future studies on SFBT may be able use research designs with a more consistent theoretical orientation that also addresses the resolution of problem areas.

A second reason that may contribute to the lack of research on solution-focused therapy involves its brief focus. An argument can be made that change may not be apparent after only a few sessions as assessed by standardized measures. In addition, requiring people to attend treatment sessions for a certain standard length of time goes against the philosophy of solution-focused therapy, which states that people choose for themselves how long to keep coming, even if it is for only one session. Brief rating scales with more frequent measurement points such as the ones described in Chapter 5 may help improve these measurement problems, although they will not completely solve them.

Probably the major explanation for the lack of research involves the constructivist origins of SFBT. The constructivist viewpoint is that knowledge about reality is constructed from social interactions (Berg & De Jong, 1996). Although, this epistemological viewpoint is often cited as a stopgap to research on SFBT, Chapter 10 of this book reviews the experiemental basis for coconstruction, suggesting that this approach is grounded in laboratory research in communication studies, thus supporting the empirical basis of the constructivist orientation of SFBT. Sharing perceptions with others through language and engaging in dialogues is the way in which reality is shaped and is an integral part of the SFBT change process (de Shazer, 1994). The constructivist change processes may be challenging to capture using positivist research methods, but as previous chapters in this book have also illustrated, quantitative procedures and treatment outcome studies on SFBT are emerging, suggesting that more research into the therapy's effectiveness with externalizing behavior may also be possible.

■ FUTURE STUDIES

The overall recommendation for future study is that more studies should be conducted on SFBT for youth externalizing problems. Future studies on SFBT should strive to be more methodologically rigorous, involving the following elements:

- Randomization to SFBT and control conditions
- Adequate sample size
- Use of standardized measurement instruments
- Assessment of treatment fidelity
- Follow-up assessment

Until at least a few large-scale studies are conducted in this matter, it will be difficult to either synthesize studies in a quantitative way via meta-analysis or claim that SFBT is an empirically supported treatment as defined by the American Psychological Association.[1] These two methods have been primary ways that evidence-based treatments have been established.

Another recommendation for future research involves the fact that students were often treatment providers in many of the studies reviewed in Corcoran and Pillai (2009) and in two out of the three studies on youth with externalizing problems. The general issues and importance of treatment fidelity have been covered in other chapters of this book and in some detail in Chapter 3. Presumably, licensed mental health professionals might obtain better outcomes with SFBT than students, so future studies should be implemented with graduated professionals who have been competently trained to deliver SFBT.

■ KEY FINDINGS TO REMEMBER

- Although SFBT has been used in individual, group, and family modalities with youth externalizing problems and has several advantages in working with this population, little research has focused on this area
- More methodologically rigorous research is needed to establish SFBT as an evidence-based treatment in this area.

■ FURTHER LEARNING

Brief Family Therapy Center in Milwaukee, Wisconsin, where SFT originated. The Web site is http://www.psyctc.org/mirrors/sft/bftc.htm

European Brief Therapy Association. The purpose of this organization is to support brief therapy in Europe by providing information and holding an annual conference. The Web site is http://www.ebta.nu

Solution Focused Brief Therapy Association. This is the North American counterpart of the European Brief Therapy Association; it also hosts an annual conference. The Web site is http://www.sfbta.org

■ ENDNOTE

1. By definition, well-supported treatments compare an experimental condition with an already established treatment for a particular problem. In addition, two or more research teams have tested the treatment and found similar positive results.

■ REFERENCES

American Psychiatric Association (2000). *Diagnostic and statistical manual of mental disorders* (4th ed., Text Revision). Washington, DC: Author.

Berg, I. K. (1994). *Family-based services: A solution-focused approach*. New York: Norton.

Berg, I. K., & De Jong, P. (1996). Solution-building conversations: Co-constructing a sense of competence with clients. *Families in Society, 77*, 376–391.

Bertolino, B., & O'Hanlon, B. (2002). *Collaborative, competency-based counseling and therapy*. Boston, MA: Allyn & Bacon.

Cade, B., & O'Hanlon, W. H. (1993). *A brief guide to brief therapy*. New York: Norton.

Clark, M. D. (1997). Interviewing for solutions. *Corrections Today, 59*(3), 98–102.

Corcoran, J. (1997). A solution-oriented approach to working with juvenile offenders. *Child and Adolescent Social Work Journal, 14*, 277–288.

Corcoran, J. (2006). A comparison group study of solution-focused therapy versus "treatment-as-usual" for behavior problems in children. *Journal of Social Service Research, 33*, 69–82.

Corcoran, J., & Pillai, V. (2009). A review of the research on solution-focused therapy. *British Journal of Social Work, 39*, 234–242.

De Jong, P., & Berg, I. K. (2008). *Interviewing for solutions* (3rd ed.). Pacific Grove, CA: Brooks/Cole.

de Shazer, S. (1994). *Words were originally magic*. New York: Norton.

Franklin, C., Moore, K., & Hopson, L. (2008). Effectiveness of solution-focused brief therapy in a school setting. *Children & Schools, 30*, 15–26.

Franklin, C., Streeter, C., Kim, J., & Tripodi, S. (2007). The effectiveness of a solution-focused, public alternative school for dropout prevention and retrieval. *Children and Schools, 29*, 133–144.

Lipsey, M., & Wilson, D. (2001). *Practical meta-analysis*. Thousand Oaks, CA: Sage Publications.

Littrell, J., Malia, J., & Vanderwood, M. (1995). Single-session brief counseling in a high-school. *Journal of Counseling & Development, 73*, 451–458.

Kim, J. (2008). Examining the effectiveness of solution-focused brief therapy: A meta-analysis. *Research on Social Work Practice, 18*, 107–116.

Newsome, W. S. (2004). Solution-focused brief therapy (SFBT) groupwork with at-risk junior high school students: Enhancing the bottom-line. *Research on Social Work Practice, 14,* 336–343.

O'Hanlon, W. H., & Weiner-Davis, M. (1989). *In search of solutions: A new direction in psychotherapy.* New York: Norton.

Seagram, B. (1997). *The efficacy of solution-focused therapy with young offenders.* Unpublished dissertation, York University, Toronto, Canada.

Selekman, M. (1993). *Pathways to change.* New York: Guilford Press.

Selekman, M. (1997). *Solution-focused therapy with children.* New York: Guilford Press.

Triantafillou, N. (2002). *Solution-focused parent groups: A new approach to treatment of youth disruptive behavior.* Unpublished doctoral dissertation, University of Toronto, Canada.

Zimmerman, T. S., Jacobsen, R. B., Macintyre, M., & Watson, C. (1996). Solution-focused parenting groups: An empirical study. *Journal of Systemic Therapies, 15,* 12–25.

9 What Works in Solution-Focused Brief Therapy

A Review of Change Process Research

■ JAY McKEEL

Ever since I (de Shazer) began practicing brief therapy in the early 1970s, my "research" question was "What do therapists do that is useful?" In the 1980s, we changed this to "What do clients and therapists do together that is useful?"

—de Shazer and Berg (1997, p. 122)

■ INTRODUCTION

Change process research looks inside the therapy room to see if and how interventions work and what clients are experiencing during their therapy. This chapter reviews change process research of solution-focused brief therapy (SFBT).

Change process research played a vital role in the development of SFBT. During the 1980s, Steve de Shazer and a team of therapists at the Brief Family Therapy Center (BFTC) began searching for and testing ideas about "what works in therapy." The BFTC team's exploration led them from existing problem-focused therapy models to a new therapy approach, which they called *solution-focused brief therapy*, that focused on solutions, exceptions to problems, and client resources. When the team began introducing SFBT through books, articles, and workshops, the change process studies they had conducted helped add credibility and confidence about this new approach to helping people in therapy.

This chapter summarizes some of the change process research conducted by the BFTC team, as well as studies by other researchers and clinicians.[1] The change process research on SFBT has investigated techniques, client optimism, and the client–therapist relationship, three factors critical to the success of psychotherapy (Duncan et al., 2010; Lambert, 1992; Norcross, 2002). The first section of this chapter examines research on several SFBT techniques. This research includes success rates, provides some suggestions derived from that research that practitioners can use to make these interventions more effective, and describes clients' views about some techniques. The second section reports on studies about clients' experiences of SFBT, including information about client optimism and the client–therapist relationship. Then some limitations of this body of research are discussed and suggestions for future research are presented.

■ RESEARCH ON SFBT TECHNIQUES

Regarding research on psychotherapy techniques, a few considerations are important to keep in mind. First, research findings on any technique can be influenced by many factors, including the therapist's skill, when the technique is used, and the fit of the technique to the client's situation, treatment goals, personality, needs, motivation, emotional state, history, etc. Second, a technique may accomplish its intended purpose and enhance, have no effect on, or even negatively impact the outcome of therapy. Third, researchers may be less likely to submit, and psychotherapy journal editors may be less likely to publish, studies that find that a technique is not successful. This possible publication bias can rob clinicians of valuable information.

For therapists, the primary advantage of change process research is learning how a majority of clients respond to a particular technique. More in-depth research can identify which clients are most likely to benefit from any particular intervention, which ones it probably would not help, and the circumstances under which a technique should do the most good.

This section reviews research on the following SFBT techniques: exploring pretreatment improvement, presuppositional questions, the miracle question, the first-session task, between-sessions change, scaling questions, and solution talk.

Pretreatment Improvement

Early in the first session of SFBT, therapists typically ask clients about changes that have already occurred in the client's problem before beginning therapy (de Shazer, 1985, 1988). Exploring *pretreatment improvements* is a common way for SFBT therapists to begin focusing on clients' strengths and resources, as well as discovering exceptions to the problems. Therapists using SFBT want to identify, acknowledge, encourage, and build on anything that has already helped or improved the client's situation. Practitioners of SFBT explain that identifying pretreatment improvement can increase clients' optimism and motivation by helping them realize that their situation can get better. Pretreatment improvements provide a guide for building solutions by identifying what clients can continue doing or do more of to accomplish their goals.

How common is pretreatment change? One study found that 30% of 200 clients reported pretreatment improvement (Allgood et al., 1995), and another study of 2,400 clients found that 15% reported significant pretreatment improvement in their problems (Howard et al., 1986). Research also shows that clients who report pretreatment change more often successfully complete therapy (Beyebach et al., 1996; Johnson et al., 1998). Clients are more likely to report pretreatment change when their therapist asks about it (Kindsvatter, 2006; McKeel & Weiner-Davis, 2009). The next section examines one technique SFBT therapists use to identify pretreatment change as well as ask about many other therapeutic issues.

Presuppositional Questions

In SFBT, *presuppositional questions* are leading questions that communicate a positive belief or expectation about clients, their situation, or their ability to accomplish treatment goals. O'Hanlon and Weiner-Davis (1989) recommend the following to SFBT therapists: "instead of, 'Did you ever do anything that worked?' ask, 'What have you done in the past that worked?' . . . The latter [question] suggests that inevitably there have been successful past solutions" (p. 80). Solution-focused therapists use presuppositional questions as interventions designed to promote hope by helping clients identify their strengths, abilities, successes, and possibilities (MacMartin, 2008; O'Hanlon & Weiner-Davis, 1989).

In a study of presuppositional questions conducted at BFTC, Weiner-Davis and colleagues (1987) asked clients at the beginning of their first session, "Many times people notice in between the time they make the appointment for therapy and their first session that things already seem different. What have you noticed about your situation" (p. 360)? This question presupposes that pretreatment changes have occurred. Twenty of the 30 clients asked this question reported pretreatment improvements and provided details about improvements in their presenting problem.

Replications of the Weiner-Davis et al. (1987) study, with many more clients, have found that more than 60% of those who were asked a similar presuppositional question reported pretreatment improvement (Lawson, 1994; McKeel & Weiner-Davis, 2009). Johnson and colleagues (1998) asked clients to complete a questionnaire before their first session that included a presuppositional question about pretreatment change; 53% reported improvements.

Therapists practicing SFBT use presuppositional questions throughout the course of therapy. In interviews following therapy sessions, MacMartin (2008) found that clients explained that presuppositional questions sometimes left them feeling that their therapist had not heard them or understood their situation. MacMartin notes that this reaction resonates with "a value that constructive or collaborative therapies uphold: the notion that clients, not therapists, are experts on their own experience" (p. 96). Based on this study, MacMartin concludes that therapists must first clearly acknowledge the client's problem before using presuppositional questions to introduce possibilities of improvement, exceptions, and/or solutions.

Miracle Question

Therapists usually ask the *miracle question*, a cornerstone of SFBT, during the first session. De Jong and Berg (1998) offer an example:

> Now, I want to ask you a strange question. Suppose that while you are sleeping tonight and the entire house is quiet, a miracle happens. The miracle is that the problem which brought you here is solved. However, because you are sleeping, you don't know the miracle has happened. So, when you wake up tomorrow morning, what will be different that will tell you a miracle has happened and the problem which brought you here is solved? (pp. 77–78)

Clients' answers to this question become a guide for therapy by helping specify the future they want and identify what will be occurring when the problem is solved (de Shazer, 2002). Therapists using SFBT rate the miracle question as the most therapeutic technique the model offers (Skidmore, 1993).

The SFBT miracle question is designed to accomplish several objectives, including developing and clarifying treatment goals, promoting hope, and preparing clients to notice exceptions (de Shazer & Dolan, 2007). Several studies have found that it does so. Dine (1995) found that the miracle question elicits responses about a wide range of issues, including concrete (e.g., a better home to live in), relational (e.g., closer relationships with loved ones), and affective/emotional (e.g., happier) improvements. Postsession interviews with clients confirm that the miracle question helped them create or clarify goals for treatment and identify specific ways to accomplish these goals (Isherwood & Regan, 2005; Shilts et al., 1994). Further, clients report feeling more hopeful after answering the miracle question (Dine, 1995; Shilts et al., 1997).

Researchers have discovered strategies for making the miracle question even more successful. Nau (1997) and Nau and Shilts (2000) observed experienced SFBT therapists conducting first sessions and discovered four factors helpful in asking the miracle question effectively. One, therapists must clearly join with the client before asking the question. Two, therapists explore exceptions to the client's problem before and while asking the miracle question. Three, during the conversation leading up to and while discussing the miracle, therapists show empathy and understanding regarding the client and his or her situation. Finally, therapists do not offer suggestions about how to achieve the miracle while the client is answering. When these strategies were used, clients were more receptive, cooperative, and detailed in their answers to the miracle question.

Three studies with small samples have identified some possible limits to the miracle question's helpfulness. Estrada and Beyebach (2007) interviewed three depressed deaf clients who completed SFBT; these clients recalled having difficulty answering the miracle question. Bowles and colleagues (2001) found that terminally ill clients tended to focus on miracle medical recoveries rather than achievable improvements in their situation. Lloyd and Dallos (2008) studied family SFBT with seven mothers whose children had severe intellectual disabilities. In interviews 2 weeks after their first SFBT session, the mothers described the question as confusing or irrelevant because of the word *miracle*. Still, these mothers reported that envisioning a hypothetical preferred future was one of the most helpful parts of their first session. These studies may suggest the need to rephrase the question when dealing with certain clients and/or clinical situations, particularly if the term *miracle* could derail the therapeutic conversation.

However, de Shazer often presented case studies and examples of successful use of the miracle question with clients facing extreme situations or challenges (e.g., de Shazer, 2002; de Shazer & Dolan, 2007). de Shazer used the miracle question not as a single question, but as a multiquestion process in which a therapist asks questions, understands the client's answers, and then follows up on these answers to elicit descriptions of observable differences that would occur after the miracle, as well as exploring past times when parts of the miracle had already occurred (de Shazer, 2002). In the three studies cited in the previous paragraph reporting possible limitations of the technique, it is not always clear whether therapists merely asked one miracle question or used a multiquestion approach to the technique.

First-Session Task

The formula *first-session task* (FFST) is the homework that SFBT therapists typically give to clients at the end of the first session. An example of the FFST is "Between now and the next time we meet, I would like you to observe, so that you can describe to me next time, what happens in your (family, life, marriage, relationship) that you want to continue to have happen" (de Shazer, 1985, p. 137). Practitioners of SFBT use the FFST to inspire hope that improvements will occur, to increase the likelihood that clients will notice exceptions or improvements, and to encourage clients to take new action to achieve their goals.

At the beginning of the second session, SFBT therapists follow up on the FFST in hopes of collecting data about clients' efforts, exceptions to the problem, and improvements since the first session and to use that information to help clients continue or develop solutions. de Shazer (1985) reported one BFTC study in which 89% of 56 clients assigned the FFST reported that something positive and worthwhile had occurred between their first and second sessions, 82% reported that something new or different had occurred that they wanted to continue, and 57% described their situation as better.

Adams and colleagues (1991) randomly assigned clients to receive either an SFBT first session, which included the FFST, or a problem-focused first session, which used a problem-focused first-session homework assignment. At the beginning of the second session, therapists in this study asked about the assigned homework. Clients given the FFST were more likely to complete the homework, were clearer about their treatment goals, and were more likely to report improvements in their problems. However, clients who received the FFST in this study were no more hopeful about accomplishing their treatment goals than clients assigned the problem-focused homework and no more likely to accomplish their treatment goals.

Jordan and Quinn (1994) conducted a similar project, comparing the FFST task with a problem-focused first-session task. As in the Adams et al. (1991) study, clients assigned the FFST more often reported improvement at the beginning of their second session. However, Jordan and Quinn found that clients assigned the FFST were more likely to expect therapy to be successful. Also, compared with clients assigned the problem-focused first-session task, those assigned the FFST rated their first session as more productive and positive.

Mireau and Inch (2009) interviewed clients about their experience of SFBT. One commented about the FFST, "your homework in the first session, noticing strengths, I was surprised to discover how well I was really handling things" (p. 66).

What's Better?

Early in the second and subsequent sessions, SFBT therapists typically ask, "What is better since our last visit?" (de Shazer, 1994). The SFBT therapists in this study, trained at BFTC, asked 129 clients this question at the beginning of each session (starting after the first session); 76% of the clients answered that something had improved from session to session (Reuterlov et al., 2000).

Scaling Questions

Therapists using SFBT ask clients to rank their problems, goals, and other relevant clinical issues on a scale of 1 to 10, with 1 typically representing the client's situation when he or she called to request the first therapy appointment and 10 representing the miracle.

Scaling questions help the client and therapist monitor progress by measuring changes from session to session. After asking the scaling question, SFBT therapists identify what led the client to move up (or down) the scale and may explore how to maintain any improvements. Therapists may then ask about what can move the rating up one number on the scale in order to explore and clarify steps to help accomplish treatment goals. For instance, if a client rates his or her situation on the scale as 3, the therapist can ask what will be different when the client is at 4 and then explore one or two things the client can do before the next session to move closer to 4 (de Shazer, 1994). Asking the scaling question is the technique most frequently used by SFBT therapists (Skidmore, 1993).

In two studies (cited previously) in which clients were critical of the miracle question (Estrada & Beyebach, 2007; Lloyd & Dallos, 2008), the same clients described scaling questions as useful. Estrada and Beyebach (2007) reported that clients easily understood scaling questions and found that the questions helped them identify specific and practical steps to improve their situation and accomplish their treatment goals. Clients in the Lloyd and Dallos (2008) study judged scaling questions, along with describing a hypothetical preferred future, as the most helpful parts of SFBT. One client in this study commented, "It [scaling] was immediately useful in making me realize that although I was feeling at 1, there had been times when I had been as high as 4 or 5. It made me remember that times would be better again" (p. 16).

Solution Talk

An overarching and defining technique of SFBT is that the therapist creates a conversation with clients about change and solutions. de Shazer (1991, 1994) describes how SFBT therapists use *solution talk*; instead of providing suggestions, advice, education, or directives, SFBT therapists rely heavily on questions to help clients discover, achieve, and maintain improvements. Therapists' questions help clients construct solutions by eliciting information about pretreatment change, exceptions, previous successes, client competencies and resources, goals, and progress toward goals. Therapists listen and absorb clients' answers, then typically ask another question to connect to, amplify, and build on the responses to work toward further progress (de Shazer & Dolan, 2007).

In the early work at BFTC as the team was exploring what works in therapy, Gingerich et al. (1988) examined transcripts of first sessions the team conducted. The researchers noticed that clients responded differently to solution talk (vs. problem talk). When therapists asked about successes and about times when the problem did not occur, or when they focused on goals, clients were also more likely to talk about positive change—exceptions to the problem, new ways of looking at the problem, improvements, and/or solutions they would like to accomplish. In other words, clients were more likely to talk about change if the therapist asked about it. The study also showed that first sessions at BFTC at that time consisted almost entirely of problem talk, whereas second and subsequent sessions consisted mainly of change talk. This prompted the BFTC team to experiment with ways to increase solution talk in the first session, which led eventually to dropping most of the usual discussion of the problem in the first session.

Tomori and Bavelas's (2007) conversational analysis demonstrates solution talk in practice. They examined four videotaped first sessions to compare the activity of two SFBT therapists, Steve de Shazer and Insoo Kim Berg, with the activity of two therapists integral in the development of client-centered therapy, Carl Rogers and Nathanial Raskin. The researchers categorized the first 50 utterances by each therapist in each session. de Shazer and Berg asked far more questions than the two client-centered therapists (29 vs. 1). Researchers rated each therapist's statements and questions as positive, neutral, or negative; positive utterances were four times higher for the SFBT therapists than the client-centered therapists (44 vs. 11). This process research study is described in more detail in Chapter 10 along with other studies based on the micro-anlaysis of conversations.

Another conversational analysis demonstrates how Bill O'Hanlon conducted a first session of SFBT marital therapy. Gale and Newfield's (1992) study describes O'Hanlon concentrating on solutions while focusing on each spouse's strengths. O'Hanlon adapted to each spouse's responses to use and build solutions while ignoring clients' responses that he deemed not useful. O'Hanlon used timing to ask questions—pausing briefly, asking "Okay?" and then offering one or a choice of solution-oriented answers, perhaps representing a blend of SFBT and Ericksonian influences (see O'Hanlon & Wilk, 1987).

A number of studies have also demonstrated that as SFBT therapists increase their solution talk, clients increase their solution talk too (e.g., Bonsi, 2005; Speicher-Bocija, 1999). Other studies have explored whether solution talk relates to the therapeutic outcome. Shields et al. (1991) found that the amount of solution talk by clients in the first session relates to clients' continuing therapy; the more clients talked about solutions or goals in the first session, the more likely they were to complete therapy rather than drop out. Similarly, Corcoran and Ivery (2004) discovered a positive association between therapists identifying clients' strengths and positive treatment outcome.

Additional information about clients' responses to solution talk is presented in the section below.

■ CLIENTS' EXPERIENCES OF SFBT

SFBT and Client Optimism

Several of the studies reviewed above found that SFBT techniques often increase clients' hopes and expectations that they will accomplish their therapeutic goals (e.g., Corcoran & Ivery, 2004; Dine, 1995; Jordan & Quinn, 1994, 1997; Shilts et al., 1997). This section reviews two studies that explored more generally how SFBT affects client optimism.

Bozeman (1999) randomly assigned 52 clients to receive either SFBT or a problem-focused therapy. Clients were interviewed after three sessions; those receiving SFBT reported having higher expectations that they would accomplish their therapeutic goals.

In Quick and Gizzo's (2007) interviews of clients receiving SFBT group therapy, clients credited the SFBT model with making them more hopeful about their situation. In these interviews, group participants specifically attributed their optimism to SFBT principles. For instance, one group member explained that the solution to his problems "might be an accumulation of small everyday victories that are known, doable, and within my grasp. Just keep doing what works, no matter how small" (p. 78).

The Client–Therapist Relationship in SFBT

Simon and Nelson (2004) interviewed 91 clients who completed SFBT to discover what clients considered most helpful about their therapist. Fifty-three said that the therapist's approach (e.g., questions, techniques, and homework) was the most important factor in their therapeutic success. Twelve clients cited encouragement and feedback as most helpful. Almost 25% reported that talking about the problem was beneficial. A follow-up analysis of videotapes of the sessions found that, on average, therapists and clients spent

15.5% (7.4 minutes of an average 41.3-minute session) of the first session discussing the problem. In subsequent sessions, the average time spent talking about the problem decreased to 1.4 minutes. The authors note that clients did not consider it necessary to devote a great deal of time talking about their problem to find that talk useful.

In other studies in which researchers interviewed clients who received SFBT, clients noted and liked the positive atmosphere of SFBT and the focus on strengths (e.g., Mireau & Inch, 2009; Monro, 1998). Clients described SFBT therapists as empowering and collaborative (Batzel, 1997; Lloyd & Dallos, 2008). Clients in several studies (e.g. Lee, 1997; Shilts et al., 1994) valued the support, validation, and positive focus they experienced in SFBT and described SFBT as empowering. In Lloyd and Dallos' (2008) interviews with recipients of SFBT, clients expressed appreciation for the fact that their skills and achievements were acknowledged by their therapist.

Speicher-Bocija (1999) compared clients receiving problem-focused therapy with clients receiving SFBT. Clients' ratings revealed no differences between the two groups for therapists' support, opportunity to discuss problems, therapists' input, and assistance. Jordan and Quinn (1994) compared SFBT with problem-focused therapy and also found no difference in the therapeutic alliance formed in the two approaches.

Specific therapist–client interactions have been linked to successful SFBT. Kowalik and colleagues (1997) conducted a conversational analysis of SFBT. They concluded that "the therapist should be sensitive to what happens, he or she should wait for 'yes-sets' and react appropriately, paying attention to the timing and 'fit' of his or her actions" (p. 210). In Beyebach and Carranza's (1997) analysis, they discovered that therapy is more likely to succeed when the therapists' questions and responses are closely related to the clients' last response.

Beyebach and his colleagues' investigations of therapists' conversational approaches have identified patterns that may influence clients to drop out of SFBT. Beyebach and Carranza (1997) found that clients were more likely to quit treatment when the therapist interrupted and talked over the client. Beyebach et al. (1996) discovered higher dropout rates when, during the information-gathering stage of therapy, clients experienced the therapist as dominating or controlling. On the other hand, clients were more likely to continue SFBT when the therapist practiced active listening, paraphrasing, and making statements such as "I understand" or "I see" to encourage clients to continue working toward their goals.

Although solution talk emphasizes asking questions instead of offering direct guidance, one study found that when therapists offered advice or suggestions in SFBT family therapy, clients valued it highly (Lloyd & Dollas, 2008).

MacDonald (2003) describes an experiment involving solution talk. For 6 months at a mental health center that primarily provides SFBT, therapists proceeded directly to SFBT techniques without asking clients about the problems for which they were seeking help. Compared to clients who had received traditional SFBT at the center, clients were much more critical of this solution-talk-only approach. For example, clients receiving the solution-talk-only treatment often explained that they did not feel heard and understood. One client commented, "The team had their own agenda" (p. 15). Interestingly, however, clients in this group had outcomes equal to those of clients at the same mental health center who had received traditional SFBT. Nevertheless, the therapists at the center returned to spending time in the first session asking about the problem; as a result, clients' critical feedback about treatment diminished.

Wettersten and colleagues (2005) found that the working alliance formed during SFBT was consistently very high and was rated higher than that of brief interpersonal therapy (BIT). The BIT therapy model places primacy on the client–therapist relationship. However, while the strength of the therapeutic relationship related strongly to success in BIT, this was not the case in SFBT. The authors suggest that the working alliance may play a different role in therapeutic success and client satisfaction in SFBT compared to BIT, a hypothesis ripe for further exploration.

■ LIMITATIONS

Despite the useful information provided by existing change process research on SFBT, the principal limitation of this body of research is the small number of studies. Multiple studies of a technique's effectiveness enhance the confidence a practitioner has in that tool; no SFBT technique has undergone enough research to strongly corroborate the findings in existing studies. In addition, not enough research exists to provide therapists with an adequate guide about if, when, how, or with whom to use SFBT interventions. Also, only a few studies have explored clients' experiences and views about if and how they find SFBT techniques to be helpful.

In light of the significant role of client optimism and the client–therapist relationship in therapeutic success, more research on these issues in SFBT is warranted. While several studies have linked SFBT and SFBT techniques to increased client expectations of accomplishing their goals, not enough is understood about how SFBT and its techniques increase client optimism or how best to implement SFBT to enhance hope and expectancy. This body of research also lacks sufficient experimental and qualitative inquiries necessary to understand the role of the therapeutic relationship in SFBT, much less provide clinicians with information and strategies for creating a beneficial client–therapist alliance when using this model.

■ FUTURE RESEARCH

Just as change process research was important in the development of SFBT, further research of this type can add to future improvements of the model. Investigators interested in conducting change process research on SFBT could consider the following:

1. Replicating studies reviewed in this chapter to increase confidence in the findings; confirmatory studies (with statistical improvements, added variables, or larger samples) are an excellent choice for many masters students' theses.
2. Creating robust studies that combine quantitative and qualitative inquiry to explore if, when, how, and with which clients to use SFBT techniques.
3. Using research and development strategies to test new techniques or refine and improve existing ones (see Bischoff et al., 1996).
4. Researching presuppositional questions about therapeutic issues other than pretreatment change and comparing presuppositional questions to other types of questions.
5. Exploring and testing the miracle question as a multiquestion technique with a variety of clients. Research could explore whether, when, and how to apply or tailor the miracle question, especially with unique or difficult clinical situations.

6. Researching other SFBT techniques (e.g., coping questions), session formats (e.g., session break, using a team), and homework assignments. For instance, Berg and Steiner (2003) offer a wealth of interventions, strategies, and homework suggestions (e.g., acting "as if") when working with children that could be investigated.
7. Further exploration of effective roles for advice and directives in SFBT.
8. Studying ways to integrate SFBT ideas into agencies' intake procedures.
9. Asking clients when they phone for an appointment to notice what happens before their first session that they would like to see continue to happen (see also Guterman, 1998).
10. Investigating how SFBT techniques may fit within other therapeutic models.
11. Research focusing solely on clients and their experiences with SFBT.

Research reviewed in this chapter regarding clients' experiences in SFBT points to opportunities to explore interesting and useful information for practitioners to continue to advance this model. Clients in many studies report that feeling heard and understood is important. However, the MacDonald (2003) and Wettersten et al. (2005) studies found that client satisfaction and a strong therapeutic relationship may not be necessary to achieve a positive outcome in SFBT. Clients' outcome, feeling heard and understood, satisfaction with treatment, and their relationship with their therapist are four distinct research variables. Further study of the association of these four variables can enhance the development and practice of SFBT.

■ KEY POINTS TO REMEMBER

- Clients frequently report pretreatment improvements and are more likely to identify these improvements when therapists ask presuppositional questions.
- Presuppositional questions, the miracle question, the first-session task, exploring what is better in second and subsequent sessions, scaling questions, and solution talk have all been found to accomplish their intended therapeutic purpose.
- Research has found that some SFBT techniques, and the model in general, engender client optimism about accomplishing treatment goals.
- The client–therapist relationship in SFBT is a frequent topic of discussion and is addressed in several other chapters in this book. Studies have found that the therapeutic alliance formed in SFBT is comparable to that in other therapy models. Research has found that clients appreciate the positive atmosphere of SFBT. They describe a validating, collaborative, and empowering experience and appreciate the focus on their strengths and success.
- In many studies, the success of SFBT techniques and the SFBT model have been linked to clients' feeling heard and understood by their therapist. Yet, two studies have found that therapists acknowledging, addressing, and understanding clients' problems, as well as the therapeutic relationship in general, do not relate to success in SFBT the way they do in some other therapeutic approaches. Further exploration of therapist–client interactions and relationships in SFBT will make a valuable contribution to the practice and further development of the model.

▪ ACKNOWLEDGMENTS

The author thanks Judy Gretsch and Wallace Gingerich for comments on earlier drafts of this chapter.

▪ ENDNOTE

1. Unless otherwise noted, findings reported in this chapter are statistically significant. To make for a smoother read, phrases such as "more likely" rather than "significantly more likely" are used.

▪ REFERENCES

Adams, J. F., Piercy, F. P., & Jurich, J. A. (1991). Effects of solution-focused therapy's "formula first session task" on compliance and outcome in family therapy. *Journal of Marital and Family Therapy, 17*, 277–290.

Allgood, S. M., Parham, K. B., Salts, C. J., & Smith, T. A. (1995). The association between pretreatment change and unplanned termination in family therapy. *American Journal of Family Therapy, 23*, 195–202.

Batzel, D. R. S. (1997). *Exploration of session perceptions in the words of clients and therapists*, Blacksburg, VA: Unpublished doctoral dissertation, Virginia Polytechnic Institute and State University.

Berg, I. K., & Steiner, T (2003). *Children's solution work*. New York: Norton.

Beyebach, M., & Carranza, V. E. (1997). Therapeutic interaction and dropout: Measuring relational communication in solution-focused therapy. *Journal of Family Therapy, 19*, 173–212.

Beyebach, M., Morejon, A. R., Palenzuela, D. L., & Rodriguez-Arias, J. L. (1996). Research on the process of solution-focused therapy. In S. D. Miller, M. A. Hubble, & B. L. Duncan (Eds.), *Handbook of solution-focused brief therapy* (pp. 299–334). San Francisco: Jossey-Bass.

Bischoff, R. J., McKeel, A. J., Moon, S. M., & Sprenkle, D. H. (1996). Systematically developing therapeutic techniques: Applications of research and development. In D. H. Sprenkle & S. M. Moon (Eds.), *Research methods in family therapy* (pp. 429–443). New York: Guilford Press.

Bonsi, E. (2005). *An empirical investigation of the usefulness of solution talk in solution-focused therapy*. Unpublished doctoral dissertation, University of Nebraska–Lincoln.

Bowles, N., Mackintosh, C., & Torn, A. (2001). Nurses' communication skills: An evaluation of the impact of solution-focused communication training. *Journal of Advanced Nursing, 36*, 347–354.

Bozeman, B. N. (1999). *The efficacy of solution-focused therapy techniques on perceptions of hope in clients with depressive symptoms*. Unpublished doctoral dissertation, New Orleans Baptist Theological Seminary.

Corcoran, J., & Ivery, J. (2004). Parent and child attributions for child behavior: Distinguishing factors for engagement and outcome. *Families in Society: The Journal of Contemporary Social Services, 85*, 101–106.

De Jong, P., & Berg, I. K. (1998). *Interviewing for solutions*. Pacific Grove, CA: Brooks/Cole.

de Shazer, S. (1985). *Keys to solution in brief therapy*. New York: Norton.

de Shazer, S. (1988). *Clues: Investigating solutions in brief therapy*. New York: Norton.

de Shazer, S. (1991). *Putting differences to work*. New York: Norton.

de Shazer, S. (1994). *Words were originally magic*. New York: Norton.

de Shazer, S. (2002). *Less is more: The discipline of brief therapy*. Presented at the Psychotherapy Networker Conference, Washington, DC.

de Shazer, S., & Berg, I. K. (1997). "What works?": Remarks on research aspects of Solution-Focused Brief Therapy. *Journal of Family Therapy, 19*, 121–124.

de Shazer, S., Dolan, Y., with Korman, H., Trepper, T., McCollum, E., & Berg, I. K. (2007). *More than miracles: The state of the art of solution-focused brief therapy*. New York: Hawthorn Press.

Dine, K. R. (1995). *Visions of the future: The miracle question and the possibility for change*. Unpublished doctoral dissertation, Boston: Massachusetts School of Professional Psychology.

Duncan, B. L., Miller, S. D., Wampold, B. E., & Hubble, M. A. (Eds.). (2010). *The heart and soul of change: Delivering what works in therapy* (2nd ed.). Washington, DC: American Psychological Association.

Estrada, B., & Beyebach, M. (2007). Solution-focused therapy with depressed deaf persons. *Journal of Family Psychotherapy, 18*, 45–63.

Gale, J., & Newfield, N. (1992). A conversational analysis of a solution-focused marital therapy session. *Journal of Marital and Family Therapy, 18*, 153–165.

Gingerich, W. J., de Shazer, S., & Weiner-Davis, M. (1988). Constructing change: A research view of interviewing. In E. Lipchik (Ed.), *Interviewing* (pp. 21–32). Rockville, MD: Aspen.

Guterman, J. T, (1998). Identifying pretreatment change before the first session. *Journal of Mental Health Counseling, 20*, 370–374.

Howard, K. I., Kopta, S. M., Krause, M. S., & Orlinsky, D. E. (1986). The dose–effect relationship in psychotherapy. *American Psychologist, 41*, 159–164.

Isherwood, K., & Regan, S. (2005). Solutions not problems: Improving outcomes in an integrated mental health rehabilitation service using a solution-focused brief therapy approach. *Social Work and Social Sciences Review, 12*, 53–71.

Johnson, L. N., Nelson, T. S., & Allgood, S. M. (1998). Noticing pretreatment change and therapeutic outcome: An initial study. *American Journal of Family Therapy, 26*, 159–168.

Jordan, K. B., & Quinn, W. H. (1994). Session two outcome of the formula first session task in problem- and solution-focused approaches. *American Journal of Family Therapy, 22*, 3–16.

Jordan, K. B., & Quinn, W. H. (1997). Male and female client perception of session two outcome of the problem- and solution-focused approaches. *Family Therapy, 24*, 23–37.

Kindsvatter, A. (2006). *Factors associated with counseling client perceptions of contributions to pretreatment change*. Kent, OH: Unpublished dissertation, Kent State University.

Kowalik, Z. J., Schiepek, G., Roberts, L. E., & Elbert, T. (1997). Psychotherapy as a chaotic process II. The application of nonlinear analysis methods on quasi time series of the client–therapist interaction: A nonstationary approach. *Psychotherapy Research, 7*, 197–281.

Lambert, M. J. (1992). Implications of outcome research for psychotherapy integration. In J. C. Norcross & M. R. Goldstein (Eds.), *Handbook of psychotherapeutic integration* (pp. 94–129). New York: Wiley-Interscience.

Lawson, D. (1994). Identifying pretreatment change. *Journal of Counseling and Development, 72*, 244–248.

Lee, M. Y. (1997). A study of solution-focused brief family therapy: Outcomes and issues. *American Journal of Family Therapy, 25*, 3–17.

Lloyd, H., & Dallos, R. (2008). First session solution-focused brief therapy with families who have a child with severe intellectual disabilities: Mothers' experiences and views. *Journal of Family Therapy, 30*, 5–28.

Macdonald, A. J. (2003). Research in solution-focused brief therapy. In B. O'Connell & S. Palmer (Eds.), *Handbook of solution-focused therapy* (pp. 12–24). London: Sage Publications.

MacMartin, C. (2008). Resisting optimistic questions in narrative and solution-focused therapies. In A. Perakyla, C. Antaki, S. Vehvilainen, & I. Leudar (Eds.), *Conversational analysis and psychotherapy* (pp. 80–99). New York: Cambridge University Press.

McKeel, A. J., & Weiner-Davis, M. (2009). *Presuppositional questions and pretreatment change: A further analysis.* Unpublished manuscript.

Mireas, R., & Inch, R. (2009). Brief solution-focused counseling: A practical effective strategy for dealing with wait lists in community-based mental health services. *Social Work, 14*, 63–70.

Monro, C. C. (1998). *Solution-focused brief therapy: A process-outcome study of positively oriented interventions.* Langley, BC: Unpublished doctoral dissertation, Trinity Western University.

Nau, D. S. (1997). *Before the miracle: The optimum use of the solution-focused miracle question.* Fort Lauderdale-Davie, FL: Unpublished doctoral dissertation, NOVA Southeastern University.

Nau, D. S., & Shilts, L. (2000). When to use the miracle question: Clues from a qualitative study of four SFBT practitioners. *Journal of Systemic Therapies, 19*, 129–135.

Norcross, J. C. (2002). *Psychotherapy relationships that work: Therapist contributions and responsiveness to patient needs.* New York: Oxford University Press.

O'Hanlon, W. H., & Weiner-Davis, M. (1989). *In search of solutions: A new direction in psychotherapy.* New York: Norton.

O'Hanlon, W. H., & Wilk, J. (1987). *Shifting contexts: The generation of effective psychotherapy.* New York: Guilford Press.

Quick, E. K., & Gizzo, D. P. (2007). The "doing what works" group: A quantitative and qualitative analysis of solution-focused group therapy. *Journal of Family Psychotherapy, 18*, 65–84.

Reuterlov, H., Lofgren, T., Nordsbrom, K., Ternstrom, A., & Miller, S. D. (2000). What is better? A preliminary investigation of between-session change. *Journal of Systemic Therapies, 19*, 111–115.

Shields, C. G., Sprenkle, D. H., & Constantine, J. A. (1991). Anatomy of an initial interview: The importance of joining and structuring skills. *American Journal of Family Therapy, 19*, 3–18.

Shilts, L., Flippino, C., & Nau, D. S. (1994). Client-informed therapy. *Journal of Systemic Therapies, 13*, 39–52.

Shilts, L., Rambo, A., & Hernandez, L.(1997). Clients helping therapists find solutions in their therapy. *Contemporary Family Therapy, 19*, 117–132.

Simon, J., & Nelson, T. (2004). Results of last session interviews in solution focused brief therapy: Learning from clients. *Journal of Family Psychotherapy, 15*, 27–45.

Skidmore, J. E. (1993). *A follow-up of therapists trained in the use of the solution-focused brief therapy model.* Vermillion: Unpublished doctoral dissertation, University of South Dakota.

Speicher-Bocija, J. D. (1999). *Comparison of the effect of solution-focused and problem-focused interviews on clients' immediate verbal responses.* Akron, OH: Unpublished doctoral dissertation, University of Akron.

Tomori, C., & Bavelas, J. B. (2007). Using microanalysis of communication to compare solution-focused and client-centered therapy. *Journal of Family Psychotherapy, 18*, 25–43.

Weiner-Davis, M., de Shazer, S., & Gingerich, W. J. (1987). Using pretreatment change to construct a therapeutic solution: An exploratory study. *Journal of Marital and Family Therapy, 13,* 359–363.

Wettersten, K. B., Lichtenberg, J. W., & Mallinckrodt, B. (2005). Associations between working alliance and outcome in solution-focused brief therapy and brief interpersonal therapy. *Psychotherapy Research, 15,* 35–43.

10 Connecting the Lab to the Therapy Room

Microanalysis, Co-construction,
and Solution-Focused Brief Therapy

■ JANET BEAVIN BAVELAS

Contemporary experimental research in psycholinguistics and communication can contribute to solution-focused brief therapy (SFBT) both substantively and methodologically. First, these experiments support a central tenet of SFBT, namely, the co-constructive nature of communication in face-to-face dialogue. Second, the methods of basic research have led to the refinement of microanalysis of dialogue, which is the moment-by-moment examination of actual communication sequences with an emphasis on how they function within a dialogue. As shown in this chapter, both of these sources are beginning to reveal the details of co-construction in psychotherapy sessions.

It may be helpful to locate these two kinds of research in a wider view of the evidence base for SFBT (e.g., Bavelas, 2006). The standard of "*the best research evidence available*" (Sackett et al., 2000) can be interpreted to mean a wide variety of methods that answer different questions and therefore complement each other. Table 10.1 outlines four such methods, each of which offers evidence that the others cannot. Outcome research (e.g., Gingrich et al., 2011, in this volume) aims for randomized controlled designs that seek to establish the effectiveness of SFBT, as measured after therapy is over. Perhaps less well known are studies that focus on the effects of specific techniques within SFBT sessions (e.g., Beyebach et al., 1996; Beyebach, 2011). The present chapter features two other approaches: first, lab experiments that provide evidence for theoretical assumptions such as co-construction and, second, the use of microanalysis of dialogue to assess the details of SFBT in practice.

■ BACKGROUND

Solution-focused therapy has a special affinity with language and communication. De Shazer and Berg were both influenced by the Palo Alto Group (e.g., de Shazer & Berg, 1991), which focused as much on communication as on psychotherapy (e.g., Jackson, 1968a, 1968b; Watzlawick et al., 1967; Watzlawick & Weakland, 1977). Both Berg and de Shazer went on to contribute their own sophisticated and detailed emphasis on language and co-construction as central to psychotherapy process (e.g., de Shazer, 1994; De Jong & Berg, 1998, 2002, 2008). A primary purpose of this chapter is to show

TABLE 10.1. *Four Corners of an Evidence Base*

Method	Setting	Focus	Purpose	SFBT Question
Outcome studies (e.g., randomized controlled trials)	Therapy	Therapy outcome	Applied research on the effectiveness of therapy	Does SFBT lead to better outcomes than a placebo or other therapies do?
Within-session studies of techniques or interventions	Therapy	Particular techniques	Applied research on the utility of specific techniques	Do key components of SFBT work as proposed?
Experimental tests of theory	Research lab	Theoretical foundation	Basic research on fundamental assumptions	Is there evidence for co-construction? How does it work?
Microanalysis of dialogue	Therapy	Therapy process	Applied research on the details of practice	Is SFBT communication consistent with its model and different from other models?

Note: Adapted from Bavelas (2006). The third and fourth methods are the topics of this chapter.

the theoretical and empirical congruence between their observations, derived from SFBT sessions, and the findings of lab experiments on dialogue.

To study communication in psychotherapy is to study face-to-face dialogue. Many scholars have proposed that face-to-face dialogue is the fundamental form of language use (e.g., Bavelas & Chovil, 2000, 2006; Bavelas et al., 1997; Chafe, 1994; Clark, 1996; Fillmore, 1981; Garrod & Pickering, 2004; Goodwin, 1981; Levinson, 1983; Linell, 2005). However, only in recent years have there been theories that focus specifically on face-to-face dialogue and are supported by experimental research; these theories and research are not widely known outside of psychology and psycholinguistics. Because of the separation of practice from research, what most practitioners have learned about communication in psychotherapy (e.g., about active listening or body language) has no research foundation. Indeed, contemporary research contradicts most of the usual curriculum on applied communication. Moreover, communication courses for psychotherapists and counselors usually start with the assumption that therapists and clients lack communication skills and therefore need to learn them from "the experts." The research described here strongly suggests that having a face-to-face dialogue is the most skillful and efficient activity that humans engage in, and they do it naturally, without formal training.

■ THE COLLABORATIVE MODEL

Psycholinguist Herbert Clark and his research group (e.g., Clark, 1992, 1996) have developed a collaborative model of dialogue, which challenges the view of language and communication that has previously dominated linguistics, psychology, and communication. They called this older tradition the *autonomous model* (e.g., Schober & Clark, 1989) because it focuses on individuals and treats dialogue as simply alternating monologues: The speaker delivers information, the listener is attentive but passive; when they take turns, they switch roles. In contrast, Clark's *collaborative model* treats communication as joint action: The speaker and listener produce the information together; they collaborate, moment by moment, to ensure mutual understanding. (See also Roberts & Bavelas, 1996.)

The isomorphism between the collaborative and constructionist models is striking, although these two models developed independently. Social construction (e.g., Berger & Luckmann, 1966) rejects the essentialist premise that meanings are "in" words and that communication is simply a neutral channel that transmits the words. Similarly, the collaborative model rejects the premise that information is independent of the details of the dialogue in which it arises. More specifically, both co-construction and collaboration focus on social interaction in dialogue as the process that inevitably shapes meaning. Meaning is created and sustained in dialogic processes. It is possible that future historians will see the autonomous and essentialist models as parts of a paradigm that went unquestioned until collaboration and co-construction offered an alternative paradigm.

This chapter proposes that experimental research within the collaborative model can provide a much-needed empirical basis for co-construction, which has otherwise remained primarily theoretical and anecdotal, seldom examining systematically *how* co-construction happens, moment by moment, in an actual dialogue. To appreciate how speakers and listeners co-construct in dialogue, it is necessary to examine their communication extremely closely, a few seconds or a few words at a time, that is, at the level of microanalysis of dialogue. It is noteworthy that this method originated with the Natural History of an Interview project, which was an intensive study of a psychotherapy session (cf. Bavelas et al., 2000b; Leeds-Hurwitz, 1987).

Experimental Evidence for Collaboration and Co-construction: The Stanford Language Use Group

Clark's program of theory and experimental research has provided evidence for a collaborative rather than an autonomous model of dialogue (e.g., Clark, 1992, 1996; Schober, 2006; Schober & Brennan, 2003). The two early articles summarized here laid the foundation for this model and still illustrate its main features.

Clark and Wilkes-Gibbs (1986). This study was a microanalysis of referential language in dialogue. Specifically, what determines the language that two individuals use to refer to things that are hard to describe? Each pair had the same set of 16 Tangram cards; see Figure 10.1. One of them (the speaker) had a subset of 12 of the cards in a particular order, and she[1] had to explain to the other person (the listener) how to put the same 12 of his cards in the same order. The cards themselves had no names, so it was necessary to invent a way to refer to each of them. There were six successive trials, each with a new subset in a new correct order. Because they were interacting through a partition, the pair could not see each other or each other's cards, but otherwise they could interact freely. Clark and Wilkes-Gibbs analyzed these dialogues and found that, even though the speakers were the ones with the correct information, they did not simply impose their own references unilaterally. A close analysis, turn by turn, revealed that the speaker and listener produced the references together. In the examples below, two different pairs were working on identifying the same Tangram (which is third in the top row of Figure 10.1).

Example 1

SPEAKER 1: "[The] third one is the guy reading with, holding his book to the left."
LISTENER 1: "Okay, kind of standing up?"
SPEAKER 1: "Yeah." (Clark & Wilkes-Gibbs, 1986, p. 22)

Figure 10.1. The full set of Tangram figures used in Clark and Wilkes-Gibbs (1986) and Schober and Clark (1989); adapted with permission.

Example 2

SPEAKER 2: "Okay, and the next one is the person that looks like they're carrying something and it's sticking out to the left. It looks like a hat that's upside down."
LISTENER 2: "The guy that's pointing to the left again?"
SPEAKER 2: "Yeah, pointing to the left, that's it!" (laughs)
LISTENER 2: "Okay." (Clark & Wilkes-Gibbs, 1986, p. 23)

Neither of these descriptions was more accurate than the other; what was important is that both pairs established that they understood each other.

All of the cards reappeared (in a new order) in later trials, and the pairs soon honed their references to the minimum features salient to both of them. As a result, they used significantly fewer and fewer words over the course of the six trials. For example, one speaker's successive descriptions of the fourth Tangram in the top row of Figure 10.1 were as follows:

Example 3

SPEAKER 3:
TRIAL 1. "All right, the next one looks like a person who's ice skating, except they're sticking two arms out in front."
TRIAL 2. "Er, the next one's the person ice skating that has two arms?"
TRIAL 3. "The fourth one is the person ice skating, with two arms."

TRIAL 4. "The next one's the ice skater."
TRIAL 5. "The fourth one's the ice skater."
TRIAL 6. "The ice skater." (Adapted from Clark & Wilkes-Gibbs, 1986, p. 12)

As their dialogue progressed, the pairs began to use shorter, often idiosyncratic terms that they both understood. This process is sometimes called *entrainment* and is easily observable in many dialogues, including in psychotherapy. In psychotherapy, it is of particular interest whose terms are adopted. Does the therapist use the client's description or does the client learn the language of the therapist's model? In SFBT in particular, does the therapist systematically introduce or entrain on more positive terms than negative ones? (The last section of this chapter points to research that has begun to answer these two questions.)

Schober and Clark (1989). This article presented two experiments demonstrating that it is specifically the moment-by-moment collaboration illustrated in Examples 1 and 2 that distinguishes dialogue from monologue. Schober and Clark began by pointing out that, in some dialogues, there are two functionally different kinds of listeners. Each listener in the Clark and Wilkes-Gibbs (1986) experiment was an *addressee* with whom the speaker was interacting. If someone else hears the speaker but cannot engage in a dialogue with the speaker, that listener is an *overhearer*. Schober and Clark used the same Tangram task as in the earlier experiment but created both kinds of listeners. For example, in one of their experiments, each group consisted of a speaker, an addressee, and an overhearer, all seated around a table (again divided by partitions). The overhearers had the same task as the addressees, which was to place their cards in the order the speaker was describing. The instructions were that the addressees could interact with the speaker, but the overhearers could not; they could only listen. So in each group of three, the addressee and the overhearer heard exactly the same information from the speaker.

If information were all that mattered, the overhearers should do as well as the addressees, but this was not the case. In both experiments, the addressees did significantly better on their task than the overhearers did. By the second trial, the addressees were already averaging close to 100% correct, whereas the overhearers did not do this well even on the last trial. The addressees' advantage could not have been due to the quality of the speakers' descriptions because, in each group of three, the addressee and overhearer heard the same description. In fact, each overhearer not only heard the same descriptions as the matched addressee, he or she also heard everything the addressee contributed. The results therefore contradicted the autonomous or essentialist view that information is all that matters.

To account for the overhearers' poorer performance, it is necessary to look closely at how the addressees and overhearers differed. The overhearers were essentially forced to act exactly as the autonomous model describes: they were passive recipients of information. In contrast, the addresses could collaborate with their speakers. They could "go beyond these autonomous actions and collaborate with each other moment by moment to try to ensure that what is said is also understood" (Schober & Clark, 1989, p. 211). This collaborative process is called *grounding,* in which the speaker and addressee ensured that the addressee had understood the speaker sufficiently for their current purposes (Clark & Schaefer, 1989; see also Clark, 1996, ch. 8). Grounding occurs constantly in the background of all dialogues. It consists of a microsequence in which

1. the speaker presents information,
2. the addressee indicates or displays understanding (or not),
3. the speaker acknowledges, explicitly or implicitly, that the addressee has understood (or not).

In its simplest form, a grounding sequence may consist of these three short steps, as in Example 1 above. However, if the addressee does not understand immediately, the process expands until they are both sure that he does. A close examination of the following example (referring to the second Tangram on the second row in Figure 10.1) shows both of them actively collaborating in the grounding process. Ensuring that they understood each other was a mutual responsibility, which they achieved moment by moment:

Example 4

SPEAKER 4: "Then number 12 is, (laughs) looks like a, a dancer or something really weird. And has a square head, and there's like, there's uh- the kinda this. . ."
ADDRESSEE 4: "Which way is the head tilted?"
SPEAKER 4: "The head is, uh—towards the left, and then th- an arm could be like up towards the right?"
ADDRESSEE 4: "Mm-hm."
SPEAKER 4: "And, it's—"
ADDRESSEE 4: (overlapping) "an- a big fat leg? You know that one?"
SPEAKER 4: (overlapping) "Yeah, a big fat leg."
ADDRESSEE 4: "And a little leg."
SPEAKER:4 "Right."
ADDRESSEE 4: "Okay."
SPEAKER 4: "Okay?"
ADDRESSEE 4: "Yeah."
By the last trial, their reference had become more compact, and the two of them took only one turn each:
SPEAKER 4: "The dancer with the big fat leg?"
ADDRESSEE 4: "Okay." (Adapted from Schober & Clark, 1989, pp. 216–217)

Notice that their final reference combined "dancer" from the speaker and "big fat leg" from the addressee. The speaker and addressee had collaborated, turn by turn, to produce a reference that worked for both of them.

The process that led the addressees to achieve near-perfect scores could not help the overhearers, because they could not participate in their own grounding with the speaker. Without the ability to interact, the overhearers could not contribute, seek clarification, or verify their understanding. Indeed, as the speaker's and addressee's descriptions became shorter and more efficient for themselves, the same descriptions became less and less helpful for the overhearer, who had had no part in creating them.

To critics who only hear anecdotal descriptions of collaboration and co-construction, these processes often seem to be insubstantial or merely hypothetical. However, Schober and Clark's (1989) experiments demonstrated significant quantitative effects of being able (or not able) to collaborate and co-construct. In effect, their procedures created one group (the overhearers) who embodied the autonomous or essentialist model and another group who had the option of collaborating and co-constructing. The addressees took advantage of the possibility of working together and achieved measurably better mutual understanding than their passively listening cohorts.

Experimental Evidence for Collaboration and Co-construction: The Victoria Microanalysis Group

Our group's program of research on the unique features of face-to-face dialogue has made use of and also contributed to collaborative theory. First, we now use the terminology of the collaborative model (rather than the earlier language of interactional systems theory; Watzlawick, et al., 1967, chs. 4 and 5) because it focuses explicitly on the linguistic details of reciprocal influence. Second, in contrast to experiments on dialogues through partitions, we have contributed our expertise on *face-to-face* dialogues, especially our research and theory on the integration of verbal and selected nonverbal acts.

In our *integrated message model* (Bavelas & Chovil, 2000, 2006), participants in a dialogue communicate with spoken words plus a specific and limited set of visible speech-related acts, namely, conversational hand gestures, facial displays, and gaze. In spontaneous dialogue, these visible acts are precisely synchronized, in both timing and meaning, with the words they accompany.[2]

Moreover, these acts are essential to understanding communication in a face-to-face dialogue, because they often convey information that supplements or complements the words. The following excerpt illustrates how a transcript of a face-to-face interaction is incomplete and even misleading. The therapist's words on their own could be read as skeptical or even as challenging what the client is saying about himself. The client was young African-American who had problems with substance abuse and the law. He was answering an earlier question about what was helpful to him:

Example 5

> CLIENT: "You s-, when I'm talking to a bunch of people and everybody laughs 'cause of somethin' you say or somethin. "
> THERAPIST: "Yeah."
> CLIENT: "You know. It make you feel good. Then it's like you don't need no drugs if you do that."
> THERAPIST: "I see. Do you have a good sense of humour?"
> CLIENT: "Yeah."
> THERAPIST: "You do?"
> CLIENT: "Yeah."
> THERAPIST: "Do– Is that what other people tell you?"
> CLIENT: "Yeah."
> THERAPIST: "You make other people laugh?"
> CLIENT: "Yeah."
> THERAPIST: "You do? Huh! Have you always been that way?"
> CLIENT: "Yeah."

THERAPIST: "Uh-huh." [slight pause]
CLIENT: "Yeah."
THERAPIST: "And you're saying that helps you."
CLIENT: "Yeah, it helps me."
THERAPIST: "Uh-huh."

In contrast to the transcript, the video shows everything that the client saw and heard. The therapist was Insoo Kim Berg (1994), and her tone of voice, facial displays, and gestures combined with her words to give an overall impression of warmth, encouragement, and being impressed by his answers. She asked her questions in a light, pleasant tone of voice that also conveyed an eager interest in the answers, even a mild surprise at discovering something positive. For example, as she began the first question ("Do you have a good sense of humour?"), she gestured out toward the client, circling her hand as if to encourage an answer. When she came to the words "sense of humour," she was nodding, looking expectant and interested, and smiling, as if already anticipating a positive answer. Each subsequent question elicited more information and affirmation from him, expanding the scope and importance of his sense of humour. The therapist's warm, slightly surprised tone of voice, her smiling, and her gestures toward him all conveyed that she was very pleased with what he was telling her. Thus, she was not doubting or challenging the client (as the transcript alone might suggest); she was engaged in co-constructing one of his positive resources.

Bavelas, Coates, and Johnson (2000a). We examined collaboration between speaker and addressee in experiments that differed from those of Clark and his colleagues in two ways: First, the pairs were in a face-to-face dialogue, not separated by a partition. Second, we created a stronger test of collaborative theory by using a task that was not as inherently cooperative as that of Clark and his colleagues. In the Tangram task, the speaker and addressee had shared knowledge (the same set of cards) and an explicit shared goal (the addressee's success). Our two experiments used a task where there was no shared knowledge and no shared or explicit goal. One stranger told another a true story about a close call from sometime in his or her past, when something bad could have happened but, in the end, everything turned out all right (e.g., a car or skiing accident, nearly missing a final exam). The addressees could only listen because they had no prior knowledge of the story. We predicted (a) that these apparently passive addressees would still contribute to the dialogue, both visibly and audibly, and (b) that their collaboration would be essential to the speaker.

Our first analysis focused entirely on the addressees. Using microanalysis, we located virtually every response each addressee made that was related to the speaker's story. Some of these responses were familiar ones, such as those illustrated in the following example, when the speaker was providing the background to her close call. (The addressee's responses are in italics and in brackets immediately below the speaker's words that they occurred with, which are indicated by underlining.)

Example 6

SPEAKER 6:
Uh, I have a single bed with a headboard <u>on the back of it</u>.
                    [*"mm, hm," nods,*
                    looks attentive]

And I got a light <u>for Christmas,</u>
> [*slight nod*]

a lamp that you clamp on <u>to the headboard.</u>
> [*slight nod*]

We called these familiar responses *generic*. Nodding, "m-hm," "yeah," and similar stereotypic responses fit almost anywhere in the story because their form is usually not specific to what the speaker is saying at the moment.

In contrast, there were also *specific* responses, such as when the same speaker began to tell what happened.

Example 6a

SPEAKER 6:
"And I guess I <u>left it on.</u>
> [*stops smiling,*
> *raises her*
> *eyebrows;*
> *looks concerned*]

And it's got a really, <u>really strong</u>, hot light"
> [*bites lip*]

Notice that the addressee's specific responses fit closely with what the speaker was saying at that moment. The speaker had just begun to hint that the close call was going to be a consequence of leaving the light on, and the addressee started to look concerned, then worried. These responses would not be appropriate, for example, during the background information in Example 6 or at the end of the story when everything had turned out all right.

It is also noteworthy that both generic addressee responses (e.g., nodding) and specific addressee responses (e.g., facial displays of alarm) were often visible instead of audible and that they were often simultaneous with the speaker's words. An apparent advantage of visible responses is that the participants do not treat them as either interruptions or a separate speaking turn.

Both generic and specific responses played a role in the addressee's grounding with the speaker, although at significantly different points in the narrative. As we had predicted, generic responses occurred mainly at the beginning, while the speaker was giving background information. Specific responses started to occur later, as the nature of the close call began to unfold. Thus, although some might describe these addressees as "merely listening," they made responses that aligned closely and appropriately with the speaker's words at a particular moment. We proposed that the addressees' responses were illustrating and co-narrating the speaker's words.

We also tested our second prediction that collaboration between the speaker and addressee was essential even in this situation where the addressee had no information to contribute. In each of the two experiments, there was also a randomly assigned condition in which listeners had to do an unrelated cognitive task during the speaker's story. For example, they had to count the number of words that the speaker said that began with the letter *t*. They were listening closely to the narrator's words but at the wrong level, focusing on an irrelevant feature rather than on the story. The first effect was that the addressees' rate of both generic and specific responses dropped significantly in this condition and their specific responses virtually disappeared. The second result was the effect on the *speakers*. Naive raters, who were unaware of the experimental conditions, rated the speakers in this condition as poor storytellers–significantly poorer than the speakers who were listening normally. Our subsequent microanalysis of the story endings showed that these endings were significantly poorer in specific ways. The speakers whose addressees were focusing on something other than the narrative became disfluent, justified their story, or needlessly repeated the ending. These speakers had neither a collaborative partner nor evidence that their addressee was understanding them and illustrating their story. They were talking to someone who was more like an overhearer than an addressee.

These experiments demonstrated, first, that an addressee's contributions in face-to-face dialogue are visible as well as audible and, second, that even what could be considered a monologue is co-constructed. The addressees who were listening normally were helping to shape the story by grounding with the speaker on background information and then providing specific illustrations of the dramatic parts of the story. Lacking this collaboration, the speakers could not tell their stories well. Most therapists to whom we describe this experiment point out the risk that a therapist can become a "*t*-counter," listening for something of theoretical interest to the therapist instead of attending to what the client is saying from the client's perspective. Another risk is for the therapist to use stereotypic and unvarying "neutral" listener responses (which are likely to be entirely generic) rather than spontaneously and naturally shaping their responses to match the moment-by-moment flow of what the client is saying.

Bavelas, Coates, and Johnson (2002). The next study examined *how* speakers and addressees coordinated their collaboration. The experiments described so far, among others, have shown that speakers and addressees interweave their contributions, moment by moment, to co-construct the dialogue. However, it was not obvious how they achieved this close timing, especially in our close-call experiment when the speaker was doing all the talking. Using an inductive approach, we reexamined the pairs in the normal listening condition, looking for what preceded and followed each listener response (whether generic or specific). Our microanalysis soon revealed that the speaker and addressee were coordinating their actions with gaze.

To understand how gaze coordinates addressee responses, it is first necessary to know how gaze works in the broader context of a dialogue. Several researchers have studied gaze in North American and European dialogues, when two participants were sitting vis-à-vis and talking back and forth (Argyle & Cook, 1976; Duncan & Fiske, 1977; Kendon, 1967). These participants do not maintain constant eye contact. Instead, whoever is the addressee at the moment looks fairly steadily at the speaker of the moment, and the speaker mostly looks away (e.g., down, around, or to the side). As they change speaking turns, their gaze roles also change back and forth, often very rapidly.

The speakers in our data were doing virtually all of the talking. As in the previous research, the addressee looked virtually constantly at the speaker, and the speaker looked only occasionally at the addressee. Each of these occasional glances by the speaker created a brief period of eye contact, which we called a *gaze window*. It was in these moments that the addressee made a generic or specific response. Statistical tests confirmed that the addressee's responses were occurring during gaze windows significantly more often than could be happening by chance. This pattern was significant, not just for the sample, but for each of the nine pairs as well. The speaker looked, and the addressee responded. However, there was more to the pattern.

The actions of the pair were not linearly determined by the speaker's glances at the addressee, because the addressee's response was followed by the speaker's looking away. That is, the addressee's responses were significantly more likely to occur in the latter half of the gaze window, which meant that the speaker looked away shortly after the addressee responded, thereby closing the gaze window. The close-call story in Examples 6 and 6a illustrated this reciprocal pattern: the speaker glanced at the addressee, who responded during the brief gaze window; as soon as the addressee had responded, the speaker looked away. The only variation (in these and other data) typically occurred when the speaker was digressing briefly to explain or add to what he or she had just said. In these cases, the speaker would continue to look at the addressee, and the addressee would continue to respond. The effect of keeping the gaze window open was to receive more feedback.

It is important to point out that these gaze patterns cannot be universal. The data were from Western cultures and from situations in which the participants were free to look at each other. Some cultures treat gaze as a matter of respect or deference or put other restrictions on it so that gaze is not available for coordinating dialogue. Even in Western cultures, there are settings that preclude the above pattern (e.g., a car driver and passenger or multi-party groups). However, as Schober and Clark (1989, p. 229) emphasized, grounding is "an opportunistic process," so we predict that participants will find alternative ways.

Summary of Research Evidence

The above studies are a sample of the experimental research that (as proposed in Table 10.1) identifies and provides experimental support for co-constructive processes in dialogue. Put more strongly, they support the view that co-construction is inevitable in dialogue, including therapeutic dialogues. Co-construction is not a theoretical option that a therapist can either adopt or reject as an epistemological preference. Rather, it is the natural way that humans have learned to do dialogue. The experimental conditions that corresponded to the autonomous or essentialist model led to significantly worse outcomes for the participants than the conditions that permitted collaboration and co-construction. Microanalytic experimental evidence also contributed to knowledge of *how* co-construction happens (e.g., grounding, generic and specific listener responses, gaze patterns). Purely theoretical arguments for co-construction do not uncover these micro-details of collaboration in dialogue, details that are often surprising, fascinating, and directly applicable to therapeutic practice and training. The rest of this chapter will describe microanalysis of dialogue as a method, as well as some of the applications that are making the details of psychotherapy process more visible.

■ MICROANALYSIS AND CO-CONSTRUCTION
IN SFBT SESSIONS

The experiments on listener responses (Bavelas et al., 2000a, 2002) required detailed analysis of video recordings of the dialogues. Since the mid-1980s, our research group has been analyzing a wide variety of video records of experimental data, which has led to the refinement of a method that we call *microanalysis of dialogue*. Microanalysis of dialogue aims for a detailed and replicable examination of observable communication sequences as they proceed, moment by moment, in a dialogue, with an emphasis on the function of these sequences within the dialogue. (Some of the methodological differences from conventional research approaches are discussed in Bavelas, 1987, 1995, 2005.)

Starting in the latter half of the 1990s, we began to apply microanalysis to psychotherapy sessions by experts in training videos, including especially the SFBT videos that Insoo and Steve were donating to us. There seems to be a natural fit between solution-focused therapists and microanalysis, presumably because of the precise focus on language and communication intrinsic to SFBT. Most SFBT trainers and practitioners would probably agree with our assumption that "communication is the tool of therapy just as physical instruments are the tools of surgery, and it is incumbent on us to treat therapeutic communication equally carefully and precisely" (Bavelas et al., 2000b, p. 6). Our projects so far have examined how three different "tools" function to co-construct therapeutic dialogues. There are many, many more possibilities to explore.

Formulations

Bruce Phillips (1998, 1999) began with a sophisticated analysis of the underlying assumptions of traditional communication approaches. One manifestation of an autonomous or essentialist approach is the *conduit metaphor* (Lakoff & Johnson, 1980; Reddy, 1979), which treats communication as a neutral conduit through which ideas, packaged in language, shuttle back and forth between minds. This assumption is implicit in the notion of active listening, which supposedly reflects or restates what the client said, sending it back without altering its meaning. Both active listening and the conduit metaphor contrast sharply with our view, which Phillips called a *collaborative-constructionist model*. Because he was particularly interested in mediation, Phillips compared a traditional problem-focused mediation session that emphasized active listening with an SFBT approach to a marital conflict (Berg, 2008).

Phillips's microanalysis of these two sessions focused on all instances of what Garfinkel and Sacks (1970), who were describing everyday conversations, had called *formulation*, that is, when one person in a conversation summarizes or talks about what the other person has said. Formulation also occurs in mediation and therapy, where it may be called *reflecting*, *echoing*, or *paraphrasing*. The following excerpt is from the problem-focused mediation session, which involved an older woman and the young man next door about whom she was complaining. The formulation is in italics.

Example 7

MEDIATOR: ". . . what brought you down here this evening?"
CLIENT: "Well, I've been to the police, and I asked them many times and called them out on this disturbance and, uh, nothing seems to happen and, uh, it just goes on just the way it was before and, uh, last time I went down to the station and complained, about these intolerable situations, why, uh, they said, well, you can take it to court, and I said, uh, I don't have money for a lawyer. What can I do? You know. And, uh, the officer down there said well, there is a

mediation process, (Mediator "M-hm") and we might be able to resolve this with your help, but I don't know. (Mediator "Well . . .") I'm at a loss, I really am. I don't know what to do."

MEDIATOR: "Well, *you mentioned disturbances and you've been to the police.*"

CLIENT: [interrupting] "Oh, it's disgusting."

MEDIATOR: "Tell me a little more about that if you would." (Adapted from Phillips, 1998, p. 52)

In the active listening model, the mediator's formulation was an objective and non-evaluative restatement of what the client had said. However, Heritage and Watson (1979) pointed out that formulations are inevitably selective and therefore transform the original statement (see also Davis, 1986). Phillips (1998, 1999) tested these contrasting views by examining whether the mediator's or therapist's formulations were neutral (as the active listening model assumes) or not (as a collaborative/constructionist model proposes). He analyzed two features of formulations: First, the topic of a formulation could be *problem focused* or *solution focused*. That is, given that both possibilities were often present in what the client had said, which one did the mediator or therapist select for emphasis in the formulation? In Example 7, the mediator chose to formulate the problems in the client's description, rather than the part that pointed toward a solution ("we might be able to resolve this with your help"). Second, Phillips examined whether the formulation invited the client's collaboration or agreement. An *open* formulation gave the client an opportunity to respond to the formulation, whether by an explicit request or implicitly (e.g., by a questioning intonation or a pause). The formulation in Example 7 was open, with the mediator allowing the client to interrupt and then explicitly asking her to continue. A *closed* formulation was one that precluded a response from the client, for example, the mediator or therapist would continue to speak immediately after the formulation, leaving no opportunity for the client to comment.

Phillips's analysis revealed that the formulations by the mediator who was using active listening were more likely to be problem focused than solution-focused. He also tended to use open formulations with one client and closed formulations with the other. Thus, one client had less opportunity to elaborate, correct, or redirect the formulations than the other did. In the SFBT session, the formulations were, as predicted by the model, almost entirely solution focused and open, and this was equally true for both clients.

Korman, De Jong, and Bavelas have made two further contributions to understanding the role of formulations in therapy. First, we elaborated on the important role of formulation in co-construction (De Jong et al., 2011) by showing how it functions within a grounding sequence. Formulations are a common way for therapists to display their understanding of what a client has said:

1. the client presents information,
2. the therapist displays his or her understanding with a formulation,
3. the client acknowledges, explicitly or implicitly, that the formulation is a correct understanding (or not).

Recall that a formulation inevitably transforms what was said to some degree, so when the client acknowledges the therapist's formulation as correct, it becomes part of their co-constructed version.

Next, we compared formulations in sessions by expert therapists from three different approaches (Korman et al., 2011). Focusing on the beginnings of these sessions, we developed a highly reliable microanalysis for identifying the parts that each therapist preserved or added to what the client had said. SFBT emphasizes the importance of using the client's language rather than inserting the therapist's interpretations. As predicted, the formulations of the solution-focused therapists contained a significantly higher proportion of the clients' own words and a lower proportion of terminology added by the therapist than did the formulations of cognitive behavioral or motivational interviewing experts. Thus, as noted in Table 10.1, microanalysis is a method that can provide evidence regarding whether SFBT practice fits its model and differs from the practice of other approaches.

Questions

Dan McGee (1999; McGee et al., 2005) focused on therapists' questions as another tool of co-construction. Rather than classify questions, he examined how they function (intentionally or not) as therapeutic interventions. Drawing on psycholinguistic principles and his own clinical experience, McGee developed a model of how questions initiate an interactional sequence that can have a powerful co-constructive effect: A therapist's question initiates a sequence that leads the client to provide answers within the framework of the therapist's theoretical approach. The main features of McGee's model will be summarized here.

The impact of a question begins with its *presuppositions*, which are assumptions that form the background of the question. Presuppositions in questions are usually implicit rather than overtly expressed. In the following excerpt, the client had been describing his long-term problem with alcohol when de Shazer (1994) asked two successive questions (in italics):

Example 8

THERAPIST: *"What about in the last few weeks? Some days have been better than others?"*

CLIENT: "Some days, yes it has. (Therapist: "M-hm") Some days've been better."

THERAPIST: "OK, and *when was the most recent good day? Without–"*

CLIENT: [interrupting] "problems 'n . . ."

THERAPIST: "M-hm." [long pause]

CLIENT: [sounding surprised] "Just about every day. (Therapist: "M-hm") It's just the physical part, really, that-that, you know, makes things uncomfortable for me when I drink. Although, you know, I- I might have problems in my life just like anybody else."

THERAPIST: "Oh, of course, (Client: "You know") Sure." (transcribed from the unpublished video, *$250,000 is enough*; also in de Shazer, 1994, pp. 246ff.)

De Shazer's first question had several presuppositions: that it is possible for things to be better; that some whole days could have been better; and that some days could have been better in the last few weeks. The question constrained the client to search for an answer within these presuppositions, that is, to search the last few weeks (not his whole life) for specific days (not the whole period) that had been comparatively better (not perfect). Although this question set the parameters, it was the client and not the therapist who provided the answer, so both contributed to this co-construction. By answering the question, the client accepted and gave evidence for the presuppositions in it. It became common ground between them that it is possible for things to be better and that some whole days have been better in the past few weeks. Therefore, the next question could go on to ask about "the most recent good day." Indeed, the client completed the second question himself and answered as if he were discovering how well the presuppositions fit his experience. A question about whether "some days have been worse than others" would probably have initiated a different sequence. (Of course, clients can and do challenge the presuppositions in questions, in which case the therapist can backtrack quickly and modify them—precisely because they had been only implicit; see McGee et al., 2005, p. 380.)

McGee (1999) applied his analysis to a wide variety of questions from different therapeutic approaches, demonstrating how the therapist's theory shapes the presuppositions in his or her questions and how the client's answers accept and contribute evidence for the theory. This analysis has a direct practical application: The therapist can choose among alternative possible questions according to the presuppositions that each would bring into the session. For example, compare a question that opens the session with "What would you say most bothers you today?" (McGee, 1999, p. 5) with a question such as "How can I be helpful today?" (De Jong & Berg, 2008, p. 55).

Positive/Negative Content

Recall that Phillips (1998, 1999) examined the content of each formulation for whether it was problem talk or solution talk (de Shazer, 1994, ch. 7). More recently, Tomori (2004; Tomori & Bavelas, 2007) also analyzed this feature, which is a distinguishing characteristic of SFBT. This study microanalyzed the content of questions and formulations in the initial stages of four demonstration videos, two by SFBT experts (Berg and de Shazer) and two by client-centered experts (Rogers and Raskin). The content of each question or formulation could be positive, negative, or neutral. The operational definition was simply whether, in the context of this client's life, the *content* of what the therapist said was in a desirable or undesirable direction for the client. For example, talking about having a "good sense of humor" (Example 5) or "the most recent good day" (Example 8) is positive, whereas talking about "disturbances and [having] been to the police" (Example 7) is negative. Neutral content would not point in either direction—for example, the mediator's opening question in Example 7. (It is important to emphasize that "positive" and "negative" in the three studies described here were not value judgements about whether what the therapist had said was appropriate or useful; these terms referred solely to content.) Independent analysts had good agreement for rating the content as positive, negative, or neutral.

The results showed striking differences between the two approaches to therapy. Consistent with the SFBT model, Berg's and de Shazer's formulations and questions were overwhelmingly positive. Surprisingly, Rogers's and Raskin's were primarily negative. The client-centered model would predict primarily neutral or positive contributions by the therapist, but this was not the case in the openings of these expert sessions.

Smock and colleagues (2011) went further and compared positive versus negative content in three SFBT and three cognitive behavioral therapy (CBT) expert sessions.

These analyses, which also had high interanalyst reliability, covered each entire session, including virtually everything the therapist and the client said. The results showed that, as predicted, the content of the SFBT therapists was significally more positive and less negative than that of the CBT sessions. Both of the above studies on positive versus negative content have illustrated the point (in Table 10.1) that microanalysis can show how SFBT practice is consistent with its model and is different from practices derived from other models.

There were two other findings of interest in Smock et al. (2011). Across all of the therapists, the clients responded in kind, that is, positive talk led to more positive talk, and negative talk led to more negative talk. Thus, a therapist's use of positive content seems to contribute to the co-construction of an overall positive session, whereas negative content would do the reverse. The third finding was that, as a group, the SFBT experts were all consistently more positive than negative, whereas the CBT experts differed widely among themselves. (Korman et al., 2011, found the same pattern in their analysis of formulations, described above; i.e., the SFBT experts were homogeneous and the CBT experts were heterogeneous.)

■ CONCLUSIONS

This chapter introduced SFBT researchers and practitioners to experimental research that confirms the inevitably co-constructive nature of language in dialogue. It also illustrated how a method that grew out of this experimental research, microanalysis of dialogue, can (a) explicate specific co-constructive processes in psychotherapy and (b) compare SFBT practice to its model as well as to other therapeutic approaches. The past decade has seen considerable evolution in this method. In particular, microanalysis of therapeutic dialogues can now achieve the same standards of operational definitions, high interanalyst reliability, and replicability as found in experimental work or randomized controlled trials. These standards should give it a place in a wider view of evidence-based research and lead to more extensive applications of the method.

■ ENDNOTES

1. For clarity of presentation, the speakers in these experiments will always be female and the addressees male. In the actual experiments, all gender combinations occurred.

2. Our theory is the opposite of the notion of a separate *body language*, a term that usually refers to an unspecified set of nonverbal actions that are unrelated to speech and are believed (without empirical evidence) to reveal unspoken emotions or thoughts.

■ REFERENCES

Argyle, M., & Cook, M. (1976). *Gaze and mutual gaze*. Cambridge: Cambridge University Press.

Bavelas, J. B. (1987). Permitting creativity in science. In D. N. Jackson & J. P. Rushton (Eds.), *Scientific excellence: Origins and assessment* (pp. 307–327). Beverly Hills, CA: Sage Publications.

Bavelas, J. B. (1995). Quantitative versus qualitative? In W. Leeds-Hurwitz (Ed.), *Social approaches to communication* (pp. 49–62). New York: Guilford Press.

Bavelas, J. B. (2005). The two solitudes: Reconciling social psychology and language and social nteraction. In K. Fitch & R. Sanders (Eds.), *Handbook of language and social interaction* (pp. 179–200). Mahwah, NJ: Erlbaum.

Bavelas, J. B. (2006, March). *Research on psychotherapy: A variety of methods.* Lecture presented to the Department of Psychology, Free University of Brussels, Belgium

Bavelas, J. B., & Chovil, N. (2000). Visible acts of meaning. An integrated message model of language use in face-to-face dialogue. *Journal of Language and Social Psychology, 19,* 163–194.

Bavelas, J. B., & Chovil, N. (2006). Hand gestures and facial displays as part of language use in face-to-face dialogue. In V. Manusov & M. Patterson (Eds.), *Handbook of nonverbal communication* (pp. 97–115). Thousand Oaks, CA: Sage Publications.

Bavelas, J. B., Coates, L., & Johnson, T. (2000a). Listeners as co-narrators. *Journal of Personality and Social Psychology, 79,* 941–952.

Bavelas, J. B., Coates, L., & Johnson, T. (2002). Listener responses as a collaborative process: The role of gaze. *Journal of Communication, 52,* 566–580.

Bavelas, J. B., Hutchinson, S., Kenwood, C., & Matheson, D. H. (1997). Using face-to-face dialogue as a standard for other communication systems. *Canadian Journal of Communication, 22,* 5–24.

Bavelas, J. B., McGee, D., Phillips, B., & Routledge, R. (2000b). Microanalysis of communication in psychotherapy. *Human Systems, 11,* 3–22.

Berg, I. K. (2008). *Irreconcilable differences.* [DVD]. (Available from the Solution Focused Brief Therapy Association, http://www.sfbta.org/SFBT_dvd_store.html).

Berg, I. K. (1994). *So what else is better?* [Videotape]. (Previously available from the Solution Focused Brief Therapy Center, Milwaukee, WI).

Berger, P., & Luckmann, T. (1966). *The social construction of reality.* New York: Penguin.

Beyebach, M. (2011). *Change Factors in Solution Focused Therapy: A Review of the Salamanca Studies.* Manuscrript submitted for publication.

Beyebach, M., Rodríguez Morejón, A. R., Palenzuela, D.L., & Rodríguez-Arias, J. L. (1996). Research on the process of solution-focused brief therapy. In S. D. Miller, M. Hubble & B. Duncan (Eds), *Handbook of Solution-Focused Brief Therapy* (pp. 299–334). Jossey-Bass: San Francisco.

Chafe, W. L. (1994). *Discourse, consciousness, and time: The flow and displacement of conscious experience in speaking and writing.* Chicago: University of Chicago Press.

Clark, H. H. (1992). *Arenas of language use.* Chicago: University of Chicago Press.

Clark, H. H. (1996). *Using language.* Cambridge: Cambridge University Press.

Clark, H. H., & Schaefer, E. F. (1989). Contributing to discourse. *Cognitive Science, 13,* 259–294.

Clark, H. H., & Wilkes-Gibbs, D. (1986). Referring as a collaborative process. *Cognition, 22,* 1–39.

Davis, K. (1986). The process of problem (re)formulation in psychotherapy. *Sociology of Health and Illness, 8,* 44–74.

De Jong, P., Bavelas, J. B., & Korman, H. (2011). *Microanalysis of formulations, Part I. Observing co-construction in psychotherapy.* Manuscript submitted for publication.

De Jong, P., & Berg, I. K. (1998). *Interviewing for solutions.* Pacific Grove, CA: Brooks/Cole.

De Jong, P., & Berg, I. K. (2002). *Interviewing for solutions* (2nd ed.). Pacific Grove, CA: Brooks/Cole.

De Jong, P., & Berg, I. K. (2008). *Interviewing for solutions* (3rd ed.). Belmont, CA: Thomson Brooks/Cole.

de Shazer, S., & Berg, I. K. (1991). The Brief Therapy tradition. In J. H. Weakland & W. A. Ray (Eds.), Propagations: Thirty years of influence from the Mental Research Institute (ch. 20, pp. 249–252). New York: Haworth.

de Shazer, S. (1994). *Words were originally magic*. New York: Norton.

Duncan, S., Jr., & Fiske, D. W. (1977). *Face-to-face interaction*. Hillsdale, NJ: Erlbaum.

Fillmore, C. (1981). Pragmatics and the description of discourse. In P. Cole (Ed.), *Radical pragmatics* (pp. 143–166). New York: Academic Press.

Garfinkel, H., & Sacks, H. (1970). On formal structure of practical actions. In J. C. McKinney & E. A. Tiryakian (Eds.), *Theoretical sociology* (pp. 337–366). New York: Appleton-Century-Crofts.

Garrod, S., & Pickering, M. J. (2004). Why is conversation so easy? *Trends in Cognitive Science, 8*, 8–11.

Gingerich, W. J., Kim, J. S., Stams, G. J. J. M., & Macdonald, A. J. (2011). Solution-Focused Brief Therapy Outcome Research. In C. Franklin, T. S. Trepper, E. McCollum, & W. J. Gingerich (Eds.), *Solution-Focused Brief Therapy. A handbook of evidence-based practice* (pp. 301–305). New York: Oxford University Press.

Goodwin, C. (1981). *Conversational organization: Interaction between speakers and hearers*. New York: Academic Press.

Heritage, J., & Watson, R. (1979). Formulations as conversational objects. In G. Psathas (Ed.), *Everyday language: Studies in ethnomethodology* (pp. 123–162). New York: Irvington.

Jackson, D. (Ed.). (1968a). *Communication, family and marriage (Human communication, Vol. 1)*. Palo Alto, CA: Science & Behavior Books.

Jackson, D. (Ed.). (1968b). *Therapy, communication and change (Human communication, Vol. 2)*. Palo Alto, CA: Science & Behavior Books.

Kendon, A. (1967). Some functions of gaze-direction in social interaction. *Acta Psychologica, 26* (22–63).

Korman, H., Bavelas, J. B., & De Jong, P. (2011). *Microanalysis of formulations, Part II:Comparing Solution Focused Brief Therapy, Cognitive Behavioral Therapy, and Motivational Interviewing*. Manuscript submitted for publication.

Lakoff, G., & Johnson, M. (1980). *Metaphors we live by*. Chicago: University of Chicago Press.

Leeds-Hurwitz, W. (1987). The social history of the Natural History of an Interview: A multidisciplinary investigation of social communication. *Research on Language and Social Interaction, 20*, 1–51.

Levinson, S. C. (1983). *Pragmatics*. Cambridge: Cambridge University Press.

Linell, P. (2005). *The written language bias in linguistics: Its nature, origins and transformations*. London: Routledge.

McGee, D. (1999). *Constructive questions. How do therapeutic questions work?* Unpublished doctoral dissertation, Department of Psychology, University of Victoria, Victoria, B.C., Canada. Available at http://www.talkworks.ca/CQ.pdf

McGee, D., Del Vento, A., & Bavelas, J. B. (2005). An interactional model of questions as therapeutic interventions. *Journal of Marital and Family Therapy, 31*, 371–384.

Phillips, B. (1998). *Formulation and reformulation in mediation and therapy*. Unpublished master's thesis, Department of Psychology, University of Victoria, Victoria, B.C., Canada.

Phillips, B. (1999). Reformulating dispute narratives through active listening. *Mediation Quarterly, 17*, 161–180.

Reddy, M. (1979). The conduit metaphor. In A. Orlony (Ed.), *Metaphor and thought*. Cambridge: Cambridge University Press.

Roberts, G. K., & Bavelas, J. B. (1996). The communicative dictionary: A collaborative theory of meaning. In J. Stewart (Ed.), *Beyond the symbol model: Reflections on the nature of language* (pp. 139–164). Albany: SUNY Press.

Sackett, D. L., Straus, S. E., Richardson, W. S., Rosenberg, W., & Haynes, R. B. (2000). *Evidence based medicine* (2nd ed.), London: Churchhill Livingstone.

Schober, M. F. (2006). Dialogue and interaction. In K. Brown (Ed.), *Encyclopedia of language and linguistics* (2nd ed., pp. 564–571). Oxford: Elsevier.

Schober, M. F., & Brennan, S. E. (2003). Processes of interactive spoken discourse: The role of the partner. In A. C. Graesser, M. A. Gernsbacher, & S. R. Goldman (Eds.), *Handbook of discourse processes* (pp. 123–164). Mahwah, NJ: Erlbaum.

Schober, M. F., & Clark, H. H. (1989). Understanding by addressees and overhearers. *Cognitive Psychology, 21,* 211–232.

Smock, S., Froerer, A., & Bavelas, J. B. (2011). *Microanalysis of Positive and Negative Content in Solution Focused Brief Therapy and Cognitive Behavioral Therapy Expert Sessions.* Manuscript submitted for publication.

Tomori, C. (2004). *A microanalysis of communication in psychotherapy: Lexical choice and therapy direction.* Unpublished honours thesis, Department of Psychology, University of Victoria, Victoria, B.C., Canada.

Tomori, C., & Bavelas, J. B. (2007). Using microanalysis of communication to compare solution-focused and client-centered therapies. *Journal of Family Psychotherapy, 18,* 25–43.

Watzlawick, P., Beavin, J., & Jackson, D. D. (1967). *Pragmatics of human communication: A study of interactional patterns, pathologies, and paradoxes.* New York: Norton.

Watzlawick, P., & Weakland, J. H. (1977). *The interactional view: Studies at the Mental Research Institute, Palo Alto 1965–74.* New York: Norton.

Solution-Focused Brief Therapy Effectiveness with Clinical Populations

11 Solution-Focused Model with Court-Mandated Domestic Violence Offenders

■ MO YEE LEE, ADRIANA UKEN,
AND JOHN SEBOLD

■ INTRODUCTION

Domestic violence has pervasive and devastating impacts on individuals, families, and children. The early efforts of the battered women's movement in the 1970s to protect the victims and their children have been expanded to include legal sanction of domestic violence as well as provision of treatment for offenders, which has become an integral part of the coordinated system response to domestic violence (Roberts & Kurst Swanger, 2002). Despite the proliferation of batterer programs across the country, the search for effective treatment models that assists offenders in living a life free of violence presents a constant challenge for service providers. Currently, the design of most treatment programs for domestic violence offenders has been based on a cognitive-behavioral approach that mainly targets individual characteristics or problems contributing to violent behaviors (e.g. Geffner & Mantooth, 1999; Saunders, 1996) and/or on a feminist perspective that focuses on the sociocultural roots of domestic violence (e.g., Martin, 1976; Pence & Paymar, 1993; Walker, 2000). The resulting psychoeducational programs usually focus on confronting participants and requiring them to recognize and admit their violent behaviors, taking full responsibility for their problems (Lindsey et al., 1993; Pence & Paymar, 1993; Russell, 1995), learning new ways to manage their anger, and communicating effectively with their spouses (Geffner & Mantooth, 1999; Sonkin, 1995; Wexler, 1999). The significant contributions of feminist-cognitive-behavioral treatment approaches in the advancement of treatment for domestic violence offenders can never be overestimated. On the other hand, questions have been raised regarding the effectiveness of such programs from both a clinical and an outcome perspective. A major therapeutic hurdle when working with this population is the issue of motivation (De Jong & Berg, 1999). A focus on confronting participants to recognize and admit their violent behaviors, take full responsibility for their problems, learn new ways to manage their anger, and communicate effectively with their spouses is a theoretically sound approach informed by cognitive-behavioral theories and feminist perspectives; although such approaches may not be a good match with clients' perception of their problems. Gondolf and White (2000) sought recommendations from more than 800 participants of four established batterer programs and asked, "'What about the men's programs should be changed or improved?'" (p. 201). Respondents commented on the critical approach and bashing received from counselors and, in general, recommendations called for more supportive counseling. Dutton (1998) suggested that "the abusive male is easily shamed and tends therefore to externalize problems by blaming others" (p. 160). Treatment that focuses on educating offenders in taking responsibility may be experienced as blaming and may unintentionally result in heightened resistance, diminished receptivity to treatment, limited ownership for one's actions (Linton et al., 2005; Mankowski et al., 2002), and high program attrition rates (Cadsky et al., 1996; Chang & Saunders, 2002).

In addition, findings from empirical studies of the effectiveness of current treatment programs are not conclusive. The recidivism rate of the Duluth Domestic Abuse Intervention Program, based on which the Duluth model is developed, was 40% (Shepard, 1992). Saunders (1996) also reported a recidivism rate of 45.9% for the feminist-cognitive-behavioral treatment models. Two experimental evaluations found batterer treatment programs to be largely ineffective in that there were no significant differences between those who received group treatment and those who did not in terms of their attitudes, beliefs, and behaviors (Feder & Forde, 2000; Feber & Wilson, 2005) or victims' reports of new violent incidents (Davis et al., 2000). In addition, conventional batterer treatment programs produced a very small effect size: .12 for experimental studies based on police reports and .09 for experimental studies based on partners' reports. The effect size for the Duluth model was .19 based on police reports and .12 based on partners' reports. In total, these programs add only about 5% more reduction in reoffense than simple arrest alone (Babcock et al., 2004). Regarding the impact of program completion on recidivism, Bennett Larry Bennett and his colleagues (2007) found that treatment completers did significantly better than treatment noncompleters in terms of reoffense. Rearrests for domestic violence involved 14.3% of completers and 34.7% of noncompleters. Completing the treatment program reduces the likelihood of rearrest by 39% to 62%. On the other hand, the attrition rate is high for these programs. In fact, on average, 50% of the participants never complete the program, regardless of whether they are court ordered (Daly & Pelowski, 2000).

The inconclusive research and clinical evaluations, on the other hand, can be an invitation for service providers to revisit the existing paradigm of treatment for domestic violence offenders and explore alternative treatment modalities.

■ WHAT WE HAVE LEARNED SO FAR: SOLUTION-FOCUSED TREATMENT OF DOMESTIC VIOLENCE OFFENDERS

The Plumas Project Domestic Violence Treatment Program, which originated in 1991, represented a radical departure in thinking and application from the treatment models of the 1970s and 1980s (Uken et al., 2007). Inspired by the work of Insoo Kim Berg, Steve de Shazer, and their associates at the Brief Family Therapy Center in Milwaukee (Berg & Kelly, 2000; de Shazer, 1991), solution-focused treatment holds domestic violence offenders accountable for solutions rather than responsible for problems. Building on a strengths perspective and using a time-limited approach, solution-focused treatment for domestic violence offenders postulates that positive, long-lasting change can occur in a relatively brief period of time by focusing on *solution talk* instead of *problem talk*. Focusing on and emphasizing solutions, competencies, and strengths in offenders must never be equated with a minimization of the destructiveness of their violent behaviors. Similar to other treatment programs, such an approach recognizes the role of offenders in instigating violence against the victims and that treatment programs are a part of the coordinated community response to domestic violence. In addition, the effectiveness of a solution-focused treatment program is contingent on the support of the legal system that provides a strong sanction against violent behaviors. Different from the cognitive-behavioral-feminist approaches, a solution-focused approach uses the language and symbols of "solution and strengths" and does not focus on the problem violence in the treatment process.

Solution-focused treatment offers a beneficial alternative perspective that addresses the clinical challenges encountered in treating domestic violence offenders in enhancing motivation and initiating a beneficial change process. First, by taking a nonblaming stance and focusing on clients' self-determined personally meaningful goals, solution-focused treatment engages offenders in the process of change more readily and enhances motivation by helping them to envision a personally meaningful and desirable future. Second, solution-focused treatment of domestic violence offenders focuses on creating beneficial change in the lives of the clients and avoids taking a social control function that emphasizes holding offenders responsible for their problems, teaching and educating them what is right or wrong. Treatment cannot effectively serve a social control function for the simple reason that therapists are not legitimized by society to control people, but rather are professionally trained to assist people in pursuing a self-initiated process of change. Benefits of using a solution-focused approach that separates punishment from treatment include the following: (a) it is easier for the therapist to engage and develop a meaningful working relationship with the offenders, as the therapist does not play a role in determining who gets what punishment but simply provides treatment to the offender who is mandated or required by the courts to receive treatment; (b) it is more likely that offenders will talk about issues they feel are relevant to changes that they need to make, rather then simply wanting to present a positive image so that they can get the court off their back; and (c) therapists are relieved of the dilemma of having to provide treatment and at the same time being a social control agent (Lee et al., 2003a). Finally, solution-focused treatment is more interested in assessing the context and observable behaviors of individual clients that are relevant in their search for and accomplishment of personally meaningful goals than in using diagnoses for determining treatment because a person is always more than the diagnosis he or she might have (de Shazer, 1994). Traditional diagnostic approaches tend to focus on problem categories that revolve around a person's deficits. Labeling can inadvertently sustain a problem reality in that the facilitator begins to make assumptions based on a diagnosis rather than on the broader reality that reflects who the participant is and what he or she is capable of (Berg & Miller, 1992). By not focusing on diagnostic categories but instead emphasizing contextual, observable behaviors, solution-focused treatment allows the client and the therapist to more easily identify and reconnect with the client's strengths, exception, and resources. Our research has shown that diagnosis is not related to successful outcomes (Lee et al., 2004).

Solution-focused interventions with domestic violence offenders are guided by the following practice assumptions (Lee et al., 2003a, 2004):

Focusing on solutions and strengths: The focus on solution talk to achieve change is supported by a systems perspective (Bateson, 1979). Because change is constant, every problem pattern includes some sort of exception to the rule (de Shazer, 1985).

These exceptions provide the clues to solutions (de Shazer, 1985) and represent the participant's 'unnoticed strengths and resources to address the problem of violence. The task for the therapist is to assist participants in noticing, amplifying, sustaining, and reinforcing these exceptions, regardless of how small and/or infrequent they may be (Berg, 1994).

Utilizing language of strengths and successes: Influenced by social constructivism, solution-focused therapists view language as the medium through which personal meaning and understanding are expressed and socially constructed in conversation (de Shazer, 1994). A major therapeutic challenge for solution-focused therapists is to initiate a "conversation of change" that helps participants to construct meanings and solutions by describing goals, observable behaviors, and progressive lives in new and beneficial ways (Miller, 1997). Solution-focused treatment does not emphasize problems of violence or its history because pathology/problem talk may sustain a problem reality through self-fulfilling prophecies, further disempower participants, and distract them and facilitators from the work of developing solutions (de Shazer, 1994; Miller, 1997). Focus on the problem tends to reify the problem.

Accountability for solutions: Not focusing on participants' responsibility for problems and/or deficits is a decisive way for treatment providers to direct all therapeutic energy toward supporting offenders' responsibility for building solutions. In this program, the solution is established in the form of a goal that is to be determined and attained by individual participants within parameters set by the facilitators. Participants are required to develop a goal by the third session and report on their efforts to reach it in every subsequent session. They are held accountable for goal accomplishment that requires hard work, discipline, and effort (Berg & Kelly, 2000).

Defining goals and constructing solutions: Influenced by social constructivism, solution-focused facilitators view solutions as private, local, meaning-making activities by individual participants (Miller, 1997). Therapeutic dialogues focus on a range of evaluative questions that assist participants in evaluating the usefulness, appropriateness, and feasibility of their goals in their personal lives.

Present and future orientation: In order to hold domestic violence offenders accountable for solutions, treatment focuses on assisting them in their present and future adjustment. The solution-focused facilitator asks questions that help participants to describe a future that does not contain the problem and to identify the first small step they can take to attain a future without the problem (De Long & Berg, 2007).

A collaborative therapeutic relationship: A constructivist view of solutions perceives participants as the "knowers" and "experts" regarding their individual experiences, realities, and aspirations (Cantwell & Holmes, 1994) who determine and achieve goals that will lead to a life that does not contain violence. The facilitator takes the role of an expert in constructing a dialogue with each participant that focuses on change and solution. The resulting relationship is egalitarian and collaborative instead of hierarchical. Such a collaborative relationship also engages participants and enhances their motivation to accomplish positive change (Lee et al, 1999; Murphy & Baxter, 1997).

Utilization as a noninstructional/educational approach: Utilizing and building on participants' strengths and exceptions is a more efficient and effective way for them to develop solutions that are relevant to and viable in their unique life circumstances. The task for the facilitator is to elicit, trigger, reinforce, expand, and consolidate exceptions that the participant generates (Berg, 1994). The facilitator avoids teaching participants skills or intervening in their lives in ways that may fit his or her model of what is good but that may not be appropriate or viable in participants' lives.

■ SOLUTION-FOCUSED INTERVENTIONS

The treatment model is a solution-focused, goal-directed program that includes eight 1-hour group sessions over a 3-month period and is co-led by one male and one female therapist. Program participants include male and female offenders who are court-mandated to receive treatment because of domestic violence charges. The treatment model primarily utilizes goals to create a context for participants to identify, notice, rediscover, and reconnect with their strengths and resources in addressing problems with domestic violence. Goals are a mandatory part of group involvement and serve as a major focus of group activity where change is expected to occur. The major task of the first session, in addition to sharing with participants the group rules, is devoted to presenting and clarifying the goal task for participants. Participants must come up with a goal that they will work on by the third session. They are required to share their goal efforts in each session.

Building on existing literature about useful goal development, we state the task of developing a goal and describe the parameters of a useful goal in the following manner (Lee et al., 2007 p. 4):

- "We want *you* to create a goal for *yourself* that will be *useful* to *you* in improving your life." (Self- determined goal to enhance commitment)
- "The goal should be one that is *interpersonal* in nature, that is to say that when you work on the goal another person will be able to *notice* the changes you've made and potentially they could be affected by the change in how you behave." (Interpersonally related, observable, and specific)
- "Another way to think about this is that if you brought us a videotape of yourself working on your goal, you would be able to point out the different things you were *doing* and maybe even note how these changes affected the other people on the tape." (Goal specificity)
- "The goal needs to be something *different*, a behavior that you have not generally done before." (Different and new)
- "The goal doesn't need to be something big. In fact, it is better to keep it small and doable." (Self-efficacy to enhance confidence to work on goal)
- "Keep in mind that since you will be expected to *report* on your goal work every time we meet so that we can keep track of the progress, it is important that your goal be a behavior you can do at least a few times a week." (Provide useful feedback to gauge progress)

The following five-phase process describes the primary tasks to be accomplished in each treatment phase (Lee et al., 2003a).

Phase One: Solution-Focused Intake Interview (prior to the beginning of the treatment group)

- Initiate a collaborative relationship
- Build initiative for change
- Plant seeds for immediate and future change efforts

- Define the expectations for the group
- Search for strengths

Phase Two: Introduction (Session 1)

- Establishing group rules and structure
- Establishing collaborative relationship
- Giving the goal task

Phase Three: Developing Useful Goals (Sessions 2 and 3)

- Assisting participants in developing useful and well-formed goals
- Assisting participants in focusing on solutions, changes, exceptions, past successes
- Assisting participants who "get stuck" in developing useful goals

Phase Four: Goal Utilization: Expanding the Solution Picture (Sessions 4, 5, 6)

- Reviewing positive changes
- Assisting participants in expanding, amplifying, and reinforcing their solution behaviors in their real life context
- Assisting participants in making the connection between their behavior and positive outcomes
- Reinforcing and complimenting participants' positive changes

Phase Five: Consolidation and Celebration of Changes (Sessions 7 and 8)

- Review goals, evaluate progress and make future plans
- Consolidate personally meaningful change descriptions and/or "new" identity
- Develop connection between participants' actions and positive outcomes
- Acknowledging and complimenting goal accomplishments
- Celebrating changes: Ownership of goal accomplishments

To facilitate the change process, solution-focused treatment of domestic violence offenders utilizes a group of questions that we call evaluative questions (Lee et al., 2003a). Evaluative questions differ from facilitator-initiated therapeutic responses. Instead of directly providing feedback to the participant, evaluative questions serve to initiate a self-feedback process within the participant. Evaluative questions ask participants to evaluate their situations in terms of their doing, thinking, and feeling. The facilitator makes no interpretation of participants' situation and suggests no ideas; she or he just asks good questions that help participants evaluate different aspects of their unique life situation. Evaluative questions operate from the stance of curiosity and convey the message that we believe that participants have the answers; we do not. We videotaped and transcribed all group sessions for the purpose of conducting process research of our program. Findings indicated that facilitators initiated 51% of all dialogues with participants, and 46% of those dialogues are in the form of questions. There is no other language form that we work harder to develop than asking good questions because change occurs when the participants begin to verbalize their search for solutions. Followings is a list of therapeutic questions that we used lavishly in our work (Lee et al., 2003a):

Exploring questions: Exploring questions are commonly asked at the beginning of the treatment process. These are simple questions designed to motivate participants to explore and play with different ideas for developing useful goals. "What have you been thinking about in terms of your goal for this group?" "Are any of these thoughts a possibility for a goal?"

Planning questions: Planning questions help participants to evaluate what action/ behavior needs to be taken for positive change to happen. These questions focus on planning for future action and anticipating what needs to be done. "Is there something you'll need to do to make sure that you stay focused on keeping yourself calm?" "So, how are you going to reach this goal of walking away from a heated argument?" More sophisticated planning questions assist participants in focusing on doing something different from what they have done before. It is also important to help participants evaluate whether what they are doing now as a goal is different from past behaviors. We believe that positive changes are usually associated with new and different behaviors. Repetitive past behaviors are more likely to maintain the problem rather than solve it (Nardone & Watzlawick, 1993). "So, what would you do different to try to get along better with your dad?" "How has being aware of your anger made a difference, helping you not to lose it rather than to say things that wouldn't be helpful?"

Indicator questions: A solution-focused approach emphasizes the establishment of a clear indicator of change early in the treatment process so that participants can clearly know when they have accomplished their goals and can stop receiving treatment. "How would you know that you have accomplished your goal?" "Yeah, but say 2 months from now, you're going to bed at night, and you can't go to sleep, and you ask yourself whether you are still focused on your goal or not? And you ask yourself, 'Am I doing okay? Am I doing what I want to do?' How would you know?"

Exception questions: In the process of developing useful goals, it is helpful to ask questions that lead participants to consider alternatives to their current behavior; questions that ask participants to search for times when things were better (de Shazer, 1985). This type of question is often a "when" question. "When was the most recent time you felt things were going well in your relationship?" Once an exception to the problem is discovered, detailed questions can be asked to help the participant expand on the exception. As implied, these questions ask for the details. "What were you doing then that you're not doing now?" "When did you do that?" "How did you do it?" "How often did you do it?"

Scaling questions: We have found the scaling question a particularly useful form of evaluative question. Scaling questions allow the participant to attach a number value to their evaluation. This is also helpful to the facilitating team, providing a unique view into the participant's vantage point that cannot be objectively defined, such as his or her motivation, confidence, commitment, progress in the change process, and so on. For example, "On a scale of 1 to 10, 1 being that it doesn't matter if you get a job and 10 being that it is the most important thing for you to accomplish, where are you at on that scale?" It is the conversation that occurs after the scaling question is asked that determines and creates the meaning of the numbers.

Effect questions: Effect questions help participants evaluate what they expect to see happen as a result of their behavior and/or goal efforts. These questions help participants think clearly about the impact of their behavior or goal efforts and what they want to accomplish by their actions. "What are you hoping will happen when you are friendlier to people?" "Do you have any thoughts of what you're hoping will happen if you do this?"

Relationship questions (Berg, 1994): Because all behaviors occur in a social context or have social implications, we find it very useful to help participants evaluate the social connections that will support desired changes. To this end, social context questions are used to help expand the solution talk into the area of relationships. Relationship questions ask for the details of the solution as it relates to others. "Who noticed what you were doing differently?" "What difference do you think it will make to your wife and your children as you spend more quality time with them?"

Helpfulness questions: Helpfulness questions assist participants in evaluating and delineating how their behavior will be useful or not in accomplishing their self-initiated goals. We have found this type of question extremely useful. "Was it helpful that you were aware that you were angry?" "What difference will it make to you when your son finishes his homework?" "How will that be helpful?

Feasibility questions: Small, sustainable, and realistic goals or behavior are more likely to be useful for participants than big, dramatic changes, as the latter may set them up for failure. Also, a realistic appraisal of the situation increases the chance of success. "Where is it easy and where is it maybe not so easy?" "Do you think that's too big a jump for you"? "Where would it be easier to start?" "Are you feeling that it's reasonable to do it?" "Have you ever done that in the past?" "How likely are you to be able to do that between now and the next session?"

Connection questions: Change is more likely to be sustained if participants can make an explicit cognitive connection between what they have done and the desired outcome. In this case, change is no longer just a result of luck or randomness. Participants will have more control in accomplishing their goal if they develop a conscious connection between useful behaviors and goal attainment. "So, how did you do that, stay out of it instead of getting in the middle of it, like you used to?" "So, how did you figure out when to stay and when it's time to walk away?"

Meaning questions: When a participant makes a change that is defined as significant, it is useful to help the participant notice and consolidate that change by bringing his or her attention to it. For example, if a participant for the first time in his life cries with his wife, evaluative questions such as "What does this crying mean about you as a person?" "What difference did it make to your wife that you were able to cry with her, do your think?" give the participant the opportunity to attribute important meaning to this event. In most cases, participants will apply positive meanings to their behavior when the opportunity occurs, such as "It means I really do care" or "It means I'm a sensitive person." This allows participants the opportunity to construct who they are and who they want to be.

Ownership questions: We believe that maximum, long-lasting therapeutic gains are more likely to occur when participants own the process of treatment and, ultimately, the successes. When a person owns the change, nobody can take it away from him or her. By asking ownership questions, we create a context in which participants can consciously and clearly verbalize and elaborate their personal decisions and therefore their ownership of the changed behaviors. Ownership questions emphasize the participant as the center of change and as the person who actively makes a decision/commitment to engage in the change process. "How did you decide to do that?" "Where do you think it comes from for you, the commitment?"

■ RESEARCH METHODS

Any intervention will need to be tested for its effectiveness. Bruce Rounsaville, Kathleen Carroll, and their associates have proposed a useful stage model to guide and implement behavioral therapy research. Stage I consists of pilot/feasibility testing, initial manual writing, training program development, and fidelity measure development for the new treatment model. Stage II primarily consists primarily of controlled clinical trials to evaluate the efficacy of manualized and pilot-tested treatments. Stage III comprises studies that evaluate the portability of the tested treatments, such as their efficacy with diverse populations, means of training therapists to use the model, cost effectiveness of the treatment, and so on (Carroll & Nuro, 2002; Carroll & Rounsaville, 2009; Rounsaville et al., 2001). Situating the development of research on solution-focused group treatment of domestic violence in this stage model, the research is primarily at Stage I, where the focus is on feasibility studies and on the development of treatment manual and fidelity measures.

A total of four studies have been conducted so far. Study 1 used a posttest design with an annual follow-up of recidivism data to investigate the role of self-determined goals in predicting recidivism in domestic violence offenders (Lee et al., 2007). Study 2 was an intervention development study in which we conducted an initial feasibility trial using a one-group pretest-posttest design with a 6-month follow-up to examine the efficacy of solution-focused treatment *for* domestic violence offenders (Lee et al., 2003a). Study 3 used *a* qualitative method to understand domestic violence offenders' and their spouses' experiences *with* a solution-focused treatment program (Lee et al., 2003b). Study 4 was an earlier study that adopted a one-group pretest-posttest design to examine the effectiveness of this group treatment model (Lee et al., 1999). Table 11.1 summarizes the research methods of these studies.

■ RESEARCH RESULTS

Table 11.2 summarizes the results of these studies. Overall, the findings provided initial empirical evidence that supported the efficacy of a solution-focused group model for treating domestic violence offenders. Study 1 indicated the positive impact of self-determined goals on reducing recidivism in these offenders. The final model [χ^2 ($df = 9$, $N = 88$) = 7.966, $p = .538$, CFI = 1.0, RMSEA = 0.0] indicated that goal specificity and goal agreement positively predicted confidence to work on goals ($r = .45$ and .20, respectively), which negatively predicted recidivism (probit coefficient = $-.08$, S.E. = .04). Goal specificity showed a direct path to recidivism and negatively predicted recidivism (probit coefficient = $-.82$, S.E. = .28). This model accounted for 58% of the variance in recidivism. Study 2 showed that domestic violence offenders who had participated in the solution-focused group demonstrated significant improvement in relational skills in intimate relationships, as evaluated by their spouses and partners using the Solution Identification Scale from pretreatment to posttreatment; this improvement was maintained 6 months after completion of the treatment program. In addition, there was a significant increase in offenders' self-esteem based on self-evaluation using the Index of Self Esteem from pretreatment to posttreatment; this increase was maintained 6 months after completion of the treatment program.

Findings of Study 3, which was a qualitative inquiry, reported offenders' and spouses' narratives regarding helpful and unhelpful treatment components, beneficial therapeutic and relational behaviors of facilitators that contributed to positive changes in offenders, and learning generated *by* attending the treatment program. Findings of Study 4 indicated a significant increase *in* Global Assessment Scale scores from pretreatment to posttreatment [$t = -17.8$, $df = 70$, $p <.001$] among those who had

TABLE 11.1. *Summary of Research Methods*

	Research Design	Samples	Measures	Source of Data	Statistical Procedures
Study 1 Lee et al. 2007	A posttest design with an annual follow-up of recidivism data to investigate the role of self-determined goals in predicting recidivism in domestic violence offenders	88 court-mandated batterers who attended a solution-focused, goal-directed treatment program 79.5% males and 21.5% females Age: 19 to 74 (mean = 37.5, SD = 9.8) Ethnicity: 87.5% Caucasians, 6.8 % African Americans, 2.3% Native Americans, 3.4% Hispanic Americans Education: Mean 12.6 (SD = 1.76; range = 8–19). DSM-IV Axis I diagnosis: 17 % DSM-IV Axis II diagnosis: 29.5% DSM-IV Axis III: 3.4 (brain injury)	Predicting variables: Goal Specificity Goal Agreement Meditating variable: Confidence Dependent variable: Recidivism	Group facilitators Offenders Victim witness office Probation office District attorney's office	Path analysis using Mplus* statistical program 3.12 (Muthén & Muthén, 2005) to test the relationships between the predictor, mediator, and dependent variables
Study 2 Lee et al. 2004	One-group pretest-posttest design with a 6-month follow-up	90 domestic violence offenders who were court-ordered to receive treatment 85.6% males, 14.4% females Age: 19 to 61 (mean = 37.2, SD = 9) Ethnicity: 84.1% Caucasians, 10.2 % African Americans, 3.4% Native Americans, 2.3% Hispanic Americans Education: Mean 12.6 (SD = 1.5; range = 9–19) DSM-IV Axis I diagnosis: 18.8% DSM-IV Axis II diagnosis: 25.5%	Solution Identification Scale (Goldman & Baydanan, 1990): Relational behavior Index of Self Esteem (Hudson, 1992) Recidivism rates Program completion rates	Partners/spouses Offenders Victim witness office Probation office District attorney's office Self-reports Administrative records	Paired sample *t*-tests Paired sample *t*-tests Descriptive Descriptive

Study	Design/Purpose	Sample	Data collection	Data sources	Analysis
Study 3 Lee et al. 2003b	Qualitative method to understand domestic violence offenders' and their spouses' experiences with a solution-focused treatment program	90 offenders and their spouses	A one-page written assignment by offenders at the end of the group about what they learned from the group. 6-month follow-up phone interview questions for offenders: (1) What things in the group did you find most helpful or unhelpful to you? (2) What did the group facilitators say or do that you found helpful or unhelpful? Six-month follow-up phone interview questions for spouses and partners: (1) In your own words, can you tell me any positive changes in your spouse/partner after s/he participated in the diversion program? (2) What things about the program did you find helpful or unhelpful to your spouse/partner?	Offenders Spouses/partners	An emergent design based on the constant comparison method was used to explore the qualitative data
Study 4 Lee et al. 1999	One-group pretest-posttest design	Study A: 117 court-ordered male domestic violence offenders who attended group treatment at a mental health center	Global Assessment Scale Self-constructed Evaluation Questionnaire on Anger Management Recidivism rates Program completion rates	Group facilitators Offenders Report from local courts regarding recidivism	Paired sample t-tests Descriptive analyses

TABLE 11.2. *Summary of Research Findings*

	Outcomes	Recidivism	Program Completion
Lee et al. 2007	Final model: The final model [χ^2 (df = 9, N = 88) = 7.966, p = .538, CFI = 1.0, RMSEA = 0.0] indicated that goal specificity and goal agreement positively predicted confidence to work on goals (r =.45 and .20 respectively), which negatively predicted recidivism (probit coefficient = −.08, S.E. = .04). Goal specificity showed a direct path to recidivism and negatively predicted recidivism (probit coefficient = −.82, S.E. =.28). This model accounted for 58% of the variance in recidivism.	10.2% (11.4% of male participants and 5.6% of female participants had re-offending records at the victim witness office, the probation office, and/or the district attorney's office)	92.8%
Lee et al. 2004	A significant improvement in offenders' relational skills in intimate relationships as evaluated by their spouses and partners using the Solution Identification Scale from pretreatment to posttreatment, which was maintained 6 months after completion of the program. A significant increase in offenders' self-esteem based on self-evaluation using the Index of Self-Esteem from pretreatment to posttreatment, which was maintained 6 months after completion of the program.	*Official records (n = 90)* District attorney (DA): 6.7% Probation office (PO): 4.4% Victim witness (WV): 15.5% Accumulative (DA, PO, or VW): 16.7% *Spouses/partners' reports (n = 22)*: 13.5% *Program participants' reports (n = 47)*: 2.1%	92.8%
Lee et al. 2003b	Offenders' and spouses' narratives described helpful and unhelpful treatment components, beneficial therapeutic and relational behaviors of facilitators that contributed to positive changes in offenders, and learning generated by attending the treatment program. *Helpful treatment components*: a goal-oriented program with a focus on the positive and on not blaming; learning that is self-focused and noninstructional; fosters new beneficial thinking and behaviors; focus is on small, attainable changes that provide indicators of progress; emphasizes solutions coming from within; a mixed group that includes males and females. *Unhelpful treatment components*: class size that is too big, class length that is too short, lack of discssuion of alcohol *Helpful therapeutic behaviors*: holding participants accountable for reaching their goals and having expectations; asking good questions that encourage thinking; focusing on doing; providing feedback; giving compliments; staying positive; being nonpunitive; being in charge of the sessions; communicating effectively; attending to individuals' needs; helping participants achieve personal understanding *Facilitative relational behavior*: engaging, encouraging, supportive, listening, giving space, being fair, being available, being sincere		

Helpful learning from the group: anger management, developing relationship skills, developing beneficial attitudes	NA	NA
Positive changes in participants as perceived by spouses/partners: improved emotional skills, enhanced relational skills, increased involvement in family, and motivation to change particularly pertaining to addiction		
Helpful treatment components as perceived by spouses and partners of participants: taking responsibility, not blaming, realization of consequences, providing hope, developing insight, focusing on the behavioral change, focus on positive		
Lee et al. 1999	A significant increase in GAS scores from pretreatment to posttreatment [$t = -17.8, df = 70, p < .001$] Evaluation Questionnaire: The average responses for all five items on a 5-point Likert scale were 4 (1 being "strongly disagree" and 5 being "strongly agree"). The items were: group helpful to me; as a result of the group; I will be less likely to use aggressive behavior; group leaders assisted me in learning to manage anger; group members assisted me in learning to manage anger; would recommend this group for others with this problem.	75%	7%

participated in solution-focused groups. See Chapter 12 for additional evidence that supports *the use of* SFBT with domestic violence cases.

Limitations of the Research Studies

These studies on solution-focused treatment with domestic violence offenders provide initial empirical evidence of its efficacy with this client population. Limitations of the studies, however, need to be first acknowledged: (a) The sample size was limited, and the sample was purposive. (b) There was no control or comparison group with randomized assignment procedures to compare the effectiveness of this approach with that of other established models of treatment. (c) The use of self-reports to measure process and outcome variables could be affected by the problem of reporting bias. For instance, participants' self-reports of their confidence to work on goals or spouses' evaluation of the offenders' relational behaviors represented only their self-evaluation, which could be different from that of a third person. On the other hand, self-report is a valid and commonly used method to examine respondents' self-evaluation and understanding of their experience. (d) While these studies used standardized measures for measuring self-esteem and relational behaviors, other variables, such as goal commitment, goal agreement, goal specificity, and confidence, were assessed by single-item, three-level Likert-scale measures. The use of single-item measures would potentially increase the likelihood of measurement errors. (e) Study 1 included only 88 out of 127 participants because of incomplete data on 39 participants. For the outcome study (Study 2), the response rates of participants and their spouses at the 6-month follow-up were about 55%. Although there were no significant differences between the completers and noncompleters for both studies on all demographic variables, childhood experiences, and DSM:IV diagnoses, findings could still be influenced by the problem of measurement attrition (Fraser, 2004). (f) There were problems in measuring recidivism. Study 1 only used official records from the district attorney's office, the victim witness office, and the probation office to define recidivism rates of program participants. Study 2 included other reporting sources, such as the spouses or partners of participants, to measure recidivism. Although both studies employed inclusive criteria to define recidivism among program participants, domestic violence could occur in other forms, such as verbal or emotional abuse, that may not be reportable. There is also the problem of underreporting of incidents of violence by victims. These limitations pose challenges to and raise suggestions for future research regarding domestic violence treatment programs.

Despite the limitations of the study design, the findings of these studies—including Study 3, which adopted a qualitative design to explore the perceptions of group participants and their spouses about the treatment program—offer useful implications for developing practice guidelines with this client population.

■ PRACTICE GUIDELINES

1. Studies have confirmed the importance of self-determined goals in reducing recidivism among domestic violence offenders. The final model of Study 1 accounted for 58% of the variance in recidivism. In particular, goal specificity and goal agreement positively predicted confidence to work on goals, which negatively predicted recidivism. In other words, professionals should help

offenders develop specific goals to be accomplished during the treatment program. In addition, the greater the agreement between program participants and facilitators about the usefulness of the goals, the greater the confidence participants have in working continuously on their goals at termination, which would negatively predict recidivism.

2. Helpful treatment components include goal-oriented treatment; focusing on the positive; being nonblaming; learning as self-focused and noninstructional; emphasis on fostering new, beneficial thinking and behaviors; helping participants to focus on small, attainable changes that provide indicators of progress; and emphasizing solutions coming from within.

3. Helpful therapeutic behaviors include holding participants accountable for reaching their goals and having expectations; asking good questions that encourage thinking; focusing on behaviors, actions, and doing; providing feedback; giving compliments; staying positive; being nonpunitive; being in charge of the sessions; providing effective communication; attending to participants' individual needs; and helping participants to achieve personal understanding.

4. Facilitative relational behaviors of the therapist include being engaging, encouraging, and supportive; listening; giving space; and being fair, available, and sincere.

5. Helpful treatment components as perceived by spouses and partners of participants include helping offenders to take responsibility; learning to avoid blame; and helping offenders to understand the consequences of their behavior and develop insight. In addition, the program should provide hope, focus on behavioral change, and focus on the positive.

6. Unhelpful treatment components include classes that are too big and class length that is too short, as participants need time to process their learning.

■ FUTURE STUDIES

Review of the limitations of existing solution-focused treatments of domestic violence offenders has led to the following recommendations for future effectiveness studies: (a) develop and standardize the treatment protocol; (b) refine and pilot-test an observation-based fidelity measurement protocol for the manual; (c) conduct controlled randomized studies and include control or comparison groups using randomized assignment procedures; (d) use multiple reporting sources to avoid reporting bias; (e) use multiple reporting sources to measure recidivism rates; and (f) carefully monitor the data collection process to reduce problems of measurement attrition.

In addition to conducting rigorous outcome studies to examine the effectiveness of this approach for treating domestic violence offenders, it is important to understand the mechanisms of actions that contribute to positive changes in offenders. Foci of research efforts should include an understanding of the process of change in domestic violence offenders (which is likely to be nonlinear), therapeutic dialogues or processes that contribute to positive changes in offenders, and the social impact of the treatment program on survivors. The use of qualitative methods would be helpful to answer these research questions. Microanalysis is another useful research method to understand how therapeutic communication works in treatment and to uncover the process of change signified by linguistic discourse in therapeutic conversation (Bavelas et al., 2000). Techniques such as interpersonal process recall (Kagan & Kagan, 1997) are helpful in helping participants and/or facilitators capture the critical process or events contributing to positive changes in offenders. It is also important to include procedures, such as a well-designed audit process and member check (Lincoln & Guba, 1985), to firmly establish the trustworthiness of these studies.

■ KEY FINDINGS TO REMEMBER

- The recidivism rate of Study 1 was 10.2% using official arrest records and including all reoffending cases that were reported by the victim witness office, the probation office, and the district attorney's office. The recidivism rate of Study 2 was 16.7%, including official arrest records and spouses' and partners' self-reports at the 6-month follow-up interviews.
- There was a significant improvement in participants' relational skills in intimate relationships, as evaluated by their spouses and partners from pretreatment to posttreatment. This improvement was maintained 6 months after completion of the program.
- There was a significant increase in the self-esteem of offenders, based on their self-reports from pretreatment to posttreatment. This increase in self-esteem was maintained 6 months after their completion of the treatment program.
- The program completion rate of 92.8%
- Goal specificity and goal agreement positively predicted confidence to work on goals, which negatively predicted recidivism. Goal specificity was also related to lower recidivism rates. The treatment model accounted for 58% of the variance in recidivism in offenders, which was 10.2%.

■ FURTHER LEARNING

- Family Research Laboratory, University of New Hampshire; the Web site is http://www.unh.edu/frl/frlbroch.htm
- Solution-Focused Brief Therapy Association; the Web site is http://www.sfbta.org/

■ REFERENCES

Babcock, J. C., Green, C. E., & Robie, C. (2004). Does batterers' treatment work?: A meta-analytic review of domestic violence treatment outcome research. *Clinical Psychology Review, 23*, 1023–1053.

Bateson, G. (1979). *Mind and nature: A necessary unity.* New York: Dutton.

Bavelas, J. B., McGee, D., Phillips, B., & Routledge, R. (2000). Microanalysis of communication in psychotherapy. *Human Systems, 11*, 47–66.

Bennett, L. W., Stoops, C., Call, C., & Flett, H. (2007). Effects of program completion on re-arrest in a batterer intervention system. *Research on Social Work Practice, 17*, 42–54.

Berg, I. K. (1994). *Family-based services: A solution-focused approach.* New York: Norton.

Berg, I. K., & Kelly, S. (2000). *Building solutions in child protective services.* New York: Norton.

Berg, I. K., & Miller, S. (1992). *Working with the problem drinker: A solution-focused approach.* New York: Norton.

Cadsky, O., Hanson, R. K., Crawford, M., & Lalonde, C. (1996). Attrition from a male batterer treatment program: Client-treatment congruence and lifestyle instability. *Violence and Victims, 11*, 51–64.

Cantwell, P., & Holmes, S. (1994). Social construction: A paradigm shift for systemic therapy and training. *Australian and New Zealand Journal of Family Therapy, 15*, 17–26.

Carroll, K. M., & Nuro, K. F. (2002). One size cannot fit all: A stage model for psychotherapy manual development. *Clinical Psychology, 9*, 396–406.

Carroll, K. M., & Rounsaville, B. J. (2009). Efficacy and effectiveness in developing treatment manuals. In A. M. Nezu & C. M. Nezu (Eds.), *Evidence-based outcome research: A practical guide to conducting randomized controlled trials for psychosocial interventions* (pp. 219–243). New York: Oxford University Press.

Chang, H., & Saunders, D. G. (2002). Predictors of attrition in two types of group programs for men who batter. *Journal of Family Violence, 17*, 273–292.

Daly, J. E., & Pelowski, S. (2000). Predictors of dropout among men who batter: A review of studies with implications for research and practice. *Violence and Victims, 15*, 137–160.

Davis, R. C., Taylor, B. G., & Maxwell, C. D. (2000). *Does batterer treatment reduce violence? A randomized experiment in Brooklyn.* New York: Victim Services.

De Jong, P., & Berg, I. K. (1999, March). *Co-constructing cooperation with mandated clients.* Presented at the 45th annual program meeting of the Council on Social Work Education, San Francisco.

Delong, P., & Berg, I. K. (2007). *Interviewing for solutions (3rd Ed.).* Belmont, CA: Brooks/ Cole.

de Shazer, S (1985). *Keys to solutions in brief therapy.* New York: Norton.

de Shazer, S. (1991). *Putting difference to work.* New York: Norton.

de Shazer, S. (1994). *Words were originally magic.* New York: Norton.

Dutton, D. G. (1998). The abusive personality: Violence and control in intimate relationships. New York: Guilford.

Feder, L., & Forde, D. R. (2000, June). *A test of the efficacy of court-mandated counseling for domestic violence offenders: The Broward Experiment.* Executive summary of the final report. Washington, DC: National Institute of Justice.

Feder, L., & Wilson, D. B. (2005). A meta-analytic review of court mandated batterer intervention programs: Can courts affect abusers' behavior? *Journal of Experimental Criminology, 1*, 239–262.

Fraser, M. (2004). Intervention research in social work: Recent advances and continuing challenges. *Research on Social Work Practice, 14*, 210–222.

Geffner, R., & Mantooth, C. (1999). *Ending spouse/partner abuse: A psychoeducational approach for individuals and couples.* New York: Springer.

Goldman, J., & Baydanan, M. (1990). *Solution Identification Scale.* Denver: Peaceful Alternatives in the Home.

Gondolf, E. W., & White, R. J. (2000). "'Consumer'" recommendations for batterers programs. *Violence Against Women, 6*, 198–217.

Gondolf, E. W., & White, R. J. (2001). Batterer program participants who repeatedly reassault: Psychopathic tendencies and other disorders. *Journal of Interpersonal Violence, 16*, 361–380.

Hudson, W. W. (1992). *The WALMYR Assessment Scales Scoring Manual.* Tempe, AZ: WALMYR.

Kagan, H., & Kagan, N. (1997). Interpersonal process recall: Influencing human interaction. In C. E. Watkins, Jr. (Ed.), *Handbook of psychotherapy supervision* (pp. 296–309). New York: Wiley.

Lee, M. Y., Greene, G. J., & Rheinscheld, J. (1999). A model for short-term solution-focused group treatment of male domestic violence offenders. *Journal of Family Social Work, 3*, 39–57.

Lee, M. Y., Sebold, J., & Uken, A. (2003a). *Solution-focused treatment with domestic violence offenders: Accountability for change.* New York: Oxford University Press.

Lee, M. Y., Sebold, J., & Uken, A. (2003b). Brief solution-focused group treatment with domestic violence offenders: Listen to the narratives of participants and their partners. *Journal of Brief Therapy, 2*, 3–26.

Lee, M. Y., Uken. A., & Sebold, J. (2004). Accountability for solutions: Solution-focused treatment with domestic violence offenders. *Families in Society, 85*, 463–476.

Lee, M. Y., Uken. A., & Sebold, J. (2007). Role of self-determined goals in predicting recidivism in domestic violence offenders. *Research on Social Work Practice, 17*, 30–41.

Lincoln, Y. S., & Guba, E. G. (1985). *Naturalistic inquiry.* Thousand Oaks, CA: Sage Publications.

Lindsey, M., McBride, R. W., & Platt, C. M. (1993). *AMEND: Philosophy and curriculum for treating batterers.* CO, Centennial: Gylantic.

Linton, J., Bischof, G., & McDonnell, K. (2005). Solution-Oriented Treatment Groups for Assaultive Behavior. *Journal for Specialists in Group Work, 30*, 5–21.

Mankowski, E., Haaken, J., & Silvergleid, C. (2002). Collateral damage: An analysis of the achievements and unintended consequences of batterer intervention programs and discourse. *Journal of Family Violence, 17*, 167–184.

Martin, D. (1976). *Battered wives.* San Francisco: Glide.

Miller, G. (1997). *Becoming miracle workers: Language and meaning in brief therapy.* New York: Aldine de Gruyter.

Murphy, C. M., & Baxter, V. A. (1997). Motivating batterers to change in the treatment context. *Journal of Interpersonal Violence, 12*, 607–619.

Nardone, G., & Watzlawick, P. (1993). *The art of change.* San Francisco: Jossey-Bass.

Pence, E., & Paymar, M. (1993). *Education groups for men who batter: The Duluth model.* New York: Springer.

Roberts, A. R., & Kurst Swanger, K. (2002). Court responses to battered women and their children. In A. R. Roberts (Ed.), *Handbook of domestic violence intervention strategies: Policies, programs, and legal remedies* (pp. 127–146). New York: Oxford University Press.

Rounsaville, B. J., Carroll, K. M., & Onken, L. S. (2001). A stage model of behavioral therapies research: Getting started and moving on from Stage 1. *Clinical Psychology, 8*, 133–142.

Russell, M. N. (1995). *Confronting abusive beliefs: Group treatment for abusive men.* Thousand Oaks, CA: Sage Publications.

Saunders, D. G. (1996). Feminist-cognitive-behavioral and process-psychodynamic treatments for men who batter: Interaction of abuser traits and treatment models. *Violence and Victims, 11*, 393–413.

Shepard, M. (1992). Predicting batterer recidivism five years after community intervention. *Journal of Family Violence, 7*, 167–178.

Sonkin, D. J. (1995). *The counselor's guide to learning to live without violence.* Volcano, CA: Volcano Press.

Uken, A., Lee, M. Y., & Sebold, J. (2007). The Plumas Project: Solution-focused treatment of domestic violence offenders. In P. De Jong & I. K. Berg, (Eds.), *Interviewing for solutions* (3rd ed., pp. 313–323). Belmont, CA: Brooks/Cole.

Walker, L. (2000). *The battered woman syndrome* (2nd ed.). New York: Springer.

Wexler, D. B. (1999). *Domestic violence 2000: An integrated skills program for men: Group leader's manual and resources for men.* New York: Norton.

12 Solution-Focused Brief Therapy in the Conjoint Couples Treatment of Intimate Partner Violence

■ ERIC E. McCOLLUM, SANDRA M. STITH,
AND CYNTHIA J. THOMSEN

■ INTRODUCTION

Intimate partner violence (IPV) remains a significant social problem—one that exacts substantial economic costs at the societal level and tremendous health and psychological costs for those in whose relationships it occurs. In national representative surveys, approximately 10% of men and women report experienced physical assault at the hands of a close partner in the past year (Straus & Gelles, 1990). See Chapter 11 for a further review of domestic violence as a significant social problem. Of particular importance for therapists is the fact that physical aggression occurs in a significant number of couples seeking outpatient treatment for general marital distress. While O'Leary and colleagues (1992) found that less than 6% of the couples in their clinic sample initially identified violence as an issue for treatment, careful assessment revealed far higher rates of physical and psychological aggression. In a recent review of the literature, Jose and O'Leary (2009) found that physical aggression occurred in 36% to 58% of couples coming to clinics, while psychological aggression (e.g., verbal abuse, threatening behavior, social isolation) occurred in 70% to 95% of couples. Thus, therapists are routinely working with couples who experience IPV, whether they are aware of it or not.

Traditional treatment of IPV has been predicated on a model of a male perpetrator and a female victim in the context of male power and privilege. Male violence was seen as one tactic for establishing and maintaining overarching and pervasive control over a female partner (Dobash & Dobash, 1979); women's violence was seen solely as a response to her male partner's attacks (Walker, 1989). Given this paradigm, treatment was delivered in separate gender tracks. Men were typically adjudicated through the court system and ordered to attend batterer intervention programs that took as their task changing the attitudes and behavior that supported male privilege and control. Women were offered sheltering and victims' support groups aimed at empowering them and helping them exit dangerous or abusive relationships. In this environment, conjoint couples treatment was seen as de facto blaming the victim, at least in part, for the abuse being done to her. It was held that systemic therapies at best diffused responsibility for a man's violence and at worst implied that the violence resulted from interactions that his female partner must help to change in order for the violence against her to subside (Bograd, 1992). Given the admonitions against it, why, then, have we come to develop and test a model of couples treatment for this difficult and emotionally charged social and relational problem? There are several reasons.

Primary in our thinking about the usefulness of conjoint couples treatment is the growing recognition among scholars and treatment professionals that not all violence between intimate partners is the same. A number of typologies of male batterers (Gondolf, 1988; Holtzworth-Monroe & Stuart, 1994) and of relationship violence (Johnson & Ferraro, 2000) have been proposed. Taken together, these typologies suggest two broad types of IPV—one that is characterological and one that is situational (Babcock et al., 2007). According to Babcock and colleagues, *characterological violence* conforms to the common view of IPV; that is, there is more likely to be a clear victim and a perpetrator; dominance and control are primary goals of the perpetrator; the perpetrator minimizes the extent and impact of the violence; and so forth. *Situational violence*, on the other hand, tends to be reciprocal, with much less clarity about who is the victim and who is the perpetrator; the partners do not minimize the violence; and the violence does not serve an overarching pattern of dominance and control. We have found, and others also report (e.g., Babcock, et al., 2007), that situational violence can be successfully treated with carefully conducted conjoint couples therapy.

A second reason for pursuing conjoint couples approaches to treating IPV springs from growing evidence that traditional treatments do not work as well as we had hoped. Male-only groups tend to have high dropout rates—as high as 50% (O'Leary, 2002). Further, such groups tend not to have an appreciable impact on violence even when men do complete the therapy. In a meta-analysis, Babcock and colleagues (2004) found that batterers' groups provided only a 5% decrease in violence over the effect of arrest alone, while Feder and Wilson (2005) found a "modest" effect in well-controlled studies using official records to assess recurrence of violence (a 7% reduction in recidivism versus no treatment). When victim reports were used as the outcome measure, no significant effect was found. Although some participants undoubtedly use their experience in batterer intervention groups to make significant changes in their lives and behavior, the lack of convincing evidence about the effectiveness of such groups certainly leaves the door open for developing and testing other approaches to ending IPV.

■ WHAT WE HAVE LEARNED SO FAR

The Domestic Violence Focused Couples Treatment (DVFCT) program represents our efforts over the past 12 years to develop and test a safe and effective approach to providing conjoint treatment to couples who wish it. Domestic Violence Focused Couples Treatment DVFCT is based on a treatment manual (Stith et al., 2007) and uses solution-focused brief therapy (SFBT; de Shazer, et al., 2007) as its conceptual basis, a choice that we feel is especially appropriate for couples who are coming for treatment for IPV. We believe that SFBT, with its focus on strengths and positive capabilities, might relieve some of the shame many couples feel when they seek help for a problem that is typically hidden from others, including close family members. In addition, by the time many couples come to treatment with us, they have been involved in encounters with law enforcement officials, the court, and other professionals that have focused intensely on the deficits in their relationship. In response, the partners then have to either agree with such negative attributions or defend their relationship. An approach that explicitly addresses areas of strength and competence clears a path for more cooperation with therapy.

While we continue to focus on issues of IPV throughout the course of treatment, we also use the SFBT principle of letting the clients' goals guide the therapy. Early in therapy, we elicit (using versions of the miracle question) the couple's view of what their life would be like without the presence of the problem. We believe that clients must have a vision of their desired future, developed along with the therapist, to help sustain them through the difficult work of addressing violence and relationship conflict. Thus, treatment focuses on the couple's needs and wishes as much as it focuses on externally prescribed goals.

We also find that SFBT is helpful in our work because, while it certainly allows for discussion of the past and of difficult emotional states, it does not require this nor does it direct a focus there. In fact, our understanding of SFBT is that it directs the therapist to help clients elaborate on their descriptions of successes, exceptions, and desired outcomes rather than problems, disappointments, and failures. Further, SFBT does not require raising emotional intensity in the session; indeed, it does not even require the discussion of conflict. Much of the communication we see in distressed couples who engage in assault and abuse of one another involves these very things—repetitive accusations, emotionally intense interactions, discussion of disappointment and failure. We believe that SFBT offers a different channel for couples to use in therapy. We have come to understand that our clients often cannot use this alternative future- and success-oriented channel until they know that we have heard and understood the suffering they have endured in their struggles. Nonetheless, once these issues have been heard, SFBT helps the couple define and move toward a future without those problems rather than keeping them immersed in the very things they are trying to escape.

Finally, we believe that SFBT is a good framework for working with IPV because it emphasizes the clients' responsibility for their own solutions and, by implication, holds them responsible for their problematic behavior as well. This is particularly important in work with IPV, where the issue of self-responsibility is seen as key to change. However, instead of focusing on evidence of lack of responsibility, as is the case in traditional confrontational approaches to IPV treatment, DVFCT looks for areas of responsibility and tries to build on them to hold clients accountable for achieving something they themselves want. In other words, SFBT approaches responsibility positively, in an affirmative manner.

While we have faith that a focus on strengths and competencies is useful to our clients, this approach is often not what the couples expect. During the first 3 years of the development of DVFCT, we routinely interviewed clients during the course of treatment to ascertain their reactions to the program. One male client described his coming to appreciate the solution-focused approach as follows:

> I had put down on one of the forms [postsession questionnaires] that I wanted to see a lot more interaction in terms of conflict, but I'm starting to see this a little differently. The counselors are taking the good things that happen, they are discussing it in the groups, and they are telling the group members, "Something good happened this week. What can you tell the rest of the group? How can you describe to the rest of the group

how these things went, so we can hopefully learn from it?" I appreciate that. I have to admit that's better than saying, "Well, she hit me, he called me a bitch, dah dah dah." That does work better than conflict.

While we were convinced that the SFBT model had much to offer a conjoint couples treatment approach, we were also concerned about the physical and emotional safety of our clients and recognized that, at times, we might need to take a more directive stance in treatment than is usually considered consistent with SFBT. As we grappled with how to meaningfully reconcile the seemingly inconsistent stances of the more therapist-directed approach that we feel is sometimes required with IPV and the less therapist-directed stance that is key to SFBT, we came across Wile's (1993) schema of primary and secondary pictures in therapy. Wile's work allowed us to thoughtfully integrate these two seemingly disparate stances and articulate when and why we would use each. For Wile, a therapist's primary picture is the set of ideas that he or she prefers to work from routinely—"the set of ideas you have in your mind most of the time: even before your clients walk into your office, even when there is no immediate evidence— even perhaps when there is *contradicting* evidence" (pp. 273–273). In our work, our primary picture is a solution-focused picture. Fundamental to this picture is a client-directed orientation in therapy—that is, clients set the goals and guide the process with our help. Thus, we believe that clients bring areas of strength and competency with them to treatment even when they are mired in seemingly endless loops of conflict and distress. According to Wile, however, all therapists also have a secondary picture—a set of beliefs that we temporarily adopt when immediate evidence suggests that they might apply. We would add that secondary pictures and their associated techniques come to the fore when constraints arise that lead us away from our primary picture. At times, we encounter what we think of as constraints that preclude our continued use of a solution-focused, client-directed stance. For us, constraints typically involve a rising risk of violence or threats to safety. At that point, in line with what we believe are best practices for conjoint couples treatment of IPV (McCollum & Stith, 2008), we shift to a more therapist-directed stance. This stance may include such things as directing the use of time out, separating the couple, sending the partners home separately, and so forth. Once the constraint is resolved, we return to our primary SFBT picture. For instance, in a case where a couple reports that during the week they had an argument and the husband grabbed his wife by the arms after she attempted to slap him, we might review the time-out procedure with them, find out what obstacles resulted in the couple's inability to use it effectively, interview each partner separately to assess his or her level of fear of subsequent physical assault, and so forth. In the absence of evidence of ongoing risk, we would then return to conjoint work within a solution-focused framework. If, on the other hand, we determined that the couple remained at risk for further physical or emotional aggression, we would continue to work directively with them until we determined that the risk had been resolved.

■ SFBT INTERVENTION

Domestic Violence Focused Couples Treatment begins with a careful assessment to determine whether a couple is appropriate for our program. We have described our assessment process in detail elsewhere (McCollum & Stith, 2007; Stith et al., 2005), as well as best practices for assessment of couples in which IPV is an issue (McCollum &

Stith, 2008). Briefly, we rely on written assessments and clinical interviews, both conducted individually. Asking couples about violence in each other's presence may increase the risk. We accept couples when we determine that neither partner is being coerced into participating in couples treatment, that both have at least some desire to make the relationship succeed, that neither is afraid of retaliation outside of therapy if difficult issues are discussed in therapy, and when each partner's independent description of the level and types of aggression in their relationship are relatively consistent. Given these criteria, we might accept a couple who described relatively severe violent assaults if neither was afraid that discussing the violence in therapy would lead to retaliation, whereas we might not accept a couple who described relatively less severe violence if the wife was afraid that bringing up her husband's assaults on her might lead him to further violence outside of therapy. We must emphasize that assessment is a cornerstone of our efforts to provide safety for the couples with whom we work. The reader is referred to our other publications for a more detailed description of the process than we can provide here.

Domestic Violence Focused Couples Treatment is delivered in 18 weekly sessions in either a multicouple group format or an individual couple format. In both cases, cotherapy teams are used. Cotherapists provide flexibility in managing risk should it arise (e.g., we can have concurrent individual meetings with partners, if needed, to manage risk). Another advantage is that cotherapists are able to support one another in the face of the emotionally intense interactions in which couples often engage. Finally, cotherapists can model appropriate cooperation and conflict resolution.

The first 6 weeks of the program have a somewhat psychoeducational aspect and provide a chance for further evaluation of a couple's appropriateness for extensive conjoint work. Much of the first 6 weeks is spent meeting separately—either in same-sex groups[1] in the multicouple format or through individual meetings with each partner in the individual-couple format. During this first phase of treatment, each session has a program-determined agenda. In the first session, for instance, we provide the partners time to tell their story and begin to build the therapeutic alliance. As noted earlier, if the clients don't believe that we have adequately understood the difficulties they have struggled with, they find it hard to shift from recounting past problems to envisioning a desired future. The second session is the only session that is conducted conjointly during the first 6 weeks. In it, we use the miracle question (de Shazer, et al., 2007) in the individual format or a modification of the miracle question—the Healthy Relationship House exercise—in the multicouple group. Using an outline drawing of a house on a flip chart to record responses, we ask the clients as a group to describe the qualities that make up a happy home. Like the answer to the miracle question for individual couples, this exercise provides the vision of the future that guides the remainder of treatment. Other topics in the 6-week psychoeducational aspect of the program include basic information about IPV, safety planning, and the teaching of negotiated time out (an interactional version of traditional time out developed over the course of our work with couples; Rosen et al., 2003), mindfulness meditation, and a self-assessment of substance abuse module based on Motivational Interviewing (Miller & Rollnick, 2002).

We have thought carefully about how to integrate a psychoeducational component into a treatment program based on solution-focused principles. Professionally led psychoeducational programs imply that the therapist has knowledge that is somehow superior to the client's knowledge and that the intervention should transmit this information to the client (McFarlane, 2005). Group psychoeducation does make room for knowledge being shared between group members, but it remains focused on the professional leaders as the primary conduits of needed information. This, of course, stands in contrast to SFBT, which assumes that clients have the knowledge needed to solve their own problems if that knowledge is effectively elicited by the therapist. To reconcile this difference, we have developed a stance we call *teach last*. In this stance, we seek first to elicit the clients' ideas, knowledge and successful strategies about the evening's topic, adding the therapist's ideas or information only as a last resort when we feel that vital information has not been contributed by the group.

As an illustration of how the integration of a psychoeducational component into a SFBT-guided program might work, we often use a videotape of the following group interaction. A male client begins to talk in group about how upsetting he finds it when his female partner accuses him of not listening. At one point, he offhandedly mentions that he is showing more self-control in these situations than he did in the past. Noting this exception, the therapist stops the clients and makes the following statement:

> Let me ask you about one of the other things you said; you said that you feel like you exercise more self-control. You went by that pretty quick. But that's a big thing, and that's really, essentially what this first issue is about, exercising self-control, so I want to ask you a little more about that. It's one thing to say, "I've had more self-control." It's another thing to actually—how have you done that? What sort of things have helped you exercise more self-control thus far?

As the client describes his efforts to exert more self-control, the therapist uses this information to begin discussion of the night's topic—the escalation ladder—with the client's own experience to illustrate strategies for recognizing and interrupting the escalation of arousal that can lead to increased conflict.

The initial 6 weeks of the program not only prepare couples for the conjoint portion of treatment by providing basic knowledge and a set of skills designed to increase safety, they also provide a longer assessment period to make sure that conjoint treatment is appropriate for a couple. The conjoint phase of treatment itself more nearly resembles traditional marital therapy either in the multicouple or individual format. In the service of ongoing monitoring and assessment of risk, we have adopted a particular structure for the conjoint sessions that differs from what one might encounter in the treatment of a couple who had not experienced violence. We begin each session with a brief meeting with each partner separately in the individual condition. In the multicouple group, we begin with brief men's and women's group meetings. During these separate meetings, the therapist leads a brief period of mindfulness meditation, asks about any areas of risk or recurrences of aggression that have occurred during the previous week, and also asks about areas of success. We use scaling questions based on the couple's miracles question or Healthy Relationship House visions to assess progress or regress. Prior to the conjoint portion of the session, the therapists confer privately—leaving the partners separate—to determine whether it is safe to proceed with conjoint work at that session. If so, we convene the conjoint session. If not, we make plans to manage risk. In the multicouple format, this may mean that one therapist meets with a struggling couple or partner alone while the other therapist works with the remaining couples conjointly. Throughout the 18 weeks, we make it clear that we may suspend conjoint work for one or many sessions at our discretion. Thus, occasional individual meetings do not occur as a surprise to the couples. During the therapist check-in, in the multicouple format, the therapists also talk about themes and commonalities that have come up in the men's and women's groups. These themes (e.g., handling disagreements about parenting) serve as the basis for the conjoint portion of the multicouple group meeting that night. The couples are encouraged to recognize their commonalities and help each other instead of each couple focusing solely on its own concerns. In this way, group cohesion is developed and maintained. At the end of the conjoint portion of the session, we again separate the partners to check in before sending them home. We want to make sure that everyone feels safe to go home together and that any risk that might have arisen during the conjoint phase has been identified and dealt with.

The work of the conjoint phase of treatment is hard to describe in a step-by-step fashion because it is directed by the clients' needs and wishes. The therapists rely on SFBT techniques like noticing and expanding exceptions, encouraging couples to find out what works and use it more frequently, and helping to punctuate movement toward the desired outcome. Throughout the conjoint phase, we use our ongoing monitoring of risk to determine how directive the therapists should be and when we must shift to our secondary picture in order to increase safety.

As an 18-week program, the goals of DVFCT are twofold. Our primary goal is to help our clients eliminate abuse of all kinds from their relationship. The tools for doing this include increasing responsibility for one's own behavior and a set of behavioral tools taught in the first 6 weeks of the program. The second goal of DVFCT is to reduce the risk of further violence by decreasing relationship distress. Pan and colleagues (1994) found that for each 20% increase in marital discord, the odds of mild partner abuse rose by 102% and the odds of severe abuse rose by 183%. We believe that the focus on the couples' relationships in the conjoint portion of the DVFCT program addresses relationship satisfaction and thereby reduces the risk for further violence. As we will describe shortly, we have some evidence to suggest that both goals can be met for our clients.

■ LIMITATIONS OF DVFCT

We must add several caveats to our description of DVFCT. This approach is not appropriate for all couples who might seek treatment. First, we carefully screen clients to make sure that they meet our eligibility criteria. As noted above, we do not accept couples when one partner is coerced to participate, when either partner fears retaliation if difficult topics are broached in sessions, or when there are major discrepancies in the reported levels of violence. In addition, DVFCT is not appropriate for couples in which one partner exerts overarching and pervasive control over the other.

While couples must want to at least find out if their relationships are viable in order to be admitted to the program, we do not see relationship preservation as necessary for a successful outcome. Some couples decide during the course of DVFCT to end their relationship; our goal then becomes helping them separate safely and, hopefully, preserve a functional coparenting relationship if they have children. Another caveat is that DVFCT is, in fact, focused primarily on IPV. In 18 weeks, it cannot address the myriad problems that couples bring to treatment. Many couples decide, at the conclusion of our program, to pursue other forms of therapy—sometimes therapy that would not have been safe until they had established a nonviolent relationship.

■ RESEARCH METHODS

To date, we have conducted two overlapping assessments of the outcome of DVFCT. The original outcome study (Stith et al., 2004) was funded by a grant from the National Institute of Mental Health (NIMH). In this phase of the study, 42 couples were randomly assigned to either the multicouple group format of DVFCT ($N = 22$) or the individual couple format ($N = 20$). A nonrandom comparison group was comprised of nine eligible couples who completed the pretests and all follow-ups but were not able to participate in treatment for reasons unrelated to violence or therapy (e.g., one couple moved out of state but completed follow-ups by mail and telephone). Outcome analyses were based on those couples who completed treatment ($N = 16$ for the multicouple format and $N = 14$ for the individual couple format).

At the end of NIMH funding for our project, we continued to provide treatment and use a subset of the original set of outcome measures to assess outcomes, thus adding to the participant pool for data analysis. The second wave of analysis was conducted with 20 couples who completed individual DVFCT and 29 who completed multicouple group DVFCT. This group included the couples from the first phase of data collection. The control group for this phase of data analysis consisted of the original nine untreated couples used in the first phase.

We used a variety of measures in this phase of the study; the two most germane to the present discussion are the Conflict Tactics Scale Revised (CTS2; Straus et al., 1996) and the Kansas Marital Satisfaction Scale (Schumm et al., 1983). The CTS2 is one of the most widely used instruments to assess IPV; it asks both partners in a couple to report on the type and amount of abuse (physical, sexual, psychological) that they have received from their partner and that they perpetrated against their partner during the referenced time period. For instance, one item pair is "My partner pushed or shoved me" and "I pushed or shoved my partner"; the respondent indicates how many times each event happened. Three of the CTS2 subscales were used in our studies—the Psychological Aggression subscale ("My partner called me fat or ugly"), the Severe Physical Aggression subscale ("My partner used a knife or gun on me"), and the Minor Physical Aggression subscale, illustrated by the pushing and shoving item above. In our analyses, we used the partner reports, rather than self-reports, of violence perpetration.

The Kansas Marital Satisfaction Scale consists of three items that assess relationship satisfaction. Responses to the three items are summed to form a scale score. Good reliability of the scale has been reported (Schumm, et al., 1983).

■ RESULTS

In the first wave of data analysis, Stith and colleagues (2004) found that participants in the multicouple group format of DVFCT had better outcomes than the control group at 6 months posttreatment, whereas the outcomes of the participants in the individual couple format did not differ significantly from those of the control group. Specifically, participants in the multicouple groups showed a significant reduction in overall abuse—that is, physical or psychological aggression by either partner—compared to those who did not receive treatment or who received individual couple treatment. Similarly, marital satisfaction increased significantly for those in the multicouple groups but not for those in the individual couple format or the control group. This increase was similar for both men and women.

In addition to demonstrating an overall decrease in psychological and physical aggression between partners at 6 months, we specifically examined the recurrence of male physical violence at 6 months and 2 years posttreatment. Male physical assault was of particular interest because it results in more injury than does female physical assault (Brush, 1990; Stets & Straus, 1990). If the women reported (on the CTS2) that their partners had committed any violent act against them, their partner was judged to have relapsed. At 6-month follow-up, using the criteria above, 67% of the men in the control group were reported to have relapsed compared to 43% in the individual couple treatment and 25% in the multicouple group treatment. Recidivism was significantly lower for men who had participated in the multicouple group than for men in the control group. Recidivism rates for men who had participated in the individual couple treatment did not differ from rates in either of the other two groups.

At 2 years posttreatment, we again contacted female partners to assess male recidivism since the 6-month follow-up. Only one woman in the multicouple group condition and no woman in the individual couple condition reported that her male partner had been physically violent toward her since the 6-month follow-up. In contrast, 50% of the control group women we contacted reported further physical assault.

As described earlier, we conducted interviews with our clients during the course of treatment to try to assess their perspective on the changes they had experienced. Examples of some of the replies we received when women were asked what changes their male partners had made during DVFCT include:

- "less likely to violent behavior [sic]."
- "talking more; compromising."
- "My spouse is more sensitive, supportive, and more there for me emotionally. He is making great efforts to lessen stress in my life."
- "no hitting; no bad language."

When men were asked what changes their female partners had made, they reported things like the following:

- "more involved"
- "greater acceptance of different opinions and anger coping mechanisms."
- "understanding me a little more; catching herself when she is getting really frustrated."

The second phase of the outcome data analysis (Stith et al., 2008) extended and refined the findings of the first phase. As shown in Table 12.1, we found that both the multicouple and individual formats resulted in significant reductions in both physical and psychological aggression for men. However, only the multicouple group format resulted in a significant increase in relationship satisfaction for men. The picture was more mixed for women; the individual couple condition resulted in a significant reduction in women's physical aggression but not in their psychological aggression. In contrast, the multicouple condition resulted in a significant reduction in women's psychological aggression but not in their physical aggression. Women in both conditions reported a significant increase in relationship satisfaction.

TABLE 12.1. *Changes in Mean Marital Satisfaction and Aggression Scores of Men and Women Participants in Individual Couple or Multi-Couple Group DVFCT*

Type of Group/Sex	Pretest	Posttest	
Individual Couples (*n* = 17)			
Perpetration of Physical Aggression			
Male	14.29	4.65	***
Female	11.53	4.65	**
Perpetration of Psychological Aggression			
Male	21.12	12.88	***
Female	17.47	14.88	
Marital Satisfaction			
Male	11.12	11.76	
Female	10.24	12.29	*
Multi-couple Groups (*n* = 27)			
Perpetration of Physical Aggression			
Male	11.21	4.79	**
Female	8.75	5.96	
Perpetration of Psychological Aggression			
Male	22.11	14.57	***
Female	17.64	13.61	*
Marital Satisfaction			
Male	13.04	14.59	*
Female	9.48	13.22	***

Note: Perpetration scores were based on partner reports.
DVFCT = Domestic Violence Focused Couples Treatment.
* $p < .05$. ** $p < .01$. *** $p < .001$. All significance tests are one-tailed.

Considering the outcome evidence to date, we believe that there is enough evidence at this point to suggest that DVFCT demonstrates at least the potential to both decrease relationship aggression and increase relationship satisfaction—especially in the multicouple group format.

■ PRACTICE GUIDELINES

Based on our experience with DVFCT and our familiarity with the literature on conjoint treatment of IPV, we have proposed a set of best practice guidelines for practitioners providing conjoint treatment regardless of the model they employ (McCollum & Stith, 2008):

- *Provide a coordinated community response to IPV*. We believe that conjoint treatment should not occur in isolation but needs to be part of a broader network of services including substance abuse intervention, batterer intervention, shelter programs, and so forth.
- *Perform careful screening*. We believe that couples need to be carefully screened before beginning conjoint treatment to prevent—to the extent possible—any increased risk for violence that might occur as a result of conjoint work. Our other publications describe our approach to screening (Stith et al., 2004, 2005).
- *Focus on IPV and relationship conflict*. We believe that conjoint treatment with couples who have been violent must focus specifically on issues of violence in addition to issues of relationship strain and conflict.

- *Adopt measures to ensure safety.* While safety can never be guaranteed, we do believe that some measures can be adopted by therapists to increase safety in conjoint treatment. Specific, regular, and intentional assessment of risk is a cornerstone of our approach, as is changing the traditional structure of treatment sessions to allow for regular individual check-ins with both partners.
- *Provide therapists skilled in both IPV and systemic couples treatment.* Therapists who provide conjoint treatment in the wake of violence must be skilled in both areas. Managing emotional intensity and deeply entrenched conflict demands a skilled couples therapist, while understanding the sometimes subtle nature of power and control in relationships and differentiating that from situational violence requires experience with IPV.

■ LIMITATIONS AND FUTURE STUDIES

Clearly, more research needs to be done. While there is preliminary evidence for the effectiveness of DVFCT, larger studies are certainly in order. Further, we would like to test the model with clients whom we have not yet served extensively but for whom we think DVFCT can be useful—gay and lesbian clients, Latino clients, and so forth. In such studies, it is crucial to include longitudinal data to look at the durability of any changes. We also suggest that a broad range of measures should be used in future studies to examine how and why DVFCT promotes change among couples, as well as what variables may lead to the durability of that change. Finally, we saw in our own work the value of both qualitative and quantitative measures to assess broad outcomes while also giving depth and meaning to the findings. We recommend that future studies of this model continue to incorporate both approaches.

■ KEY FINDINGS TO REMEMBER

- Our developing understanding of IPV suggests that not all violence is the same and that no one treatment approach is appropriate for all instances of IPV.
- Despite historical controversy about its use, we believe the evidence supports the use of conjoint couples treatment for IPV, with careful assessment and monitoring throughout treatment to increase safety.
- Solution-focused brief therapy offers a useful vantage point from which to approach IPV in work with couples. With a focus on competencies and strengths as well as not purposefully eliciting emotional intensity, it provides potential new perspectives from which couples can view their interactions.

■ FURTHER LEARNING

Hamel, J., & Nicholls, T. L. (2007). *Family interventions in domestic violence: A handbook of gender-inclusive theory and treatment.* New York: Springer.
O'Leary, K. D., & Woodin, E. M. (Eds.). (2009). *Psychological and physical aggression in couples: Causes and interventions.* Washington, DC: American Psychological Association.
Stith, S. M., McCollum, E. E., Rosen, K. H., Locke, L., & Goldberg, P. (2005). Domestic violence focused couples treatment. In J. Lebow (Ed.), *Handbook of clinical family therapy* (pp. 406–430). New York: Wiley.

■ ENDNOTE

1. To date, DVFCT has been used only with heterosexual couples, although we believe it could be useful with same-sex couples as well.

■ REFERENCES

Babcock, J. C., Canady, B. E., Graham, K., & Schart, L. (2007). The evolution of battering interventions: From the dark ages to the scientific age. In J. Hamel & T. Nicholls (Eds.), *Family intervention in domestic violence: A handbook of gender inclusive theory and treatment* (pp. 215–246). New York: Springer.

Babcock, J. C., Green, C. E., & Robie, C. (2004). Does batterers' treatment work? A meta-analytic review of domestic violence treatment. *Clinical Psychology Review, 23,* 1023–1053.

Bograd, M. (1992). Values in conflict: Challenges to family therapists' thinking. *Journal of Marital and Family Therapy, 18,* 245–256.

Brush, L. D. (1990). Violent acts and injurious outcomes in married couples: Methodological issues in the National Survey of Families and Households. *Gender & Society, 4*(1), 56–67.

de Shazer, S., Dolan, Y., Korman, H., Trepper, T. S., McCollum, E. E., & Berg, I. K. (2007). *More than miracles: The state of the art of solution-focused brief therapy.* New York: Haworth Press.

Dobash, R. E., & Dobash, R. P. (1979). *Violence against wives: A case against the patriarchy.* New York: Free Press.

Feder, L., & Wilson, D. B. (2005). A meta-analysis of court-mandated batterer intervention programs: Can courts affect abusers' behavior? *Journal of Experimental Criminology, 1,* 239–262.

Gondolf, E. W. (1988). Who are those guys? Toward a behavioral typology of batterers. *Violence and Victims, 3*(3), 187–203.

Holzworth-Munroe, A., & Stuart, G. (1994). Typologies of male batterers: Three subtypes and the differences among them. *Psychological Bulletin, 116,* 476–497.

Johnson, M. P., & Ferraro, K. J. (2000). Research on domestic violence in the 1990s: Making distinctions. *Journal of Marriage and the Family, 62,* 948–963.

Jose, A., & O'Leary, K. D. (2009). Prevalence of partner aggression in representative and clinic samples. In K. D. O'Leary & E. M. Woodin (Eds.), *Psychological and physical aggression in couples: Causes and interventions* (pp. 15–35). Washington, DC: American Psychological Association.

McCollum, E. E., & Stith, S. M. (2007). Conjoint couple's treatment for intimate partner violence: Controversy and promise. *Journal of Couple and Relationship Therapy, 6* (1&2), 71–82.

McCollum, E. E., & Stith, S. M. (2008). Couples treatment for IPV: A review of outcome research literature and current clinical practices. *Violence and Victims, 23,* 187–201.

McFarlane, W. R. (2005). Psychoeducational multifamily groups for families with person with severe mental illlness. In J. Lebow (Ed.), *Handbook of clinical family therapy* (pp. 195–227). Hoboken, NJ: Wiley.

Miller, W. R., & Rollnick, S. (2002). *Motivational interviewing: Preparing people to change addictive behavior (*2nd ed.*).* New York: Guilford Press.

O'Leary, K. D. (2002). Conjoint therapy for partners who engage in physically aggressive behavior: Rationale and research. *Journal of Aggression, Maltreatment & Trauma, 5,* 145–164.

O'Leary, K. D., Vivian, D., & Malone, J. (1992). Assessment of physical aggression against women in marriage: The need for multimodal assessment. *Behavioral Assessment, 14,* 5–14.

Pan, H. S., Neidig, P. H., & O'Leary, K. D. (1994). Predicting mild and severe husband-to-wife physical aggression. *Journal of Consulting and Clinical Psychology, 62,* 975–981.

Rosen, K. H., Matheson, J., Stith, S. M., & McCollum, E. E. (2003). Negotiated time-out: A de-escalation tool for couples. *Journal of Marital and Family Therapy, 29*(3), 291–298.

Schumm, W. R., Nichols, C. W., Schectman, K. L., & Grigsby, C. C. (1983). Characteristics of responses to the Kansas Marital Satisfaction Scale by a sample of 84 married mothers. *Psychological Reports, 53,* 567–572.

Stets, J. E., & Straus, M. A. (1990). Gender differences in reporting marital violence and its medical and psychological consequences. In M. A. Straus & R. J. Gelles (Eds.), *Physical violence in American families: Risk factors and adaptations to violence in 8145 families* (pp. 151–166). New Brunswick, NJ: Transaction.

Stith, S. M., McCollum, E. E., & Rosen, K. H. (2007). *Domestic violence focused couple treatment: Multi-couple treatment manual.* Unpublished manuscript, Marriage and Family Therapy Program, Virginia Tech – Northern Virginia Center, Falls Church, VA.

Stith, S. M., McCollum, E. E., Rosen, K. H., Locke, L., & Goldberg, P. (2005). Domestic violence focused couples treatment. In J. Lebow (Ed.), *Handbook of clinical family therapy* (pp. 406–430). New York: Wiley.

Stith, S. M., McCollum, E. E., & Thomsen, C. J. (2008, July). *Effectiveness of domestic violence focused couples treatment.* Paper presented at the International Family Violence Research Conference, Portsmouth, NH.

Stith, S. M., Rosen, K. H., McCollum, E. E., & Thomsen, C. J. (2004). Treating intimate partner violence within intact couple relationships: Outcomes of multi-couple versus individual couple therapy. *Journal of Marital and Family Therapy, 30*(3), 305–318.

Straus, M. A., & Gelles, R. J. (1990). *Physical violence in American families: Risk and adaptations to violence in 8,145 families.* New Brunswick, NJ: Transaction.

Straus, M. A., Hamby, S. L., Boney-McCoy, S., & Sugarman, D. B. (1996). The revised Conflict Tactics Scales (CTS2): Development and preliminary psychometric data. *Journal of Family Issues, 17,* 283–316.

Walker, L. (1989). Psychology and violence against women. *American Psychologist, 44,* 695–702.

Wile, D. B. (1993). *After the fight: Using your disagreements to build a stronger relationship.* New York: Guilford Press.

13 Solution-Focused Brief Therapy and Medication Adherence with Schizophrenic Patients

■ PLAMEN A. PANAYOTOV, BOYAN E.
STRAHILOV, AND ANETA Y. ANICHKINA

■ INTRODUCTION

Patient adherence to prescribed medication treatment for chronic health problems is a common issue in medical practice. Many efforts and diverse methods have been used by medical professionals to ensure their patients' cooperation with proposed treatment strategies, with varying results and long-term stability (Janssen et al., 2006; Koop, 2007; Starner, 2006).

Psychotherapy and psychoeducation to increase adherence to medication therapy for chronic mental health problems are increasingly becoming of interest to psychiatrists. Many in the field of psychiatric medicine believe that if patients become more invested in their treatment, they are more likely to cooperate with medication regimens (Bäuml et al., 2006; Hogarty et al., 1991). These approaches often involve the patient's family as well as the patient in the belief that these significant others will in some way encourage the patient to take his or her medication.

In our experience, traditionally trained psychiatrists try to make their patients speak the professional jargon of medicine and accept the traditional psychiatric language picture of their own mental conditions. To paraphrase the philosopher Ludwig Wittgenstein (1953, aph.2), psychiatric patients are asked to play the professional language game of the psychiatric trade. This is a difficult task for patients, similar to learning a foreign language. The result is that patients are often confused, resistant, and ultimately less likely to comply with the medication regimen.

We wondered if there was an alternative possibility. Could psychiatrists help their patients adhere to their medical treatment regimen by using a solution-focused brief therapy (SFBT) approach? Using SFBT, psychiatrists could encourage their patients to use their personal perspectives on their lives and problems and, using uninfluenced, everyday language, develop their own goals for therapy, which most likely would include taking their medication.

Using Wittgenstein's view, three different language games, or perspectives, are involved in the usual psychiatric situation: the psychiatrist's, the patient's, and the family's

perspectives.

196

descriptions of the problem situation. These linguistic pictures are usually simultaneously present in the common psychiatrist–patient–family member encounter.

What is

–*a symptom*, that is, a brain disease manifestation, for the psychiatrist,
is also
–*a fact of life*, and one of many personal identifiers, for the patient,
and
–*a set of problem behaviors to be overcome*, for the patient's family.

It is no wonder these three participants in the conversation often disagree as to what should be done next. Psychiatrists usually propose some kind of medical treatment (to justify their involvement in the case), while patients insist on living their lives free of medication, even though this is usually not to the taste of family or friends. And often the family of the patient wants something to be done by the psychiatrists so that the "bothersome" behaviors of the patient will disappear.

"*Patient resists his therapy*" and "*Family does not cooperate*" are common notes in a patient's chart, which suggest the collision of these three very different standpoints:

Psychiatrist: "Your mental disease is . . ., and we will cure it with . . ."
Patient: "This is how my life is."
Important Others: "We want him to behave better."

From a solution-focused perspective, this triangle can be reframed in a new and nonconflicting way: Defining realistic, personally meaningful *patient* goals (rather than those of the psychiatrist), and the ways of achieving these goals, leads to coconstructing the patient's symptoms as obstacles to reaching these goals. Medication then often becomes a "helping tool" on this road toward the patient's goals. This changes the patient's attitude toward medical treatment considerably. When the goals are agreed upon and shared by the family, the conversation is built on a common ground without challenging the viewpoints of both patients and their relatives. No special language is needed to do this, since the patient's goals are always constructed using the patient's own language.

■ WHAT WE HAVE LEARNED SO FAR

Some case examples from our clinical practice illustrate the importance of developing goals that are meaningful to patients' decisions to take or not take their prescribed medications.

Patient A, a 44-year-old divorced father of one daughter, was permitted by the civil court to see her only once a month, always in the presence of her mother. This decision was made by the court for safety reasons, given his schizophrenia. In the course of a solution-focused interview, the patient said that he wanted to see his daughter more often—"at least every couple of weeks, and not necessarily with her mother." When setting goals during his SFBT sessions, he decided that what he needed to do was to find and keep a job, earn money for legal assistance, convince the court that he was in a good and stable condition, and reach a new decision on better scheduling of his meetings with the child. In order to accomplish these things, Mr. A decided on his own that he needed to take his oral neuroleptic medication regularly, and he did so for more than 2 years.

However, in a subsequent hearing, the court rejected his appeal to see his daughter more often. Two days after this was announced, Mr. A stopped taking his medication.

After that, SFBT was reinstituted. Mr. A's primary goal remained the same. It was redefined, however, to convince his ex-wife to let him see his daughter more often, independent of the court decision. The patient considered redirecting some of the money he earned at work from "useless lawyers" to "my daughter." Mr. A decided to resume taking his medication, kept on working, and eventually succeeded in seeing his daughter almost weekly. He is still on his medication.

Patient B is a 54-year old man who was diagnosed with paranoid schizophrenia more than 30 years ago. He lives with his wife. Mr. B had a history of not taking his medication; however, now he does not miss a date for his monthly depot neuroleptic treatment. The change took place after his wife told him some 6 years ago that she would leave him if he didn't take his medication. Mr. B indicated that he wanted to preserve his marriage, saying that he loved his wife and was ready to do whatever it took to keep their relationship going well. In his own words, "My medication calms *her* down, and I want her to be always like this."

Mr. C is in his mid-40s and had experienced six episodes of schizoaffective disorder. He has been in stable remission for 4 years, visits his psychiatrist regularly, and says that he almost never misses taking the prescribed combination of tablets. Sometimes the patient proposes his own dosage change to his psychiatrist, who tries to accommodate his wishes. Mr. C wanted to retain his job as a taxi driver, and keeping his driver's license depended on his adherence to treatment. Driving his taxi requires freedom both from psychotic and/or serious depressive symptoms and from the side effects of the medication. He has continued to work with his psychiatrist to maintain just the right dosage so that he can maintain these goals.

We have noted many similar observations of a meaningful *goal-setting–medication adherence* relationship. We wanted to know more about this relationship and to see if the SFBT approach, when offered as part of psychiatric treatment, would prove useful in medication adherence in regular psychiatric clinical settings. This led us to conduct a pilot study to examine this issue more fully.

Rationale for the Study

Psychotropic medication is part of the standard of practice for long-term symptom management in patients with schizophrenia. The most commonly used antipsychotic drugs are well tolerated and have generally reasonable side effects. However, chronic psychiatric patients take their prescribed medication on an average of 4.6 months before stopping (Lewis & Lieberman, 2008).

Pilot Study

We wondered if SFBT would help support patients in taking their antipsychotic medication by helping them to change their perception of their schizophrenia from an *identity marker* to a set of obstacles or stumbling blocks that can be overcome with medication and thus allow them to reach their specific goals. Solution-focused brief therapy is an extremely popular approach worldwide that, because of its positive orientation, resiliency, and focus on client strengths, is thought to be an excellent approach to increase medication adherence. Numerous studies have shown an average client satisfaction level of 70%–85%, independent of the nature of the presenting problems (Gingerich & Eisengart, 2000; Kim, 2008).

We were fortunate to have had access to patient records at two clinics in Bulgaria, where SFBT was part of the treatment program for some of the patients. This allowed us to conduct a naturalistic observation of the possible effects of SFBT on medication adherence. We had access to patient records before, during, and after their SFBT interventions, which allowed us to do some preliminary analyses.

■ METHODS

Sample. Fifty-one schizophrenic patients (28 male and 23 female) between 19 and 65 years of age (mean, 38 years), who were receiving outpatient treatment in two psychiatric clinics in Bulgaria, and who had had at least one SFBT session, were included in the study. To be included, each subject had to have been diagnosed with schizophrenic disorder (DSM-IV-TR 295.0), be between the ages of 19 and 65 years, and have psychotropic medication prescribed for them as part of their treatment regimen. In addition, each subject had to have taken psychotropic medication at least once prior to his or her SFBT interventions and had had at least one of the common side effects associated with that drug. This was to ensure that there would have been at least some discomfort with the medication, which could have been used as a reason to stop taking it. Each subject also had to have had at least one SFBT session sometime during the course of the medication treatment.

We used a retrospective, naturalistic observation, single-case study with subjects as their own control. We collected data on medication adherence before, during, and after SFBT intervention. Up to 42 years of previously recorded reliable clinical data for the patients were collected from clinical records and from patient and family reports. The patients' adherence to medical treatment was determined by the available information about how often and how long they took their psychotropic medication. The data were derived from (a) the subjects' medical case records (37 subjects); (b) the subjects' own reports (32); (c) their relatives (32); and (d) other sources (4). Each subject was used as his or her own control, as every subject's pre-SFBT compliance behavior was compared to his or her post-SFBT behavior.

Solution-focused brief therapy was provided for each of the patients, along with members of their families, by one of the three coauthors, according to the European Brief Therapy Assocation treatment manual (Beyebach, 2000). The team paid special attention to developing well-formed goals in the course of therapy, using de Shazer's (1980, p. 112) description of workable goals as (a) small, clear and noticable; (b) having details included; (c) described in action terms; (d) appearing to be realistic for the client; (e) describing the "presence/development of something" instead of the "absence/lack of something"; (f) useful for clients and achievable by them; and (g) perceived by clients as requiring "heavy work" to reach them. Medication was discussed in the course of the SF interventions only if patients themselves brought up the subject in conversation. Taking medication was not, therefore, the topic of conversation during the SFBT sessions, nor was it suggested to be the goal of the SFBT by the psychiatrist. Instead, as is the case with standard SFBT practice, the patients' goals were scaled, followed by discussions concerning the times when the goals were met ("exceptions to the problem"), ways in which the patients could move up the scale toward their goals (which may or may not have included taking their medication), and ways in which other persons, such as family members and friends, would know that they were moving up the scale.

■ RESULTS

Descriptive statistical analyses were performed to examine the changes in medication regimen adherence before and after SFBT administration. Before receiving SFBT, the subjects took their medication for a mean of 244 days. After SFBT, they adhered to their medication regimen for a mean of 827 days. This is more than a threefold increase in the rate of medication adherence after SFBT intervention. In addition, at the time the data were collected, 39 subjects (76%) had continued taking their medication (see Figure 13.1).

■ PRACTICE IMPLICATIONS AND SUGGESTIONS FOR FUTURE RESEARCH

The study results suggest that SFBT may have an important role in psychiatry, not only as a useful approach for psychotherapy, but also as an adjunct to medication management. Solution-focused brief therapy with chronic psychiatric patients has the advantage of using the patients' own language and goals. This, in turn, makes the taking of their medication meaningful to the patients themselves.

Limitations

There were a number of limitations in this pilot study. First, while using subjects as their own controls allowed us to see changes that occurred within the patients as a result of the SFBT intervention, the study would have been strengthened by being able to compare subjects *between* groups. Based on the results of this pilot study, we would recommend that, in future studies, an experimental design be used, comparing a group who had SFBT intervention prior to measurement of medication adherence with a group who did not. This would allow greater control of potential extraneous variables and allow for the use of inferential statistics to help determine the actual effects. Another limitation of this study was its retrospective nature, which limited the accuracy of the information gathered. A prospective rather than a retrospective design is suggested for future studies to allow for more controlled collection of the medication adherence information. Finally, a larger sample should be used, This would be determined by the statistical requirements of the experimental design and would allow the

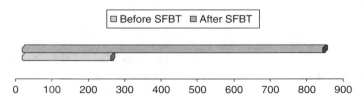

Figure 13.1. Duration (days) of medication intake.

examination of other independent variables, such as different subtypes of schizophrenia, duration of the disease, gender of the patient, and so on.

■ KEY FINDINGS TO REMEMBER

The dominant language in psychiatric settings today is centered on the biology of mental disorders. While mostly useful among psychiatrists in the field, this language is often of limited value when talking to psychiatric patients themselves. We believe that SFBT can be a very useful therapeutic conversational practice with psychiatric patients, enabling them to become more actively involved in their own medical treatment.

Our conclusions are as follows:

- Medication works only if the patient takes it. Therefore, adherence to the medication regimen is an important concern in both research and practice.
- Solution-focused brief therapy may be helpful to increase medication adherence among psychiatric patients.
- The usefulness of SFBT in terms of medication adherence is most likely due to the fact that it employs the patients' own goals and language, uses positive rather than negative language, and is future oriented.
- The pharmaceutical industry may be interested in providing SFBT training for psychiatrists and other medical staff.

■ ACKNOWLEDGMENTS

The study described in this chapter was supported by a research grant from the European Brief Therapy Association.

■ FURTHER LEARNING

The Solutions Brief Therapy and Counseling Centre in Rousse, Bulgaria, http://www.solutions-centre-rousse-bulgaria.org/, and PIK (Psychological Research and Counseling) Centre, in Sofia, Bulgaria, http://www.pikcenter.eu/, are organizations founded on the principles of solution-focused thinking, speaking, and action. New tools and ways of applying SFBT principles in diverse social fields are being developed at the two centers.

■ REFERENCES

Agassi, A. (2009). *Open: An autobiography*. New York: HarperCollins.

Bäuml, J., Fröböse, T., Kraemer, S., Rentrop, M., & Pitschel-Walz, G. (2006). Psychoeducation: A basic psychotherapeutic intervention for patients with schizophrenia and their families. *Schizophrenia Bulletin, 32* (Suppl 1), S1–S9.

Beyebach, M. (2000). *EBTA outcome research definition*. Retrieved 20 June 2009 from http://www.ebta.nu/sfbtresearchdefinition.pdf

de Shazer, S. (1980). *Putting difference to work*. New York: Norton.

Gingerich, W., & Eisengart, S. (2000). Solution-focused brief therapy: A review of the outcome research. *Family Process, 39*, 477–498.

Hogarty, G. E., Anderson, C. M., Reiss, D., et al. (1991). Family psychoeducation, social skills training and maintenance chemotherapy in the aftercare treatment of schizophrenia: II. Two-year effects of a controlled study on relapse and adjustment. *Archives of General Psychiatry*, 48, 340–347.

Janssen, B., Gaebel, W., Haerter, M., Komaharadi, F., Lindel, B., & Weinmann, S. (2006). Evaluation of factors influencing medication adherence in inpatient treatment of psychotic disorders. *Psychopharmacology (Berlin)*, 187(2), 229–236.

Kim, J. S. (2008). Examining the effectiveness of solution-focused brief therapy: A meta-analysis. *Research on Social Work Practice*, 18(2), 107–116.

Koop, C. E. (2007). *Drugs don't work in patients who don't take them*. Retrieved 14 June 2010 from http://www.cadexwatch.com/clinicals.html

Lewis, S., Lieberman, J. (2008) CATIE and CUtLASS: can we handle the truth? *The British Journal of Psychiatry*, 192, 161–163.

Starner T. (2006). *The price of noncompliance*. Retrieved 12 June 2010 from http://www.amcp.org/data/jmcp/JMCPSuppB_JulyAug08.pdf

Wittgenstein, L. (1953/1973). *Philosophical investigations*. New York: Prentice Hall.

14 Signs of Safety and the Child Protection Movement

■ JOHN WHEELER AND VIV HOGG

■ INTRODUCTION

Child protection workers in most jurisdictions are under immense pressure to do a vast amount of work in a very short period of time. They have to work primarily with people who do not want to work with them, people who are angry, resent the intervention, and are skilled at pulling the wool over workers' eyes if they choose to do so. A high proportion of these people are poor, unemployed, without positive experiences of education, and without good role models for parenting. Some of them are engaged in criminality and substance misuse to get by. These are people who, on the face of it, don't have many resources in terms of social support and finance, whose lives can look very gloomy and without hope. Child protection workers enter family situations where they are often bombarded by information, much of which is contradictory; they have to decide very quickly who is telling the truth and what they need to do to keep the children safe. They have to figure out very quickly what's really going on and take actions that can have lifetime implications. If they get it wrong, in the most extreme situations, they face the prospect of being publicly criticized by the media and the government.

On the face of it, this is a particularly challenging environment for workers to use solution-focused brief therapy (SFBT), an approach that usually depends on clients collaborating with the worker and drawing on their personal resources to achieve the future they want. Experience also tells us, however, that successful outcomes in child protection typically depend on workers' ability to stay energetic, hopeful, and optimistic so that they can approach every family believing that they can achieve a good outcome for the children and build respectful relationships despite the involuntary position of most clients.

De Jong (2003), drawing on the experience of adapting SFBT to child protection services in Michigan in the United States, found that "All groups emphasized that it is the careful and respectful exploration of the allegations of abuse or neglect combined with the respectful gathering of information about family strengths, diversity, and resources that is the single most important force for promoting change that ensures the safety of children and strengthens those families in which abuse or neglect has been substantiated" (p. 8).

Our own study (Hogg & Wheeler, 2004) showed us that SFBT can help workers to elicit detailed descriptions of events, balance what is working well in families against what isn't, establish cooperation around shared goals for change, keep the work on track, and ensure that professional power is used creatively to increase the safety of children. A number of accounts further illustrate how SFBT can be used effectively by child protection workers (Berg 1991; Berg & Kelly, 2000; de Vries, 2002; Mylan & Lethem, 1999; O'Neill & McCashen 1991; Walsh 1997).

Full-scale implementations of SFBT without additional protocols in child protection work, however, has been rare. More typical has been the positioning of SFBT in the Child, Youth and Family Enhancement Act of Alberta in Canada (2004), for example, where the approach is recommended for cases with only low to moderate risk.

■ WHAT WE HAVE LEARNED SO FAR

Child protection can be a challenging field in which to carry out research, especially in terms of what can be done and what counts as evidence. Gold standard randomized, controlled studies, for example, can't be done if there is a risk that children in a control group could come to harm. When potentially better practices are discovered, they are usually adopted as soon as possible for the sake of the children who are currently in danger, and when services do find funds to evaluate, it is sometimes too late to measure what was happening prior to the initiative. In terms of what counts as evidence, researchers have typically looked at the impact on practitioners, the impact on families, the impact on engagement between practitioners and families, and the impact on service outcome data: and even this has not been without complications. Good engagement between workers and carers doesn't necessarily mean that the children are safer, for example (Dale et al., 1986). Fewer children being removed from families might mean that workers and carers are working together more effectively to keep children safe, but an increase in their removal might mean that workers have a more detailed understanding of what's really going on and are in a better position to know when to seek the removal of the children.

Sundman (1997) and deVries (2009) studied the impact of training in SFBT on the workers' experience of practice and the degree of engagement with service users. Although both researchers studied workers with typical caseloads, the outcomes indicate that SFBT could have something useful to contribute to child protection.

Sundman (1997) studied the impact of SFBT on 11 social workers in Finland compared to a group of 9 who had not been trained in the approach, using before and after qualitative and quantitative measures. Ten clients from the caseload of each social worker were chosen at random, generating a sample of 382 clients. Social workers were asked to complete a questionnaire concerning each of their clients to explore the current work, goals for the work, and means for achieving these goals. Clients were sent questionnaires to explore the helpfulness of the involvement with the social worker. Questionnaires were repeated at 12-month and 18-month intervals. Each social worker also recorded one randomly chosen interview for qualitative analysis by independent researchers to explore the extent to which the conversation was connected to the client's concerns and goals.

Sundman (1997) concludes that a number of benefits to practice emerged. Clients tended to be more satisfied with the involvement, became more focused on their own goals for change, and tended to be more engaged in problem solving with their social workers. The social workers began with a broader focus and with a greater awareness of their clients' strengths. The engagement was more positive, more focused, and geared towards fewer goals for change, with the result that clients did more for themselves and their social workers needed to do less.

Another important outcome of this study is that some light was shed on the interactions between workers and clients when goals for the work were defined. This raises the important question of what else might need to be in place so that workers using SFBT in child protection can do more to maintain their focus on the safety of the children and seek explanations from carers in a robust way while maintaining a good relationship with them.

De Vries (2009 personal communication), looking back on the training of over 900 Dutch social workers in SFBT, reports on four evaluations of the impact on workers. Of the 70 workers who were interviewed a month after being trained, almost all had started using the approach and many reported that it helped them to be more direct in their work. A significant proportion of them reported that the work was easier to manage; it was also more structured, more effective, and empowering of clients. Many of the 80 workers followed up 8 months after training were found to be more experimental in their use of the approach, with most finding the work to be lighter and more effective. When they were asked to reflect on what SFBT had contributed to their practice, they identified changes in work attitude, increased job satisfaction, feeling less responsible for finding solutions to clients' problems, having a better grip on the conversations with clients, and experiencing a shift from a problem-oriented focus to empowerment. Workers also reported clients being more positive and hopeful, being quicker at finding their own solutions and putting them into action, and being more aware of their responsibilities and opportunities. A sample of workers who completed questionnaires 18 months after training in SFBT reported that they were all using the approach intensively. When de Vries sought the views of 23 workers 3 years after training, he found that earlier changes had been maintained and some had increased. A significant proportion found that their work was more structured, easier, more effective, and briefer, and that they had more grip on their conversations with clients.

Put together, the Sundman (1997) and DeVries (2009) studies suggest that SFBT could equip workers to carry out child protection work in a balanced and rigorous manner. However, there remains a concern that use of SFBT may cause workers to lose their focus on child safety. Child protection services need to be sure that all workers are doing all they can to ensure the safety of all the children in their caseloads. DeVries had trained workers over a 4-month period, which may help to explain the high proportion subsequently using the approach confidently and with a better grip on their conversations. Our own experience (Wheeler, 2005) has shown that the amount of training in SFBT can make a marked difference to workers' confidence in using the approach and may increase their ability to address difficult issues. In child protection other factors, such as the degree of support, rigorous supervision from supervisors, and team morale, are also likely to have a bearing on how each worker uses SFBT with each family each time they meet.

■ SFBT INTERVENTIONS

De Jong and colleagues (2003) give an account of the adaptation of SFBT to Children's Protective Services in Michigan in the United States. In 1999, protocols for using Strengths Based interviewing were developed through focus groups with workers, supervisors, and clients, drawing on what each had to say about what constituted effective investigations and follow-up visits in substantiated cases. Protocols were refined through discussions with workers about the step-by-step processes describing how they went about their work. Further refinements through field testing developed the tools to a point where they dovetailed with existing documentation, including structured decision making, and could then be recommended to workers across the service. These protocols actively encourage workers to be completely clear about the concerns that have been raised, drawing partly on practice wisdom about the necessity of doing so and also on clients' stated wish to know why the worker is involved. While this might seem to contradict the usual emphasis in SFBT on problem-free talk, evidently this adaptation had to be made for workers to be confident that their involvement with families was both balanced and rigorous.

In a similar manner, Turnell and Edwards (1999) had found that while the child protection workers they trained in western Australia during the 1990s were enthusiastic about using SFBT with families, they too wanted a collaborative assessment to keep the work on track. Out of careful discussions with workers regarding what they thought needed to be captured in such a template to be able to make constructive use of solution-focused ideas in child protection work came the Signs of Safety assessment and planning framework, as shown in Figure 14.1. As Turnell (2008, p. 11) explains, "At its simplest this framework can be understood as containing four domains for inquiry:

- What are we worried about? (Past harm, future danger and complicating factors)
- What's working well? (Existing strengths and safety)
- What needs to happen? (Future safety)
- Where are we on a scale of 0 to 10 where 10 means there is enough safety for child protection authorities to close the case and 0 means it is certain that the child will be (re)abused (Judgement)"

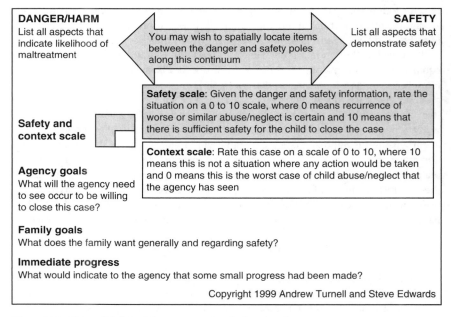

Figure 14.1. Signs of Safety risk assessment and planning form.

Turnell (2008, p. 5) reports that "since 2000 . . . tens of thousands of child protection practitioners have been trained in the approach [Signs of Safety] in Finland, Sweden, Denmark, Netherlands, France, United Kingdom, Canada, USA, Japan and New Zealand." Many have been trained as part of sustained implementations of the approach. The growing use of Signs of Safety in such a variety of jurisdictions has allowed a number of studies on the usefulness of this approach to strengths-based work in child protection.

■ RESEARCH ON SIGNS OF SAFETY: METHODS AND RESULTS

Turnell and Edwards (1999) used questionnaires to take a "before" and 6 months "after" measure to assess the impact of training in SFBT and Signs of Safety on 15 practitioners in Perth, Australia, using a 10-point rating scale to measure workers' self-evaluations of their expertise and skillfulness. They reported that "on average, the group increased the rating of their own practice and role by almost a full point" (p. 200). The study was limited by the size of the group, the size of the improvement, and reliance on workers' own judgment compared to external evaluation. Analysis of the data by the originators of the approach also introduced a potential degree of bias. However, the study did provide early signs that this way of structuring SFBT might more reliably equip workers to use SFBT with balance and rigor.

Sundman (2002) studied a pilot of the Signs of Safety approach in a child protection service in Finland. Several methodologies were used to explore the impact of Signs of Safety on child protection work and the impact on the workers. Self-rating scaling questions were used to ascertain the atmosphere in the workplace, workers' enthusiasm for their work, their concentration on their cases, their ability to cope with their workload, and their sense of solidarity. Workers rated each of the items once every 2 weeks over a 1-year period. The impact of Signs of Safety on practice was explored through single-case studies and semistructured interviews with workers and carers.

Signs of Safety was not found to make a difference to workers' professional lives. Individual differences between workers remained substantial, and where coping had changed, this was attributed to what was happening in their personal lives. The impact on practice, however, was of some significance, with workers reporting that Signs of Safety helped to make the work with families clearer and more goal focused, and made it easier for workers to talk about danger to children more openly with carers.

Interviews with workers and carers indicated that the working relationships had become more open. Some workers did comment, however, that it was difficult to make agreements with carers when goals were conflicting, and the model was impossible to use with carers who were mentally unstable or in situations where children had to be removed immediately. Sundman (2002) judged that a significant benefit from the piloting of Signs of Safety was that workers were finding time to reflect, and that the learning of new skills had facilitated a degree of personal processing.

The overall approach was action research, with the study developing and evolving over time as different stages of the pilot came about and as different lines of inquiry emerged. This made it possible for the research to be an integral part of the embedding of Signs of Safety in the service. A limitation of this study is that the manager who initiated the pilot was also directly involved in exploring the impact of Signs of Safety on practice and on workers, which may have biased the interpretation of data and influenced the degree to which workers could be open about their experience.

Westbrock (2006) used a qualitative design to evaluate the impact of Signs of Safety in Carver County, Minnesota, in the United States. Child Protective Services supervisors interviewed nine parents who had undergone two separate child protection assessments using a schedule designed by Westbrock to explore the client–worker relationship from the perspective of the clients and any differences they saw between the two assessments each family had experienced. The first assessment utilized a traditional model, while the second occurred 6 months later—after workers had been trained in Signs of Safety. Interviews were audio recorded and passed to Westbrock for analysis. Data were analyzed according to themes discerned by Westbrock from a review of the literature as being important in creating a positive working relationship: Did the respondents feel understood and respected by the assessment worker? Did the respondents feel that the assessment worker was honest about the process? Did the respondents feel that they had input and choices concerning the assessment? Did the respondents know what the agency wanted for case closure? Westbrock also explored whether or not the respondents had noticed a difference between the two assessments.

Seven of the nine respondents did report differences between the first and second assessments, indicating an improvement in the working relationship and noting in particular that workers were more caring, taking their time, explaining more, not judging, being more personable, being warmer, listening more, being more patient, offering more options, and being less intrusive. In some cases, respondents had been assessed both times by the same worker, which meant that the changes had taken place within the worker. Westbrock saw this as "strong evidence that the implementation of Signs of Safety appears to have had a positive impact on the delivery of child protective services in Carver County" (2006, p. 43).

Westbrock (2006) notes several limitations to the study. The interviewers all had a potential vested interest in the results of the outcome of the interviews, and respondents may not have felt completely comfortable giving honest answers to a representative of the agency that had recently investigated abuse in their family. The study did not test for interrater reliability, and the accuracy of the information obtained by the respondents depended on their ability to recall the experience of the earlier assessment. Finally, at the time of the study, Signs of Safety was still a new approach that was not yet well integrated into local practice, so this may not have been a fair test.

Appleton and Weld (2005) reported on a national initiative in New Zealand to find out how strengths-based practice (SBP) could be applied to the Child Youth and Family Services (CYF), the National Child Protection Agency, and the part played by Signs of Safety. The initiative was jointly sponsored by the CEO and the Chief Social Worker of CYF in New Zealand. The project team chose a "learning lab" approach to test the application of SBP, defined by the project as "a practice development process driven by the frontline staff, where they are invited to co-create the practice approach, within the parameters defining it, with the project team" (Jack et al., 2005, p.11). Tauranga, one of New Zealand's fastest-growing cities, was chosen as a test site, and training in SBP, Signs of Safety, and other strengths-based frameworks was delivered to front-line workers, including five teams of social workers and their supervisors. Facilitators were trained to use Signs of Safety to structure action reflection sessions, which were held regularly every fortnight for approximately 2 hours for a period of several months.

Two qualitative evaluations were completed by independent researchers Hall (2004) and Latham (2004). The evaluations drew on semistructured face-to-face interviews with workers, access to case notes, and interviews with partner agencies such as police, the courts, and nongovernmental organizations to seek their views on the practice.

The following comments specific to Signs of Safety emerged (Appleton & Weld, 2005, p. 25):

[W]orkers described Signs of Safety as a useful framework for addressing the danger and harm factors in a case and clarifying the concerns, especially for the more difficult cases and during periods of crisis; Signs of Safety was considered to be a useful way to gather information, assess it and to help create a plan; workers particularly mentioned how the use of scaling questions in Signs of Safety helped them to measure change and ascertain the level of safety.

The overall conclusion was that it was reasonable to assume that a strengths-based approach had provided a viable framework for effective child protection practice in a statutory organization. This was based on the following findings: SBP was well received and enthusiastically applied by staff in Tauranga, and was known to be contributing to staff recruitment and retention; staff morale improved, and there was clear support for the approach from staff members, management, and community providers; SBP was assisting staff to organize and structure practice toward a focus on the safety and well-being of children and the involvement of their families in generating outcomes even when the ultimate sanction of removing a child was necessary; SBP was complementing the agency protocols that workers needed to use; there was a steady increase in Family/Whanau agreements where there were concerns about the likely danger and harm to children; an increase in the use of voluntary agreements as opposed to custody orders was noted, with more families willingly placing their children in care where this was necessary and working on reunification plans.

Turnell and colleagues (2007) used a single-case design to explore the workings of Signs of Safety in a metropolitan borough in Gateshead, UK from the point of view of the worker, her manager, and the parents. The mother had contacted Social Services when she became pregnant, knowing that she might not be able to keep the baby because seven previous children had been adopted when she and her husband had lived elsewhere. Signs of Safety had contributed to an assessment that there were grounds for the parents and baby to be further assessed in a residential facility rather than to have the baby removed at birth. Turnell and colleagues used a Grounded Theory approach to explore and describe the worker's decision-making process, the manner in which Signs of Safety organized her thinking, and the role taken by her manager. They also used a Grounded Theory approach with the parents to explore their experience of the assessment. The interview with the parents was carried out when the child was almost 2 years old and thriving in her parents' care. The interviews with the worker and carers indicated that the practice had been founded on a working relationship in which the parents felt understood and respected; the worker had been able to maintain a "purposive focus," including a rigorous focus on the child safety concerns balanced by recognition of the parents' strengths and changes; honesty from the worker from the outset about the possibility of the parents either keeping or losing their child; hope and a sense of opportunity for the parents; and careful attention by the worker to maintain the working relationship at a time when the parents were highly anxious. The interview with the manager highlighted the worker's thorough reading of documentary materials to juxtapose risk and safety factors; her use of team consultation using Signs of Safety as a shared framework, ensuring that her professional judgment was based on available evidence; and the manager's encouragement of the worker's confidence and competence balanced with a readiness to provide a safety net when necessary.

As this examination of the contribution of Signs of Safety to a particular case was carried out by the originator of the approach, along with a worker and a manager who were both committed to using the approach, there is an inevitable degree of bias. However, while the parents may have been biased toward speaking positively about members of a service that had supported them in keeping their child, they were not necessarily expected to be loyal to the approach used to assess them. So, when the parents commented on features taken to be typical of the approach, they could be said to be doing so with a degree of independence.

Keddell (2009 personal communication), from the Department of Social Work and Community Development of the University of Otago in New Zealand, is currently examining social workers' decision making and judgment in child protection, asking social workers about how they use the Signs of Safety approach and how it contributes to the decisions they make. Keddell has also interviewed a small number of children and young people, parents, and foster parents, asking them about their perceptions and input into the decisions made about their families. Keddell hopes to shed light on the following issues: How does the Signs of Safety approach affect social workers' information gathering, reasoning, case interpretation, and attribution of meaning? How does the Signs of Safety approach affect the ability of social workers and clients to form collaborative working relationships (including perceptions of clients and social workers)? How do collaborative working relationships, based on the Signs of Safety approach, influence the creation of agreed-upon meanings? How do these meanings in turn influence decisions, and what are the consequences of this for children, families, social workers, and ongoing relationships?

Preliminary findings are pointing to the importance of the worker–client relationship as mediating the decisions made, in particular the relative riskiness or safety of these decisions. Signs of Safety provides a particular way of informing collaborative relationships and showing respectful attitudes to clients. It allows clients to position themselves as competent within the worker–client relationship. This assists parents in demonstrating safety and tends to contribute to client engagement.

Between 2005 and 2008 in Denmark, the Borough of Copenhagen Child and Family Services undertook a 3-year training program and implementation of the Signs of Safety approach and SFBT skills throughout all social services offices, involving almost 380 workers in three successive 1-year programs. The project has been independently evaluated by Holmgård Sørensen (2009), who interviewed 171 workers. Of the workers involved in the project, 87% reported that the training had changed their work with families with children at risk; 75% of workers reported that the approach provided more useful tools and skills set than were previously available; 72% reported an increased focus on the family's resources; 55% reported greater inclusion of families' strategies and solutions; and 49% noticed that they were giving families more responsibility. The Signs of Safety framework had created more purposive, positive meetings with colleagues and families for 96% of the workers, and 79% reported regular use of Signs of Safety at team meetings. Also, 69% of the workers reported that they were using Signs of Safety together with families, and 66% were using it at network meetings with other professionals. Finally, 88% of the workers reported that the training had increased their sense of the professionalism and the quality of their work, in particular increasing constructive communication with families, decreasing their sense of isolation, and increasing their engagement in their work.

Three Child Protection social work teams of a County Children and Young Peoples Services in the United Kingdom have been trained in SFBT and Signs of Safety as a pilot, and the impact of this training has been evaluated prior to a countywide rollout (Alcock et al., 2009). The success of the pilot was measured against three success criteria: children are safe/safety is improved; relationships are respectful; and there is a shared understanding of concerns. The views of children, young people, social workers, and members of other services were initially sought through a series of scaling questions. The questions concerned three child protection involvements with each of the trained teams and two with a team who had not been trained as a control group. The interviews were carried out by four social workers, one from each of the trained teams and one from the control group, each exploring the work of a team in a different area from where they worked. The results were independently analyzed, and the research was supported by the Children's Workforce Development Council, a U.K. government agency. Preliminary findings are as follows: children and young people did not understand Signs of Safety as well as adults, and it might be useful to have a different template for them; Signs of Safety had encouraged children and families to participate in the process of resolving difficulties in their lives; outcomes for families appeared to have improved as a result of using Signs of Safety; and there was some evidence that Signs of Safety helped agencies to work together, though there was a need to share the methods, goals, and techniques of the approach more fully with partner agencies.

A limitation to this evaluation is that teams in the study group were left to choose which families to name for interviews, which left them open to nominate families who had been most engaged with Signs of Safety. The strengths of the evaluation are that the results were compared against a control group and the evaluation drew on the views of partner agencies and the children themselves.

Case Outcome Data Sets

Currently, two data sets have emerged from services using Signs of Safety that can be used to deduce the potential impact on clients with regard to case outcomes.

Turnell (2008, pp. 6–7) reports that "Olmsted County Child and Family Services (OCCFS) have utilised their version of Signs of Safety to organise all child protection casework since 2000. . . . In the 12 years to 2007 during a period in which OCCFS has tripled the number of children the agency works with, the agency has halved the proportion of children taken into care and halved the number of families taken before the courts. . . . It would be possible to suggest that this may be the result of a system that is focused on cost cutting or is lax on child abuse except that in 2006 and 2007 the county recorded a recidivism rate of 2% as measured through state and federal audit with the expected federal standard in the US being 6.7%." These are clearly impressive outcomes, and Signs of Safety has played a part. However, as Turnell acknowledges, these outcomes have occurred in a context of radical changes to the structuring of teams, case conferencing, and court proceedings. Consequently, it is difficult to ascertain the extent to which the outcomes correlate with the use of Signs of Safety in particular.

Turnell (2008, p. 7) also reports that "Carver County Community Social Services (CCCSS) began implementing Signs of Safety in late 2004 . . . and some trends were emerging. In 2004 and 2005 the Carver system terminated parental rights in 21 families, in 2006/7 only four families experienced the ultimate sanction. . . . Carver's out of home placements and children in long term care has been trending downwards over the past two years but it is too early to say whether this trend is significant and will be maintained. The next two to three years will be critical in ascertaining whether the

Signs of Safety implementation at CCCSS is having a significant impact in casework data." Koziolek (2009 personal communication) notes that the number of children being placed as a result of a maltreatment report in Carver County is about half what it was before the service started using Signs of Safety. Analysis of the number of children involved in new placements within 60 days of a child protection assessment has shown a significant decrease from 2006 on, with placements in 2006 being 57, those in 2007 being 35, and those in 2008 being 26.

A 3-year period is too small a time frame to be certain about the direction of an outcome trend, and in an organization as large as a child welfare service, it is possible that many other factors could be responsible for this change. However, the findings so far have encouraged the service to develop its use of Signs of Safety.

■ PRACTICE GUIDELINES

- Equipping child protections workers with relevant practice tools helps them face the challenges of their work with enthusiasm and hope for good outcomes for the children. Studies are showing that training in SFBT can equip workers to some extent. Most studies are showing that the impact of SFBT and the sustainability of the outcomes are increased when workers are provided with congruent frameworks and protocols such as the Signs of Safety.
- When child protection workers discuss service concerns in a clear, nonjudgmental manner, clients are more likely to share these concerns and commit themselves to goals for change that address concerns about the safety of their children. Studies are showing that this can sometimes be achieved when workers use SFBT in a skillful manner, but it is more likely to happen when workers use a framework such as the Signs of Safety, clearly naming and exploring current dangers.
- When child protection workers actively seek the views of clients, the degree of engagement increases even when the clients would prefer not to be involved with the service. Studies are showing that training workers in SFBT helps to increase engagement to an extent, but that this is increased still further when workers use a framework such as the Signs of Safety to map the conversations and ongoing work in a joint and focused manner.
- Signs of Safety and SFBT are not specifically targeted at eliciting the voice of the child during the course of child protection assessment and intervention. New Zealand practitioners Nicki Weld and Maggie Greening (Weld, 2008; Weld & Greening2005), inspired by the Signs of Safety framework and strengths-based ideas, created a tool called the Three Houses (using drawn Houses of "Worries," "Good Things," and "Dreams") to achieve this objective. Nicki Weld presented the Three Houses tool and process at the first Signs of Safety Gathering in 2005, and Andrew Turnell has trained many in its use around the world. Since that time, child protection practitioners have been consistently reporting that this tool offers them a practical and powerful means for bringing the child's voice into the Signs of Safety assessment and planning processes (Weld, 2008).
- When child protection workers use a coherent framework to assess risk and plan action, there is a greater likelihood that other services with concerns for children's safety will be able to use that framework to add their voice in a constructive manner to the risk assessment and action planning. Studies are showing early

signs that when Signs of Safety is used in network meetings, services are better able to work together and in partnership with clients.

- When child protection services embrace a strengths-based approach to practice throughout the organization, workers are more likely to deliver balanced and rigorous service, compared to training initiatives that only equip workers with new skills and protocols. Studies are showing that when implementations put in place a parallel process, whereby supervisors and managers are trained to use solution-focused supervision, as in Michigan, or appreciative inquiry, as in several Signs of Safety implementations, it is much more likely that workers will develop and sustain SBP with confidence and creativity.

■ LIMITATIONS

While results are promising, each study performed to date has limitations. Early studies and some more recent ones draw on small samples, though, as interest in the approach has grown, larger studies have become feasible. Many have been conducted by people who have supported the approach, who have trained practitioners, or are at least sympathetic. In some of the studies, however, efforts have clearly been made to ensure a degree of independence. Early studies had explored the impact of solution-focused methods on generic caseloads, making it difficult to tease out the impact on child protection in particular. Over time, interest has focused more specifically on implementations in child protection services, allowing more opportunity to draw setting-specific conclusions. Service data sets, while providing encouraging outcomes, draw on complex environments with many variables that make it difficult to draw definite conclusions about the causal connections between how practitioners have been trained and what happens to the children with whom they have worked.

■ FUTURE STUDIES

Legislatures with systems in place to log changes in child protection service outcomes over time could provide more long-term evidence of the differences that emerge when workers are equipped to use SFBT and Signs of Safety. While the interpretation of the changes in such data may not always be straightforward, this would make a useful contribution to the overall picture of what might be improving when workers use these approaches.

Workers play a pivotal role in the delivery of child protection services. Further studies on how SFBT and Signs of Safetu impact on workers and how this impact shows up over time would help services to understand how best to equip workers to meet the complex challenges they face.

Overall, the clarification of what works well in child protection is likely to depend on the readiness of services and researchers to make good use of the opportunities that are available or could be made available fairly easily, and this may be different from setting to setting. For some, it may involve using existing outcome data or exploring the impact on workers, as identified above. For others, it may involve capturing the rich practice wisdom that emerges from single-case studies. For some, it may be finding methodologies that service users are willing to use to shed light on their experiences. For others, it may be through realizing, as in Westbrock's (2006) study, that an opportunity has arisen to carry out "before" and "after" measurements. Put together, a variety of methodologies will then help to generate a fuller picture of what SFBT and Signs of Safety can contribute to child protection practice.

■ KEY FINDINGS TO REMEMBER

- The SFBT approach and Signs of Safety appear to offer workers a specific set of skills for engaging clients that they value.
- The SFBT approach and skill set appear most useful to child protection workers when integrated within protocols that allow and guide them in solution building in direct relation to child safety concerns.
- The SFBT approach, particularly when offered to child protection workers in a way that integrates problem exploration with solution building, appears to consistently enhance their capacity to involve clients more directly in the casework and increases their sense of satisfaction with the work.
- The SFBT methods, underpinned by the framework of Signs of Safety, when used within a sustained systemwide implementation, such as is occurring in Olmsted and Carver counties in Minnesota, appears to make a significant difference in case outcome data.

■ ACKNOWLEDGMENTS

To Andrew Turnell for supporting us throughout our writing of this chapter and offering us ideas from his extensive experience of developing Signs of Safety and supporting implementations in many places.

To child protection workers making a difference in the lives of children.

■ FURTHER LEARNING

The main Web site for the Signs of Safety approach is http://www.signsofsafety.net. The Web site for documents developed in Michigan Child Protective Services is http://www.SFBTA.org/trainingdl.html.

Turnell A. & Edwards S. (1999). Signs of Safety: A safety and solution oriented approach to child protection casework, New York: WW Norton.

■ REFERENCES

Alcock, H., Wilcockson, S., Donaldson, G., & Barnes, J. (2009). *Does the Signs of Safety Social Work model focus upon highlighting strengths as well as difficulties, improve the participation of and outcomes for children and their families whilst ensuring that agencies adopt integrated, common approaches?* Children's Workforce Development Council,London HMSO.

Appleton, C., & Weld, N. (2005). *The journey of strengths-based practice and integration of the Signs of Safety tool within the Learning Lab at Tauranga service delivery site for the Department of Child Youth and Family Services, New Zealand.* Presented at the Signs of Safety Gathering, Gateshead, England, August 2005.

Berg, I. K. (1991). *Family preservation: A brief therapy workbook.* London: Brief Therapy Press.

Berg, I. K., & Kelly, S. (2000). *Building solutions in child protective services.* New York: Norton.

Child, Youth and Family Enhancement Act. (2004). Retrieved from http://www.southwestalbertacfsa.gov.ab.ca/home/514.cfm

Dale, P., Davies, M., Morrison, T., & Walters, J. (1986). *Dangerous families: Assessment and treatment of child abuse.* London: Tavistock.

De Jong, P. (2003). *Field guide for Strengths-Based Interviewing protocols for use in CPS investigations and safety/service planning, and CPS follow-up contacts. State of Michigan Children's Protective Services.* Retrieved from http://www.sfbta.org/handouts/field.pdf on 14.4.09.

DeVries, S. (2002). Kortdurende oplossingsgerichte therapie. *Maatwerk, 3,* 15–20.

Hall, K. (2004, July). *Evaluation of strengths-based practice for Child Youth and Family. Qualitative report.* Wellington, New Zealand: Kathryn Hall Research and Evaluation Limited.

Hogg, V., & Wheeler, J. (2004). Miracles R them: Solution-focused practice in a social services duty team. *Practice: The News Magazine for the British Association of Social Workers, 16*(4), 299–314.

Holmgård Sørensen, T. (2009). *Familien I Centrum, Socialcentrenes Implementering af Løsningsfokuserede Metoder, Mål og Rammekontoret for Børn og Familier(The Family in Focus, Social service centre for implementation of Solution-focused methodologies, gol orientations of the office for children and families)P.* Socialforvaltningen (Social Services Department), Københavns Kommune Copenhagen, Denmark.

Latham, J. (2004). *The Tauranga experience—a qualitative evaluation of the development of strengths based practice for statutory social work by Child Youth and Family Tauranga,.* Palmerston, North New Zealand: School of Sociology, Social Policy and Social Work, Massey University.

Mylan, T., & Letham, J. (1999). *Searching for strengths in child protection assessment: From guidelines to practice.* London: Brief Therapy Press.

O'Neill, D., & McCashen, W. (1991). Competency based family support: Brief therapy as a tool in goal setting and family valuing in child protection work. *Family Therapy Case Studies, 6*(2), 3–12.

Sundman, P. (1997). Solution-focused ideas in social work. *Journal of Family Therapy, 19*(2), 159–172.

Sundman, P. (2002, July). *How to get an evaluation process going in social* work. Presented at the Fourth International Conference Evaluation for Practice, Tampere, Finland.

Turnell, A. (2008). *Adoption of Signs of Safety as the Department for Child Protection's child protection practice framework: Background paper.* Internal report. Department for Child Protection, Western Australia. Retrieved from http://www.signsofsafety.net/?q=node/54 on 14.4.09.

Turnell, A. (in press). *Building safety in child protection practice:. working with a strengths and solution-focus in an environment of risk,* London: Palgrave.

Turnell, A., & Edwards, S. (1999). *Signs of Safety: A safety and solution oriented approach to child protection casework.* New York: Norton.

Turnell, A., Elliott, S., & Hogg, V. (2007). Compassionate, safe and rigorous child protection practice with parents of adopted children. *Child Abuse Review, 16*(2), 108–119.

Walsh, T. (Ed.). (1997). *Solution focused child protection— towards a positive frame for social work practice.* Dublin: University of Dublin Press.

Weld, N. (2008). The three houses tool: Building safety and positive change. In M. Calder (Ed.), *Contemporary risk assessment in safeguarding children* (pp.224-231). Lyme Regis, England: Russell House.

Weld, N., & Greening, M. (2005Issue 29, December). The three houses: A new tool for gathering information. *Social Work Now,* 34–37.

Westbrock, S. (2006). Utilizing the Signs of Safety framework to create effective relationships with child protection service recipients. St. Paul, MN: MSW Clinical Research, University of St. Thomas.

Wheeler, J. (2005). *Summary account of the delivery of Solution Focused training in Passport to Services.* Internal report. Gateshead UK Social Services.

15 Solution-Focused Family Therapy for Troubled and Runaway Youths

■ SANNA J. THOMPSON

AND KATHERINE SANCHEZ

■ INTRODUCTION

Solution-focused brief therapy (SFBT) is more than the trademark techniques it employs. It is an optimistic therapeutic process in which the therapist focuses on developing a strong therapeutic alliance, trusting the client, and exploring the clients' competencies (Watts & Pietrzak, 2000). De Jong and Berg (1998) describe the therapist–client relationship as "cooperative," "collaborative," "respectful," and "shared," basic skills that they note are not exclusive to SFBT. Littrell (1998) adds that "strategies and techniques are ineffectual if the facilitative conditions of warmth, genuineness, and empathy do not permeate the counseling process" (p. 8).

Regardless of the type of treatment offered, researchers and practitioners have noted barriers to families seeking and engaging in services, such as the lack of reliable transportation, inconsistent or late work schedules, few financial resources, and childcare difficulties (Kazdin & Wassell, 1999; Sanders, 1999). These barriers often interfere with attendance at office-based sessions; therefore, services delivered in naturalistic settings, such as the family's home, have been undertaken as a potentially important treatment option. Community-based services have increasingly moved to provide services in the therapist's office; however, it is unclear whether providing these services in the home might produce improved satisfaction and client participation in therapy sessions. Thus, the purpose of this study was to evaluate whether families receiving solution-focused family therapy (SFFT) in home-based versus office-based settings differed on various treatment outcomes with troubled and runaway youth. Families were recruited from among those who sought family-based services at a community agency that focused on treating issues of family conflict. Families also sought assistance for difficulties associated with their adolescent child's runaway, truant, and/or delinquent behaviors. This study evaluated differences between families receiving home-based versus office-based services on measures associated with the treatment process, including retention, goal attainment, engagement, counselor rapport, and satisfaction with services.

■ WHAT WE HAVE LEARNED SO FAR

Research has shown that youth with complex risk profiles often reside in families characterized by poor parental caretaking practices, chaos, violence, neglect, and physical and/or sexual abuse (Dumas et al., 2005; Kilpatrick et al., 2000). Family environmental stressors and adolescent–parent conflict are typically cited by youth as their major reasons for running away (Johnson et al., 2005), using drugs and alcohol (Thompson & Pillai, 2006), and engaging in other high-risk and delinquent behaviors (Dembo et al., 1990). It has been argued that families are central to the process of youth developing emotional and behavioral problems when poor intrafamilial relationships, poor communication, poor problem solving, and unresolved conflict co-occur with dysfunctional family relationships (Paradise et al., 2001). Poor and inconsistent parenting and family dysfunction can place children in danger of developing high-risk behaviors, such as drug abuse and delinquency (Paschall et al., 2003).

Conversely, emotional and physical support by family members results in positive adjustment in childhood and adolescence, suggesting that family support is a protective factor that buffers against adolescents engaging in high-risk behaviors (Wills et al., 1994). Given the family's fundamental influence on children's lives, research has consistently suggested the potential benefits of including families in the treatment of troubled youth, especially those who have run away (Hawkins et al., 1992; Thompson & Pillai, 2006). Considerable empirical support confirms that including families in the treatment of troubled teens is effective, even necessary.

Family-oriented intervention models often include effective parenting and family-strengthening strategies in an effort to reduce many types of adolescent behavioral and emotional adjustment problems (Kumpfer & Kaftarian, 2000). Family-based interventions compared to other forms of service delivery have demonstrated reductions in youths' behavior problems (Liddle et al., 2000; Rowe et al., 2002; Spoth & Day, 2002; Waldron et al., 2001) and have increased engagement and retention in treatment (Henggeler et al., 1999; Liddle et al., 2001). Family-focused interventions have been shown to be more effective than peer group therapy, parent education, multifamily interventions, and individual counseling (Liddle & Hogue, 2000).

Family preservation services were among the first to provide services within the home environment. The underlying assumption of this service is that the best way to protect children is to strengthen the family, as the well-being of children is intricately connected to the welfare of the family unit (Mosier et al., 2001; Scannapieco, 1994). In a review of family-based, empirically supported treatments (Alexander et al., 2000), particularly strong support was found for interventions delivered to "living units as they exist in the natural environment" (p. 186). This finding suggests that family therapy is a treatment methodology whose effectiveness may increase when delivered in the home environment (Mosier et al., 2001).

Home-based family therapy is often employed with multiproblem adolescents and their families who have not responded to traditional forms of therapy (Yorgason et al., 2005), such as families where abuse/neglect has occurred or where adolescent children are engaged in delinquent acts and running away (Mosier et al., 2001). Home-based treatment has also been shown to significantly reduce externalizing symptoms and secure compliance among adolescents (Lay et al., 2001), a notoriously difficult population to engage in treatment. The growing empirical support for home-based services suggests that it is a valuable clinical strategy for improving clients' engagement, motivation, and commitment to the treatment process (Slesnick et al., 2006). It appears to be especially effective in engaging and retaining adolescents in therapy and leads to fewer dropouts from treatment compared to other therapeutic approaches (Liddle et al., 2001). Therapists who provide services in the home also note a greater therapeutic alliance with family members, a factor closely tied to long-term positive outcomes (Mattejat et al., 2001). Therefore, services delivered in naturalistic settings, such as the family's home, may improve client outcomes (Thompson et al., 2009).

Principles of solution-oriented approaches or SFBT fit well with the basic tenets of family-oriented interventions. Among nine studies with well-controlled methods, four were conducted with children and youth (LaFountain & Garner, 1996; Litrell et al., 1995; Triantafillou, 2002) and another study evaluated parenting skills (Zimmerman et al., 1997). All of these studies showed statistically significant effects that favored the solution-focused condition. In a recent meta-analysis of experimental or quasi-experimental studies of solution-focused methods used in community settings, results indicated that this approach demonstrated a small (effect sizes = .11–.26) but significant improvement in outcomes compared to control groups (Kim, 2008). Two studies examining family and relationship problems (Adams et al.,1991; Cockburn et al., 1997) also showed significant differences in treatment outcomes for solution-focused treatment compared to control groups, favoring the solution-focused condition (Kelly et al., 2008). While the results from these reviews are not definitive due to methodological weaknesses, they suggest that the solution-focused approach achieves positive results in community-based settings.

■ SFBT INTERVENTION

Social service agencies throughout Texas that receive state funds to deliver services to families with high-risk adolescents are required to receive training and utilize SFBT methods when conducting family therapy sessions. Family-focused sessions are typically provided in office-based settings by masters of social work (MSW)-level therapists who receive monthly training and supervision concerning implementation of solution-focused methods.

In this study, solution-focused sessions were centered on family and youth needs. Therapists helped families develop a detailed and carefully articulated vision of what it would be like if their difficulties were resolved. Goals and outcomes were developed with all family members, not just the identified youth. During each family therapy session, discussions between family members and therapists were directed by the solution-focused approach. Goals were set and completion was determined by the parent, the youth, and other family members during each session. Goal attainment scaling, a particularly helpful and simple means for monitoring goal achievement over time (Kiresuk & Sherman, 1968), was used during each session to identify the outcomes of at least two goals. Each consecutive session included follow-up to the previous session's goals and the level of attainment of the specified goals.

Following goal specification, therapists led family discussions guided by solution-focused, strengths-based methods. These sessions focused on the unique needs of families and youths, including topics related to substance use, peer relationships, educational problems, and a variety of family relationship, communication, and conflict difficulties. Based on these individualized discussions, therapists helped the family construct and identify the part each member played in the sequence of behaviors leading up to an identified problem. The therapist helped the family examine exceptions to the sequence of events or behaviors leading to the development of the problem and used exceptions to construct a sequence of behavior changes to solve the difficulty.

As this study's primary aim was to evaluate how the setting of family therapy sessions influenced the family's perceptions of the treatment process, sessions were conducted either in the therapist's office or the family's home. Both settings included family therapy with the same SFFT methods described above. Sessions in both settings were typically 1–1½ hours in length and were held weekly. The program provided funding for up to 12 sessions; however, since SFBT techniques were used, fewer sessions were expected.

Although both office-based and home-based family therapy sessions utilized SFBTmethods, there were some differences in the way therapists employed these methods in each setting. For example, families receiving office-based therapy were treated more formally, which was typical of meetings held in agency settings. On the other hand, family therapy sessions delivered in the home required creative methods to draw the family together once the therapist arrived. Experiential activities or "ice breakers" were used to encourage more interaction among parent(s), adolescents, and therapist. These activities helped create a relaxed, positive environment for the family's therapeutic sessions, as they involved experiential interactions and skill-building exercises that encouraged active participation from all family members. One of the experiential activities is presented in Box 15.1.

Solution-focused techniques included therapists' expanding on topics that came up during the experiential activities. For example, therapists continually focused discussions using positive, strengths-based conversation and questions. Conversations were coconstructive; therapists and clients together created descriptions of the problem and its solutions, which were augmented by the strengths and capabilities of the family. Solution-focused questions emphasized the positive aspects of clients' actions or goals without dwelling on problems. Discussions during therapeutic sessions built cooperation and rapport between therapists and clients as information concerning the family's functioning was divulged and the client's frame of reference, strengths, and resources were identified. As information was presented, therapists continually encouraged clients to explore what they wanted to be different in their lives (goals). Resources and strengths possessed by family members to achieve those goals were then identified, and past successes and abilities were affirmed. The therapist helped the family form small, concrete goals that were likely to lead to positive changes in the lives of individual family members, as well as for the family as a unit. Basic listening skills such as paraphrasing and summarizing were employed by therapists to reframe information by commending clients on their strengths and capabilities.

▪ RESEARCH METHODS

Design and Participants

The current exploratory study utilized a quasi-experimental design with intervention (home-based SFFT) versus comparison (treatment as usual, office-based SFFT) groups. Prior to seeking each family's consent to participate, research assistants used an overflow design to determine which option would be offered to a particular family. If one of the two home-based counselors had an available opening, the family was offered

BOX 15.1 ▪ Example of Experiential Activity—Meaningful Events

Implementation Description

The therapist provides a large sheet of paper with the title "Meaningful Events in Our Family." Each person receives a pad of post-it notes. The family members are directed to write a memory of a meaningful event on one post-it note and stick it on the large sheet of paper to create an events collage. Post-it notes are added for each event by every person involved in the group until everyone has had ample opportunity to describe each event that was important to them. Adolescents, in particular, tend to interpret *meaningful* as *positive*, so discussion of the difference between these words is a good preface to this activity. For example, the death of a loved one is meaningful but not necessarily positive, while an enjoyable family vacation is positive and meaningful. The therapist should encourage at least three contributions from each individual. Ideally, discussion will flow from these memories. From the written post-it notes, the family will have a record of memories that individual family members felt were important to them. Discussion of the family's conception of *meaningful* can be an interlude to this activity. Therapists must encourage free expression of meaningful events by each individual.

Once everyone has recorded their events on the post-its, family members read them to each other and the therapist encourages discussion.

Some ideas to talk about are:

- What emotions a person felt at the time of the event
- What a person actually did at the time
- What a person learned or can now learn from the event
- How many of the events overlap between family members
- Themes that seem to surface, such as beginnings, endings, transitions, and enjoyable events.
- What might have surprised family members about the other members' responses
- Perception of each other's recollection of the same events

The meaningful events collage is left with the family. The therapist can encourage the family to keep it in a place where family members can refer to it often.

Clinical Impressions from Counselors Who Implemented This Activity

The meaningful events collage provides family members with the means to begin disclosing and sharing their mutual history. It begins the process of building a shared vision and a mutual understanding of what has been important for the family. This activity can lead to surprising disclosures, giving family members a chance to learn something new about one another.

This activity often turns family members' attention to positive and constructive aspects of their family and themselves. It is this change in energy and atmosphere that often sets a new tone and draws families seamlessly into connection with each other and with the therapist. Simply sharing memories appears to build bonds and connections between family members.

This activity encourages families to disclose a great deal of family history that is not typically revealed in family counseling. This can provide more insight into family

BOX 15.1 ■ (*continued*)

dynamics, such as the family structure and hierarchy, which is revealed when family members share the evolution of the formation of their family.

Specific events are likely to be both positive and negative, such as births, significant illnesses, loss of a job and the family's standard of living, divorce, death of a loved one, and so on. Events may also center on the beginnings and endings of life transitions and situations, such as the death of a parent or a significant other. Though these events may provoke sadness, they also provide an opportunity to recognize family members' similar reactions to the same event and give the therapist an opportunity to praise the family for their resiliency at a time of loss.

Activities like the meaningful events one can remind family members of what they have in common. This shared experience can help to reestablish positive communication patterns. If cultivated by the therapist, these patterns can strengthen trust in family relationships and provide much-needed support for family members struggling to find common meaning in the experiences and perceptions of experiences among other family members. It ca n encourage them to try to find more positive ways to communicate and resolve the inevitable conflicts that arise.

home-based SFFT; otherwise, families were recruited for services delivered in the standard office-based setting, or treatment as usual.

Participants in the study were recruited from among families seeking services at a social service agency in central Texas. The multiservice agency offered a targeted program for families with adolescent children struggling with delinquency, truancy, family conflict, and/or running away. Agency staff in this program presented families with the opportunity to learn about the study if (a) the identified youth was 12–17 years of age and was living at home, (b) the family resided within a 30-mile radius of the social service agency, and (c) at least one parent was willing to participate in family therapy sessions and provide consent for the child's participation.

Parents and youths who agreed to be contacted by research staff for possible participation in the study were provided a full explanation of the study. Those parents and youths who agreed to participate were visited in their home to complete the written consent/assent form. Methods for this study were reviewed and approved by the affiliated university's Institutional Review Board.

Once family members provided written consent/assent, pretests were completed. One parent and the identified youth completed questionnaires that included various standardized measures. Following completion of treatment (up to 12 weeks), a posttest was conducted that included measures nearly identical to those on the initial questionnaire. The number of sessions each family attended over the 12-week period was also documented. Youths and parents in both conditions received compensation for completing the questionnaires.

Measures

In addition to being monitored for retention (number of sessions attended), goal attainment scaling was used during each session as required by the agency (see Figure 15.1).

```
┌─────────────────────────────────────────────────────────────────────┐
│ Goal Attainment Scaling Form                                          │
│                                            Session # _____       │
│                                                                       │
│ Client_____ Case #_____ Counselor _____│
├─────────────────────────────────────────────────────────────────────┤
│ What is better?                    Level of attainment                │
│                                                                       │
│ Level of Coping. ............................................ 0-1-2-3-4-5-6-7-8-9-10 │
│                                                                       │
│ Goal 1 _____ 0-1-2-3-4-5-6-7-8-9-10 │
│                                                                       │
│ Goal 2 _____ 0-1-2-3-4-5-6-7-8-9-10 │
│                                                                       │
│ New Goal _____│
├─────────────────────────────────────────────────────────────────────┤
│ New Concerns:                                                         │
│                                                                       │
│ New steps this week _____│
│                                                                       │
│ Who will accomplish_____ │
│                                                                       │
│ Review date _____ │
│                                                                       │
│ What is working _____ │
├─────────────────────────────────────────────────────────────────────┤
│ Family Member's Signatures_____               │
│                                                                       │
│ Therapist's Signature_____                │
└─────────────────────────────────────────────────────────────────────┘
```

Figure 15.1. Goal Attainment Scaling Form.

This form was a helpful and simple means of monitoring goal achievement over time (Kiresuk & Sherman, 1968). Goals were listed with a time frame suggested for achievement. During each session, parents and youths reported the level of attainment for a specific goal on a scale from 1 to 10 (1 = not at all attained; 10 = fully attained).

The Client Evaluation of Self & Treatment (CEST) (Joe et al., 2002) was used to monitor clients' treatment needs and determine their perceptions of various dimensions of the treatment process. The CEST consists of 144 items that measure five dimensions of treatment: treatment motivation, treatment process, psychological functioning, social functioning, and social network support. Examination of the psychometric properties of the CEST has shown adequate reliability (alpha > .70) for all subscales and good construct validity (Joe et al., 2002). For the current analysis, only the treatment process variables of satisfaction, engagement in treatment sessions, and counselor rapport are reported.

Data Analysis

Following descriptive analyses of youth and parent characteristics, chi-square and *t*-tests were conducted to determine the differences between office-based and home-based treatment groups for youths and parents. Retention rates were calculated based on the number of sessions the family attended. T-tests were then conducted to determine the differences between groups on measures of goal attainment and treatment process variables.

■ RESULTS OF RESEARCH

Sample Demographics

The study sample included 83 families: 42 receiving home-based SFFT and 41 receiving office-based SFFT. Youths in both groups averaged 14 years of age ($SD + 1.5$); parents were, on average, 42 years of age ($SD + 9.4$). Families were predominantly Hispanic/Latino ($n = 44$; 53%), White ($n = 14$; 17%), or African American ($n = 11$; 13%). Most parents were employed full-time ($n = 42$; 52%), had some college education ($n = 39$, 47%), and were members of two-parent families ($n = 49$; 59%). Few significant differences were found on family characteristics based on receiving home-based or office-based SFFT; however, parents who received home-based SFFT were significantly older ($M = 44.1$, $SD + 9$ years) than parents receiving office-based SFFT ($M = 39.8$, $SD + 9.5$ years), [$t(81) = -2.03$, $p < .05$]. In addition, families receiving home-based SFFT had fewer children ($M = 2.14$, $SD + 1.0$) than did families receiving office-based SFFT ($M = 2.61$, $SD + 1.1$), [$t(81) = 2.05$, $p < .05$], and more families receiving home-based SFFT consisted of single parents (52.4%) compared to families receiving office-based SFFT (29.3%), [χ^2 (1, $N = 83$) = 4.58, $p < .05$].

Session Completion

Analysis of the number of sessions completed by all participating families showed that those who received home-based SFFT engaged in a greater number of sessions than the office-based SFFT group. The average number of sessions was 9.6 ($SD + 3.1$) for the home-based SFFT group and 4.4 ($SD + 3.9$) for the office-based group, a statistically significant difference, $t(81) = -6.66$, $p < .001$. The majority of office-based families (53%; $n = 23$) completed or terminated services after session 3.

Goal Attainment

Goal attainment was assessed for all families at the sixth session or at the last session if the family terminated services before 6 weeks. It was found that the level of goal attainment (on a scale from 1 to 10) was similar for the office-based and home-based SFFT groups. Figure 15.2 depicts families' average goal achievement across six sessions. Note that for both office-based and home-based groups, the average level of goal attainment reported was nearly identical for the first session (office-based family's score = 4.3; home-based family's score = 4.2), $t(81) = -.53$, $p = .59$. Both groups improved fairly consistently throughout the six sessions, with very similar reports of goals attained through session 6 (office-based family's score = 7.4; home-based family's score = 7.1), $t(73) = -.62$, $p = .54$. It should be noted that since nearly half of the office-based SFFT families completed/terminated services after three sessions, Figure 15.2 also shows nearly identical goal attainment for both groups at week 3 as well (office-based family's score = 6.2; home-based family's score = 6.4), $t(54) = -.73$, $p = .47$.

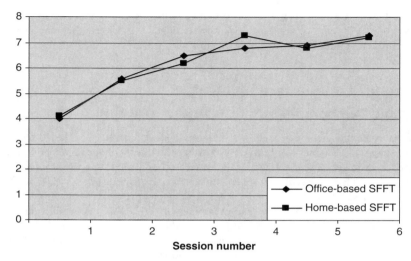

Figure 15.2. Average goal attainment for six sessions of office-based and home-based SFFT.

Treatment Process

Perceptions of the treatment process for families in home-based SFFT and office-based SFFT were assessed following each family's final session. Findings indicated that parents in the home-based SFFT group reported greater satisfaction with treatment ($M = 41.6$, $SD + 6.4$) than did parents in the office-based group ($M = 38.4$, $SD + 6.9$), [$t(81) = -2.18$, $p = .03$]. Parents in the home-based SFFT group also reported greater rapport with their counselor ($M = 42.5$, $SD + 5.1$) than did parents in the office-based group ($M = 39.7$, $SD + 6.6$), [$t(81) = -2.19$, $p = .03$]. However, no differences were found between parents in the home-based versus office-based SFFT groups on their level of participation in treatment sessions. Youths' responses to all measures of the treatment process were not significantly different based on the treatment setting.

■ PRACTICE GUIDELINES

The findings of this comparison study of SFFT in office-based versus home-based settings provided a unique opportunity to evaluate the impact of treatment setting on families' session completion, goal attainment, and engagement in and satisfaction with the treatment process. The most obvious difference between the treatment settings and the use of SFFT was the length of time families remained in treatment. As noted, families receiving home-based treatment received, on average, three times as many sessions. Their retention in treatment is likely due to the ease of receiving services in the family's home compared to the need to travel to the therapist's office. Confirming previous research (Scannapieco, 1994; Slesnick et al., 2006), parents and youth in this study noted that receiving services in their home created an environment conducive to remaining engaged in treatment, as barriers to treatment access such as transportation, child care, and financial constraints were alleviated. Some families reported that they would not have participated in as many treatment sessions if they had been required to meet with a counselor in the office. In addition, families voiced appreciation for the willingness of therapists to work within the family's environment, the flexibility in scheduling sessions, and the high level of therapist commitment and respect for the family as the therapist integrated into the family's surroundings, cultural traditions, living arrangements, and neighborhood context.

Counselors providing SFFT in families' homes noted that they often had to work within a context of limited private and quiet spaces. One family of nine, with multiple small children, lived in a three-bedroom home with only a kitchen and living room as shared space. Although the setting was at times a distraction, the therapist felt that she was able to experience family members' interactions and develop insights that would not have been possible in a more formal, office-based setting where the environmental context was not observable.

Previous research has suggested that willingness to participate in treatment is among the strongest predictors of positive outcomes in family therapy (Karver et al., 2006; Lay et al., 2001). However, in this study, the increased level of families' engagement, as measured by session completion, did not appear to be a key factor in positive treatment outcomes. Families that received office-based services did not remain in treatment as long as those receiving services in the home, but similar levels of goal attainment were noted. Although engagement in the therapeutic process appeared increased for families receiving home-based treatment, as evidenced by their attendance at a greater number of sessions, it is possible that solution-focused methods of identifying solutions to specified problems requires fewer sessions to improve outcomes. It appears that although family members felt more positive and satisfied with their therapist and the treatment provided when services were delivered in the home, these positive attitudes did not result in greater attainment of goals.

During SFBT sessions in both groups, the focus was on what the family wanted to achieve rather than delving into problems. Therapists recognized that the greatest source of change is the client—his or her strengths, resources, and motivations (Tallman & Bohart, 1999, p. 91); therefore, session content included the essential concept of recognizing and encouraging the client's strengths. Through a strong therapeutic alliance, the therapist acted as a collaborator in helping the family seek solutions (Watts & Pietrzak, 2000). It may be that sessions delivered in the home made it easier for families to continue in treatment, but this did not lead to better outcomes.

Another issue that therapists had to manage in this study was scheduling of office or home visits. Requiring families to meet in agency-based settings can be less challenging than scheduling home-based visits, as office visits are scheduled with the expectation that families will arrive at the specific time allotted for the meeting. Recognizing that a chaotic household can distract family members from fully engaging in the therapeutic process, office-based services inherently address obstacles to the therapeutic milieu, such as distractions during sessions and the safety of the therapist. On the other hand, in this study, sessions provided in the home often occurred in the evening or on weekends as therapists attempted to meet the demands and scheduling needs of the family. The in-home sessions also provided a prime opportunity for therapists to observe behaviors and actions within their true context, enhancing their ability to understand the family dynamics (Thompson et al., 2007).

Although most families in both treatment conditions assessed in this study were able to build a positive alliance with their therapist, engaging in the therapeutic process presented various challenges for building that alliance with each family member. For example, difficulties due to varied levels of commitment among family members were evident, as some family members were more committed to making changes than others. In addition, some family members were less able to cope with the intense emotions or sensitive subject matter often brought out during family therapy sessions and simply disengaged from the treatment process. Previous studies suggest that confronting negative client responses to therapists can improve alliance development and engagement (Beck et al., 2006; Digiuseppe et al., 1996). Thus, transforming resistance and reluctance into a collaborative relationship with the therapist is one of the first and most critical tasks in the therapeutic process (Diamond et al., 1999).

Limitations

Various methodological limitations are common in intervention research (Thompson et al., 2006) and should be considered in interpreting the results of this exploratory research. Although a true random assignment design was attempted, it was not possible due to various constraints. However, analyses demonstrated that the two groups were comparable across key variables, including demographics. One major difficulty in the current study was the lack of posttest data from some of the families. Once families completed or terminated treatment, agency counselors notified the research team. At that point, the research team attempted to contact these families to collect posttest information. However, some families relocated and four were eventually lost to follow-up. Thus, implementing more rigorous research methodologies is needed to evaluate more fully the effectiveness of SFFT.

■ FUTURE STUDIES

While preliminary research has indicated that it is an effective intervention, SFFT still lacks the empirical support to be considered evidence-based (de Shazer et al., 2007; Kim, 2008). The demand for empirical support for well-defined, specific interventions is likely to remain the dominant trend in social science research. To address the limitations of this study and extend its findings, there are several directions for future research. A large randomized clinical trial measuring the impact of the treatment setting as a mechanism of change in family therapy is needed. The greater satisfaction and rapport among the home-based participants supports the need for a larger, more controlled, and sufficiently powered study of SFFT as a mechanism of change in family therapy delivered in various treatment settings. Furthermore, studies with larger samples should be conducted to determine whether SFFT significantly improves families' ability to reach a broad range of individual and family-oriented outcomes.

■ KEY FINDINGS TO REMEMBER

- The majority of families receiving office-based services engaged in fewer sessions than did families receiving home-based services. The average number of sessions for the office-based group was four, compared to nine for families in the home-based SFFT group.

- The level of goal attainment reported was nearly identical for the first session (an average score in both groups of 4) and remained fairly consistent throughout the six sessions for both groups (an average score of 7.25).
- Parents in the home-based SFFT group reported greater satisfaction with treatment than did parents in the office-based group.
- Parents in the home-based SFFT group reported better rapport with their therapist than did parents in the office-based group.
- No differences were found between parents in the home-based versus the office-based SFFT group on their participation in treatment sessions.
- Youths' responses to all measures of the treatment process were not significantly different based on the treatment setting.

■ FURTHER LEARNING

The European Brief Therapy Association (EBTA) continues to study the connection between SFBT and objective measures of progress through the EBTA Multi-Center Research Project (European Brief Therapy Association, 2011). Therapies to be included in the EBTA Outcome Study should meet the criteria for the SFBT model as developed by Steve de Shazer and Insoo Kim Berg. A "minimum sufficient" manual has been developed for the research study and is available at no cost (http://www.ebta.nu/page2/page30/page30.html). All of the features of the model must be present, and data must be collected with the instruments provided by EBTA in order to be included in the study.

The Ohio Youth in Transition (OYIT) Alumni Support and Assistance (ASAP) Solution Focused Intervention Pilot project aims to develop and test a solution-focused group intervention for youth in transition from foster care, formerly in foster care, and/or runaway/homeless (http://csw.osu.edu/research/key/interventions/youth/). This SFBT small-group intervention aims to help youth in transition to shift focus from problems and deficits to solutions and existing skills. Due to its relatively simple and low-cost focus, it is more feasible and accessible for a large number of youths in transition who need assistance and/or support.

■ REFERENCES

Adams, J. F., Piercy, F. P., & Jurich, J. A. (1991). Effects of solution-focused therapy's formula first session task on compliance and outcome in family therapy. *Journal of Marital and Family Therapy, 17,* 277–290.

Alexander, J., Robbins, M., & Sexton, T. (2000). Family-based Interventions with older, at-risk youth: From promise to proof to practice. *The Journal of Primary Prevention, 21*(2), 185–205.

Cockburn, J. T., Thomas, F. N., & Cockburn, O. J. (1997). Solution-focused therapy and psychosocial adjustment to orthopedic rehabilitation in a work hardening program. *Journal of Occupational Rehabilitation, 7,* 97–106.

De Jong, P., & Berg, I. K. (1998). *Interviewing for solutions.* Pacific Grove, CA: Brooks/Cole.

de Shazer, S., Dolan, Y., Korman, H., McCollum, E., Trepper, T., & Berg, I. K. (2007). *More than miracles: The state of the art of solution-focused brief therapy.* New York: Haworth Press.

Dembo, R., Williams, L., la Voie, L., Berry, E., Getreu, A., Kern, J., et al. (1990). Physical abuse, sexual victimization and marijuana/hashish and cocaine use over time: A structural analysis among a cohort of high risk youths. *Journal of Prison & Jail Health, 9*(1), 13–43.

Diamond, G. M., Liddle, H. A., Hogue, A., & Dakof, G. A. (1999). Alliance-building interventions with adolescents in family therapy: A process study. *Psychotherapy, 36*(4), 355–368.

Digiuseppe, R., Linscott, J., & Jilton, R. (1996). Developing the therapeutic alliance in child-adolescent psychotherapy. *Applied & Preventive Psychology, 5*(2), 85–100.

Dumas, J. E., Nissley, J., Smith, E. P., Prinz, R. J., & Levine, D. W. (2005). Home chaos: Sociodemographic, parenting, interactional, and child correlates. *Journal of Clinical Child & Adolescent Psychology, 34*(1), 93–104.

European Brief Therapy Association. (2011). *European brief therapy association outcome study: Research definition description of the treatment* . Retrieved 2011, from http://www. ebta.nu/page2/page30/page30.html.

Hawkins, J., Catalano, R. F., & Miller, J. Y. (1992). Risk and protective factors for alcohol and other drug problems in adolescence and early adulthood: Implications for substance abuse prevention. *Psychological Bulletin, 112*(1), 64–105.

Henggeler, S. W., Rowland, M. D., Randall, J., Ward, D. M., Pickrel, S. G., Cunningham, P. B., et al. (1999). Home-based multisystemic therapy as an alternative to the hospitalization of youths in psychiatric crisis: Clinical outcomes. *Journal of the American Academy of Child and Adolescent Psychiatry, 38*(11), 1331–1339.

Johnson, K. D., Whitbeck, L. B., & Hoyt, D. R. (2005). Substance abuse disorders among homeless and runaway adolescents. *Journal of Drug Issues, 35*(4), 799–816.

Joe, G. W., Broome, K. M., Rowan-Szal, G. A., & Simpson, D. D. (2002). Measuring patient attributes and engagement in treatment. *Journal of Substance Abuse Treatment, 22*(4), 183–196.

Karver, M. S., Handelsman, J. B., Fields, S., & Bickman, L. (2006). Meta-analysis of therapeutic relationship variables in youth and family therapy: The evidence for different relationship variables in the child and adolescent treatment outcome literature. *Clinical Psychology Review, 26*(1), 50–65.

Kazdin, A. E., & Wassell, G. (1999). Barriers to treatment participation and therapeutic change among children referred for conduct disorder. *Journal of Clinical Child Psychology, 28*(2), 160–172.

Kelly, M. S., Kim, J. S., & Franklin, C. (2008). *Solution-focused brief therapy in schools.* New York: Oxford University Press.

Kilpatrick, D. G., Acierno, R., Saunders, B., Resnick, H. S., Best, C. L., & Schnurr, P. P. (2000). Risk factors for adolescent substance abuse and dependence: Data from a national sample. *Journal of Consulting and Clinical Psychology, 68*(1), 19–30.

Kim, J. S. (2008). Examining the effectiveness of solution-focused brief therapy: A meta-analysis. *Research on Social Work Practice, 18*(2), 107–116.

Kiresuk, T., & Sherman, R. E. (1968). Goal attainment scaling: A general method for evaluating comprehensive mental health programs. *Community Mental Health Journal, 4,* 443–453.

Kumpfer, K., & Kaftarian, S. (2000). Bridging the gap between family-focused research and substance abuse prevention practice: Preface. *Journal of Primary Prevention, 21*(2), 169–184.

LaFountain, R. M., & Garner, N. E. (1996). Solution-focused counseling groups: The results are in. *Journal for Specialists in Group Work, 21*(2), 128–143.

Lay, B., Blanz, B., & Schmidt, M. H. (2001). Effectiveness of home treatment in children and adolescents with externalizing psychiatric disorders. *European Child & Adolescent Psychiatry, 10*(Suppl 1), 80–90.

Liddle, H. A., Dakof, G. A., Parker, K., Diamond, G. S., Barrett, K., & Tejeda, M. (2001). Multidimensional family therapy for adolescent drug abuse: Results of a randomized clinical trial. *American Journal of Drug and Alcohol Abuse, 27*(4), 651–688.

Liddle, H. A., & Hogue, A. (2000). A family-based, developmental-ecological preventive intervention for high-risk adolescents. *Journal of Marital and Family Therapy*, 26(3), 265–279.

Liddle, H. A., Rowe, C., Diamond, G. M., Sessa, F. M., Schmidt, S., & Ettinger, D. (2000). Toward a developmental family therapy: The clinical utility of research on adolescence. *Journal of Marital and Family Therapy*, 26(4), 485–500.

Littrell, J. M. (1998). *Brief counseling in action*. New York: Norton.

Litrell, J. M., Malia, J. A., & Vanderwood, M. (1995). Single session brief counseling in a high school. *Journal of Counseling and Development*, 73, 451–458.

Mattejat, F., Hirt, B. R., Wilken, J., Schmidt, M. H., & Remschmidt, H. (2001). Efficacy of inpatient and home treatment in psychiatrically disturbed children and adolescents. *European Child & Adolescent Psychiatry*, 10(Suppl 1), 71–79.

Paradise, M., Cauce, A. M., Ginzler, J., Wert, S., Wruck, K., & Brooker, M. (2001). The role of relationships in developmental trajectories of homeless and runaway youth. In B. R. Sarason & S. Duck (Eds.), *Personal relationships: Implications for clinical and community psychology* (pp. 159-180). New York: Wiley.

Paschall, M. J., Ringwalt, C. L., & Flewelling, R. L. (2003). Effects of parenting, father absence, and affiliation with delinquent peers on delinquent behavior among African-American male adolescents. *Adolescence*, 38(149), 15.

Rowe, C., Liddle, H. A., McClintic, K., Quille, T. J., & Kaslow, F. W. (2002). Integrative treatment development: Multidimensional family therapy for adolescent substance abuse. In F. W. Kaslow, J. J. Magnavita, & T. Patterson (Eds.), *Comprehensive handbook of psychotherapy: Integrative/eclectic* (Vol. 4, pp. 133–161): New York: Wiley.

Sanders, M. R. (1999). Triple P-Positive Parenting Program: Towards an empirically validated multilevel parenting and family support strategy for the prevention of behavior and emotional problems in children. *Clinical Child and Family Psychology Review*, 2(2), 71–90.

Slesnick, N., Bartle-Haring, S., & Gangamma, R. (2006). Predictors of substance use and family therapy outcome among physically and sexually abused runaway adolescents. *Journal of Marriage and the Family Therapy*, 32(3), 261-281.

Spoth, R., & Day, S. (2002). Universal family-focused interventions in alcohol-use disorder prevention: Cost-effectiveness and cost-benefit analyses of two interventions. *Journal of Studies on Alcohol*, 63(2), 219–229.

Tallman, K., & Bohart, A. C. (1999). The client as a common factor: Clients as self-healers. In M. A. Hubble, B. L. Duncan, & S. D. Miller (Eds.), *The heart and soul of change* (pp. 91–131). Washington, DC: American Psychological Association.

Thompson, S. J., Bender, K., Lantry, J., & Flynn, P. (2007). Treatment engagement: Building therapeutic alliance in family-based treatment. *Contemporary Family Therapy*, 29(1/2), 39–55.

Thompson, S. J., Bender, K., Windsor, L. C., & Flynn, P. (2009). Keeping families engaged: The effects of in-home family therapy enhanced with experiential activities. *Social Work Research*, 33(2), 121–126.

Thompson, S. J., & Pillai, V. K. (2006). Determinants of runaway episodes among adolescents using crisis shelter services. *International Journal of Social Welfare*, 15, 142–149.

Thompson, S. J., Windsor, L. C., Lantry, J., Bender, K., & Maddox, G. (2006). The quagmires of conducting clinical research: One team's quest for creative solutions. *Reflections*, 12(2), 36–45.

Triantafillou, N. (2002). *Solution-focused parent groups. A new approach to the treatment of youth disruptive behavior*. Unpublished doctoral dissertation. University of Toronto, Canada.

Waldron, H. B., Slesnick, N., Brody, J. L., Charles, W., & Thomas, R. (2001). Treatment outcomes for adolescent substance abuse at 4- and 7-month assessments. *Journal of Consulting & Clinical Psychology, 69*(5), 802–813.

Watts, R. E., & Pietrzak, D. (2000). Adlerian "encouragement" and the therapeutic process of solution-focused brief therapy. *Journal of Counseling & Development, 78*(4), 442–447.

Wills, T. A., Schreibman, D., Benson, G., & Vaccaro, D. (1994). Impact of parental substance use on adolescents: A test of a mediational model. *Journal of Pediatric Psychology, 19*(5), 537–555.

Yorgason, J. B., McWey, L. M., & Felts, L. (2005). In-home family therapy: Indicators of success. *Journal of Marital and Family Therapy, 31*(4), 301–312.

Zimmerman, T. S., Prest, L. A., & Wetzel, B. E. (1997). Solution-focused couples therapy groups: An empirical study. *Journal of Family Therapy, 19*, 125–144.

16 Solution-Focused Brief Therapy in School Settings

■ CYNTHIA FRANKLIN, JOHNNY S. KIM, AND KAITLIN STEWART BRIGMAN

■ INTRODUCTION

School counselors and social workers started using solution-focused brief therapy (SFBT) techniques in schools during the 1990s, with the first publications and small research studies appearing in print in the mid-1990s (e.g., Kral, 1995; LaFountain & Garner, 1996; Metcalf, 1995; Murphy, 1996; Sklare, 1997). Since that time, SFBT has been implemented in schools in both the United States and Europe (Kelly et al., 2008), and the SFBT literature for school practitioners across disciplines has been advancing (e.g., Berg & Shilts, 2004; Franklin & Gerlach, 2007; Kelly et al., 2008; Metcalf, 2008; Murphy & Duncan, 2007; Webb, 1999). Commensurate with the growth of SFBT in schools has been an increase in research examining the outcomes of SFBT on externalizing and internalizing behavioral and academic problems of students. The purpose of this chapter is to summarize the outcome research on SFBT in school settings. Results of a recent systematic review on school studies (Kim & Franklin, 2009) will be summarized, along with the future implications for both practice and research. In addition, the types of SFBT interventions that are used in schools are highlighted along with the need for future studies.

■ WHAT WE HAVE LEARNED SO FAR

We have learned enough about the practice of SFBT to determine that it is a therapy approach that can be used in school settings. The solution-focused brief therapy (SFBT) approach shows transportability to schools because it has been successfully implemented at different levels of school programs and with diverse groups within the school environment. For example, the techniques of SFBT have been used to:

- Help at-risk students in individual, group, and family interventions (Franklin et al., 2001; Murphy, 2008
- Coach teachers in using solution-building talk in special education classrooms (see the Working on What Works [WWOW] program that is summarized in; Kelly et al., 2008)

- Change interactions between parents, teachers, and students, such as in parent–teacher meetings (Metcalf, 1995, 2008)
- Change school outcomes with students at risk for dropout, such as Hispanic pregnant and parenting mothers (Harris & Franklin, 2008)
- Change the school culture, such as when an entire school adopts the solution-focused change philosophy and trains all staff (including teachers and principals) in SFBT techniques (Franklin & Streeter, 2003, cited in Kelly et al., 2008)

There are several reasons that SFBT may work well in a school. First, many students experiencing problems in school match the description of *involuntary clients* with high-risk characteristics, such as those with multiple social problems, dropout prone due to academic failure and missed days of school, or homeless, as well as immigrants and teen parents. While these are only a few of the issues that schoolchildren face, there is no doubt that school systems are the de facto mental health and social agency for the underserved in Western society and a hub of mental health prevention for the most vulnerable students. As a therapeutic approach, SFBT evolved out of brief family therapy, which was developed to achieve efficient and effective change with complicated cases. In fact, the first sessions of SFBT were conducted in a clinic in Milwaukee, and many of the clients had characteristics of at-risk populations. See Chapter 1 for a description of the origins of SFBT.

Second, schools often have students with very challenging issues but have little time or money for long therapeutic interventions. What school counselors and school social workers require instead are brief, practical solutions to the day-to-day problems that may prevent a student from learning. Third, SFBT focuses on the resolution of problems using strengths, positive behaviors that already exist, goal setting, and client-selected behavior plans known as *solutions*. In addition, SFBT facilitates collaboration with others involved in the student's life. This therapeutic approach works well with the other team approaches used in the schools, such as the Response to Intervention (RTI) and the Individual Education Plans (IEPs) used in special education because each perspective has a practical, behavioral, and goal-oriented approach. Finally, SFBT is very flexible; it uses different ways of helping and can be used by teachers and other professionals within the school (Franklin & Gerlach, 2007; Kelly et al., 2008).

Research evidence is starting to emerge that shows that SFBT is a promising intervention that achieves good results in school settings. In a recent meta-analysis on SFBT that is discussed in Chapter 6, for example, Kim (2008) reported that the outcome studies completed in school settings had medium effect sizes (e.g., Franklin et al., 2007, 2008; Springer et al., 2000); this means that when SFBT is applied in schools, it achieves promising outcomes. More recently, Kim and Franklin (2009) completed a systematic review on the effectiveness of SFBT interventions in schools. In the subsequent sections of this chapter, this review will be discussed further to gain a better understanding of the interventions used in schools and the current state of the outcome research for SFBT in schools.

■ SFBT INTERVENTIONS IN SCHOOLS

In order to understand the types of SFBT interventions that are being used in schools, we examined the literature on SFBT in schools with special attention to systematic reviews on SFBT outcomes in those settings (Kim & Franklin, 2009). While we did not code every SFBT technique or intervention that has ever been discussed in the school literature, we did survey several research articles that were identified through searches in PsycINFO, Expanded Academic Search Premier, Social Services Abstract, and ERIC databases using the keywords *solution-focused brief therapy* cross-referenced with *schools*. In addition, we reviewed several books on the topic of SFBT in schools (e.g., Duncan & Murphy, 2007; Kelly et al., 2008; Mahlberg & Sjoblom, 2004; Metcalf 2008; Webb, 1999). We found that most of the SFBT interventions being used in schools were consistent with the treatment manual recently developed by the Research Committee of the Solution-Focused Brief Therapy Association (see Chapter 2 in this book for a review of the manual). The treatment manual identifies three general characteristics of SFBT: (a) use of conversations centered on clients' concerns; (b) conversations focused on coconstructing new meanings around clients' concerns; and (c) use of specific techniques to help clients coconstruct a vision of a preferred future and draw on past success and strengths to help resolve issues (Trepper et al., 2008).

Previous books and articles on SFBT in schools describe approaches that are consistent with the following core components, which have also been identified by Gingerich and Eisengart (2000): (a) using the miracle question; (b) using scaling questions; (c) using a consultation break and giving the client a set of compliments; (d) assigning homework tasks; (e) looking for competencies, strengths, or solutions; (f) setting goals; and (g) looking for exceptions to the problem. Currently, these core components remain important techniques for change in SFBT and are an integral part of SFBT interventions in schools. The following case examples, taken from the authors' work in school settings, highlight some different ways in which counselors, social workers, teachers, and administrators use SFBT to help students. Other examples of SFBT school interventions are also discussed in the Results section of this chapter.

Example 1. A school counselor describes how she uses the scaling question in individual sessions with students.

> Scaling can often stop the storytelling about the students' problems, which can take an hour, and it makes it quicker to move toward finding solutions. It's amazing to me how quickly students understand how to use the scaling. They know exactly what I mean when I say "On a scale from 1 to 10, how are you coping?" They can put a number on it right away, and it's so nice because they will seldom say it's a 0 or a 1. So, that allows me to say, "Wow, so it's a 5. What makes it that high?" They can tell me what makes it a 5 instead of a 1, which allows us to focus on the positive stuff and go from there.

In this example, the counselor describes how solution building can help counselors work with students who have multiple difficulties, build on their strengths to give them a feeling of competence, and work toward returning the students' focus to their academic goals.

Example 2. A school social worker describes how she changes the focus with a teacher to times when the unproductive behavior of a student did not happen, providing valuable information about a student's assignments.

> TEACHER: I have tried to listen and be understanding, but Alice continues to spend most of her class time surfing the Web instead of writing her history report. I don't know why she insists on doing this.

SCHOOL SOCIAL WORKER: I don't know why either. Was there any time this week that you noticed she was working on her class assignment?

TEACHER: (After a long pause.) You know, she did some work on her report Tuesday morning.

SCHOOL SOCIAL WORKER: What was different about Tuesday morning?

TEACHER: She found a Web site about fashion in the Roaring Twenties. She's doing her report on that era. I could tell she was really interested in the flapper and her style. She asked me if I thought there were any books in the library.

SCHOOL SOCIAL WORKER: Can you think of any other times when she's been that engaged in researching her report?

TEACHER: She had a lot of questions when another student presented a report on the life of the pioneer women. Alice was more animated than I've seen her since the first of the year. There may have been some other times, too.

SCHOOL SOCIAL WORKER: Well, if you see a pattern to those times, you might be able to come up with a way to alter the assignment and capture that interest and animation.

TEACHER: I know there have been other times when she showed that excitement. I'll have to do some thinking about this.

In this example, the conversation shifted from complaint about a student to a focus on a solution when a teacher saw some new options for engaging the student in her schoolwork.

Example 3. A principal uses solution-focused therapy techniques with a student.

PRINCIPAL: I deal with kids on a regular basis all the time. I'm dealing with a student who's been in a residential treatment for substance abuse. She came to visit me in my office, and here is a sample of the conversation between us.

STUDENT: I haven't felt a lot of these emotions in a long time.

PRINCIPAL: So, you are aware of a lot of feelings inside. Now you can see the difference between when you're loaded and when you're not . . .

STUDENT: (long pause) Yeah, kind of tough some days but that is really different.

PRINCIPAL: Of course . . . It is hard to deal with tough feelings some times. But that is great because you could not do that before. Is that right?

STUDENT: Yeah, not before my stay in the center.

PRINCIPAL: What else can you do better now that you could not do before?

STUDENT: (pause) Well, I can concentrate on my schoolwork.

PRINCIPAL: How does that help you?

STUDENT: It is easier to finish and get a good grade.

PRINCIPAL: You're making better grades now. That is great! What other ways does doing your work help you?

STUDENT: Well, it helps me focus and stay sober.

PRINCIPAL: You can do that now? You can focus and stay sober?

STUDENT: Yeah. So far . . . I am good.

In this example, the principal focuses on strengths and compliments to help a student sustain the progress that he gained during his substance abuse recovery program.

By focusing on strengths rather than problems, the principal reinforces the point that this student has the skills and knowledge to stay sober and succeed in school, and gives the student credit for that success. This builds confidence that a solution is possible even if there are some days when the student deals with distressing feelings.

SFBT Research in Schools

As the examples above demonstrate, the application of SFBT in schools can be very useful, but it is also important to examine empirically how effective SFBT is in school settings. In order to evaluate the outcomes of a school intervention, it is best to use experimental or quasi-experimental designs that are carefully controlled so that researchers can develop the causal inferences necessary to determine if an intervention is working. This type of research is sometimes called *efficacy* or *intervention research*. The term *intervention research* may be applied when outcome research is conducted with fewer controls in an applied setting like a school. What is needed for outcome research and the criteria for good experimental designs are discussed in Chapters 6 and 7. While all research is challenging, outcome studies using well-controlled experimental designs are a most difficult type of research because of the longitudinal, large-scale, rigorous nature of these studies, as well as their high costs (Frazer et al., 2009). Controlled, randomized experiments or clinical trials are the gold standard for outcome studies, but these types of research are not often used in school settings (Franklin et al., 2009; Hoagwood & Erwin, 1997; Roans & Hoagwood, 2000). Due to the applied nature of the field setting of a school and the often limited resources, researchers have more frequently applied quasi-experimental designs when evaluating school mental health interventions. While this unfortunately weakens school outcome studies, it is important to maintain a focus on the overall status of school mental health research when examining current SFBT studies and deciding what is needed to advance and improve the SFBT research base.

Outcome studies on SFBT interventions in schools are a new development, and most studies have appeared in the past 10 years. The recent Kim and Franklin (2009) systematic review on SFBT outcomes in schools only included the most rigorous outcome studies that used experimental and quasi-experimental designs with standardized measures and met criteria for a solution-focused intervention. This is the most up-to-date review of SFBT outcome studies in schools, and we will elaborate on its key findings in this chapter.

■ **RESEARCH METHODS**

This section summarizes methods used in school outcome research drawing from Kim and Franklin's (2009) systematic review on outcome studies of SFBT in schools. Effect size estimates from this review are presented to further examine the effectiveness of SFBT interventions. Research designs and issues with the research are further discussed.

The research methods for Kim and Franklin's (2009) systematic review involved tracking down published studies on SFBT in schools through searches in PsycINFO, Expanded Academic Search Premier, Social Services Abstract, and ERIC databases using the keywords *solution-focused brief therapy* cross- referenced *with schools*. To be included in the review, only published primary studies using experimental designs that examined the effectiveness of SFBT conducted in either a school setting or with students were reviewed. Studies reviewed were conducted in the United States from 1988 to 2008. It was decided that due to the limited resources and practical issues with language barriers, studies outside the United States and dissertations would not be reviewed. To be included in the systematic school review, one or more core components of SFBT mentioned earlier must have been studied. This decision was based on the Gingerich and Eisengart's (2000) article, which used this same selection criterion. When the studies did not report effect sizes (d), the authors of the systematic review calculated them when enough statistical information was provided.

Research Methods for School Studies: Strengths and Limitations

Seven SFBT school studies were included in the systematic review of Kim and Franklin (2009). See Table 16.1 for a review of the studies and their research methods. Of the school outcome studies, one employed an experimental design, six were quasi-experimental designs, and one used a single-case design. It is very encouraging to see that SFBT interventions have been studied with experimental and quasi-experimental designs that meet rigorous research criteria. This is a step in the right direction in developing the evidence base for SFBT interventions. Strengths of the current research include the following: The studies were conducted by more than one investigator, using treatment manuals or protocols, employing standardized measures and a fidelity evaluation. The research also took place in the real-world setting of schools, and this usually bodes well for transportability and effective usage of the methods by school practitioners.

Limitations of the Current SFBT School Research

We would be remiss if we did not mention some of the weaknesses of the current SFBT school studies and the limitations of the research methods used. We hope that a review of the weaknesses may help future researchers improve upon SFBT studies in schools. First, only a few studies are available, which makes it difficult to draw definitive conclusions about whether SFBT works. More studies should be developed that also have improved quality. Along with the limited number of studies, samples tended to be small, which limits statistical power to detect treatment effects and generalizability. Moreover, most of the studies used a quasi-experimental design; only one study (Froeschle et al., 2007) employed a true experimental design with randomization, which has the highest controls for threats to internal validity (Kazdin, 2002; Rubin & Babbie, 2005). The limitations of small samples and weak designs are not unusual given the fact that all of these studies were conducted in school settings, thus increasing our confidence in generalization of clinical findings but making randomization difficult to implement. Future research would be improved if researchers employed randomized experimental designs with larger samples. A small improvement would be a randomized design with a sample size of 200 or more in each group, for example.

Despite these limitations, SFBT is achieving effective outcomes when compared to other therapeutic and educational interventions that are being delivered in a community setting (Weisz et al., 2004). Of particular note is the fact that most of the studies were conducted under real-world practice conditions. Therefore, the results show promise in typical school-based practice situations, unlike the optimal clinical trial or

TABLE 16.1. *SFBT Studies in Schools*

Study	Design	Sample Size	Sample Population	Outcome Construct	Effect Size (Hedges' g)
Springer, Lynch, & Rubin (2000)	Quasi-experimental	10	Hispanic elementary students	Self-esteem	Hare Self-Esteem Scale = 0.57
Franklin, Biever, Moore, Clemons & Scamardo (2001)	Single case	7	Middle school students	Behavioral problems	Not applicable
Newsome (2004)	Quasi-experimental	52	Middle school students	Academic issues	Grades = 0.43; Attendance = Not enough information to calculate
Corcoran (2006)	Quasi-experimental	86	Students aged 5-17	Behavioral problems	Conners' Parent Rating Scale = 0.08; Feelings, Attitudes, and Behaviors Scale for Children = 0.48
Franklin, Streeter, Kim, & Tripodi (2007)	Quasi-experimental	85	At-risk high school students	Academic issues	Credits = 0.47; Attendance = -1.63; Graduation Rate = Not applicable
Froeschle, Smith, & Ricard (2007)	Experimental design	65	8th grade females	Drug use, self-esteem, behavioral problems, and academic issues	American Drug and Alcohol Survey = 0.65; Substance Abuse Subtle Screening Inventory Adolescent-2 = 0.76; Knowledge exam on physical symptoms of drug use = 1.76; Piers-Harris Children's Self Concept Scale-2 = 0.17; Home & Community Social Behavior Scales = 0.63; School Social Behavior Scales 2nd Edition = 1.16; Referrals = 0.38; Grade Point Average = 0.35
Franklin, Moore, & Hopson (2008)	Quasi-experimental	59	Middle school students	Self-esteem, behavioral problems	Child Behavior Checklist - Youth Self Report Form • Internal = 0.08; • External = 0.86; Child Behavior Checklist- Teacher's Report Form • Internal = 1.40; • External = 0.61

efficacy studies that have been shown to be ineffective when the model was transferred to a community practice setting like a school (Kim, 2008).

Results of the School Research

As Table 16.1 indicates, sample sizes from the school studies ranged from 7 to 86 students, with four studies (Franklin et al., 2001, 2008; Froeschle et al., 2007; Newsome, 2004) conducted with middle school students, one study (Springer et al., 2000) with elementary school students, one study (Franklin et al., 2007) with high school students, and one study (Corcoran, 2006) crossing all three school levels. The SFBT school studies therefore crossed different ages and grade levels. In addition, the studies used several SFBT techniques and worked with diverse problems involving externalizing behaviors, internalizing behaviors, self-esteem, and academic outcomes. All outcomes assessed in the studies are relevant to schools and, even with the mixed findings achieved, make it possible for us to determine some areas in which SFBT may be getting the best results and other areas where the outcomes are less clear. We summarize the findings below.

Key Findings in School Studies. Referrals for students with learning disabilities and externalizing behavioral issues are prevalent in schools. Two different teams of therapists and researchers (Corcoran, 2006; Franklin et al., 2001) applied SFBT with students who had serious behavioral problems. Corcoran (2006) examined the effectiveness of SFBT in behavior problems such as aggression, conduct problems in schools, and impulsivity using an intervention protocol similar to the one used by the Franklin team, which is described below. Corcoran's (2006) study involved a total of 86 students ages 5–17 who received either a SFBT intervention or treatment as usual, which consisted of a family treatment program incorporating many cognitive-behavioral techniques. Participants were assessed on the Conners' Parent Rating Scale and the Feelings, Attitudes, and Behaviors Scale for Children. The SFBT intervention was administered by 20 second-year masters-level field student interns who were trained by the author through videotaped demonstrations by Insoo Kim Berg, lectures, discussions, and role play. Students and their families received between four and six SFBT sessions at a school of social work–sponsored mental health clinic.

Results show that both the SFBT and the comparison group improved at posttest; however, the statistical test comparing group differences on the behavioral outcome measures found no significant differences between the groups. There were small effect sizes for both the Conners' Parent Rating Scale scores ($d = 0.08$) and the Feelings, Attitudes, and Behaviors Scale for Children scores ($d = 0.48$). Corcoran (2006) notes, however, that this lack of difference in outcome might be expected since the treatment as usual incorporated many cognitive-behavioral therapy components that have been empirically validated. And while both groups had high attrition rates, SFBT had better treatment engagement and fewer dropouts than the treatment as usual group (Corcoran, 2006).

Franklin and colleagues (2001) conducted a study with middle school students who received 5–10 sessions lasting 30–45 minutes per session based on a SFBT treatment protocol that used exception questions, miracle question, and scaling questions in every session. Additionally, consultations were conducted with teachers using the collaborative meeting process and specific questions and forms developed by Metcalf (1995) to discuss the progress of the cases. The study used an AB single-case design study with seven children who were referred with learning disabilities and behavioral problems. Outcomes were measured using the Conners' Teacher Rating Scale to examine behavioral changes in students as reported by their teachers. The researchers observed the students twice per week during the 4-week baseline phase (6–8 observations) and once a week for the duration of therapy (5–10 observations).

Franklin et al. (2001) report that five of the seven students (71%) showed improvement on previous clinically significant subscales of the Conners' Teacher Rating Scale. In this study, hyperactivity, conduct problems, emotional indulgence, and asocial behavior were outcomes that teachers frequently rated as moving out of the clinical range on the Conner's measure. Individual positive outcomes were supported by movement out of the clinical range and the magnitude of change achieved based on the subscale scores that changed for each case. Due to the research design and the available data, effect size results could not be calculated for this study. However, the percentage of nonoverlapping data (PND) between the baseline and treatment phases in single-subject graphs provides an index of treatment effectiveness, and was calculated for this study and reported in Chapter 7 of this book (see that chapter for more information). Several PND scores of the Conners' Teacher Rating subscales showed that the Hyperactivity intervention was ineffective, the Hyperactivity and Daydream Attention interventions were mildly effective, and the Asocial and Conduct Problem interventions were moderately effective.

Besides behavioral problems, internalizing problems have been examined in the SFBT school studies. One study used the SFBT model with students to try to improve their self-esteem. In an effort to determine the effects of a group intervention on the self-esteem of children of prisoners, Springer and colleagues (2000) used a SFBT group approach with children whose parents or other family members have been incarcerated. Ten elementary school students participated, five in the experimental group and five in the wait list comparison group. The experimental group leader used specific SFBT techniques such as scaling questions and miracle question to help facilitate the six-session group. The group leader also used mutual aid group processes and interactional approaches.

The study results were mixed. On the positive side, students in the SFBT group had statistically significant increase scores on the Hare Self-Esteem Scale after the group intervention, whereas the comparison group's scores were unchanged. A medium effect size ($d = 0.57$) was reported; however, the small sample size suggests cautious interpretation of this effect size. Despite the medium effect size, a covariance analysis of posttest scores found no significant differences between the SFBT and comparison groups on the Hare Self-Esteem Scale at the end of the 6-week study.

One recent study examined both behavioral problems and internalizing outcomes with students who received SFBT intervention. Franklin and colleagues (2008) conducted a quasi-experimental design study with 67 middle school students using the Teachers Report and Youth Self-Report Forms of the Achenbach Child Behavioral Checklist to assess outcomes.

Results showed that the SFBT group declined below the clinically signficant level on the standardized measure by posttest and remained there at follow-up for both the Internalizing and Externalizing scores on the Teachers Report Form. As for the comparison group, there was little change between pretest, posttest, and follow-up. Franklin et al. (2008) reported a large effect size ($d = 1.40$) for the Internalizing score and a medium effect size ($d = 0.61$) for the Externalizing score. Results for the Youth

Self-Report showed no difference between the SFBT and comparison groups for the Internalizing score, but the Externalizing score showed that the SFBT group dropped below the clinical level and continued to drop at follow-up. The study reported a small effect size ($d = 0.08$) for the Internalizing score but a large effect size ($d = 0.86$) for the Externalizing score.

Regarding academic outcomes, two studies (Franklin et al., 2007; Newsome, 2004) used SFBT to try to improve school and academic outcomes. Newsome (2004) studied the effectiveness of SFBT on middle school students identified as at risk due to academic and attendance problems. Fifty-two students participated in this pretest-posttest comparison group study, with 26 students receiving the SFBT intervention and 26 students comprising the comparison group. The SFBT group met for one class period (35 minutes) for 8 weeks, during which the group facilitator used various SFBT techniques such as scaling questions, miracle question, goals, and homework tasks. Students in the SFBT group increased their grades from a mean pretest score of 1.58 to a mean posttest score of 1.69, while the comparison group's grades decreased from a mean pretest score of 1.66 to a posttest score of 1.48. Newsome (2004) reported a medium effect size ($d = 0.43$) for grades. For the other dependant variable, attendance, there was no statistical difference between the SFBT and comparison groups.

Franklin and colleagues (2007) also conducted a quasi-experimental study but applied it to two groups of high school students to examine if SFBT could help improve credits earned, attendance measures, and graduation rates. The purpose of the study was to evaluate the effectiveness of an academic alternative school that focuses on dropout prevention using a SFBT framework. The SFBT group consisted of 46 students, and the comparison group consisted of 39 students from another school who were matched on at-risk characteristics similar to those of the SFBT students. Analysis using repeated measures ANOVA found that over time, there was a change in the number of credits earned as a proportion of credits attempted for both the experimental and comparison groups. While both groups increased their proportion of credits earned, independent samples t-tests showed that the experimental group had statistically significant higher average proportion of credits earned to credits attempted than the comparison group. A medium effect size of 0.47 was reported for the dependent variable credits earned. The students at the comparison school, however, did better than those who received SFBT in terms of attending classes, with a large effect size reported ($d = -1.63$) favoring the comparison group. Franklin et al. (2007) suggested that the comparison of attendance between the groups may not be fair because the SFBT students worked on a self-paced curriculum and could decrease their attendance when the curriculum was completed. Therefore, in this study, attendance may not be an accurate measure for determining the effectiveness of the intervention.

To examine the graduation rate, Franklin et al. (2007) looked at all students in their sample who were classified as being in 12th grade in the spring semester of 2004. Of the 37 students from the SFBT group, 23 (62%) graduated in the 2003–2004 academic year, while 27 (90%) graduated from the comparison group. While 14 students in the SFBT group did not graduate at the end of the academic year, 9 of these students were still enrolled in high school the following fall, with 7 of the 9 graduating the following year, bringing the total percentage of graduated students in the SFBT group to 30 (81%). Furthermore, of the remaining five students not enrolled in the high school, three were attending another alternative school and one was attending a traditional public high school (Franklin et al., 2007).

One recent study examined the effectiveness of SFBT on behavior problems, self-esteem, academic issues, and substance use. Froeschle and colleagues' (2007) randomized experimental design study used SFBT group sessions, mentorship, and action learning techniques to reduce substance use and behavioral problems among adolescent girls. The univariate statistical analysis found statistically significant differences on drug use, attitudes toward drugs, knowledge of physical symptoms of drug use, and competent behavior scores (parent and teacher reported) favoring the SFBT group. The Knowledge exam and the School Social Behavior Scales (Second Edition) both indicated great improvement, with some improvement indicated on the American Drug and Alcohol Survey, the Substance Abuse Subtle Screening Inventory Adolescent Version 2, and the Home and Community Social Behavior Scale measures. However, no group differences were found on negative behaviors, as measured by office referrals (Referrals). Since effect sizes were not reported by Froeschle et al. (2007), Kim and Franklin (2009) calculated the effect sizes based on the available data in the article. Small effect sizes were calculated for the Piers-Harris Children's Self-Concept Scale-2 ($d = 0.17$), grade point averages ($d = 0.35$), and office referrals ($d = 0.38$). Both the Home and Community Social Behavior Scale ($d = 0.63$) and the American Drug and Alcohol Survey ($d = 0.65$) outcomes had medium effect sizes. Lastly, three outcome measures had large effect sizes: the Substance Abuse Subtle Screening Inventory Adolescent Version 2 ($d = 0.76$), the School Social Behavior Scales (Second Edition) ($d = 1.16$), and the Knowledge exam on physical symptoms of drug use ($d = 1.76$).

■ **PRACTICE GUIDELINES**

Solution-focused brief therapy may be effectively applied to a range of academic and behavioral problems in school. Age ranges for applications in schools also appear to be flexible, with one of the strongest-designed studies showing positive outcomes with fifth and sixth graders (Franklin et al., 2008). Positive results were also achieved with adolescents, suggesting that SFBT may be used effectively with both older children and adolescents. While the SFBT research in schools is not sufficiently advanced to develop guidelines for evidence-based practice, enough research now exists for us to examine the different studies and to be cognizant of the major issues as we move forward with SFBT practice and research. We can gain a better understanding of the positive applications of SFBT and some of the areas in which SFBT did not do well when we look at the major themes across the school studies.

Themes Across Studies

Academic Performance: Solution-focused brief therapy may help students earn academic credits and improve their grades. In two studies, SFBT demonstrated school outcomes such as credits earned (Franklin et al., 2007) and better grades (Newsome, 2004), which may be especially relevant to the school practice setting (Hoagwood et al., 2007).

Externalizing Behavior Problems: Solution-focused brief therapy may reduce externalizing behavioral problems. Several of the school studies found that SFBT helped students decrease these problems (Franklin et al., 2001, 2008; Froeschle et al., 2007). The Franklin et al. (2008) study, for example, showed that SFBT improved the outcomes of children who had classroom and behavioral problems that could not be resolved by teachers, principals, or school counselors. Both teachers' and children's ratings improved, and effect sizes were found to be in the medium to large range. Positive outcomes with behavioral problems have considerable clinical significance for school-based practitioners because of the effect sizes achieved and because most of the studies involved important issues (e.g., conduct problems, hyperactivity, substance use).

These positive school findings, however, need to be replicated in larger studies and evaluated against other research on SFBT. Corcoran's evaluation of the research literature on externalizing behavior problems (see Chapter 8 in this volume), for example, suggests that there is not enough research yet to conclude that SFBT is effective with externalizing behavior problems. The Kim (2008) meta-analysis reported in Chapter 6 also failed to find effective outcomes with externalizing behaviors. Another meta-analysis conducted by Stams and colleagues (2006) suggested that SFBT was effective with conduct disorder, oppositional defiant disorder, attention deficit/hyperactivity disorder, and other externalizing behavior problems, and the results suggested that larger effects could be achieved in institutional settings. As this chapter suggests, positive outcomes have been found in schools with externalizing behavior problems. It is important to note that the reviews of SFBT used different criteria and review methods, resulting in these different findings. The use of different research methods in the studies limits comparisons between the reviews and their findings. Currently, the reason for the mixed results is unclear. In addition, there are not enough controlled studies available to investigate statistically possible moderator differences (i.e., samples and settings) between the different studies.

Brief Results: Solution-focused brief therapy may produce quick results when applied in schools The majority of studies examined in this review revealed that about four to eight sessions of SFBT were delivered and achieved favorable outcomes. Only two studies (Franklin et al., 2001; Froeschle et al., 2007) suggested that more than eight student sessions were used. Successes achieved through brief interventions suggest the clinical utility of SFBT for school settings, which often require brief, practical responses for changing student behavior and solving academic problems (Franklin & Gerlach, 2007).

Attendance and Graduation Rates: More research is needed. Practitioners should not necessarily discount SFBT for use with attendance problems or to increase graduation rates; at the same time, however, no evidence exists to supports the approach. Two studies suggest that SFBT did not improve student attendance (Franklin et al., 2007; Newsome, 2004), but flaws in the research designs may have contributed to this negative result. Newsome's (2004) study found no difference between the experimental and control groups on attendance, but it cites sample issues as a possible explanation for the nonsignificant results. Franklin et al. (2007) looked at the attendance of at-risk high school students and found that the comparison group did better in terms of school days attended for the semester. The results may be misleading, however, due to the self-paced curriculum design of the high school attended by the SFBT students, which allowed them to achieve their credits early but still be counted absent in the school district's records. This same study, using a high-risk sample of students prone to dropout, found that SFBT helped at-risk students graduate but did no better than standard academic practice.

Self-Esteem: Student self-esteem does not improve with the use of SFBT, but this finding may not be very relevant to student success. Springer et al. (2000) and

Froeschle et al. (2007) found that SFBT did not improve self-esteem in their studies. However, the generalizability of using self-esteem as an outcome has become a recent concern. Recent research has questioned the validity of using self-esteem as a measure for behavioral and academic improvement, and studies done by Baumeister and colleagues (2003) found that high self-esteem does not lead to improved school performance. In fact, elevated self-esteem may actually increase risky behaviors, such as smoking, drug use, and early sexual activity in adolescents.

■ FUTURE STUDIES

While SFBT shows promising results, school-based professionals and researchers must provide more studies on this approach if a strong evidence base is to be developed. Future studies need to examine more carefully which school-based populations and problem areas SFBT would be best suited to help. Researchers should also work to improve the research designs of school-based studies of SFBT and continue using better measures as they replicate existing findings and explore new applications of SFBT in school settings. The top outcome priority for schools continues to be school achievement, involving problems that are known to sabotage a student's school career, like poor school motivation and engagement, low attendance, dropout, poor academic performance, and low career readiness. Future research should give attention to studying these performance outcomes with SFBT in order to demonstrate the greatest relevance and clinical utility for school settings (Franklin et al., 2009; Hoagwood et al, 2007).

Future studies may also continue to focus on assessing both internalizing and externalizing behavioral outcomes. Externalizing behaviors are particularly egregious in schools, and the positive outcomes reported in the school research by different observers (e.g., students and teachers) should be replicated and may be of great interest to both practitioners and researchers. Behavioral outcomes, in particular, are important to measure when compared to internal psychological constructs such as self-esteem, which showed no increase with SFBT and has not been found to be a good measure for predicting school performance. Substance use appears to be another area that can be measured with good clinical utility for outcomes in schools.

Another area of research might be to create a treatment manual for schools addressing different levels of intervention. Solution-focused brief therapy in schools is very complex. It may be applied as prevention and remediation tools, as well as treatment for difficult populations. In addition, SFBT may be delivered using different modalities, such as individual, group, family, or even organizational interventions by diverse personnel, including mental health therapists, school counselors or social workers, or teachers and administrators. Future studies can assess the levels of intervention at which SFBT appears to be most effective.

More attention also needs to be given to clinical process issues and assessment, as well as the mechanisms of change in school settings. As was pointed out in Chapter 9, process research that can guide clinicians on the implementation of different solution-focused techniques is definitiely needed. Mixed-design studies may address the complex change issues encountered in a school setting better than strict applications of outcome research or process studies alone. Researchers may wish to develop outcome designs that also assess process variables and to further study the best school context in which SFBT interventions are delivered.

■ KEY FINDINGS TO REMEMBER

- As a brief intervention, SFBT may be useful because it tries to engage with children, families, and teachers to focus on quick improvements in the target problem. The majority of studies examined in this review revealed that about four to eight sessions of SFBT were delivered to achieve favorable outcomes.
- The solution-focused practice of defining small, concrete goals is also more realistic is a school situation, where those involved have limited time and resources (Murphy, 1996).
- Positive outcomes in the school research suggest that SFBT can be beneficial in helping students reduce the intensity of their negative feelings, manage their conduct problems, improve academic outcomes like credits earned, and reduce externalizing behavioral problems and substance use.
- In one study, SFBT was just as effective as cognitive-behavioral therapy in producing behavioral change, and was more effective in engaging clients and retaining them in the therapy process.
- Future studies need to examine more carefully which school-based populations and problem areas SFBT would be best suited to help.

■ FURTHER LEARNING

BRIEF in London, Solutions in Education
http://www.brief.org.uk/training-details.php?item_id=65&CourseCode=21
Garza High School
http://www.austinschools.org/campus/garza/html/aboutgarza.htm
School Social Work and Research Special Interest Group Web site: http://www.luc.edu/sswsig

■ REFERENCES

Baumeister, R. F., Campbell, J. D., Krueger, J. I., & Vohs, K. D. (2003). Does self-esteem cause better performance, interpersonal success, happiness, or healthier lifestyles? *Psychological Science in the Public Interest, 4,* 1–44.

Berg, I. K., & Shilts, L. (2004). *Classroom solutions: WOWW approach.* Milwaukee: Brief Family Therapy Center Press.

Corcoran, J. (2006). A comparison group study of solution-focused therapy versus "treatment-as-usual" for behavior problems in children. *Journal of Social Service Research, 33,* 69–81.

Duncan, B. L., & Murphy, J. J. (2007). *Brief interventions for school problems* (2nd ed.). New York: Guilford Press.

Franklin, C., Biever, J. L., Moore, K. C., Clemons, D., & Scamardo, M. (2001). Effectiveness of solution-focused therapy with children in a school setting. *Research on Social Work Practice, 11,* 411–434.

Franklin, C., & Gerlach, B. (2007). Clinical applications of solution-focused brief therapy in public schools. In T. S. Nelson & F. N. Thomas (Eds.), *Handbook of solution-focused brief therapy: Clinical applications* (pp. 168–169). Philadelphia: Haworth Press.

Franklin, C., & Hopson, L. (2009). Involuntary clients in public schools: Solution-focused interventions. In R. H. Rooney (Ed.), *Strategies for work with involuntary clients* (2nd ed., pp. 322–333). New York: Columbia University Press.

Franklin, C., Kim, J. S., & Tripodi, S. J. (2009). A meta-analysis of published school social work intervention studies: 1980–2007. *Research on Social Work Practice, 19*(6), 667–677.

Franklin, C., Moore, K., & Hopson, L. (2008). Effectiveness of solution-focused brief therapy in a school setting. *Children & Schools, 30*, 15–26.

Franklin, C., Streeter, C. L., Kim, J. S., & Tripodi, S. J. (2007). The effectiveness of a solution-focused, public alternative school for dropout prevention and retrieval. *Children & Schools, 29*, 133–144.

Franklin, C. & Streeter, C. L. (2003). Solution-focused Accountabilty Schools for the Twenty-first Century: An Evaluation of Garza High School. The University of Texas at Austin, Hogg Foundation for Mental Health.

Frazer, M. W., Richmond, J. M., Galinsky, M. J., & Day, S. H. (2009). *Intervention research.* New York: Oxford University Press.

Froeschle, J. G., Smith, R. L., & Ricard, R. (2007). The efficacy of a systematic substance abuse program for adolescent females. *Professional School Counseling, 10*, 498–505.

Gingerich, W., & Eisengart, S. (2000). Solution-focused brief therapy: A review of outcome research. *Family Process, 39*, 477–496.

Harris, M. B., & Franklin, C. (2008). *Taking charge: A school based life skills program for adolescent mothers.* New York: Oxford University Press.

Hedges, L. V., & Olkin, I. (1985). *Statistical models for meta-analysis.* New York: Academic Press.

Hoagwood, K. E., & Erwin, H. D. (1997). The effectiveness of school-based mental health services for children: A 10-year research review. *Journal of Child and Family Studies, 6*, 435–451.

Hoagwood, K. E., Olin, S. S., Kerker, B. D., Kratochwill, T. R., Crowe, M., & Saka, N. (2007). Empirically based school interventions targeted at academic and mental health functioning. *Journal of Emotional and Behavioral Disorders, 15*, 66–92.

Hopson, L. M., & Kim, J. S. (2005). A solution-focused approach to crisis intervention with adolescents. *Journal of Evidence-Based Social Work, 1*, 93–110.

Kazdin, A. E. (2002). *Research design in clinical psychology* (4th ed.). Boston: Allyn & Bacon.

Kelly, M. S., Kim, J. S., & Franklin, C. (2008). *Solution-focused brief therapy in schools: A 360-degree view of the research and practice principles.* New York: Oxford University Press.

Kim, J. S. (2008). Examining the effectiveness of solution-focused brief therapy: A meta-analysis. *Research on Social Work Practice, 18*, 107–116.

Kim, J. S., & Franklin, C. (2009). Solution-focused brief therapy in schools: A review of the literature. *Children and Youth Services Review, 31*(4), 464–470.

Kral, R. (1995). *Solutions for schools.* Milwaukee: Brief Family Therapy Center Press.

LaFountain, R. M., & Garner, N. E. (1996). Solution-focused counseling groups: The results are in. *Journal for Specialists in Group Work, 21*, 128–143.

Mahlberg, K., & Sjöblom. M. (2004). *Solution-focused education.* Stockholm, Sweden Smedjebaken: Mahlberg & Sjöblom.

Metcalf, L. (1995). *Counseling toward solutions: A practical solution-focused program for working with students, teachers, and parents.* San Francisco: Jossey-Bass.

Metcalf, L. (2008). *A field guide to counseling toward solutions.* San Francisco: Jossey-Bass.

Murphy, J. J. (1996). Solution-focused brief therapy in the school. In S. D. Miller, M. A. Hubble, & B. S. Duncan (Eds.), *Handbook of solution-focused brief therapy* (pp. 184–204). San Francisco: Jossey-Bass.

Murphy, J. J., & Duncan, B. S. (2007). *Brief interventions for school problems* (2nd ed.). New York: Guilford Publications.

Murphy, J. J. (2008). *Solution-focused Counseling in Schools.* Alexandria, Virginia: American Counseling Association.

Newsome, S. (2004). Solution-focused brief therapy (SFBT) groupwork with at-risk junior high school students: Enhancing the bottom-line. *Research on Social Work Practice, 14,* 336–343.

Roans, M., & Hoagwood, K. (2000). School-based mental health services: A research review. *Clinical Child and Family Psychology Review, 3,* 223–241.

Rubin, A., & Babbie, E. (2005). *Research methods for social work* (5th ed.). Belmont, CA: Brooks/Cole-Thomson Learning.

Sklare, G. B. (1997). *Brief counseling that works: A solution-focused approach for school counselors.* Thousand Oaks, CA: Sage Publications.

Solution-Focused Brief Therapy Research Committee. (2007). *Solution-focused therapy treatment manual for working with individuals.* Retrieved July 15, 2007, from http://www.sfbta.org/

Springer, D. W., Lynch, C., & Rubin, A. (2000). Effects of a solution-focused mutual aid group for Hispanic children of incarcerated parents. *Child & Adolescent Social Work Journal, 17,* 431–432.

Stams, G. J. J. M., Dekovic, M., Buist, K., & De Vries, L. (2006). Effectiviteit van oplossings-gerichte korte therapie: een meta-analyse [Efficacy of solution focused brief therapy: A meta-analysis]. *Tijdschrift voor Gedragstherapie, 39,* 81–94.

Trepper, T. S., McCollum, E. E., De Jong, P., Korman, H., Gingerich, W., & Franklin, C. (2008). *Solution focused therapy treatment manual for working with individuals.* Solution Focused Brief Therapy Association Research Committee. Retrieved April 22, 2010, from http://www.sfbta.org/Research.pdf

Webb, W. H. (1999). *Solutioning: Solution-focused interventions for counselors.* Philadelphia: Accelerated Press.

Weisz, J. R., Chu, B. C., & Polo, A. J. (2004). Treatment dissemination and evidence-based practice: Strengthening intervention through clinician–researcher collaboration. *Clinical Psychology: Science and Practice, 11,* 300–307.

17 Taking Charge

A Solution-Focused Intervention for Pregnant and Parenting Adolescents

■ MARY BETH HARRIS AND CYNTHIA FRANKLIN

■ INTRODUCTION

Adolescent pregnancy occurs across all social, economic, religious, racial, and cultural groups and is a serious social problem of our time. Once an adolescent woman becomes pregnant, her world changes abruptly and profoundly. Adolescence, a time for gradually moving out of childhood and developing the skills one needs for adult living, has been cut short for her. The social and life skills that an adolescent mother needs that she might have developed when she entered her 20s she now needs immediately—at the age of 17, 15, or even younger. Women bearing children in their adolescence have extra challenges in order to prepare themselves to be good parents and to grow into self-sufficient adults. Many of the actions and decisions that a young mother makes during her pregnancy and the first year of her child's life will profoundly affect the quality of both their lives for many years to come.

Governments in diverse countries recognize the challenges of adolescent pregnancy and the risks that exist for both the mother and her child. As a result, considerable resources have been used to both prevent adolescent pregnancy and avert the deleterious consequences of having babies at a young age. Yet, in spite of all of these efforts, adolescent pregnancy continues to grow. For example, in the United States, nearly 800,000 adolescents become pregnant each year and 400,000 give birth, giving the United States the highest teen birth rate of any industrialized nation (Guttmacher Institute, 2006, 2010; Hamilton et al., 2007). Of course, adolescent pregnancy is not just a problem for the United States. It is a significant issue for other countries in Europe and Canada, and most industrialized nations are funding programs to lower the teen pregnancy rate and to assist adolescents with their parenting, health, and social and economic welfare.

The purpose of this chapter is to describe the solution-focused Taking Charge (TC) intervention, a school-based program designed to help adolescent mothers. Taking Charge is a multimodal, brief cognitive behavioral curriculum that was developed within solution-focused and developmental frameworks, utilizing the strengths, resources, life goals, and developmental tasks of adolescent mothers. The goals of the curriculum are to construct a solution-focused approach that can help adolescent mothers develop the solutions they need in order to achieve good outcomes in four targeted life domains: (a) the mother's education, (b) social support/personal relationships, (c) parenting, and (d) employment/career preparation. This chapter describes the importance of these four life domains to the future outcomes of adolescent mothers and how the major components of the solution-focused TC intervention help adolescent women who are pregnant and parenting develop their own goals and solutions in these areas. The chapter also highlights how the TC program was created, using research evidence on what works to help adolescent mothers be self-sufficient, and describes the research studies where the program was tested in schools with adolescents.

■ WHAT WE HAVE LEARNED SO FAR

One of the biggest problems surrounding teen pregnancy is poverty, which creates circumstances fostering social problems such as school dropout, substance abuse, gang involvement, and teen pregnancy (Haveman et al., 1997). Adolescents who become pregnant face various social problems that may reinforce each other in an endless feedback loop. For example, adolescents who become pregnant are more likely to be struggling academically and to drop out of school (National At-Risk Education Network, 2006), and those who have dropped out or abuse substances or who were maltreated as children are even more likely to become pregnant and have a child than their peers who stay in school (Kirby, 2002; National Center on Addiction and Substance Abuse at Columbia University [CASA], 1997; 2002b). For example, 72% percent of adolescents who have had sex use drugs compared to 36% of those who have never used drugs (CASA, 2002c). Studies also suggest that about 50% of teenage girls who become pregnant were sexually abused as children (Raj et al., 2000), and as many as 96% were physically abused (Herrenkohl et al., 1998).

Focusing on Strengths: Predictors of Life Quality for Adolescent Mothers

In developing the TC intervention, we believed it was important to offer a strengths-based approach to best help teen mothers. Instead of focusing on the complexity of the problems in the adolescent mother's life, we emphasized what would be different in her life when she had positive outcomes despite having one or more children at a young age. We searched the research literature and identified factors that predicted the self-sufficiency, economic success, and well-being of both mothers and their children. We discovered four important life domains that predict the quality of life for adolescent mothers:

1. Education: whether or not she is able to finish high school or obtain a GED by the time she turns 20.
2. Social support/personal relationships: whether or not she is able to sustain supportive relationships with her family and friends, particularly with her parents and her partner or the father of her baby.
3. Parenting efficacy: whether or not she gains a deep sense of confidence and belief in herself as a mother and can use these attitudes in caring for her child

and advocating for the child's needs with the community systems that affect his or her education, health, and social development.

4. Readiness for employment or a career: whether or not she explores, plans, and gains work experience or additional training or education for a career or employment that will provide for herself and her child.

Research tells us that these four life domains—education, social support/personal relationships, parenting, and employment/career preparation—all interact and affect one another (Harris & Franklin, 2008, 2009; Zupicich, 2003) and are essential to the positive life outcomes of teenage mothers and their children. For a review of this research, see Harris and Franklin (2008). Following are some examples of how these four factors work together and affect the life outcomes of teenage mothers. The more social and support and positive relationships a teen mother has with family members, the baby's father, and peers, for example, the more likely she is to be able to increase her competencies to be a good mother and at the same time go to school. Her family, the baby's father, and friends can help relieve her burden, compensate for her lack of experience with child care, and provide the extra emotional, social, and financial support the mother needs to keep progressing in her parenting and school experiences. The more consistently a teen mother attends school, the more likely she is to achieve passing marks and feel committed to her education. This is extremely important because more than 60% of teenage girls who become pregnant and have a child drop out of school and do not graduate (Laird et al., 2007). This means that more than 240,000 adolescent girls in the United States drop out of school each year because they have become mothers. The fact that so many teen mothers do not finish high school and thus do not qualify well for the job market means that they and their children are more likely to live in poverty (Zill & O'Donnell, 2004). More than anything else, these young women must have an education that prepares them to be productive wage earners.

To continue our example, the more an adolescent mother achieves academically, the more likely she is to consider postgraduation training or college and a career. On the other hand, when the young mother is unsupported by her family or in conflict with the father of her baby, or when she is not able to communicate her academic needs to her teachers or counselor, her hope and motivation concerning can shrink until she simply gives up and drops out. When this happens—and statistics tell us that it often does—this young mother's life and her future become limited in a way that is difficult to overcome.

Best Approaches and Strategies for Helping

The good news is this: As challenging as young mothers' lives may be, in general they are more resilient and have more strengths, stamina, and determination than one might assume. We say this after studying and observing hundreds of these young women and seeing their strengths firsthand (Harris & Franklin, 2002, 2008, 2009). After studying the best practices with adolescents that we could find in the disciplines of social work, psychology, and education, we developed a strengths-based approach that we believe is effective for our work with teen mothers.

Even though we as a society expect more of adolescent mothers than of other teenagers and treat them differently when they become pregnant, they are still teenagers.

They are still dealing with all the stresses that teenagers encounter—and now much more. Now they have an immediate need for a new set of skills that their peers will not develop for 3 to 5 more years. Our job is to help them learn how to identify the adult skills they need by providing a learning process in which they can set their own goals and work toward solutions in areas requiring improved school outcomes, social support, parenting, and career readiness. We then coach and support them in developing their own competencies and solutions.

In developing the TC intervention, we used both a solution-focused brief therapy (SFBT) approach and cognitive behavioral interventions that focused on learning new behaviors and changing the young mother's thinking—her assumptions about herself and the world around her—in ways that alter her behavior and her methods for dealing with her life. Without reservation, we approach our work with adolescent mothers from a solution-focused perspective, with the assumption that they are clearly competent and capable and either already possess or can learn the skills they need in order to take charge of their own lives. We assume that, with encouragement and support, teen mothers can and will rise to the challenge. By and large, from our experiences with teen mothers, our assumption has been correct.

Importance of Learning New Life Skills Quickly: We have already stated that teen mothers have to learn adult life skills quickly. What life skills does a young mother need in order to become a self-sufficient adult and parent? How does a social worker, counselor, or teacher help her gain confidence in enacting new roles and skills? In this section, we discuss three skills that we consider primary: (a) goal setting, (b) social problem solving, and (c) active coping. We used both solution-focused therapy and cognitive behavioral interventions to help young mothers identify, learn, and practice these three skills as they relate to their personal life challenges across the four essential life domains that were mentioned above and were found to be important to the mother's self-sufficiency. We helped these teenagers to practice new solutions and to master new behaviors and skills across these life domains by using the following cognitive behavioral interventions that have been found in other research to help teenagers with behavior problems (Hogue & Liddle, 1999):

1. The professional (social worker, counselor, etc.) models the skill in session with the teenager.
2. The teenager role-plays and practices the skill in session.
3. The teenager is assigned homework to continue practicing the skill in the real world.
4. The professional discusses with the teenager her success in practicing the skill and adjusts the practice according to the first results.

We further used solution-focused therapy to focus on the teen mothers' strengths and resources while they were learning the skills and to help them gain confidence in working out difficulties in their everyday lives.

Social Problem-Solving and Coping Skills: Adolescent mothers have many stressors to deal with in their daily lives. In addition to going to school, doing homework, and managing daily responsibilities, they have another person—their child—to take care of. They have well-baby appointments to keep, diapers to change, feeding, bathing, and dressing to do, bouts of 2:00 a.m. colic to get through, and negotiations about all of this with parents, siblings, and the baby's father. Research has shown us that teenagers typically cope with stresses such as these in a variety of ways: (a) Many simply avoid the problems and hope that they will go away. (b) Some just accept the problems as unchangeable and out of their control and accommodate them. (c) A few focus on acting to change or resolve the problems (Harris & Franklin, 2008).

With daily stressors that are central to the present and future well-being of the mother and her child, avoidance and passive acceptance are no longer real options. Solution-focused brief therapy helps these mothers address the stressors by focusing on what changes they want to make in their lives and what solutions are needed to effect these changes. Research has shown that young mothers who can focus on the future and develop solutions by taking action to solve problems experience less stress, do better in school, and show greater acceptance, warmth, and helpfulness in dealing with their children (Harris & Franklin, 2008; Passino et. al, 1993). Our goal is for young mothers to *have a deep conviction* that they can take charge of their problems and build their own solutions with less avoidance and passivity. We do this by showing them how to use the social problem-solving process, described in Box 17.1, to break down and tackle problems that seem overwhelming. In the TC intervention, we integrate the social problem-solving approach with a solution-building approach in which the mothers identify their own goals across the four life areas of education, social support, parenting, and career preparation. Once the mothers identify these goals, they create their own solutions.

■ SFBT INTERVENTION: THE TC GROUP

The TC intervention is presented in an 8- to 12-week school-based program that is offered within a task-centered group. The tasks of the TC group focus on building new solutions that strengthen the adolescent mother's active problem-solving and coping abilities. In turn, enacted solutions are used to gain better outcomes across the four life domains of education, social support/personal relationships, parenting, and employment/career. In other words, every time the mother builds a solution in one of the life domains, the more that domain may improve. We have published a treatment manual that guides therapists and educators through a step-by step process for offering each group session and includes other instructions for making the group intervention a success in school settings (Harris & Franklin, 2008). We summarize the change process

---

BOX 17.1. ■ The Social Problem-Solving Process

1. Identify the situation that is currently a real problem for me.
2. Identify the smaller problems that underlie this situation.
3. Describe my goal for solving this problem.
4. Identify barriers that could keep me from reaching my goal.
5. Identify the resources I have to help me reach my goal.
6. List as many possible strategies as I can to help me reach my goal.
7. Pick a strategy from these that I believe has the best chance to succeed.
8. Decide on two tasks I can do immediately to carry out my strategy.
9. Now . . . JUST DO IT!

and the core treatment components of TC below, but practitioners should read the treatment manual to gain a better understanding of this approach.

Taking Charge Change Group Process

The TC group intervention combines behavioral incentives with goal setting and solution building, and is delivered using a task-centered group process with 8–12 pregnant and parenting adolescents. The task-centered group process engages the adolescents in actively setting their own goals and tasks that lead to self-selected behavioral changes across the domains of school, personal relationships, parenting, and career preparation. The core components of the intervention include personal goal setting; learning and applying social problem-solving, active coping, and solution-building skills; and the use of incentives through compliments and a point system. The task-centered group further provides peer and group support for constructing and performing specific behavioral tasks leading to achievement of the self-selected goals across the four life domains. See Figure 17.1 for a summary of the core components of the TC intervention.

Implementing the Major Components of the TC Intervention

Personal Goal Setting and Solution Building. In the solution-building and goal-setting change processes, each group participant forms a goal that is solution focused in each

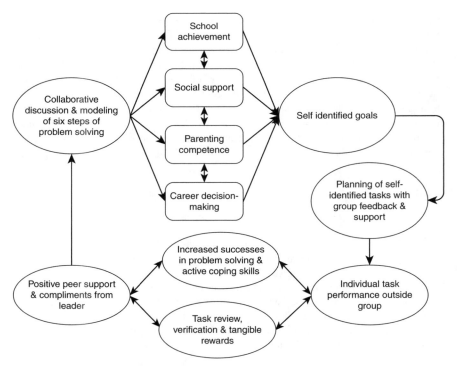

Figure 17.1. Core components of the Taking Charge intervention.

of the four life domains. Participants are taught the social problem-solving process through a collaborative discussion, and the group leader facilitates the learning of active coping and solution-building skills while participants identify strategies and specific tasks to help them achieve their goals. Each adolescent carries out her self-selected tasks between group sessions and then reports her results back to the group. Goal setting leads to the development of self-identified solutions for areas that the mother identifies as important to her everyday life.

Learning how to develop goals and actively follow a plan to accomplish them is central to the development of the life skills needed by teenage mothers. In our work, we focus on the strengths of young mothers and help them find their own solutions. We believe it is also essential to help teen mothers establish their own goals, and we use the following process in setting goals with them:

> *The goal must be behaviorally defined and be important to the young mother. It must also be set with a commitment to follow through and must be perceived as hard work. Finally, it must be described in a series of steps that are part of a social process—in other words, what the mother will do with whom to make this happen by when. The mother also must make a commitment to the group to report back on how her solution worked.*

In setting goals, we are careful to support the *mother's* process of identifying *her own* goals, strategies, and tasks rather than imposing our own, even though at times we may have reservations about her goal. We want the mother to find her own competencies to succeed. When we supply the "right answer," we deny her the motivation and responsibility for her own experience. Box 17.2 illustrates how a young woman in one of our groups worked through the social problem-solving steps in setting a goal and developing her own solution.

Compliments and Incentives. In the TC program, adolescent mothers are frequently complimented for their efforts, both directly and indirectly. For example, a group leader might say, "I am amazed at how patient you were with your mother-in-law" or "You are a good student to make those grades!" Or a leader might say something like "How did you make that happen? Tell me the steps again. That's incredible that you can do that at such a young age."

Incentives are provided to strengthen participation and maximize the benefits of the group. A point system provides motivation for performing tasks and increasing school attendance and participation. Group participants earn points toward an award at the end of the intervention for school and group attendance, tasks completed, homework, and extra-credit assignments. Participants who earn a set minimum number of points are presented with an award, such as a gift certificate, at the end of the intervention. Lunch or a snack is served at the beginning of each session, and small surprise gifts are presented at two of the sessions. Beyond these tangible incentives, the group focuses on frequent compliments both from the leaders and from other group members.

The Importance of Tasks and Building Competencies. Taking Charge uses the processes of goal setting, solution building, and task performance to show the mother her own competencies. Carrying out tasks that adolescent mothers set for themselves is an important process for mastering new life skills. Tasks are as essential to this change process as flour is to bread! Whereas goal setting is where changes in thinking begin to happen, actually *performing the tasks* needed to achieve the goal is where real change—in thinking and behavior—is driven home. When the adolescent mother

---

BOX 17.2. ■ Social Problem-Solving Example

Sonia: My Personal Relationship Goal

1. MY PROBLEM: My mother-in-law and I don't get along. She's cold to me and criticizes the way I look and dress, how I cook, and especially the way I take care of my baby.
2. SMALLER PROBLEMS: My husband won't stand up to her. I think he's afraid of her. Neither does my father-in-law, even though I get along fine with him. She takes care of my baby while I'm at school, so she's with him as much as I am. My husband is in welding school and only makes [a] minimum wage 20 hours a week at his job, so we're financially dependent on his parents for another year. I don't have a car, so she has to take me to appointments for the baby.
3. MY GOAL: For my mother-in-law to like me better and stop criticizing me so much.
4. POSSIBLE BARRIERS: If I try to change anything between us, it may just make things worse. I'm scared of her and try to stay away from her. I don't know how to talk to her. I don't like her at all.
5. MY RESOURCES: My boyfriend loves me and wants me to stay. Another resource is my cousin, who's a probation officer. She tries to help me understand my mother-in-law better. Another is my boyfriend's sister, who is cool with me when she drops by, and tells me to ignore my mother-in-law.
6. POSSIBLE STRATEGIES: (1) Confront my mother-in-law and threaten to move out if she doesn't change. (2) Go out of my way to please her without talking about it. (3) Get to know her better. (4) Clear the air with her to find out what I can do to make things better between us. (5) Take my baby and move back to my mother's house.
7. I CHOOSE: The strategy of clearing the air with my mother-in-law and finding out how I can make things better between us.
8. MY TASKS: (1) To talk to my boyfriend's sister about my goal and get her advice on how to talk to her mother. (2) To tell my mother-in-law that I want to have a good relationship with her and ask her what I can do to help that happen.

Source: Harris and Franklin (2008). Page 114.

---

faces her problem and *acts to change and resolve it*, this experience creates a deep sense of confidence in her. Our job in facilitating this solution-oriented, life-altering process is to encourage her to take the risk, assure and remind her that she is capable of solution building in this situation, and support her when things do not go as she hoped the first time and it is necessary to try again.

■ RESEARCH METHODS: STUDIES TO TEST THE EFFICACY OF THE TC GROUP INTERVENTION

Harris and Franklin (2002, 2008, 2009) developed the TC group intervention in response to a request from school social workers on the U.S.–Mexico border. The social workers asked for help in reducing the absenteeism and failing grades that were leading to school dropout among adolescent mothers in the district high schools. To date, three efficacy studies of TC have been conducted in high school settings with leaders who were teachers, school support professionals, or school interns and with former adolescent mothers. The following studies provide initial support for the use of TC. Currently there is one randomized clinical trial (RCT; Study 1) and two quasi-experimental studies. See Table 17.1 for a discussion of the demographics across the three studies.

Study 1

The original TC study was an RCT completed in El Paso, Texas, in the Ysleta School District ($n = 73$) in five high schools. All participants identified themselves as Mexican or Mexican American and were randomly assigned to either the intervention or the standard school practice condition. Results indicated a significant improvement in outcomes for school attendance (ES .47), grades (ES .48). Specifically, at pretest, the treatment group (.83 attendance) and the comparison group (.84 attendance) were nearly identical in school attendance, both groups having missed an average of about 5 days during the previous 6 weeks. At posttest, the treatment group (.90 attendance), with a 7% increase in school attendance, had missed an average of only 3 days compared to the control group (.83 attendance), which had dropped 1% in attendance and had again averaged about 5 days missed over the previous 6 weeks. At the beginning of Study 1, the treatment group's grade point average (GPA; 78.75) was nearly identical to the comparison group's GPA (78.52), both classified as a C average. At posttest 9 weeks later, the treatment group had gained over 2 points (80.79), rising from a C average to

TABLE 17.1. *Demographic Characteristics from the Three Taking Charge Studies*

| | Study 1: $n = 73$ | | Study 2: $n = 46$ | | Study 3: $n = 19$ | |
	Treatment $n = 33$	Control $n = 40$	Treatment $n = 27$	Comparison $n = 19$	Treatment $n = 12$	Comparison $n = 7$
Age						
Mean	17.89	17.97	16.93	16.84	16.66	17.14
SD	1.44	1.39	1.38	1.11	2.32	1.53
Range	6.00	6.00	6.00	5.00	4.00	4.00
Grade in School						
Ninth	2 (6%)	4 (10%)	3 (11%)	3 (16%)	2 (17%)	1 (14%)
Tenth	8 (24%)	3 (8%)	2 (7%)	2 (11%)	5 (42%)	1 (14%)
Eleventh	7 (21%)	14 (35%)	9 (33%)	6 (32%)	2 (17%)	2 (29%)
Twelfth	16 (48%)	18 (45%)	13 (48%)	8 (42%)	3 (25%)	3 (43%)
Other	—	1 (2%)	—	—	—	—
Culture/Race						
Mex Am	26 (79%)	37 (93%)	4 (15%)	5 (26%)	10 (83%)	7 (100%)
Mex Citizen	–5 (15%)	–2 (5%)				
African Am	—	—	12 (44%)	–5 (26%)	—	
Asian Am	—	—	2 (7%)	–1 (5%)	—	
Anglo Am	—	—	8 (30%)	6 (32%)	–2 (17%)	
Am Indian	—	—	—	2 (11%)		
Other	2 (6%)	1 (2%)	1 (4%)	—		
Parenting Status						
Pregnant	7 (21%)	10 (26%)	9 (33%) x	5 (42%)	v	v
Have a child	24 (73%)	26 (67%)	13 (48%)	10 (53%)	4 (33%)	3 (43%)
Pregnant+child		2 (5%)	5 (19%)	5 (26%)	3 (25%)	1 (14%)

a B- average. This was significantly higher than the posttest comparison group GPA (72.63). Similar findings were replicated in Studies 2 and 3. In addition to these school outcomes, the TC intervention improved the indicators of .social problem solving (ES 1.0) and active coping (ES .79) in relation to the changes in the comparison group (Harris & Franklin, 2002). Social problem solving was measured using the Social Problem Solving Skills Inventory-Revised (SPSI-R Short Form; D'Zurilla & Nezu, 1990). At posttest the intervention group score was significantly higher (ES 1.0) than the comparison group score, showing that the TC intervention positively impacted the social problem-solving skills of participants. These results held at the 6-weeks follow-up. Active coping was also measured with three subscales of the Adolescent Coping Orientation for Problem Experiences (A-COPE; McCubbin & Thompson, 1991). These subscales measured problem-focused (active) coping behaviors in three domains: self-reliance, social support, and solving family problems. At posttest, significant changes were found in the intervention group, and the effect size was .79. These findings show that the Latina adolescents had increased their use of active coping behaviors, and these results held at the 6-week follow-up.

Study 2

The second study ($n = 46$) was quasi-experimental in design but identical to Study 1 in outcome variables. The study was conducted in a north Texas school district with culturally diverse students (Harris & Franklin, 2008). African American (37%), White (30%), Hispanic (20%), Asian American (7%), and American Indian (6%) adolescent mothers comprised the sample in this study. Researchers adjusted statistically for possible differences in the purposive sample. Study 2 results favored the intervention group over the "business as usual" group and were statistically significant for school attendance (ES .55), academic achievement (ES .57), problem solving (ES .71), and active coping (ES .73). Social problem solving was measured with the okay SPSI-R Short Form (D'Zurilla & Nezu, 1990). At posttest, the intervention group score was significantly higher (ES .71) than the comparison group score, suggesting that the intervention was positively impacting the social problem-solving skills of participants. These results held at the 6-week follow-up. Active coping was also measured in Study 2 with three subscales of the Adolescent Coping Orientation for Problem Experiences (A-COPE; McCubbin & Thompson, 1991). These subscales measured problem-focused (active) coping behaviors in three domains: self-reliance, social support, and solving family problems. At posttest, significant changes were found in the intervention group, and the effect sizes was .73. These findings held at the 6-week follow-up, showing that the adolescents had increased their use of active coping behaviors. See Table 17.2 for more information on the outcomes.

Study 3

Study 3 ($n = 23$) was conducted in a semirural school district in New Mexico. The participants in this study identified themselves as 89% Latina and 11% Anglo. Due to the small purposive sample, only school-related data on grades and attendance were collected and analyzed. Results of the study showed significant improvements in the intervention group on attendance (ES .93) and grades (ES .26; Harris & Franklin, 2009).

See Table 17.2 for a more detailed picture of the outcomes across the three studies. This table also highlights the statistical analysis.

TABLE 17.2. *Results from the Three Taking Charge Studies by Outcome Measures*

Adolescent Coping Orientation for Problem Experiences (A-COPE) Subscales Pretest, Posttest, and Follow-up Means and Standard Deviations

	Study 1		Study 2	
	Treatment	Control	Treatment	Comparison
	Pretest			
Mean	58.52	58.35	53.88	57.58
SD	10.41	9.05	9.03	7.04
	Posttest			
Mean	65.58	56.85	61.48	55.58
SD	10.47	11.09	8.42	7.61
	Follow-up			
Mean	64.07	56.62	59.37	56.21
SD	9.57	12.55	7.78	6.50

Study 1 ANOVA results: F = 15.98; $d.f.$ = 1,70; p < .000; eta squared = .19.
Study 2 ANOVA results: F = 24.47; $d.f.$ = 1,43; p < .000; eta squared = .36.

Social Problem Solving Inventory-Revised (SPRI-R) Short Form Pretest, Posttest, and Follow-up Means and Standard Deviations

	Study 1		Study 2	
	Treatment	Control	Treatment	Comparison
	Pretest			
Mean	12.88	12.98	12.53	11.70
SD	3.14	2.85	3.71	3.94
	Posttest			
Mean	14.94	12.08	13.92	11.35
SD	3.17	2.86	3.26	3.88
	Follow-up			
Mean	14.93	12.88	13.46	11.00
SD	3.56	3.43	2.56	3.69

Study 1 ANOVA results: F = 19.49; $d.f.$ = 1,70; p < .000; eta squared = .22.
Study 2 ANOVA results: F = 5.48; $d.f.$ = 1,41; p < .024; partial eta squared = .29.

School Attendance (Percent) Pretest, Posttest, and Follow-up Means and Standard Deviations

	Study 1		Study 2		Study 3	
	Treatment	Control	Treatment	Comparison	Treatment	Comparison
	Pretest					
Mean	.83	.84	.78	.81	.80	.80
SD	.14	.17	.14	.11	.08	.16
	Posttest					
Mean	.90	.83	.86	.77	.88	.78
SD	.01	.15	.12	.20	.06	.14
	Follow-up					
Mean .86	.75	.86	.75	—	—	
SD	.12	.20	.14	.21	—	—

Study 1 ANOVA results: F = 9.791; $d.f.$ = 1,70; p < .003; eta squared = .12.
Study 2 ANOVA results: F = 5.373; $d.f.$ = 1,43; p < .025; partial eta squared = .11.
Study 3 ANOVA results: F = 15.178; $d.f.$ = 1,16; p < .001; partial eta squared = .49.

(Continued)

TABLE 17.2. *(continued)*

Academic Achievement Pretest and Posttest Means and Standard Deviations

	Study 1		Study 2		Study 3	
	GPA		Curriculum Units		GPA	
	Treatment	Control	Treatment	Comparison	Treatment	Comparison
	Pretest					
Mean	77.84	77.45	7.26	8.00	80.62	83.43
SD	9.52	7.89	5.77	3.74	4.95	7.19
	Posttest					
Mean	79.59	71.63	12.44	8.58	82.66	80.73
SD	11.03	16.48	8.72	3.89	.34	9.48

Study 1 ANOVA results: $F = 7.07$; $d.f. = 1,64$; $p < .010$; eta squared = .10.
Study 2 ANOVA results: $F = 21.66$; $d.f. = 1,43$; $p < .000$; eta squared = .34.
Study 3 ANOVA results: $F = 25.625$; $d.f. = 1,16$; $p < .000$; partial eta squared = .62.

Follow-up Analysis on Staying in School

Post hoc analyses of dropout statistics were conducted for all three studies. These analyses suggest that participating in the TC group has a positive impact on staying in school for the adolescents who were pregnant and parenting. This was measured by the dropout status (not having a diploma or GED and not being enrolled in school) of each person in the study (Harris & Franklin, 2008). Of the 73 students who initially entered Study 1, 8 (20%) members of the comparison group dropped out of school before the end of the school year compared to 1 (3%) in the TC intervention group. Of the 46 students who entered Study 2, 3 (16%) in the comparison group dropped out of school during the study, while all participants in TC were in school at the end of the school year. In Study 3, four students (36%) in the comparison group dropped out during the study compared to no dropouts in the TC group.

Study Limitations

The experimental design of Study 1 and the quasi-experimental design of Studies 2 and 3 controlled for several competing explanatory factors, especially as the treatment and comparison groups were found to be equivalent on most identified demographic and outcome variables at pretest. However, a design weakness is the fact that a quasi-experimental design such as those used in Studies 2 and 3 suggests potentially unrecognized differences between the two groups, which could impact the degree of difference in the groups at posttest.

A limitation of Study 3 is the small sample size ($n = 23$), although the sample for this study is typical of the numbers available to practitioners in evaluating local programs and practices. Another weakness is that the two groups in Study 3 were unequal in size due to the withdrawal of four members of the comparison group during the study. Even though only two outcomes were analyzed and a Bonferroni adjustment set alpha at .01, the small sample reduces confidence that the statistical results would hold up with a larger sample.

Generalizability is limited in Studies 1 and 3 by the homogeneous Latina sample. In addition to being primarily Mexican American, these adolescent mothers lived primarily with their family or the family of their baby's father, or in their own home. No participants in the three studies lived in residential or foster care, and none had identified physical or mental disabilities. It should not be assumed that TC would be effective with Hispanic adolescent mothers in other locations or with adolescents who differed from these samples in other ways, even within the current locations. Even so, Study 2, with a broadly culturally diverse sample, suggests that TC is effective with adolescent mothers across cultures. As well, research on the effectiveness of solution-focused and cognitive-behavioral skills-building approaches with adolescents in schools (Dupper, 1998; Harris & Franklin, 2007; Kim & Franklin, 2009) provides evidence that these types of interventions may be effective with adolescents fromdiverse cultures. This suggests that the TC curriculum should generalize if appropriate cultural modifications are made in its delivery.

■ FUTURE STUDIES

Future studies need to replicate the findings of Studies 1 to 3 using an RCT with a large sample and evaluate the ultimate outcome of high school completion. Future studies might also examine the mediating effects of solution building, social problem solving, and active coping on study outcomes. In prior studies, we showed that indicators for social problem solving and active coping significantly improved, but we were not able to examine the mediating effects of these variables on the outcomes of school achievement. In the three studies mentioned previously we also focused on measuring changes in social problem solving and coping and on school outcomes like improved grades and attendance, but we did not directly investigate the intervention's impact on parenting and career readiness. Other studies may wish to focus more on these other outcomes, as well as continuing to measure the intervention's effectiveness on school outcomes. The importance of any SFBT intervention will be its staying power, so longer follow-ups with adolescent mothers will also be important in future studies.

■ PRACTICE GUIDELINES

The results of the studies so far suggest that the solution-focused TC group is a promising intervention for the school population of adolescent mothers. The U.S. Office of Juvenile Justice also rated TC as a promising practice. Adolescent mothers who participated in the treatment groups showed both statistically and substantively significant improvement over comparison group participants in school attendance and grades. These tangible results are especially important because they provide evidence of behavioral changes that support improved school performance. The following practice guidelines are based on the TC research findings and an examination of the strengths and weaknesses of the studies:

1. Use the TC treatment manual. Become knowledgeable and comfortable with the manual, and follow it faithfully.
2. Modify the TC program so that it fits with the local community and population. A program that is effective with young mothers vastly different from those in the local school (urban vs. rural, Southwest vs. Northeast, Latina vs. Asian American) may not be effective locally.

3. Know the culture(s) of group members and ensure that your program delivery aligns with the cultural orientations of the group.
4. In designing an evaluation of the program, try to obtain the largest group of participants possible, but understand that evaluation with even the smallest group is an important step in demonstrating effectiveness.
5. Try to obtain a comparison group in evaluating the program. If this is not feasible, measure the outcomes at several points before pretest and after posttest in order to develop an adequate single-case evaluation design.

Strengths of the TC Intervention to Keep in Mind

First, TC has been tested in clinical studies and demonstrated to be promising in improving school attendance, grades, social problem solving, and active coping with participants who represent not only Latino youth but also other primary cultural and racial groups in U.S. public schools. Further, it is based on a solution-focused theoretical framework and is relevant to the developmental needs and current life issues of the young mothers in school.

A second strength observed in the three studies was participants' exceptional receptivity to the TC group. Young mothers who participated in the group responded with a great degree of interest and motivation, reflected by the fact that most treatment participants in the three studies earned enough points for an award, and fewer than 20% missed more than one group session.

Third, TC helps group leaders focus on cultural competence as an important treatment component. One probable factor influencing the positive response in Studies 1 and 3 was the integration of culturally relevant activities and values of these primarily Latina groups. It is important that the culturally relevant components for Latina adolescents were delivered as directed by the treatment manual. For example, the ritual of having lunch or snacks together during group sessions parallels a strong Hispanic cultural tradition. Planning, preparing, and sharing food is a primary cohesive activity in Mexican groups, for example, especially among women. Lunches shared during the sessions, often provided by the school cafeteria, were anticipated by participants and contributed to a comfortable, culturally familiar environment. Although the program is written and generally delivered in English, bilingual leaders frequently spoke in Spanish to participants in Spanish-dominant groups and used colloquial sayings known in Spanish as *dichos* and cultural metaphors in leading the group.

Finally, treatment fidelity is supported by the availability and use of a treatment manual. The manual provides precision and depth of training for group leaders, as well as consistent and detailed guidance in facilitating group sessions. Leaders in all studies used the manual to prepare for sessions each week and reported that they referred to it often during sessions. The onsite program supervisor in Study 2 reported that use of the manual provided social work and counseling interns with a more grounded understanding of the intervention, as well as guidance in mastering the group process and solution-focused leadership skills.

■ KEY FINDINGS TO REMEMBER

- Adolescent pregnancy occurs across all social, economic, religious, racial, and cultural groups and is a worldwide social problem. Most industrialized countries are funding programs to combat teen pregnancy and to adolescent mothers with their parenting, health, and social and economic welfare.

- Statistics suggest that there is a continued need to offer effective interventions to assist adolescents who continue to give birth. Taking Charge is a solution-focused and a cognitive behavioral curriculum that was developed within solution-focused and developmental frameworks, utilizing the strengths, resources, life goals, and developmental tasks of adolescent mothers.
- Research tells us that there are four life domains that predict self-sufficiency and positive life outcomes for adolescent mothers and their children: education, social support/personal relationships, parenting, and employment/career preparation.
- The TC intervention is presented as an 8- to 12-week school-based program that is offered within a task-centered group. The tasks of the TC group focus on building new solutions that strengthen the adolescent mother's active problem-solving and coping abilities. In turn, enacted solutions are used to gain better outcomes across the four important life domains that are essential for the self-sufficiency and success of the teenage mother and her child.
- To date, three efficacy studies of TC have been conducted in high school settings with leaders who were teachers, school support professionals, or school interns and with former adolescent mothers. They include one RCT and two quasi-experimental studies, and these studies provide initial support for the use of the solution-focused TC intervention.
- A published treatment manual is available to help practitioners and researchers learn how to implement and perform further research on TC (Harris & Franklin, 2008).

■ FURTHER LEARNING

The following are additional resources for the TC program and other research, program planning, and service delivery with adolescent mothers:

Franklin, C., Corcoran, J., & Harris, M. B. (2004). Risk and the protective factors for adolescent Pregnancy: Basis for effective intervention. In M. W. Fraser (Ed.), *Risk and resilience in childhood: An ecological perspective* (pp. 281–314). Washington, DC: NASW Press.

Harris, M. B., & Franklin, C. (2008). *Taking charge: A school-based life skills program for adolescent mothers.* New York: Oxford University Press.

The National Campaign to Prevent Adolescent Pregnancy: http://www.thenational campaign.org

United States Health and Human Services, Office of Population Affairs: http://www.hhs.gov/opa/familylife/

■ REFERENCES

Dupper, D. R. (1998). An alternative to suspension for middle school youths with behavior problems: Findings from a "school survival" group. *Research on Social Work Practice*, 8(3), 354–366.

D'Zurilla, T. J., & Nezu, A. (1990). Development and preliminary evaluation of the Social Problem Solving Invenory. *Psychological Assessment: A Journal of Consulting and Clinical Psychology*, 78, 104–126.

Guttmacher Institute. (2006). *U.S. teenage pregnancy statistics national and state trends and trends by race and ethnicity*. Retrieved from http://www.guttmacher.org/pubs/2006/09/12/USTPstats.pdf

Guttmacher Institute. (2010). *U.S. teenage pregnancy statistics national and state trends and trends by race and ethnicity*. Retrieved from http://www.guttmacher.org/pubs/USTPtrends.pdf

Hamilton, B. E., Martin, J. A., & Ventura, S. J. (2007). *Births: Preliminary data for 2006*. National Vital Statistics Reports, 56(7). Hyattsville, MD: National Center for Health Statistics. Retrieved February 25, 2008, from http://www.cdc.gov/nchs/data/nvsr/nvsr56/nvsr56_07.pdf

Harris, M. B. (2008). Best school-based practices with adolescent parents. In C. Franklin, M. B. Harris, & P. Allen-Meares (Eds.) *The school practitioner's concise companion to preventing dropout and attendance problems* (pp. 101–110). New York: Oxford University Press.

Harris, M. B., & Franklin, C. (2002). Effectiveness of a cognitive-behavioral group intervention with Mexican American adolescent mothers. *Social Work Research 17*(2), 71–83.

Harris, M.B. & Franklin, C. (2008). Taking Charge: A life skills group curriculum for adolescent mothers. New York: Oxford University Press.

Harris, M. B., & Franklin, C. (2009). Helping adolescent mothers to achieve in school. *Children & Schools, 31*(1), 27–34.

Haveman, R. H., Wolfe, B., & Peterson, E. (1997). Children of early childbearers as young adults. In R. A. Maynard (Ed.), *Kids having kids* (pp. 257–284). Washington, DC: Urban Institute.

Haveman, R., Wolfe, B., & Wilson, K. (1997). Childhood poverty and adolescent schooling and fertility outcomes: Reduced-form and structural estimates. In G. J. Duncan & J. Brooks-Gunn (Eds.), *Consequences of growing up poor* (pp. 419–460). New York: Russell Sage Foundation.

Herrenkohl, E. C., Herrenkohl, R. C., Egolf, B. P., & Russo, M. J. (1998). The relationship between early maltreatment and teenage parenthood. *Journal of Adolescence, 21*, 291–303.

Hogue, A., & Liddle, H. A. (1999). Family-based preventive intervention: An approach to preventing substance abuse and antisocial behavior. *American Journal of Orthopsychiatry, 69*, 275–293.

Kim, J., & Franklin, C. (2009). Solution-focused, brief therapy in schools: A review of the outcome literature. *Children and Youth Services Review, 31*, 461–470.

Kirby, D. (2002). The impact of schools and school programs upon adolescent sexual behavior. *Journal of Sex Research, 39*(1), 27–33.

Laird, J., DeBell, M., Kienzl, G., & Chapman, C. (2007). *Dropout rates in the United States: 2005* (NCES 2007–059). U.S. Department of Education. Washington, DC: National Center for Education Statistics. Retrieved February 25, 2008, from http://nces.ed.gov/pubs2007/2007059.pdf

McCubbin, H. I., & Thompson, A. (1991). *Family assessment inventories for research and practice* (2nd ed.). Madison: University of Wisconsin.

National At-Risk Education Network (2006). *Who is at-risk?* Retrieved July 12, 2006, from http://www.atriskeducation.net

National Center on Addiction and Substance Abuse at Columbia University (CASA). (1997). *Back to school 1997 – National survey of American attitudes on substance abuse III: Teens and their parents, teachers and principals*. New York: Columbia University.

National Center on Addiction and Substance Abuse at Columbia University (CASA). (1999). *Dangerous liaisons: Substance abuse and sex, 1999 analysis of 1997 YRBS data.* New York: Columbia University.

National Center on Addiction and Substance Abuse at Columbia University (CASA). (2002a). *CASA 2002 teen survey.* New York: Author.

National Center on Addiction and Substance Abuse at Columbia University (CASA). (2002b). *National survey of American attitudes on substance abuse III: Teens parents, and siblings.* New York: Columbia University.

National Center on Addiction and Substance Abuse at Columbia University (CASA). (2002c). Youth Knowledge and Attitudes on Sexual Health: A national survey of adolescents and young adults. In *Dangerous liaisons: Substance abuse and sexual behavior, 2002.* New York: Columbia University.

Passino, A. W., Whitman, T. L., Borkowski, J. G., Schellenbach, C. J., Maxwell, S. E., & Keogh, D. R. (1993). Personal adjustment during pregnancy and adolescent parenting. *Adolescence, 28*(109), 97–123.

Raj, A., Silverman, J. G., & Amaro, H. (2000). The relationship between sexual abuse and sexual risk among high school students: Findings from the 1997 Massachusetts Youth Risk Behavior Survey. *Maternal and Child Health Journal, 4*(2), 125–134.

Zill, N., & O'Donnell, K. (2004). *Child poverty rates by maternal risk factors: An update.* Unpublished manuscript. Rockville, MD: WESTAT.

Zupicich, S. (2003). Understanding social supportive processes among adolescent mothers. *Dissertation Abstracts International Section A: Humanities and Social Sciences, 63*(11-A), 3869.

18 Solution-Focused Brief Therapy in Alcohol Treatment

■ STÉPHAN HENDRICK, LUC ISEBAERT,
AND YVONNE DOLAN

■ INTRODUCTION

Underlying almost all psychotherapy approaches since Freud, traditional psychotherapy focuses on problem formation and problem resolution. Solution-focused brief therapy or (SFBT; de Shazer et al., 2007; Isebaert & Cabie, 1999) constitutes a paradigm shift away from traditional approaches. SFBT focuses on client strengths and resiliencies. The therapist examine the previous solutions and exceptions to the problem with the client. He then encourage the client to do more of those behaviors. Solution-focused brief therapy has been applied with success in clinical settings with clients who abuse alcohol (Berg & Miller, 1992; Miller & Berg, 1996).

This chapter explores SFBT as a potentially effective approach for alcohol treatment, analyzes SFBT principles, demonstrates how SFBT incorporates proven therapeutic principles for effective alcohol treatment, and describes how we use the SFBT approach and SFBT principles in our alcohol treatment program at St. John's Hospital in Bruges, Belgium. Finally, we report on three small pilot studies that have been done on the effectiveness of SFBT with alcohol problems in our treatment facility.

■ WHAT WE HAVE LEARNED SO FAR

Miller and colleagues (2003) reviewed 381 alcohol treatment outcome studies and discovered that brief therapy models are effective in the treatment of alcohol problems. As part of their review, they developed a cumulative index score (CES). The CES is a quality index that takes into account the quality of the design (e.g., with or without a control group) and the quality of the methodology (e.g., randomization or not, follow-up completed, blind interviewer, etc.). Forty-seven treatment modalities were ranked according to the outcome, the quality of the methodology of the study, and the mean severity of the problems in the cohort. Several interesting points emerged from this study. First, brief therapy models received the highest CES score. People with drinking problems often drop out of treatment after a few sessions. Consequently, decisive interventions should be concentrated in the first sessions.

Second, Miller and colleagues (2003) found that common, or nonspecific, therapeutic factors (i.e., empathy, hope, and self-efficacy) appeared to exert a strong influence on the outcome. Common factors can be understood as the effective processes of therapy that account for client change irrespective of the approach. While common factors may be shared by myriad psychotherapy models, specific therapeutic factors are used only in a particular intervention approach.

Empathy is a key common factor (Miller, 1995) in successful alcohol treatment. Miller et al. (2000) asked three independent observers to rate the degree of empathy of nine clinicians during 8 months of treatment for excessive alcohol drinkers. The raters were blind concerning the outcome. The results indicated that empathy and outcome were highly correlated ($r = -.819$, $p < .01$). That is, the more empathic the therapist was, the less the client drank. What was rated as accurate empathy of therapists accounted for 67% of the outcome variance.

Motivational Enhancement Therapy (MET) has been shown to be effective with substance abusers, especially with less motivated clients. Miller (1995) developed a manualized MET treatment protocol designed to enhance the motivation of drugs abusers based on the stages of change theory. The manual describes the motivational interview guidelines designed to help clients move from one stage to the next.

Miller et al. (1993) have shown the importance of a supportive, nonconfrontational style with subjects who have a drinking problem. For these authors, motivation is the key issue in helping alcohol abusers. In their view, motivating the client is the main task of the therapist. They first devised the Drinker's Check Up (DCU), which is composed of 34 measures including self-reports, a breath test, a blood test, and neuropsychological tests. In order to corroborate client self-reports, significant others were also interviewed. Subjects were recruited through the press. The authors randomized 42 subjects with a drinking problem into three conditions: (a) directive-confrontational feedback, (b) client-centered feedback, and (c) a waiting list control. Each group received the DCU feedback after 6 weeks.

The interviewers were trained to deliver both directive and client-centered feedback. The sessions were videotaped. The three main dependent variables measured were the average weekly consumption, the weekly peak blood alcohol concentration (BAC), and the number of weekly drinking days. A follow-up was scheduled at 6 weeks and at 12 months. At 12 months, 35 subjects (83%) participated in the interview.

Among the results, the following are particularly interesting. Agreement between subjects' and collaterals' reports was significant at both intake and 12 months. Groups (a) and (b) reported less weekly consumption, a lower peak BAC, and fewer drinking days relative to the waiting list group. No difference was found between directive and client-centered feedback for the three dependent variables. Nevertheless, the two counseling styles were discriminant. That is, the directive-confrontational style induced significantly more resistance from clients, which in turn predicted a poorer outcome at 12 months. Finally, a single therapist behavior was predictive of the 1-year outcome in the sense that the more the therapist confronted, the more the client drank.

We will now discuss the relationship between SFBT and the research reviewed in the previous section and go on to describe how various principles of the SFBT approach reflect and utilize proven therapeutic principles of effective alcohol treatment. We begin by distinguishing between two concepts: principle and technique (Hendrick, 2007a & b). A *principle* is a set of rules that guide the therapeutic process. Principles describe *what* needs to be done and *why*. A principle is applied throughout the whole course of therapy. An example of principle in SFBT is "Use and enhance client competence." Whereas a principle is a set of rules, a *technique* is a specific procedure used to get a specific result. In SFBT, the miracle question (de Shazer, 1988) is a good example of a technique. While a principle is always applicable, a technique may be used or not. In other words, a principle is more general, while a technique is more specific. All these assumptions characterize the SFBT model.

In alcohol treatment, the SFBT approach makes use of several effective therapeutic principles that have been described in both in Common Factors and MET research. For example, as described earlier, brief therapy has been found to be an effective treatment modality for substance abusers, and research indicates that alcoholics often drop out of therapy after a few sessions. The SFBT approach, in addition to being a form of brief therapy, is ideally suited for accommodating alcoholic clients who are likely to drop out early. This is because, instead of spending the first sessions doing a lengthy evaluation of the client, gradually developing a diagnosis, and only then beginning treatment, as is commonly done in the traditional medical model of treatment (Berg & Dolan, 2001) SFBT therapists focus on what the client needs to have happen in order to be able to say afterward that the therapy had been useful and that it had been a good idea to come (de Shazer et al., 2007).

As described earlier, accurate empathy is a key factor in effective substance abuse treatment. Because SFBT therapists incorporate the client's exact words, deliberately refrain from making interpretations, and phrase questions based on the assumption that from the client's perspective, there is likely a "good reason" (Berg & Dolan, 2001) for the behaviors and perceptions he or she brings to therapy; accurate empathy typifies the SFBT approach.

We will now analyze some of the basic principles of the SFBT approach. For each SFBT principle we address, we provide a short description, show how the principle has been found to be effective in therapy research, discuss the pertinence and efficacy of each SFBT principle specific to alcohol treatment, and describe how we have incorporated these principles in our Bruge model alcoholic treatment program at St. John's Hospital.

Start Where the Client Is, or Adapt to the Stage in Which the Client Exists

De Shazer (1988) proposed three types of patients: the complainant, the visitor, and the customer. The complainant suffers from a situation without making any clear request for help (e.g., a woman states that she has an alcohol problem but that she cannot do anything about it as long as her husband rejects her). Conversely, the customer asks for help (e.g., a client with an alcohol problem contacts a therapist personally). The visitor, however, makes no such request. Visitors are referred by social workers and other mental health professionals, or by the court system, or are brought to therapy by a family member. In the Bruges model of alcohol treatment that we use, these ways of categorizing clients are not seen as characteristics of the client, but rather as phases in the therapeutic relationship (Isebaert 2004, 2007), and this relationship approach is important to engaging clients.

Adapting to the change processes of a client has also been supported by other research on substance abuse treatment. Prochaska and colleagues (1992) propose six stages in the process of change: precontemplation, contemplation, determination, action, maintenance, and sometimes relapse. These stages in the process of change have also been widely applied in substance abuse treatment and found to be effective (Velasquez et al., 2001). The precontemplative stage corresponds to the visitor position, or the nonengaged relationship, the contemplative stage to the complainant position (or the searching relationship), and the determination and action stages to the customer position (or the consulting-an-expert relationships).

Failure is often related to an error in the choice of a therapeutic action that is not adapted to the stage in which the client exists. These stages are part of a cycle. The client may move from one stage to another. In case of relapse, he or she may reenter the cycle at any point. Thus, the SFBT principle of adapting to the stage in which the client engages (or doesn't engage) in the therapeutic relationship is strongly supported by empirical studies.

Use and Enhance the Client's Competence

One of the assumptions of SFBT is that clients have competencies and resources; they are the experts (Berg & Dolan, 2001). As a result, the therapy focuses more on positive experiences than on negative ones. Indeed, as Yapko (2001) points out, focusing on a specific idea amplifies the importance of that idea in one's mind. Conversely, focusing on one's problems, one's incompetence, and one's failures amplifies these in our minds. Focusing on competenceis and achievements and reexperiencing them in the therapeutic setting enhances the client's ability to use them in the problem situation.

Every person has abilities and coping strategies prior to any therapeutic intervention. This implies that the therapeutic process does not consist of the therapist designing "solutions" for the client's problems. Instead, it consists of bringing forward and implementing solutions that are already present in the client's life and relationships. Boosting the client's competence and self-efficacy has been shown to be one of the core factors necessary for therapeutic change. While many therapeutic models emphasize the importance of fostering client competence and self-efficacy, the SFBT approach focuses specifically on this principle.

Also in line with the SFBT approach is the common factors research finding that therapy works better if the solution suggested by the therapist is based on the natural healing processes of the patient. In other words, efforts to help will be useful only if the therapist uses the client's own experience.

Defining Clear Goals and Obtaining the Client's Collaboration

As de Shazer and Isebaert (2003) stated, emphasis is consistently placed on clear and specific goals. These goals are derived from the client's vision of how life will be at some point in the future when the problem that brought them to therapy is gone Solution-focused brief therapy, as used in our Bruges model substance abuse treatment program at St. John's, includes techniques especially designed to define clear goals, such as the miracle question (de Shazer, 1988) and Yvonne Dolan's letter from the future (1991), whereas scaling questions (Berg & Dolan, 2001) help clients assess their progress toward attaining their goals. The first session formula task (FSFT; de Shazer et al., 2007) and the " three questions for a happy life" (Isebaert, 2007) are devised to help clients identify what they are already doing that is congruent with their existential choices.

Chapter 9 of this book described research on the use of the solution-focused FSFT that was originally described by de Shazer (1991). Research on FSFT suggests that the SFBT approach does indeed help clients with drinking problems define clear goals and collaborate with the therapist. The FSFT asks clients to identify what is working, and the therapist tells clients to continue to use that behavior between sessions. Adams & et al. (1991) investigated the impact of a SFBT intervention alone or in combination with a structural-strategic intervention. In this study, study, 60 families were assigned randomly to one of the following three group conditions during the two first sessions: (a) the solution-focused FSFT followed by problem-focused therapy, (b) the FSFT followed by solution-focused therapy, or (c) a problem-focused task (PFT) followed by structural-strategic treatment.

After the two first sessions, the therapy was conducted as usual. Both self-rating scales and observer rating scales (used by the therapist and blind independent observers) were used to gather data. Assessment was conducted after the second session and at discharge. The following dependent variables were addressed: compliance, goal clarity, optimism, and improvement. The main results show that FSFT was an effective intervention in the initial stage of treatment for compliance, goal clarity, and outcome and improvement but was not effective in increasing family optimism. That is, the two FSFT groups (a and b) were superior to the PFT group (c) for these outcomes. Important to our point here is that FSFT enhanced the goal clarity and compliance of the clients involved in this study.

Change the Client's Perceptions and Experience

Dewan et al. (2004) believe that the ability to create experiences in which the client has an opportunity to learn something new is an essential ingredient of brief therapy. The term *corrective emotional experience* has evolved over the years to include the development of new cognitions and/or behaviors. Greenberg et al. (1988) have further identified the corrective emotional experience as being more about experiencing something new than about attaining a new insight.

When working with clients in the Bruge alcohol treatment model, we focus on new behaviors and experiences. In SFBT, allowing clients to identify their own solutions and face their own consequences are ways in which the corrective emotional experiences happen.

Using a Family Therapy Approach

As described in the first chapter of this book, SFBT originated from a brief family therapy approach. In the Bruges model of alcohol treatment, partners and family members are included and we use a family therapy approach (Isebaert, 2004, 2007), drawing from some of the best practices in family therapy described by Sexton et. al. (2003). These interventions, which are all used in our solution-focused treatment approach, include reframing, reducing negative interactions, creating new solutions to previous road blocks to change, and improving interactions and behavioral competencies. We will now describe these in further detail.

Reframing. At the first meeting, people usually arrive with a theory of their problem. This theory is generally a causal explanation, which often consists of blaming the partner, a parent, or another family member. Reframing the problem (i.e., getting people to consider it from a new angle) appears to be linked to better outcomes. Reframing is much easier if it occurs early (if possible at the first meeting).

We use reframing to lessen blame in the same way that is suggested in MET. In the study by Miller et al. (1993), for example, results show that in the client-centered condition, clients believing alcoholism to be a bad habit drank on significantly fewer days per week ($m = 1.33$, $s.d. = 1.41$) than did clients viewing alcoholism as a disease. This view is central to the Bruges concept of alcohol abuse (Isebaert, 2004, 2007).

Reducing Negative Interactions. Reducing negative interactions during the sessions naturally increases solution-focused *exceptions*—times when relational problems are absent or happening less often.

Overcoming Obstacles to Change. In a solution-focused model, we move beyond therapeutic obstacles to change by developing solutions that will cause the obstacles to shrink or disappear. In their process research, Diamond and Liddle (1996) showed that moving from a focus on the problem to a focus on the solution made it easier to distinguish successes from failures. The study also indicated that moving from a control problem to a relational problem made change easier. More specifically, these authors developed an intervention that shifted "the content and the emotional tone of the conversation to topics and affective states that engender a more productive therapeutic dialogue" (p. 481). This approach is an excellent example of more general principles of SFBT in our work. In our program at St. John's hospital, we use SFBT exception questions (de Shazer et al., 2007) to shift from problem talk to solution talk, and we repeatedly ask questions about past, current, and potential exceptions and solutions during all of our therapy sessions and conversations with patients and family members. .

Improving Interactional and Behavioral Competencies. Improving communication and interaction within the family is essential for improvement, but it is not enough to stop the negative interactions, so we also use SFBT systemic questions (de Shazer et al., 2007) to further encourage positive relationships and interactions. In particular, as has been shown by in family research, there is a relationship between improvements in family interaction and treatment outcomes in situations with adolescents abusing drugs. In particular, improving communication and attachment, and working on roles, boundaries, and rebuilding relationships, are important to family-based outcomes (Dennis et. al., 2004).

■ IMPORTANCE OF SOLUTION-ORIENTED LANGUAGE

Solution-focused brief therapy helps clients to discover their own solutions and expects the therapist to adopt a trusting and respectful attitude. The style of the therapist is never confrontational or directive.

Consistent with other family therapy approaches, speaking the client's language is a way to establish rapport. The therapist adopts the words, the intonation, and other linguistic characteristics of the client. As to content, the therapist does not confront the beliefs and the worldview of the client. He or she avoids attempts to persuade. Instead, the therapist just offers an alternative, and more positive, perspective.

As we mentioned earlier, we have observed that solution-oriented language is very similar to the style of interviewing found to be effective in studies on motivational interviewing. We were impressed with the similarity between the basic principles described in the MET manual and those of SFBT. For example, here are some of the basic assumptions of the manual: express empathy, avoid argumentation, support self-efficacy, give the client freedom of choice, never attempt to sell a diagnostic label, enhance hope and optimism, rely on the client's own natural change processes and resources, elicit ideas from the client (not from the therapist), and recognize that client resistance is a therapist problem, not a client problem.

■ RESEARCH CONDUCTED AT ST. JOHN'S HOSPITAL, BRUGES, BELGIUM

St. John's is a regional public hospital that serves a population of 120,000 in the Bruges area. It has 900 beds, of which 80 are acute psychiatric beds. A ward of 26 beds is reserved for substance abusers, 90% of whom are alcohol abusers. In addition, there are facilities for 18 patients in the day clinic. Outpatient follow-up is typically for 4 to 6 weeks following discharge.

All the personnel in the psychiatric department have SFBT training. The treatment model is SFBT according to the Bruges model (de Shazer & Isebaert, 2003; Isebaert, 2004, 2007). We have described some aspects of our approach to treatment throughout this chapter, but a more detailed description in English can be found at http://www.korzybski.com. The mean duration of hospitalization, including detoxification and day care, is 3 to 4 weeks. The inpatient program consists of the detoxification and information phase (5 to 10 days), inpatient group therapy (1 to 3 weeks), and day-care group therapy (1 to 2 weeks). Ambulatory follow-up is offered, though not insisted upon. Clients generally come back two to four times before stopping treatment.

Three follow-up studies have been conducted on cohorts of patients who had been treated in the substance dependency ward at St. John's Hospital. These studies will now be described.

Study 1

In 1999, we studied the predictive value of a number of social and personal variables on the outcome of patients hospitalized in 1994 and 1995[1].

Sample: Out of a total of 635 admissions, after excluding patients for whom no alcohol use severity measures were available and those for whom no telephone number had been noted (essentially emergency room patients who had been admitted while intoxicated and who left the following day), 195 were selected at random. Of these, 115 could be readily contacted by telephone. From the remaining 80, 15 were selected at random after extra efforts were made to trace them. Four of them could be found and were included in the cohort. Although this number is, of course, too small to permit definite conclusions, their results were not different from those of the rest of the cohort.

In addition, 13 patients had died in the interval, and the cause of their death was obtained through their family physician. The total for the cohort was 132. Of the 132 patients, 67.4% were male and 32.6% were female. The median age was 46 years, the youngest patient being 19 and the oldest 74.

Procedure: At T1, two weeks into treatment, the severity of alcohol abuse was established by the Munich Alcohol Test (MALT) score. The MALT is a well-validated German questionnaire. It is comprised of both a client's (MALT-Z) and a physician's (MALT-A) part. A score of 0–5 indicates "no problem with alcohol," 6–10 "heightened risk," and 11–52 "alcohol abuse." At T2 a telephone interview was conducted. The information gathered included the patient's marital status, living environment, source of income, satisfaction with the personal and family situation, and daily functioning. Alcohol consumption at T2 and its stability over the last 6 months was also assessed (see Table 18.1).

At T2, 63.9% of the patients were married or living with a partner, 26.9% were living alone, 7.6% were living with their parents, and 1.7% were in an institution. In this patient group, 58.5% were working, 7.3% were on welfare, 11.9% were receiving a pension, and 19.5% were on sick leave.

Of the 132 patients, 108 had completed the entire (4-week) treatment program, while 24 left earlier. The results showed no statistical difference between the two groups.

At T1, the mean MALT score was 27.39, with a standard deviation of 7.82. Ninety-eight percent of the patients had a MALT score higher than 10. The MALT score ranged from 4 to 49.

Hypothesis: First, there would be a change in the alcohol consumption pattern such that at T2, clients would either be abstinent or drinking in a controlled way (defined as <30 g/day for men and <20 g/day for women, with increased drinking only on special occasions). This change would be stable over the last 6 months. The higher the MALT score, the worse the results would be. Patients who opted for abstinence would achieve better results than those who opted for controlled drinking.

Second, if the change was simply due to the time elapsed between T1 and T2, and not to specific effects of the therapy, a number of personal or environmental factors would influence it. The following results would appear: (a) stable recovery would occur more often with men than with women, (b) stable recovery would occur more often with married people if they were male but not if they were female, (c) stable recovery would occur more often with people who were gainfully employed than with jobless or

TABLE 18.1. *Results at T2*

Outcome	N	%
Abstinent	60	45.45%
Drinking in a controlled way	40	30.30%
Drinking too much	19	14.39%
Died*	13	9.85%
Of those who died:	9	6.82%
– Still drinking excessively at time of death	2	1.52%
– Not drinking at time of death	2	1.52%
– Not known		

*Cause of death: suicide, five; hepatic cirrhosis, two; pancreatitis, one; accident, two; cancer, two; cardiac arrest, two.

pensioned people, (d) stable recovery would occur more often with people who functioned well on a daily basis (who did their daily chores), (e) stable recovery would occur more often when there were no partner problems or family disharmony, (f) those who drank in a controlled way had a higher socioeconomic status and more family harmony than those who practiced abstinence, and (g) alcohol-related mortality would be higher in women than in men by a factor of 1.5 to 2.

Seventy-four percent of patients were not hospitalized again after this treatment. For the first hypothesis, there was no statistically significant difference in success rate between persons with high or low MALT scores. Although more persons who originally opted for abstinence achieved better results than persons who originally opted for controlled drinking, the difference was not statistically significant (chi(1) = 2.177). In addition, it is interesting to note that 26.66% of those who originally opted for controlled drinking reported at follow-up that they had since changed their option to abstinence.

For the second hypothesis, there was no statistically significant difference between (a) men and women (chi(1) = 1.469), (b) married men and women (chi(1) = 0.069 for men, 0.494 for women), or (c) gainfully occupied and not gainfully occupied persons (chi(1) = 1.084). There was, however, a statistically significant difference for persons who function well on a daily basis. They had a higher success rate than those who do not function well (chi(1) = 5.314, $p < .05$). The investigation into the relation between success rate and family harmony found that there was no statistically significant difference based on family (dis)harmony for abstainers compared to controlled drinkers. In addition, there was no statistically significant difference between success rate and support from the partner during therapy. Moreover, there was no statistically significant difference according to socioeconomic status for those who were abstinent and those who drank in a controlled way. Finally, among the 13 deceased patients, there was only one woman. As a result, the hypothesis regarding alcohol-related mortality being higher for women than men by a factor of 1.5 to 2 was not supported.

Discussion of Study 1. There are a number of limitations of this study. First, there was no control group. This limitation is, however, mitigated by the fact that the hypotheses tested are taken from the generally accepted literature. A second limitation of the study is that comorbidity is not taken into account. This, however, makes for a more naturalistic study, alcohol abusers being among the champions of comorbidity. Another limitation of the study is that no distinction is made between alcohol-dependent and alcohol-abusing patients. The mean MALT score, however, is high. Lastly, the study is limited in that the results at T2 rely on self-reporting. This limitation is somewhat reduced by the fact that most patients had achieved good results and confidentiality was guaranteed, which, according to several studies, ensures reasonably reliant information. In addition, whenever possible, family members were asked to confirm the answers.

The strengths of the study are (a) the large number of persons interviewed and (b) no exclusion criteria. Even clients who left immediately after detoxification were used, which made for a more naturalistic study.

There are four main points of interest. First, apart from one personality factor (daily functioning), none of the personality or environmental factors researched had a statistically significant influence on the outcome. This seems to indicate that the treatment, and not just the time elapsed between T1 and T2, had a positive impact on the outcome. Second, the same conclusion may be drawn from the fact that there was no statistically significant difference in outcome between heavy drinkers and less heavy ones. Third, the relatively high percentage of patients who achieved stable recovery and the low percentage of those who had to be hospitalized again point in the same direction. Finally, there was no statistically significant difference in outcome between patients who, at the time of treatment, opted for abstinence and those who chose controlled drinking as their goal.

Study 2

In 2002, we studied a number of sometimes unrelated hypotheses[2]. Her subjects also were patients at the Alcohol Clinic at St. John's Hospital, Bruges, Belgium.

Sample. In 2001–2002, 73 randomly selected patients were asked if they would consent to participate in a follow-up study. Of these, 50 accepted. In the third week of hospitalization, a battery of tests and questionnaires was administered. At T2, 1 year after discharge, they were contacted by letter and telephone and asked if they would consent to do the same battery of tests. Thirteen could not be traced and 7 refused, bringing the remaining total to 30. The tests and questionnaires were administered at the subject's home or in the hospital.

Of the 30 research participants, 60% were male and 40% were female. The median age was 45, the youngest being 21 and the oldest 70. Forty percent were married or living with a partner, and 60% were living alone: 30% divorced, 20% single, 10% widowed.

Method. Nine measures were taken at week 3 of hospitalization and at T2, 1 year after discharge:

The neo-Five Factor Inventory (FFF)
The SCL-90 Symptom Checklist
The Utrecht Coping List (UCL; distinguishes seven patterns of coping with difficulties)
The Dyadic Adjustment Scale (DAS)
The OQ-45 Outcome Questionnaire
The MINI International Neuropsychiatric Interview
The Global Assessment of Functioning Scale (GAS)
The Global Assessment of Relational Functioning Scale (GARF)
The Timeline Follow-Back (Sobell & al, 2003).

Hypothesis. For this study, there were six hypotheses. The first hypothesis stated that there would be a significant reduction in alcohol consumption at T2. Second, there would be a correlation between certain personality traits and the results at T2, which would include the following: (a) There would be a positive correlation between neuroticism and alcohol consumption. (b) There would be a negative correlation between conscientiousness and alcohol consumption. (c) There would be a negative correlation between altruism and alcohol consumption. (d) The correlation between extraversion and alcohol consumption remains to be established, the results in the literature being inconsistent. The third hypothesis states that sociodemographic factors, such as age and sex, should have the following impact: (a) At T2, there should be no correlation between age and rate of alcohol consumption. However, older people should drink more frequently, whereas younger people should drink more on drinking days. (b) As anxiety and depression predict negatively, and as women who abuse alcohol tend to be more anxious and depressed than men, women should show a higher rate of relapse. (c) Patients with comorbid anxiety disorders at T1 should show a higher rate of relapse. (d) Patients with comorbid depression at T1 should also show a higher rate of relapse, albeit less higher than that of patients with anxiety disorders. (e) Patients with relational problems at T1 should show a higher rate of relapse. The study also hypothesizes that the influence of the choice for abstinence or for controlled drinking on relapse remains to be determined. Additionally, it is hypothesized that a longer hospitalization (4–6 weeks) should ensure better results than a shorter one (1–3 weeks). The final hypothesis of the study states that global and relational functioning should be better at T2 than at T1.

Results. There were significant improvements in drinking habits. The maximum number of units per day decreased from 21, 20 to 15, 13. The maximum number of days with zero units increased from 10, 67 to 14, 00. The median number of units/day decreased from 11, 93 to 7,76. The percentage of days with zero units increased from 31, 87 to 70, 02.

The results indicate that patients with high conscientiousness, as measured by the neo-FFI, scored less well at T2 on all the items in 1 than those with moderate or low conscientiousness. In addition, none of the other factors in the neo-FFI (neuroticism, extraversion, openness, and altruism) had an impact on the outcome. Moreover, there was no influence on relapse from age or gender of the participants. Furthermore, the coping strategies of the participants, as measured with the UCL, had no influence on the outcome. Also, comorbid depression (as measured by the MINI) at T1 had no influence on the outcome in terms of alcohol consumption. The percentage of depressed patients went from 70 at T1 to 30 at T2. Those who were depressed at T2 tended to drink less than the nondepressed (Pearson corr. −.383). The results of the study also indicate that comorbid anxiety disorders (panic disorder, agoraphobia, social phobia, and generalized anxiety; as measured by the MINI and SCL-90) had no influence on the outcome (the numbers of patients, of course, was very small here). Here again, those with a high score for anxiety and agoraphobia on the SCL-90 at T2 were drinking less than those without an anxiety disorder (Pearson corr. -.369). Relational problems at T1, as measured by the DAS and the GARF, had no influence on the outcome. Global functioning was better at T2 than at T1 (OQ-45: 84.23 to 66.00; GAF: 35.27 to 64.30). Whether, at T1, patients made the choice of abstinence or of controlled drinking had no influence on the frequency of relapse. Lastly, a longer hospitalization did not have an influence on the frequency of relapse, but it did lead to a lower maximum number of units for those who continued drinking.

Discussion of Study 2. There are some limitations of this study. The study was limited in the small overall number of participants, which leads to very small numbers when different traits or comorbidity issues are measured. Second, some of the tests and questionnaires are well validated (e.g., the neo-FFI, the MINI, the SCL-90, the OQ-45, the UCL), others less so (e.g., the GAS and GARF). A strength of the study is that it used well-established tests and questionnaires, some of which are well validated.

Together with the study by Sylvie Buyse, this study shows that 1 year after treatment, recovery has not progressed as far as after 4 years, but it is already significant. It also confirms that personality traits and comorbidity have little influence on the outcome after SFBT.

Study 3

A third research study was made in 2007 at St. John's Hospital by Dr. Thariax Opperman in the substance dependency ward.(Dr. Thariax Opperman).

Sample. This study focused on the heaviest drinkers, with a median consumption of 168 g/day. Ninety-five percent of these patients showed liver steatosis on echography (20% mild, 33% moderate, and 26% severe). Pancreatic lipomatosis was evident in 46%, with 16% showing pancreatic calcifications. None of the patients were positive for HIV or hepatitis B or C or showed evidence of acute infection. One patient was known to have used illegal substances in the past, but no patients were using them now. Only patients who participated in the 3-week inpatient program and who intended to continue follow-up after discharge were included. Of 50 initially targeted patients, 6 (12%) discontinued inpatient treatment in the first 10 days, 7 (14%) moved away and were unavailable for follow-up, and 7 (14%) refused the follow-up offer. The remaining group of 30 consisted of 18 (60%) men and 12 (40%) women. The patients included had limited support from family members. Eighty-three percent were living alone and 23% had no support from anyone. Thirty-eight percent were separated, 33% were divorced, 10% were single, and 3% were widowed. Seventy-three percent were unemployed.

Method. Patients were followed for a period of 12 months at 6–12 weekly intervals after discharge. Timeline follow-back reports (Sobell & al, 2003) in which patients reported on the number on days that they stayed abstinent (percentage of days abstinent, or PDA), on daily alcohol intake during drinking days (drinks per drinking day, or D/DD), and the number of heavy drinking days (defined as >50 g/day for males and >40 g/day for females; percentage of heavy drinking days, or PHDD). These measures were obtained shortly before discharge, referring to the month before admittance, and at T2, 1 year after discharge. The biomarkers used were gamma glutamyltransferase (GGT), alanine aminotransferase (ALT), aspartate aminotransferase (AST), and mean corpuscular volume (MCV).

Hypothesis. This study put forth two hypotheses: (a) Although neither total abstinence nor persistent controlled drinking would be achieved, there would be an overall reduction of drinking days and of alcohol consumption on drinking days, and (b) this improvement might or might not be reflected in the biological markers investigated.

Results. Nineteen patients (63.3%) reported an overall improvement in drinking behavior, with an increase in abstinent days, a statistically significant decrease in absolute daily intake (168 to 79 g/day), and a nonstatistically significant decrease in binge drinking days (12.3 to 9.3). Of the 19 patients who showed an improvement, 8 showed a return to normal in all biomarkers, while in the 11 remaining patients, three out of four biomarkers returned to normal. However, the numbers involved were too small to allow for statistical significance.

Discussion of Study 3. The limitations of this study include the small number of participants, the absence of a control group, and the fact that the investigator was also the therapist. In addition, although the Sobells' timeline follow-back is a reasonably accurate measure, alcohol intake was assessed by self-reporting.

There are two interesting points in the study. First, the cohort consisted of the heaviest drinkers, with a history of years of heavy drinking and social isolation. Second, although the small numbers involved did not allow for statistical significance, the reported decrease in alcohol abuse was echoed by a marked improvement in the biological markers.

■ FUTURE RESEARCH

The small studies completed at St. John's Hospital in Bruges, Belgium, provide a foundation on which future larger quasi-experimental and randomized clinical trials may be conducted. The studies appeared to show reduced drinking behaviour, but at this time we cannot draw any definitive conclusions about the overall effectiveness of the SFBT approach in alcohol treatment. One process issue of interest is the importance of the treatment components themselves and how they may or may not be similar to those of other effective approaches to substance abuse, such as MET. Future studies may also want to investigate the similarities, differences, and complementary uses of SFBT and MET in alcohol treatment.

■ TREATMENT GUIDELINES

In the solution-focused Bruges treatment model at St. John's Hospital, the focus is on client-related factors and the therapeutic relationship. Client-related factors include (a) helping clients to define positive goals (i.e., existential choices), (b) understanding that bringing alcohol consumption under control is not so much a goal as a means to achieve these positive goals, (c) helping clients to realize what they are already doing to achieve their goals, (d) helping to focus on all resources, competencies, and achievements of the clients/partners/family/environment that can be used to achieve these goals, (e) helping to solve any problems that can be solved (anxiety, depression, loneliness, etc.) and to accept what cannot be changed (genetic factors, certain comorbid disorders, trauma, loss and mourning, etc.), and (f) fostering hope. The therapeutic relationship includes the following: (a) respect for the client's existential choices, (b) unconditional acceptance of the client's habits, even if they are not helpful, (c) a caring attitude toward the client and the partner/family, and (d) empathy for the client's and partner's/family's feelings.

There are four main themes in the therapeutic procedure. The first is offering clients choices. For instance, clients are offered the choice between abstinence, controlled drinking, and controlled relapses. *Abstinence* is defined as not drinking any alcohol; *controlled drinking* as drinking not more than 3 units/day for men and 2 units/day for women, with at least 1 abstinent day per week; and *controlled relapses* as short (1 to 3 days), infrequent (not more than four times a year), and light (not more than 7 units/day). In addition, clients and their families are helped to redefine as concretely as possible their existential choices (goals) with the use of future-oriented techniques (e.g., the miracle question).

The second theme in the therapeutic procedure is giving adequate and personalized information. A series of five information sessions covering all aspects of alcohol abuse is offered to all hospitalized clients in the form of interactive group sessions. A similar series is organized for clients, their partners, and other family members.

Accessing competences and solutions is the third theme. Much emphasis is placed on instances of control, however partial, that the client exerts already: how has he managed to stop on the days when he has drunk less than usual? How has she sometimes managed to abstain from drinking although the urge was there? In regard to relapse management, the team helps the client develop strategies to prevent or limit relapses. Whenever relapse occurs, the discussion is about how the client limited it in time and severity. Finally, compliments are given to partners and family members as well as to clients.

The last theme is specific to chronic clients. With very heavy drinkers who relapse immediately after discharge, emphasis is placed on restoring satisfactory habits in daily life and rebuilding family or friendship ties. Through a longer stay in the day clinic, the transfer of more satisfying habits to the home life is facilitated.

■ KEY FINDINGS TO REMEMBER

- In alcoholism treatment, SFBT implements many of the common factors that have been found in process research to be effective in therapeutic change. The SFBT interventions are specifically designed to boost certain common factors such as relationship enhancement, clear goals, hope, and expectancy for change.
- Many principles used in SFBT treatment have been found in therapy research to be effective in substance abuse treatment.
- Solution-focused brief therapy and MET are complementary in their approach to alcohol treatment, especially in regard to their relationship style and the interviewing style of the therapist. The relationship style proposed by SFBT, for example, has been found to be effective in studies on MET.
- When partners and family members are included in alcohol treatment, SFBT uses a family therapy approach (Isebaert, 2004, 2007) that includes reframing, reducing negative interactions, overcoming roadblocks to change, and improving interactions and behavioral competencies.
- The staff of St. John's Hospital in Bruges, Belgium, has been trained in SFBT and has developed a SFBT treatment program. This program has conducted three small pilot studies that support the effectiveness of SFBT with clients with alcohol problems.

■ FURTHER LEARNING

The SFBT treatment approach used at St. John's Hospital in Bruges, Belgium, can be found at http://www.korzybski.com

■ ENDNOTES

1. with the collaboration of Sylvie Buyse
2. with the collaboration of Eva de Stecker.

■ REFERENCES

Adams, J. F., Piercy, F. P. & Jurich, J. A. (1991). Effects of solution focused therapy's "Formula First Session Task" on compliance and outcome in family therapy. *Journal of Marital and Family Therapy, 17*(3), 277–290.

Berg, I. K., & Dolan, Y. (2001). *Tales of solution: A collection of hope-inspiring stories.* New York: Norton.

Berg, I. K., & Miller, S. D. (1992). *Working with the problem drinker.* New York: Norton.

Bergin, A. E., & Garfield, L. (2003). *Handbook of psychotherapy and behavior change.* London:Wiley.

Dennis, M. L., Godley, S. H., Diamond, G. S., Tims, F. M., Babor, T., Donaldson, J., Liddle, H. A., Titus, J. C., Kaminer, Y., Webb, C., Hamilton, N., & Funk, R. R. (2004). The cannabis youth treatment (CYT) study: Main findings from two randomized clinical trails. *Journal of Substance Abuse Treatment, 27*, 197–213.

de Shazer, S. (1988). *Clues: Investigating solutions in brief therapy.* New York: W.W. Norton & Company Inc., New York.

de Shazer, S. (1991). *Putting difference to work.* New York. W.W. Norton & Company Inc., New York.

de Shazer, S., Dolan, Y., Korman, H., Trepper, T., McCollum, & Berg, I. K. (2007). *More than miracles: The state of the art of solution-focused brief therapy*. New York: Haworth/Taylor-Routledge.

de Shazer, S., & Isebaert, L. (2003). The Bruges model: A solution-focused approach to problem drinking and Susbstance Abuse. *Journal of Family Psychotherapy, 14*(4), pp. 43–52.

Dewan, M. J., Steenbarger, B. N., & Greenberg, R. P. (2004). *The art and science of brief psychotherapies. A practitioner's guide*. Arlington, VA:American Psychiatric Press.

Diamond, G. S., & Liddle, H. A. (1996). Resolving a therapeutic impasse between parents and adolescents in Multidimensional Family Therapy. *Journal of Consulting and Clinical Psychology, 64*(3), 481–488.

Dolan, Y., (1991). *Resolving sexual abuse: Solution-focused therapy and Ericksonian hypnotherapy for adult survivors*. New York: Norton.

Greenberg, L. S., James, P. S., & Conry, R. F. (1988). Perceived change in couples therapy. *Journal of Family Psychology, 2*, 5–23.

Hendrick, S. (2007a). *Un modèle de thérapie brève systémique*. Paris: Eres.

Hendrick, S. (2007b). Un modèle de thérapie brève systémique. *Thérapie Familiale, 28*(2), 121–138.

Hester, R. K., & Miller, W. R. (Eds.). (2003). *Handbook of alcoholism treatment approaches: Effective alternatives* (3rd ed.). Boston: Allyn & Bacon.

Isebaert, L. c.s. (2004). *Kurzzeittherapie, ein praktisches Handbuch. Die gesundheitsorientierte kognitive Therapie*. Stuttgart: Thieme Verlag.

Isebaert, L. c.s. (2007). *Praktijkboek oplossingsgerichte cognitieve thérapie*. Utrecht: De Tijdstroom.

Isebaert, L., & Cabie, M.-C. (1999). *Pour une thérapie brève: Le libre choix du patient comme éthique en psychothérapie*. Ramonville Saint-Agne: Eres.

Miller, W. R. (1995). *Motivational enhancement therapy with drug abusers*. Albuquerque: Department of Psychology and Center on Alcoholism, Substance Abuse, and Addictions (CASAA), University of New Mexico.

Miller, W. R., Benfield, R. G., & Tonigan, J. S. (1993). Enhancing motivation for change in problem drinking: A controlled comparison of two therapist styles. *Journal of Consulting and Clinical Psychology, 61*(3), 455–461.

Miller, S. D., & Berg, I. K. (1996). *The miracle method: A radical approach to problem drinking*. New York: Norton.

Miller, W. R., Taylor, C. A., & West, J. C. (2000). Focused versus broad-spectrum behavior therapy for problem drinkers. *Journal of Consulting and Clinical Psychology, 48*(3), 590–601.

Miller, W. R., Wilbourne, P. L., & Hettema, J. E. (2003). What works? A summary of alcohol treatment outcome research. In R. K. Hester & W. R. Miller,. (Eds.), *Handbook of alcoholism treatment approaches: Effective alternatives* (3rd ed., pp 13–63). Boston: Allyn & Bacon.

Prochaska, J. O., DiClemente, C. C., & Norcross, J. C. (1992), In search of how people change: Applications to addictive behaviors. *American Psychologist, 47*(9), 1102–1114.

Sexton, T. L., Weeks, G. R., & Robbins, M. S. (2003b). *Handbook of family therapy*. New York: Brunner-Routledge.

Sobell, L.C., Agrawal, S., Sobell, M. B., Leo, G. I., Young, L. J., Cunningham, J. A., Simco, E. R. (2003), Comparison of a Quick Drinking Screen with the Timeline Followback for Individuals with Alcohol Problems. *J. Stud. Alcohol 64*: 858–861.

Velasquez, M. M., Gaddy-Maurer, G., Crouch, C., DiClemente, C. C. (2001), *Group Treatment for Substance Abuse: A Stages of Change Therapy Manual*. New York, NY: The Guilford Press.

Yapko, M. (2001). *Treating depression with hypnosis*. Philadelphia: Brunner-Routledge.

Research on Innovative Practice Programs

19 From Solution to Description

Practice and Research in Tandem

■ GUY SHENNAN AND CHRIS IVESON

■ INTRODUCTION

Practice-based evidence has been important to the development of solution-focused brief therapy since its inception at the Brief Family Therapy Center (BFTC) in Milwaukee. The purpose of this chapter is to illustrate the importance of using practice-based research data to shape solution-focused practices in a clinical setting by chronicling the developments at one clinic, BRIEF, in London, and showing how research data was used there to guide and improve the delivery of solution-focused therapy. We will also discuss both the challenges of collecting practice-based research data and the benefits and uses of this type of data in a clinical setting. We hope that this account of our journey will inspire other therapists to collect practice-based research data on solution-focused brief therapy.

Practice-based evidence is important to the development of therapy for a number of reasons, the following all being relevant in the case of BRIEF:

- An evidence base rooted in practice can complement data from controlled research settings and "together yield a more robust knowledge base for the psychological therapies" (Charman & Barkham, 2005).
- Evidence arising from practice in real-world settings is important for practitioners working in real-world settings, for whom the "external validity" of research findings is just as important as the internal validity required in controlled research settings (Midgeley, 2009).
- Research findings also have to be judged by the standards of values and utility (Weick, 2000), and data generated by researching what practitioners are actually doing can help to produce usable practices.
- It has been shown that outcomes improve where practitioners consistently seek out their clients' views on outcome (Bringhurst et al., 2006).
- The proximity of the research to practice enables practice to be responsive to the data, thus creating the type of recursive relationship between practice and research exemplified by BFTC (de Shazer, 1985, 1988, 1991).

- Developing "research-mindedness" as practitioners encourages a reflective and critical stance towards taken-for-granted ways of doing things (Everitt et al., 1992).
- As the purpose of research is to change and modify practice in the light of results, being constantly alive to one's effectiveness is conducive to a developmental approach to practice. And being prepared to make changes is important, if only because, to quote Thom Gunn, "one is always nearer by not keeping still."[1].

Five outcome studies of different shapes and sizes have been undertaken at BRIEF thus far, between 1990 and 2008, while we have been continuously examining, developing, and refining our solution-focused practice in the years in between and since. In the next section, we describe the five studies and what we have learned from their results.

■ WHAT WE HAVE LEARNED SO FAR

The five studies are not evenly spread out in time. The first two took place in quick succession at the beginning of BRIEF's journey, and the third study was carried out nine years later. During this period, BRIEF made many of the main developments that have led to a distinctively minimal and noninstrumental version of solution-focused brief therapy. These developments were in some ways responses to the second study and were tested out by the third. In the years that followed we continued to make further refinements to our practice, and the fourth study was carried out in 2006–2007. The relatively disappointing outcomes in this study in comparison to the first three led to the fifth being undertaken soon afterwards. The results of this study were encouraging once more, but the slight dip in outcomes in the fourth study has led to a redoubled commitment to constantly check and evaluate the effectiveness of our practice.

Study 1: Preliminary Findings

In the late 1980s the three founders of BRIEF, then working as family therapists in a public mental health clinic in central London, decided to teach themselves solution-focused brief therapy so that they could add it to both their clinical and teaching repertoires. They were given permission by their managers to begin the Brief Therapy Project pending research evidence that the approach worked at least as well as other models used at the clinic. The very first evidence that was presented to the clinic concerned the outcomes for the 62 clients with whom therapy had been completed between February 1989 and March 1990 (see Table 19.1) Although the outcomes here were based largely on therapist judgement —unlike the later studies, which were based solely on the client's view—on their own terms the figures were seen as encouraging enough. Where the client's view could be taken into account, there was at least a 66% success rate, and if the therapists' views when clients stopped attending are added in, then the positive outcome rate becomes 79%. In any event, the study fulfilled its purpose, as this was accepted as sufficient evidence for the continuation of the project. A few months later, the team published the first account of its work (George et al., 1990) with an appendix that detailed this first survey and heralded the start of a more formal outcome study.

TABLE 19.1 *Outcomes of Study 1 (February 1989–March 1990)*

Assessment of Outcome	Number (total = 62)
Outcome at completion seen as positive by both client and therapist	41 (66%)
Outcome seen as positive by therapist when client discontinued therapy	8 (13%)
Outcome seen as negative by client at completion or by therapist when client discontinued therapy	13 (21%)

Study 2: It Works

The other four studies all shared the main features of the naturalistic studies characteristic of early solution-focused brief therapy research (Macdonald, 2007). In particular, they sought the client's view of the outcome of the therapy at some point after completion. The second study (Iveson, 1991) was the most rigorous of the five. The outcomes (83% "better" - see Table 19.2) matched almost exactly those in the Milwaukee study of the early 1980s (de Shazer, 1985) and in doing so taught us the useful lesson that therapists are an unreliable source of outcome information. The outcomes we had anticipated were significantly more modest than the study showed. This first formal study also marked the beginning of BRIEF's divergence from BFTC. The data showed no significant outcome differences related to the client–therapist relationship categories suggested by de Shazer (1988). On the contrary, the clients thought to be in complainant and visitor relationships with the therapist were just as likely to report a positive outcome as the "customers" (Table 19.3).

These results gave a great boost to the team's confidence and started to shape the practice developments made throughout the 1990s. Two aspects of the study were perhaps most influential. First, the positive results came from a sample that included seemingly entrenched and intractable problems such as long-term depression, child abuse, and alcoholism. What this showed was that problem and prognosis could be unhooked. It appeared that what the client came with in terms of problem history had no predictive value in terms of outcome. So if every referral is more than likely to end with a positive outcome, the start of each treatment can be accompanied by

TABLE 19.2 *Outcomes of Study 2*

Outcome related by the client	Number (total 24)
Better	20 (83%)
Same	3 (12.5%)
Worse	1 (4%)

TABLE 19.3 *Outcomes of Study 2 by Customer, Complainant, and Visitor Relationships*

	Customer	Complainant	Visitor
Better	12	5	2
Same	2	1	0
Worse	0	1	0

Note: The figures reported here (Iveson, 1991) total 23, whereas the sample was 24.

hopefulness and optimism on the part of the therapist. Even as a client tells a story that breaks the heart, the therapist can listen with genuine "evidence-based" hope. Second, the findings that cast doubt on the predictive value of the client–therapist relationship categories led the team to drop this attempt to categorize motivation and instead work from the premise that all clients are motivated, that is, anyone who for any reason is speaking with us in our professional role is doing so for a good reason. These research-informed notions of therapist hope and client motivation create instant energy from the very start of the first meeting.

Study 3: Checking Developments

Having spent the 1990s expanding its training activities and focusing on practice development, BRIEF decided it was time to put these developments to the test and commissioned another follow-up study. The outcomes of this third study, carried out in 2000, were almost identical to those of the second, with 80% of the clients reporting improvement (see Table 19.4). Once again, although this was a smallscale study and not undertaken in a rigorously controlled setting, clinically its findings were of great value. That the outcomes were virtually identical to those of the second study confirmed to us that the changes set in train by that study had not reduced our effectiveness.

Study 4: Food for Thought

Six years later we were approached by a master's student, who had attended courses with BRIEF, who wanted to inquire into what clients found effective in solution-focused brief therapy. In order to do this, he carried out a two-part study using a sample of BRIEF's clients (Henfrey, 2007, 2010). The first part was a simple outcome study similar to the second and third studies. In the second part, the group of "improved" clients were asked about which aspects of the model they had found helpful and why. The outcomes for the 57 people who completed the first part are shown in Table 19.5.

TABLE 19.4 *Outcomes of Study 3*

Outcome Related by the Client	Number (total 39)
Considerable improvement	17 (44%)
Some improvement	14 (36%)
No change	6 (15%)
Worse	2 (5%)

TABLE 19.5 *Outcomes of Study 4*

Outcome related by the client	Number (total 57)
Much improved	11 (19.3%)
Improved	23 (40.4%)
The same	21 (36.8%)
Worse	2 (3.5%)

Study 5: Briefer and Still Effective?

The dip in outcomes (60% improved) of the fourth study compared to the previous studies spurred us on to put systems in place to enable more regular and systematic evaluations of our work. Because we wanted to check our practice as quickly as possible after the fourth study, the fifth was undertaken about a year later. Eighty-four percent of the clients reported that they had made progress towards their "best hopes" from the work on average a year after its completion, with an average of 1.8 sessions per client (see Table 19.6). The questions asked in this study differed from those in the previous studies, the measure being about achievement of hopes rather than resolution of problems. This reflected the significant practice developments that had been set in train by the earlier studies, and it is to these that we now turn.

■ **SOLUTION-FOCUSED BRIEF INTERVENTIONS**

The Late 1980s: Beginning Solution-Focused Brief Therapy

In the late 1980s, in common with other therapists, those at BRIEF were learning to do solution-focused brief therapy from the books and articles coming out of Milwaukee (de Shazer, 1985, 1988; de Shazer et al., 1986). In following this emerging model, the work whose effectiveness was evaluated by the first two studies consisted of the following practices. The first session had eight stages: (a) "problem-free talk": building rapport and locating strengths; (b) statement of the problem pattern; (c) exploration of exceptions to this pattern; (d) goal setting —the miracle question; (e) establishing small steps of change; (f) taking a break; (g) compliments; and (h) task setting. Subsequent sessions followed a similar pattern, with a focus on further exceptions and the next steps for change, and were ended in the same way (George et al., 1990).

The 1990s: A Developing BRIEF Version of Solution-Focused Brief Therapy

From 1991 onwards, BRIEF adopted a developmental approach to its practice so that, by the third study in 2000, our version of solution-focused brief therapy showed some marked differences from the model sketched above. Although a number of factors other than our research data influenced these developments, as we will see shortly, the second study was fundamental in two respects. Firstly, it produced the confidence without which a developmental approach could not have been taken. Secondly, its results drew our attention to Ockham's razor, which we had come across in the writings of de Shazer (1985) but whose value we had not fully appreciated up to that point. William of Ockham, a medieval philosopher, held that "what can be achieved with

TABLE 19.6 *Outcomes of Study 5*

"Best hopes" achieved according to the client	Number (total 25)
Completely	2 (8%)
A lot	12 (48%)
A little	7 (28%)
Not at all	4 (16%)

fewer means is done in vain with many." If there was no need to categorize client–therapist relationships as customer, complainant, or visitor, we began to wonder if we were engaging in other potentially superfluous therapeutic activities. In particular, seeing the disconnect between outcome and problem was our first step towards a practice that left problems behind altogether.

We therefore decided to use Ockham's razor as a central philosophy to guide our practice developments. This led to a dynamic minimalist process whereby the removal of one unnecessary practice, rather than limiting the whole, would create space in time and the imagination for new ideas and new practices to emerge. Between the second and third studies, along with dropping the categorization of client–therapist relationships, this led to four other significant changes to the way we thought about and did solution-focused brief therapy.

From Goals to Preferred Futures

This was an example of a small change making a very significant difference. The team was talking, writing, and teaching about "goals," where the client wanted to be instead of "in the problem." At this time, we were working to replace the problem rather than to reach a hoped-for outcome, the crucial distinction between the two still to be fully grasped. Yet our "miracle" sequences, which we had understood to be a "frame for helping clients set goals" (de Shazer, 1988, p. 5), were gradually leading to something else. The original idea behind the miracle question made sense: The clearer the destination, the more likely you are to recognize it when you arrive, thus providing an antidote to endless therapy. And if clarity was important, then time spent achieving this was justified, so the team found that their clients' "miracles" were becoming increasingly rich in their descriptions of their lives without the problem.

Following de Shazer's developing blueprint, the miracle question would almost invariably be followed by a scale in which 10 represented "the day after the miracle" (Berg & de Shazer, 1993, p. 22). As descriptions grew richer, it became increasingly difficult to see the "miracle day" as a goal or even a set of goals. As a single goal it was too broad and multifaceted, and as a collection of goals there were far too many to be realistic. The descriptions might include certain specific thoughts on waking; ways of looking at and talking to any number of household members, colleagues, and friends; ways of eating toast at breakfast or the evening meal on the Sabbath; the most apparently insignificant to the most outrageously different behaviors, all of which could not possibly be defined by the narrow term *goal*. What, in fact, they were describing were entire ways of being, located within a hypothetical future. Seeing these miracle descriptions as preferred ways of living, the team began to refer to them as *preferred futures* (Iveson, 1994).

From Exceptions to Instances

Although we will always see the decision by the BFTC to focus on "exceptions to the rule" rather than problems as the pivotal moment that led to the revolution in therapy which began in Milwaukee in the 1980s, exceptions have gradually moved away from the center to the very edges of our practice. In Chapter 1 there is an account of how solution-focused brief therapy evolved in Milwaukee from a problem-focused brief therapy to a conversation about exceptions and future possibilities. The shift at BRIEF away from exceptions began as soon as we started to expand our future-focused questions. Amplifying the detail of their preferred future descriptions often led clients to refer to aspects of them that were already happening.

> What else would your partner notice about you?
> He'd see me smile.
> What else?
> Maybe that I'd be asking about his day. A bit like last night perhaps. We had a pleasant conversation then.

We started to see an equivalence between "times when the miracle is already happening" and "times when the problem is not happening," and the more we heard our clients talk about bits of their miracle days that were already in place, the less we felt the need to ask about exceptions. We were only able to let exceptions go more or less completely once our focus on "best hopes" took us beyond problems altogether, as we shall see shortly, but this was the starting point. More recently, we have decided to use the word *instances* in our teaching as an alternative to *exceptions* to highlight this shift, which was made in practice long before the language used to describe our approach caught up.

Best Hopes: Leaving the Problem Behind

As the increasing part descriptions of preferred futures were playing in BRIEF's first sessions was leading us away from the need to elicit exceptions, we looked next at how we began the session. If we were not asking about exceptions to the problem, we questioned the need to start with a statement of the problem pattern. Realizing that our focus was shifting and simplifying from "What does the client want instead of the problem?" to "What does the client want?" we began to set the scene instead by asking the client at the start of the work what he or she wanted from it: "What needs to happen for this to be useful to you?"

While this question provided a more coherent entry into the detailed descriptions of what was wanted, its wording sometimes led to a muddle (for both client and therapist) between outcome and process. The intention to focus on what needs to happen in the client's life was often heard as what needs to happen in the work between client and therapist. This muddle persisted until 1998, when a client, stuck on the "what needs to happen" question, indirectly suggested an alternative to the therapist that led to the opening question that has directed BRIEF's work ever since: "What are your best hopes from our work together?"

A person can have hopes or ambitions quite independently of any problem, and beginning work with a focus on the client's hopes led to a further adjustment in practice that took us beyond problem (and therefore solution) altogether. Up to this point, we had been defining the miracle as "all the problems that bring you here are gone." As the discontinuity between hopes and problem removal became clearer, the framing of the preferred future became the realization of the client's best hopes, and a more seamless flow was established:

> What are your best hopes from our work together?
> To be able to get on with my life

Suppose a miracle happened... and you were getting on with your life in the way that you wish to. What's the first thing you would notice about yourself?

With this question, there was no need to refer to the existence of a problem and certainly no need for the therapist to know of one. A client might choose to talk about his or her problems and then the therapist would need to listen, but since this time, defining a solvable problem has not been a part of our practice.

From End-of-Session Tasks to In-Session Conversation

As we were starting to assimilate the implications of the shift from goals to preferred futures, our thinking was helped further by a question posed surprisingly by a 17-year-old client at the end of a session in 1993. "How does this therapy work? Are you collecting information in order to advise us what to do or is it in the questions and answers?" Not only was this one of the greatest questions of all time, but it marked a turning point in how BRIEF thought about its practice. The therapist answered: "Great question! We have always worked the first way—collecting information and giving advice—but we are now beginning to think that it may be in the conversation itself that the therapy takes place." "Definitely!" said the young man. From that point on, BRIEF began to focus on the conversational process rather than on the construction of tasks. Until then, the team had been practicing an essentially traditional form of therapy. Certainly a looking glass was in place, so old assumptions had been turned on their heads, but the glass had not yet found its Alice-like powers of transformation. All that was reflected was an opposite image in which the therapist still collected information from the client, assessed its meaning and value from the therapist's own standpoint, and then gave an opinion, albeit a complimentary one, and instructions. The reflection in the mirror was still of a very "doing to" model. The content might be radically different, but the process was much the same. The notion of preferred futures started to put the magic in the looking glass, and a 17-year-old client helped us to see it!

Bringing research-mindedness to bear on this issue, the team began to notice what had probably always been there. Clients who did not perform their tasks seemed often to improve anyway, as did clients to whom no task was given. Was the evidence suggesting that tasks were not essential to the process of effective solution-focused brief therapy? What was becoming clear was that the two activities—the coconstructing of conversations on the one hand and the giving of tasks on the other—did not sit well together. The process of task construction must begin well before the conclusion of a session. Tasks do not come out of the ether; the conversation needs to elicit information for the therapist to decide on a doing task, an observational task, or no task at all. To collect this information, the therapist has an agenda and purpose of his or her own, and this diverts the conversation from other possible courses.

So, gradually, task setting was dropped. The difference this made to practice was not to shorten session time but to allow more emphasis on eliciting details of the client's preferred future and about what the client was already doing that might contribute to that future. Leaving tasks behind also released us from a sense that it was our job to get the client to change. Instead, the therapist's role was seen more as helping the client lay out straightforward, doable possibilities and leaving them simply as choices. A specific change resulting from this was to avoid implying that the client should take any action. To this end, the wording of questions about 1 point up the scale was changed, the emphasis shifting from "steps" ("What do you need to do to move up from 3 to 4?") to "signs" ("If you moved from 3 to 4, what might you notice?"). BRIEF was thus moving towards a minimally instrumental version of solution-focused brief therapy.

The 2000s: Continuing Developments

The results of the third study in 2000 confirmed that the practice changes made since the second study had not reduced our effectiveness. We therefore entered the new decade continuing to wield Ockham's razor with confidence. In 2005 BRIEF began its diploma training, a 1-year advanced course, and this also provided a very creative stimulus to the team. Assessing students' assignment tapes and looking ever more closely at the conversational process, we became increasingly committed to the idea that the most powerful therapeutic elements at work were the client's descriptions. We became more conscious of when we were using our own language and attempted to minimize the introduction of our own ideas in therapy sessions. This led us to realize more clearly the influence of Insoo Kim Berg and her injunction to "leave no footprints" in our clients' lives,[2] and one effect of this was to intensify the attention we had been paying to how we ended sessions.

From Compliments to Summaries

For many years, the team had been aware that compliments do not sit well with respect for the client's own self-knowledge. If the influence of therapy is somewhere in the conversation, then why add something else at the end? And if it is the client's knowledge that is paramount, why does the therapist then make an assessment of his or her own? On the other hand, when the team asked clients, they tended to say that they valued the feedback. Perhaps what made the difference was the recollection that compliments were originally intended to create a yes set through which the client was believed more likely to comply with a task (de Shazer, 1982). If that was their purpose, then, having already relinquished tasks, the team came to the view that compliments were dispensable. Instead, the team began to end their sessions either more or less after the client's last answer or, more commonly, with a summary of the client's preferred future and what the client was already contributing towards it.

Dropping the Break

The main impact that the fourth study has had on our practice thus far has been in relation to taking a break. Having dropped tasks and replaced compliments with summaries, it had appeared that taking a break before the end of the session was becoming redundant. In the second part of the fourth study, clients who had improved following therapy were asked to comment on what they had found useful (Henfrey, 2010). The one aspect of practice that they appeared dubious about was the break. This finding reinforced our thinking, and we have since largely discontinued taking a break before summarizing at the end of sessions.

Into the 2010s: BRIEF's Current Version: A (Minimal) Summary

So, at the end of the first decade of the new century, the lessons from our research, our use of Ockham's razor, and our desire to leave no footprints in our clients' lives have led to a practice that can be summarized as follows. The starting point in our therapy is to help the client articulate his or her best hopes from it, and we see this desired outcome as providing a contract for the work. From this point on, we simply invite the client to describe what the realization of those hopes would look like (the preferred future) and what is already in place (instances of the preferred future). We suspect that participants on our training courses keep waiting with interest to hear what else we do, however hard we try to reassure them that there really is nothing else. The results from the third study and, with some reservations, from the fifth study have confirmed our view concerning the usefulness of Ockham's razor, while the results of the fourth study have put us on our mettle to continue putting our practice developments to the test.

Case Examples

A comparison of two cases, one from 1990 and the second from 17 years later, will illustrate these shifts in practice. In the earlier case Miss Bonchance,[3] age 23, was referred by her general practitioner due to eating and weight difficulties. Full details of this case can be found in George et al. (1990, pp. 69–85), and the quotes that follow are taken from this account. The therapist spent some time early in the first session hearing about the problem, as the view then was that "like anyone coming for therapy Miss Bonchance needs to have her problem heard." She had recently stopped eating and had lost 35 pounds and her parents were taking time off from work to be with her at home to prevent her from vomiting and taking laxatives. The therapist sought to define the problem as solvable—a "new development" that Miss Bonchance wanted to "nip in the bud"—and then started a search for exceptions.

Exception finding was helped considerably when Miss Bonchance said, "it's awful because you have your good days and you have your bad. You have those days when you just don't want to do anything like that" (make yourself vomit). The therapist was then able to ask about the differences on good days, "with the most important question being 'what else?'." This produced four activities: window shopping, walking, watching videos, and contacting friends, which later formed the basis for a homework task. After developing more specific goals and exploring Miss Bonchance's past experiences of problem solving, the therapist took a break and with the team constructed compliments and the task. As she could not predict the good days, Miss Bonchance was advised to toss a coin each evening to decide whether the next day would be one when she would do something about her difficulty and, if so, to do the easiest of the good-day activities listed earlier. A week later, Miss Bonchance reported that every day since had been good, and the therapy came to an end.

Seventeen years later, Ben,[4] age 15, was referred by a worker from the youth justice service. This time, rather than defining a problem and then looking for exceptions, the therapist's starting point was to ask Ben about his "best hopes" from the work. Not unexpectedly, Ben's first few responses consisted of "I don't know," and persistence was required. Eventually, Ben said that he would know he had been helped if he stopped his offending behavior. He was asked what he wanted to do instead, which turned out to be getting a job, plumbing perhaps. A contract had been established for the work, based on Ben's hope of shifting from a life of offending to a life of work. The therapist's task for the rest of the work would consist only of inviting Ben to describe (a) how he would know that he had made this shift and (b) ways in which he was already making it.

When Ben was asked to describe the differences that turning his life around would make tomorrow morning, it soon became apparent that he was only saying things that he was already doing—for example, asking the staff at the youth offending team about going to college and socializing with nonoffending friends. It transpired that Ben had come out of prison 3 weeks before, having been inside for 9 months, and wanted to "go straight". The therapist made the reasonable point that a lot of people come out of prison and say that they want to go straight but do not manage to do so. What did Ben know about himself that told him he meant business? Ben replied that he was doing it for himself and for his dad. The therapist then decided to leave the discussion of the future and devote the rest of the session to descriptions of what Ben was doing already that was helping him turn his life around.

He asked Ben to write his first answer—"socializing with the right friends"—on a flipchart in the room and then went out to adjust the camera filming the session. On returning to the room, the therapist asked the question that focused the rest of the session: "What else? And we're just going to do fifty things!" For the next 35 minutes, the therapist asked questions that enabled Ben to write on the chart 50 things he had done and had noticed about himself in the past 3 weeks, and in prison before that time, that had helped him get on and stay on the right track. All that was left to do was for the therapist to summarize by reading Ben's words on the chart back to him: asking about college, going to the youth offending center every day, being self-disciplined, coming home on time, learning to cook, and so on. Ben did not turn up for a second session, and the outcome was not known until a chance meeting a couple of years later with the worker who had referred him. In the weeks following the first session, the youth offending team had decided that Ben was doing well enough not to need further therapy.

The session with Ben, having very little "preferred future" description, was somewhat unusual and yet, set alongside the work with Miss Bonchance, some of the major differences between early and late BRIEF interventions are brought into sharp relief. In particular, it is clear from the original summary of the earlier session (George et al., 1990) that great importance was attached to the eliciting of four or five things that Miss Bonchance did that helped her have good days. The possibility of eliciting 50 constructive actions from a client would have been hard to imagine then. The space to do this was opened up by the relinquishing of other and perhaps more therapist-led activities, such as taking a break to devise compliments and task setting.

■ RESEARCH METHODS

The methods employed in the studies also developed over time. As the first study had to be put together quickly to provide data to convince managers to allow the Brief Therapy Project to continue, the team relied heavily on the therapist's assessment of outcome, and outcomes were judged on completion of the work rather than being followed up at a later point. A third factor affecting the validity of these figures is that they also depended on the therapist's prediction of outcome in the cases of "dropout", and as already noted, we were to learn that therapists are not particularly good predictors of outcome.

It is difficult now to remember how radical the idea of letting the client be the sole judge of outcome was. It was an idea that was entirely consistent with solution-focused brief therapy and, grasping more fully the implications of the approach, the team went on to ensure that future studies would be based on asking the client. The questions asked about outcome developed over time and are summarized in Table 19.7. As we were initially attempting to follow the Milwaukee template closely, the second study used the BFTC measure (de Shazer, 1985) to indicate whether we were on the right track. In the third study a similar measure was used, except that four potential answers were offered instead of three, following a development seen in Milwaukee (de Shazer, 1991), and this was replicated in the fourth study. Another difference in the third and fourth studies reflected one of our practice developments. As naming a problem was no longer part of our process, clients were not reminded of the specific "complaint" that brought them to therapy, but were simply invited to consider improvement (or not) in the "problem" or "issue". A significant change was made for the fifth study measure, again to follow developments in practice. We decided to vary the questions asked of the clients, as we considered that there might be a lack of congruence between the therapy and its measure. The research questions had been about problem resolution, yet the therapy was now directed towards the clients' best hopes from it. The clients were therefore asked whether or not they had achieved their best hopes (at least in part) and, if so, whether they had achieved them "completely," "a lot" or "a little."

The sample sizes varied due to a number of factors, including the time available to the researcher and the number of clients who could be found to respond. The samples were arrived at by simply selecting a period of time and then attempting to contact, by telephone, all clients who had completed therapy during that period. Sample sizes for the second to the fifth studies are shown in Table 19.8.

The follow-up period is an important factor in naturalistic studies of this type. It has been argued that clients should be contacted about 1 year after completion, as before that time there might be a "honeymoon" effect and after that time there is a greater

TABLE 19.7 *Follow-up Questions (Measures) Used in Studies 2 to 5*

	Measure
Study 2	When you came to therapy, your main complaint was… Is this better? Is this the same? Is it worse?
Study 3	Thinking of the problem that brought you to therapy, has there been considerable improvement, some improvement, no change, or is it worse?
Study 4	Are the issue(s) that resulted in your accessing SFBT much improved, improved, the same or worse?
Study 5	Have you achieved your best hopes from the therapy completely, a lot, a little, or not at all?

TABLE 19.8 *Sample Sizes and Follow Up Periods of Studies 2 to 5*

	Sample size	Follow-up period
Study 2	24	6 months to a year
Study 3	39	Minimum 6 months, average 18 months
Study 4	57	Minimum not known, maximum 3 years
Study 5	25	8 to 16 months

chance that subsequent life events might have interfered with the effects of the therapy (Macdonald, 2007). In the second, third, and fifth studies the follow-up period varied, but the average was either 1 year or 18 months post completion (see Table 19.8). In the fourth study, the researcher wanted a large original sample to ensure that he received a sufficient number of completed questionnaires in the second part of the study, which contributed to a decision to contact clients who had completed their therapy as far back as 3 years previously. So, as with all the studies reported here, which have limitations of varying kinds, the results of this study need to be treated with caution.

■ LIMITATIONS OF PRACTICE-BASED RESEARCH

The literature concerning practice-based research tends to be positive, with the references cited in the introduction to this chapter being typical. However, limitations of practice-based research studies have also been well documented. One of the main limitations arises from the competing demands on practitioners' time, which are often managed by the prioritizing of service delivery, with research, perhaps viewed as less of a necessity, taking a back seat (Garland et al., 2008; Peake et al., 2005). This partly explains the length of time that elapsed here between the second and third studies. Pressures on practitioners' time are also a contributory factor to the small sample sizes in studies such as these. Contacting research populations takes time. Another potential limitation that can slow clinicians down further is their lack of research expertise, which can lead to a number of other difficulties. These include a limit on the types of data that are collected and demands being made on the monitoring of reliability and validity (Zarin et al., 1997).

A limitation of all the studies reported in this chapter is a common one in producing practice-based evidence, namely, the potential effect of researcher allegiance (Luborsky et al., 1999). Each study was undertaken by a person who was positive about the solution focused approach, though this arose out of necessity rather than choice. Research projects take time and resources, and in a small team neither is readily available. The second study came about when the partner of one of the therapists needed a research project for her master's degree, and this person was also turned to for the third study. Such an association might taint the research as far as its external value is concerned, though within the clinic at the time there was no conflict, as information was wanted for ethical confirmation and for pointers it might give for practice development rather than for external justification.

■ RESEARCH RESULTS

BRIEF has been established for 21 years, and its founders had started using solution-focused brief therapy prior to this time while working in the public sector. It is hard to imagine that this longevity could have been achieved in the absence of studies evaluating the effectiveness of what was being done. The effects of the research carried out in the five studies can be grouped under two main headings. Firstly—and initially this was of greater importance—the research has provided confirmation that clients were being effectively served by the approach. Secondly—and this was particularly the case following the second study —it has provided the impetus to take a developmental approach to practice and suggested a direction in which developments could be taken.

The confirming effects of the research have been important in a number of ways. Firstly, the evidence from the first study enabled our then managers to support the use of solution-focused brief therapy in a public mental health clinic. This, in turn, enabled us to devote an increasing amount of time to learning and practicing the approach, which led eventually to the creation of BRIEF as a private practice and training center. The second study was a seminal moment in the development of BRIEF. The confidence arising from it led the team members to begin teaching the approach in earnest, and the learning from teaching, together with some of the thought-provoking findings of the study, created the developmental ethos that has remained with BRIEF ever since.

When we were first learning how to do solution-focused brief therapy, it had seemed not only simple but finite. We supposed that we would fully learn and grasp the approach, and then therapist boredom and model ossification would drive us to move on. Being drawn to Ockham's razor by the results of the second study meant that we did indeed keep moving, but within what turned out to be an infinitely elastic model. The practice developments triggered by the second study can be summarized as follows:

- Dropping the categorization of client–therapist relationships as either customer, complainant, or visitor and instead assuming client motivation —every client is a customer for something
- Working towards the client's hopes from the therapy rather than problem resolution
- Inviting detailed descriptions of preferred futures rather than setting goals
- Focusing on instances—times when the preferred future is happening —rather than on exceptions to the problem
- Dropping task setting and focusing more on the conversation during the session

The third study was also crucial in that it offered confirmation that these developments had not detracted from the effectiveness of our work, and thereby simultaneously encouraged developments to continue:

- Summarizing rather than complimenting

A further development was consolidated by the fourth study:

- Dropping the break

Notwithstanding its lengthy follow-up periods, the less favorable outcomes of the fourth study led to much clinical discussion and soul searching among the team. We were unsure how to read the results: Were they "just one of those things"? Did they reflect too much experimentation? Did they reflect complacency? Our first response was to commit ourselves to more regular evaluations of our work and to search for the best ways to carry out these evaluations.

The fifth and most recent study was more encouraging, though due to the different questions asked, it is hard to compare the findings with those of the previous studies. That 28% of clients described their best hopes as being achieved only "a little" has given us food for thought about the questions asked at follow-up as well as about the therapy. We will consider some ideas concerning future follow-up studies below. Regarding the therapy, we frequently now have as our starting point with clients a contract based on aspirational "best hopes" such as getting on with one's life or being happy. The preferred future is often then framed as "moving towards" the achievement of these hopes, in which case perhaps it is unsurprising if clients judge that they are making only "a little progress" toward these aspirations.

An unexpected finding of the fifth study was that the average number of sessions across the 25 clients was as low as 1.8. This by no means reflects BRIEF's overall average, which over the past 10 years has been closer to three sessions (reduced from an average of four in the team's early days), but it does suggest that lasting changes can be set in motion with minimal therapist input. Our best guess about the reason for the reduction in the number of sessions is that it is related to our attempt to become noninstrumental in our conversations with clients. Though overall our intention is to be successful therapists by helping clients move forward in their lives, client by client, the team endeavors to remain neutral about what the client does. Our hunch is that if clients are confronted in any way by our ideas concerning possible actions to take, then they will need to take time to consider these ideas. Conversely, the more we are able to keep out of their way, by simply inviting clients to describe future possibilities and whatever aspects of these possibilities are already in place, the more quickly they will be able to get on with whatever they choose to do.

■ PRACTICE GUIDELINES

In this section, we will summarize what we have learned from doing practice-based research and hope that this can be of some use to other therapists who are thinking of doing their own.

Before beginning any research, we recommend thinking carefully about its purpose. Who is the intended audience? Are you seeking to check the direction of your work for your own benefit or to convince managers or an outside body of the value of your approach? In the United Kingdom, the National Institute for Health and Clinical Excellence (NICE) issues guidelines for National Health Service practitioners regarding treatments and approaches that should be followed. In order to approve treatments under these guidelines, NICE needs to be convinced that they are effective with specific client populations. The evidence that they are most keen to see is that produced by randomized controlled trials, though they are apparently realizing that such research is often unrealistic and not necessarily the most useful in the mental health field. Notwithstanding this relaxation, NICE still wants to see evidence of effectiveness with specific client groups. To this end, BRIEF intends to include some form of diagnostic formulation for each client in future studies.

Including such a formulation involves planning ahead. Once the results of the fourth study came in, we immediately began to prepare for future studies, for example by seeking permission from all new clients to contact them after the end of the work for research purposes and clearly recording useful contact details.

For our fifth study, we began to think more carefully about the most suitable measures to use, measures that are simple and at the same time valid and reliable. Berg and Steiner (2003) suggest a way forward by substituting the word helpful or useful for successful as a criterion for the effectiveness of therapy. "The problems of living are far too complex to divide into such simple categories as success or failure, and we are aware that what one person would consider a success could easily be a failure for someone else" (p. 230). They point, therefore, to the use of scales in eliciting clients' sense of progress toward their goal. There is evidence that simple solution-focused scales can be used as a valid measure of outcome (Franklin et al., 1997), and we plan to use scales as the measure in our next study.

While we have focused in this chapter on five discrete studies, we have also referred to research-mindedness. We have not had the space here to refer to all the experimentation that we have engaged in. Suffice to say that we have become aware that some of our developments did not work simply by paying careful attention to their effects in sessions and by frequent discussions in the team. Research-mindedness can help us to start small and continuously evaluate all that we do rather than rely only on planned studies.

More planned and formal research takes time and resources. We have found it important to nurture relationships with potential researchers and to look for opportunities to collaborate. We have been fortunate to find master's students who needed to undertake research, and forging connections with academia will be helpful.

■ KEY FINDINGS TO REMEMBER

- Practice-based research can be carried out by a small team of therapists.
- The original (Milwaukee) form of solution-focused brief therapy can be practiced effectively by therapists working in a public mental health clinic in the United Kingdom.
- A more minimal and noninstrumental version of this therapy can be practiced equally effectively.
- Effective therapy can be undertaken with a wide range of clients without a problem having to be stated or even known by the therapist.
- Tasks are not a necessary component of solution-focused brief therapy.
- Undertaking research encourages a developmental approach to practice, and this, in turn, can maintain practitioner interest and enthusiasm over an extended period of time.
- Outcomes can fluctuate over time, and it is therefore important to remain vigilant about the effectiveness of new developments and committed to their evaluation.

■ FURTHER LEARNING

- The BRIEF Web site is http://www.brief.org.uk
- BRIEFER: A Solution-focused practice manual (George et al., 2009) is published by BRIEF and given to all participants in our introductory courses. The manual is available from BRIEF either by visiting the Web site or by calling +44(0)20 7600 3366.
- The Web site of NICE, the National Institute for Health and Clinical Excellence, is http://www.nice.org.uk

■ FIRST AUTHOR'S NOTE

Chris Iveson was a founding member of BRIEF and was present during the whole period described in this chapter. First trained by BRIEF in 1995, Guy Shennan joined the team in 2004. The other two founding and current members of the team are Evan George and Harvey Ratner, who together with Chris Iveson pioneered the use of solution focused brief therapy in the United Kingdom. Between them, they are responsible for the (in my view) groundbreaking developments described here.

■ ENDNOTES

1. "On the Move" in Thom Gunn (1994), *Collected Poems*. New York: Farrar, Straus and Giroux.
2. This is an often cited but little referenced remark of Insoo's. In the second edition of *Problem to Solution* (George et al., 1999) we acknowledged its source as a posting on an Internet list.
3. Not her real name.
4. Not his real name.

■ REFERENCES

Berg, I., K., & de Shazer, S. (1993). Making numbers talk: Language in therapy. In S. Friedman (Ed.), *The new language of change: Constructive collaboration in psychotherapy* (pp. 5–24). New York: Guilford Press.

Berg, I. K., & Steiner, T. (2003). Children's solution work. New York: Norton.

Bringhurst, D., Watson, C., Miller, S., & Duncan, B. (2006). The reliability and validity of the Outcome Rating Scale: A replication study of a brief clinical measure. *Journal of Brief Therapy*, 5(1), 23–30.

Charman, D., & Barkham, M. (2005). Psychological treatments: Evidence-based practice and practice-based evidence. In *Inpsych*. Retrieved April 30, 2010, from http://www.psychology.org.au/publications/inpsych/treatments/

de Shazer, S. (1982). *Patterns of brief family therapy*. New York: Guilford Press.

de Shazer, S. (1985). *Keys to solution in brief therapy*. New York: Norton.

de Shazer, S. (1988). *Clues: Investigating solutions in brief therapy*. New York: Norton.

de Shazer, S. (1991). *Putting difference to work*. New York: Norton.

de Shazer, S., Berg, I. K., Lipchik, E., Nunnally, E., Molnar, A., Gingerich, W., & Weiner-Davis, M. (1986). Brief therapy: Focused solution development. *Family Process*, 25(2), 207–222.

Everitt, A., Hardiker, P., Littlewood, J., & Mullender, A. (1992). *Applied research for better practice*. Basingstoke, UK: Macmillan Education.

Franklin, C., Corcoran, J., Nowicki, J., & Streeter, C. (1997). Using client self-anchored scales to measure outcomes in solution-focused therapy. *Journal of Systemic Therapies*, 16(3), 246–265.

Garland, A., McCabe, K., & Yeh, M. (2008). Ethical challenges in practice-based mental health services research: Examples from research with children and families. Clinical Psychology: Science and Practice, 15(2), 118–124.

George, E., Iveson, C., & Ratner, H. (1990). *Problem to solution*. London: BT Press.

George, E., Iveson, C., & Ratner, H. (1999). *Problem to solution* (2nd ed.). London: BT Press.

George, E., Iveson, C., Ratner, H., & Shennan, G. (2009). *BRIEFER: A solution focused practice manual*. London: BRIEF.

Henfrey, S. (2007). *A client-centred evaluation of what people find effective about solution focused brief therapy*. Unpublished master's thesis, University of Birmingham, Birmingham, United Kingdom.

Henfrey, S. (2010). *A client-centred evaluation of what people find effective about solution focused brief therapy*. Solution Focused Research Review, 1(2), 19–34. Retrieved March 31, 2010, from http://www.sfrr.co.uk/issues/sfrr1-2.pdf

Iveson, D. (1991). *Outcome research: What is it and who for?* Unpublished master's thesis, University of London, Birkbeck College, United Kingdom.

Iveson, C. (1994). *Preferred futures, constructive histories.* Presentation at the European Brief Therapy Association conference. Stockholm, Sweden.

Luborsky, L., Diguer, L., Seligman, D. A., Rosenthal, R., Krause, E. D., Johnson, S., et al. (1999). The researcher's own therapy allegiances: A "wild card" in comparisons of treatment efficacy. Clinical Psychology: Science and Practice, 6(1), 95–106.

Macdonald, A. (2007). *Solution-focused therapy: Theory, research and practice.* London: Sage Publications.

Midgeley, N. (2009). Editorial: Improvers, adapters and rejecters—the link between "evidence-based practice" and "evidence-based practitioners." *Clinical Child Psychology and Psychiatry*, 14(3), 323–327.

Peake, K., Mirabito, D., Epstein, I., & Giannone, V. (2005). Creating and sustaining a practice-based research group in an urban adolescent mental health program. *Social Work in Mental Health*, 3(1), 39–54.

Weick, A. (2000). Hidden voices. *Social Work*, 45(5), 395–402.

Zarin, D., Pincus, H., West, J., & McIntyre, J. (1997). Practice-based research in psychiatry. *American Journal of Psychiatry*, 154(9), 1199–1208.

20 Outcomes of Solution-Focused Brief Therapy for Adolescents in Foster Care and Health Care Settings

■ RYTIS PAKROSNIS AND VIKTORIJA ČEPUKIENĖ

■ INTRODUCTION

Adolescence is one of the most charming and promising but at the same time challenging periods in human life. Ongoing rapid and at times extensive biological, psychological, and social changes require from adolescents (and their social environment) much inner as well as outer resources and coping efforts. However, the adjustment process is rather complex and does not always lead to desired outcomes (Brown, 2005; Compas, 2004; McMahon et al., 2003).

Some adolescents have very specific life conditions, such as living apart from their biological families or having a physical or mental illness, which can further reduce their ability to employ required recourses, so they might need some assistance in evoking them. This chapter is devoted to three of these specific adolescents groups: those living in foster care, those having physical health problems, and those having mental health problems.

A review of the literature indicates that foster care usually involves very vulnerable children who need special attention, care, and help from many professionals. However, despite the services that are available, mental health problems among children living in foster care are prevalent to the same extent as before they enter the foster care system (Simms et al., 2000; Taussing, 2002). On the other hand, there is evidence that the difficulties of these adolescents are not permanent or "fixed" by the early negative experience of neglect or loss of parents. There are data suggesting that a foster care environment and adolescents' efforts to achieve better adaptation in this environment can decrease the prevalence of psychosocial difficulties (e.g., Davidson-Arad, 2005; Cepukiene & Pakrosnis, 2008).

Data show that the prevalence of psychosocial adjustment problems among adolescents experiencing health disorders is 10%–15% higher than among adolescents from the general population (Garralda, 2004). Mental health disorders are related to more severe problems of psychosocial adjustment than physical health disorders. However, the type of health disorder is a weak predictor of adolescents' psychological functioning problems (Bishop, 2005; McMahon et al., 2003; Schmidt et al., 2003). This indicates that there must be other factors—such as availability of resources, coping strategies, and the quality of family relationships—that account for the prevalence of psychosocial difficulties among these adolescents (Bishop, 2005). This idea is promising because it indicates that these factors are more "flexible" and thus can be altered.

This short review of the literature suggests that despite difficult life conditions, the problems among adolescents in foster care and health care settings are not fixed and thus can be altered by therapeutic interventions.

While these adolescents may be helped by extensive professional assistance, data suggest that providing therapy for them can often be a challenge for mental health professionals due to their low motivation to seek and receive help, unwillingness to be criticized, difficulty forming and maintaining close relations with adults, and a tendency to terminate therapy early (Kazdin, 2002, 2003; Kazdin & Nock, 2003; Smith, 2002). The recent literature on psychotherapy outcomes suggests that when working with adolescents, it is most beneficial to stay brief, foster collaboration, and take into account and value their opinions and point of view (Kazdin, 2002, 2003). This could be one of the explanations for the growing popularity of solution-focused brief therapy (SFBT) among professionals working with young people (Corcoran & Stephenson 2000; Gingerich & Wabeke, 2001). See Chapters 8 and 16 for discussions of other potential advantages of using SFBT with children and adolescents who have behavior difficulties.

The SFBT approach emphasizes a positive attitude toward the client and develops cooperation between therapist and client. This approach also avoids confrontation, which helps to minimize adolescents' resistance to therapy and enhances the therapeutic alliance. In addition, it tends to decreases adolescents' self-blame. Finally, SFBT increases adolescents' satisfaction and motivation to continue therapy, stimulates their thinking, and helps to name and clarify the changes the client desires (Corcoran & Stephenson 2000; Lethem, 2002; Simon & Berg, 2004). However, despite the growing popularity of SFBT and the increasing body of research supporting its use, there is a notable lack of reliable knowledge about the effectiveness of SFBT for adolescents, especially in specific settings such as foster care and health care.

In this chapter, we will introduce and discuss the state of SFBT research in these groups of adolescents. We will also present the results of a study with this population conducted in Lithuania that was aimed at evaluating the effectiveness of SFBT for adolescents in foster care[1] and health care settings.

■ WHAT WE HAVE LEARNED SO FAR

In the last few decades, the body of SFBT research has grown dramatically. For example, during the last 5 years, the number of published studies included in the SFBT evaluation list provided by the European Brief Therapy Association (http://www.ebta.nu) has increased by 76%, most of them showing that the model benefits the clients. In this section, we will discuss existing evidence of the effectiveness of SFBT for adolescents in foster care and health care settings. We will present a theoretical model (providing a possible explanation) of the action mechanisms involved in SFBT as well as a review of the research conducted in these client groups.

Review of multiple sources discussing the SFBT process led to the need to summarize theoretical principles, therapeutic processes, and possible change mechanisms embedded in the model. As the result of this analysis, the model presented in Figure 20.1 was designed. This model is the basis for the questions and methodology of the study that will be presented in the following sections of the chapter.

As the model suggests, it is often stressed that the therapeutic process in SFBT proceeds in a cooperative atmosphere, which is essential for those striving to find solutions. Cooperation is the result of the interaction between a therapist and a client in which each makes a significant contribution. The therapist assumes a "not-knowing" position, which means being curious and making efforts to understand the client's frame of reference without prejudice about the problem, its origins, and possible solutions. The therapist's not-knowing position lets the client take the "expert" position—knowing and providing the therapist with valuable information regarding the problem and the possible solutions. While the therapist is responsible for the process of keeping the conversation focused on solutions, the client is responsible for the content of the conversation and for taking actions that lead to positive changes. The SFBT sessions involve specific steps, including analyzing exceptions; listening for the client's strengths and resources; formulating measurable, small, achievable behavioral goals; searching for alternative behaviors and meanings; planning the first steps; formulating therapeutic tasks leading to changes in the client's perception of the situation; and increasing the client's motivation and hope for change. At the same time, most changes in the client's life occur between sessions (De Jong & Berg, 1998). It is expected that the perception of changes and therapeutic tasks will lead to positive changes in the client's behavior. It is assumed that the social system plays an important role in the client's behavioral changes, responding to positive changes in the client's behavior, reinforcing them, and changing itself.

Three assumptions can be drawn from this model. First, due to the emphasis on cooperation, the client's resources, respect for the client's frame of reference, fostering

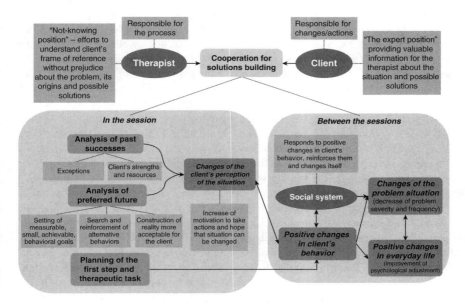

Figure 20.1. Theoretical model of SFBT process and change mechanisms.

of hope and motivation, searching for multiple alternatives, and maintenance of systemic thinking can be keys to the effectiveness of SFBT. This model can help an adolescent stay in therapy and strive for positive changes. Second, it can be hypothesized that positive changes are not limited to the situation (or the theme of the therapeutic conversation) but also have the potential to affect positively the broader context of the client's life. Finally, it can be hypothesized that positive changes in the situation and in the broader context of the client's life are interrelated.

Let us now turn to the existing empirical evidence of the effectiveness of SFBT in foster care and health care settings, where, out of a comparatively large and quickly growing body of SFBT research, only a few studies have been conducted on the adolescent population. Many of these studies focus on SFBT in a group setting (Franklin et al., 2001; LaFountain & Garner, 1996; Newsome, 2004; Tyson & Baffour, 2004; Viner et al., 2003) or in family therapy (Franklin et al., 1997; Wilmshurst, 2002). We will offer a brief review of those studies where SFBT was applied as an *individual* intervention for adolescents in foster care and health care settings. See Chapters 13 and 25 for other examples of how SFBT may be useful in health care settings when applied to adult clients.

Research on Adolescents in Foster Care

Only two studies examined SFBT with adolescents in foster care. Van Dyk (2004) studied the impact of SFBT on the foster care recidivism rate of adolescent offenders. The results of this study showed that 2 years after SFBT intervention, adolescent offenders experienced significantly fewer returns to foster care. However, in this study no standardized measures were applied, there was no control group, and the aim and purpose of entering the foster care system were different from those in our study. In another study Koob and Love (2010) found that after residential treatment applying SFBT, the number of disruptions among foster care adolescents decreased significantly. The authors concluded that SFBT has potential to promote foster care placement stability with adolescents. The results of both studies could be interpreted as indirect demonstration of improvement of foster care adolescents' psychosocial functioning during the SFBT. However, these studies do not provide knowledge on what specific effects SFBT has on foster care adolescents' emotions, behaviour, interpersonal relationship etc. Summarizing, we can conclude that there are almost no available data on the outcome of SFBT with adolescents living apart from their biological families.

In the literature, we found four studies conducted in mental health care settings where SFBT was applied as an individual intervention. In two of these studies (Burr, 1993; Lee, 1997), only clients' satisfaction with the outcomes of SFBT was measured. The results revealed that 77% and 54% of clients, respectively, reported that the problem situation improved or that the therapy helped them to meet their goals. Lee (1997) stated that in most cases, positive changes in family relationships and in the child's behavior were reported. In two other studies (Corcoran, 2006; Corcoran & Stephenson, 2000), standardized outcome evaluation methods were applied.Corcoran (2006) compared the outcomes of SFBT and treatment as usual for children with behavior problems. This study used the Feelings, Attitudes, and Behaviors Scale for Children (FAB-C) and the Conners Parent Rating Scales at a university outpatient mental health clinic. The results revealed that parents reported significant improvements between pretest and posttest scores for the following categories: conduct problems, learning problems, psychosomatic problems, and impulsivity-hyperactivity. The children reported significant improvement in self image but worsening conduct problems. However, the authors did not analyze the relations between outcome and clients' age (which ranged from 5 to 17 years); thus, the applicability of the findings to the adolescent population is not clear. Corcoran and Stephenson (2000) also reported on a similar study using the same measures. Parents and children reported similar improvement, with no differences between both treatment conditions. These experimental studies and others similar to them were previously reviewed in some detail in Chapters 8 and 16. They are mentioned here again because they represent examples of intervention in the individual behavior problems of children.

Few studies, however, have analyzed the outcome of SFBT as an individual intervention for adolescents in a rehabilitation setting or for those experiencing physical health problems. From the review of the current research on child outcomes we conclude that SFBT may be of value for these adolescent groups, but we cannot conclude that a large amount of evidence exists. Most of the studies we reviewed, however, suggest that SFBT leads to positive changes in problem situations and child behavior. This corresponds with the theoretical model presented above. However, this small number of studies does not provide sufficient evidence for the effectiveness of SFBT in these settings. Other chapters in this volume also report that there are mixed findings on the effectiveness of SFBT with children who have behavior problems, and previous systematic reviews suggest that we need well-designed studies with larger samples to sort out the differences. See the previous reviews in Chapters 6, 7, 8, and 16.

The Current Study

In this context, we can highlight some distinctive features of our current study. First, in this study, the outcome of SFBT was gauged using a range of measures, including subjective evaluation by adolescents, evaluation by the therapist, and standardized measures, while other SFBT studies in given settings usually employ only one of them. This enabled us to compare these measures and evaluate whether changes in psychological adjustment were related to changes in the problem situation. It also allowed us to gain some insight into the therapeutic change mechanisms discussed earlier in the theoretical model (see Figure 20.1).

Second, employing the same research design in two different client samples allowed direct comparison of the outcome of SFBT among the three different subgroups.

Finally, professionals studying the effectiveness of psychotherapy for adolescents point out the lack of studies conducted in clinical settings, which would consider not only the changes in symptoms or problems but also the changes in the child's general functioning (Kazdin & Nock, 2003; Nock, 2003). Therefore, this study is relevant in the context of psychotherapy effectiveness studies, because it takes into account the above-mentioned references. The study was carried out in a clinical as opposed to an experimental setting, and it analyzed not only changes in the presenting problem but also changes in broader psychosocial functioning.

The research questions for our study were as follows:

- Does the severity of problems among adolescents in foster care and health care settings decrease in the course of SFBT?
- Do adolescents in foster care and health care settings who participate in SFBT experience improved psychological adjustment?

- Is there any evidence that the changes in problem severity and psychological adjustment experienced by adolescents during SFBT are interrelated?
- Do adolescents from different settings achieve similar outcomes after receiving SFBT?

■ SFBT INTERVENTION

In this study, SFBT intervention involved the components of the model as described by the developers of the model without modification of the principles and techniques or combination with other therapeutic models.

For research purposes, a SFBT manual was developed based upon the requirements of the European Brief Therapy Association (Beyebach, 2000) and methodological suggestions by De Jong and Berg (1998). In the manual the therapeutic procedure, including specific techniques, their sequence and its variations, depending on the client's responses, were described.

In each case, the SFBT process was recorded using a SFBT protocol (developed by the authors and provided in the case example). It included information about the presenting problem, various circumstances related to the problem, therapeutic contact, observation of the client's physical and emotional condition and behavior during the session, the client's expectations, therapeutic goals, planned interventions, the course of each session, and evaluation of the outcome (changes occurred, results achieved, and recommendations given).

Compliance with the SFBT manual was evaluated by reviewing the SFBT protocol after the completion of therapy. In order to be included in the data analysis, the interventions in each case had to meet specific criteria provided by the European Brief Therapy Association (Beyebach, 2000). In the first session, an exception question, a miracle question, and scaling questions (aimed at evaluating the severity of the problem and the client's motivation to change, as well as planning the client's actions necessary to move toward established therapeutic goals) had to be asked and explored in detail. In addition, a feedback message was provided that included compliments and an intervention task assignment for the client before the end of the session. In the second and following sessions, the SFBT protocol had to describe instances of the use of the "what's better?" question (discovering and exploring the changes occurring between sessions) and scaling questions, as well as a discussion of the next small steps toward the desired solution, a feedback message including compliments, and an intervention task assignment.

■ RESEARCH METHODS

Subjects

The study was conducted in Lithuania at seven foster care homes and three health care institutions: two primary mental health care centers (participants were outpatients with mental health problems) and a rehabilitation hospital (participants were inpatients with long-term physical health problems).

The number and average age of the adolescent participants from the different study settings are provided in Figure 20.2. There were 112 subjects in the treatment condition and 91 in the control condition.

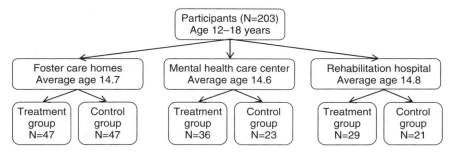

Figure 20.2. The number and average age of participants in different settings.

No significant differences in age, gender, and psychological adjustment between the treatment and control groups in each of three settings were found at pretreatment evaluation.

Psychological Adjustment Evaluation Method

Our study used the Adolescent Behavior Checklist (Pakrosnis & Cepukiene, 2009), which includes 54 dichotomous items that have been developed through content analysis. The checklist was completed by the adolescents. Based on a factorial analysis, five subscales were composed: Emotional Difficulties, Adjustment at School Difficulties, Social Insensibility, Nonadaptive Behavior, and Self-esteem Difficulties. Cronbach alpha values ranged between .63 and .85.

Outcome Evaluation Methods

The outcome of SFBT was measured using two types of methods:

1. Methods for the assessment of therapeutic progress (for practical application see the Case example)
   - *The Client's Evaluation of Progress.* According to the SFBT manual, during every session each client was asked to evaluate the severity of his or her problem on a scale from 0 to 10 (where 0 stands for the problem that brought the client in at its worst and 10 stands for the solved problem). The difference between problem severity in the first and last sessions was used as an indicator of progress as evaluated by the client.
   - *The Therapist's Evaluation of Improvement.* After termination of each client's therapy, the therapist estimated the client's improvement on the basis of the following criteria:
     Changes in the client's perceptions of the problem (changes in the client's view of his or her role in the origin of the problem and possible solutions; discovering possible solutions)
     Changes in the client's behavior related to the problem (indications of the client's actions toward developing possible solutions)
     Changes in the client's problem/situation and related circumstances (changes in the problem's character, severity, and frequency; changes in the client's

emotional state; changes in other people's reactions and behavior toward the client)

These criteria were used to evaluate the progress of each client in solving his or her problem, and progress was rated as one of five improvement levels:

No change (no changes in the client's perceptions of the problem, behavior, problem/situation and related circumstances)

Slight improvement (clear changes in the client's perceptions of the problem, no changes in the client's behavior, problem/situation and related circumstances)

Average improvement (changes in the client's perceptions and behavior related to the problem, no changes in the problem/situation and related circumstances)

Considerable improvement (changes in the client's perceptions and behavior related to the problem, partial changes in the problem/situation and related circumstances)

Problem solved completely (changes in the client's perceptions and behavior related to the problem, disappearance of the problem)

2. Methods for evaluation of changes in psychosocial adjustment
   • The Checklist of Adolescent Behavior Changes, consisting of the same 54 items included in the Adolescent Behavior Checklist and assessing changes in five subscales of psychological adjustment: Emotional Difficulties, Adjustment at School Difficulties, Social Insensibility, Nonadaptive Behavior, and Self-esteem Difficulties. In the data analysis, the total index of psychological adjustment changes was used as well. When completing the checklist, a respondent had to choose one of three possible answers describing changes in the frequency of given behavior during the last month: "more often" "less often," or "no change." If the answer indicated that the respondent's behavior had changed in a positive direction (e.g., if the item "I behave in line with the school rules" was answered "more often"), it was considered a positive change.

Study Design

Figure 20.3 outlines the study design along with the application and timing of the measures. In the stage of pretreatment evaluation, the adolescents' psychosocial functioning was evaluated using the Adolescent Behavior Checklist. All 12- to 18-year-old adolescents living in foster care institutions, and those using services at health care institutions between November 2003 and February 2005, participated in pretreatment evaluation. Every adolescent was informed about the opportunity to participate in the SFBT. Some adolescents were self-referred, while others were referred by parents, medical doctors, or foster care staff.

The second stage of the study involved SFBT for the treatment group and no intervention for the other participants. Control groups were selected from this group without intervention; they were matched to the treatment group by age, gender, and psychological adjustment level at the pretreatment evaluation. Each adolescent participating in SFBT had an opportunity to attend a maximum of five sessions (one session per week). Adolescents who terminated early (terminating without giving

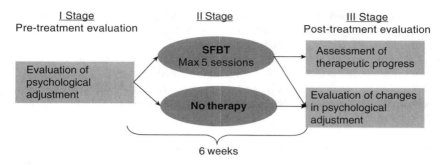

Figure 20.3. Study design.

notification after attending one or two to four sessions or refusing to continue therapy) were considered dropouts. We should note that the therapy was provided by two therapists (female in the foster care setting, male in the health care settings). Bearing in mind that therapist-related factors (such as gender or personal characteristics) could influence the outcome, we conducted a pilot study; it showed no difference in outcome for the same client group. In addition, the two therapists had similar education and training in SFBT as well as similar amounts of clinical experience (more than 5 years). Thus, the assumption can be made that differences between the treatment groups (this will be established) should not be attributed to therapist-related factors.

In the last stage of the study, a posttreatment evaluation was conducted using the Checklist of Adolescent Behavior Changes. In addition, for the treatment group, the client's evaluation of progress and the therapist's evaluation of improvement were provided. The time period between pretreatment and posttreatment evaluation was 6 weeks.

■ RESULTS OF RESEARCH

General Results

A total of 139 adolescents in all three settings started SFBT. However, 27 (19%) dropped out early: missed an appointed session without any notification and did not return to therapy or refused to continue therapy in spite of the absence of clear indications of improvement. Accordingly, 112 participants completed SFBT. It should be noted that the dropout rate is much lower than those given in other studies, where it ranges between 40% and 60% (Kazdin, 2003). This difference could be considered indirect evidence that SFBT, possibly due to the collaborative clinical atmosphere and emphasis on the client's expertise rather than the therapist's, decreases adolescents' resistance and increases their motivation to continue therapy (Bertolino, 2003; Corcoran & Stephenson, 2000; Lethem, 2002).

The types of problems presented for therapy were grouped according to the dominant topic and included interpersonal relationship problems (32%), problems caused by adolescents' inappropriate behavior (35%), and emotional problems (33%). Data comparison revealed that interpersonal relationship problems were more prevalent among foster care adolescents, while behavior problems were least prevalent among patients from rehabilitation hospital. Finally, the prevalence of emotional problems was almost identical among all three groups. In addition, as could be expected, boys usually presented for behavior-related problems, while girls more often came because of emotional and relationship problems.

The average number of sessions for participants who completed therapy was 3.11 ($SD = 1.09$). Out of the 112 completers, 38 (34%) required four to five sessions, 72 (64%) needed two to three sessions, and only 2 (2%) completed therapy after a single session. The number of sessions in this study are similar to those found in other studies on SFBT, which range from 2.9 to 5.5 (McKeel, 2000).

Changes in the Presenting Problem During SFBT

As mentioned in the methodology section, the changes in the problems that brought adolescents to therapy were assessed by both the clients and the therapists. The improvement levels ascribed using the Therapist's Evaluation of Improvement in all three treatment groups can be seen in Figure 20.4. As the figure shows, in all groups the largest percentage of clients achieved considerable improvement. The following success rates (problems evaluated by the therapist as considerably improved or solved completely) were achieved: foster care group, 77%; mental health care group, 67%; and rehabilitation hospital group, 52%. These results are in line with those of other SFBT outcome studies conducted in children and adolescents, which show that success rates usually range between 55% and 77% (Burr, 1993; Cruz & Littrell, 1998; Lee, 1997; Shennan, 2003).

Although Figure 20.4 shows that the distribution of clients in different categories of improvement differs slightly among the three treatment groups, statistical analysis showed no significant difference (Pearson $\chi^2 = 9.83$; $p = .28$). Thus, we can conclude that SFBT, even though it was applied by two different therapists in three different client groups, resulted in very similar outcomes as evaluated by the therapists.

Adolescents in all treatment groups evaluated their therapeutic progress positively as well. Using the Client's Evaluation of Progress, the mean scores of problem severity, obtained in the first and last sessions, were compared using the paired-samples t-test. As shown in Figure 20.5, problem severity in all three treatment groups decreased significantly ($p < .0001$).

However, Figure 20.5 also shows that foster care adolescents, although they started at a lower level, made greater progress (5.5 points) than both health care groups

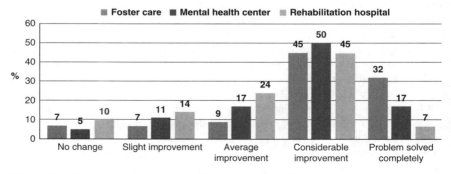

Figure 20.4. The therapist's evaluation of improvement in three treatment groups.

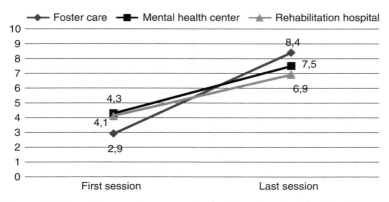

Figure 20.5. Differences between the mean scores of clients' evaluation of problem severity in the first and last sessions on a scale from 1 to 10, where 0 is the problem at its worst and 10 indicates that the problem has been solved.

(2.8 points for the rehabilitation hospital group and 3.2 for the mental health centers group). This difference was statistically significant (Kruskal-Wallis test = 20.83; $p < .0001$).

Changes in Psychological Adjustment During SFBT

In order to view the broader picture of changes in psychological functioning that allow comparison of the changes in different domains between the treatment and control groups as well as within each group, profiles of positive changes have been drawn (mean scores of the groups have been transformed into t-scores; these changes have been standardized on the basis of all available data on the changes in psychological functioning).

The results achieved in each setting are shown separately in Figures 20.6, 20.7, and 20.8. In Figure 20.6 we can see that during the 6-week therapy period, foster care adolescents in the treatment group achieved statistically significantly more positive changes in all areas of psychological adjustment than those in the control group.

Figure 20.7 shows that patients from the mental health care centers, after participating in the SFBT, reported significantly more positive changes on all scales except the Adjustment at School Difficulties scale. Nevertheless, even this difference was very close to statistical significance ($p = .053$). Thus, we can probably conclude that the treatment group did better on all indicators of psychological adjustment than the controls.

Moving to the last group (from the rehabilitation hospital), Figure 20.8 shows significant differences between treated adolescents and controls in the areas related to behavior difficulties. By contrast, change patterns related to internalized difficulties, such as emotional and self-esteem difficulties, were not distinct in either group.

The results obtained in the rehabilitation hospital group are worthy of remark. In Figure 20.8 we can see that the profile of positive changes in the control group is not as flat as that of the other two control groups (see Figures 20.6 and 20.7) and has a shape very similar to that of the treatment group—more changes in internalized difficulties and not as many in externalized difficulties. Different amounts of positive change in

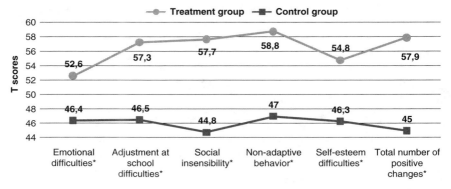

Figure 20.6. Comparison of positive changes in psychological adjustment between foster care treatment and control groups (* *p* < .005).

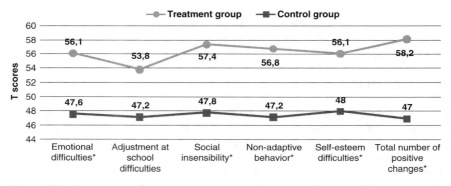

Figure 20.7. Comparison of positive changes in psychological adjustment between mental health care centers' treatment and control groups (**p* < .01).

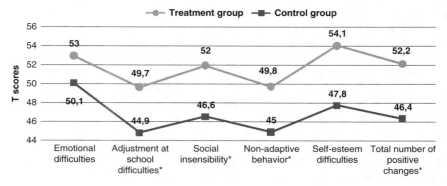

Figure 20.8. Comparison of positive changes in psychological adjustment between the rehabilitation hospital treatment and control groups (**p* < .05).

different areas (and no such pattern in control groups from other settings) could suggest that being at the rehabilitation hospital (which involves having various health restoration procedures) can improve psychological adjustment in some areas. Thus, we think that SFBT had the effect of amplifying these positive effects of rehabilitation services, while in other settings it can be considered more as an initiator of changes in the structure of psychological adjustment.

Additionally, we estimated the effect sizes, which indicate the magnitude of the differences found. The estimated effect sizes and their interpretation (effect sizes between 0.2 and 0.4 are considered small, those between 0.5 and 0.7 medium, and those above 0.8 large) are provided in Table 20.1.

These results are in line with those discussed earlier and indicate that the effect sizes in foster care and mental health care settings are generally large, while those achieved in the rehabilitation hospital are mostly medium. It is established that effect sizes for psychotherapy in children and adolescents range between 0.7 and 0.8 (Kazdin, 2003; Weisz et al., 1995). Thus, the effect size (considering the total number of positive changes) in the rehabilitation group reaches the lower limit of this range, while in the foster care and mental groups it far exceeds the upper limit, demonstrating the great benefit of SFBT for adolescents.

Finally, as mentioned earlier, we did between-group comparisons of the outcome. The results of the analysis are shown in Figure 20.9. Two main points can be highlighted. First, there is some evidence that the number of positive changes in some areas differs significantly between groups. Statistical analysis revealed no differences between the foster care and mental health care treatment groups. However, both of these groups differed significantly from the rehabilitation hospital group when positive changes were compared in the area of nonadaptive behavior. In addition, the foster care treatment group reported significantly more positive changes in the areas of adjustment at school and social insensibility as well as higher total numbers of positive changes. Second, the shape of the profile is different in all three groups: positive changes in externalized problems (adjustment difficulties at school, social insensibility, nonadaptive behavior) prevail in the foster care treatment group, while in the rehabilitation hospital treatment group the greatest positive changes involved internalized problems (emotional and self-esteem difficulties). In the mental health care treatment group, positive changes in different areas are not as marked as in the other two groups.

Changes in the problem situation and in psychological adjustment revealed some evidence of SFBT outcome differences in all three treatment groups, and some possible explanations can be proposed. First, the differences in outcome could be explained by

TABLE 20.1. *Effect Sizes (Cohen's d with Hedges correction) of Positive Changes Obtained During the SFBT in Different Settings*

Areas of Psychological Adjustment	Foster Care	Mental Health Center	Rehabilitation Hospital
Emotional difficulties	0.7 (medium)	1.0 (large)	0.3 (small)
Adjustment at school difficulties	1.2 (large)	0.6 (medium)	0.6 (medium)
Social insensibility	1.4 (large)	1.1 (large)	0.6 (medium)
Non-adaptive behavior	1.2 (large)	1.0 (large)	0.6 (medium)
Self-esteem difficulties	0.9 (large)	0.8 (large)	0.6 (medium)
Total number of positive changes	1.4 (large)	1.2 (large)	0.7 (medium)

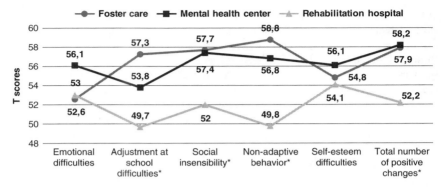

Figure 20.9. Comparison of positive changes in psychological adjustment among all three treatment groups (*p < .05).

the client-related factors (e.g., gender, age, type of problem, motivation for change) often mentioned in the psychotherapy literature as variables to be considered when conducting a study (Kazdin, 2003; Eyberg et al., 1998; Weersing & Weisz, 2002). Interestingly, SFBT outcome literature has little if anything to offer concerning the impact of such factors on the therapy outcomes in adolescents. This prompted us to conduct additional regression analysis aimed at defining the prognostic value of the research setting (foster care, mental health care, rehabilitation) on the outcome of SFBT in the context of some client-related variables, such as gender, age, type of problem, psychological adjustment before treatment, presence of a diagnosed somatic or mental disorder, and motivation for change (as evaluated on a 10-point scale). Regression for both dependent variables (the client's evaluation of progress and the total number of positive changes in psychological adjustment) revealed that the only significant prognostic factor was the research setting. These results confirm the results of our previous analysis, showing that there were significant outcome differences between groups of clients, while client-related factors showed no significant influence. On the other hand, the goodness of fit of both models in the population was low (the models explained only 7% and 15% of the data distribution), indicating that there are other significant factors besides those included in the analysis.

Second, when interpreting the above-mentioned differences, we cannot eliminate the fact that the study was conducted by two therapists, each working in a different setting (one working with clients in foster care homes, the other in health care settings). Thus, some therapist-related factors could have had an impact on the outcome; however, the study was not primarily aimed at a comparison of the groups, so we did not analyze this further.

Third, between-group differences could be explained by various characteristics of the studied groups, such as different social experience and current life circumstances in all three settings: foster care adolescents experiencing great loss in their lives and living under very specific circumstances with no close family relations; adolescents in rehabilitation experiencing serious health difficulties and at the same time temporarily being away from their usual social environment; and finally, adolescents from mental health care settings living in their ordinary environment but at the same time experiencing severe psychosocial problems. Such differences could lead to different possibilities in the formation and implementation of solutions in these three groups. We should not forget, however, that adolescents in all groups were able to build solutions successfully; despite the between-group differences, all three treatment groups achieved significant improvement on all applied measures.

Relation between Positive Changes in the Problem Situation and Psychological Adjustment

The final question we address is: Can we say that therapeutic improvement in problem situation is related to positive changes in client's psychological adjustment? To answer this question, correlation analysis was conducted. It revealed that a decrease in the severity of the problem correlates significantly with the number of positive changes in some areas of psychological adjustment: adjustment at school difficulties ($r = 0.33$; $p = .001$), social insensibility ($r = 0.28$; $p = .006$) and nonadaptive behavior ($r = 0.20$; $p = .048$) as well as with the total number of positive changes ($r = 0.27$; $p = .009$). We can conclude that improvement in the problem is related to changes in the areas of psychological adjustment reflecting behaviour, while no such correlation was established with the scales of psychological adjustment reflecting inner psychological states (emotions and self-esteem).

This is an interesting outcome that warrants further discussion. As the theoretical model (see Figure 20.1) suggests, established correlations were something we could expect: It was hypothesized that conversation about actions possibly leading to solutions initiates *actual* changes in the client's behavior that, mediated by the social system, could lead to improvement in the problem and in the broader life context. What is especially interesting is the *absence* of the correlation between improvement in the problem and positive changes in the areas of emotions and self-esteem. Such findings provide interesting insights into the possible mechanisms and process of SFBT.

On the one hand, these findings could reflect the systemic processes whereby, as clients start acting differently in the course of SFBT, their proximate social system catches up quickly, reinforcing these positive changes and thus allowing clients to interpret the situation as improving. Changes in the clients' inner world cannot be observed by the system so quickly; thus, the lack of positive feedback from the system in some cases could be maintained by perceiving the situation as improved. On the other hand, solution building in SFBT is mainly about clients' actions, even in cases where the conversation is about inner states. It could be that constructing solutions as consisting mainly of behavior-related elements prompts client to concentrate on actions: to experiment with them and to keep track of behavior changes, while inner states stay on the edge of the solution picture and the client's scope of attention. This could be especially applicable to adolescents, who at times might have difficulty connecting different elements of their existence (action–consequence, word–action, action–feeling etc.). This raises the question: Would it be helpful if,during solution building, we could help adolescents not only to construct potentially useful actions but also tolink them to the consequences/benefits related to their inner states? Well-known SFBT questions, such as "How might that be helpful?," "How it will be different?," and "What will you notice that's different?" are usually followed by action-oriented questions such as "What will you do differently?" What might happen if, after talking about actions, we also ask questions like "What will be different in your inner life?," "How will you feel differently?," "What will it reveal about your situation?," "What will you do differently then?," "How will you think differently about yourself?," and "How would it change your actions?" Maybe such circling back and forth between actions and inner states could help link these important segments of adolescents' experience, potentially resulting in a broader picture of the solution, more possibilities for chang,e and higher satisfaction with the outcome of SFBT. It should be noted that similar ideas have already been proposed in the SFBT literature (Kiser et al., 1993; Lipchik, 1999, 2002; Miller & de Shazer, 2000). Of course, these issues require additional research and may be answered in the future.

Concluding the results section, we can state that adolescents from all three settings, within three sessions on average, achieved significant improvement in their problems and in most areas of psychological adjustment (some pathways of individual changes are demonstrated in the Case example). In addition, the correlation between these changes was established. Finally, we found some differences in outcome between adolescents from different settings.

■ PRACTICE GUIDELINES

Some practical implications of the results can be defined. The findings of this study and of previous research suggest that SFBT can be considered not only an effective but also an appropriate method for treating adolescents living under different specific conditions. Most of the adolescents seemed to appreciate the nonexpert position of the therapists. As a result, we recorded a comparatively low dropout rate. Also, in most cases, an increase in motivation for change was observed during solution-building conversations. Finally, the treatment groups from the three different settings achieved significant improvement on all measures; the outcome was not related to the type of problem that brought them to therapy. This supports the assumption that SFBT is not about problem solving but rather about solution building and that the person's limitations are far less important than the person's resources. Thus, we strongly believe that SFBT can meet the needs of troubled adolescents and can be recommended as one of the first choices when working with adolescents from foster care and health care settings.

The results suggest that, when applying SFBT for adolescents, practitioners can consider providing additional help by linking their actions with their inner states when constructing solutions. Such links could possibly help an adolescent to broaden the solution picture by incorporating changes in both the outside and inside worlds, thus providing more possible clues for noticing changes. Additionally, our practical experience shows that helping adolescents link together different elements of their experience by noticing, for example, the relation between their actions and the responses of others (by asking relationship questions) is very beneficial. Thus, we can hypothesize that the more links between different elements of the experience an adolescent makes, the more alternative ways of perceiving the situation and ongoing changes he or she has.

Limitations of the Study

The present research was designed as a clinical study (rather than a clinical trial or a laboratory study), leading to typical but serious limitations. First, no random assignment to different experimental conditions was applied. Second, when assessing the outcome of SFBT, we did not obtain outcome data from other persons related to the subjects, such as family members, teachers, foster care staff, medical personnel, and so on. This additional evaluation would have provided increased outcome information. Third, the posttreatment assessments were conducted shortly after the end of therapy; further follow-up could provide useful information about the continuity of the results achieved. Finally, the study was not aimed exclusively at a comparison of the outcome between different client groups. This made it difficult, if not impossible, to control some potentially significant factors (such as therapist-related factors; client group–related factors, etc.) as well as to interpret the results.

■ FUTURE STUDIES

The findings of our study and the previous research suggest the need for further studies to answer the following questions:

- Are the positive changes in the adolescent's life achieved during SFBT noticeable to significant others (family, teachers, medical staff, etc.)?
- Do the improvements in the problem situation, and especially in psychological adjustment, achieved during SFBT persist over time?
- What factors (related to the client, the therapist, or thetherapeutic process) contribute most to the effectiveness of SFBT in these populations?
- Are the established differences between client groups from different settingsconsistent? If so, does this say something about the responsiveness to the therapy of different groups of clients or should we look for the explanation in the mechanisms and processes of SFBT?
- Does the therapeutic conversation about the links between different elements of the adolescent's experience (e.g., actions and the following feelings; actions and the system's response) amplify the positive outcomes of SFBT when helping adolescents to build solutions?

■ KEY FINDINGS TO REMEMBER

- In the literature on SFBT, we found only five studies on the outcome of the model (as an individual intervention) in these settings: one for foster care, four for the mental health care setting, and none for the rehabilitation setting. These few studies provide evidence that SFBT can be of value for these groups of adolescents. However, this small number of studies is not sufficient to prove the effectiveness of SFBT in these settings.
- The dropout rate in our study was only 19%, which is lower than that with other approaches, demonstrating that SFBT can be considered useful for treating troubled adolescents.
- Although the number of sessions in the study was limited to 5.0, the average number of sessions needed to reach a desired improvement was 3.11.
- Success rates (percentage of clients evaluated by the therapists as improved considerably or as having solved their problems completely) among the three groups were as follows: foster care group, 77%; mental health care group, 67%; rehabilitation hospital group, 52%.

- During the 6 weeks between pretreatment and posttreatment evaluation, problem severity evaluated by the clients decreased significantly in all three treatment groups. However, foster care adolescents, although they started at a lower level, achieved significantly greater progress than both health care groups.
- In comparison with the control group, the SFBT groups showed more positive changes in most areas of psychological adjustment. The effect sizes in the foster care and mental health care groups were mostly large, while those in the rehabilitation hospital group were mostly medium. Statistical analysis revealed no differences between the foster care and mental health care treatment groups. However, both of these groups differed significantly from the rehabilitation hospital group when positive changes in the area of behavior difficulties were compared.
- Regression analysis for clients' evaluation of progress and total number of positive changes in psychological adjustment confirmed the differences in outcomes between the study groups. By comparison, client-related factors (gender, age, type of problem, psychological adjustment before treatment, presence of diagnosed somatic or mental disorder, motivation for change) had no significant prognostic value.
- Correlations between positive changes in the problem situation and changes in the areas of psychological adjustment reflecting behavior were established.

■ FURTHER LEARNING

- For more information on SFBT research, see http://www.ebta.nu; http://www.octir.nl/r/index.asp; http://www.solutionsdoc.co.uk/sfb.html; and http://www.gingerich.net/SFBT/Default.htm
- For SFBT applications with adolescents, see:

  Selekman, M. D. (2005). *Pathways to change: Brief therapy with difficult adolescents* (2nd ed.). New York: Guilford Press.
  Simon, J. K., & Berg, I. K. (2004). Solution-focused brief therapy with adolescents. In F. W. Kaslow & R. F. Massey (Eds.), *Comprehensive handbook of psychotherapy* (Vol. 3, pp. 133–152). New York: Wiley.

■ CASE EXAMPLE

To illustrate the practical application of the methods used in this study and the process of therapeutic change, we will present one of the cases from the pool of those analyzed in the study.

Context of the Therapy

The counseling took place at a typical children's foster care home in Lithuania that participated in the study. The client, a 15-year-old boy, came willing to discuss his situation with the counselor.

The boy had been living in foster care for 12 years. His parents lost parental rights because of their dysfunctional lifestyle (alcohol abuse, neglect and abuse of their children). He had a younger brother living in the same foster home (although brothers were not close emotionally) and visited his grandparents several times a month.

Problem Situation

In the first of four sessions, the client complained about his lack of self-confidence. He considered himself to be weak and worthless. He mentioned that he usually gave up easily when facing challenges and difficulties in his relations with others. This led to a low social status among his peers and problems at school resulting in bad marks, skipping school, and finally pressure (reproaches, lectures, and penalties) from foster care staff. He also complained about being teased by other children at the foster care home. In these situations he usually talked back, provoking conflicts in which he was lost, as he put it, because of physical weakness. This again eroded his self-confidence.

Therapeutic Process

In talking about his expectations for therapy, he expressed the hope of becoming more self-confident. The discussion of the miracle question revealed that, for this client, being more self-confident meant being able to get up earlier, get to school on time, concentrate more on listening and completing assignments during the lessons, and doing his homework. He also wanted to be able to stop peers from teasing him. However, at this point, he had no specific ideas about how to achieve these goals. However, he came up with very good ideas during later sessions. Meanwhile, he decided to devote himself to his studies. And as we can see from the description of following sessions, his efforts were successful; his ability to concentrate during his classes, as well as to study more, increased gradually from session to session. As a result, he became more successful at school. In this case, keeping track of exceptions was extremely useful: It helped the client to notice the range of possibilities and resources, try out new behaviors, and experience their outcomes. This is especially evident in the area of teasing: Observing those moments when he was not teased by peers, he developed a new and very successful strategy to prevent teasing by not giving the desired feedback.

Therapeutic Changes and Outcome

The model provided earlier in this chapter (see Figure 20.1) suggests that therapeutic changes involve several areas: the client's perception and behavior leading to changes in the problem situation itself as well as in functioning in everyday life. Detailed changes in each of these areas can be seen in the SFBT protocol provided below. Here we will highlight the main changes in each area, comparing the first and the sessions (Figure 20.10, 20.11, and 20.12).

As Figure 20.10 shows, in the first session the client expressed low motivation for change, and perceived the situation as being out of his control and somewhat hopeless. This perception resulted in the tendency to give up easily when facing challenges, which led to inappropriate behavior in other areas, such as school performance and relations with peers. Thus, the problem situation as presented by the client involved

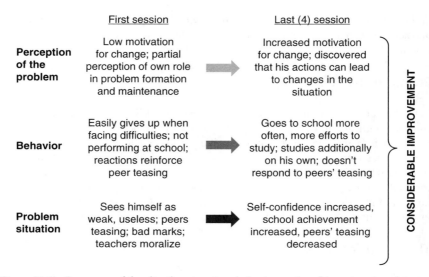

First session   Last (4) session

Perception of the problem
Low motivation for change; partial perception of own role in problem formation and maintenance
Increased motivation for change; discovered that his actions can lead to changes in the situation

Behavior
Easily gives up when facing difficulties; not performing at school; reactions reinforce peer teasing
Goes to school more often, more efforts to study; studies additionally on his own; doesn't respond to peers' teasing

Problem situation
Sees himself as weak, useless; peers teasing; bad marks; teachers moralize
Self-confidence increased, school achievement increased, peers' teasing decreased

CONSIDERABLE IMPROVEMENT

Figure 20.10. Summary of the client's perception, behavior, and problem situation changes.

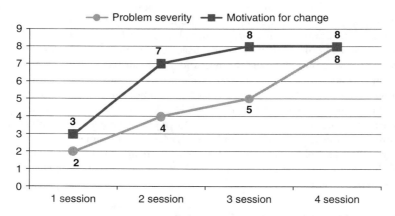

Figure 20.11. Changes in the client's motivation for change and subjectively evaluated problem severity.

low self-esteem, peer teasing, and difficulties at school. The situation had lasted for at least 5 years.

Let's look at how this situation changed after four SFBT sessions. The client's willingness to take actions in order to improve the situation increased dramatically (by 5 points; see Figure 20.11) and he discovered that his actions could lead to changes in the situation.

The client indicated clear changes in behavior as well: During therapy, he saw improvement in school performance as the ground for regaining his self-esteem. Thus, he put a lot of effort into going to school and studying. In addition, he ignored peers'

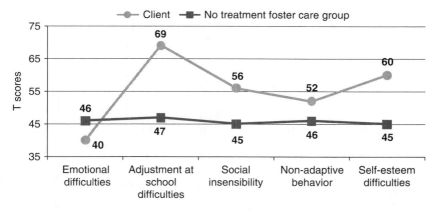

Figure 20.12. Client's psychological adjustment changes compared to those of the no-treatment foster care group.

teasing by not showing his irritation. As a result, the problem situation improved significantly. The boy indicated that he gained more self-confidence, performed better at school, and was happy because the teasing had decreased.

The therapist evaluated the client's changes in this case as considerable.

The client's evaluation of progress demonstrated significant improvement as well. Figure 20.11 shows that problem severity, as evaluated by the client, decreased by 6 points (where 0 stands for the problem at its worst and 10 stands for the problem solved).

In Figure 20.12 t-scores of positive changes in the client's psychosocial adjustment are presented in comparison to those of a nontreatment group of adolescents ($n = 180$) living in foster care. We can see that changes in the areas of adjustment at school, interpersonal involvement, and self-esteem are considerably higher than the average changes in the nontreatment group. Clear links between these results and those discussed earlier can be seen. Although the main topic of the therapeutic conversations was the issue of self-esteem, the change process was closely related to the areas of school achievement and interpersonal relations. Thus main changes in these areas are reflected in the evaluation of the client's psychosocial adjustment when standardized methods are applied.

SFBT PROTOCOL

Code	Birth Date	1-Male; 2-Female	Age	Grade	Date of First Session	Date of Last Session	Number of Sessions
		1	15	7			4

First session   date

Client information

Living in foster care institution for 12 years. Has a younger brother living in the same foster care institution.

Problem

Type of referral:

☐ Referred (by whom, reason) _____

☒ Self-referred

Contact description: *Slightly tense, willing to communicate, talkative but has difficulty expressing thoughts.*

Complaints/problem as presented by client: *Low self-confidence, easily gives up when facing difficulties; some peers teasing; his reactions (usually talks back) provoke conflicts in which he loses because of physical weakness.*

How problem affects client's life: *Sees himself as weak, useless, bad marks. Teachers moralize.*

Client's attempts to solve the problem/what was useful: *Doesn't recall any attempts to change the situation.*

Does client see him/her-self as a part of the problem?
☒ Yes ☐ No

Client's evaluation of the problem severity on a scale from 0 to 10 *2*.

What is needed for this number to increase? *Doesn't know.*

Goal formation

Client's expectations/goals: *To become more self-confident. He would know that he's more self-confident if he felt better, would be more committed to achieving goals, overcoming difficulties, would be able to defend himself when peers teased him.*

Exceptions   ☐ Exception question not used (why?) _____

☒ No exceptions

☐ Exceptions:

☐ Due to client's actions

☐ Due to others' actions/situation

Miracle   ☐ Miracle question not used (why?) _____

☐ Not able to describe the miracle day

☒ Description of the miracle day: ☒ Related to client's different behavior: *Will wake up early, eat, get dressed, will go to school on time which will prevent teachers from moralizing, keep him in a good mood, will let him concentrate on studying, be able to defend himself if someone teased him.*

☐ Related exceptionally to others' different behavior

Coping question ☐ Not used ☐ Not answered ☒ Client's answer: *Sometimes doesn't pay attention to teasing—leaves the room or stays for a couple of days at grandfather's place.*

Additional notes: *Looks physically weak, observable physical defect: squint (strabismus).*

Summary (Problem/complaint → goals → solution behavior): *Low self-confidence → increased self-confidence which will lead to increased ability to defend himself → coming to school on time, studying harder.*

Motivation for change

Client–therapist relationship evaluation (scaling question) 3.
What is needed for this number to increase? If he saw any results of his attempts to change the situation, he'll be more willing to keep trying.

Type of client: □ Customer ☒ Complainant □ Visitor
Feedback □ Session brake □ Applied ☒ Not applied
Compliments: Able to stand peers' teasing sometimes, which means that he can be strong sometimes; agreed to participate in the counseling, which shows that he wants to change the situation.
Bridge: Situation is not easy, and time and effort will be needed to change it.
Task: First session formula task

Second session   date

Contact description: Less tense, good contact.
Positive changes (What's better?): Went to school more often, made more of an effort to study, peer teasing decreased.
Client's actions causing positive changes (How did you do that?): Studied during lessons, did all the homework assignments, doesn't know exactly why teasing decreased, maybe peers just stopped teasing.
Reinforcement of positive changes (How does it help/What is different now?): Less conflicts with teachers, better marks at school, self-confidence slightly increased.
What is needed for positive changes to continue? Needs to keep studying harder, make more time for studying, increase school attendance.
Evaluation of confidence in continuation of positive changes (on a scale from 0 to 10)___
What is needed for this number to increase? ___

Client's evaluation of problem severity on a scale from 0 to 10 4.

What is needed for this number to increase? Two hours per day for homework assignments, manage to prevent peers from teasing him if they start.
Coping question ☒ Not used □ Not answered □ Client's answer

Additional notes Likes foreign languages, studies Russian on his own. He is thinking about the future—wants to become an animal doctor because likes animals.
Client–therapist relationship evaluation (scaling question) Z.
What is needed for this number to increase? To get more good marks at school.

Feedback □ Session brake □ Applied ☒ Not applied
Compliments: Being so young, thinks about the future and takes steps to have a better future despite all the difficulties.
Bridge: Once he's willing to continue creating a better future for himself.
Task: Continue doing what was useful last week and keep track of those moments when peers do not tease—how these moments happen, what's different at these moments?

Third session   date

Contact description: Not changed.
Positive changes (What's better?): Does better at school, felt better because peers' teasing has decreased.
Client's actions causing positive changes (How did you do that?): Spends more time studying, studies additionally on his own, when peers start teasing, doesn't show irritation, tries to escape the place, noticed that such behavior leads to decrease in peers' efforts to tease him.
Reinforcement of positive changes (How does it help/What is different now?): Gets better marks; as a reward, foster care staff took him to a shop to

buy new clothes, feels more self-confident because he has found the way to defend himself.

What is needed for positive changes to continue? Keep doing things that helped him last week.

Evaluation of the confidence in continuation of positive changes (on a scale from 0 to 10) 8

What is needed for this number to increase?

Client's evaluation of problem severity on a scale from 0 to 10 5.

What is needed for this number to increase? Keep getting good marks at school, attend school regularly, keep preventing peers from teasing him.

Coping question ☒ Not used   ☐ Not answered   ☐ Client's answer

Additional notes

Client–therapist relationship evaluation (scaling question) 8.

What is needed for this number to increase?

Feedback   Session brake   ☐ Applied   ☒ Not applied

Compliments: Creative because he has figured out how to fend for himself, seems very committed to creating a better future for himself.

Bridge: Once he's willing to continue doing things that are useful.

Task: Continue doing what is useful, keep track of those moments when he feels self-confident— how these moments happen, what's different at these moments?

Fourth session   date

Contact description: Not changed.

Positive changes (What's better?): Everything is okay— marks at school improved, peers don't tease anymore.

Client's actions causing positive changes (How did you do that?): When studying, concentrates on the task, tries to understand the text when reading, listens to teachers' explanations during the lessons; as for peers, he doesn't react to their teasing attempts, so they get bored and find someone else to tease.

Reinforcement of positive changes (How does it help/What is different now?): Feels lively, more self-confident, willing to study and has more hope for the future.

What is needed for positive changes to continue? Continue doing things that have been useful so far

Evaluation of confidence in continuation of positive changes (on a scale from 0 to 10) 6 What is needed for this number to increase?

Client's evaluation of problem severity on a scale from 0 to 10 8.

What is needed for this number to increase?

Coping question ☒ Not used   ☐ Not answered   ☐ Client's answer

Additional notes: Client and counselor agreed upon termination of the counseling.

Client–therapist relationship evaluation (scaling question) 8.

What is needed for this number to increase?

Feedback   Session brake   ☐ Applied   ☒ Not applied

Compliments: Seems strong-willed—doesn't give up and seeks to achieve his goals despite all difficulties.

Bridge: Because he has courage and knows what to do for a better future.

Task: Continue doing what is useful and at hard times remember how he managed to change the situation this time.

Case summary

Type of termination: ☐ Early termination _____

☒ Completed _____

☐ Unclosed (more sessions needed) _____

Changes in the client's perceptions of the problem (changes in client's view of his/her role in the problem origin and solution possibilities; discovering possible solutions, motivation for change) _Turned from complainant into customer—motivation to change increased dramatically, discovered that his actions can lead to changes in the situation._

Changes in the client's behavior: _Employed solution behavior discussed during the sessions._

Changes in the client's problem/situation and related circumstances (changes in problem's character, severity, frequency; changes in the client's emotional state; changes in other people's reactions and behavior toward the client): _Self-confidence increased, school achievement increased and was noticed by teachers, peers' teasing decreased._

Outcome evaluation:

Client's evaluation of progress (The difference in problem severity in the first and last sessions): _8 – 2 = +6_

Counselor's evaluation of progress:

☐ **Problem solved due to objective (independent) changes in the situation**

☐ **Problem solved** (changes in the client's perceptions and behavior; the problem does not occur anymore)

☒ **Considerable improvement** (changes in the client's perceptions and behavior, partial changes in the problem/situation and related circumstances)

☐ **Average improvement** (changes in the client's perceptions and behavior; no changes in the problem/situation and related circumstances)

☐ **Slight improvement** (obvious changes in the client's perceptions of the problem; no changes in the client's behavior, problem/situation, and related circumstances)

☐ **No improvement** (no positive changes in the client's perceptions of the problem, behavior, problem/situation, and related circumstances)

■ ENDNOTE

1. Foster care refers to institutions with 40–100 children of different ages living in the same building, divided into groups of 6 to 10. Each group had separate accommodation facilities and three or four adult caregivers who took care of them on an alternating schedule. In Lithuania, about 3,500 children every year are placed in foster care because of restricted parental rights. Most of these children are taken from dysfunctional families. According to the data from the Lithuanian Statistical Department, children and adolescents in foster care constitute 9% of the general population of children (Cepukiene & Pakrosnis, 2008).

■ REFERENCES

Bertolino, B. (2003). *Change-oriented therapy with adolescents and young adults: A new generation of respectful and effective process and practices.* New York: Norton.

Beyebach, M. (2000). *European Brief Therapy Association outcome study: Research definition.* Retrieved 14 05 2002 from http://www.ebta.nu/page2/page30/page30.html

Bishop, M. (2005). Quality of life and psychosocial adaptation to chronic illness and acquired disability: A conceptual and theoretical synthesis. *Journal of Rehabilitation.* Retrieved 20 09 2007 from http://www.findarticles.com/p/articles/mi_m0825/is_2_71/ai_n13820423

Brown, B. B. (2005). Moving forward with research on adolescence: Some reflections on the state of JRA and the state of the field. *Journal of Research on Adolescence, 15*(4), 657–673.

Burr, W. (1993). Evaluation der Anwendung Iosungsorientierter Kurztherapie in einer kinder- und jugendpsychiartischen Praxis [Evaluation of the use of brief therapy in practice for children and adolescents]. *Familiendynamik, 18,* 11–21.

Cepukiene, V., & Pakrosnis, R. (2008). Vaikų globos namuose gyvenančių paauglių psichologinio ir socialinio funkcionavimo sunkumus lemiantys veiksniai: asmenybės savybių ir gyvenimo globos namuose ypatumų sąveika [Factors influencing psychosocial difficulties of adolescents living in foster care: Interaction between personality traits and foster home characteristics. *Specialusis ugdymas* [Baltic Journal of Special Education], *2*(19), 31–44.

Compas, B. E. (2004). Processes of risk and resilience during adolescence. In R. M. Lerner & L. Steinberg,. (Eds.), *Handbook of adolescent psychology* (pp. 263–296). Hoboken, NJ: Wiley.

Corcoran, J. (2006). A comparison group study of solution-focused therapy versus "treatment-as-usual" for behavior problems: A preliminary report. *Journal of Social Service Research, 33*(1), 69–81.

Corcoran, J., & Stephenson, M. (2000). The Effectiveness of Solution-Focused Therapy with Child Behavior Problems: A Preliminary Report. *Families in Society, 81*(5), 468–474.

Cruz, J., & Littrell, J. M. (1998). Brief counseling with Hispanic American college students. *Journal of Multicultural Counseling and Development, 26,* 227–238.

Davidson-Arad, B. (2005). Fifteen-month follow-up of children at risk: Comparison of the quality of life of children removed from home and children remaining at home. *Children and Youth Services Review, 27,* 1–20.

De Jong, P., & Berg, I. K. (1998). *Interviewing for solutions.* Pacific Grove, CA: Brooks/Cole.

Eyberg, S. M., Schuhmann, E. M., & Rey, J. (1998). Child and adolescent psychotherapy research: Developmental issues. *Journal of Abnormal Child Psychology, 26*(1), 71–82.

Franklin, C., Biever, J., Moore, K., Clemons, D., & Scamardo, M. (2001). The effectiveness of solution-focused therapy with children in a school setting. *Research on Social Work Practice, 11*(4), 411–434.

Franklin, C., Corcoran, J., Nowicki, J., & Streeter, C. (1997). Using client self-anchored scales to measure outcomes in solution-focused therapy. *Journal of Systemic Therapies, 16*(3), 246–265.

Garralda, M. E. (2004). The relations between physical and mental health problems and medical help seeking in children and adolescents: A research perspective. *Child and Adolescent Mental Health, 9*(4), 146–155.

Gingerich, W. J., & Wabeke, T. (2001). A solution-focused approach to mental health intervention in school settings. *Children & Schools, 23*(1), 33–48.

Kazdin, A. E. (2002). The state of child and adolescent psychotherapy research. *Child and Adolescent Mental Health, 7*(2), 53–59.

Kazdin, A. E. (2003). Psychotherapy for children and adolescents. *Annual Review of Psychology, 54*(1), 253–276.

Kazdin, A. E., & Nock, M. K. (2003). Delineating mechanisms of change in child and adolescent therapy: Methodological issues and research recommendations. *Journal of Child Psychology and Psychiatry, 44*(8), 1116–1129.

Kiser, D. J., Piercy, F. P., & Lipchik, E. (1993). The integration of emotion in solution-focused therapy. *Journal of Marital and Family Therapy, 19*, 233–242.

Koob, J. J., & Love, S. M. (2010). The implementation of solution-focused therapy to increase foster care placement stability. *Children and Youth Services Review, 32*, 1346–1350.

LaFountain, R. M., & Garner, N. E. (1996). Solution-focused counseling groups. *Journal of Specialists in Group Work, 21*(2), 128–143.

Lee, M. Y. (1997). A study of solution-focused brief family therapy: Outcomes and issues. *American Journal of Family Therapy, 25*(1), 3–17.

Lethem, J. (2002). Brief solution focused therapy. *Child and Adolescent Mental Health, 7*(4), 189–192.

Lipchik, L. (1999). Theoretical and practical thoughts about expanding the solution-focused approach to include emotions. In W. R. Ray & S. de Shazer (Eds.), *Evolving brief therapy: In honor of John H. Weakland.* (pp. 157–177). Galena, IL, and Iowa City, IA: Geist & Russell Companies.

Lipchik, L. (2002). *Beyond technique in solution-focused therapy: Working with emotions and the therapeutic relationship.* New York: Guilford Press.

McKeel, A. J. (2000). *A selected review of research of solution-focused brief therapy.* Retrieved 05 11 2002 from http://www.enabling.org/ia/sft/Review%20McKeel.htm

McMahon, S. D., Grant, K. E., Compas, B. E., Thurm, A. E., & Ey, S. (2003). Stress and psychopathology in children and adolescents: Is there evidence of specificity? *Journal of Child Psychology and Psychiatry, 44*(1), 107–133.

Miller, G., & de Shazer, S. (2000). Emotions in solution-focused therapy: A re-examination. *Family Process, 39*(1), 5–23.

Newsome, W. S. (2004). Solution-focused brief therapy groupwork with at-risk junior high school students: Enhancing the base line. *Research on Social Work Practice, 14*(5), 336–343.

Nock, M. K. (2003). Progress review of the psychosocial treatment of child conduct problems. *Clinical Psychology: Science and Practice, 10*(1), 1–28.

Pakrosnis, R., & Cepukiene, V. (2009). Paauglio psichologinio funkcionavimo sunkumų klausimynas: sudarymas ir pirminė psichometrinė analizė [Adolescent Psychological Functioning Difficulties Questionnaire: Composition and primary psychometric analysis]. *International Journal of Psychology: A Biopsychosocial Approach, 3*, 9–32.

Schmidt, S., Petersen, C., & Bullinger, M. (2003). Coping with chronic disease from the perspective of children and adolescents—a conceptual framework and its implications for participation. *Child: Care, Health and Development, 29*(1), 63–75.

Shennan, G. (2003). The Early Response Project: A voluntary sector contribution to CAMHS. *Child and Adolescent Mental Health in Primary Care, 1*, 46–50.

Simms, M. D., Dubowitz, H., & Szilagyi, M. (2000). Health care needs of children in the foster care system. *Pediatrics, 106*(4), 909–918.

Simon, J. K., & Berg, I. K. (2004). Solution-focused brief therapy with adolescents. In F. W. Kaslow & R. F. Massey (Eds.), *Comprehensive handbook of psychotherapy* (Vol. 3, 133–152). New York: Wiley

Smith, S. (2002). What works for whom: The link between process and outcome in effectiveness research. *Australian Social Work, 55*(2), 147–155.

Taussing, H. N. (2002). Risk behaviors in maltreated youth placed in foster care: A longitudal study of protective and vulnerability factors. *Child Abuse & Neglect, 26*(11), 1179–1199.

Tyson, E. H., & Baffour, T. D. (2004). Arts-based strengths: A solution-focused intervention with adolescents in an acute-care psychiatric setting. *The Arts in Psychotherapy, 31*(4), 213–227.

Van Dyk, M. (2004). *The impact of solution focused brief therapy on the foster care recidivism rate of adolescent offenders* (a doctoral thesis). Retrieved 02 03 2005 from http://www.proquest.com

Viner, R. M., Christie, D., Taylor, V., & Hey, S. (2003). Motivational/solution-focused intervention improves HbAlc in adolescents with Type 1 diabetes: A pilot study. *Diabetic Medicine, 20*(9), 739–742.

Weersing, V. R., & Weisz, J. R. (2002). Mechanisms of action in youth psychotherapy. *Journal of Child Psychology and Psychiatry, 43*(1), 3–29.

Weisz, J. R., Donenberg, G. R., Han, S. S., & Kauneckis, D. (1995). Child and adolescent psychotherapy outcomes in experiments versus clinics: Why the disparity? *Journal of Abnormal Child Psychology, 23*(1), 83–98.

Wilmshurst, L. A. (2002). Treatment programs for youth with emotional and behavioral disorders: An outcome study of two alternate approaches. *Mental Health Services Research, 4*(2), 85–96.

21 Solution-Focused Approaches in Management

■ MARK McKERGOW

■ INTRODUCTION

One feature of the spread of solution-focused (SF) approaches over the past 15 years has been the many applications found in the area of management and organizational change. In many ways, this is not a surprising development; the pragmatic and effective nature of the approach matches the desire for efficient ways to make progress found in most organizations. From the time of early experiments in the mid-1990s, the SF approach has become increasingly influential.

This book is mainly concerned with research results. While controlled studies are possible in the field of therapy, applications in the organizational sphere are much more often carried out on an ad hoc basis; the main concern is to make progress, and whatever helps to do this is welcomed. There is far less emphasis on recording, writing up, and publishing accounts of the work.

This chapter is not, therefore, an account of a research study. It is a collection of what has been recorded and documented thus far. We can safely assume that the impact of SF approaches on management is even more widespread than anyone currently knows.

■ WHAT WE HAVE LEARNED SO FAR

It seems very likely that some clinicians exposed to SF therapy will have also noticed that the approach can be used in a more general way to make progress under difficult circumstances. They will then presumably have made use of it to help themselves in managerial roles. It is therefore very difficult to say when this approach first appeared in the context of management.

As far as I am aware, the first training course to address SF coaching explicitly was run by British practitioner Harry Norman at Bristol University in 1996. Others around the world were discovering the advantages of the SF model independently. The earliest books appeared in German (Schmitz & Billen, 2000), and Dutch (Cauffman, 2001).

The first book to specifically address SF management in English (Jackson & McKergow, 2002) helped to spread the word even further, and the SOLWorld community (http://www.solworld.org) started by these authors and their Bristol Solutions Group colleagues has gone on to become a worldwide network of consultants, managers, coaches, and facilitators developing myriad applications and variations. The SOLWorld community now includes, remarkably, a thriving Japanese network with its own local conferences and events. A new, more formal professional body, the Association for the Quality Development of Solution-Focused Consulting and Training (SFCT; http://www.asfct.org), has been founded to support the development of SF practitioners within the consulting, coaching, and training world.

■ SF INTERVENTIONS IN MANAGEMENT: VARIED CONTEXTS

One of the challenges of translating the SF therapy approach into management contexts is that these contexts are much more varied than the usual client–helper situation of therapy and counseling. Situations range from coaching (which may involve an external coach, a manager coaching a worker, or peer coaching) through workplace conversations including reviews and appraisals, team development, quality groups, organizational development, leadership development, outplacement, conflict resolution, career guidance, and many more. As will become apparent, these many different contexts have brought a reappraisal of how SF practice can be defined and described.

While the usual question-based descriptions taken from the therapy world provide a good start, the different relationships found in the workplace give rise to different needs; how (for example) to ask questions from a not-knowing position if one is the manager, has known all those involved for many years, and will need to continue the relationship long after the conversation has finished. Jackson and McKergow (2002) offered six "solutions tools" and six SIMPLE principles to guide managers:

- Solutions—not problems
- In between—not individual
- Make use of what's there—not what isn't
- Possibilities—from the past, present, and future
- Language—simply said
- Every case is different—beware ill-fitting theory

Hjerth (in Klingenstierna, 2001) addressed the same issue in a different way with the PLUS model:

- Platform—what is the issue
- Look from the preferred future—what is wanted
- Utilize successes and resources—use what is already working
- Stepping the scales—next steps forward

Cauffman and Dierolf (2006) have offered the metaphor of a dance between those involved, with seven steps (socializing, contextualizing, goal setting, uncovering resources, giving compliments, differentiating through scaling, future orientation).

All these efforts highlight the challenge in translating the subtle simplicity of SF practice for an audience that wants something quick and easy with which to work. None of these translations is definitive; indeed, their variety shows how challenging it can be to describe SF practice. The impossibility of developing a complete and definitive model of SF practice has brought challenges in spreading the word in management circles, as compared to approaches such as Appreciative Inquiry (see, for example, Cooperider & Whitney, 2001). However, it has also helped to generate many interesting variations, each of which may work well in particular circumstances. For a comparison between SF, Appreciative Inquiry, and Positive Psychology see McKergow (2005).

Solution-focused work is a very practice-oriented field, which may have resulted in the relative underdevelopment of the academic side (Gale Miller, as quoted in McKergow, 2009b). There are signs that this situation is also starting to change: David Weber is now teaching the SF approach as a consulting and communication methodology at the University of North Carolina at Wilmington, and the SFCT journal *InterAction* publishes peer-reviewed papers.

■ RESEARCH METHODS

As I mentioned in the Introduction, there tends to be less focus on standardized testing/research in the organizational field than in therapy. Most organizations are primarily concerned with results in their own context rather than with adding to global knowledge, and even outcome research—trying the same intervention over and over and logging the results—is not a feature of the landscape. This fact may be connected to less rigorous adherence to a diagnostic paradigm; after all, a diagnosis is supposed to provide valuable information for treatment, and the therapeutic conventions about diagnosis may lead researchers down the path of testing interventions against certain diagnoses. In the world of the manager, progress now—in whatever messy and confused situation—is of overriding importance.

In general, the research data that exist are more like case studies of bespoke interventions in specific situations. In some cases there are measured outcomes, in others simply a satisfactory conclusion from the organization's point of view. However, some projects have been written up and published with enough detail for the reader to be able to place confidence in the results, and it is these projects that I summarize here. There are many more interventions with anecdotal evidence of success.

■ RESULTS OF RESEARCH

Coaching

Coaching has been one of the earliest fields to pick up on the possibilities offered by the SF approach. This may well be due to the contextual similarities between therapy and coaching: A helper talks to a client with the overall aim of helping the client make progress in a challenging situation. Anthony Grant of the Coaching Psychology Unit at the University of Sydney was one of those to grasp some of the possibilities early on (Greene & Grant, 2003), although his work features much else besides SF ideas. Peter Szabó of Weiterbildungs Forum in Switzerland has been teaching SF coaching since about 1997, and his book with Insoo Kim Berg (Berg & Szabó, 2005) has been influential in the international coaching community. He has recently presented an even more brief and clear version of these ideas (Szabó & Meier, 2009). This chapter looks at coaching as a management tool. Chapter 22 offers a more detailed look at the coaching field and, in particular, the use of the SF approach in life coaching.

The development of coaching as a management tool during the 1990s was greatly helped by the work of John Whitmore (Whitmore, 1992), whose GROW model proved popular with managers. The easy-to-remember framework helped those learning to coach to stay on track during their conversations. Recognizing this, Jackson and McKergow (2007) devised the OSKAR model around the turn of the millennium to serve a similar purpose in SF coaching conversations:

- *Outcome*—what is wanted, for the client, the topic, and the session?
- *Scale*—on a scale from 1 to 10 where 10 is the outcome, where are you now?
- *Know-how*—what is getting you that high already? What other relevant know-how can you find elsewhere in the organization?
- *Affirm* and *Action*—what impresses the coach? What are some small next steps?
- *Review*—what's better since last time? How did you do that?

The OSKAR model has been used in many organizations as a simple way to engage managers with SF processes and ideas. Some projects that have been reported include those of Walkers Snackfoods (Jackson, 2005), the Metropolitan Police in London, and the London Borough of Merton (Sked & Waldman, 2006). Readers may note the element of sharing know-how contained within OSKAR; this was deliberately included at the request of clients and offers another dimension of finding "what's working."

Godat (2006) has worked with some 50 SF questions on cards. He reports that simply using these questions, drawn in a random way without any skill or design, can be an effective solution-building aid for managers.

Team Development

Helping teams work more effectively together is a key task for managers. Often an external facilitator will be brought in to design and run group processes to help the team make progress in challenging situations, and the SF approach provides an excellent framework for this kind of practice. For example, Henden (2005) reports on remotivating a team facing a difficult future by using a "time-quake" to imagine themselves at a later date, having weathered the storm. This process serves as an equivalent to a miracle question; a better future is imagined without any consideration of what caused it to come about.

Meier (2005) has produced the SolutionCircle, an eight-phase process for managers and facilitators working with teams that has been used in educational (Szabó & Meier, 2007) and corporate contexts. The Solution-Focused Reflecting Team format (see Norman et al., 2005) has proved popular with teams around the world. This format is a way of sharing group wisdom and bringing experience to bear on an issue that is held, on behalf of the group, by one of its team members.

Röhrig and Clarke (2008) have assembled a collection of activities used by SF facilitators from around the world. The number and range of contributions are indicative of the increasing acceptance of these methods.

Jackson and Coombs (2009) have reported on a team event with art handlers from TATE in London. Interestingly, these very practical people seem to have been engaged well by the SF processes employed, indicating that such methods may be used with a wide range of work levels and staff. Korn (2006) has used SF ideas combined with the psychodrama of Moreno in developing a departmental team from an information technology (IT) service provider.

Organizational Development and Performance

Moving up from teams, SF methodology is also being used at the level of organizational change. Organizational development (OD) is an area where SF ideas can be readily applied. Clarke and McKergow (2007) report on the successful use of SF methods in a restructuring/reorganization project at a semiconductor factory. Glass (2007) shows how one manager can make small changes that ripple through a whole department, making sizable improvements to morale in a billion-pound conglomerate in the United Kingdom. Intriguingly, Glass identifies the power of many tiny interventions as opposed to one big and much-trumpeted change program; if small actions are made guerrilla style as part of the normal flow of work, then there can be no resistance.

Making a more effective organization is one thing. It is often argued that making a more profitable organization is quite another. Although the bottom line is easy to measure, there are typically many factors involved, and singling out the effects of particular interventions is challenging. Hoffman and Luisser (2007) report on a fascinating direct comparison study from two Scandinavian food production factories. In one factory, shift leaders at the middle management level received SF leadership training—6 days in four modules, spread across some 3 months, with three additional coaching sessions during the period. The impact on their performance, and on the performances of their subordinates, was measured using a mix of qualitative interviews, self-rating forms, and questionnaires including subordinates' perceptions. Five "hard" indicators of overall performance were also used—returns by customers, absence, loss of packaging materials, faults in production, and overall equipment efficiency. Results from this plant were also compared to those of the other "control" plant, producing the same goods in the same company and in the same overall environment.

Improvements were seen in the areas of communication, time management, and leadership ability as perceived by subordinates. Even more remarkably, statistically significant improvements were seen in returns by customers and loss of packaging materials. Many small changes resulting from the training were being made as the study was being concluded, leading the authors to suggest that further improvements can reasonably be assumed. This study is unusual in its rigor.

Other senior managers have linked SF working to overall company results. Van Hogh (2009) introduced the management team of the Dutch IT company Hogendoorn to SF ideas via a workshop and a strategic planning exercise. The resulting changes to business plans and implementation led to a doubling in profit and halving of stocks and debtors in just 3 months. Van Hogh links this success with the way that SF methods helped connect the management and workforce and channeled energy and motivation into next-day action. He advised managers not to attempt to "convert" all staff to SF processes; starting at the top and engaging people was the way to go.

On a smaller scale, Bauer and Lueger (2007) used SF ideas to help increase the profitability of a small chain of sportswear retailers in Austria, using Lueger's (2006) idea of the power of positive differences—what makes things better, which is not the same as the opposite: what makes things worse—in time (sales in one shop over different periods) and in space (between different shops in the same chain). They found that this helped the staff move beyond statements of what was wrong (in this case, extended roadworks outside the shop in question) and focus on what helped (layout, furnishings, chat with the customers). Turnover increased by 20%.

SF Approaches in Everyday Management

The applications considered so far have related to attempts to improve specific aspects of personal and organizational performance. However, one aspect of management, as opposed to therapy, is that there are continuing relationships between those involved that may last for many years where there is no clear helper–helped context; those involved are supposed to be working together in the interests of the organization. It appears that introducing aspects of SF practice into this context can have a positive effect on the productivity of everyday operations.

One common feature of introducing managers to SF ideas seems to be that they will then apply these ideas in a flexible way to whatever they are working on at the time. This can result in all kinds of different tactics, from simply asking a single refocusing question in a meeting to tackling a whole project in an SF way. One reason for this might be that "what works?" conversations are by definition positive conversations.

Mona Hojab (2007) relates her experience of using SF ideas in everyday management in her role in a London housing association. She found many ways to use SF ideas, in particular the application of small steps in difficult situations. She describes this tactic as Trojan Mice: Like the famous Trojan Horse of legend, these small steps do not attract great attention but can lead to all kinds of interesting progress. Each small step is viewed as a kind of experiment rather than a done deal. It's impossible to tell which small steps will have an impact; the key thing is to watch what happens and learn. This is a good example of how one element of SF practice can find multiple novel applications in different contexts.

International human resources (HR) manager Antoinette Oglethorpe related her many uses of SF in an interview (McKergow, 2008). She identified as a key benefit the way in which SF methods provide a framework for working alongside managers in a process way while keeping discussions focused and on track. Along with many other applications, Oglethorpe mentions employee management and retention; she argues that SF ideas offer an excellent way to encourage disgruntled employees who are thinking of leaving to change their minds, providing major cost savings in recruitment and training for organizations.

Hans Zeinhofer (2007) describes how he used SF ideas in his role as managing director of an electricity company in Austria. He was asked to lead a review of a near disaster in customer communication—and did so by simply asking, "What did we do right?" and "What will we do better next time?" This was not at all what his senior colleagues expected—they anticipated an exploration of what had gone wrong—but it proved eminently satisfactory.

Leadership Development

Exactly where management ends and leadership begins is something of a moot point in the organizational world. One old adage has it that "management is doing things right; leadership is doing the right things." While studies such as that of Hoffman and Luisser (2007) contain elements of leadership, other authors and practitioners have considered the question of leadership in more detail.

Mussman (2006) examined ways in which SF leadership showed in day-to-day work in a Swiss health clinic. Using interviews and questionnaires, she concluded that

SF leadership can live alongside more conventional classical and authoritarian behaviors. The idea of "leading from behind," appreciating the work of others, and working in a process orientation were noted. Mussman also found that the managers saw their own SF abilities in a much more critical way than did their subordinates.

Garssen (2006) describes a top-level leadership development program in the city of Apeldoorn in the Netherlands. Taking inspiration from Stephen Covey's "Seven Habits" work (Covey, 1993) as well as SF, Garssen and his team worked with 120 managers with positive results. Johansson and Persson (2007) describe their work with the leader of a 40-strong Social Security team in Sweden, resulting in improvements in performance across the board.

One aspect of leadership involves working with messy and ambiguous situations. Röhrig (2007) describes working with those involved in ensuring that patients' views are taken into account in the German health care system. The Cologne Local Health Conference had commissioned a report, for which there were several hundred pages of data. Using a very simple SF approach combining an eye on the finished document and small steps along the way, Röhrig describes a successful way to work with a confusing mess of data without attempting to simplify it. In a similar vein, Dierolf (2007) reports on using SF methods to help an international chemical company pick a path through a maze of regulatory and stakeholder issues.

Brent and McKergow (2009) have addressed the application of SF coaching as a leadership tool. They see SF as an excellent practical strategy for dealing with complex interconnected situations (a description that can be applied to much of organizational life!). They have found capable managers trained in subjects like engineering, who naturally attempt to apply the same analytical skills to these complex situations. Solution-focused methodology offers a valuable alternative, stressing observation, awareness, and small steps over direction and false confidence in an unknowable position.

McKergow (2009a) has extended the idea of SF leadership with the metaphor of the leader as host. Although the idea of the SF therapist as one who hosts conversations has been around for many years, McKergow finds this metaphor as one with a rich resonance in the organizational community. Host leaders use the power of invitation, create spaces, and move backward and forward as demanded by the situation, producing a rich and flexible set of ideas for practice.

Performance Management

A key part of most managers' role is to appraise and review the performance of their subordinates, often as part of an organizationwide review process. Lueger (2005) has rethought this conversation from an SF perspective in a way that has proved influential in many organizations. Lueger's novel approach of preserving evidence of difference by allocating scores across several performance grades, rather than the more conventional practice of choosing a single grade to represent performance, can make possible a much wider range of conversations between the manager and the employee.

This approach has been applied in a number of large organizations. Powell and Coombs (2006) describe the application of this approach at TATE, the United Kingdom's main modern and British art galleries. These authors applied a variety if SF interventions, including coaching and performance reviews, with positive results. One measurable outcome was that the proportion of staff having a formal review increased from about 70% to about 90%. Powell and Coombs discuss the power of the "ripple effect"—also discussed by Kay (2006)—where change starts from small actions that then ripple through the organization through a variety of (mainly) informal channels. This is another example of an SF idea—making use of what's there—finding an interesting home in an organizational context. Fink (2006) reports on the application of Lueger's (2005) approach in a Finnish university.

Quality Management

The use of analytical (and problem-focused) processes to improve quality has been an important feature of life for manufacturing companies and others over the past 30 years. These methods usually involve the measurement and elimination of defects, aiming to achieve preset levels of quality. As such, this movement has been very effective.

Durnford (2007) reports on applying SF methods alongside these more traditional approaches. Working in the UK satellite TV business British Sky Broadcasting, he found that the different and positive flavor of SF applications could make a valuable contribution. In situations where conventional problem analysis was failing to produce progress, Durnford found that he could apply SF methods to open up new avenues and ideas. Also, classical processes sometimes shed light on what is to be done—but not on how to engage people in doing it. Durnford concludes that SF processes can play a good part in engaging workers in implementing new work practices. Clarke (2006) described a similar process as "clearing up after McKinsey" when she assisted with the implementation of a new manufacturing system devised by the leading consultancy firm. Heilbrunn (2009) describes how SF methods helped add great value to quality and make auditing more effective and efficient in his role as quality auditor with an aerospace component manufacturer.

Conflict Resolution/Mediation

The use of SF ideas in conflict resolution and mediation is not, of course, limited to management applications. Bannink (2009) has been a leading figure in developing SF mediation models. She describes a three-meeting mediation between a team of nurses, as well as surveying many connections between SF ideas and the mediation literature. Working in a similar situation, Macdonald (2006) describes his use of SF ideas to "find co-operation quickly" in challenging circumstances. Schienecker (2006) used SF ideas in an organizational conflict situation with very positive results.

Stellamans (2006) describes his use of SF ideas in international conflict situations—Northern Ireland, Congo, and Kosovo. He makes the important point that while peace building is often preceded by an analysis and categorization of the conflict (based on previous conflicts), an SF approach looks instead for exceptions and small signs of progress and willingness in the present. Oglethorpe (2009) has developed the PARTNER framework to help managers, HR professionals, and mediators prepare for and handle conflict discussions.

Sales

The process of selling goods and services is a key part of any business, and one that is often approached with trepidation by newcomers. Although it is a long way from its original therapeutic roots, the collaborative ethos of SF practice provides a useful framework for conversations aimed at finding out what people want and helping them achieve it. Sproson (2010) took an early lead in this area, reframing selling as "client recruitment." Regele and Regele (2006) used SF processes to help refocus a sales and marketing team from a multinational chemical company on attractive opportunities. Hofstetter (2008) has gone even further and drawn together much research from the SF and sales fields into a new approach to selling.

Strategy

Strategic planning was famously described by McGill University's Professor Henry Mintzberg (1994) as "an oxymoron." He argued that it was clearly a misnomer to apply the word *planning* to something as complex and fluid as the long term. The SF approach, with its focus on useful change and positive difference, is clearly a candidate for some kind of "new strategic planning." Woodings (2006; discussed in Stewart, 2009) has developed and performed a trial of a form of strategic intervention based on alignment (of the people) and direction (of the organization) rather than the more conventional analysis, goals, and action plans. His work, first in a vast multi-billion-dollar oil project and subsequently with the BBC's Performing Groups, has shown that there is great potential for SF ideas to permeate further into these high-level organizational processes.

Training

The positive pragmatism of the SF approach has found ready use in the training department of a number of organizations. Learning and development professionals have been quick to take on aspects of SF; encouragement to look at "what's working" when examining the presentations skills of a novice, for example, can provide a much firmer base for skill development than a detailed analysis of "things to do differently." McKergow (2007) cataloged 11 different kinds of application of SF ideas by the training department of a U.K. building society. These included uses in course design, facilitation, sales training, training needs analysis, e-learning, and strategic impact (working with the organization's executives).

The way in which SF (and anything else) is trained can also include SF ideas. Hankovzsky and Szabó (2002) have written about how they construct training courses using SF ideas where the content is better "caught" (by practice and demonstration) than "taught" didactically. The work of Hirschburger (2006) in developing SF evaluation approaches has also been influential. He argues that any kind of training or intervention can be evaluated in a way that not only measures the impact, but also reinforces and builds on it. The use of SF questions in these processes gives a remarkable new aspect to this field.

Limitations

The studies and cases mentioned above show wide applicability of the SF approach to management and organizational contexts. However, this should not be taken to indicate that SF ideas will work wonders in any situation irrespective of the manner in which they are used. The authors cited above are mostly experienced and skilled SF practitioners who could be expected to carefully fit their actions to the context at hand, in keeping with the principle that "every case is different" (Jackson and McKergow, 2002).

The lack of any peer-reviewed material showing SF to be an ineffective or, worse, a damaging approach is notable but perhaps not surprising. It is unlikely that any SF practitioner, sensing that his or her work was going nowhere, would see it through to the bitter end and then write it up! This is surely not to say that there have been no disappointments along the way—just that, as in any organizational change process, nothing works all the time. The SF mantra of "stop doing what doesn't work and do something different" is helpful in ensuring that the frustrations of management are merely the ordinary frustrations of life rather than the repeated roadblocks of dysfunction.

■ PRACTICE GUIDELINES

One aspect of the results presented above is that these many applications seem to have all been extremely successful. The way in which the SF approach seems to fit all the different areas is remarkable. This should encourage others to carry on and develop their own new applications and mini-models to build on the basic SF framework in other areas. It seems unlikely that an SF intervention—done with care, respect, and skill—could cause real and lasting harm.

Many of the interventions and projects described above were undertaken by managers and consultants with strong experience in their specialist field (coaching, conflict management, or whatever). Within this, it seems to me that they have by and large kept the flexibility of the SF approach rather than assembling something overcodified and mechanical.

Practice guidelines therefore include the following:

- Build on your own speciality and experience; don't expect to go from SF coach to master conflict mediator overnight.
- Stay flexible and encourage others to stay flexible; this is a pragmatic approach stressing the uniqueness of each case.
- Be bold; develop new applications and models for SF within the management field.

■ FUTURE STUDIES

As the SF approach becomes more widely known and used in the management world, it will become increasingly important both to position what we do in relation to other management approaches and to be clear about what makes SF unique and different. This will be a challenge. The next steps might involve working with people more accustomed to other approaches, to see how they view SF and what their views are about where SF might or might not be useful.

Longer-term follow-up studies would also be interesting. We know that SF therapy has good long-term results; is this also true in the organizational sphere? Do managers who learn SF keep on using it, and do they get better results as they become more experienced with the approach?

Another possibility is to make more connections between the relatively underdeveloped academic philosophical side of SF methodology and the well-developed practical side. Many business schools seem to me to be uncomfortable with an approach that is so flexible and under continuing development. Clearly, we do not wish to ossify and prevent further developments of SF approaches; and yet, if the field does not begin to find its place alongside other known approaches, there is a risk that it will disappear completely from the wider world and become the domain of a few dedicated followers. This would be a great shame; the insights and sharpness of the SF approach can make a big contribution over the decades to come.

■ CONCLUSION

This chapter has outlined some of the ways in which SF ideas have been used in management thus far. There are many others for which there was no space, including applications relating to workplace environments, branding, health and safety improvement, and project management. There are also many other applications that have been used, but not yet published formally, such as the work of Yasuteru Aoki with Canon Finetech Inc. in Japan (recently published as Aoki, 2010), applications in career guidance and outplacement, and negotiation. There is no doubt a host of uses that will never see the light of day, aside from their benefit to those involved.

There are several important messages to take from all these developments. The first is that the SF approach, as a general philosophy of change, has applications far beyond its original therapeutic use. The developments led by the Brief Family Therapy Center (BFTC team), described as "serendipitous" by Steve de Shazer and Insoo Kim Berg (1995), have opened the door to a new and valuable way to approach challenging situations. The sheer variety and quantity of experience in the organizational field alone attest to this.

Secondly, the ways in which experience has been written, shared, and used has shown that the organizational SF community is one where the original values of modesty, care, sharing credit, and appreciating success are alive and well. Visitors to SOLWorld conferences often comment on the overwhelmingly generous and appreciative nature of the gathering, often coupled with remarks about how unusual and refreshing this is.

Finally, in a business world that thrives on protecting knowledge and intellectual property, the SF community has strived to keep an open-source ethos. Practitioners have their own favourite ways to present what they do, but by making everything open and encouraging people to apply these ideas and share what they have learned, there has been no successful attempt to trademark or claim ownership of these ideas; one attempt to claim ownership (not from anyone referred to here) in the United Kingdom was rejected by the Patent Office. The SOLWorld charter clearly states that "SF ideas and principles belong to everyone." By placing so much of our work in the public domain, I hope we have made it impossible for anyone to successfully claim ownership in the future, leaving the field clear for further development, sharing, and results. The Association for the Quality Development of Solution-Focused Consulting and Training (http://www.asfct.org), with its journal InterAction, is now acting as a focal point for new research and writing in this area.

■ KEY FINDINGS TO REMEMBER

- The SF approach has relevance far beyond the original therapeutic setting.
- The SF approach has been successfully applied in many management settings.

- Broader definitions of the SF approach have been pioneered in the organizational field, which may help the field develop across the board.
- The use of SF is becoming increasingly important in the coaching world.
- The pragmatism, flexibility, and results of SF are welcomed by leaders and managers around the world.
- The international SF community has a reputation for openness, generosity. and appreciation, and is seeking to keep the approach open source in an age of licensing and intellectual property.

■ FURTHER LEARNING

- The Association for the Quality Development of Solution Focused Consulting and Training (SFCT) is the professional body for those using the SF approach in organizations, with professional reviews, accreditation, the academic journal *InterAction*, and national chapters worldwide. The Web site is http://www. asfct.org
- The SOLWorld community offers conferences, discussions, and an online community for those applying SF in management. The Web site is http://www. solworld.org
- The Centre for SF at Work has a large library of resources, articles, and other materials. The Web site is http://www.sfwork.com

■ REFERENCES

Aoki, Y. (2010). "Creating a workplace where we all wanna go every morning!", *InterAction*, *1*(2), 113–119

Bannink, F. P. (2009). SF Conflict management in teams and organisations. *InterAction*, *1*(1), 11–25.

Bauer, K., & Lueger, G. (2007). Back to the future: Increasing sales with positive differences. In M. McKergow & J. Clarke (Eds.), *Solutions focus working* (pp. 63–72). Cheltenham, UK: Solutions Books.

Berg, I. K., & Szabó, P. (2005). *Brief coaching for lasting solutions*. New York: Norton.

Brent, M., & McKergow, M. (2009). Acting in uncertainty: Solution focused coaching and leadership. *Coaching at Work*, *4*(5), 44–48.

Cauffman, L. (2001). *Oplossingsgericht Management: Simpel werkt het best* (Solution-focused management: Simple works the best). Amsterdam: Lemma.

Cauffman, L., with Dierolf, K. (2006). *The solution tango: Seven simple steps to solutions in management*. London: Marshall Cavendish.

Clarke, J. (2006). Turning clients into customers for change. In G. Lueger & H.-P. Korn (Eds.), *Solution-focused management* (pp. 357–362). Munich: Reiner Hampp Verlag.

Clarke, J., & McKergow, M. (2007). Optimising the organisation. In M. McKergow & J. Clarke (Eds.), *Solutions focus working* (pp. 93–103). Cheltenham, UK: Solutions Books.

Cooperrider, D., & Whitney, D. (2001). *Appreciative inquiry*. Berrett-Koehler.

Covey, S. R. (1993). *The seven habits of highly effective people*. New York: Free Press.

de Shazer, S., & Berg, I. K. (1995). The brief therapy tradition. In J. Weakland & W. Ray (Eds.), *Propagations: Thirty years of influence from the Mental Research Institute* (pp. 249–252). Binghamton, NY: Haworth Press.

Dierolf, K. (2007). Solutions focus tackles complexity. In M. McKergow & J. Clarke (Eds), *Solutions focus working* (pp. 105–117). Cheltenham, UK: Solutions Books.

Durnford, T. (2007). Turning the tables on quality. In M. McKergow & J. Clarke (Eds), *Solutions focus working* (pp. 49–62). Cheltenham, UK: Solutions Books.

Fink, B. (2006). Making performance rating relevant, informative and meaningful. In G. Lueger & H.-P. Korn (Eds.), *Solution-focused management* (pp. 213–222). Munich: Reiner Hampp Verlag.

Garssen, B. (2006). Dancing with your boss. In G. Lueger & H.-P. Korn (Eds.), *Solution-focused management* (pp. 135–145). Munich: Reiner Hampp Verlag.

Godat, D. (2006). Random micro solution-focused work. In G. Lueger & H.-P. Korn (Eds.), *Solution-focused management* (pp. 421–426) Munich: Reiner Hampp Verlag

Greene, J., & Grant, A. M. (2003). *Solution-focused coaching: Managing people in a complex world*. London: Momentum.

Glass, C. (2007). The power of one. In M. McKergow & J. Clarke (Eds.), *Solutions focus working* (pp. 13–31). Cheltenham, UK: Solutions Books.

Hankovszky, K., & Szabó, P. (2002). Elements of solution-focused training methodology. *Lernende Organisation, 9,* 29–32.

Heilbrunn, M. (2009). *Solutions focus in auditing. INFORM,* e-journal of the International Registry of Certified Auditors, 21. Retrieved from http://www.irca.org/inform/issue21/MHeilbrunn.html (retrieved 17 March 2011)

Henden, J. (2005). Team remotivation. In M. McKergow & J. Clarke (Eds.), *Positive approaches to change* (pp. 39–52). Cheltenham, UK: Solutions Books.

Hirschburger, F. (2006). The formula for resourceful evaluation of training and coaching. In G. Lueger & H.-P. Korn (Eds.), *Solution-focused management* (pp. 287–295). Munich: Reiner Hampp Verlag.

Hoffman, K., & Luisser, P. (2007). *Effects of solution-focused training on leadership behaviour and productivity.* Munich: Rainer Hampp Verlag.

Hofstetter, D. (2008). *Solution-focused selling.* Munich: Rainer Hampp Verlag.

Hojab, M. (2007). Small steps and Trojan mice. In M. McKergow & J. Clarke (Eds.), *Solutions focus working* (pp. 83–92). Cheltenham, UK: Solutions Books.

Jackson, P. Z. (2005). How to improve your management skills. In M. McKergow & J. Clarke (Eds.), *Solutions focus working* (pp. 141–154). Cheltenham, UK: Solutions Books.

Jackson, P. Z., & Coombs, C. (2009). Making it happen in your organisation. *InterAction, 1*(1), 66–77.

Jackson, P. Z., & McKergow, M. (2002). *The solutions focus: The SIMPLE way to positive change.* London: Nicholas Brealey.

Jackson, P. Z. & McKergow, M. (2007). *The solutions focus: Making coaching & change SIMPLE.* (second edition) London: Nicholas Brealey

Johansson, B., & Persson, E. (2007). Change is in the eye of the beholder. In M. McKergow & J. Clarke (Eds.), *Solutions focus working* (pp. 159–173). Cheltenham, UK: Solutions Books.

Kay, A. (2006). The use of solutions focus in branded customer experience implementation. In G. Lueger & H.-P. Korn (Eds.), *Solution-focused management* (pp. 159–168). Munich: Reiner Hampp Verlag.

Klingenstierna, C. (2001). *Lösningsfokuserad gruppterapi vid långtidssjukskrivning—en jämförande studie med deltagare sjukskrivna mer än sex månader.* (Solution-focused group therapy with long term sickness absence – a comparative study with participants on sick leave more than six months) Unpublished MSc. Psychology thesis, Uppsala University, Uppsala, Sweden.

Korn, H.-P. (2006). Staging of strategic solutions for the future business. In G. Lueger & H.-P. Korn (Eds.), *Solution-focused management* (pp. 169–183). Munich: Reiner Hampp Verlag.

Lueger, G. (2005). Solution focused rating. In M. McKergow & J. Clarke (Eds.), *Positive approaches to change* (pp. 81–92). Cheltenham, UK: Solutions Books.

Lueger, G. (2006). Solution-focused management: Towards a theory of positive differences. In G. Lueger & H.-P. Korn (Eds.), *Solution-focused management* (pp. 1–13). Munich: Reiner Hampp Verlag.

Macdonald, A. (2006). Solution-focused situation management. In G. Lueger & H.-P. Korn (Eds.), *Solution-focused management* (pp. 61–66). Munich: Reiner Hampp Verlag.

McKergow, M. (2005). Positive approaches to organisations and people. In M. McKergow & J. Clarke (Eds.), *Positive approaches to change* (pp. 1–11). Cheltenham, UK: Solutions Books.

McKergow, M. (2007). Listing and letting go: Transforming a training department. In M. McKergow & J. Clarke (Eds.), *Solutions focus working* (pp. 147–157). Cheltenham, UK: Solutions Books.

McKergow, M. (2008). *Solutions focus: How to change everything by changing as little as possible*. Retrieved from http://www.sfwork.com/jsp/index.jsp?lnk=6d7 (retrieved 17 March 2011)

McKergow, M. (2009a). Leader as host, host as leader: Towards a new yet ancient metaphor. *International Journal for Leadership in Public Services, 5*(1), 19–24.

McKergow, M. (2009b). Gale Miller: The man behind the mirror behind the mirror at BFTC. *InterAction, 1*(1), 78–88.

Meier, D. (2005). *Team coaching with the SolutionCircle*. Cheltenham, UK: Solutions Books.

Mintzberg. H. (1994). *The fall and rise of strategic planning*. London: Prentice Hall.

Mussan, C. (2006). Solution-focused leadership. In G. Lueger & H.-P. Korn (Eds.), *Solution-focused management* (pp. 99–110) Munich: Reiner Hampp Verlag.

Norman, H., Hjerth, M., & Pidsley, T. (2005). Solution focused reflecting teams in action. In M. McKergow & J. Clarke (Eds.), *Positive approaches to change* (pp. 67–79). Cheltenham, UK: Solutions Books.

Oglethorpe, A., & Oglethorpe, D. (2009, June 10). *Resolving conflict in the workplace: PARTNERing for success*. Presented at the 10th International Conference on Human Resource Development Research and Practice across Europe, Northumbria University Business School, Northumbria, UK.

Powell, V., & Coombs, C. (2006). Using SF to accelerate a performance and development culture. In G. Lueger & H.-P. Korn (Eds.), *Solution-focused management* (pp. 307–314). Munich: Reiner Hampp Verlag.

Regele, D., & Regele, W. (2006). Solution-focused improvement of the customer segmentation process. In G. Lueger & H.-P. Korn (Eds.), *Solution-focused management* (pp. 185–192). Munich: Reiner Hampp Verlag.

Röhrig, P. (2007). Making sense of information. In M. McKergow & J. Clarke (Eds.), *Solutions focus working* (pp. 147–157). Cheltenham, UK: Solutions Books.

Röhrig, P., & Clarke, J. (2008). *57 SF activities for facilitators and consultants.* Cheltenham, UK: Solutions Books.

Scheinecker, M. (2006). SF-conflict management in conflict consulting in organisations, In G. Lueger & H.-P. Korn (Eds.), *Solution-focused management* (pp. 317–324). Munich: Reiner Hampp Verlag.

Schmitz, L., & Billen, B. (2000). *Mitarbeitergespräche. Lösungsorientiert - klar–konsequent.* Vienna: Uebereuter Wirt.

Sked, C., & Waldman, J. (2006). Working in partnership to introduce SF as a management tool. In G. Lueger & H.-P. Korn (Eds.), *Solution-focused management* (pp. 443–452). Munich: Reiner Hampp Verlag.

Sproson, J. (2010). *They call it selling—we call it client recruitment*. Burghfield, UK: Sales Mentor.

Stellamans, A. (2006). Solution-focused peace building. In G. Lueger & H.-P. Korn (Eds.), *Solution-focused management* (pp. 339–343). Munich: Reiner Hampp Verlag.

Stewart, A. (2009, April 25). Riding the storm. *Classical Music*, 22–25.

Szabó, P., & Meier, D. (2007). Getting a team working together. In M. McKergow & J. Clarke (Eds.), *Solutions focus working* (pp. 135–146). Cheltenham, UK: Solutions Books.

Szabó, P., & Meier, D. (2009). *Coaching plain & simple: Solution-focused brief coaching essentials*. New York: Norton.

Van Hogh, M. (2009). *SF management in an IT company*. Presented to the SOLWorld 2009 conference, Texel, the Netherlands.

Whitmore, J. (1992). *Coaching for performance*. London: Nicholas Brealey.

Woodings, B. (2006). Aligning large multi-cultural teams performance with a solutions focused approach. In G. Lueger & H.-P. Korn (Eds.), *Solution-focused management* (pp. 371–382). Munich: Reiner Hampp Verlag.

Zeinhofer, H. (2007). What went well? In M. McKergow & J. Clarke (Eds.), *Solutions focus working* (pp. 187–190). Cheltenham, UK: Solutions Books.

22 Solution-Focused Life Coaching

■ SUZY GREEN

■ INTRODUCTION

Solution-focused life coaching is an increasingly popular approach aimed at assisting individuals to make desired changes in their personal or work life or to enhance their overall level of happiness and well-being. Research is currently embryonic; however; the studies conducted so far are encouraging and suggest that this is a promising approach for mental health professionals to consider. It offers an evidence-based methodology for those practitioners already providing coaching services and also for those working within a traditional counseling model who may wish to expand their practices and offer life coaching as an additional service. Early research suggests that evidence-based life coaching may have the potential to be a useful change methodology (Grant et al., 2010; Green et al., 2006, 2007; Spence & Grant, 2007).

■ WHAT WE HAVE LEARNED SO FAR

While the term *coaching* has many definitions and uses, it is popularly referred to as sustained cognitive, emotional, and behavioral change that facilitates goal attainment and performance enhancement, either in one's work or in one's personal life (Douglas & McCauley, 1999). The term *coaching* has been utilized for decades in the corporate setting, where it is perceived as a "perk" for higher-level management (Williams, 2000). However, life coaching did not have a real presence until the early 1990s (Williams & Davis, 2002). Chapter 21 discussed solution-focused coaching as a management tool; this chapter focuses more on life coaching as a method to help individuals restructure their lives to achieve their goals. Life coaching is a systematized, structured approach to helping people make changes in their life, and has become a popular means of helping nonclinical populations set and reach goals and enhance their well-being (Green et al., 2006). It is important to note, though, that the coaching industry is unregulated in many countries; currently, anyone can identify themselves as a life coach (Grant, 2001). It has been claimed that executive and life coaches number in the tens of thousands in the United States (Hall et al., 1999) and there are also many unregulated coach training schools. The International Coach Federation (ICF), a large coaching association, has established certification guidelines, though currently certification is not required to work as a coach and training programs are not standardized. Grant (2003), commenting on the current status of coaching, claimed that "coaching is far from meeting the basic delineations of a true profession" (p. 3).

Dr. Anthony Grant, considered to be the father of coaching psychology, defined coaching (encompassing life, personal, and workplace coaching) in his doctoral dissertation "Towards a Psychology of Coaching" (2001) as "a solution-focused, results-orientated systematic process in which the coach facilitates the enhancement of the coachee's life experience and performance in various domains (as determined by the coachee), and fosters the self-directed learning and personal growth of the coachee" (p. 20).

■ SOLUTION-FOCUSED BRIEF THERAPY INTERVENTION: SOLUTION-FOCUSED COACHING

Despite variations in definitions, the term *coaching*, whether *executive*, *business*, or *life*, is often described as being "solution-focused." The solution-focused approach underpins many coaching interventions and is utilized in many attempts to define coaching. Finding solutions may be considered the basic premise of coaching, and the solution-focused approach includes rules such as "if it works, don't fix it" and "if it does not work, do something different" (Berg & Szabo, 2005). Such key approaches in coaching can assist a coachee to make desired changes. So, while the definition of coaching continues to be debated, there appears to be agreement among those attempting a definition that any definition of coaching should include reference to it as being solution-focused.

Solution-focused coaching (SFC) has also recently been defined by O'Connell and Palmer (2007) as an outcome-oriented, competence-based approach. They claim that it "helps clients to achieve their preferred outcomes by evoking and co-constructing solutions to their problems" (p. 278). O'Connell and Palmer state that SFC developed an international following since the late 1990s, building on the solution-focused approach adopted in primarily therapeutic settings by therapists such as Steve de Shazer and Insoo Kim Berg. In its early days, solution-focused therapy was utilized for families with multiple and complex problems. It was noted that when families were encouraged to focus on things that were working, as opposed to those that weren't, they made faster progress. Since then, solution-focused therapeutic approaches have been utilized in a variety of contexts outside of mental health, including parent training, supervision, education, business, management, and organizational change. They have been used extensively with complex systems such as couples, families, groups, and teams.

Thanks largely to the coaching industry embracing and promoting the solution-focused approach, it has now been extended from its primarily therapeutic use to personal growth and development and the enhancement of well-being. In the early 1990s, when the coaching industry emerged, many coaches utilized the solution-focused approach. In 2000, the University of Sydney, Australia, established the world's first Coaching Psychology Unit, which embraced both solution-focused and cognitive-behavioral approaches in its teaching and associated research. The director of the unit, Dr. Anthony Grant, in his formulation of a psychology of coaching (2001), utilized theories and techniques from clinical and counseling psychology with a cognitive-behavioral, solution-focused framework applied to a nonclinical adult population.

Grant's model includes theories and techniques including the Transtheoretical Model of Change (Prochaska & DiClimente, 1984), a model of self-regulated learning, and both cognitive-behavioral and solution-focused theories and techniques. All these components having long and extensive research histories in psychology (see Grant, 2001, for a review). Grant (2001) suggested that solution-focused theories and techniques could be utilized in a coaching framework where the focus is on client strengths and solutions rather than problems.

In an initial evidence-based coaching study, Grant (2003) utilized a cognitive-behavioral and solution-focused life coaching program adapted from a self-help book, *Coach Yourself* (Grant & Greene 2001). This program is based on principles drawn from cognitive-behavioral clinical and counseling psychology (Beck et al., 1979), brief solution-focused therapy (O'Connell, 1998), and models of self-regulated learning (Zimmerman, 1989). The solution-focused component of this program encourages participants to identify the benefits of focusing on solutions rather than problems and to identify exceptions to the problem, and utilizes a number of solution-focused questions that the participants can draw on to identify alternative pathways to their goals (i.e., the miracle question; de Shazer, 1988). In Grant's initial study, 20 adult participants focused on attaining goals that had eluded them for an average of 23.5 months. Grant (2001) found that participation in the program was associated with significantly enhanced mental health, an improved quality of life, and increased goal attainment.

Grant and his associates at the Coaching Psychology Unit have continued to conduct further research on cognitive-behavioral solution-focused coaching (CB-SFC) since that time. This research will be reviewed later in the chapter.

While solution-focused therapy continues to be popular and utilized as a mental health treatment intervention, there is a need for more interventions that focus on mental health promotion given the increasing rates of mental illness in the community. Solution-focused life coaching fits the bill well and has been suggested as one such approach (Green et al., 2006).

Mental health professionals such as psychologists, social workers, therapists, and counselors should be encouraged to adopt a proactive rather than a reactive approach (i.e., waiting until mental illness develops and then offering treatment). It is suggested that mental health professionals should expand their focus from treatment of mental illness to prevention and promotion of mental health and well-being. This approach aligns well with the positive psychology movement, whose focus is on the promotion of well-being and the prevention of mental illness (Seligman & Csikszentmihalyi, 2000). In fact positive psychology and coaching psychology are complementary sciences and perfect partners in a solution-focused therapeutic or coaching scenario (Green & Spence, 2008; Kaufmann, 2006; Linley & Harrington, 2005).

Solution-focused life coaching can provide mental health professionals, who are well equipped to work within this realm, with an evidence-based intervention to offer clients who may be "languishing" (for a definition and review, see Keyes, 2002) or who may be seeking assistance to solve "life problems" or explore "unused opportunities" (Egan, 1988).

Solution-focused coaching provides an intervention for those clients seeking help who may not fit a clinical diagnosis but who require an evidence-based change program to enhance their overall well-being. It also provides mental health professionals with the opportunity to expand their practices and to work with individuals who historically may not have utilized the services of a mental health professional.

Key Elements of an SFC Intervention

Pure solution-focused coaching interventions that have been rigorously scientifically tested are not currently available. Even the studies conducted at the Coaching Psychology Unit utilize a mixed approach with both solution-focused and cognitive behavioral elements. This section will attempt to outline the key elements of a SFC intervention.

Shift in Mindset. First and foremost, the SFC approach involves a shift in mindset. This shift in mindset and the assumptions that underlie it are the foundation for working within a SFC approach. Key assumptions include (1) that the client is the expert in his or her own life and (2) that the client is capable of change. The solution-focused coach, like the solution-focused therapist, does not take the role of expert. The coach does not offer solutions or tell the coachee what he or she should do. The coach may offer a solution if the coachee has exhausted all options; in that case, the coach would request permission to do so. The role of the solution-focused coach is more of a facilitator. O'Connell and Palmer (2007) suggest that this occurs through a "process of supporting questioning and reflection" enabling clients to "tap into their own resources and realize that they have a reservoir of skills, strengths and strategies which are relevant to their current challenges" (p. 283).

The solution-focused mindset is also complementary to the strengths-based approach of positive psychology and the applied positive psychology practitioner. Similarly to the solution-focused approach, which focuses on solutions rather than problems, positive psychology focuses on strengths rather than weaknesses. Most important to note, though, is that the solution-focused and strengths-based approaches are underpinned by a strong working alliance, which has been shown to be a strong predictor of psychotherapeutic outcomes (Horvath & Symonds, 1991).

Skills and Strategies. The specific skills and strategies utilized in a SFC intervention may include many of the approaches utilized in a solution-focused therapeutic setting, such as the following:

- *Problem-Free Talk.* This is an opportunity for the client to talk about his or her life holistically, including the parts that are progressing relatively well. It also gives the client an opportunity to identify values and strengths that can be drawn on in a solution-focused approach to assist in enacting change.

- *Competence Seeking.* This is an opportunity to identify the client's strengths, talents, and any areas of competence in general. The use of strengths assessment tools such as the VIA Character Strengths Assessment Peterson & Seligman (2004) might assist this effort, given many clients' struggle to identify and/or describe their own strengths.

- *Exceptions.* This is an opportunity to identify exceptions to the rule. This approach highlights the reality that most circumstances are never all or nothing (e.g., "I always fail"). Solution-focused questions can help identify exceptions to these global statements (e.g., "When in the past have you been successful in overcoming obstacles?") Exceptions to the rule provide rich information about how the client might do things differently or create the changes he or she desires.

- *The Miracle Question.* Most solution-focused therapists will be familiar with this technique. Its usual form is: *"Imagine one night when you are asleep, a miracle happens and the problems we've been discussing disappear. Since you are asleep, you do not know that a miracle has occurred. When you wake up, what will be the first signs that a miracle has happened?"* A related approach involves the magic wand: *"If a magic wand was waved and things were exactly as you'd hoped for, what would be happening?"* Both of these techniques allow the client to define a clear picture of the future and help the client and coach to develop specific goals to focus on in coaching.

- *Scaling.* This may be used in numerous ways in coaching. For example, scaling questions may assist in the measurement of goal importance, goal commitment, and goal progress (e.g., *"On a scale from 1 to 10, where 1 is the worst-case scenario and 10 is the best you could hope for, where are you now and where would you like to be by the end of our intervention?"*). Scaling may also be used to assess the client's confidence in his or her ability to carry out agreed-upon action tasks in wrap-up (e.g., *"On a scale from 1 to 10, where 1 means no confidence at all and 10 means complete confidence, how confident are you right now about completing all the actions you have committed to prior to our next session?"*).

- *Goal Setting.* Any SFC intervention usually includes a goal-setting component, with goals being a key component of coaching generally. This is due to a strong research basis highlighting the benefits of goal setting, not only in terms of attainment but also in terms of well-being (Emmons, 1999). Additionally, goals that are specific, measurable, attractive, realistic, and time-framed have been found to increase goal attainment (i.e., SMART goals; Locke & Latham, 1990). Goals that are "authentic" or "self-concordant" (i.e., consistent with a person's core values or developing interests) have been found to increase well-being (Sheldon & Elliot, 1999).

- *A Structured Approach.* Many coaches utilize a structured approach in their sessions. While many models are available, the one most commonly used is the GROW Model (Whitmore, 1999). This involves the client identifying the **G**oal for the session (linked to the overarching SMART goal/s); the **R**eality of where the client currently exists; the **O**ptions as the client sees them; and the **W**rap-up, the opportunity to commit to homework assignments that will be done prior to the following coaching session. The **O**ptions section is where the solution-focused approach is utilized heavily in the form of solution-focused questions and language to identify potential pathways to the client's goals.

- *Feedback.* Feedback is an essential component of coaching. The coach provides it at the beginning and end of each session. If the coachee has been unable to complete the homework identified in the **W**rap-up, a solution-focused approach is again utilized rather than focusing on the "why" of this situation. Coachees are encouraged to attend sessions despite not having completed homework and to use the SFC approach to identify solutions to the obstacles they have encountered between sessions. In other words, the coachee is constantly socialized to the SFC approach. The coachee learns to "self-coach" and shift his or her own mindset from a problem-centered to a solution-focused one.

- *Cognitive-Behavioral Approaches.* Since the research identified earlier is both solution-focused and cognitive-behavioral, SFC coaches are encouraged to adopt cognitive-behavioral theory and strategies. This is particularly useful in the *reframing* process that often occurs in a solution-focused approach whereby the client is asked to "change the viewing" (O'Hanlon & Beadle, 1996). Drawing on cognitive-behavioral methods will enhance this approach.

An SFC intervention includes the creation of a strong working alliance, adoption of a solution-focused and strengths-based mindset, a toolkit including competent use of solution-focused-language and questioning techniques, and use of the complementary cognitive-behavioral approach. These methods are all underpinned by goal-setting theory and a coaching model that enhances the self-regulation process and supports goal attainment (e.g., GROW). An example of an SFC intervention, outlining a step-by-step approach, can be found in the last chapter of Grant and Green's (2001) book *Coach Yourself: Make Real Change in Your Life.*

■ RESEARCH ON SFC

There is a considerable literature on coaching generally. In the preparation of this chapter, there were 4,118 citations on coaching using the database PsychInfo. However, that literature included no rigorous scientific studies conducted solely on SFC. Using the term *solution-focused coaching,* only six references were identified; all of them were book citations based on the topic. Currently, research on SFC is embryonic. It is important to note, though, that the search utilizing the term *coaching* provided references to a very broad range of applications, many of which we might assume included a solution-focused approach, given its foundational status in coaching.

Corcoran and Pillai (2007) also noted the difficulties involved in synthesizing the research for their solution-focused therapy review due to the different populations and problems areas. While this is not necessarily the primary problem when it comes to SFC research, synthesis is an issue and the above findings raise an important question: How many coaching studies have been conducted that utilized a solution-focused approach that was not explicitly identified in the methodology or the research design and potentially, in many cases, not identified but subsumed under the actual definition of coaching? In any case, research is limited and there is a great need for further research in SFC.

While coaching research has been rapidly growing, the body of evidence is still emerging (refer to the annotated bibliography in Grant, 2009). In this review of coaching research, Grant found that there were 156 outcome studies published since 1980, including 104 case studies, 36 within-subject studies, and 16 between-subject studies. Of the 16 between-subject studies, only 12 were randomized. Grant concluded, "The knowledge base underpinning coaching appears to be growing at a substantial rate. To further move towards a solid evidence-based approach to coaching, more between subject studies, and particularly randomised outcome studies, are needed" (p. 1).

At this time, rigorous scientific research focused solely on SFC is not available. In terms of research that may be useful to consider for the purposes of this chapter and for the purposes of practical application, the rigorous evidence-based coaching studies conducted by researchers at the Coaching Psychology Unit of the University of Sydney (see Table 22.1) will be utilized. It should be noted that these studies utilized a combined approach involving both solution-focused and cognitive-behavioral coaching.

All of the studies in Table 22.1 are randomized controlled trials (between-subject studies). Randomized controlled trials are considered the gold standard of research and are a rigorous means of testing the efficacy of an intervention, particularly when compared to a wait-list control group. All studies have clearly articulated theoretical underpinnings and researched models of change (e.g., hope theory, the transtheoretical model of change, the generic cycle of self-regulation, cognitive behavioral theory).

TABLE 22.1. *Summary Table of Between-Subject SF-CB coaching studies*

Study	Intervention Overview	Key Findings
Green et al. (2006)	RCT Community sample CB-SF coaching Group-based life coaching Wait list control	Statistically significant increases in goal striving, well-being, and hope
Spence and Grant (2007)	RCT Community sample CB-SF coaching Professional coaching Peer coaching Wait list control	Statistically significant increases in goal attainment, goal commitment, and environmental mastery
Green et al. (2007)	RCT Senior student sample CB-SF coaching Individual coaching Wait list control	Statistically significant increases in cognitive hardiness, hope, and mental health
Grant et al. (2009)	RCT Executive sample CB-SF coaching Individual coaching Wait list control	Statistically significant increases in goal attainment, resilience, workplace well-being; reduced depression and stress
Grant et al. (2010)	RCT Teacher sample CB-SF coaching Individual coaching Wait list control	Statistically significant increases in goal striving, workplace well-being, and cognitive hardiness; significant decreases in stress

All studies were manualized or followed a well-articulated evidence-based coaching approach. For example, Grant's initial study (2001) was based on the self-help program "Coach Yourself". This program is underpinned by a cognitive-behavioral, solution-focused framework.

Green, Oades, and Grant's (2006) study was a group-based life coaching program that was also derived from Grant and Green's *Coach Yourself* (2001) program and manualized. Spence and Grant's (2007) study was also manualized and derived from the *Coach Yourself* program. Green, Grant, and Rysaardt's (2007) study, conducted with senior high school students, was based on a training program for teachers who were to be coaches in the study and again was based on the *Coach Yourself* program. In the Grant, Frith, and Burton (2009) study with executives, individual coaching sessions were conducted by coaches with tertiary qualifications in coaching psychology from the Coaching Psychology Unit at the University of Sydney and who also utilized a cognitive-behavioral solution-focused approach. Finally, in the Grant, Green, and Rynsaardt (2010) study, all coaches (coaching psychologists) had completed the masters of applied science (in coaching psychology); adhered to the same theories, models, and techniques; and were supervised during the intervention by a lecturer in the Coaching Psychology Unit.

Outcome measures in these studies included numerous reliable and valid measures including psychological well-being (Ryff, 1989b) and subjective well-being (Satisfaction with Life Scale: Diener et al., 1985; Positive Affect Negative Affect Scale: Watson et al., 1988), hope (Snyder et al., 1991), cognitive hardiness (Nowack, 1990), workplace well-being (Page, 2005), and mental health (Depression Anxiety &

Stress Scale 21: Lovibond & Lovibond, 1995). (Refer to Table 22.1 for the measures utilized in each of these studies and to the original studies for a full description of the outcome measures.)

■ RESULTS OF RESEARCH

The studies outlined in Table 22.1 all utilized an evidence-based coaching approach and, as noted, were not strictly SFC but a combination of solution-focused and cognitive-behavioral approaches. In none of the studies was an attempt made to factor out the impact of the solution-focused techniques compared to the cognitive-behavioral techniques. Each of these studies was based on the evidenced-based coaching model developed by Dr Anthony Grant is his doctoral dissertation on coaching psychology, "Towards a Psychology of Coaching" (2001).

Green, Oades, and Grant's (2006) study was a randomized controlled trial (RCT) based on Grant's initial study. This study involved training participants in the key components of coaching psychology in a 1-day workshop, which was followed by weekly 1-hour meetings where a review of one of the key components was conducted followed by peer coaching to monitor and evaluate goal striving progress. The results of this study were that a CB-SF coaching intervention was found to significantly increase participants' self-reported levels of goal attainment, well-being, and hope from pre- to postintervention. Many of these increases were maintained at the 30-week follow-up (refer to the study for a full description of the results).

Spence and Grant (2007) also utilized an RCT to compare peer group coaching with individual professional coaching (in which participants were coached one-on-one by a coaching psychologist). Both groups were compared to a wait-list control group. The results of this study were that a CB-SF coaching intervention was found to significantly increase participant's self-reported levels of goal commitment, goal attainment, and environmental mastery.

Green, Grant, and Rysaardt (2007) targeted a population of senior high school students. This study was also an individual coaching intervention in which teachers coached students over a period of 10 weeks. Teachers were trained to be coaches in a 1-day "Teacher as Coach" program developed by the researchers. This training was supplemented by regular supervision by the school counsellor (who had completed a masters in applied science, coaching psychology). The results of this study were that a CB-SF coaching intervention was found to have a significant increase on participants' self-reported levels of cognitive hardiness, hope, and mental health.

Grant, Frith, and Burton's (2009) study involved 41 executives in a public health agency. This study was not manualized; however, it was based on a CB-SF approach, with all coaches having tertiary qualifications in coaching psychology. The results of this study show that participants reported self-reported increases in goal attainment, resilience, and workplace well-being, as well as reduced depression and stress.

Finally, Grant, Green, and Rynsaardt (2010) undertook an executive coaching study utilizing teachers. This intervention was again a CB-SF coaching intervention that involved teachers being coached individually by coaching psychologists (all of whom had completed a masters of applied science, coaching psychology). This study did not utilize a manual. However, all coaching psychologists had been rigorously trained in the evidence-based coaching approach taught in the Coaching Psychology Unit at the University of Sydney. The initial results of this study show that participants reported increases in goal striving, workplace well-being, and cognitive hardiness, as well as significant decreases in stress.

Overall, while the research is still in its infancy, these early studies show that SFC has the potential to be a powerful methodology for change. While there is still a long way to go, the research is growing. A rigorous foundation for coaching utilizing solution-focused and other evidence-based approaches will help to validate this nonstigmatized and increasing popular approach to helping people change and improve their lives.

■ PRACTICE GUIDELINES

Based on the limited research conducted so far, the following practice guidelines are suggested:

1. Practitioners of SFC should adhere to the traditional solution-focused approach utilizing techniques and language that can be drawn from selected resources (e.g., O'Hanlon & Beadle's 1996 *Field Guide to Possibility Land*).
2. Similarly to SFT, SFC practitioners are encouraged to adopt a solution-focused and strengths-based mindset: focusing on solutions rather than problem and on strengths rather than weaknesses, and asking more than telling.
3. Practitioners of SFC should utilize the growing body of evidence emerging from positive psychology, particularly concerning strengths-based identification and development.
4. Practitioners of SFC should be encouraged to consider the benefits of embracing cognitive-behavioral theory and techniques as being complementary to their solution-focused approach, as shown by the research provided in this chapter.

■ CURRENT LIMITATIONS AND FUTURE RESEARCH

There are a number of limitations that need to be considered when interpreting the results of the studies reviewed in this chapter. First, the participants in all studies were self-selected members of specific samples (e.g., teachers from one school, members of a specific community), who therefore may not be representative of the general population. Second, the majority of participants were of English background with limited cultural variance. Once again, the generalizability of study results to the population as a whole or to other populations needs to be tested.

As volunteers for research, participants may also have been particularly motivated to achieve their goals. However, one could argue that the majority of coaching clients will be voluntary and motivated, the only exception being mandatory coaching, where clients are required by an external authority to attend (e.g., workplace coaching).

Finally, the studies reviewed in this chapter utilized one approach to solution-focused coaching, namely, solution-focused, cognitive-behavioural coaching; research on other solution-focused coaching approaches is sorely needed. While the research reviewed in this chapter is encouraging, it is clear that much more rigorous research is required to establish SFC's effectiveness. Practitioners should understand that there is no strong evidence base for SFC at this time.

Hopefully, future research will allow for meta-analyses and confirmation of what many practitioners already believe to be true: that SFC is a powerful approach for change or enhancement of life experience.

Further studies could examine a strictly solution-focused intervention versus a cognitive- behavioral intervention. Research is also required to compare the effects of SFC on different populations and for different purposes (i.e., children, adolescents, and adults; personal and career goals).

■ KEY FINDINGS TO REMEMBER

- There is currently limited evidence to support the efficacy of SFC.
- Studies so far suggest that the solution-focused approach is useful to consider in a coaching context.
- Studies so far highlight the benefits of combining a cognitive-behavioral approach with a solution-focused approach.
- Solution-focused language and techniques developed in a therapeutic context are easily adaptable to a coaching context.

■ FURTHER LEARNING

Coach Yourself: Make Real Changes in Your Life by Grant and Greene (2001).
Coaching Psychology Unit, University of Sydney, Australia. The Web site is http://www.psych.usyd.edu.au/coach
Handbook of Coaching Psychology: A Guide for Practitioners, edited by Palmer and Whybrow (2007).
Solution-Focused Coaching:Managing People in a Complex World by Greene and Grant (2003).

■ REFERENCES

Beck, A. T., Rush, A. J., Shaw, B. F., & Emery, G. (1979). *Cognitive therapy of depression*. New York: Guilford Press.
Berg, I. K., & Szabo, P. (2005). *Brief coaching for lasting solutions*. New York: Norton.
Corcoran, J., & Pillai, V. (2007). A review of the research on solution-focused therapy. *British Journal of Social Work, 39*, 234–242.
de Shazer, S. (1988). *Clues: Investigating solutions in brief therapy*. New York: Norton.
Diener, E., Emmons, R. A., Larsen, R. J., & Griffin, S. (1985). The Satisfaction with Life Scale. *Journal of Personality Assessment, 49*, 71–75.
Douglas, C. A., & McCauley, C. D. (1999). Formal developmental relationships: A survey of organisational practices. *Human Resources Development Quarterly, 10*(3), 203–220.
Egan, G. (1998). *The skilled helper* (6th ed.). Pacific Grove, CA: Brooks/Cole.
Emmons, R. A. (1999). *The psychology of ultimate concerns: Motivation and spirituality in personality*. New York: Guilford Press.
Grant, A. M. (2001). *Towards a psychology of coaching: The impact of coaching on metacognition, mental health and goal attainment*. Unpublished manuscript, Macquarie University, NSW, Australia.
Grant, A. M. (2003). The impact of life coaching on goal attainment, metacognition and mental health. *Social Behaviour and Personality, 31*(3), 253–263.
Grant, A. M. (2009). *Workplace, executive and life coaching: An annotated bibliography from the behavioral science and business literature*. Coaching Psychology Unit, University of Sydney, Australia.

Grant, A. M., Frith, L., & Burton, G. (2009). Executive coaching enhances goal attainment, resilience and workplace well-being: A randomised controlled study. *Journal of Positive Psychology*, 4(5), 396–407.

Grant, A. M., & Greene, J. (2001). *Coach Yourself: Make real change in your life*. London: Momentum Press.

Grant, A. M., Green, L., & Rynsaardt, J. (2010). Developmental coaching for high school teachers: Executive coaching goes to school. *Consulting Psychology Journal: Practice and Research*, 62(3), 151–168.

Greene, J., & Grant, A. M. (2003). *Solution-focused coaching: Managing people in a complex world*. London: Momentum Press.

Green, L. S., Grant, A. M., & Rynsaardt, J. (2007). Evidence-based coaching for senior high school students: Building hardiness and hope. *International Coaching Psychology Review*, 2(1), 24–31.

Green, L. S., Oades, L., & Grant, A. M. (2006). Cognitive-behavioral, solution-focused life coaching: Enhancing goal striving, well-being and hope. *Journal of Positive Psychology*, 1(3), 142–149.

Green, L. S., & Spence, G (2008). *Coaching psychology and positive psychology: Perfect partners at work*. Presented at the First Australian Positive Psychology Conference, Sydney.

Hall, D. T., Otazo, K. L., & Hollenbeck, G. P. (1999). Behind closed doors: what really happens in executive coaching. *Organizational Dynamics*, 39–53.

Horvath, A., & Symonds, D. (1991). Relation between the working alliance and outcome in psychotherapy: A meta-analysis. *Journal of Counseling Psychology*, 38, 139–149.

Kauffman, C. (2006). Positive psychology: The science at the heart of coaching. In D. R. Stober & A. M. Grant (Eds.), *Evidence based coaching handbook: Putting best practices to work for your clients* (pp. 219–253). Hoboken, NJ: Wiley.

Keyes, C. L. M. (2002). The mental health continuum: From languishing to flourishing in life. *Journal of Health and Behavior Research*, 43, 207–222.

Linley, P. A., & Harrington, S. (2005). Positive psychology and coaching psychology: Perspectives on integration. *The Coaching Psychologist*, 1(1), 13–14.

Locke, E. A., & Latham, G. P. (1990). *A theory of goal setting and task performance*. Englewood Cliffs, NJ: Prentice-Hall.

Lovibond, S. H., & Lovibond, P. F. (1995). *Manual for the Depression Anxiety Stress Scales*. Sydney: Psychology Foundation of Australia.

Nowack, K. (1990). Initial development of an inventory to assess stress and health risk. *American Journal of Health Promotion*, 4, 173–180.

O'Connell, B. (1998). *Solution-focused therapy*. London: Sage Publications.

O'Connell, B., & Palmer, S. (2007). Solution-focused coaching. In S. Palmer & A. Whybrow (Eds.), *Handbook of coaching psychology: A guide for practitioners* (pp.). London: Sage Publications.

O'Hanlon, B., & Beadle, S. (1996). *A field guide to possibility land.*: BT Press.

Page, K. (2005). *Subjective well-being in the workplace*. Unpublished honours thesis, Deakin University, Melbourne, Australia. Retrieved http://www.deakin.edu.au/research/acqol/instruments/index.htm

Palmer, S., & Whybrow, A. (2007). Coaching psychology: An introduction. In S. Palmer & A. Whybrow (eds.), *Handbook of coaching psychology: A guide for practitioners* (pp.). London: Sage Publications.

Peterson, C., & Seligman, M. E. P. (2004). *Character strengths and virtues: A classification and handbook*. NewYork: Oxford University Press. Washington, DC: American Psychological Association.

Prochaska, J. O., & DiClemente, C. C. (1984). Toward a comprehensive model of change. In J. O. Prochaska & C. C. DiClemente (Eds.), *The transtheoretical approach: Crossing the traditional boundaries of therapy* (pp.). Homewood, IL: Dow-Jones.

Ryff, C. D. (1989). Happiness is everything, or is it? Explorations on the meaning of psychological well-being. *Journal of Personality and Social Psychology, 57,* 1069–1081.

Seligman, M. E. P., & Csikszentmihalyi, M. (2000). Positive psychology: An introduction. *American Psychologist, 55*(1), 5–14.

Sheldon, K., & Elliot, A. J. (1999). Goal striving, need satisfaction, and longitudinal well-being: The self-concordance model. *Journal of Personality and Social Psychology, 76,* 482–497.

Snyder, C. R., Harris, C., Anderson, J. R., Holleran, S. A., Irving, L. M., Sigmon, S. T., Yoshinobu, L., Gibb, J., Langelle, C., & Harney, P. (1991). The will and the ways: Development and validation of an individual differences measure of hope. *Journal of Personality and Social Psychology, 60,* 570–585.

Spence, G. B., & Grant, A. M. (2007). Professional and peer life coaching and the enhancement of goal striving and well-being: An exploratory study. *Journal of Positive Psychology, 2*(3), 185–194.

Watson, D., Clark, L. A., & Tellegen, A. (1988). Development and validation of brief measures of positive and negative affect: The PANAS scales. *Journal of Personality and Social Psychology, 54,* 1063–1070.

Whitmore, J. (1999). *Coaching for performance.* (2nd ed., pp. 48–51). London: Nicholas Brealey.

Williams, P. (2000). *Personal coaching's evolution from therapy.* Retrieved September 11, 2009, from http://www.consultingtoday.com.

Williams, P., & Davis, D. C. (2002). *Therapist as life coach: Transforming your practice.* New York: Norton.

Zimmerman, B. J. (1989). A social cognitive view of self-regulated academic learning. *Journal of Educational Psychology, 81*(3), 329–339.

23 Making Classrooms More Solution-Focused for Teachers and Students

The WOWW Teacher Coaching Intervention

■ MICHAEL S. KELLY, MICHELE LISCIO,

ROBIN BLUESTONE-MILLER, AND LEE SHILTS

■ INTRODUCTION

The WOWW (Working on What Works) program strives to empower teachers in regular and special education settings to recognize their own strengths as well as their students' strengths in setting goals and to work together in a collaborative manner. It was first developed by solution-focused brief therapy (SFBT) pioneers Insoo Kim Berg and Lee Shilts in Florida in 2002. After starting in Florida, the program was pilot tested in other states, including several schools the chapter authors have worked with in Chicago. The authors have also partnered with Metropolitan Family Services of Chicago as we worked in some Chicago Public Schools (CPS) Community in Schools Programs. In this chapter, we will share some of these preliminary findings on WOWW's success in helping students and teachers, as well as identifying challenges in implementing WOWW successfully in schools that may not yet be solution-focused settings for teachers and students. Specifically, we are interested in discussing here how WOWW can begin to address three crucial areas in today's schools: (a) increasing the classroom management skills of teachers to produce (b) less burnout and higher teacher retention in challenging schools and ultimately (c) better academic and social/emotional/behavioral outcomes for students.

■ WHAT WE HAVE LEARNED SO FAR

In his best-selling book *The Tipping Point: How Little Things Can Make a Big Difference*, Gladwell (2002) discusses the many factors that eventually cause something to change and "tip" into something altogether new and exciting. While most of his examples addressed trends in marketing, business, and organizational development, his book does ask questions about how "little changes" in educational settings like today's K-12 schools can become their own tipping points. And while his work doesn't specifically address SFBT ideas (one wishes that he had interviewed some SFBT thinkers for the book), his subtitle comes straight from one of the central tenets of SFBT: that observing and encouraging small changes in our clients can eventually produce larger changes (Kelly et al., 2008). This chapter will describe the SFBT classroom intervention WOWW, which seeks to inspire a series of tipping points in classrooms to prevent teacher burnout and improve specific educational and behavioral outcomes for the students in the classroom. There is no doubt that one of the most promising areas of SFBT intervention research is school settings. See Chapters 16, 17, and 24 for other examples of SFBT interventions that are used in schools.

Some of the most exciting areas currently being debated in K-12 education policy and research today involve the question "What factors can form the tipping point in creating effective and positive educational settings?" This overarching question can be made even more specific when we ask, "What makes a school tip from failing to becoming successful?," "What makes a classroom learning environment tip from negative to positive,?" and "What makes a teacher tip from deciding to leave the profession to deciding to stay?" While the pilot data on implementation of WOWW in schools in Florida and Chicago only allow for tentative conclusions, the empirical and anecdotal evidence gleaned from our pilot studies indicates that WOWW may prove to be a SFBT-based education intervention that might begin to facilitate more positive tipping points in the nation's K-12 classrooms.

According to Kathleen Cotton (1990), "During most of its twenty-two year existence, the Annual Gallup Poll of the Public's Attitudes Toward the Public Schools has identified 'lack of discipline' as the most serious problem facing the nation's educational system" (p. 1). For this reason, students and teachers may lose valuable learning time while the teacher attempts to handle discipline problems.

An investigation of the current literature on our educational system has revealed similar views. It is still believed that improving teacher–student relationships and reducing discipline issues are primary in establishing a productive learning environment. In the Gallup poll of September 2006, these themes continue to resonate. Rose and Gallup (2006) report the followings findings:

- Discipline is one of the top problems in public schools.
- Seventy-three percent of Americans blame societal factors for school problems.
- The top three reasons teachers leave within 5 years are lack of support, poor working conditions, and lack of respect.
- Seventy-one percent of Americans believe in the need to reform the public school system.

Researchers believe that school reform or restructuring continues to fail because the basic principals of human relationships are overlooked. Improving the relationships between teachers and students might be the start of school reform and/or restructuring that our society has sought for the last 100 years. As Russell L. Ackoff and Sheldon Rovin (2003) point out in their book *Redesigning Society*, the education system needs to take a systemic view of dealing with the issues in schools today. They also share their thoughts on the ingredients of learning, which are "(1) a desire to learn and (2) caring and skilled facilitators of learning who recognize that the learners' interests should come before their own, that conformity and creativity are not the same thing, and that creativity is the greater of these—and that without fun and inspiration learning is an unpleasant chore" (p. 109).

Teachers are integral parts of the school culture that we seek to serve, and in our own school social work practice, we often serve them in collaborative and consultative relationships. We do this in part because we see teachers as some of our most vulnerable clients; so many of them are trying to do an extremely difficult job under very challenging conditions (Glasser, 1992). Teachers enter schools excited to give their students a love of learning and with the belief that students want to learn. Again and again, beginning teachers report a "love of children" and a passion for teaching as part of their reason for choosing to teach (Roehrig et al., 2002). Yet research also shows that 50% of those same excited, idealistic teachers will leave the profession within 5 years (NEA, 2007) According to survey research, teachers who leave report that classroom management and school organizational factors (e.g., relationship factors) are more important reasons than low pay (NEA, 2007).

As in any multifaceted and complicated profession, there is no one way that teachers become burned out and decide to leave (indeed, some of the 50% who leave do so for family or personal reasons, and don't cite burnout and stress as factors). Still, when a profession as important as teaching continues to have such great turnover, it seems fair to hypothesize that at least part of the reason is the lack of helpful tools that will allow teachers to better manage their classrooms and create more positive and engaged relationships with their students. These problems are especially acute in schools in low-income rural and urban areas, where researchers and policymakers have long documented a severe shortage of highly qualified teachers who can be recruited and retained in these potentially challenging educational environments (NEA, 2007).

Growing evidence suggests that the classroom environment impacts social, behavioral, and academic outcomes, even after family, individual, and school characteristics are accounted for (e.g., Barth et al., 2004; Beaver et al., 2008; Hoglund & Leadbeater, 2004; Kellam et al., 1998; Wang et al.,1990). Prosocial behavior and limited victimization in the classroom can have a positive impact even on children with previously maladaptive behavior (Vitaro et al., 1999). Classrooms that promote positive behaviors and supportive relationships encourage social competence among students (Brody et al., 2002; Criss et al., 2002; Hoglund & Leadbeater, 2004). Additionally, evidence of fewer aggressive behaviors (Kellam et al., 1998), improved self-control (Beaver et al., 2008), better peer relationships, and heightened academic focus have been noted (Barth et al., 2004). Creating a positive classroom environment plays an important role in influencing behavior and learning and in meeting the multiple challenges of today's classroom.

Teacher–student relationships also have a direct impact on student learning. The qualities of these relationships influence school adjustment and student behavior (Baker et al., 2008; Hamre & Pianta, 2001) Students whose teachers are responsive and are able to spend more time on academic activities have more successful academic outcomes (McDonald Connor et al., 2005). Conversely, teacher–student conflict in the classroom increases problem behaviors and teacher stress (Mantzicopoulos, 2005). Additionally, teacher support has been linked to achieving educational goals (Wilson & Wilson, 1992; for a review, see Lynn et al., 2003). Taken as a whole, this research suggests a strong association between teacher–student relationships and academic, social, and behavioral outcomes.

■ SFBT INTERVENTIONS

The SFBT philosophy that underlies WOWW includes a list of assumptions about teachers, children, and parents (Berg & Shilts 2005a). We assume that teachers want to have a positive influence on students and feel like good teachers. Also, as practitioners, our mission is to support teachers as much as we support students and parents. The research discussed in the next section indicates that enhancing and improving the teacher–student relationship may be the most powerful thing we can do.

As mentioned earlier, WOWW is an extension of the SFBT model aimed at improving student–teacher relationships and classroom behaviors. Our theory of change will provide guidance on how this intervention may be able to achieve these outcomes and what factors will promote them.

The WOWW intervention was developed as a collaborative project between SFBT creator Insoo Berg Kim, SFBT expert Lee Shilts, and doctoral student Michele Liscio, as well as classroom teachers in one school district in Fort Lauderdale, Florida. It has been pilot tested in Florida and for 3 years (2006–2008) in CPS. The WOWW program is a coaching and consultation intervention involving the collaboration of mental health professionals and classroom teachers. The mental health professional, who is trained in solution-focused principles, operates primarily in a consultative role with the teacher and his or her her class and is referred to as the *WOWW coach*. When the program is implemented at scale, the WOWW coach would ideally be the school social worker; however, for one of our research study (in Florida), outside professionals were used.

The WOWW coach is responsible for observing the classroom, facilitating group discussions, and offering coaching to the teacher. The coach does not lead the group the way a group treatment approach would function; that is; he or she she does not deliver a specific therapeutic intervention in a specific sequence. Right away, in WOWW, the basic tenets of SFBT are revealed in contrast to other approaches, as the clients (in this case, the teacher and his or her students) are put in charge of setting the goals for the WOWW class discussions and for changes to the learning environment. Box 23.1 describes how the WOWW coach uses debriefing times with the teacher to amplify the teacher's strengths. Using SFBT techniques including, observation, compliments, exceptions, and coping questions, the coach leads the students and teachers to reenvision the class in a more positive way. The WOWW coach, who sometimes functions in the school as a social worker, must wear a different hat when working in the WOWW classroom. In this role, he or she does not intervene in changing student behaviors or try to coax individual students to do better. Details of the phases and steps of the WOWW program are provided in Box 23.2.

■ RESEARCH METHODS: TRANSFORMATION THROUGH WOWW

As described above, the WOWW intervention provides teachers with the training and skills to manage their classrooms differently. Testing this intervention is predicated on a theory of change: the theory that providing teachers with tools for coping with students' behavioral and emotional difficulties, improving teacher–student relationships, and positively changing the classroom environment are pivotal to enhancing student outcomes, particularly given the complex makeup of today's classrooms. As part of school reform, we must address barriers to learning, and engaging teachers is part of this process (Adelman & Taylor, 2000). Teachers note students' distractibility, aggression, excessive demands for their attention, and disruption as some of the major challenges in today's classrooms (Stephenson et al., 2000). These difficulties are

BOX 23.1 ■ Focusing on the Teacher's Strengths: WOWW Debriefing Sessions

Teacher debriefing times are another crucial component of the WOWW program. In these confidential sessions, the teacher is given the same opportunities as the students to reflect on the classroom and to identify his or her own capacities and strengths. Here is an example of a WOWW coach debriefing from a third-grade class.

School Social Worker: Thanks for meeting with me today. How's the day been?

Mrs. Smith: Really good; the kids have been great. It's one of those days where you keep wondering when the other shoe's going to drop when they get back from lunch. It's almost too perfect . . .

SSW: Those kinds of days are amazing but also a little nerve-wracking. Have you noticed anything you were doing differently this morning to help the kids be so well behaved?

MS: No, I can't think . . . well, I did wind up singing to them this morning.

SSW: Wait, you . . . sang?

MS: Yeah, today the principal made an announcement about the class song contest for the spirit day, and I was telling the class about my favorite song, "Dancing Queen," by Abba. The kids said they had never heard of it, and I told them that they needed to hear it before they got to fourth grade. Billy dared me to sing it, so I did. The kids just fell out laughing, and then they gave me a standing ovation.

SSW: You just sang, just like that?

MS: I did; I've never done that before. I mean, I like to sing with my family and at church, but I don't think the kids ever heard me sing before.

SSW: Awesome. What makes you think that might have affected their behavior today?

MS: I'm not sure, maybe because the kids were having fun and it was only 8:15 in the morning! Or maybe they were able to see that I was in a good mood and that they could relax with me today.

SSW: What do you mean by "relaxing with you"? Are there times when you're more relaxed that you notice you get a different response from the kids?

MS: Totally. The kids totally take their cue from me; if I'm loose and having fun, we all do better together.

One of the major goals of WOWW coaching is to end the tendency of classrooms with a few difficult students to lose cohesion and a sense of mutual purpose by bringing the conversation back to what the whole class sees as things they value in their classroom and the other things they want to change. Additionally, an effort is made to point out the strengths of the more challenging students, as well as to validate the students who are already following the teacher's rules and working well with others. In addition to the importance placed on getting students to mobilize around their inherent strengths, ample attention is paid in the WOWW intervention to what the teacher hopes to change about his or her classroom. In the spirit of collaboration, there are whole-class discussions as well as debriefings at another time between the WOWW coach and the teacher. Unlike other classroom management models that try to use gimmicks or external rewards, the WOWW coaching intervention focuses on teachers and students discovering the small gains they are making and then "doing more of what's working" to turn those successes into larger gains for the whole classroom environment.

BOX 23.2 ■ WOWW Program Phases and Steps

Phase 1: Compliments Phase

Weeks 1–3: Sessions consist of about 40 minutes of observation and 15 minutes of feedback.
Timing depends on each school's schedules.

1. Introduce yourself to students, saying, "I'm going to be visiting your room to watch for all the things the class does that are good and helpful. I will report back to you what I see that's going well."
2. Note class strengths by giving group and individual compliments to students and teachers.
3. Meet with the teacher in a confidential debriefing session to discuss observations and create classroom goals.

Phase 2: Scaling Phase (Building the rubric for self-assessment)

Weeks 4–6: Observe for about 40 minutes. Allow 15 minutes for feedback and discussion.

1. Continue giving positive feedback.
2. Define in behavioral terms, such as "Best Class in _____School. (Rubric)
3. Decide on the scaling method (e.g., 1–10, 1–5, smiling faces).
4. Discuss the "best" classroom and ask, "What would a 10 look like?," "What would a 5 look like?," and so on.
5. Help the students and teacher understand the scaling method and practice scaling at each meeting. Draw a consensus from the teacher and class and record the results every week.
6. Keep noticing students who are exhibiting the positive behaviors that make this the best class.
7. Make prediction for the next meeting. Discuss what behaviors are needed to improve on the scale to move toward the "best class" score.
8. Continue debriefing sessions with teachers as needed.

Phase 3: Goal Setting

Define the concepts in goals (i.e., what does paying attention look like, how does your teacher know you are listening, what will you be doing when you are being respectful, and so on. Michele Liscio found that often it meant just a difference in expectations; for example, one teacher may require no talking, whereas another may say that whispering is fine.
Continuing the same routine as for the above WOWW sessions
Week 7–end

1. Decide with the teacher and class which of the behaviors on the rubric need to improve.
2. Choose only one or two manageable goals to start, and then see if the class has additional goals to work on and how motivated they appear to be in working together on them.
3. Encourage the teacher to use scaling at least once per day and post a chart in class.

(continued)

BOX 23.2 ■ (continued)

4. The WOWW coach continues to give positive feedback, noticing strengths, amplifying changes, and applying compliments toward the identified goals.
5. New goals can be added when other goals are accomplished or something needs to be changed; constant attention is paid to finding ways to involve the students directly in deciding what still needs to be changed. (SFBT basic tenet: Do something different if it is not working!)
6. Continue debriefing sessions with teachers as needed.

Source: Adapted from Berg, I., & Shilts, L. (2004). *Classroom Solutions: WOWW Approach*. Milwaukee: BFTC Press.

---

coupled with problems related to discipline, violence, and a changing classroom context that includes more demands for teachers and a wider range of student problems (Hennessy & Green-Hennessy, 2000; Rose & Gallup, 2007). Additional challenges of low-performing schools, higher testing standards, and increases in students' needs require teachers to meet multiple social, behavioral, and academic demands. An ecological-mediational model of student outcomes suggests that teacher factors including classroom organization, practice strategies, support for students, and stress level have a direct impact on students' mental health, behavior, educational engagement, and academic performance (Lynn et al., 2003). Given these challenges and the potential for teacher impact, new strategies are needed to help teachers deal with these demands, improve the classroom environment, and create better teacher–student relationships. What follows are summaries of two pilot studies we have conducted on WOWW, as well as some of the implications of these studies for future WOWW study and practice.

■ METHOD FOR THE FLORIDA WOWW STUDY

Participants

The records of 12 classroom teachers from the 2004–2005 school year were collected and analyzed. The data included 105 students in the WOWW intervention group that were collected from six classrooms; 101 students were used as the comparison group, again collected from six classrooms. The total sample size for the pilot study was 12 classroom teachers and 206 students. The teachers selected for this study were from New River Middle School (NRMS) who had volunteered as participants. Classroom teachers who did not receive the treatment were selected randomly. The demographic designations of the study were gender (male/female), ethnicity (Black, White, Hispanic, other), grade level (6, 7, and 8), and age of participants.

Teacher Training

Training was made available to teachers who wanted to volunteer their classes to participate in this study. At the start of the school year, these teachers received an introduction to and brief training in the program. The coaches were introduced at this time, and met briefly with the teachers to explain their role in the classroom and to schedule a date and a time to begin implementing WOWW. During the course of the year, several consultations were offered to teachers to update and inform them of the program's status. Throughout the program, the teachers were encouraged to e-mail coaches regarding any issues that arose on the days when coaches were not in their classroom.

Measures and Administration

With permission and assistance from the personnel at NRMS, I (Michele Liscio) accessed and researched the records of the 2004–2005 academic year. The records were retrieved from the Broward County School Board database. As the principal investigator, with assistance from school personnel, I collected the students' data without identifiers. The dependent variables for students in classes who had the treatment (WOWW) were compared and contrasted to those of students in classes that did not participate in the treatment.

The data were collected for the entire 2004–2005 school term, as well as for the length of the WOWW intervention. To determine statistical significance, we hoped to reduce the number of student absences, reduce the amount of student tardiness, decrease suspensions, and increase the standardized test score on the Florida Comprehensive Acheivement Test (FCAT) for the 2003–2004 school term.

Intervention

As stated earlier, the WOWW approach utilized three main practices of SFBT: client compliments, goal setting, and scaling. Prior to the coach's visits to the classrooms, teachers participated in training and consultations. Once rapport was established, a coach was assigned to multiple classrooms and was scheduled to observe in each class, for one class period (approximately 50 minutes), once per week. The only time needed for teachers and students to participate in WOWW was a few minutes at the beginning of the class to introduce the coach and a few minutes at the end of the class for the coach to read his or her observations of the class in the form of compliments. After the first week, the time taken at the beginning of the class was not necessary and was eliminated. Coaches were greeted as part of the class and took a seat to observe the class period. We continued to observe and compliment at the end of a class period, and once this was accepted, the teacher and students were asked to begin thinking about goals they would like to implement in their class. After approximately 3 to 5 weeks of classroom observation, the teacher and students were ready to negotiate and specify their goals.

A very important aspect of goal setting was to define the meaning of words such as *respect*, *participation*, and *quiet*. When observing, coaches needed to know exactly what they were looking for when taking notes. This process defined observable behavior and established clear expectations for goals established by the class. It also helped the coaches to compliment when they observed the achievement of a goal.

Our shift in language from classroom rules to classroom goals was significant and purposeful. It conveyed the idea that goals can be negotiated and attained, while rules are set and followed. The idea of influence may be partly embedded in language, as

SFBT co-creator Steve de Shazer emphasized in his ongoing discussions of how language creates expectations that can directly influence client reality (Braus et al., 2003).

Once the goals were negotiated and memorialized on poster board, they were placed in a prominent area of the classroom. A success scale was also produced on poster board and hung in the classroom. This chart helped to track the teacher's and students' daily scaling of their performance for each class period.

Data Analysis

Descriptive and graphical techniques were used to review data. To account for the variation among students and classes, nested Generalized Estimating Equations (GEEs) were used. These are methods of parameter estimation for correlated data. When data on repeated observations are collected on the same units across successive points in time, these repeated data are correlated over time. If this correlation is not taken into account, then the standard errors of the parameter estimates will not be valid and hypothesis-testing results will be nonreplicable.

In this pilot study entitled, "Effectiveness of Classroom Solutions: WOWW Approach in a Middle School Setting". The demographics and moderator variables were:

1. Individuals in groups with and without the WOWW program
2. Gender designation of groups on two levels: male/female
3. Ethnicity designation of groups on three levels: Black, Hispanic, other
4. Grade for groups on three levels: sixth, seventh, and eighth grades
5. Age of group participants—continuous

The outcome measures were:

1. To increase students' grades for the 2004–2005 calendar year
2. To reduce the number of excused absences from school
3. To reduce the number of unexcused absences from school
4. To reduce the amount of student tardiness
5. To decrease the number of in-school suspensions
6. To decrease the number of out-of-school suspensions
7. To increase students' FCAT performance from the 2004 to 2005 school year

■ RESULTS

The demographics in this study were as follows: 50% of the students were male, the average age was 13, and the majority of students were black. One hundred five students were given the treatment (WOWW), while 101 students did not receive it. Table 23.1 shows the results for the research questions of the study.

This pilot study shows that the WOWW program and its use of SFBT techniques were effective in several of the research areas. It also supports other studies indicating that SFBT is effective when applied to a school setting (Franklin et. al., 2001; Kelly et al., 2008; LaFountain & Gardner, 1996; Litrell, 1995). The study also demonstrates positive implications for the improvement of student performance by improving the teacher–student relationship and creating a positive, collaborative classroom environment. Classes in the experimental group showed significant fewer excused absences and tardiness compared to those in the comparison group. The study failed to show

TABLE 23.1. *Results from the Florida WOWW Pilot Study*

Research Questions	Intervention Group (WOWW): Sixth–Eighth Graders, $N = 105$	No Intervention Group: Sixth–Eighth Graders, $N = 100$
Increase grades*	NS	NS
Reduce excused absences	**	
Reduce unexcused absences	**	
Reduce tardies	**	
Decrease in-school suspensions*	NS	NS
Decrease out-of-school suspensions*	NS	NS
Increase achievement on standardized tests	NS	NS

*Though not statistically significant, intervention group results trended toward the goals of intervention.
**$p < .01$.
NS = nonsignificant differences between groups.

statistically significant differences between the experimental and comparison groups on grades, suspensions, or FCAT performance. However, though statistically significant group differences in these areas were not found, emerging trends were noted. Grades in the experimental group were higher than those in the comparison group. In-school and out-of-school suspensions were lower in the experimental group than in the comparison group.

Additional analysis revealed gender, age, and ethnic differences across certain measures. For example, Black and Hispanic students were more likely to have unexcused absences, males were more likely to be suspended (out of school or in school), and students in the upper grades were more likely to be tardy (especially males) or have an unexcused absence. The results indicate that further study is needed to determine whether the WOWW program may be better equipped to intervene with the aforementioned high-risk student groups and improve learning in the classroom.

Limitations

Several aspects of the convenience sample were a limitation in this pilot study. With pressure to add to current research on the effects of SFBT in school settings, it was decided to evaluate the WOWW program in only its second full year of implementation. For this reason, coaches implemented WOWW in only six classrooms at the start of the 2004–2005 school term. This contributed to the small sample size of this pilot study. Another limitation of the sample was controlled for before the statistical analysis was run; however, it warrants mention. Initially, there was an unequal distribution of ethnicities, and the data were recoded.

Another limitation of this study involved the collection process and the reliability of the data retrieved from the NRMS database. In both the experimental and comparison groups, there were students whose records had missing and/or unreported data. These students had to be removed from the study, which lowered our sample size. Also, although gathering outcome data on students in the school's database is standard practice in this school district, the researcher was probably unable to substantiate the validity or reliability of the data.

Lastly, all teachers involved in this pilot study volunteered their classes' participation. Teachers who show more interest in new approaches to classroom management may already be invested in making positive changes. Therefore, teachers with more interest in new approaches could be responsible for better results.

■ THE CHICAGO PILOT STUDY

Preliminary Data from the Pilot study of WOWW in Chicago

From 2006 to 2008, our Loyola Family and Schools Partnership Program (FSPP) brought WOWW to eight K-8 public elementary schools in Chicago. The pilot study described here was conducted with 27 teachers who agreed to participate voluntarily.

A pretest-posttest design was used, and a brief scale designed by the researchers was completed by the participating teachers. Items were scaled from 1 to 5, and assessed how teachers perceived their own classroom management skills and how WOWW had impacted their students' behavior. Repeated-measure t-tests revealed that WOWW produced statistically significant outcomes, indicating its effectiveness in improving the classroom climate. The findings are as follows:

- The WOWW program increased teachers' perception of their class as better behaved, $t(26) = 2.6$, $p < .01$, one-tailed.
- The WOWW program increased teachers' perception of themselves as effective classroom managers, $t(26) = 1.9$, $p < .05$, one-tailed.
- The WOWW program increased teachers' view of students as better behaved, as well as their sense that students would also report better behavior, $t(26) = 3.22$, $p < .05$ and $t(26) = 2.8$, $p < .05$, one-tailed.

These pilot data ($N = 27$) show the promise of WOWW as an effective classroom management and staff development program (Kelly & Bluestone-Miller, 2009; Kelly et al., 2008). We have also partnered with Metropolitan Family Services while doing a quasi-experimental study with WOWW at Marsh Elementary school. We found that seventh grade classes receiving WOWW significantly reduced detentions and suspensions compared to control classrooms (Kelly & Ridings, 2008).

■ PRACTICE GUIDELINES

1. Work only with teachers who voluntarily participate in the program. I (Robin Bluestone-Miller) worked with two classes that were selected by the principal. The teachers didn't see any need for help. They allowed me to come into the classes and talk to the students about their behaviors and scaling, but they never used any scaling when I wasn't in the classroom. Box 23.3 describes our work with a class that had been described as one of the "baddest" in the school.
2. Don't forget to compliment the teacher or the teacher's aides in front of the class. It helps the students see their teachers in a positive light and helps the teacher feel the afterglow of a compliment.
3. When using scaling, whether it is 1–5 or 1–10 or smiling faces, help the class and the teacher understand that the best score does not have to be 100% perfect. Otherwise, scaling leads to frustration and a feeling of never being able to be good enough. No one is perfect, so help set the expectation that one or two students might not reach the goal of 100%.
4. During the scaling process, some teachers start using scaling language in communicating with their class. In one class that used a stoplight system

(green, yellow, red), the teacher would tell the class that they were having a "Yellow Day," and they would know what that meant and what they needed to do to improve to a "Green Day." In another class that used a 1–5 scale, the teacher would hold up her fingers to signal where students were on the scale as they were walking down the hallway. Since their goal was to be quiet in the hall, walk single file, and keep their hands to themselves, she could look at them and and hold up a few fingers. By holding up three fingers, she was able to communicate with her class without saying a word.

5. It is not always necessary to see the class in the same room or with the same teacher. Sometimes it is beneficial to see them in a different environment, like the lunchroom or the physical education class. This also helps younger children generalize the scaling to other places besides their homerooms.

6. Teaching the "special teachers" how to scale is also helpful. For example, teaching the lunchroom aides or monitors how to scale could become a whole-school intervention. Each table could be scaled separately and given privileges or allowed to leave first by having a high number on the scale.

7. Set up the expectation that there will be some dropoff in scaling from time to time. This can be disappointing to the teacher and staff, but it is normal. Everyone has a bad day.

8. In a special education class, the WOWW coach took pictures of the students when they were using the chosen goals and posted them in the room. Other coaches had the students role-play the behaviors of the "best class" in their school.

9. Our WOWW training with the CPS social workers has taken on a life of its own. The group members have become very supportive of each other. The enthusiasm of those doing the training has spread like wildfire. It seems to help them stay excited about the work they are doing and may even prevent some burn out.

■ FUTURE STUDIES

With both of the studies summarized in this chapter, the small sample size and lack of a randomized comparison classroom group, as well as lack of information on the benefits of the WOWW program for other classroom performance variables (e.g., test scores, attendance), precludes the conclusion at this point that WOWW can have a significant impact on the many school performance variables that other classroom management techniques have claimed to address (Marzano, 2003).

Nevertheless, WOWW has an intuitive appeal to school social workers trying to find positive and nonthreatening ways to help teachers and students function better together in the classroom. It is a promising new idea that involves using the ingredients of SFBT to make a meaningful impact on classroom behavior, teacher resilience, and student achievement. It also fulfills many of Illinois' Social Emotional Learning Standards in the classroom without the need to learn an entirely new curriculum. It is far too early to say whether WOWW can positively impact such important variables in schools, though we hope, in the years to come, to bring the WOWW program to more classrooms in Chicago and its suburbs. We hope to study the program in those settings with a larger sample size and classrooms acting as comparison groups. In the meantime, we are training a number of social workers and counselors so that they can work more consistently with the teachers beyond the scope of this research program.

BOX 23.3 ■ The "BADDEST Class in the School"

One of our chapter authors (Robin Bluestone-Miller, referred to here as the *WOWW coach*) was invited to work with two fifth-grade classes that had originally been one class that was split into two due to the many behavior problems. The teachers were very appreciative of the help and wanted pointers on classroom management and control.

When the WOWW coach first started working with one of the classes, they responded very well to compliments. They were an active class that needed to move around, but they were fun and engaging when she was in the classroom. The coach enjoyed working with this class. The teacher seemed burned out.

When the WOWW coach entered this class for the third session, there was a substitute teacher in the classroom, along with two security guards. Some of the kids were running around the room, not doing their work, and talking very loudly; one student put glue all over the chairs to prank other students. This student was removed from the class just before the WOWW coach entered. She did not intervene, but walked around the class making notes.

As she was watching, more of the students settled down and began doing their work. The WOWW coach began giving compliments to the students who were working and ignoring the distractions around them. She told them that she saw some students doing good work by themselves and in small groups. The substitute teacher interrupted the coach and said that this was a horrible class and wondered how anyone could say anything good about them. The WOWW coach answered that she disagreed.

When the WOWW coach came back to this class for the fourth session, the regular teacher had returned. Later, she told the coach that because of this class, she had decided to quit teaching after this year. She said that she would complete the year, however, because she needed the health insurance. When the WOWW coach asked the class how the rest of their week had gone, they said that they were yelled at by their teacher, their principal, and their assistant principal. They also said that they didn't like the substitute teacher, who made some of them very angry. They said that they were purposely acting out because they didn't like her. The WOWW coach continued to look for ways to compliment them when she was in the classroom.

During session 5, the teacher said that the class had improved and that they were especially good on Thursday, the day the WOWW coach came to do the WOWW program. She asked the students how they were able to be so well behaved on Thursdays. The WOWW coach told them that she couldn't believe that other teachers were saying so many bad things about them. They answered that they liked getting the coach's compliments. They said that all of the teachers in their school saw them as a "bad class." They didn't like having this bad reputation. The WOWW coach asked what they wanted to do about it. One student suggested trying to accumulate compliments and keep track of them by hanging a paper clip on the board at the front of the room for every compliment they were given by anyone in the school.

The teacher and students were excited by this idea of tracking compliments. They had previously told the coach that they did not like the music class that they went to after their WOWW meetings. They said that the music teacher was very negative.

BOX 23.3 ■ (continued)

She asked them what they thought they could do to get a compliment from her. They said they needed to bring in their music books and a pencil and read their books during music class. The WOWW coach responded that this seemed to be an easy task; did they think they could do it? Yes, they wanted to try and would report back to the coach the following week.

When the WOWW coach returned to the class for session 7, the entire class and the teacher were all smiles. They had received a compliment from the music teacher. One of the students said that the teacher was nicer to them and "not in your face."

The class continued to keep track of their compliments with the paper clips and accumulated 18 compliments during the next 2 weeks. They were very proud of themselves. They reported that the principal had complimented them on their behavior in the halls and that their physical education teacher said they were one of his best classes. The homeroom teacher reported that they were between a 7 and an 8 on a 10-point scale during the week.

By the end of the 10-week session, the class was doing much better. They weren't perfect and didn't always get 7's and 8's, but their improvement was good. The teacher felt very positive about the WOWW program and about how much it helped her complete the school year. She wrote a thank-you note to the coach that said, "You are definitely needed to bring light back into learning." She did decide to leave the field of education, however.

These studies, along with other research on SFBT applied in school settings, have promising implications for improved teacher–student relationships and enhanced student outcomes. Additional research should be conducted on the WOWW program using SFBT at NRMS to substantiate and further explore this pilot study's results. In addition, other schools that have adopted WOWW, both in the United States and in other countries, should conduct a study on student outcomes after successful implementation of the program. Any subsequent research study should include a larger sample size with a larger number of classes in both the experimental and comparison groups. The sample size should be at least double that of this pilot study's population to increase the possibility of achieving statistically significant outcomes in each of the research areas. Also, it is suggested that qualitative interviews and/or pretests and posttests be conducted in the next study. Lastly, WOWW is a practical program that school social workers, guidance counselors, family therapists, and others could use to promote this research and practice in their school. In doing so, it is hoped that the voices of the teachers, students, and staff participating in the program will provide additional support for the quantitative data. It is also hoped that further research on WOWW and SFBT will continue to transform the model into a more evidence-based practice. This may cause solution-focused programs to be accepted and widely used within school settings. A true experimental design is also suggested for future research.

The results of our pilot studies provide support for the effectiveness of the WOWW approach in school settings. They call attention to the possible benefits of having WOWW coaches and/or training school personnel to become coaches. In doing so,

WOWW may help facilitate a more collaborative school environment with improved student outcomes. During these studies, coaches noted a quick shift in teacher–student relationships shortly after WOWW was implemented in a classroom (i.e., after three to five visits). These studies support the coaches' observation of a shift and show that in some areas it has affected student outcomes significantly. Teachers are looking for successful classroom management tools that are not time-consuming, and school districts are looking for programs that are cost effective. The WOWW program and its SFBT techniques can provide tools that are both inexpensive and easy to use.

■ KEY FINDINGS TO REMEMBER

- The WOWW program is designed to help teachers become better classroom managers, not to transform them into therapists or school-based clinicians.
- The WOWW coach uses compliments and scaling questions to help students and teachers set their own classroom goals.
- When WOWW works, it has been shown to reduce students' unexcused absences and tardiness and to improve teachers' view of themselves as effective classroom managers.

■ FURTHER LEARNING

- http://www.solutionsdoc.co.uk/sft.html (a nice Web site that collects all the recent empirical work on SFBT effectiveness)
- http://www.luc.edu/socialwork/fspp_caps_091.shtml (the Web site of Loyola's Family and School Partnership Program, where trainees can get additional training in the WOWW approach through consultation groups and on-site workshops)
- http://www.oxfordscholarship.com/oso/public/content/socialwork/9780195366297/toc.html (the official Oxford Scholarship Online Web site for our book on SFBT in schools, including additional information about the WOWW approach and other ways to implement SFBT interventions in schools)

■ ACKNOWLEDGMENTS

The authors wish to thank Patrick C. Hardigan, PhD, Executive Director for Health Professions Research and Educational Assessment, Nova Southeastern University, for his work on an earlier draft of an article that was incorporated into this chapter.

■ REFERENCES

Ackoff, R. L., & Rovin, S. (2003). *Redesigning society*. Stanford, CA: Stanford University Press.

Adelman, H., & Taylor, L. (2000). Shaping the future of mental health in schools. *Psychology in the schools*, 37(1), 49–60.

Baker, J., Grant, S., & Morlock, L. (2008). The teacher-student relationship as a developmental context for children with internalizing or externalizing behavior problems. *School psychology quarterly*, 23(1), 3–15.

Barth, J., Dunlap, S. T., Dane, H., Lochman, J. E., & Wells, K. C. (2004). Classroom environment influences on aggression, peer relations, and academic focus. *Journal of School Psychology*, 42(2), 115–133.

Beaver, K., Wright, J. P., & Maume, M. O. (2008). The effect of school classroom characteristics on low self-control: A multilevel analysis. *Journal of Criminal Justice*, 36(2), 174–181.

Berg, I. K., & Shilts, L. (2005a). *Classroom solutions: WOWW coaching*. Milwaukee: BFTC Press.

Berg, I. K., & Shilts, L. (2005b). Keeping the solutions within the classroom: WOWW approach. *School Counselor*, July/August, 30–35.

Braus, S., Cole, J., & Berg, I. K. (2003). *Supervision and mentoring in child welfare services: Guidelines and strategies*. New York: Norton.

Brody, G. H., Dorsey, S., Forehand, R., & Armistead, L. (2002). Unique and protective contributions of parenting and classroom processes to the adjustment of African American children living in single-parent families. *Child Development*, 73(1), 274–286.

Cotton, K. (1990). *Schoolwide and classroom discipline. Close-Up No. 9*. Portland, OR: Northwest Regional Educational Laboratory.

Criss, M. M., Pettit, G. S., Bates, J. E., Dodge, K. A., & Lapp, A. L. (2002). Family adversity, positive peer relationships, and children's externalizing behavior: A longitudinal perspective on risk and resilience. *Child development*, 73(4), 1220–1237.

Franklin, C., Biever, J., Moore, K., Clemons, D., & Scamardo, M. (2001). The effectiveness of solution-focused therapy with children in a school setting. *Research on Social Work Practice*, 11(4), 411–434.

Gladwell, M. (2002). *The tipping point: How little things can make a big difference*. Boston: Back Bay Books.

Glasser, W. (1992). *The quality school: Managing students without coercion*. New York: Harper Books.

Hamre, B. K., & Pianta, R. C. (2001). Early teacher-child relationships and the trajectory of children's school outcomes through eighth grade. *Child Development*, 72, 625–638.

Hoglund, W. L., & Leadbeater, B. J. (2004). The effects of family, school, and classroom ecologies on changes in children's social competence and emotional and behavioral problems in first grade. *Developmental Psychology*, 40, 533–544.

Kellam, S. G., Ling, X., Merisca, R., Brown, C. H., & Ialongo, N. (1998). The effect of the level of aggression in the first grade classroom on the course and malleability of aggressive behavior into middle school. *Development and psychopathology*, 10(2), 165–185.

Kelly, M. S., Kim, J., & Franklin, C. (2008). *Solution-focused brief therapy in schools: A 360-degree view of practice and research*. New York: Oxford University Press.

Kelly, M. S. & Bluestone-Miller, R. (2009). Working on What Works (WOWW): Coaching teachers to do more of what's working. *Children & Schools*, 31(1), 35–38.

LaFountain, R. M., & Garner, N. E. (1996). Solution-focused counseling groups: The results are in. *Journal for Specialists in Group Work*, 21(2), 128–143.

Littrell, J. M., Malia, J. A., & Vanderwood, M. (1995). Single-session brief counseling in a high school. *Journal of Counseling and Development*, 73, 451–458.

Lynn, C., McKay, M. M., & Atkins, M. S. (2003). School Social Work: Meeting the Mental Health Needs of Students through Collaboration with Teachers. *Children & schools*, 25(4), 197–209.

Mantzicopoulos, P. (2005). Conflictual relationships between kindergarten children and their teachers: Associations with child and classroom context variables. *Journal of School Psychology*, 43(5), 425–442.

Marzano, R. J. (2003). *What works in schools: Translating research into action.* Alexandria, VA: Association for Supervision and Curriculum Development.

McDonald Connor, C., Son, S.-H., Hindman, A. H., & Morrison, F. J. (2005). Teacher qualifications, classroom practices, family characteristics, and preschool experience: Complex effects on first graders' vocabulary and early reading outcomes. *Journal of School Psychology, 43*(4), 343–375.

National Education Association (2007). *Attracting and keeping quality teachers.* Retrieved August 4, 2007 from http://www.nea.org/teachershortage/index.html

Roehrig, A., Presley, M., & Talotta, D. (2002). *Stories of beginning teachers: First-year challenges and beyond.* South Bend, IN: Notre Dame Press.

Rose, L. C., & Gallup, A. C. (2006). *The 38th annual Phi Delta Kappa/Gallup Poll of the public's attitudes toward the public schools, 41–53.* Retrieved January 24, 2007, from http://www.pkdmembers.org/e_GALLUP/kpoll_pdfs/ pdkpoll38_2006.pdf.

Rose, L. C., & Gallup, A. M. (2007). The 39th annual Phi Delta Kappa/Gallup Poll of the public's attitudes toward the public schools. *Phi Delta Kappan, 89*(1), 33(13).

Stephenson, J., Linfoot, K., & Martin, A. (2000). Behaviours of Concern to Teachers in the Early Years of School. *International journal of disability, development, and education, 47*(3), 225–235.

Vitaro, F., Brendgen, M., Pagani, L., Tremblay, R. E., & McDuff, P. (1999). Disruptive behavior, peer association, and conduct disorder. Testing the developmental links through early intervention. *Development and Psychopathology, 11,* 287–304.

Wang, M., Haertel, G. D., & Walberg, H. J. (1990). What influences learning? A content analysis of review literature. *The Journal of Educational Research, 84*(1), 30–43.

Wilson, P. M., & Wilson, J. R. (1992). Environmental influences on adolescent educational aspirations: A logistic transform model. *Youth & Society, 24,* 52–70.

24 Research and Development of a Solution-Focused High School

■ CYNTHIA FRANKLIN, KATHERINE L.
MONTGOMERY, VICTORIA BALDWIN,
AND LINDA WEBB

■ INTRODUCTION

Solution-focused interventions have been found to be promising in changing the behavior of at-risk youth in school settings (Kim & Franklin, 2009). See Chapter 16 in this book for a review of school studies. Utilizing a solution-focused approach, an alternative high school in Austin, Texas, has been able to impact multiple risk factors in the lives of youth identified as at risk of dropping out of school. Garza High School has become known as a solution-focused alternative school (SFAS) and has participated in various research investigations. The solution-focused approach has been developed into a model school program, recognized by the Texas Education Agency (TEA) as a model dropout prevention program and as providing high academic success for its students. For example, for the past few years, Garza High School has produced the highest SAT college examination scores in the Austin Independent School District. Garza has also been studied and visited by numerous people both from within the United States and from other countries who were interested in studying how the school translated solution-focused techniques into its daily educational practices. For more information on the specific solution-focused practices of Garza High School, see Kelly et al. (2008), Franklin et al. (2007a), and Franklin and Streeter (2003).

The purpose of this chapter is to provide specific information on how Garza High School became and sustained its status as an SFAS, as well as a summary and critical review of the research investigations. Finally, the chapter offers suggestions and implications for future research on building solution-focused school programs for at-risk students.

■ WHAT WE HAVE LEARNED SO FAR

In the United States, approximately 7,000 students drop out of school each day (Alliance for Excellent Education, 2009). The national high school dropout rate has become a top government priority in recent months due to the economic ramifications and consequences of uneducated youth (Obama, 2010). In fact, it is estimated that the current dropout rate will be responsible for a potential $3 trillion loss to the U.S. economy over the next decade (Alliance for Excellent Education, 2009). High school dropout prevention researchers have identified specific factors that place an adolescent at risk of dropping out. Some of the major factors are teenage pregnancy, substance use, delinquency, mental health issues, school behavior and attendance problems, academic problems, failure to be promoted to the next grade level, involvement in special education programs, and a feeling of disconnection from school and normally achieving peers (Franklin et al., 2006). These issues are similar to those of the student body at Garza High School, and because of the diverse needs of the dropout population, it became imperative for us to create and research a solution-focused school that was designed to help students graduate.

Important School Characteristics

At Garza High School, solution-focused therapy became a philosophy and a set of principles from which several effective educational practices were applied. Garza incorporated many characteristics from the research literature on what constitutes an effective school and dropout prevention program. The characteristics were not derived from the solution-focused brief therapy model, but they are highly congruent with the model's underlying assumptions and techniques. Important characteristics of Garza are as follows:

1. The strong leadership style of the principal is considered to be an important component of effective schools and alternative schools (Mendez-Morse, 1992; Reynolds, 2001). Strong leadership encourages stability in the school environment and, in the case of Garza, helps teachers and staff to utilize the solution-building model in their work. While some school administrators support the use of solution building by school social workers and counselors, few actually practice and encourage these techniques throughout the school. Administrators at Garza lead by example and use solution-building techniques with students, facilitators, and staff.

2. Positive student relationships and a low teacher-student ratio are also important characteristics of Garza (Van Heusden, 2000; Waxman et al., 1997). Solution building is a relationship-oriented approach, emphasizing collaborative relationships between students and staff. Smaller classes allow these personal relationships to form as well as provide attention to educational solutions for individual students.

3. The use of an alternative school approach to dropout prevention is an important characteristic of Garza. Although research is limited, alternative schools have been cited as being one of the most effective ways to graduate students who are prone to dropout (Reimer & Cash, 2003). Dupper (2006) describes two different and opposing models of alternative schools. One model is disciplinary or correctional in nature; it aims to fix problem students. The othe model is academic and creative, promoting a more effective way to educate students. Garza offers the second approach by creating an alternative school environment that is challenging, caring, and supportive. The Garza approach is consistent with other academic alternative school programs designed to help students with diverse

learning styles and backgrounds become successful. Staff in this type of setting are working by choice and are dedicated to helping students with diverse learning styles take responsibility for their own learning. The curriculum and instruction within alternative schools like Garza offer learning that is individualized, engaging, and relevant. The academic alternative school, by design, is one that fosters a full instructional program by a multidisciplinary team.

Readers are directed to the Garza training manual developed by Franklin and Streeter (2003) or to Franklin et al. (2007) and Kelly et al. (2008) for a more detailed exploration of Garza and its educational programs. It is also important to note that the Garza High School described in the publications is not exactly what you will find in the school today because, as in any organization, some of these practices have evolved or have been amended over time. The publications suggested, however, describe the school in which we performed our research studies.

A School's Readiness to Learn and Apply a Solution-focused Approach

Garza High School was very successful in both learning and applying solution-focused interventions. However, multiple factors influence the successful implementation of an intervention in an organization like a school (Hogue et al., 2008; McHugh et al., 2009). We call the factors that assisted the successful training of solution-focused therapy at Garza *school readiness factors*. We believe that these factors are helpful in the adoption of solution-focused techniques or any innovative practice within an organization. We will now discuss some of the readiness factors and how they promoted the adoption of the solution-focused approach at Garza.

Research on organizations indicates that the culture of an organization can determine whether a new intervention like the solution-focused approach is likely to be used (Glisson, 2002; Jaskyte & Dressler, 2005). Franklin and Hopson (2007b) identified several characteristics of organizations that have been found in research to be helpful when training staff in evidence-based practices. These characteristics were also believed to be part of the organizational culture of Garza and helped facilitate its use of the solution-focused model.

1. *The presence of a constructive organizational culture.* Constructive cultures in organizations promote staff autonomy and positive, proactive behavior that also encourages positive interactions among staff. This type of culture is characterized by norms of achievement, which encourage taking on challenging tasks, and *self-actualization*, which refers to developing one's full potential, utilizing the norms of humanism and support for each other. Because Garza was an alternative school, it already had the mission of educating the school district's most at-risk students. As an academic alternative school, Garza was already creative in its approach, and the staff were given considerable autonomy and support in coming up with new and innovative interventions. In fact, the staff were already exploring solution-focused techniques before the solution-focused consultants and trainers became involved with Garza (Kelly et al., 2008).

2. *A decentralized management structure in which staff collaborate in decision making and are open to innovative ideas and willing to incorporate them into their practices.* This is in contrast to a centralized management structure that has a

clear chain of command through which decisions are made and passed down to lower-level staff. The principal at Garza involved many people in the development of Garza, such as the teachers, students, parents, community members, researchers, and even the data management staff, which provided a participatory approach to the governance of the school. As the school evolved, it became more and more student led as a positive peer culture was developed throughout the school.

3. *An organization characterized by staff participation, flexibility, and risk taking.* The Garza staff created a school that was highly flexibile, with flexible hours and many choices of learning styles with self-paced, diverse, and integrative curriculums to meet the needs of its students. Staff were given support to carry out new ideas and were willing to take considerable risks, such as making home visits, jail visits, and general community outreach efforts to assist at-risk students. They also became advocates for students and frequently found ways to work around inflexible school district policies that might not be helpful to the at-risk students they served. For example, Garza had an open campus rule that allowed students who had already graduated to come back to the school when that was forbidden by other high schools. They also had more open sex education programs than is used in other district high schools.

4. *Adequate funding of the organization to carry out new and innovative practices.* The principal made a contract with the school district stating that she would not take on the task of developing Garza High School unless they provided the funds to create a top-notch and innovative school. The school district agreed to fund a first-rate school with the best practices in education. The University of Texas researchers also obtained a training and research grant from the Hogg Foundation for Mental Health that aided the school in developing its solution-focused practices.

5. *Supervision, consultation, and ongoing technical assistance to support the learning of new practices.* Garza had the benefit of a resident solution-focused coach while being initially trained in the solution-focused practices. Garza also has more counselors than much larger high schools have available, and those counselors were experts in solution-focused brief therapy (SFBT). In addition, Garza staff had ongoing training and consultations from Insoo Kim Berg and Cynthia Franklin from 2000 to 2006.

These organizational readiness factors created a school climate to which solution-focused interventions could be transferred and thrive in the school's educational programs. Below we describe how the solution-focused approach was taught at Garza and what was done to sustain the training.

■ SFBT INTERVENTIONS

Training of School Staff

Principal Vicki Baldwin, now retired, made a decision to train all Garza staff in the solution-building approach. Ms. Baldwin's forthright character and determination were directed to this task. Ms. Baldwin displayed a sign in her office that reads, "Show Me the Money"; thus, there was little questions regarding the fact that she wanted the job completed. In November 2001, the first training was a half-day of professional development training for Garza staff. From that time on, the training evolved so that teachers and staff, called *facilitators* at Garza, assumed ownership of the process and become actively involved in designing and delivering the training. Several strategies were developed by the teachers, staff (facilitators), and research team that helped facilitate learning of the solution-focused philosophy and techniques. These strategies are as follows:

1. A library of solution-focused resources was made available to facilitators.
2. Facilitators organized themselves into groups and formed a book club of readings.
3. Brown bag meetings were scheduled for teachers, staff, and administrators to watch videotapes of solution-focused interventions.
4. In-service trainings were also organized, with Insoo Kim Berg serving as the trainer. Insoo also met with individuals and smaller groups (such as the principal, administrators, and counselors) for additional training and consultation. Throughout the school's training process, other solution-focused trainers were also brought in to enhance the annual in-service training sessions.
5. A solution-focused coach worked in the school and was available for classroom consultations and modeling of the solution-focused approach as needed.
6. Facilitators were provided with quick reference sheets for solution-focused techniques that they could use with students.
7. Principal Baldwin also added competencies in solution-focused intervention to her annual performance evaluation with faculty and staff (Kelly et al., 2008).

The experience gained from training Garza High School staff in solution-focused techniques revealed several strategies that other schools can employ when introducing the solution-focused model to a school. Some of these ideas include:

1. Determining the overall readiness of a school to learn the solution-focused model.
2. Creating specific learning steps in a training process—for example, first teaching the philosophy of solution building and then developing the steps to facilitate the learning and application of techniques.
3. Using a solution-building coach for the school.
4. Applying the solution-building philosophy and techniques to administrative and classroom forms used regularly in the school.
5. Creating partnerships with administrators, counselors, and teachers in the use of the model.

It is important to acknowledge that throughout the training process, it was the sharing across professional lines that defined the emergence of solution building at Garza. School social workers, counselors, teachers, staff, and administrators learned a new approach to helping and educating students and combined their areas of expertise to create a unique application of solution building. In this approach, different team members share knowledge and expertise with each other to create new methods for intervention by adapting that shared knowledge. Streeter and Franklin (2002) call this type of learning a *transdisciplinary team approach* to solving problems. Also noteworthy is that the students were included as part of the team effort in developing the solution-focused approaches at Garza. Because it is a solution-building school, listening to students and integrating their suggestions is part of the culture at Garza.

Garza as a Solution-building School

Garza High School began evolving into a solution-building school over the summer of 2000 when the administrators, the school social worker, and a group of teachers and staff started incorporating SFBT techniques in their work with at-risk students. It is important to mention that the solution-building approach was not forced into Garza High School. Instead, it evolved out of the intrinsic work of administrators, faculty, and staff along with student motivation and behavior focused on their mutual interest in dropout prevention. Solution building ultimately became a philosophy guiding their work and success with at-risk students and represented the primary intervention model undergirding their school mental health practices.

Solution-Building Skills and Techniques. This strengths-based philosophy places emphasis on choosing hopeful, positive, empowering language, experimenting with new behavior, and celebrating incremental change. The assumptions and beliefs that inform SFBT in school settings can be divided into four groups of concepts, as outlined by Murphy (1997):

Solution Driven

- The purpose of the communication is to uncover clues to a new possible course of action that will reduce the severity of the problem.
- A small change in any part of the problem can create a solution.
- Complex problems do not warrant complex solutions, nor are there logical connections between the problem and the solution.
- Successful solutions are conceived as taking new action rather than ceasing previous behaviors.

Asset Based

- Students, teachers, and parents have the strengths and abilities to change school difficulties in the lives of at-risk youth.
- Any solution-focused goal must be developed by the person experiencing the difficulty.
- It is considered highly motivating when facilitators recognize and affirm the student's competence and ability to change.

Focus Shift

- Concentration on future possibilities supports change and success.
- Having or fostering insight into the nature of the problem is not necessary for building solutions.
- There are always exceptions to the difficulty: a time or place when the problem was not as great or was even absent.
- In a school setting, the emphasis on solutions enhances personal development, academic success, and progress toward graduation.

Experimental Action

- Change is inevitable.
- There is no single correct way to build a solution.
- There are multiple possible meanings and ways in which one can understand any given behavior; therefore, if one view is not working, try another.
- If it works, repeat it; if it does not work, try something different.

Garza's administrators, teachers, and staff used the solution-building model to guide the school to facilitate positive relationships with students. They were trained to view the students as experts in identifying their own solutions to their problems and difficulties. This view is opposed to the usual approach of expert-driven strategies that are used in most educational settings. Because Garza's administrators and teachers believe students have the knowledge and abilities to solve their own problems, student input is valued and actively sought. Here are some ways that Garza's facilitators use the solution-building intervention skills to help students:

- Assisting students to come up with a realistic solution
- Looking for ways in which the solution is already occurring in the student's life
- Helping the student to create small, measurable goals toward the solution
- Taking immediate steps that impact educational and life outcomes

This strengths-based approach is a central theme throughout the solution-building school, and SFBT offers all facilitators specific skills for recognizing and fostering strengths in students. Identifying the student's strengths is necessary to build confidence so that the student can believe that a solution is possible. This helps create positive changes for the student quickly and allows the student to shift the focus away from the problems.

Transition of Leadership

In the spring of 2008, after providing 11 years of leadership to Garza and 41 years of service to public education, Principal Vicki Baldwin retired and leadership of the school shifted to Dr. Linda Webb. Because Ms. Baldwin had invested a great deal of energy in creating the unique school philosophy upon which the SFAS had been built, she played an active role in recruiting, hiring, and training the new principal.

The selection process of principals varies, depending upon the superintendent in large districts. The Austin independent school district (AISD) is an urban district with 83,000 students. The current district procedure for selecting principals was followed. This meant that the associate superintendent for high schools, Dr. Glenn Nolly, met with each stakeholder group, staff, parents, and students to hear what characteristics of they wanted the next principal to possess. In the meantime, the position was posted on the AISD Web site.

According to Dr. Nolly, the district received more applications for the Garza position than any other school listing. This was amazing and encouraging, but Ms.Baldwin believed that many who had applied did not understand the complexities and culture of Garza; further, she was concerned that they thought it might be an easy job.

Ms. Baldwin only had one request, which was to select the principal in a timely manner so that she could help his or her transition. Garza looks easy to the outsider, but it is very complex. Unlike most schools, where students must fit into the organization, Garza is an ever-evolving organization that fine-tunes itself based on students' needs. Garza's students have not been successful with the standard school-system structure, so the structure offered at Garza needed to be different. The next principal needed to love and respect all students. He or she required a strong background in curriculum and also had to be willing to ask "Why not?" when wrestling with decisions to be made. All decisions had to be made in terms of what was in the best interest of each student. Most of all, the principal had to believe unequivocally that all people have strengths and that it is the job of the school to help students identify their strengths.

Ms. Baldwin often called the Garza students the "walking wounded." They need to be nurtured and empowered to regain respect for themselves and the decisions they make. The solution-focused model is at the core of all of these attributes.

Various principals called Ms. Baldwin to inquire if they might be a good fit. Some might have been, but most were not. Ms. Baldwin also encouraged a few principals to apply; one of them was an elementary school, principal, Dr. Linda Webb. Dr. Webb was the principal of Pillow Elementary in Austin ISD. She had taken that school to Blue Ribbon status nationally and was responsible for its exemplary state rating (the highest award). She and her staff met the needs of children with over 24 nationalities and many special needs students (both identified special education students and students who received free and reduced-price lunch). Dr. Webb and Ms. Baldwin had been friends for years, and they had had dinner from time to time to discuss the state of education and how to make a difference in a broken system. While Dr. Webb initially rejected Ms. Baldwin's request, she ultimately reconsidered and applied.

Because the principal "buy-in" was integral to sustaining the solution-focused model throughout Garza, Ms. Baldwin made it a priority to be heavily involved in the transition. Dr. Webb and Ms. Baldwin had been meeting for the past 2 years (just before the transition and throughout Dr. Webb's first years) and continue to meet monthly to share ideas, work through any problems, and maintain their friendship. They both believe that this process has been crucial in promoting a successful transition. Additionally, they both recognize and respect their variations in approach and style. Through this mutual respect, Dr. Webb was encouraged and had the freedom to look at Garza with fresh eyes.

Dr. Webb's new perspective allowed her to look at Garza and ask three questions: (a) What is working? (b) What is not working? and (c) How can we do things better? She organized individual meetings with each of the faculty and staff members and asked these three questions. The answers led her to recognize that solutions were needed to solve four primary problems: (a) smoking on school property, (b) poor attendance, (c) tardiness, and (d) teachers' feeling of disempowerment. Dr. Webb creatively worked with the faculty, staff, and students to seek solutions to these problems. See Boxes 24.1 and 24.2 for examples of how Dr. Webb offered solutions to existing problems and to continued improvement of Garza. She also applied her solution-focused training to teaching her staff more advanced solution-focused skills and help

---

BOX 24.1 ■ Looking for a Solution to the Problem of Poor School Attendance

Upon discovering that attendance was a problem at Garza High School, the new principal, Dr. Webb, called a school assembly. During the assembly, each student was provided with an individual envelope addressed to him or her. The students were asked to open their envelopes at the same time. Each student found a piece of paper with an individually calculated number representing the amount of money the school lost as a result of the number of days he or she chose not to come to school. Dr. Webb used this exercise to emphasize the importance of all students attending school and hoped that they would consider the impact they had as individuals on Garza as a result of the choices they make when considering attending or skipping school.

BOX 24.2 ■ Looking for a Solution to the Problem of Teacher Empowerment

Several teachers reported to Dr. Webb that they believed the solution-focused model prevented them from enforcing the consequences for unacceptable classroom behavior (tardiness, speaking disrespectfully to teachers, etc.). To learn more about the solution-focused model herself and to clarify the situation for the faculty, Dr. Webb had a solution-focused trainer come to the school and offer additional training. Many questions were answered, and teachers and staff left with a greater understanding of the solution-focused model.

---

them improve their abilities— for example, how to apply and be more consistent with holding students accountable for their behavior.

■ RESEARCH METHODS

To date, three studies have been conducted on Garza High School employing three different methodologies: a quasi-experimental design (Franklin et al., 2007c), a qualitative design (Lagana-Riordan et al., 2010), and concept-mapping methodology (Streeter et al., in press). What follows is a summary of the research designs and procedures employed for the three Garza studies.

Study 1

Design, Participants, and Procedures. This first study utilized a quasi-experimental pretest-posttest comparison groups design. Participants ($n = 46$) in the experimental group all attended Garza High School. Because no additional alternative school was available, the comparison group ($n = 39$) was recruited from a traditional local public high school. The comparison group was matched with the experimental group on the following characteristics: attendance, number of credits earned, participation in the free lunch program, race, gender, and whether the student was defined as at risk according the Texas Education Code (TEC).

Three dependant variables were observed in this study: credits earned, attendance, and graduation rates. Data for these three variables was obtained through the AISD records using each student's school identification number. The data for *credits earned* was a reflection of the relationship between the credits attempted and the credits completed over a four-semester period. Each student was given a proportion score for *credits earned* that ranged between 0 and 1.0, where 1.0 meant the student had competed all of the credits he or she attempted. The data for *attendance* was a number indicating the proportion of days attended out of the school calendar days. This proportional variable also ranged from 0.0 to 1.0, where 1.0 meant that the student was in attendance during all of the school calendar days being observed over a four-semester period.

Study 2

Design, Participants, and Procedures. The second study employed a qualitative case study methodology and recruited participants from the experimental group in the first study. Of the 46 students who were asked to participate, 33 elected to do so. The students were primarily Caucasian (54.6%) or Hispanic (39.9%), and more than half were female (57.6%). Each participant answered 36 questions in a 45- to 60-minute semistructured interview. The interview questions were a combination of scaling questions, list items, and open-ended questions. The interviewers used probes to gather additional information.

The questions and probes coalesced around topics related to satisfaction with current and previous schools, family history, and relationships with peers and family. Responses were transcribed, coded, and theoretically grouped using a thematic analysis. Methods to provide rigor and trustworthiness included triangulations with quantitative data, persistent observation, and prolonged engagement.

Study 3

Design, Participants, and Procedures. The third study utilized a concept-mapping design with the intent to quantitatively understand qualitative data. "The purpose of [the] concept mapping exercise was to help examine the program's fidelity towards its guiding theory and philosophy, and to evaluate the most important program features that contribute to the program's mission to graduate at-risk students" (Streeter et al., in press, p. 9). Fourteen students and 37 adults (teachers, administrators, and staff) participated in the concept-mapping sessions and generated a combined total of 182 unique answers in response to the following statement: *Describe the specific characteristics of the alternative school that helps students achieve their educational goals.* Once the 182 answers had been compiled, the participants were asked to divide them into like groups. A total of 15 clusters emerged from this process. Once the clusters were identified, participants were asked to rate them by level of uniqueness, importance, and connectedness to the solution-focused model. These levels were analyzed through pattern-matching analysis.

■ RESULTS OF THE RESEARCH

Study 1

The results of the quasi-experimental study (Franklin et al., 2007c) offer researchers and practitioners insight into understanding the potential impact of a SFAS on students' school credits earned, attendance, and graduation rates. Repeated measures analysis of variance (ANOVA) revealed that there was no significant difference between the comparison group (matched students attending a regular local public high school) and the SFAS participants during the 2002–2003 academic school year; however, a significant difference was found between the groups during the 2003–2004 academic school year, indicating that students enrolled in the SFAS earned a greater proportion of credits than those in the comparison group (Hedge's $g = .47$). One important factor to consider is the pace at which students progress through the SFAS program compared to the comparison group's traditional high school setting. The SFAS is a self-paced, individualized program that allows students the flexibility to attend school for half-days and work part time; it also gives some students the flexibility to be a parent as well. One possible conclusion is that while SFAS students may take slightly longer, they are more likely to complete their credits than the regular high school students.

When calculating repeated measures ANOVA to observe the difference between the groups' attendance, there was a significant difference between groups at each of the observed time periods. This difference, however, indicated that the comparison group had a higher level of attendance than the SFAS group. As mentioned above, the new principal, Dr. Webb, found attendance to be one of the problems at Garza High School. Additionally, the format of Garza's flexibility may contribute to this statistical difference.

Researchers also calculated the graduation rate percentages of 12th-grade students from both groups. It was found that 62% of SFAS 12th graders and 90% of comparison group 12th graders graduated in the spring semester of 2004. One important difference to consider when interpreting these results is that Garza High School does not have an annual graduation. Rather, students graduate throughout the year as they complete their coursework on their own individualized timeline. For this reason, researchers also followed the 14 SFAS students who did not graduate and found that 9 graduated in the fall of 2004 (bringing the experimental group percentage up to 81%). Similar to the influence of the findings on attendance, it may be that researchers were not able to capture the true impact of the SFAS because of the structure and format of this alternative school.

Study 2

The thematic analysis results of the qualitative study (Lagana-Riordan et al., 2010) revealed several differences in students' SFAS and traditional school experiences. The majority of the students' perceptions of the SFAS were positive. The major positive themes that emerged were positive student–teacher relationships, improving maturity level and responsibility, alternative structure, understanding of social issues, and positive peer relationships. Participants in the study explained that the SFAS atmosphere was one in which teachers and peers offered understanding, support, and increased individual attention. Additionally, students described the school's flexibility and expectations of empowering responsibility to be central to their success.

Several themes regarding the students' perceptions of the major weaknesses of traditional schools emerged: problems with teachers, lack of safety, overly rigid authority, inadequate school structure, and problems with peer relationships. Students expressed the feeling of being judged by peers and teachers. Additionally, they felt that traditional schools could not offer the individual attention or safety necessary to foster effective learning. The findings from this study offer researchers and practitioners important characteristics to consider when intervening in the lives of students at risk of school dropout. Consistent with previous research, the impact teachers have on academic motivation is great (Darling-Hammond, 2004; Tuerk, 2005). Additionally, the quality of the school environment, flexibility, and individual attention all appear to be important in the lives of at-risk youth. This solution-focused model at the SFAS allows students to take charge of and be more engaged in their academic success.

Study 3

The results of the concept-mapping evaluation (Streeter et al., in press) offered 15 clusters reflecting participants' description and understanding of the SFAS: relationships, professional environment, respect evident throughout the school, strength based, sense of community, student–student interaction, empowering culture, cutting-edge practices, organizational foundation, school size and structure of the school day, admission and exit policies, resources directed to student success, preparation for life, student success, and continuous improvement. See Table 24.1 for a description of each cluster and cluster groups.

The results of the pattern-matching analysis revealed how teachers, administrators, and staff rated the uniqueness and importance of the 15 clusters. Researchers found that cutting-edge practices, admission and exit polices, and the structure of the school were believed to be unique. When the importance of these unique features was rated, clusters related to school culture and relationships were rated higher by teachers, administrators, and staff. Thus, "the most unique factors tended to be concrete organizational aspects of the school while the most important features in helping students achieve their academic goals were relationships and school culture" (Streeter et al., in press, p. 16).

TABLE 24.1. *Description of Clusters from SFAS Concept-Mapping Research*

Cluster Grouping	Individual Cluster	Cluster Description
Theme of Community	Respect Evident Throughout the School	Trust and respect evident throughout school relationships (students, staff, faculty, administration)
	Sense of Community	School's close, supportive, and nurturing relationships
	Student–Student Interaction	Students' respect for each other and appreciation for differences
	Empowering Culture	Individual freedoms coupled with encouragement of personal responsibilities
Theme of School Organization	Organizational Foundation	How the school is organized: class schedule, academic plans, school staffing.
	School Size and Structure of the School Day	This cluster provides specific examples of school days' schedule and classroom characteristics
	Cutting Edge	Nontraditional techniques at the school not normative of alternatives schools
	Admission and Exit	Unique features of admission criteria and graduation requirements
Additional Clusters	Relationships	Reflects broad relationships among principal, students, and staff
	Professional Environment	Reciprocal recognition and appreciation of strengths, skills, and ability to work with each other
	Strengths-Based	School's focus on strengths of individuals
	Resources Directed Toward Student Success	Services individualized to assist students in meeting academic requirements, continuing on to postsecondary education, and obtaining employment skills and experiences
	Preparation for Life	This cluster focuses on specific programs for increasing postsecondary education and employment for the students
	Student Success	Assisting students to define and achieve personal goals and recognize their success upon meeting these goals
	Continuous Improvement	Continually examining practices and willingness to make changes in efforts to assist students in achieving success

Source: Adapted from Streeter, C. L., Franklin, C., Kim, J. S., & Tripodi, S. J. (in press). Using concept mapping to examine school dropouts: A solution-focused alternative school case study. *Children and Schools.*

Pattern-matching analysis was also used to observe the difference in students' versus teachers,' administrators,' and staffs' perspectives on individual clusters' level of importance. Both groups believed *respect evident throughout the school* and *sense of community* to be among their three most important clusters. Students, however, believed *interaction with other students* to be most important. Research supports the notion that when students bond with conventional peers, they are more likely to be protected from school dropout (Franklin et al., 2006) and delinquency (Montgomery et al., 2010). One conclusion to be drawn from this finding is that the SFAS fosters an environment that offers this protective factor. In contrast to students' top responses, teachers, administrators, and staff believed *student success* to be the third most important cluster. In line with the solution-focused model, those working with students at the school felt that student's achievement of success and goal attainment are of great importance.

Finally, pattern-matching analysis provided an understanding of teachers,' administrators,' and staffs' perception of an individual cluster's importance in relation to their understanding of the solution-focused model. Results indicated that they believed *respect evident throughout the school* to be of the highest importance *and* to be most closely related to the solution-focused model. Additionally, they believed both *strengths-based perspective* and *sense of community* to be among the five most important clusters as well as the five most closely related to the solution-focused model. An important point to note regarding these findings is that what they viewed as most important is also most closely related to the solution-focused model. Research indicates that one of the greatest challenges in implementing a new treatment or model is obtaining the "buy-in" of the service providers. Having the support of the teachers, administrators, and staff is central to the successful implementation of the solution-focused model at Garza High School.

■ PRACTICE GUIDELINES

The aforementioned research studies have several implications for researchers and practitioners desiring to understand more about the use of a solution-focused approach with students at risk of dropping out. Despite their limitations, these studies suggest that there are several specific characteristics necessary to the development and implementation of a solution-focused model in a school. They also provide insight into specific characteristics that students and teachers find important and valuable in a solution-focused model.

Limitations

Study 1. The two primary limitations of the quasi-experimental study concern the sample size and the comparison group. Due to the small sample size, these results are probably not generalizable. To understand more fully the extent to which schoolwide solution-focused interventions impact attendance, academic performance, and graduation, a much larger study is necessary. Another limitation of the study is the use of students from a traditional public school as a comparison group. It is possible that many of the differences between the groups can be explained simply by the different type of school. The pace, individualized curriculum, and timeline students experience in an alternative school is very different from those of a traditional public school.

Study 2. The uniqueness of their design makes qualitative studies virtually impossible to generalize to a broader population. While it offers a deeper and richer understanding of students' beliefs, we cannot use this study to say what the experience would be for participants in another study. However, although the findings are specific to the participants' experiences, the information provided by students seems to be consistent with those reported in school social work and education literature and, thus, may possibly reflect experiences of at-risk students across different geographic locations.

Study 3. Like Study 1, the concept-mapping study is comprised of a small, nonrandomized sample and the results may not be generalizable. Additionally, the use of a group setting to gather data may have prevented some individuals from offering information out of fear of others' responses or reactions. A final limitation of this study is the large number of statements provided ($n = 182$). Ideally, a brainstorming session should be limited to 80 statements for the sorting ease of the participants. Sorting through this large number of statements may have been a tiresome process, and some participants may have offered less true responses toward the end of the brainstorming exercise.

Despite their limitations, current research from the SFAS offers researchers and practitioners a greater understanding of the characteristics of a schoolwide solution-focused model. The pace, individualization, and empowerment of the SFAS seem to be significant characteristics that emerged from all of the studies. Additionally, as noted in the second and third studies, the relationships and support described by participants seemed to be important characteristics.

Characteristics of the SFAS

Goals and Future Orientation. One of the important attributes of Garza that was identified during the concept-mapping study was its focus on students' academic goals. Garza kept students focused on the future rather than the past and continuously used goal setting and techniques like scaling to help students progress academically, even if only in small steps.

Pace. At-risk students seem to thrive in an environment where they can slow the pace or vary the schedule of schooling, depending on their environment. Self-paced learning means that some students who are far behind in school can catch up, while others can take the extra time they need to finish. The research that has been done on Garza supports the fact that some students could earn credits much faster than those in a traditional high school and that other students, when given more time to graduate, could do so. Box 24.3 offers a few quotes and examples from recent Garza graduates that also shows the importance of the self-paced school. Those offering solution-focused services to at-risk students should consider ways in which students can have the option to control the pace of their learning. Further, as is consistent with SFBT, finding an alternative pace might be an exception to the problem, and the service provider can assist the student in identifying strengths that become available when the academic pace is individualized to the student.

Individualization. Students at the SFAS not only choose a pace individualized to them, but also choose the order in which they can take classes and a class schedule that works best for them. Additionally, the SFAS offers a large variety of practical life skills, as well as preparation for future employment and secondary education opportunities that are tailored to the individual. Consistent with research literature, at-risk students

---

BOX 24.3 ■ SFAS Graduating Students' Quotes: The Pace of School

"Throughout my stay at Garza, I realized that learning is fun! Seriously! I always did my work and I would want to know more about what I was doing, so I looked it up. Then I would wonder about something a little off of the subject and before I knew it, I was trying to learn about things that were completely unrelated! By the end of every school day, I learned so many new things. This made me have an idea of what I want to do with my life and eventually I figured out that I have talents that I didn't know I possessed. When I get out in the big bad Texas world, I don't want to grab it by its big ol' Texas horns because I am not ready. I am going to take it slow. In January next semester I will start one class at [a local community college]. While only taking one class, I will be working at [a local sandwich shop]. If I am not working, then I will be at school. Since I am only taking one class, I would spend most of my time making sandwiches. This will go on for the next year, but as time goes on and I get the hang of it, I will take more and more classes and eventually become a police officer, social worker, or veterinarian, whichever comes first."

"I can say that I am graduating six months early and starting college in the summer. My life is beginning to take off and get exciting, and I thank Garza for helping me get to this point."

"Being in a self-paced environment allowed me to gain more knowledge from my courses than I ever could have gained in a traditional high school setting. Not only was I able to allow myself the time I needed to fully understand difficult concepts, but I was also blessed with the most incredible teachers."

---

often need individualized learning plans to accommodate their complex situations and needs. Thus, for those providing services, at-risk students need to be offered an education plan (to the extent possible) that they can control and organize.

Building on Competencies. One characteristic evident from the above studies that is central to the solution-focused model is the focus on building one's competencies. Garza focused staff on building competencies by helping each student to take responsibility for his or her choices and actions. Students at Garza are given the responsibility to control their own learning and are empowered to make choices that will allow them to succeed. Box 24.4 provides statements from students regarding this experience.

Relationships and Support. The importance and value of relationships was central in the research studies. Support and reciprocal respect among teachers, administrators, staff, and students were identified as two of the most important aspects of the SFAS. Box 24.5 presents graduating students' remarks regarding relationships and support. For those employing solution-focused interventions with at-risk students, these studies suggest that a focus on supportive and respectful relationships (from both adults and peers) is of great importance.

■ FUTURE STUDIES

The studies presented in this chapter offer a foundation for future research. As previously noted, these studies are limited by their small sample size and may not be generalizable to larger populations. Additionally, the experimental study is limited by

---

BOX 24.4 ■ SFAS Graduating Students' Quotes: Empowerment

"The philosophy at Garza is a very unique one, and I know it will stay with me through-out my life. This school has inspired me to be self-motivated, proactive, and optimistic in all aspects of my life."

"I am graduating after only attending this school for five months. . . . Even the work the teachers give you challenges you to use your brain more, and I really like that."

"{I have learned] that I have control of my success and failure even if I don't feel like I don't sometimes."

BOX 24.5 ■ SAFS Graduating Students' Quotes: Relationships and Support

"Never had I been to a school where almost everyone was accepting of me, as they were at Garza. . . . The facilitators at Garza have been very influential on me. I can tell that they really love what they do, and I know I will continue to let them inspire me throughout my life. . . . I have come to realized that the students and staff who are here influence the atmosphere much more than the curriculum or activism we do here."

"Before I attended Garza . . . the teachers couldn't keep track of anyone. They only knew you if you were a troublemaker or their best students. When I started attending Garza, it was great. I felt welcomed. The teachers and principals know everyone's name, and if not, they at least greet you and try to get to know you. I remember before I went to Garza I wanted to drop out of school."

---

the inability to compare the SFAS to another alternative school. More rigorous designs with larger samples sizes are needed to better understand the use of solution-focused interventions as a schoolwide model. Also, because Garza High School is one of the only schools in the entire educational system employing the solution-focused model, additional research is needed to understand the extent to which the school context, administrators, and leadership roles affect the implementation of the SFBT model. The current research, for example, does not address the issues many practitioners face when trying to train and use SFBT in traditional high schools. Because Garza was an academic alternative school, it had many school readiness characteristics in place that allowed it to more easily accept and use solution-focused practices, Future studies should focus on what might be needed to increase the readiness of a traditional school to accept solution-focused practices and facilitate schoolwide applications of this approach.

■ KEY FINDINGS TO REMEMBER

- Garza High School shows that it is possible to create a schoolwide solution-focused model within an academic alternative school environment. The results of the concept-mapping study appear to support adherence to solution-focused principles from administrators, staff, and students. School staff were successfully trained in how to use solution-focused interventions and, with the support of their principal, found ways to both share and use the solution-focused approach in the school.

- The culture of a school organization is important in deciding whether a school will learn and apply new and innovative practices like solution-focused therapy. Prior to the training in solution-focused interventions, Garza High School possessed several school readiness factors that have been associated with the acceptance and implementation of innovative practices.

- Support and reciprocal respect among teachers, administrators, staff, and students were identified in the research on Garza as two of the most important aspects of the solution-focused school, showing high congruity with the solution-focused model.

- The studies at Garza show that central to the solution-focused school is the importance of continuously building student competencies and moving students toward academic success, even if that happens in smaller steps than students in traditional schools are expected to achieve. The small steps finally do lead to academic success and high school graduation for many students, as indicated by the research on Garza.

- The at-risk students who matriculated at Garza seemed to thrive in an environment that is focused on the future and allowed them to set their own goals and slow or expedite the pace of schooling, depending upon their environment. The research on Garza supports the importance of the self-paced curriculum. Some students attending Garza could earn credits much faster than those in a traditional high school, while other students needed more time to progress and, when given more time to graduate, could do so.

- Consistent with the research literature, at-risk students often need individualized learning plans tailored to their complex situations and life needs. The research on Garza suggests that students also responded favorably to the attention that teachers gave to their social and life needs.

■ FURTHER LEARNING

- Lagana-Riordan, C., Aguilar, J. P., Franklin, C., Streeter, C. L., Kim, J. S., Tripodi, S. J., & Hopson, L. (2010). At-risk students' perceptions of traditional schools and a solution-focused public alternative school. *Preventing School Failure. 55* (1) 1–10.

- Streeter, C. L., Franklin, C., Kim, J. S., & Tripodi, S. J. (in press). Using concept mapping to examine school dropouts: A solution-focused alternative school case study. *Children and Schools.*

- For more information on the solution-focused approach at Garza High School, go to: http://www.austinisd.org/schools/website.phtml?id=024

■ REFERENCES

Alliance for Excellent Education. (2009). *High school dropouts in America*. Washington, DC: Author.

Darling-Hammond, L. (2004). Standards, accountability, and school reform. *Teachers College Record, 106*, 1047–1085.

Dupper, D. (2006). Guides for designing and establishing alternative school programs for dropout. In C. Franklin, M. B. Harris, & P. Allen-Meares (Eds.), *The school services sourcebook: A guide for school-based professionals* (pp. 413–422).

Franklin, C., Garner, J., & Berg, I. K. (2007a). At-risk youth: Preventing and retrieving high school dropouts. In R. Greene (Ed.), *Social work practice: A risk and resiliency perspective* (pp. 115–139). Pacific Grove, CA: Brooks/Cole.

Franklin, C., & Hopson, L. M. (2007b). Facilitating the use of evidence-based practices in community organizations. *Journal of Social Work Education, 43*(3), 377–404.

Franklin, C., Kim, J. S., & Tripodi, S. J. (2006). Solution focused, brief therapy interventions for students at-risk to dropout. In C. Franklin, M. B. Harris, & P. Allen-Meares (Eds.), *School Social Work and Mental Health Workers Training and Resource Manual.* London: Oxford University Press.

Franklin, C., & Streeter, C. L. (2003). *Creating solution-focused accountability schools for the 21st century: A training manual for Garza High School.* The University of Texas at Austin. Austin: Hogg Foundation for Mental Health, The University of Texas at Austin.

Franklin, C., Streeter, C. L., Kim, J. S., & Tripodi, S. J. (2007b). The effectiveness of a solution focused, public alternative school for dropout prevention and retrieval. *Children and Schools, 29,* 133–144.

Glisson, C., & James, L. R. (2002). The cross-level effects of culture and climate in human services teams. *Journal of Organizational Behavior, 23,* 767–794.

Hogue, A., Dauber, S., Barajas, P. C., Fried, A., Henderson, C. E., & Liddle, H. A. (2008). Treatment adherence, competence, and outcome in individual and family therapy for adolescent behavior problems. *Journal of Consulting and Clinical Psychology, 4,* 544–555.

Jaskyte, K., & Dressler, W. W. (2005). Organizational culture and innovation in nonprofit human service organizations. *Administration in Social Work, 29,* 23–41.

Kelly, M. S., Kim, J. S., & Franklin, C. (2008). *Solution-focused brief therapy in schools: A 360 degree view of research and practice.* New York: Oxford University Press.

Kim, J., & Franklin, C. (2009). Solution-focused, brief therapy in schools: A review of the outcome literature. *Children and Youth Services Review, 31,* 461–470.

Lagana-Riordan, C., Aguilar, J. P., Franklin, C., Streeter, C. L., Kim, J. S., Tripodi, S. J., & Hopson, L. (2010). At-risk students' perceptions of traditional schools and a solution-focused public alternative school. *Preventing School Failure.* 55.1–10

McHugh, R. K., Murray, H. W., & Barlow, D. H. (2009). Balancing fidelity and adaptation in the dissemination of empirically-supported treatments: The promise of transdiagnostic interventions. *Behaviour Research and Therapy, 47,* 946–953.

Mendez-Morse, S. (1992). *Leadership characteristics that facilitate school change.* New York: Teachers College Press.

Montgomery, K. L., Barczyk, A. N., Thompson, S. J. (2010). Evidence-based practices for juvenile delinquency: Risk and protective factors in treatment implementation. In F. Columbus (Ed.), *Youth Violence and Juvenile Justice: Causes, Intervention and Treatment Programs.* Hauppauge, NY: Nova Publishers.

Murphy, J. J. (1997). *Solution-focued counseling in middle and high schools.* Alexandria, VA: American Counseling Association.

Obama, B. (2010, March). *White House press conference.* Speech presented at the White House, Washington, DC.

Reimer, M. S., & Cash, T. (2003). *Alternative schools: Best practices for development and evaluation.* Clemson, SC: National Dropout Prevention Center/Network.

Reynolds, D. (2001). *Effective school leadership: The contributions of school effectiveness research.* Nottingham, UK: National College for School Leadership.

Streeter C. L. & Franklin, C. (2002). Standards for school social work in the 21st century. In A. Roberts & G. Greene (Eds.). *Social worker's desk reference.* Oxford University Press.

Streeter, C. L., Franklin, C., Kim, J. S., & Tripodi, S. J. (in press). Using concept mapping to examine school dropouts: A solution-focused alternative school case study. *Children and Schools.*

Tuerk, P. W. (2005). Research in the high-stakes era: Achievement, resources, and No Child Left Behind. *Psychological Science, 16*(6), 419–425.

Van Heusden, H. S. (2000). *Comprehensive school reform: Research strategies to achieve high standards.* San Francisco: WestEd.

Waxman, H. C., Anderson, L., Huang, S. L., & Weinstein, T. (1997). Classroom process differences in inner city elementary school. *Journal of Educational Research, 91,* 49–59.

25 Applying a Solution-Focused Approach to Health Interviews in Japan

■ NORIO MISHIMA

■ INTRODUCTION

Insoo Kim Berg visited Japan many times to hold workshops on solution-focused therapy (SFT). In the mid-1990s, she began to regularly visit Fukuoka City, a big city in the western part of Japan where the author's office is located. Since then, she came here almost every year to teach SFT and shared the newest information on its application in psychotherapy and related fields with Japanese people until her passing. She continued to make a profound impression upon participants because she not only demonstrated her genius in psychotherapy, but also showed her generous attitude of imparting invaluable information. Her workshop encouraged many participants to apply SFT to their own work. Many of her books on SFT have been translated into Japanese and have come to be some of the most important resources for Japanese learners of SFT (Berg, 1994; Berg & Dolan, 2001; Berg & Kelly, 2000; Berg & Miller, 1992; Berg & Reuss, 1998; De Jong & Berg, 2008). This chapter describes how a solution-focused interviewing approach in Japan assists nurses in increasing interviewees' satisfaction, and also how solution-focused techniques increase nurses' job satisfaction.

■ WHAT WE HAVE LEARNED SO FAR

In Japan, SFT is mainly used as a psychotherapeutic method in clinical psychology and medicine. It has also attracted the attention of school counselors and teachers because Insoo Kim Berg imparted information on Garza High School and WOWW to participants from the early stages of their development. Textbooks on WOWW were translated into Japanese by some of the participants (Berg & Shilts, 2004, 2005). The application of SFT in job coaching has also attracted much attention. See Chapters 23 and 24 for reviews of Working on What Works (WOWW) and the Garza High School program.

In medicine, SFT's application has been limited only to psychiatry and psychosomatic medicine in Japan[1]. To the best of my knowledge, only a small number of doctors are interested in continuing to improve their interviewing skills, although communication skills are very important in clinical medicine. Hence, most doctors in Japan are not knowledgeable about SFT. They do not even know that there is an interviewing method that is not based on the medical model.

Compared to clinicians, occupational health (OH) physicians and nurses may be interested in improving their interviewing skills. In Japan, every employee in the workplace has to take a medical examination annually. After the examination, many workers are interviewed on their health conditions either by an OH nurse or by an OH physician. Most nurses seem to have made persistent efforts to be helpful to workers in health interviews, but they are not always welcomed by interviewees. One of the reasons may be that the interviews are typically problem-focused, and that the nurses talk about current or future health problems even when the problems are insignificant.

These situations that nurses face can be attributed to the education on interviewing that they have received during college and at work. According to the stories that I have heard directly from some nurses and in an article in a Japanese journal (Japanese Society of Public Health, 2007), nurses have not been educated enough on the practical skills needed in their job. Hence, they may have sufficient knowledge on what to talk about in interviews, but not on how to have a useful interview with clients. It is likely that nurses have failed to meet the expectations of workers in interviews, even though the nurses have worked very hard.

■ SFT INTERVENTION

Working under the aforementioned circumstances, a group of OH nurses contacted me to ask for help in improving their interviewing skills. In response to their request, a workshop was held to teach active listening and give additional information on techniques such as SFT. At that time, I was very curious to know about the strengths and resources that nurses had already acquired through their daily work. So, at the beginning of the workshop, I asked several solution-focused questions and made them delve into their experiences of health interviews. This revealed that each of them had very useful experiences (Box 25.2), although they had not shared such information previously with each other.

After the workshop, a lead nurse started thinking that the nurses should take more time to learn the basics of SFT. She believed that SFT would provide useful tools allowing nurses to draw out the details of interviewees' subtle, but important, positive efforts in maintaining health. These efforts would not be elicited by the conventional interviewing method, because nurses had not learned how to focus on positive aspects of workers in their previous training based on problem-focused interviewing. She believed that SFT would enable nurses to learn how to do this.

The lead nurse was also interested in proving the effect of learning SFT scientifically. Hence, the purpose of this study is to investigate whether or not significant changes occur in health interviews when OH nurses learn SFT and utilize it in their job. The hypothesis of this study is that the solution-focused health interview enhances not only interviewees' satisfaction with interviews, but also nurses' satisfaction with their job. In the following sections, I explain the results of analyzing data and discuss how helpful SFT can be in health interviews.

BOX 25.1 ■ Feedback from the Nurses

Active listening

1. I bear in mind that active listening is important, and my listening has improved.
2. I noticed that I had been giving workers explanations and instructions one-sidedly and had viewed them from a distance. When I put myself in workers' shoes, talking with someone like me, an OH nurse, about what they think and feel in their daily lives probably clarifies vague ideas that they didn't notice, helps them identify problems, and relieves them. It seems that SFT has a lot of good ideas to make workers talk about these things.

Complimenting

3. Learning SFT makes me communicate more easily with workers, and I have become able to help them to find their strengths and see themselves differently. This enables me to have a wonderful time in the interview. After the interview, they usually have a cheerful expression.
4. Instead of finding reasons why a worker has abnormal test results, I start the interview by finding his/her positive aspect and complimenting the worker on it. Many workers leave the room with a smile on their face, saying, "I thought I would hear you criticize me for my behavior, but actually you don't!"

Respecting the feelings and ideas of workers

5. I have come to interview workers by keeping in mind the idea that "they must have already been thinking about their own health."
6. I used to think negatively about workers. I thought that they must have bad lifestyles. Now that I have realized that workers have their own goals and ideas, I can feel more comfortable when I have to interview workers who might not be convinced why they should have a health interview.
7. I have come to realize that many people have been doing something good for their health. I think it is the attitudes of us, the OH nurses, believing that workers must have kept doing something good that allow us to get this information. SFT is a meaningful method that also makes OH nurses change.
8. When I asked, "What would be different if you were at one point higher?" in the scaling question, I sometimes received unexpected answers. This made me notice that I had been seeing workers only from the viewpoint of test results.

SFT

9. I have come to use questions that make workers answer by thinking in depth about themselves, instead of answering with a yes or a no. Then, I use "How?" and "What else?" to further explore their ideas.

■ METHOD

Participants

There were two groups of participants, interviewees and interviewers, in this study. The interviewees were employees of small to medium-sized enterprises in Fukuoka

Prefecture, Japan. The interviewers were OH nurses who worked at the Fukuoka branch of an organization subsidized by the Japanese government. They were in charge of conducting health interviews with workers whose companies held a contract with the organization. Every interview was given after an annual medical examination.

The interviewees who participated in the study were the workers who were interviewed and allowed us to use their data. All of them were divided into two groups based upon the period when they were interviewed. During the control period, 911 interviewees (69.3%) out of 1,315 workers agreed to participate in the study. During the SFT period, 975 interviewees (68.2%) out of 1,429 workers participated.

Regarding the interviewers, all of the OH nurses at the branch, 21 women with an average age of 40.8 years, agreed to take part in the study. The branch manager of the organization supported it as one of the activities for improving nurses' interviewing skills.

Questionnaires

The study used four questionnaires, all of which were developed for the study by the author and the lead nurses. Table 25.1 shows the outline of the questionnaires. Most questions in them are similar to the scaling question. Participants were requested to check a number between 1 and 10 in each question, where 1 means the worst and 10 means the best. Every worker filled in questionnaire 1 before the interview and questionnaire 2 just after the interview. Every nurse rated the result of every interview by herself immediately afterward and filled in questionnaire 3. At the end of the study, the nurses evaluated their own attitudes toward interviewing in questionnaire 4 and also provided feedback on the changes that they experienced after learning SFT.

Procedure

All workers were requested to fill in the questionnaires before and after the interview during the control and SFT periods. They filled in questionnaire 1 and gave written consent before the interview, and filled in questionnaire 2 just after the interview.

During the control period (December 2002 to February 2003), the nurses interviewed the workers in a conventional way based on the medical model and answered questionnaire 3 just after each interview. After this period, they attended a 1-day training workshop to learn solution-focused interviewing for the first time in March 2003. They attended a second training workshop one and a half months later in April. The SFT training was given by the author. During the SFT period (from April 2003 to July 2003), they interviewed workers in the solution-focused way. Except for the interviewing method, other conditions, including the questionnaires, were the same as those for the control period.

When the study was finished, the nurses evaluated themselves regarding how their interviewing had changed by answering questionnaire 4 with written feedback to the author.

Training of SFT

In their daily practice, nurses can spend only 15 to 20 minutes for a regular interview, and its main purpose is decided by law. The purpose is to give workers an opportunity to understand their health conditions and motivate them to take action to improve their health. Hence, I adjusted the solution-focused interviewing process to these limitations, as shown in Table 25.2.

TABLE 25.1. *The Outlines of the Questionnaires Used in the Study*

Question No.	Answerer	Content	Response
		Questionnaire 1: Answered Before the Health Interview	
1–1	Worker	How necessary is it for you to take care of your health?	1———10
1–2	Worker	Have you changed something about your lifestyle after you received the results of your medical examinations this year?	yes/no
1–3	Worker	How much do you expect a health interview by a health nurse to be helpful for thinking about your health?	1———10
		Questionnaire 2: Answered Just After the Health Interview	
2–1	Worker	How necessary is it for you to take care of your health?	1———10
2–2	Worker	How helpful was the interview for you to think about your health?	1———10
2–3	Worker	How well do you think the nurse tried to listen to you to understand you?	1———10
2–4	Worker	How much did today's interview motivate you to begin doing something for your health from tomorrow?	1———10
2–5	Worker	How much do you want to have a health interview by an occupational health nurse next year?	1———10
		Questionnaire 3: Answered Just After the Health Interview	
3–1	Nurse	How helpful do you think your interview was for the worker to think about his/her health?	1———10
3–2	Nurse	How well do you think the worker understood the necessity of taking care of his/her health?	1———10
3–3	Nurse	How likely do you think it is for the worker to begin doing something for his/her health from tomorrow?	1———10
		Questionnaire 4: Answered At the End of the SFT Period	
4–1	Nurse	How much attention do you pay to workers' positive behavior even though it is very subtle?	1———10
4–2	Nurse	How actively do you listen to workers?	1———10
4–3	Nurse	How much do you trust that workers think about their health in their own way?	1———10
4–4	Nurse	How often do you compliment workers on their health behavior?	1———10
4–5	Nurse	How much have you changed your ways of interviewing, ideas and attitudes after learning SFT?	1———10

TABLE 25.2. *The Process of the Solution-Focused Health Interview*

1. Create good relationships with the worker.
   - Acknowledge his/her efforts to come to the interview.
   - Identify what the worker wants to talk about.
2. Find out what's good for the worker.
   - Find his/her health behavior that the worker had already been doing.
   - Compliment the worker on his/her efforts to keep doing it.
3. Find out what the next step would be.
   - Who is important to the worker?
   - What is important to the worker?
4. Think about his/her next behavior.
   - What is the worker willing to do?
   - What is the worker able to do?
5. Summary
   - Feedback to the worker.

In the first training workshop, nurses learned the basic philosophy and ideas of SFT. Then they did several exercises in small groups in which they found out their own strengths and resources as OH nurses. They also practiced complimenting and asking the scaling question. I always stayed solution-focused in the training and attempted to let them think about and experience the solution-focused process by themselves rather than lecture them about it. Between the two workshops, I also supported their learning by e-mail or by fax. In the second workshop, the nurses were invited to ask questions to clarify vague points, and then some basic practices were repeated.

Statistical Analyses

The data from the four questionnaires were analyzed to compare the answers in the SFT period with those in the control period. Almost all questions in these questionnaires were answered by choosing a number on a scale from 1 to 10. These numbers are treated as a metric value.

Regarding the interviews, questionnaires 2 and 3 were used to find out how differently the workers responded to the interview and how differently the nurses evaluated it between the control and SFT periods. In these analyses, the same data could be used in two ways. When a worker was seen as one sample, the answers to all questions in the interview with the worker were used as they were, and comparisons were made by the two-sample t-test, because the workers were different between the two periods. This analysis will be referred to as the *worker-based analysis*; its sample sizes are 898 to 911 for the control period and 957 to 975 for the SFT period.

Secondly, when a nurse was seen as one sample, the answers regarding specific workers who were interviewed by the same nurse were averaged in each question, and an average was used as a value for the question. Comparisons were made by the paired t-test, because the same nurses interviewed in both periods. This analysis will be referred to as the *nurse-based analysis*; its sample size is 21 (the number of nurses participating in the study).

In terms of choosing data, all data were evaluated in the first analysis of each comparison. In order to confirm the stability of the results, two additional analyses were conducted by changing conditions to choose data. In the second analysis, the workers interviewed in the latter half of the SFT period were chosen as the sample of the SFT period, because nurses' interviewing skills might have improved in the latter half of this period. In the third analysis, the comparisons were made only among the workers who had answered in questionnaire 1 that they had not changed anything about their lifestyle after receiving the results of their medical examinations. This analysis is considered to indicate how useful solution-focused interviewing would be in helping less motivated workers.

For questionnaire 4, no comparison was made, and only its descriptive statistics were calculated. Information from questionnaire 1 was mainly used to confirm that workers' basic attitudes toward health interviews had not changed between the two periods.

Statistical analyses were carried out using SAS V8.2.

■ **RESULTS**

Comparisons of the Two Periods Regarding Conditions Before the Interviews

As explained in the method section, the sample was comprised of different workers between the control and SFT periods. In the control period, their average age was 49.2 years; 633 were male and 278 were female. In the SFT period, their average age was 49.5 years; 646 were male and 329 were female. There were no significant age and gender differences between the two groups.

If the conditions of the workers before the health interviews were different, it would be inappropriate to discuss the study results based only on the comparisons of questionnaires 2 and 3 that were answered just after the interview. In order to confirm that workers' pre-interview conditions were similar, the two groups were compared by analyzing questionnaire 1. It revealed that there were no significant differences in the answers to questionnaire 1 between the two periods. Hence, it can be concluded that the two groups were similar regarding their pre-interview attitudes about health and expectations about health interviews.

Comparisons of the Answers to Questionnaires 2 and 3 Between the Two Periods

The main purpose of the study is to investigate whether or not the workers showed different attitudes about their health after the nurses learned SFT and changed their ways of interviewing the workers. Hence, the answers to questionnaires 2 and 3 were analyzed in detail.

When all data were analyzed by considering a worker as one sample (the worker-based analysis), there were significant differences in several questions. As shown in Table 25.3, workers in the SFT period answered that the nurses had listened to them better ($p < .005$) and that they were more motivated to begin doing something to improve their health ($p < .05$). They tended to feel that the health interviews were more helpful ($p < .1$) and that it was more likely that they would have an interview next year ($p < .1$).

TABLE 25.3. *Comparisons of the Questionnaires to the Workers and the Nurses After Health Interviews by the Worker-Based Analysis*

Question	Control period			SFT period			p
	N	Mean	(SD)	N	Mean	(SD)	
Answers from the workers							
2–1 How necessary?	908	8.03	(1.92)	970	8.09	(1.94)	.4999
2–2 How helpful?	905	8.42	(1.75)	970	8.57	(1.64)	.0553
2–3 How well listened?	903	9.01	(1.42)	966	9.20	(1.31)	.0018
2–4 How motivated?	909	8.15	(1.68)	965	8.30	(1.67)	.0485
2–5 Have an interview next year?	898	8.61	(1.75)	957	8.75	(1.69)	.0849
Answers from the nurses							
3–1 How helpful?	911	6.12	(1.40)	975	6.26	(1.29)	.0278
3–2 How well understood?	911	6.42	(1.50)	975	6.51	(1.43)	.1612
3–3 How likely to do something?	911	6.05	(1.62)	975	6.18	(1.37)	.0498

The nurses also rated the workers more favorably in the SFT period than in the control period. They believed that the interviews were more helpful to the workers ($p < .05$), and that the workers were more likely to do something to improve their health ($p < .05$).

The worker-based analysis has a few disadvantages, although it has the advantage of high statistical power due to the large sample size. Because the number of workers participating in the study was not constant among the nurses, it is possible that only a few of the nurses who interviewed many workers had improved their interviewing markedly, whereas the other nurses had not. To deal with this issue, all of the data were analyzed again by the nurse-based analysis. The results are shown in Table 25.4. As predicted from the small sample size ($n = 21$), statistical significance tended to be lower in this analysis. Nevertheless, the workers in the SFT period answered that they felt that the health interviews were more helpful ($p < .05$) and that the nurses listened to them better ($p < .05$). The nurses also believed that the workers were more likely to do something to improve their health ($p < .1$).

Further Analyses

The same data were analyzed further to confirm that similar results were obtained in the subgroups of workers. Because the nurses had learned solution-focused interviewing just before the SFT period began, it was likely that their interviewing skills improved more in the latter half of the SFT period, and that differences were more marked when the workers in that period were compared with the workers in the control period. As shown in the second column of Table 25.5, the results of this comparison with the worker-based analysis confirmed that the differences in the workers' answers were more marked, although those of the nurses were not. The results of the nurse-based analysis are omitted in describing the further analyses, because they are similar to those of the worker-based analysis.

The third column of Table 25.5 shows the results of comparisons regarding the workers who answered in questionnaire 1 that they had not changed anything about their lifestyle after receiving the results of their medical examinations. These workers were considered to be less motivated to do something to improve their health.

TABLE 25.4. *Comparisons of the Questionnaires to the Workers and the Nurses After Health Interviews by the Nurse-Based Analysis*

Question	Control Period			SFT Period			p
	N	Mean	(SD)	N	Mean	(SD)	
	Answers from the Workers						
2–1 How necessary?	21	8.00	(0.38)	21	8.05	(0.29)	.5279
2–2 How helpful?	21	8.32	(0.46)	21	8.50	(0.45)	.0125
2–3 How well listened?	21	8.96	(0.35)	21	9.18	(0.32)	.0130
2–4 How motivated?	21	8.09	(0.44)	21	8.24	(0.46)	.1431
2–5 Have an interview next year?	21	8.53	(0.42)	21	8.65	(0.48)	.2101
	Answers from the Nurses						
3–1 How helpful	21	6.01	(0.91)	21	6.26	(0.90)	.1575
3–2 How well understood?	21	6.33	(0.95)	21	6.51	(0.98)	.2419
3–3 How likely to do something?	21	5.91	(0.98)	21	6.19	(0.71)	.0727

TABLE 25.5. *Comparisons of the Questionnaires to the Subgroups of the Workers After Health Interviews by the Worker-Based Analysis*

Questions	Control Period	All Workers	All Workers	Workers Without Prechanges
	SFT period	All Workers	Workers in the Latter Half	Workers Without Prechanges
Answers from the Workers				
2–1 How necessary?		ns	ns	$p < .05$
2–2 How helpful?		$p < .1$	$p < .05$	$p < .05$
2–3 How well listened?		$p < .005$	$p < .005$	$p < .001$
2–4 How motivated?		$p < .05$	$p < .05$	$p < .05$
2–5 Have an interview next year?		$p < .1$	$p < .05$	$p < .05$
Answers from the Nurses				
3–1 How helpful		$p < .05$	$p < .1$	$p < .005$
3–2 How well understood?		ns	ns	$p < .05$
3–3 How likely to do something?		$p < .05$	ns	$p < .0005$

(ns: not significant)

Hence, if the differences in these workers were remarkable, it could be concluded that solution-focused interviewing is very useful. As shown in Table 25.5, the differences were more significant among these workers both in the answers from the workers and in the answers from the nurses.

Nurses' Own Evaluation of Changes After They Learned SFT

Table 25.6 shows how the nurses rated themselves at the end of the study. There were no data for comparison purposes; these are just nurses' subjective evaluations. In general, they evaluated themselves very highly on most questions. They came to compliment workers more often and to trust workers more in particular.

Along with these answers, the nurses were asked to give the author feedback about their experience of learning SFT and taking part in the study. Their comments were generally positive; this will be discussed later.

■ PRACTICE GUIDELINES

There are two important questions to be answered in understanding the interpretation of the results. The first question is whether or not SFT can provide useful tools for

TABLE 25.6. *The Results of the Questionnaire to the Nurses After the SFT Period*

Question	Worst									Best
	1	2	3	4	5	6	7	8	9	10
4–1 Paying attention to workers' behavior						1	7	9	4	
4–2 Active listening		1		1	4	8	7			
4–3 Trusting workers					1	4	9	4	3	
4–4 Compliment							1	9	9	2
4–5 Changes in heath Interviews				3		8	6	4		

(the number of nurses)

health interviews so that nurses can improve their interviewing skills by learning it. The second one is why and how SFT tools can be useful in health interviews. These questions are considered in the following discussion.

Can SFT Provide Useful Tools for Health Interviews?

To answer this question, it is necessary to carefully examine the study results in detail. Because the data were analyzed in two ways, the worker-based analysis and the nurse-based analysis, I should consider the respective results separately. However, there were only subtle differences between the two analyses, and overall tendencies in the changes between the two periods were similar. Hence, I will discuss the results by putting these together.

The most consistent change in the comparisons of the workers' answers is that they felt they were heard better in the SFT period; they also felt that the interview was more helpful in motivating them to think about their health. When the analysis focused on the workers who answered that they had not changed anything about their health status before the interview, the differences were more notable. In addition to the above-mentioned changes, the workers in the SFT period better understood the necessity of taking care of their health and became more motivated after the interview. These results suggest that solution-focused interviewing has great potential for health interviews, because these workers were considered to be less motivated to do something to improve their health and to be an important target of health interviews.

The nurses' evaluation of the interviews also changed in a similar manner. In the SFT period, they felt that the interviews were more helpful to the workers and that the workers were more likely to start doing something for their health. However, the changes in the nurses' evaluation were smaller than those in the workers.' In addition to the smaller changes, the average scores in both periods were generally lower than those of the workers. This may mean that the nurses were stricter about evaluating themselves.

In spite of the statistically significant differences found in many questions, the actual differences in scores were not remarkable, as shown in Tables 25.3 and 25.4. This can be understood as an indication that learning SFT made only small differences. However, if the fact that the workers in the control period already rated the interviews very highly is taken into account, these differences are considered to be of greater importance, because it is generally understood that increasing values that are initially high is difficult. Hence, it can be concluded that the improvement in interviewing that the nurses indicated after they learned SFT was more meaningful than it appeared, and that SFT provided useful tools for health interviews.

Before answering the second question about the reason why SFT was useful, it is necessary to carefully examine the changes in the nurses' attitudes toward the health interviews. So, I will now analyze the data concerning their attitude changes and their feedback after the study.

At the end of the SFT period, the nurses reported remarkable changes in many aspects of the interviews, as shown in Table 25.6. Regarding trusting and complimenting workers, most nurses thought highly of themselves. Many of them came to pay much attention to workers' behavior and to listen actively to them. The nurses also gave positive feedback reports to the author. Box 25.1 describes some of these reports.

All of them indicate that the nurses came to view workers more positively and tried to find out their resources and strengths.

Although I believe strongly that the nurses' learning SFT is the most significant reason for their improvement in interviewing, there are other factors to consider. One of the factors is that the nurses were highly motivated from the outset. The level of their interviewing skills was also very high, as shown by the high values in the control period in Tables 25.3 and 25.4. These may have had positive influences on the results. Without their motivation, it would have been impossible even to plan the present study because of their busy work schedules.

As explained briefly in the introduction, I had held a training workshop to help the nurses improve their interviews 2 years before the study. At that time, I did not deal with SFT in detail, but instead concentrated on finding the nurses' strengths and resources and encouraged them to make use of their findings by themselves. The nurses then revealed their remarkable potential. This could explain why their interviews were highly rated by the workers even in the control period. For the information of readers, I have summarized briefly the experiences they had already acquired in Box 25.2.

BOX 25.2 ■ Strengths and Resources That the Nurses
Already had before learning SFT

In the training workshop, OH nurses were divided into groups of four or five. In each group, they talked about answers to the following questions and summarized their discussion and insights, which were finally shared among the nurses.
The questions asked to the OH nurses to elicit their possibilities:

1. "Think back on your experience of receiving advice from a leader or a teacher or someone in a similar position. When did you think that you should accept and follow the advice? How did the advisor guide you so that you thought that following the advice was a good idea? Please remember as many things or conditions as possible regarding the situations, the advisor's actions, your conditions, the types of issues, and so forth."
2. "What efforts do you think the advisor made to guide you that way? Please remember as many things as possible regarding the advisor's efforts and behavior in particular."
3. "What efforts do you need to make, if you utilize these things or actions in your work of guiding people?"

The summary of information found by the nurses:
   a. Useful things and conditions that the OH nurses found as an advisee
      The advisor should:
      • Give us greetings, new information, evidence, and what we have wanted to hear.
      • Show empathy and respect for our experience.
      • Talk with a soft voice, and explain concretely and seriously.
      • Allow us to talk, listen to our story, and have no preconception.
      • Give us acknowledgment and encouragement.
      • Leave us some room for an excuse
      • Compliment us, especially on coming to the interview in particular.

BOX 25.2 ■ (*continued*)

b. Useful things and conditions that the OH nurses wanted to utilize as an advisor:

We should:

- Find out what the person wants to hear.
- Not use technical terms and use words that are easy to understand.
- Be careful about the person's reaction.
- Begin the session by asking about easy subjects for the person to answer, and then move gradually to core subjects.
- Give advice that is doable, and set a goal that fits the person.
- Compliment the person naturally.
- Do not use the phrase "have to…"
- While talking with the person, make eye contact.
- Ask questions that the person can understand.
- Find the person's goal that can be achieved with a little effort.

Why and How Can SFT Tools Be Useful in Health Interviews?

The usefulness of SFT as an interviewing method in general has been discussed in many references. Here I would like to concentrate on its usefulness in the application to health interviews. Since SFT has several advantages in helping nurses improve their interviews, the following discussion deals with the advantages first by focusing on the interviewees' experiences and then by focusing on the interviewers' experiences.

It is obvious from the results that SFT has definite potential for giving nurses new skills to fully utilize interviewees' strengths and resources. In general, many nurses' interviews based on the medical model might have difficulty creating productive relationships with interviewees, because most people usually do not like to be cautioned about health conditions that are not problematic to them at present. A target population for health interviews is ordinary workers who are healthy enough to go to work and do their job, whether or not they have health problems. It seems that interviewing by the medical model has put too much emphasis on finding and correcting health problems and has almost ignored the healthy part of workers' lives. For this reason, OH nurses may not have learned enough about how to focus on the positive aspects of workers' health and may have difficulty utilizing workers' strengths. Some nurses have told me that even if they found workers doing something good for their health, such as exercising a little and being somewhat careful about their diet, they did not know how best to connect such behavior to a more healthy lifestyle. It is obvious from the nurses' feedback at the end of the study that learning SFT has enabled them to utilize the workers' strengths.

From the standpoint of an interviewer learning a new method, an important advantage of SFT is that it can be taught in a solution-focused way, and that it fully utilizes trainees' strengths and expertise. This means that the training itself provides a very useful opportunity for trainees to recognize their unconscious strengths and resources, as well as to learn SFT skills as a new way of interviewing. Another advantage is that once trainees have learned SFT, they can practice it to solve not only their own health problems, but also their daily life problems. If a workshop is conducted based on the medical model, trainees are unlikely to utilize the knowledge and skills they have learned to solve personal problems that were not dealt with in the training, because training using the medical model is based on the results of analyzing problems, which usually differ depending on the types of problems considered.

The fact that SFT is applicable in solving different kinds of problems is worth repeating. If a trainee applied SFT to solving his or her own problem and achieved a satisfactory result, this experience would provide compelling evidence that it really works, which would make the trainee more confident in practicing SFT effectively at work. This suggests that the learning experiences of nurses during the training are very important. In order to provide nurses with these experiences, a trainer has to pay close attention to their experience during the training.

I had had a great deal of experience in teaching active listening (AL) to middle managers before I started learning SFT. From my experience as a trainer, I strongly believe that a trainer should be very careful in creating an experiential environment so that the training is effective, and that SFT has a great advantage in this sense, too. Hence, I would like to discuss the advantage of SFT from the standpoint of a trainer as well by describing my experience.

In Japan, middle managers are expected to learn AL as an important skill for better communication so that they can have good relationships with subordinates and help them maintain good mental health. However, managers are not usually motivated to learn it well, because in the past an expert trained them based on the medical model. This means that the expert pointed out the problems with managers' current listening styles and tried to convince them to change their styles from the expert's standpoint. Some managers disagreed with the expert and had a hard time learning the expert's style.

I adopted a completely different approach. Kubota, Mishima, and Nagata (2004) developed a new AL training method, called *inventive experiential learning* (IEL), and proved that it was very effective in encouraging managers to learn AL. In IEL, AL is taught by AL. Its basic philosophy is very similar to that of SFT. A trainer listens attentively to trainees while focusing on a positive aspect of their current listening style, however small it is. This enables the trainees to realize their strengths and improve their listening skills. The results of our studies on AL were explained in detail in the above report.

Based on this experience, I believe that the training would be more productive if the target skills taught were congruent with trainees' experience during their learning. The way the nurses were trained in this study was congruent with SFT in this sense. They learned SFT not in a critical environment but in a solution-focused environment. I believe this is why the nurses understood the philosophy of SFT in a relatively short period of time.

Limitations of the Interviewing Study

This study has shown that SFT is worth learning for OH nurses to improve their interviewing skills, although the study is considered to be preliminary in a strict sense. This method might be useful even to nurses whose interviewing skills are already very high, because it would enable them to discover strengths and resources in themselves as well as in interviewees, a discovery that would not be possible with the conventional interviewing method. The small sample size and lack of standardization of the study, however, limit its generalizability. In Japan, I also cannot envision a rapid broadening of the applications of SFT in medicine. However, I hope this small study makes an important first step toward the future, because solution-focused therapists know that "take small steps and go slow" is one of the important philosophies of SFT.

■ FUTURE APPLICATIONS

This study dealt only with health interviews, which are an important but small part of nurses' activities. There are other areas where communication plays a significant role in nurses' daily practice. If they could communicate more effectively with patients using SFT, it would enhance cooperation between patients and health care professionals.

This change would not be limited to nurses' activities. Mishima, Kubota, and Nagata (2005) have reported that SFT is also very useful to OH physicians. It can be expected that better communication between physicians and patients will contribute to better practice in clinical medicine in general, although only a small number of physicians may be currently interested in learning SFT in Japan.

The group of nurses who participated in the study continue to learn, and some nurses have even received advanced training in SFT. This shows that once a person has learned SFT to some extent, he or she never stops learning. It is possible that these nurses will continue to improve their skills so that other nurses around them may also consider learning SFT.

■ KEY POINTS TO REMEMBER

- In Japan, the use of solution-focused interventions is primarily reserved for therapeutic settings and is not often considered in medicine. Because workers in Japan are required to receive annual medical examinations and interviews, nurses frequently conduct routine interviews.
- Workers in the SFT period believed that the nurses had listened to them better ($p < .005$), and they were more motivated to begin doing something to improve their health ($p < .05$). Additionally, they tended to feel that the health interviews were more helpful ($p < 0.1$), and it was more likely that they would have an interview next year ($p < .1$).
- Because these workers were considered to be less motivated to do something to improve their health and to be an important target of health interviews, these results suggest that solution-focused interviewing has great potential for improving health interviews.
- Although the study is considered preliminary, it has shown that SFT is worth learning for OH nurses to improve their interviewing skills.

■ FURTHER LEARNING

Japanese Society of Public Health (2007). A committee report on what the public health nursing should be (originally in Japanese, translated by the author). *Japanese Journal of Public Health, 34,* 399–406.

Kubota, S., Mishima, N., & Nagata, S. (2004). A study of the effect of active listening on listening attitudes of middle managers. *Journal of Occupational Health, 46,* 60–67.

Mishima, N., Kubota, S., & Nagata, S. (2005). Applying a solution-focused approach to support a worker who is under stress. *Journal of University of Occupational and Environmental Health, 27,* 197–208.

■ **ACKNOWLEDGMENTS**

The author would like to express his deep appreciation for the support and cooperation of Keiko Kamimura, R.N., P.H.N., her colleagues, and the Fukuoka Branch of The Social Insurance Health Project Foundation, Fukuoka, Japan. Without their assistance, this study would not be possible.

■ **ENDNOTE**

1. Psychosomatic medicine in Japan is part of clinical medicine and is rather similar to mind-body medicine in the United States.

■ **REFERENCES**

Berg, I. K. (1994). *Family-based services: A solution-focused approach.* New York: Norton.

Berg, I. K., & Dolan, Y. (2001). *Tales of solutions: A collection of hope-inspiring stories.* New York: Norton.

Berg, I. K., & Kelly, S. (2000). *Building solutions in child protective services.* New York: Norton.

Berg, I. K., & Miller, S. D. (1992). *Working with the problem drinker: A solution-oriented approach.* New York: Norton.

Berg, I. K., & Reuss, N. H. (1998). *Solutions step by step: A substance abuse treatment manual.* New York: Norton.

Berg, I. K., & Shilts, L. (2004). *Classroom Solutions: WOWW approach.* Milwaukee: BFTC Press.

Berg, I. K., & Shilts, L. (2005). *Classroom solutions: WOWW coaching.* Milwaukee: BFTC Press.

De Jong, P., & Berg, I. K. (2008). *Interviewing for solutions* (3rd ed.). Belmont, CA: Thomson Brooks/Cole.

Japanese Society of Public Health (2007). A committee report on what the public health nursing should be (originally in Japanese, translated by the author). *Japanese Journal of Public Health, 34,* 399–406.

Kubota, S., Mishima, N., & Nagata, S. (2004). A study of the effect of active listening on listening attitudes of middle managers. *Journal of Occupational Health, 46,* 60–67.

Mishima, N., Kubota, S., & Nagata, S. (2005). Applying a solution-focused approach to support a worker who is under stress. *Journal of University of Occupational and Environmental Health, 27,* 197–208.

Epilogue

The Future of Research in Solution-Focused
Brief Therapy

■ TERRY S. TREPPER AND CYNTHIA FRANKLIN

Over the past 10 years, the number of research studies on solution-focused brief therapy (SFBT) has increased exponentially; this book updates both practitioners and researchers concerning these developments. Even though, as researchers, we have noted throughout this book the limitations in the number and quality of studies that exist in different areas of practice, it is equally important to emphasize that SFBT is grounded in research evidence and continues to improve upon its mechanisms of change and outcome research. Practice-based evidence has always been integral to the development of SFBT. Lipchick et al. noted in Chapter 1 that SFBT had its origins as a true-evidence-based approach and was *developed* by observing carefully what worked and didn't work for master therapists. Then changes were made, interventions were discarded, and more evidence was compiled until what was left was the essence of "what worked." Using qualitative and intensive case study process methods, these practitioner/researchers tried to discover what works in brief family therapy and created SFBT. We believe, therefore, that it is helpful for practitioners of SFBT to think of the studies reported in this book as being part of a program of empirical work on SFBT practices that has been present since the inception of SFBT, has improved over time, and may continue to improve.

The purpose of this final chapter is to summarize the state of the art of empirical work in SFBT as described in this book and to propose some future directions for SFBT research. Based on the worldwide popularity of SFBT alone, popularity that is only increasing, there is no doubt that significant research will continue to be developed to test SFBT's mechanisms of change and efficacy. More research is certainly needed, but we want to take this opportunity to point out the important trends and implications of the research that has been presented.

The Evidence Basis of SFBT. Cinical practitioners have often asked, "Is SFBT an evidence-based practice?" This question presupposes an absolute yes or no answer; however, research evidence that supports psychotherapies is more of an ongoing process, and it is continuously developed, evaluated, and reevaluated in consideration of many factors. We strongly believe that the contents of this book support the evidence base of SFBT. Another question we are frequently asked is "Does SFBT work as well as other psychotherapies, such as cognitive-behavioral therapy (CBT)?" This question presupposes that there need to be some studies on SFBT indicating that it performs as well as other approaches to psychotherapy. Fortunately, as indicated in different chapters of this book, these types of studies now exist. In their careful review in Chapter 6 of the empirical literature, including two recent meta-analyses, Gingerich et al. concluded that "the outcome research to data shows SFBT" to have a small to moderate positive outcome (meta-analytic reviews), and when compared with established treatments in well-designed studies, is the equivalent of other evidence-based approaches, sometimes producing results in substantially less time and at less cost." So, we feel confident in stating that SFBT *is* an approach that is comparable to other psychotherapies and will continue to strengthen its evidence base as new and even better-designed studies are added to those that already exist.

That said, it is also imperative that the field continue to conduct high-quality, well-controlled studies using when possible the gold standard of randomized, controlled, double-blind clinical trials. The quality of the studies must be considered in any systematic review, so by designing better-quality studies, we will improve our research on SFBT. As was pointed out throughout this book, larger clinical trials on its efficacy instead of smaller experimental and quasi-experimetnal studies are the next step for SFBT research. This is not to discount the well-controlled studies that now exist because the number of well-controlled studies has been growing. The findings from the better-controlled studies have important implications for clinical practice, especially the fairly consistent outcome that SFBT effects changes in *less* time than comparative therapies, which potentially creates fewer time demands, less stress, and lower costs for the client. By analogy, if a drug were found in smaller-scale research to be as effective as other drugs for the same condition, but worked more quickly and with fewer side effects, then this would be considered a very important finding, certainly worthy of continued research. What follows is a summary of the trends in SFBT research that we observed during our review of this book and suggestions for future empirical research on SFBT.

■ TRENDS IN SOLUTION-FOCUSED PRACTICES RESEARCH AND SUGGESTIONS FOR THE FUTURE

Methods and Instruments

Treatment Manuals and Fidelity Instruments. One of the foundations of well-controlled clinical studies is standardized procedures and instrumentation. It is particularly important that researchers in such studies use treatment manuals as the basis of their interventions to allow for a greater likelihood of meaningful replication in future studies. Both the European Brief Therapy Association and the Solution-Focused Brief Therapy Association have developed treatment manuals for SFBT; the latter appears in this book. Treatment manuals, of course, should be dynamic, changing as refinements in an approach and new information about the approach become available. We would recommend that the official treatment manuals of both associations be updated regularly, perhaps semiannually, and reflect the newest research on the practice of SFBT.

Also foundational in clinical research is the assumption that the therapists in the research study are *doing* SFBT. To that end, fidelity instruments can help determine the degree of adherence to the approach that is present. In Chapter 3, Lehman and Patton described the initial development of one such instrument. It was shown to be reliable, and further studies should be undertaken to determine the validity of the instrument, both convergent and discriminant, and should use observers rather than self-ratings.

Strength-Based Outcome Measures. Solution-focused brief therapy should perform as well on standard problem-focused measures as other models of psychotherapy for its effectiveness to be meaningful determined. At the same time, this approach appears to have as its important mechanisms of change *strengths, hope, expectations,* and *resiliency.* It would seem important to make certain that future research utilizes strength-based measures as well as other measures assessing change. It may also be useful to examine the mediating effects of increasing client strengths on client outcomes to further test the change theory of SFBT. It is fortunate that there is already a large number of psychometrically sound strength-based instruments, which are listed and described in Chapter 4 by Smock. Unfortunately, of the 41 instruments she reviewed, only 9 have been used in SFBT research. Future SFBT outcome studies should be encouraged to use these instruments and other standardized strength-based outcome measures, since these are theoretically consistent with the approach. It would be especially useful to pair strengths-based with non-strengths-based instruments. For example, in a study of the effects of SFBT on the treatment of depression, researchers could pair a standardized hope scale with a depression inventory to determine if, as a result of the intervention, hope *increases* while depression *decreases.*

Outcome and Session-Rating Scales. Of recent interest is the use of scales that are given to clients during their session to monitor client feedback on the session. There is evidence to suggest that not only does this feedback help the clinician make informed in-session decisions, but it also leads to improved client outcomes. In Chapter 5, Gillaspy and Murphy describe two such scales, the Outcome Rating Scale and the Session Rating Scale, which are given to tclients either at the beginning or at the end of the session, and are scored and discussed with the client during the session. Further research should be done using these and other in-session instruments with SFBT versus other non-solution-focused approaches to test both the mechanisms of change in SFBT and the discriminant validity of the measures.

Single-Case Studies and Research Occurring as Part of Practice. Single-case study designs have been used for many years in clinical research. There are far fewer impediments to single-case studies than to larger-scale large-sample designs, not the least of which is cost. Single-case studies also allow practitioners to become involved with the research process both in conducting their own studies and in monitoring the effects of their clinical practices. And while historically single-case studies have fallen under the rubric of descriptive research, some approaches can make single-case studies experimental or quasi-experimental. In particular, multiple-baseline designs that compare each client outcome to other clients using a time series analysis across settings or behaviors qualify as well-controlled experimental designs yet are still flexible enough to be used in clinical practice settings (Bloom et al., 2005). In Chapter 7, Kim also describes a procedure using the percentage of nonoverlapping data (PND), which can be very valuable in analyzing the results of single-case designs. This method provides better understanding of the effectiveness of individual case studies than a mere presentation of graphical evidence, and it can more easily be combined with other single-case studies to determine the effectiveness of groups of single-case studies. The advantage is that it "can add to the empirical base on SFBT and can be viewed in context with other empirical studies and systematic reviews." We would recommend further research, both on this method and using this method for adding to the archive of research on SFBT.

The experiences of BRIEF in London, as described in Chapter 19 by Shennan and Iveson, beautifully demonstrate the importance and possibilities of practitioners doing empirical research on their own work, using the results of that research to improve their services and also to provide important information that can be added to the empirical archive for use by other researchers. While the methods used by these researchers did not provide the stringent control that is found in experimental research studies, this limitation is balanced by the importance of program evaluations in real-world settings. While practioner-based research cannot be the only method of researching the efficacy of SFBT because of its possible threats to internal and external validity, it certainly has a place both for practicing clinicians and for the field in general, and should be done—and the results published—more in the future.

Microanalysis and Process Outcome Research. One of the most exciting developments in psychotherapy research has been emerging from communication laboratories. Bavelas and her associates have been conducting experimental research, described in Chapter 10, that demonstrates that there is an empirical, rather than an anecdotal, basis to the important SFBT constructs of *coconstruction* and *collaboration*. This supports one of the foundational mechanisms of change in SFBT. This team's current work is demonstrating that it will be possible to test some of the fundamental tenets of SFBT, such as that solution talk has a different effect on the client than does problem talk. Microanalysis also may hold an important key in ferreting out the actual effects of the so-called common factors (Lambert 1992; Sprenkle & Blow, 2004) by demonstrating the specific communication mechanisms occuring in the therapist–client interaction. These mechanisms could then be analyzed in relation to specific theraputic outcome measures, the effects of which could be measured. The work of Bevales and her team so far suggests that some of the factors of SFBT are measurably different from those of other therapeutic approaches. These findings are particularly important for demonstrating the theory and mechanisms of change that are inherent in solution-focused practice. It remains to be seen whether those SFBT factors are contributing to therapeutic change, but this is certainly one of the most exciting and important areas of basic psychotherapy research to come along in decades.

Considerable other process and process/outcome research also exists on SFBT techniques and awaits larger studies. As indicated by McKeel in Chapter 9, many SFBT techniques have been studied using process research, and this research is especially instructive to clinical practice. At present, however, not enough process/outcome research on SFBT exists to guide clinical practitioners on what to do with their clients, and on the specifics of how and when to use certain techniques and procedures One possible future research project would be to conduct prospective process/outcome studies using systematic methods like microanalysis so that therapist–client interactions and client outcomes might be simultaneously studied.

Populations and Problems

SFBT in the Schools. The SFBT approach has been adapted to school settings, and the results have been very good. The basic tenets of SFBT are quite applicable to educational settings, and as Franklin, Kim, and Brigman noted in Chapter 16, applying solution-focused practices to school settings has shown quite promising results.

The authors also noted some specific areas that are important to better refine our knowledge of using these practices in schools. These include (a) understanding which school-based populations and problem areas SF practices would be best suited to help; (b) testing the effects of these practices on school achievement; (c) examining the usefulness of SF practices for improving behavioral outcomes; (d) developing treatment manuals so that more schools could both utilize the approach and be part of interschool research; and (e) conducting studies on the differential effects of SF intervention at the classroom, school, family, and even community level.

One of the most promising developments in the educational application of SF in the schools is the Working on What Works (WOWW) program to improve classroom management, described in Chapter 23 by Kelly, Liscio, Bluestone-Miller, and Shilts. This program directly applies the principles of SF practices to the individual classroom setting by providing an SF-trained coach in the classroom for both the teacher and the students. The coach's job, like that of the good SF psychotherapist, is to help the class find what is working and encourage more of it through the use of the SF-based techniques of compliments, goal setting, and scaling. The two pilot studies described in the chapter, one in Florida and one in Chicago, found significant improvements in WOWW classrooms on a variety of behavioral and interactional measures. Qualitative data also suggested that both students and teachers enjoyed the WOWW program and found it extremely helpful. The problems with these studies were the lack of randomized control groups, possible experimenter and respondent bias because of the lack of blind evaluations, and small sample sizes. Still, these results are extremely important and suggest that educational researchers should conduct well-controlled studies on the efficacy of the WOWW Program.

Domestic Violence and Abuse. Lee, Uken, and Sebold in Chapter 11 and McCollum, Stith and Thomsen 12 have described exciting and controversial programs using SFBT with domestic violence offenders. As Lee et al. noted:"Solution-focused treatment holds domestic violence offenders accountable for solutions rather than responsible for problems." This rather simple statement reflects a revolutionary view of treatment for domestic abuse, in which *solutions* take precedence over blame. Solution-focused brief therapy may be seen as another clinical option to help individuals, couples, and families make significant changes so that abuse does not recur, but do so in a respectful, caring, collaborative way. Given the promising preliminary results of both sets of projects, there clearly should be larger-scale clinical trials with randomized controls to determine the effects of SFBT, along with continued efficacy studies showing the usefulness of this alternative approach on the front lines of clinical practice.

Child Protection Services. One area that could benefit most from a more positive psychological view is the child protection area. In Chapter 14, Wheeler and Hogg (along with the earlier work of De Jong and Berg, 1998) have documented some important strides being taken around the world to incorporate SF practices and other similar stremgths-based approaches in the usually heavily problem-focused child protection area. They have outlined some of the serious ethical and practical problems in doing contolled studies with such populations, and have offered important suggestions for researchers wanting to demonstrate the usefulness of these new approaches. We believe that, given the continued empirical support for SF practices in other areas, like psychotherapy, medicine, and education, using SF practices in various aspects of the child welfare system, such as training of social workers and providing direct services to child victims and their families, should be systematically studied. We think it will offer a chance to greatly improve the system and increase social workers' satisfaction and retention, improve social worker–client interactions, increase the likelihood of more colleagial relationships between social worker and families, and ultimately improve outcomes.

Medication Adherence. An increasing number of psychiatrists worldwide have adopted SFBT both as their clinical orientation and as a way to improve their patients' adherence to their medication regimen. Certain mental health problems, such as schizophrenia and bipolar disorders, are best treated with a combination of medication and nonmedical interventions, such as psychotherapy. The problem for many psychiatrists is that patients often do not take their medication. In Chapter 13, Panayotov, Strahilov, and Anichkina described a study conducted in their clinic that found that patients, after receiving SFBT, were far more likely to take their medication than before. These researchers believe that SFBT is more likely to encourage patients to take personal responsibility because they set their own goals instead of having them set by the psychiatrist; they further believe that this is the most important finding of their study. This preliminary study used a quasi-experimental design with subjects as their own controls. We would highly recommend that future experimental studies be conducted to determine if SFBT can indeed improve adherence to medication regimens.

Adolescents. Psychotherapy with adolescents, while often very rewarding, can prove a significant challenge to many clinicians. Solution-focused brief therapy has been used with this population since its early development and continues to be extremely popular. Because of its collaborative, cooperative, respectful, and shared therapist–client stance, along with honest, nonmanipulative use of clients' goals, adolescents often embrace SFBT much more than other approaches, and as a result show gains in fewer sessions. In this book, several researchers have described studies supporting SFBT with a number of adolescent populations, including homeless and runaway youth (Thompson and Sanchez, Chapter 15); adolescents displaying externalizing behavioral problems (Corcoran, Chapter 8); pregnant and parenting adolescents (Harris and Franklin, Chapter 17); and adolescents in foster care and health care institutions (Pakrosnis and Čepulcienė, Chapter 20). Most of the studies supporting claims that SFBT works with adolescent problems were descriptive, quasi-experimental, and qualitative in nature. However, Harris and Franklin described a small randomized, experimental study followed up by two quasi-experimental studies that showed that the solution-focused Taking Charge intervention for adolescent mothers improved social problem solving, coping, attendance, and grades and reduced high school dropout of teens who are pregnant and parenting. Given the strong interest in adolescent issues and the support from the studies reviewed in this volume, we conclude that SF practices may be extremely useful when working with high-risk adolescent populations, but more research is needed to determine the problem areas where it might be most useful. It is clearly time to determine the effectiveness and efficacy of SF practices with important issues like externalizing problems, as well as other concerns frequently encountered in adolescent populations.

Substance Abuse. Solution-focused brief therapy has been used for the treatment of alcoholism and substance abuse around the world for decades and has been studied empirically in some treatment programs. In Chapter 18, Hendrick, Isaebert, and Dolan describe their clinical work of using SFBT in alcohol treatment and the clinical studies that were completed at St. John's Hospital in Bruges, Belgium. All published studies have found significant changes in drinking or drug use after SFBT intervention, but only Smock et al. (2007) used a randomized, controlled design (and she and her colleagues found significant improvements in most measures for the SF group vs. the control group). However, other researchers using descriptive and quasi-experimental designs also found improvements as a result of SFBT intervention. In light of these studies and the empirical support for motivational interviewing (e.g. Lundahl et al, 2010), which shares some but not all of the critical components of SF therapy, it is clearly time to conduct large-scale clinical studies with SFBT. There is certainly good clinical evidence that SFBT is effective in the treatment of alcoholism, especially because it tends to lead to improvements sooner than other approaches. Also, because of its collegial and collaborative stance, it may be a useful approach for clients who have not found the Alcoholics Anonymous or medical model–based approaches helpful. Certainly, the positive outcomes achieved so far suggest that larger studies are warranted.

Management and Coaching. Chapter 21, by McKergow, describes the exciting application of SF practices to business, especially management. Solution-focused tenets are particularly applicable to specific areas of business such as coaching (as described by Green in Chapter 22 of this book); team development; organizational development; performance and performance evaluations; quality management; leadership development; and day-to-day management of employees, including conflict resoloution and mediation. There has also been increased interest in the use of SF practices in sales. Unfortunately, while there have been many *descriptions* of the use of SF in management, there have been few empirical or programatic evaluations to support its effectiveness. While this is not uncommon in business, it would seem that given the preliminary success of the SF approach in management and coaching, the time has come to expand beyond the descriptive, and for business and management researchers to conduct empirical studies to test SF practices in the business environment, especially comparing them to other, more common approaches. In terms of life coaching, Green has noted several empirical studies on the use of SF practices, and while research in this area is in its infancy, there is good beginning evidence to support its efficacy.

■ CONCLUSIONS

We started this Epilogue by noting that SFBT developed in an evidence-based fashion, where very closely watching what worked and doing more of it, and watching what didn't work and doing less of it, led to the development of this approach. Since then, we have seen almost 30 years of research, including basic research from communication laboratories, as well as descriptive, correlational, and experimental studies, which, taken as a whole, supports the effectiveness of SFBT. An overall review of this book suggests that SFBT has considerable empirical support and has sought to continuously ground itself in research evidence. We now believe that SFBT is ready to take the next steps in its research development toward larger and even better-controlled research studies. For this to happen, researchers and practitioners must continue to work together to do the studies and to seek funding from governments, foundations, and other private sources in order to advance SFBT research. International efforts to increase research planning and funding are defintely needed because research advances more quickly when considerable infrastructure and resources are available to carry out the work. Of particular interest to many present-day funders might be studies on the specific mechanisms of change that may be operating with SFBT and their respective outcomes, as well as how SFBT differs from other approaches. A review of this book also suggests that there should be more research on the specific elements of SFBT and how these may help certain populations or treatment problems under specific conditions.

As almost every author in this book has stated, more rigorously designed research studies are needed for all types of SFBT research. The cumulative research over time has advanced the evidence base of SFBT even if some pilot studies were only able take one small step. In the future, however, we hope for high standards in SFBT research studies. For example, we should encourage large studies with randomized control and double-blind assessment because as this is best way to determine the effectiveness of a given approach.

Finally, as the medical, neuroscience, and genetics fields continue to offer advances concerning mental health problems, SFBT should be prepared to grow and accommodate to those changes as well. All of these studies will help to further develop the evidence base of SFBT as an effective therapeutic approach and to continue its expansion beyond psychotherapy to education, social services, business, and other areas yet to be discovered.

■ REFERENCES

Bloom, M., Fischer, J., & Orme, J. (2005). *Evaluating practice: Guidelines for the accountable professional* (5th ed.). Boston: Allyn & Bacon.

De Jong, P., & Berg, I. K. (1998). *Interviewing for solutions.* Pacific Grove, CA: Brooks/Cole.

Lambert, M. J. (1992). Implications of outcome research for psychotherapy integration. In J. C. Norcross & M. R. Goldstein (Eds.), *Handbook of psychotherapeutic integration* (pp. 94–129). New York: Wiley-Interscience.

Lundahl, B. W., Kunz, C., Brownell, C., Tollefson, D., & Burke, B. L. (2010). A meta-analysis of Motivational Interviewing: Twenty-five years of empirical studies. *Research in Social Work Practice, 20* (2), 137–160.

Smock, S. A. (2007, October). *Further Development of the Solution Building Inventory.* Poster session presented at the annual meeting of the American Association for Marriage and Family Therapy, Long Beach, CA.

Sprenkle, D. H., & Blow, A. J. (2004). Common factors and our sacred models. *Journal of Marital and Family Therapy, 30,* 113–129.

■ INDEX

Note: Page numbers followed by "*f*" and "*t*" denote figures and tables, respectively.